Originally from the London suburbs, Brian J. Rance now lives and works in Birmingham. He has a Diploma in Town Planning from Oxford Brookes University, is a member of the Royal Town Planning Institute, and has a Masters degree in Social Science from Birmingham University. He has worked in local government, and as an academic at Birmingham City University, where he is currently Assistant Director of Estates (planning).

By the same author:

Finding My Place, Book Guild Publishing, 2012

WALKING MY PATCH

Seven More Journeys through Kent and East Sussex

Brian J. Rance

Book Guild Publishing

Sussex, England

First published in Great Britain in 2013 by
The Book Guild Ltd
Pavilion View
19 New Road
Brighton, BN1 1UF

Typesetting in Garamond by
YHT Ltd, London

Printed and bound in Great Britain by
CPI Antony Rowe

A catalogue record for this book is available from
The British Library.

ISBN 978 1 84624 942 6

Contents

Acknowledgement

Once again I am indebted to Allan Buxton and Neil Parfrement. Allan has produced the excellent maps and Neil and I have worked together closely in the design and presentation of the illustrative plates. As before I thank all those people of Kent and East Sussex I have met on my journeys who have provided material for this book. Finally I would like to thank my daughters Jessica and Eleanor for their encouragement, and my partner Wendy for her forbearance and support in this ambitious project.

Introduction

This volume, comprising a further seven marathon walks, together with my first book, completes a project I embarked upon over ten years ago. As I began to walk through Kent and East Sussex, gradually the idea of documenting these walks took hold of me, and now it is finished. I can't help sharing with you that I now feel a great sense of relief.

This volume of walks commenced in 2008 as my endeavour gained pace. As such, it is less retrospective than the first book. In writing about these fourteen walks, I guess I have been like the gypsy scholar in Matthew Arnold's epic poem of the same name, 'nursing his project in unclouded joy', but unlike him, not waiting for 'the spark from heaven to fall'.

The gypsy scholar roamed the area to the north and west of Oxford, in the Cumnor Hills, much as I did when I was a student in that fair city. Latterly, I have felt the need to compose one of my place poems to celebrate the fact.

Oxford
Fondly remembered
Student sojourn
Opened doors to
A life forlorn
Worrying about that which I could not control.

This poem is an example of many dotted throughout both books, which is my attempt to summarise the essence of a place and its meaning to me in a standard, five-line format. I believe this experimental, five-line format is original, and whilst not having the provenance of a seventeen-syllable haiku or a limerick, it consists of four lines in a 5/4/5/4 pattern, the second and fourth rhyming, with a free fifth line at the end. The discerning reader will be able to identify the two occasions, one in each book, when I have indulgently departed from this format.

I have made a conscious effort in this book to widen my area of interest to include more splendid parts of East Sussex, including the East Sussex Weald and Rother Valley. I always seem to be ending up in the many jewelled town of Rye. However, these walks also give a much more comprehensive coverage of the ground in Kent, as the following maps will hopefully demonstrate.

Whilst this is the end of this particular project, I have no doubt that I have further walks in me, even if they are somewhat less driven and not strung together as a route march. I'm sure I will need to walk again and fall prey to the sentiments expressed by W.H. Auden in his domestic lament, in his poem, 'Atlantis': 'All the little household gods have started crying, but say good-bye now, and put to sea.' I thought the god of the ironing board, closely followed by the dishwasher, would complain the most.

After a quick reckoning, I am sure that I have walked over 1,000 miles in completing both volumes. The pure physical challenge of this enterprise has been considerable and my body, after a number of running repairs, is now pretty much worn out. I believe that this aspect has perhaps not come through very strongly, particularly in the first volume. The mental challenge, in common with many endurance activities, has been equally demanding, constantly fighting against the desire to give up, in the face of painful knees and bad weather. With this type of activity it is not possible to choose to walk only on fine days, since one is always trying to reach a pre-booked destination, and it is rare to have more than a few consecutive good days in a typical British summer.

I have tried to provide a deeper understanding of the landscape and its formation but I imagine that landscape archaeologists would cringe at some of my half-baked statements. My only intention here is to inform and popularise the fundamental structures and processes of the landscape, much like science writers seek to popularise the wonders of our world. I am reminded of Pope's seminal poem, 'An Essay on Criticism', which suggests that 'a little learning is a dangerous thing', as follows:

> A little learning is a dang'rous thing
> Drink deep, or taste not the Pierian Spring
> There shallow draughts intoxicate the brain
> And drinking largely sobers us again.

Whilst I can't claim to have come across a Pierian Spring, (the Chalybeate Spring in Tunbridge Wells doesn't quite fit the bill), I have tried to provide background information on: the places visited on my journey, the flora and fauna I have observed, and the beneficial organisations that play a huge part in maintaining the countryside. I also share the sentiments of Woody Guthrie about his homeland America, when he says, 'This land is your land, this land is my land', and I might add, 'from the London suburbs to the Channel waters,' 'This land is meant for you and me'. I have shamelessly plagiarised his song and the results of this enterprise are shown at the end of this book.

I am amazed, given that I am an atheist, how much this and my previous book refer to churches. I guess this can be explained by the immense importance of churches in the landscape and in our social history. Another key ingredient in the traditional village scene is the village pub, and latterly I have become greatly concerned at its demise. In this book I catalogue the rash of pub closures and conversions in the countryside that I have stumbled across in my travels. There is nothing so dispiriting and detrimental to the maintenance of community spirit than a derelict village pub. However, my concern here is essentially with the visual effect of this increasingly common occurrence, and its negative effect on tourism.

I hope that you, the reader, have enjoyed my first book *Finding My Place: Seven Long Distance Walks in Kent and East Sussex*, and will equally enjoy this volume. I am very well aware that readers may not agree with the opinions expressed, or may have further information that could usefully be added to the narrative; if this is so, I invite serious comments via my publisher.

Map showing walks in this book

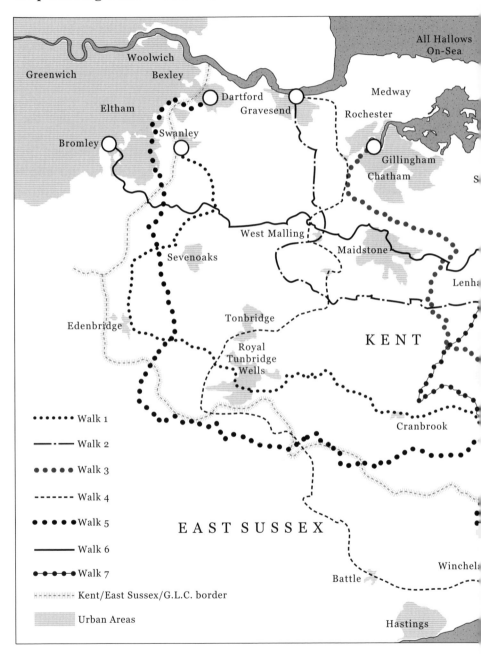

All Hallows
On-Sea

Woolwich
Greenwich
Bexley

Medway

Eltham
Dartford
Gravesend
Rochester

Swanley

Bromley

Gillingham
Chatham

West Malling

Maidstone

Sevenoaks

Lenh

Edenbridge

Tonbridge

KENT

Royal
Tunbridge
Wells

•••••• Walk 1

Cranbrook

—·—· Walk 2

•••• Walk 3

------ Walk 4

•••• Walk 5

EAST SUSSEX

—— Walk 6

•••• Walk 7

Winchel

Kent/East Sussex/G.L.C. border

Battle

Urban Areas

Hastings

x

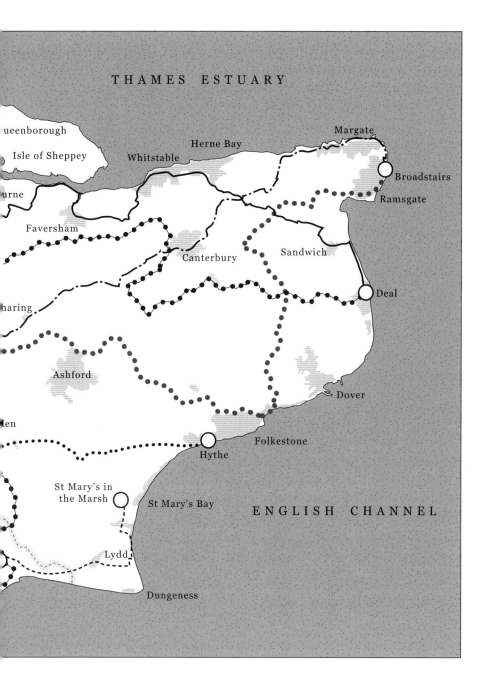

THAMES ESTUARY

ueenborough

Isle of Sheppey

urne

Faversham

haring

Ashford

len

St Mary's in
the Marsh

Lydd

Dungeness

Whitstable

Herne Bay

Margate

Broadstairs

Ramsgate

Canterbury

Sandwich

Deal

Dover

Folkestone

Hythe

St Mary's Bay

ENGLISH CHANNEL

Map showing walks in both books

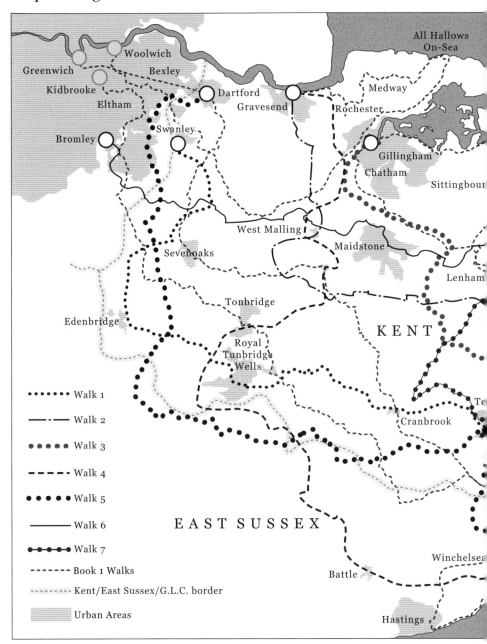

Legend:

- • • • • • • Walk 1
- — · — Walk 2
- • • • • Walk 3
- - - - - Walk 4
- ● ● ● ● Walk 5
- —— Walk 6
- ●–●–●–● Walk 7
- - - - - - Book 1 Walks
- ⊞⊞⊞⊞⊞ Kent/East Sussex/G.L.C. border
- Urban Areas

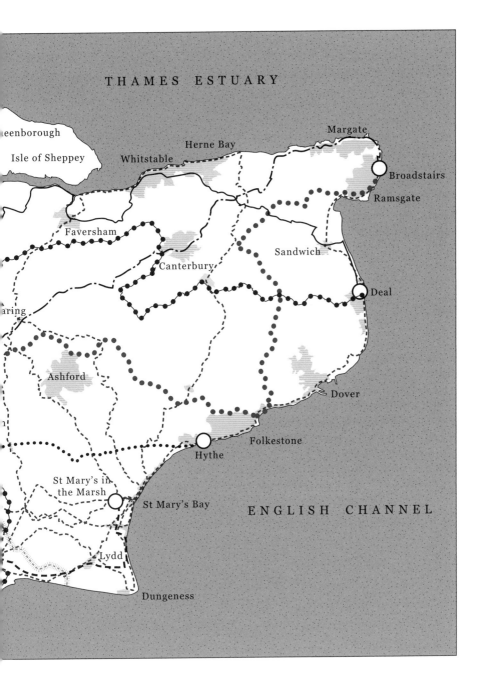

THAMES ESTUARY

eenborough

Isle of Sheppey

Whitstable

Herne Bay

Margate

Broadstairs

Ramsgate

Faversham

Canterbury

Sandwich

Deal

aring

Ashford

Dover

Folkestone

Hythe

St Mary's in
the Marsh

St Mary's Bay

ENGLISH CHANNEL

Lydd

Dungeness

1

Swanley to Hythe (Summer 2009)

At the ripe old age of 59, having more ambition than sense, I embarked on another marathon trek through the Kent countryside, from the London suburbs to the Channel coast. On this occasion I started at Swanley, arriving in that dormitory settlement about mid-morning. There were heavy showers on the way up, and the weather looked most unpromising for the rest of the day.

When I got off the train I made the cardinal error of not noting which way the train had come into the station. As a consequence, I was unable to orientate myself when coming out of the concourse and set off in the wrong direction. I even gave wrong directions to a young, smartly dressed, Asian man who was seeking the town centre. He was obviously a stranger to the place and my guess was that he was going to a job interview; I do hope that I didn't cause him to be late.

Realising my mistake, I had to retrace my steps back towards the station before setting off along the road to Crockenhill. I trudged out through the scruffy outskirts of Swanley to Crockenhill, which consisted of the usual church, pub and houses, and many graveyards. It seemed as though this was a popular place for burials, with relatives from the suburbs choosing to bury their dead in more pleasant surroundings, on the edge of the countryside. There was a stiff climb out of the village, uphill all the way to the bridge over the M25.

When I reached the motorway, after Wested Farm, I donned wet gear against the impending shower blowing up from the west, and carried on down Crockenhill Lane, another example of a narrow lane that had become exceedingly busy. As a consequence, the banks at each side of the lane were damaged and polished smooth by countless tyres, like the ice walls of a bobsleigh run, and I had to be very careful of oncoming traffic flying round blind corners on the way down to Eynsford.

While striding down the lane there were impressive views to the south, across the valley of the River Darent and, on balance, I was pleased to be out again, walking in the countryside. Soon I reached Sharepenny Lane, the small road to the west of the river from Farningham, which I had trod before. That time I walked on past Lullingstone to Shoreham, but today I turned east through the village alongside the River Darent.

Eynsford is a pretty little village with its river and ford leading to the church. Alongside the wide river is a strip of open space that is used extensively for families picnicking at the weekend. Indeed, when I drove down on the previous Sunday, the place was crowded with people sitting by and wading in the shallow, pebble-dressed river. I crossed over the bridge with its contiguous ford and paused in the lych gate of the fine church on the main A225 to Sevenoaks. To the south of the church, just down the main road, was the previously referred to, and fondly remembered, Malt Shovel pub. But it had now met an unfortunate fate; it had been converted into a gastro pub.

The newer, residential part of Eynsford also lay to the south, strung out towards the railway station along the road to Otford. To the north, down by the river, on the Farningham road, is the exceptional Eynsford Castle, one of the most complete Norman castles in the country, which is looked after by English Heritage. I remember cycling out from Welling with my old school friend, to visit the castle on one of our first bike rides.

My way lay to the north of the church, where I picked up Bower Lane, and there was a stiff climb out of the valley past Polyhaugh Farm. It is nearly 3 miles from Eynsford to Romney Street, my next target. It was a hard slog up the long dip slope of the North Downs, rising from about 30 feet at Eynsford to 180 feet at Romney Street. For most of the time the lane was hollow, deeply incised below banks and hedges with very little to see out. I'm not complaining because I find hedgerows fascinating. Just looking at the fauna and observing and naming the variety of plant species is rewarding in itself. However, I couldn't help comparing this lane with the adjacent lane to the east, going down into Knatt's Valley. That was a superb walk with a wonderful sense of the valley closing in. Here, I was walking on the ridge which should have afforded wonderful views but I was hemmed in by the hedge for the most part.

I mused on the thought that what sometimes appears to be a good route on the map doesn't always live up to expectations. However, the converse is really rewarding when an unpromising route turns out to be surprisingly good. Later, looking at the Ordnance Survey map again, I

Swanley to Romney Street

[Map showing Swanley, A20, Crockenhill, M25, R.DARENT, Castle, Eynsford, North Downs, Airfield, Romney Street, 210M]

History of Bar Billiards

The origins of the game are unknown, but its similarity with Bagatelle, a game that was popular in the eighteenth century, suggests that it may be derived from this game. During the 1930s bar billiard tables were manufactured for the first time, and pubs seemed keen to buy tables due to their economical use of space.

Eynsford

Is a picturesque village on the River Darent with a crossing consisting of a ford and an attractive humpback bridge. There are many old buildings including the Plough Inn by the river, the Old Mill and the church dedicated to St Martin. In about 1163, Thomas Becket is reputed to have excommunicated William de Eynsford, the owner of Eynsford Castle. The action was cancelled by King Henry II and the issue became part of the quarrel that led to Becket's murder in 1170. Eynsford Castle, on the north eastern edge of the village, dating from 1088, is one of the most complete Norman castles in England. Ransacked in the fourteenth century, it fell into decay and is now in the care of English Heritage and open to the public.

Eynsford village

The first pub league was established in Oxford in 1936, but shortly afterwards another influential league was established in Canterbury. Before the Second World War there was apparently an organisation called the National Bar Billiards Association, and the now defunct Canterbury league team won its challenge cup, beating the team from Oxford, just before the war. The All England Bar Billiards Association now supervises the game across eighteen counties, mainly in the south of England.

Bar billiards

1

noticed a parallel footpath to the west, which might have been a better option, but it would have been slower going. Sometimes, when pushing the body to walk longer distances, one has to forgo interesting local footpaths and stick to the direct hard surface where one can make better time.

As I was walking up the slope to Romney Street, I kept seeing small fragments of metal glinting in the surface of the road. It was as though the original surface of the road had worn off, and well it might have, for the metal showing through was the evidence of a 'metalled' surface. I realised then that a metalled road contained pieces of metal, and the evidence was under my feet.

I carried on up to Romney Street, past the flat top that was still used as an airfield, to the Fox and Hounds public house. I reflected on the probability that this airfield would have been a hive of activity during the Battle of Britain, which was fought in the skies above. I repaired in the pub, an entirely satisfactory experience, and struck up an immediate rapport with the landlady. It came to light that she had lived in Welling, just like me, and had gone to the same Bexley Grammar school. This part of Kent is full of exiles from the south and south-east suburbs of London. The landlady volunteered the information that many walkers passed this way, being quite close to The North Downs Way. Also, one of the highest points in Kent, at over 210 feet, was just down the road.

I left the pub after a decent interval and carried on along the lanes, up to this high point. Romney Street was nothing more than a pub, a few cottages and a small mobile home park. I was tempted to take local footpaths through Magpie Bottom but thought better of it, since this route seemed to push me more down to Shoreham and I wanted to get to Otford. As I was hiking along the lane, a lady motorist with a Maltese accent stopped and offered me a lift into Otford. I declined, explaining that if I were to accept a lift it would be tantamount to cheating. It is ever thus, on these occasions, but I have often wondered what might happen if one day I was tempted, and accepted the proffered lift.

I walked on to the point where The North Downs Way joins from the right, and where the footpath issues out across Otford Mount. This was a pleasant walk and it made an agreeable change to be off a hard surface. I anticipated fabulous views from Otford Mount but was largely disappointed, since the vegetation had grown up unchecked and largely obscured any views. Some sterling efforts had been made to clear the shrubbery at the top of the scarp slope to provide viewing points by some strategically placed benches, but the overall effect, in the absence of any grazing animals, was of the whole area reverting to its climax vegetation of deciduous woodland. I only caught glimpses of that curious paperclip-shaped housing development shown on the map, set back into the hillside to the north of Otford Mount.

I careered off the mount down into Otford and rested on a welcome bench at the bottom of the hill, on a green patch by the side of the main Sevenoaks Road. I was feeling pretty rough. I was struggling with the effort of the first day's walk at this point, and beginning to suffer with a burgeoning head cold. I had deliberately walked somewhat less on the first day, just to give a chance to get my legs in gear. I knew from previous experience that later on in the week, my legs would get used to walking longer distances. But sitting on this bench it did cross my mind that I might be too old to undertake this marathon. One day, I thought, hopefully in the distant future, I would have to admit to myself that enough is enough and hang up my boots for good. All that remained was for me to walk down into Otford, take a quick look at the disappointing duck pond graced by a couple of moorhens, and seek out my bed and breakfast accommodation. In the evening I met some old friends in the historic Crown Inn and we talked over old times, including the visits to the Malt Shovel in Eynsford, referred to earlier.

Romney Street to Chipstead

Chipstead

Is a small, attractive village in the parish of Chevening, nestling below the North Downs, and located on the headwaters of the River Darent, which is rapidly becoming part of the north western suburbs of Sevenoaks. The village has two public houses: the George and Dragon, a sixteenth-century coaching inn on the High Street, and the Bricklayers Arms on Chevening road, opposite Chipstead (or Longford) Lake. The 74-acre lake is man-made, the result of extensive gravel extraction during the twentieth century.

Lavender
(Lavandula angustifolia)

The common lavender, which is also known as true lavender, narrow-leaved lavender or English lavender, is native to the western Mediterranean region. It is a strongly aromatic, evergreen flowering plant growing up to 2 metres tall. It is commonly grown as an ornamental plant and tolerant of dry conditions. The leaves and flowers are used as a culinary herb and produce essential oil which has extensive medical and cosmetic value.

Otford

Darent under Downs

Duck pond chalice

In the valley's throat

Ruined palace

Once as grand as Hampton Court.

Otford Palace

The Archbishop's palace was one of the chain of houses belonging to the Archbishop of Canterbury. It was rebuilt around 1515 by Archbishop Wareham to rival that of Wolsey at Hampton Court. Henry VIII forced Archbishop Thomas Cranmer to surrender the palace in 1537. When Henry died the palace fell into ruin and the principal surviving remains are the North-West Tower, the lower gallery, now converted to cottages, and a part of the Great Gatehouse. The entire site of about four acres is designated as an ancient monument.

The ruins of Otford Palace

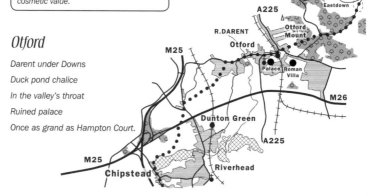

2

The next morning, after posting my box, containing dirty clothes, back home I strolled through the grounds of the ruined Otford Palace, astonished at the one-time importance of this crumbling edifice, once rivalling Hampton Court. I carried on, back into the centre of the village, along a track that would have been the main approach to the palace, and noted that parts of the ruins had been converted into a row of comfortable cottages. Passing out of Otford, down the High Street and across the River Darent, bathed in sunshine, I noted that a large part of the straggly village lies to the west of the river, away from the historic part.

Climbing out of the valley, I picked up the Darent Valley Path. I had already completed the Dartford to Dunton Green section of this long-distance footpath on a previous journey, but today I was going to the headwaters of the river. I strode on through fields dedicated to lavender, crossed over the railway and on up to the top of the unnamed hill of 109 feet. From the top of the hill, a much denuded outlier of the North Downs, I took the time to gaze around. I could see what we used to call Polhill and the chalk scarp with its massive chalk quarry quite clearly. The roads in this vicinity had been drastically reshaped after the construction of the M25, and I could clearly hear the hum of nearby motorways, but still the grand prospect was pleasing. I descended to Dunton Green or at least that part north of the M26, since the motorway cuts the village in two. Still following the designated path I passed under the motorway and across a dismantled railway line to arrive on the shores of the large lake, between Riverhead and Chipstead, called variously Chipstead or Long-ford Lake. The land about here was largely uncultivated; I couldn't work out whether it was in fact unfarmed or whether it was just being rested, but as in all such places, it was quickly being colonised by plants, and the birds and butterflies were returning.

I skirted the massive lake, which presumably was created by gravel extraction or the like, an integral part of the headwaters of the River Darent, fed by streams leading west, all the way back to Westerham. As I came up into Chipstead I passed by the back of a school and the noise from the playground sounded like a flock of scolded seagulls on a council rubbish tip.

At the head of the lake, I was surprised by the neat, linear village of Chipstead. This was a place I had not been to before, and this quiet backwater on the road to Chevening was delightful. I guess, in times gone by, before the construction of the motorways hereabouts and the

Chipstead to Westerham

The Life and Times of General Wolfe

Major General James P. Wolfe (1727–1759) was a British army officer, born in Westerham, and known for his training reforms but remembered chiefly for his victory over the French in Canada. He had received his first commission at a young age and saw extensive service in Europe where he fought during the War of the Austrian Succession. His service in Flanders and Scotland, where he took part in the suppression of the Jacobite Rebellion, brought him to the attention of his superiors. The advancement of his career was halted by the Peace Treaty of 1748, and he spent much of the next eight years in garrison duty in the Scottish Highlands.

The outbreak of the Seven Years' War in 1756 offered Wolfe fresh opportunities for advancement. His part in the aborted attack on Rochefort in 1757 led William Pitt to appoint him second-in-command of an expedition to capture Louisbourg. Following the success of this operation he was made commander of a force designated to sail up the Saint Lawrence River to capture Quebec. After a lengthy siege he defeated the French force under Montcalm allowing British forces to capture the city by scaling the Heights of Abraham.

Wolfe was killed at the height of the battle by a French cannon shot. His part in the taking of Quebec in 1759 earned him posthumous fame and he became an icon of Britain's victory in the Seven Years' War and subsequent territorial expansion. With the fall of Quebec, French rule in North America, outside Louisiana and the tiny islands of St Pierre and Miquelon, came to an end.

Quebec House, Westerham

Quebec House

Was the family home in Westerham of the Wolfe family where General James P. Wolfe was born on the 2nd January 1727, and lived for eleven years before the family moved to Greenwich. The house is now a grade I listed building owned by the National Trust and has been restored to appear much as it did when the Wolfes lived there. The adjacent coach house contains an exhibition concerned with the Battle of Quebec in 1759.

Brasted High Street

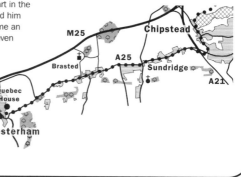

consequent disruption to the local road network, the village would have been more at the centre of things on route to Chevening Park. Now it is largely passed by, a pretty settlement on the north-western outskirts of Sevenoaks.

From Chipstead, I carried on to the west of Bessels Green before crossing over the busy junction with the A21 and slogging along the A25, past the turning to Dry Hill, to Sundridge. Along this stretch, the river ran through a marshy swamp just to the north, beside the road. I was thinking that this patch of land with the youthful river could be tamed to make a fashionable, accessible watery wildlife area. I sat on a seat in the centre of Sundridge, by the war memorial, and rested for a while in the burning sun.

Striding along the road to Brasted, I was conscious that the day seemed to be overheating and as I approached the village, a magnificent thunderstorm was brewing up in the west. As the heavens opened, I dived into the first pub to avoid the deluge. The first lightning strike was right overhead, taking out the power, and the pub was thrown into darkness. Some of the customers were unhappy about the fact that lunch was off, seeking to cast blame on somebody for the inconvenience caused, suggesting it was unreasonable that the pub did not have a backup generator. As far as I know, nobody resorted, in their desperation, to bothering the Almighty about this event.

When the rain eased up I made a dash for Westerham. I had intended to pick up the footpath to Westerham lying to the north of the A25 but it was not clearly marked on the ground and I felt disinclined to search for it. If the footpath was poorly used it would be overgrown and I would have got soaking wet from brushing through, so I slogged along the main road instead. I came into Westerham via the church, by the elegant Quebec House, and arrived at the back of the sloping village green that houses the recumbent statue of Winston Churchill, a local lad who lived nearby at Chartwell. The distinctive, triangular green was also graced by a second, older statue: that of General Wolfe, who was a central player in the Seven Years' War with France over territories in North America and fought a famous battle at the Heights of Abraham in Quebec. Nearby Quebec House, his boyhood home, was open to the public and I thought I would visit one day.

In Westerham, the weather gave a repeat performance and I duly dived into The George and Dragon. I decided I would have something to eat

9

and wanted to sit at the bar and have a bar snack, but this offended house rules. A waiter ushered me to a small round table in an out of the way corner and as I didn't want a full meal, just to be awkward, I ordered a soup and roll, which of course, with all its accessories, was quite adequate. The poor foreign waiter had great difficulty comprehending my simple requirements, but got his own back with the palaver of the bill. He feigned ignorance when I asked for 'l'addition, s'il vous plait, monsieur,' and got his revenge by not allowing me to pay at the bar. He made me sit in my allotted seat until he was ready to bring me the bill, casually strolling over, after engaging other groups in extended conversation on the way to me. His demeanour reminded me of that exhibited by the waiter Manuel, played by Andrew Sachs, a character from the television programme *Fawlty Towers.*

When the elements settled down again I set out for Crockham Hill on the Greensand Ridge, blind, for I had run out of map, thinking I knew the way by heart. Just out of Westerham I sought advice about the best way to get to Crockham Hill from two women with four black dogs, who pointed me in the right direction. Shortly afterwards, to confirm the way, I asked directions of a bloke, modestly with only one dog, and proceeded hopefully on my way. I carried on up the valley and observed this kind gentleman walking beside woods, way over to my right. At a confusing gaggle of signposts, I selected what I thought was the right track and carried on along it for 100 yards or so. I was startled by the chap, with his dog, running up behind me to tell me I had taken the wrong path. I couldn't believe that he had run across the valley just to tell me that if I proceeded on this path it would take me to Chartwell. After this overly athletic and kind intervention I regained my desired route.

I climbed up through a valley given over to rough pasture, through the parkland associated with Squerryes Court and passed a dead tree that looked as though it had been sculpted into the shape of a birds head. I took a photograph. It was so striking that I'm sure it must have been well known locally, and it might even have had a name; maybe it was not entirely a work of nature. It was a pleasant walk up into the woods on top of the hill, that is, until it decided to rain again. Having judiciously avoided two downpours, this time, I knew I was going to get soaking wet as there was no shelter for some way. I went over the top of the ridge and picked up the B269 road, before diving down into the village of Crockham Hill. I'm afraid to say that in my wet and bedraggled state, the obvious charms of the place were lost on me and I pushed on, head down, along the long road to Marlpit Hill and Edenbridge.

After a rest and a change of clothes, I had a look around Edenbridge. For the most part, the buildings in the High Street, and the street scene generally, were of high quality. The inner ring-road, named Mont Saint Aignan Way, takes traffic out of the High Street and gives the opportunity for partial pedestrianisation and environmental improvement. I'm not sure of the French connection with this road name, but it did strike me as somewhat clumsy and out of place; it is probably the result of some town twinning folly. The ring-road also avoids traffic squeezing through the narrow gap by the Old Crown Inn. The road at this point is spanned by one of those elaborate, wrought-iron inn signs. However, the lower part of the High Street towards the river is diminished by disconnected buildings, punctuated by access ways to derelict yards, which back onto the massive retail development surrounded by a sea of car parking off the ring-road. Also, there is an appalling 1960s, flat-roof, concrete development adjacent to the Old Crown, opposite the attractive Church Street, which seriously detracts from the scene. If ever there was a candidate for the worst building in the town this would be it. Someone should seriously consider demolishing it and replacing it with a better-designed complex.

11

Westerham to Edenbridge

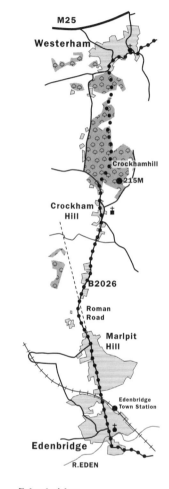

M25

Westerham

Crockhamhill

215M

Crockham
Hill

B2026

Roman
Road

Marlpit
Hill

Edenbridge
Town Station

Edenbridge

R.EDEN

Westerham

Is a small town in the shadow of the North Downs lying on the headwaters of the river Darent. The town is mentioned in the Domesday Book, but there is evidence that the area around has been settled for thousands of years. By 1227 Henry III granted the town a market charter, making the new village a major player in the buying and selling of cattle in Kent, a tradition that survived to 1961 when the last cattle market was held. The Warde family have lived at nearby Squerryes Court since 1731, and their home has become a tourist attraction. General James Wolfe was born in the town in 1727 and lived in Quebec House. His statue adorns the Town Square in front of the church, where more recently a statue to Sir Winston Churchill has been erected. In 1922 Winston Churchill MP purchased Chartwell Manor on the outskirts of the town, which was his home for the rest of his life. Chartwell is now administered by the National Trust.

Westerham town square

Sir Winston Churchill, Westerham

Edenbridge

I cycled here from
Suburban Kent
Loved the high street then
Now, faded, spent
By-passed and badly neglected.

4

Indeed, the whole lower High Street area, from the High Street to the ring-road, including the environs of the large supermarket, urgently need the attention of a good urban designer and investment in a new development programme. This achieved, Edenbridge could become a very attractive place. As it stands, it is a job half done. It is perfectly possible to blend old and new buildings and attractive, functional public spaces in a comprehensive scheme, but it needs vision. A scheme that removes ugly buildings, provides good links between the old High Street and the supermarket, contains the sea of car parking around the supermarket, rationalises existing servicing arrangements for the supermarket, redevelops the redundant spaces off the High Street and maximises the use of the river frontage for public recreation would be very welcome. I wondered whether the local planning authority had any such plans for this area.

After an extravagant meal of fish and chips in the buildings just castigated, I returned to The Star Inn, where I spent a pleasant evening. I was even tempted to perform on the pool table, an experience that was rendered unique by the crazy antics of the resident pub dog; a sheep dog that insisted on chasing the balls around the table as though he were rounding them up.

In the morning I left Edenbridge in the rain, found the road to Hever and morosely trudged on, passing eastwards through the verdant valley of the River Eden. Hever is an attractive little village consisting of a pub, church and a car park for visitors to the historic castle down the road, the home of the Boleyn family in Tudor times. Even at this relatively early hour there were many foreign tourists preparing to immerse themselves in English history. I amused myself by wishing them all good morning in a hearty English way while trying to guess their nationality by their response.

I passed through the churchyard and picked up the Eden Valley Walk, which took me all the way to Hill Hoath, through delightful, pleasantly wooded countryside. I took off my wet gear as the day began to warm up. After Hill Hoath, I left the main footpath and made for Weller's Town with the elegant spire of Chiddingstone Church dancing above the hedgerows to the north. I realised that I had lost the background hum of traffic noise, maybe for the first time. After Weller's Town, I cut across the fields to a track high up on the ridge beyond Wat Stock, which brought me back on the designated walk.

While leaning on a gate, admiring the stunning view down the Eden Valley, I fell into conversation with a fellow walker who came up behind me from Wat Stock. We walked on together, comparing notes all the time, down into Penshurst, a village dominated by another significant, historical stately home. My new companion and I had a couple of pints in the Leicester Arms, located directly opposite the church and Penshurst Place. We had many similar interests and got on famously, and like Stanley and Livingstone at Ujiji, we considered ourselves well met. We discussed the discipline needed in retirement, writing, poetry, golf and Betjeman (not many people would have been familiar with Betjeman's poems). We could have stayed in the pub all afternoon, but reluctantly we concluded that we had to move on and go our separate ways, like the aforementioned explorers, never to meet again.

Coming out of Penshurst I crossed over the River Medway, recently joined by the River Eden, and strode up the hill along the B2176, before taking the lane south to Speldhurst. I was kicking myself later when I checked the map more thoroughly because I could have taken the lower and no doubt more pleasant track, via Old Swaylands, avoiding a 75-foot climb up and down the bluff in a big bend of the river. I came down to the hamlet of Poundsbridge and climbed steeply again to the village of

Edenbridge to Penshurst

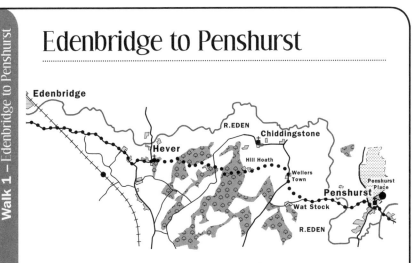

Edenbridge

Is a town near the Surrey border on the upper floodplain of the River Medway, which derives its name from the River Eden, a major tributary. The old part of the town grew up along a section of a disused London to Lewes Roman road at a point where it crosses the river. In the Middle Ages it became a centre of the wealden iron industry, and there are many medieval timber buildings in the town, one of which houses the Eden Valley Museum. With the coming of the railway the town expanded, swallowing the original separate settlement of Marlpit Hill to the north. Edenbridge is twinned with Mont-Saint-Aignan in France, and a by-pass of the same name was built in the twenty-first century to relieve traffic pressure on the old, narrow High Street.

Penshurst

Is a village consisting of an attractive group of buildings at the confluence of the Medway River and its major tributary, the River Eden, that grew up around the stately home of Penshurst Place, the historical home of the Sidney family. There are many Tudor-looking buildings in the village, although some are Victorian in age. The evocative Leicester Arms, once part of the Penshurst Estate, was owned by Sir William Sidney, grandfather of the poet and statesman Sir Philip Sidney. His other grandson, the Viscount De L'isle, was appointed Earl of Leicester in 1618, and it was shortly after that The Leicester Arms, formerly known as The Porcupine, was renamed in his honour. The Inn is now a privately owned free house.

Edenbridge High Street

Penshurst village

Speldhurst. The terrain on this stretch was, not surprisingly, quite hilly as I had reached the Weald with its many places ending in 'hurst', denoting the top of a hill. But I thought that Speldhurst was disappointing and lacked presence as a place. I ate lunch in the George and Dragon, a gastro pub opposite the church. The ploughman's lunch I ordered was expensive and served up pretentiously on a block of wood, but it was very good despite that.

From Speldhurst there was another stiff climb along the lane up to Rusthall, a distinct settlement with its own common on the outskirts of Tunbridge Wells. I skirted the edge of Rustall Common, making a short detour to observe the distinctive Toad Rock, a popular tourist attraction in Victorian times. After a short stretch along the A264, I strolled across the more extensive Tunbridge Wells Common, which reminded me of Chislehurst Common. They had the same management problems; reverting to woodland due to the lack of grazing by 'commoners' exercising their ancient rights and privileges. I passed another of the distinctive rock outcrops that adorn these commons, viewed across a well-tended cricket ground. These rock outcrops consist of Ardingly Sandstone, a variety of Tunbridge Wells sand containing small pebbles. They were originally laid down in the Lower Cretaceous period, around 136 million years ago, as deposits from a vast freshwater lake covering much of southern Britain. These are some of the oldest rocks in the Weald and formed the lowest strata of the Wealden anticline, which has since been eroded and exposed on the surface as it is today.

It was a pleasant stroll across the common to the adjacent Pantiles, the historic heart of Tunbridge Wells, to check into the Swan Hotel where I was to spend the night. In the evening, out and about in the Pantiles, I paid due respect to the slightly grubby, iron-stained, Chalybeate Spring, the reason for the town's existence. It occurred to me that Tunbridge Wells, with a population of 56,000, according to the mid-year estimate in 2006, was one of the few large towns in Kent that did not have a significant river, although the River Teise does rise in its eastern suburbs.

I was treated to an open-air play performed by the local amateur dramatics society. I didn't have a clue what the play was about but I enjoyed the spectacle, which contributed to a lively, cultured street atmosphere. I got talking to a chap in a bar about my project, suggesting that it should not be about my experiences of walking and about how difficult it was to pitch this narrative. He maintained that I should not

Penshurst to Royal Tunbridge Wells

Rusthall and Toad Rock

Rusthall is a modern village, largely built after the trains arrived in Tunbridge Wells during the mid-1800s. It was created as a tourist spot, with visitors coming up from the station in charabancs to see the 'Toad Rock' on the common to the east of the village. Toad Rock is a natural rock formation which looks like a sitting toad, standing on an outcrop of sandstone. Other outcrops of sandstone can be seen throughout the Tunbridge Wells and Rusthall Common areas. The village has two centres; the first near to the Toad Rock, which is really an old Victorian resort, and the second main shopping area further to the west, which is slowly, along with the neighbouring village of Langton Green, being absorbed into the large urban area that is Tunbridge Wells.

Tunbridge Wells and Rusthall Commons

Consist of 250 acres of woods and heathland which abut Tunbridge Wells town centre and the village of Rusthall. The commons are owned by the Manor of Rusthall (the title is now held by Targetfollow (Pantiles) Ltd.), and managed by the Commons Conservators in accordance with the County of Kent Act 1981, and is funded by the Borough Council. Originally a lowland heath, much of the area has reverted to dense woodland due to the absence of grazing animals. The current management plan seeks to open up parts of the commons and regain more of the heathland habitat.

Toad Rock

The Weald

Eroded hub of

An anticline

A French connection

In long past time

Now showing up in sandstone outcrops.

water it down by taking out all the personal bits, because he felt it would become just another limited, boring guide book. I have taken considerable comfort from this conversation and was greatly encouraged to stick to my guns.

The next morning, after a detour to the south-western suburbs of Tunbridge Wells to find a post office to offload my box, I managed to find the High Weald Landscape Trail out of the town to the east. I walked through elegant suburbs to Camden Park, and out to Hawkenbury on the edge of town. Settling into the day's walk, I followed the path along the high ridge, past Little Bayhall, all the way to Pembury. This was a pleasant stroll in the morning sunshine with impressive views out across the undulating contours of the Weald, nurturing the headwaters of the River Teise.

I had another look at Pembury, just to give it another chance to impress, but unfortunately it failed again. Maybe this was because the hard walk up to the village, crossing the A21, had left me damp and it was not warm enough to compensate; Pembury sent a chill through my body, just like the last time I was here. There was the imposing inn of course, and a church by the triangular green, but very few useful shops in the centre. Indeed, the general store/post office is further down the hill going east. I left via Henwood Green, which would have been a separate hamlet once, and walked on through the lanes to the north of the dreaded A21, a road to be avoided at all costs.

There was an awkward stretch north, along the busy B2160 south of Matfield, before picking up lanes to the right, through the hamlet of Kingsmead. I stopped to ask a man who was struggling with a gate padlock whether there was still a pub at Petteridge, and he answered enthusiastically in the affirmative, so I headed that way. Petteridge was a curious mixture; there were some vital, affordable council houses for the rural workforce and some quaint cottages towards and around the pub. I went in the Hop Bine pub for lunch, but found it hard to settle there. At first I went outside and sat on a seat hard against the lane. There was a group of locals already seated who made no effort to make me welcome. I went back inside and sat at the bar feeling damp and cold. The middle-aged barmaid, struggling to control an ample bosom, seemed more interested in strutting around on high heels, and making herself busy moving glasses around, than striking up a civil conversation with a weary traveller.

Royal Tunbridge Wells to Petteridge

Royal Tunbridge Wells

Is situated at the northern edge of the High Weald in Kent, hard up against the East Sussex border, and is the source of the River Teise. The town came into being as a spa in Georgian times, and had its heyday as a tourist resort under the patronage of Richard (Beau) Nash when the Pantiles and its chalybeate spring attracted visitors who wished to take the waters. The popularity of this activity waned with the advent of sea bathing, but the town still remains a popular tourist attraction. This significant town has a population of 56,500 at the last census, and has the reputation of an archetypal conservative 'middle England' town, a stereotype that is typified by the fictional letter-writer 'Disgusted of Tunbridge Wells'.

Chalybeate Spring in the Pantiles, Royal Tunbridge Wells

High Weald Landscape Trail

Is a 90-mile footpath running between Horsham, West Sussex, through parts of Kent, to Rye, East Sussex, designed to pass through the main landscape areas of the High Weald Area of Outstanding Natural Beauty, but it also traverses the area known as the Low Weald in the east. This footpath is not a National Trail within the meaning of the National Parks and Access to the Countryside Act 1949, but a trail of regional importance.

The Pantiles, Royal Tunbridge Wells

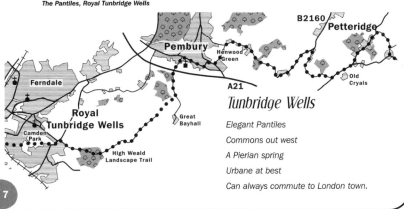

Tunbridge Wells

Elegant Pantiles

Commons out west

A Pierian spring

Urbane at best

Can always commute to London town.

7

Leaving the pub, somewhat disgruntled, I made my way by back lanes to Tibb's Court, Brattles Grange and Marle Place, a satisfying walk with sharp little rises in the northern foothills of the Weald. This whole area around the villages of Matfield, Brenchley and Horsmonden is given over to orchards and hop fields. At Marle Place there was a garden which was open to the public. Bathed in sunshine, for a fleeting moment I rested against the garden's brick wall, grateful to soak up its warmth across my damp back.

Further down the lane, which also doubled up as a cycle route, I crossed another north-east/south-west, former drove road, the B2162. I carried on along the cycle route to Rectory Park, but never came across a cyclist. The grand rectory in question was associated with Horsmonden Church, which was at least a mile from the current settlement of the same name to the north. There clearly is a story to tell here; one assumes that the village and church are within the same parish but the arrangement needs investigating. Normally, in these circumstances, the original settlement would have been by the church, but for some reason the village has been abandoned and migrated to another position. One factor which is often suggested to be the cause of this is the massive depopulation occurring in the Middle Ages from the ravages of the Black Death in 1348, and successive plagues.

I carried on down Smallbridge Lane into the broad valley of the River Teise. I had to avoid, on a number of occasions, the ample proportions of flying 4x4s, driven by women collecting kids from school. I crossed over the river, one of the main tributaries of the Medway, and observed the impressive prospect of Goudhurst perched on its hill, getting ever closer. I prepared myself for the final stiff climb of about 100 feet up into the village. Arriving in the centre of the village, I sojourned for a while by the large duck pond. By the inaccessible side of the pond, floating mats had been strung across the water to encourage the wildfowl. I identified a number of common ducks including moorhens and coots. I then ambled up the quaint High Street, with a mixture of attractive shops and houses, and sought out the splendid Star and Eagle Hotel below the church.

After resting for a while, I sat out in the beer garden, which afforded fantastic views south over the Weald. I was writing up the day's events, when I was joined again by the same friends I had met a few days before. We carried on where we had left off in Otford, talking over old times.

Petteridge to Goudhurst

Goudhurst

Is an ancient village at the end of a ridge of over 100 feet on the northern foothills of the Low Weald, with a large distinctive village pond and attractive High Street. The place name of Goudhurst is derived from the Old English *guo hyrst*, meaning battle hill, commemorating a battle fought on this high ground in Saxon times. The ancient church probably existed before 1119, its earliest recorded date, and has been altered and rebuilt many times. The battle of Goudhurst in 1747 led to the demise of the infamous Hawkhurst Gang of smugglers. Today this pleasant village is dogged by traffic problems in its narrow streets on the route of the increasingly busy A262 road from the A21 to Tenterden.

Goudhurst High Street

Moorhen
(*Gallinula chloropus*)

Is a common, medium-sized, ground dwelling bird that is usually found near water. From a distance it looks black with a ragged line along its body. Up close it is olive-brown on the back and the head and underparts are blue-grey. It has a red bill with a yellow tip and breeds in lowland areas in the UK.

The River Teise

Is a major tributary of the River Medway originating in Dunorlan Park in Tunbridge Wells. It flows eastwards past Bayham Abbey, and then through Lamberhurst, being joined soon after by the small River Bewl, on which the reservoir Bewl Water is built. Thereafter, downstream from Marden, it unusually bifurcates, passing either side of a low ridge; the Lesser Teise to the east joining the River Beult south of Hunton, and the Greater Teise to the west, joining the River Medway at Twyford Bridge. Like many other rivers in southern England the river was subject to a Land Drainage Improvement Scheme in the 1950s. The Lesser Teise was widened, straightened and deepened and now carries the majority of the flow of the river. While this work effectively drained the land, it has impoverished the ecology of the river and led to a loss of flood plain habitat.

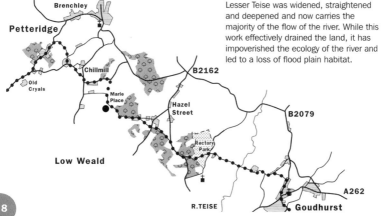

After a pleasant meal and a few drinks, my friends returned home. I had a few more at the bar before retiring to bed.

I left Goudhurst feeling fit and well, and picked up the High Weald Landscape Trail to the south of the village. I came down into a shallow valley, containing a tributary of the River Teise. I then climbed back up along a well-marked footpath to a prominent ridge that took me all the way to Glassenbury. It was a lovely walk along the ridge and I passed many natural ponds inhabited by a multitude of different kinds of ducks. As I progressed along the track I drove flocks of quail in front of me. They would scamper along the track before finding a place to dive for cover. Occasionally, I would pass a pond that was completely dead, covered with a stinking weed and devoid of life. Maybe, if this was a spring line, these unfortunate ponds were not well served, missing the life-giving water welling up from below.

I crossed over the B2085 below Glassenbury, another one of the sumptuous historical houses littered around the Kent countryside, and on through Angley Wood. It occurred to me that this wood, like most of the patches of woodland in these parts, including Hemsted Forest further east, would once have been part of the vast and impenetrable Forest of Anderida, which covered the Weald in Roman times, and supplied one of the vital raw materials for the growth of the Wealden iron making industry.

Passing through the wood, I came to the bottom end of Cranbrook, the so-called capital of the Weald. Although I had probably been there half a dozen times before, the charming town was never a disappointment. I strolled along the High Street, with its raised pavement, and bought some cherries. I then sat on the seat at the bend in the road by the Town Hall, where I traditionally contemplated my life. I shared my cherries with a young woman who sat on the seat next to me, a shop worker who had popped out for a smoking break, and I resisted the temptation to berate her about her disgusting habit.

At this point I had a big decision to make; should I take the longer and no doubt more enjoyable route, along the High Weald Landscape Trail to Tenterden via Benenden, Rolvenden and Rolvenden Layne, or should I take the straight route north of Hemsted Forest? I chose the second option, and it proved to be a bad decision, as I was forced to slog along a fairly featureless road, on through Golford, continually assailed by local traffic. I passed the northern entrance to Hemsted Forest and observed

Goudhurst to Cranbrook

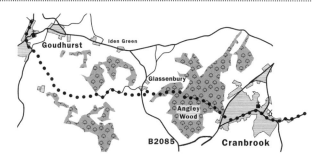

The Forest of Anderida

Through Roman times, the Dark Ages and right up to the Norman Conquest a vast, dense, impenetrable, sparsely populated oak woodland covered the Weald. It extended for 30 miles between the North and South Downs, and 90 miles from east to west between Kent and Hampshire. In Saxon times it was known as Andredes Weald, meaning 'the forest of Andred', derived from the name of the Roman fort at Pevensey, that is, Anderida. The oak woodlands scattered throughout the Kent and Sussex Wealds are the remnants of this great forest, as indeed is Ashdown Forest. During historical times the forest was opened up by farmers driving their livestock from the chalk hills to the north and south into the Weald for summer pasture, creating clearings in the forest, called dens, which now is a common place name. These forests formed one of the essential ingredients for the development of the Wealden iron industry.

Cranbrook High Street

Coot
(Fulica atra)

Is an all black duck, larger than its cousin, the moorhen, with a distinctive white beak and 'shield' above the beak which earns it the title 'bald as a coot'. It is a common bird of lakes, rivers and ponds when deep enough. It patters noisily over the water before taking off, and can be very aggressive towards other ducks.

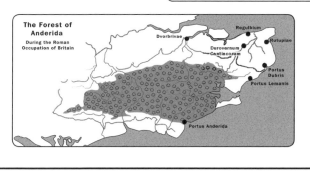

The Forest of Anderida
During the Roman Occupation of Britain

9

the avenue of mature pine trees planted in 1941, ushering the track south through the forest.

When I reached Clapper Hill, the promise of a rest in a pub did not materialise as it was out of action, another example of the rash of closures affecting this wonderful institution. I had little choice but to carry on and as a consequence, I arrived in Tenterden early, after a long, hard, continuous trek of about eight miles from Cranbrook. After Clapper Hill, I had passed from the watershed of the River Medway into that of the Rother, and I came into Tenterden at its lower end, across the Kent & East Sussex Light Railway, a mecca for steam train enthusiasts.

Naturally, I called into the first pub I came to, but I felt as if I was intruding in some private world, with two punters mutually flirting with a buxom barmaid in the intimate, tactile activity of playing a quiz machine. After eventually managing to attract attention and get served, I left after a single pint of mediocre beer. I then strolled into the centre of the village and sat outside the White Lion, drinking and relaxing, people-watching and writing for a very pleasant couple of hours.

Tenterden has a very attractive High Street, with many fine buildings set back from the road as one comes in from the west. This allows for an all-important strip of roadside verge with mature London plane trees,

Cranbrook to Clapper Hill

Hemsted Forest and The Forestry Commission

Hemsted Forest is a large area of coniferous woodland lying between Cranbrook and Tenterden, which is managed by The Forestry Commission. The forest was a victim of the hurricane of 1987 and has subsequently had many trees replanted by the community. Areas were also cleared of mature conifers in 2000 and replanted with douglas fir. The dense foliage attracts numerous birds, and dormice are known to thrive in this habitat. A north/south walk of 3.8 miles, popular with horse riders, traverses the forest from the vicinity of Goddard's Green to the east of Cranbrook, to the Tenterden road between Golford and Clapper Hill.

The Forestry Commission is a government department that was set up in 1919, immediately after the First World War, to protect and expand Britain's forests and woodlands, and increase their value to society and the environment. The commission manages almost one million hectares of land in Britain, making it the country's biggest land manager, and some of our best-loved and most spectacular landscapes are in its care. Afforestation was the main reason for its creation, since concern was felt that little of the country's original forests remained after the First World War.

The commission is also the largest provider of outdoor recreation in Britain, and works with many groups to promote the use of its land for various activities such as hillwalking, cycling and horse riding. Britain's forests and woodlands are a valuable habitat and species resource, and biodiversity conservation is now an integral part of sustainable forestry. Many areas of mature conifer woodland have been felled to provide the opportunity to plant a more diverse range of broad-leaved trees.

Dormouse
(Muscardinus avellanarius)

The hazel dormouse or common dormouse is the only dormouse native to the British Isles, although the edible dormouse (Glis glis), accidentally introduced, has an established population. It is a small omnivorous mammal, unrelated to mice, of 6 to 9cm long that hibernates from October to April/May, with golden-brown fur and large black eyes that is nocturnal in habit, feeding on fruits, berries, flowers, nuts and insects. If the weather is cold and wet, and food scarce, it saves energy by going into torpor; it curls up in a ball and goes to sleep, and its name is derived from the French word dormir, meaning to sleep.

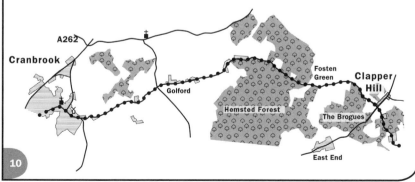

Clapper Hill to Tenterden

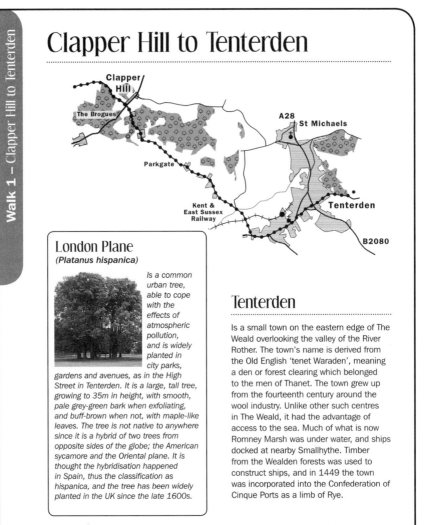

London Plane
(Platanus hispanica)

Is a common urban tree, able to cope with the effects of atmospheric pollution, and is widely planted in city parks, gardens and avenues, as in the High Street in Tenterden. It is a large, tall tree, growing to 35m in height, with smooth, pale grey-green bark when exfoliating, and buff-brown when not, with maple-like leaves. The tree is not native to anywhere since it is a hybrid of two trees from opposite sides of the globe; the American sycamore and the Oriental plane. It is thought the hybridisation happened in Spain, thus the classification as hispanica, and the tree has been widely planted in the UK since the late 1600s.

Tenterden

Is a small town on the eastern edge of The Weald overlooking the valley of the River Rother. The town's name is derived from the Old English 'tenet Waraden', meaning a den or forest clearing which belonged to the men of Thanet. The town grew up from the fourteenth century around the wool industry. Unlike other such centres in The Weald, it had the advantage of access to the sea. Much of what is now Romney Marsh was under water, and ships docked at nearby Smallhythe. Timber from the Wealden forests was used to construct ships, and in 1449 the town was incorporated into the Confederation of Cinque Ports as a limb of Rye.

Tenterden High Street

Tenterden High Street

11

which add immeasurably to the quality of the urban scene. Towards the church, opposite the White Lion, the road narrows and provides the building angles that age the settlement. At the eastern end of the High Street is a pleasant recreation ground with various amenities. Car parking and modern shopping and leisure facilities are discreetly located to the south of the High Street behind the quality frontage. The adjoining settlement of St Michaels, to the north, has none of these advantages and seems a somewhat ordinary place on the road to Maidstone.

When I thought sufficient time had passed in this self-indulgent activity, I retired to my room in the same pub and rested. I spent most of the evening nearby, in The Woolpack, a pub whose name gives a good indication of the economic history of Tenterden. After sufficient lubrication, I returned to my base pub for a long night's sleep.

I crawled timidly out of Tenterden in the morning, under lowering skies threatening rain. I decided to make as much progress as possible, with my first objective being Woodchurch. I left the town by the B2067 and picked up the footpath that runs across the West Kent Golf Course to Robhurst via Brissenden Farm. Golf courses are notoriously difficult to navigate across because the managers of such establishments tend not to be great respecters of public rights of way, given that a passing pedestrian can easily distract players from the serious business of guiding a little white ball around the course in the least shots possible. This time I managed the traverse successfully, reaching the desired exit point on the far side without a problem. However, after Brissenden Farm, I did lose the way in sheep-damaged fields and ended up in the lane below Swain Farm. When I worked out where I was on the map, I retraced my steps and crossed over the headwaters of the Tenterden Sewer, reaching Robhurst without too much sweat. From there, I took the pleasant footpath across fields to Townland Green, part of the settlement of Woodchurch.

I reached Woodchurch by the middle of the morning and observed the attractive houses, including the timber-framed Hendon Place, located around the ample village green, on which the locals were setting up their summer fete. I strolled across the green, admiring the fortitude of the inhabitants who were undaunted by the miserable weather. They seemed to be having as much fun in the setting up as in the execution of the various activities. It demonstrated to me a very healthy, and very British, community spirit. I am often amazed at how much time and effort goes

Walk 1 – Tenterden to Woodchurch

Tenterden to Woodchurch

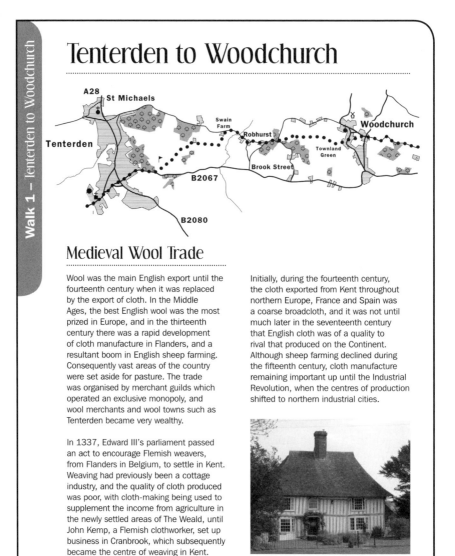

Medieval Wool Trade

Wool was the main English export until the fourteenth century when it was replaced by the export of cloth. In the Middle Ages, the best English wool was the most prized in Europe, and in the thirteenth century there was a rapid development of cloth manufacture in Flanders, and a resultant boom in English sheep farming. Consequently vast areas of the country were set aside for pasture. The trade was organised by merchant guilds which operated an exclusive monopoly, and wool merchants and wool towns such as Tenterden became very wealthy.

In 1337, Edward III's parliament passed an act to encourage Flemish weavers, from Flanders in Belgium, to settle in Kent. Weaving had previously been a cottage industry, and the quality of cloth produced was poor, with cloth-making being used to supplement the income from agriculture in the newly settled areas of The Weald, until John Kemp, a Flemish clothworker, set up business in Cranbrook, which subsequently became the centre of weaving in Kent.

Successive monarchs taxed the wool trade heavily. Edward III, realising the importance of these taxes to his royal coffers, actually went to war with France, partly to protect the wool trade with Flanders. The burghers from the rich Flemish cloth-towns had appealed to him for help against their French overlords, which gave rise to the Hundred Years War which actually lasted for 116 years from 1337 to 1453.

Initially, during the fourteenth century, the cloth exported from Kent throughout northern Europe, France and Spain was a coarse broadcloth, and it was not until much later in the seventeenth century that English cloth was of a quality to rival that produced on the Continent. Although sheep farming declined during the fifteenth century, cloth manufacture remaining important up until the Industrial Revolution, when the centres of production shifted to northern industrial cities.

Henden Place, The Green, Woodchurch

Woodchurch

Community alive

On village Green

Optimistic fete

Has to be seen

As a success in spite of the awful weather.

12

into the planning of such activities when the vagaries of the British summer weather can make such efforts completely redundant. I too had suffered in this way when I used to sell plants in my local summer fete in Kings Heath Park, Birmingham; for two years running it was totally washed out.

As I could not linger, I passed on to the east with the music from the village fete vibrating through the air. I carried on along the lane that petered out at the back of The Rare Breeds Centre, a popular local tourist attraction, but no doubt doing valuable work as well. The lane became progressively more unkempt as it approached the centre, and I could have gained access by the back door, and had a look at the animals therein for free if I was so inclined. I got caught up in the new extension, which offered ancillary adventure play and extended nature walks, spilling out into the fields to the north. The footpath was difficult to follow, and I had to make an illegal exit from an orchard north of Hunts Wood to the adjacent lane in the vicinity of Hatch. The weather was warming up but it was still overcast.

I rambled down the quiet, undulating lane to The Leacon and crossed over the B2067 to the village of Warehorne. The old village grouped around its pub and church exuded antiquity. It was situated on a bluff, looking out over Romney Marsh on the line of the old sea cliffs, which the Romans would have recognised. It was possibly once as important as Appledore, further along the Saxon Shore Way, but now it was just a sleepy hamlet. There were fabulous views from the back of the church, across the marsh, over the low-lying area of land called The Dowells, a large section of which is included in the parish.

I repaired to The Woolpack Inn, a building of considerable presence. Having been into a few pubs over the years, I have noticed that there are rare occasions when the proprietors contrive to make you feel uncomfortable and unwelcome. So it was in this case. It was as though it was too much of an effort for them to serve me. It may be that, in that snobbish sort of way, they needed to establish their superiority over a mere, less than sartorial, walker. I ordered a drink and a ploughman's lunch, sat outside and reflected on the experience. The lady serving behind the bar, who I presumed to be the landlady, brought the food out to me and as if to compensate from the frosty reception inside, was ridiculously attentive. I thought they were unsuited to the pub trade.

I rested for a while outside the pub, but knew I couldn't tarry for long,

Woodchurch to Ruckinge

Hamstreet and the Ordnance Survey

Hamstreet is known as the 'gateway to the marsh', being located on a low, heavily wooded, ridge of clay hills on the edge of Romney Marsh. The village was by-passed in 1994, and is now a quiet backwater, with some pleasant cottages along the main High Street. Along with Warehorne, it is in the parish of Orlestone, the original village being located in the hamlet of Orlestone about one mile to the north. The main claim to fame of the village came in 1991 when maps of the village appeared on postage stamps to mark the bicentenary of the Ordnance Survey, because the area around Hamstreet was the first to be systematically mapped.

Hamstreet postage stamps to mark the bicentenary of the Ordnance Survey

Warehorne

Is a small village standing on a ridge overlooking Romney Marsh on the Saxon Shore. The village was first mentioned in a charter of King Egbert in AD 820, where it is called 'Werehornas', meaning the place on the bend by the weir. Presumably this bend was on the ancient course of the river variously called Limen, Lymne and Rother.

Warehorne church

Warehorne

Atmospheric inn

Church on a bluff

View south over marsh

It is enough

To imagine the flat lands covered by a shallow sea.

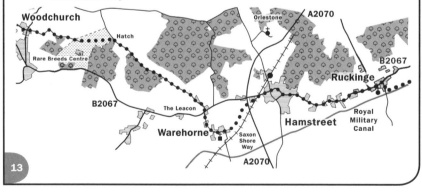

since I still had a long way to go before reaching my destination at Hythe. I considered that the pub, just like the one I patronised in Tenterden, would have got its name from the medieval wool trade occasioned by the vast expanse of reclaimed sheep pastures stretching to the sea, and the world-famous Romney breed of sheep. The riches generated by the wool trade created many fine towns, villages and buildings that grace the Kent countryside.

I walked up to Hamstreet, along the quaintly organised Saxon Shore Way, through old-fashioned, sized fields, by well-appointed styles and gates. Although I had passed through Hamstreet many times before, slipping down onto Romney Marsh, mainly as a child with my family en route to the caravan at St Mary's Bay, I felt it was an unremarkable place. On this Saturday afternoon it felt dead. The pub where we used to break our journey was closed and the weather was closing in. Hamstreet's main claim to fame was that the village appeared on the postage stamps issued to commemorate the one hundredth anniversary of the Ordnance Survey in 1991, because it was evidently the first place to be systematically mapped. I had the stamps in my own not-insubstantial collection at home. Hamstreet is in the parish of Orlestone, with the parish church in the hamlet of that name lying 1 mile to the north, the original site of the settlement. This occurrence, with the main village being detached from the parish church, was now becoming common, and similar to my observations in relation to Horsmonden. Again, I wondered whether the Black Death had had a hand in creating this settlement pattern.

I pressed on along the relatively busy B2067 to Ruckinge. Pacing along this undulating road, there were good views out across the marsh. Although in this vicinity the land shelved down gently into the marsh, one could still imagine that the waves would be lapping on the shore here a few centuries ago. The relatively gentle slope of these former sea cliffs is explained by the fact that they are composed of the weaker mud and clay layers of the Wealden formations. I reached Ruckinge about mid-afternoon and had another pint in the Blue Anchor. I left the pub at 4.00 p.m. to walk the remaining 8 miles or so along the Royal Military Canal to Hythe. It would take me the best part of three hours before I made it to the hotel, right down on the front at Hythe.

I picked up the path along the banks of the yellow, lily-covered canal. The first part, from Ruckinge to Bilsington, was hard going and overgrown, as if rarely used. The Cosway monument at Bilsington was clearly

Ruckinge to Marwood Farm

[Map showing route from Ruckinge to Marwood Farm, with labels: B2067, Aldington Knoll, Marwood Farm, St Rumwolds Church, Bilsington, Cosway Monument, Ruckinge, Royal Military Canal, Saxon Shore Way]

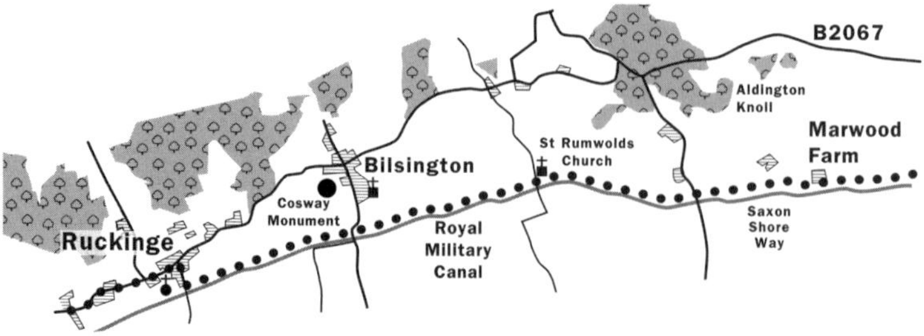

The Royal Military Canal

Is a unique military Scheduled Ancient Monument, built between 1804 and 1809 to protect England from the threat of invasion from the Continent by Napoleon Bonaparte. It runs for 28 miles from Seabrooke, near Hythe, to Cliff End, near Fairlight, following the old sea cliffs bordering Romney Marsh and Pett Level. It was constructed in two sections: the longest section in Kent from Seabrooke to Iden Lock; the second shorter section in East Sussex from the foot of Winchelsea Hill to Cliff End. The two sections are linked by the Rivers Rother and Brede, making the total length of the defensive system 35 miles.

Gun positions along the canal were generally located every 500 yards, with the canal being doglegged to improve the line of fire along the length of the canal. Any troops stationed or moving along the military road along its northern edge would have been protected by the earthen bank of the parapet, which was thrown up during construction. Despite the fact that the canal never saw military action, it was used in the attempt to control smuggling, and guard houses were erected at each bridge along its length. Although a commercial barge service was established from Hythe to Rye, the canal was abandoned in 1877 and leased to the Lords of the level of Romney Marsh. During the early stages of World War II, when a German invasion seemed likely, the canal was again fortified by the iconic concrete pillboxes.

The tree-lined canal is now used by the Environment Agency to regulate the water levels on the Marsh, and is managed as an important environmental site, containing several Sites of Special Scientific Interest. It is a valuable habitat for fish and other wildlife, including kingfishers, dragonflies and marsh frogs.

Yellow Water Lily
(Nuphar Lutea)

Sometimes called spatterdock, cow lily or yellow pond lily is an aquatic plant of the northern hemisphere and grows in freshwater with its roots fixed into the ground and its leaves floating on the water's surface. The plant has a single, terminal flower, pollinated by insects, which blooms from June to September. Spatterdock was used extensively in traditional medicine and the seeds and root are edible.

An iconic concrete pillbox

14

32

visible and this was evidently an important landmark for pilots returning across the Channel in World War II. Past Bilsington, the going was easy as the footpath ran along a broad, sheep-grazed bank, which formed the inner ramparts of the Royal Military Canal. I began to make good progress. All the while there were captivating glimpses of the substantial canal to my right. To my left were cultivated, arable fields sloping down to the marsh, topped by a line of distinctive churches from west to east; Warehorne, Ruckinge, Bilsington and the tiny chapel of St Rumwolds.

Further on, it was more convenient to trudge along below the rampart on the gravel of the back path, strewn with watery craters that required some agility to avoid. All the while the old sea cliffs were coming closer, and below Court-at-Street, they began to look like cliffs as the harder greensand rocks of the Wealden formations began to make their presence felt.

Below Lympne, the cliffs were occupied by the famous wild animal park. The way past the zoo became difficult with muddy bogs, and the only distraction in this dark tunnel of vegetation was the occasional glimpses of exotic animals that did not belong in the British countryside, behind miles of chain-link fencing, topped, mercifully, by vicious-looking

Marwood Farm to Hythe

A Cinque Port

Below the down the stranded town
What may betide forlornly waits,
With memories of smoky skies,
When Gallic navies crossed the straits;
When waves with fire and blood grew bright,
And cannon thundered through the night.

With swinging stride the rhythmic tide
Bore to the harbour barque and sloop;
Across the bar the ship of war,
In castled stern and lanterned poop'
Came up with conquests on her lee'
The stately mistress of the sea.

Where argosies have wooed the breeze,
The simple sheep are feeding now;
And near and far across the bar
The ploughman whistles at the plough;
Where once the long waves washed the shore,
Larks from their lowly lodgings soar.

Below the down the stranded town
Hears far away the rollers beat;
About the wall the seabirds call;
The salt wind murmurs through the street;
Forlorn the sea's forsaken bride
Awaits the end that shall betide.

John Davidson (1857–1909)

Barbed Wire

Is an important invention of the nineteenth century which is used to construct inexpensive fences, on top of walls surrounding secured property, and extensively as a feature of the fortifications in trench warfare. A person trying to pass through or over barbed wire will suffer discomfort and possible injury. As fencing it requires only fence posts, wire and fixing devices such as staples, and is simple to construct and quick to erect.

The first patent in the US for barbed wire was issued in 1867 to a Lucien B. Smith of Kent, Ohio, who is regarded as the inventor. It was the first wire technology capable of restraining cattle. As it became widely available and easily affordable, it made it possible to fence much larger areas than before, which ushered in animal husbandry on a much greater scale, and contributed to the opening up of large areas of North America and other continents to grazing and agriculture.

Hythe

A military place
And stranded town
Of rifles popping
Below the down
As John Davidson may have put it.

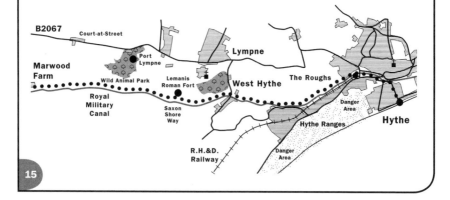

barbed wire. I mused for a while on the significance of barbed wire. It had been suggested to me that barbed wire had been one of the most significant inventions of modern times, which had allowed the control of grazing animals and allowed many parts of the world to be opened up for animal husbandry. Barbed wire is one of the most useful and functional of commodities but one of the least attractive, particularly when it becomes discarded in a tangled rusty heap. At the furthest extent of the zoo I had a good view of the Roman port of Lemanis, now a con-glomeration of confusing white stones sliding down the hillside into the marsh. The old church and manor house at Lympne looked impressive, picked out against the skyline on top of the cliff.

When I reached the small settlement of West Hythe, I was still 2.5 miles from Hythe and my knees were beginning to hurt. The distinctive greensand sea cliffs from now on were grazed sparsely by sheep. From the West Hythe sluice, the canal was navigable to Hythe, but is only ever used by rowing boats and canoes. The north bank from here on in had been laid out as a country park with a sinuous canal-side walk, decked out with carefully placed benches, children's play equipment and barbecue stations to encourage picnicking. Frequent milestones ushered me wearily into Hythe, the outskirts of which gathered itself on the southern bank of the canal first, as the town tucked itself neatly under its burgeoning cliff, known as the Hythe escarpment. I was reminded of Davidson's poem called '*A Cinque Port*,' about a 'stranded town below the down', and wondered whether he could have been thinking of Hythe.

Eventually, I reached the terminus of the Romney, Hythe & Dym-church Light Railway, much beloved of my childhood, and plunged into the plain park beside the last stretch of canal, before arriving in the centre of the town. I walked down Stade Street to the seafront where my hotel was located. I was on my last legs and I felt that I had been a bit ambitious with the day's walk of nearly 30 miles. In the evening, I spent a pleasant couple of hours in the Hope Inn on Stade Street as I didn't have the energy to walk back into the town centre. Reading the history of the pub proffered by the friendly barman, I was surprised by the extent to which Hythe's origins were as a military base camp.

I staggered back to the hotel and took a couple of drinks up to my room, where I started to write up this adventure. My curious room was on two levels with a narrow staircase, giving access to an attic room overlooking the sea. I sat for a while in the attic room, writing, drinking and admiring the raw sea view with the window wide open so I could feel the elements. As had been promised throughout the day, as I was sitting there, a storm blew in from the west. The angle of the building meant that I could sit by the open window without getting wet. I was able to admire the full majesty of the storm, as the guttering immediately below my window gurgled in its efforts to disperse the rapidly accumulating torrents of water. I retired, eventually, feeling somewhat satisfied with the week's exploits.

In the morning, I returned to St Mary's Bay, said hello to my mother, picked up my car and drove back to Birmingham to return to the necessary world of work.

2

Gravesend to Broadstairs (Autumn 2009)

Starting another walk at Gravesend, I came out of the station to the small square at the head of the High Street. I selected one of the roads going south, away from the river this time, and climbed up through the urban penumbra of Gravesend to the newly constructed A2. Between the new road and the town was a strip of parched land planted up with trees and laid out with paths. The road had been shifted away from the houses and in time, if the trees survived, they would form a barrier to help moderate the intrusive traffic noise. There was an ugly, disused petrol station indicating the original route of the road, which needed to be demolished, and I considered that the remaindered edge of the urban area needed tidying up.

I crossed over the new road and rail corridor by footbridges on the way to St Margaret's Church. Thereafter, I took a footpath across a ploughed field diagonally to Jeskyns Farm. I made ground steadily on three fellow walkers up ahead of me. In the far corner of the field the farmer had meticulously prepared a patch of ground for planting crops. A huge, mechanical, watering contraption was on standby, having thoroughly soaked the ground. The footpath went straight across this prepared plot. The farmer had taken no account of the footpath and the three walkers in front had bravely ploughed straight across. I guiltily slithered after them, concerned more about spoiling the pristine, ridged preparation of the ground. I caught up with the three fellows in Jeskyns Farm. They were elderly friends out for a leisurely walk; what an excellent way for retired gentlemen to pass the day. This encounter evoked a comparison with the three chaps in the television programme *The Last of the Summer Wine*. We exchanged pleasantries and I moved on, down Jeskyns Lane, towards Cobham.

I passed through a massive country park, which swept down from the new trunk road and across the lane. It was heavily planted and decked out

with children's play areas and barbecue stations. I doubted whether the trees would ever become established in this area, as it was one of the hottest and driest parts of the country, and whether this massive area would really work as a successful open space. On the south side of Jeskyns Lane they had planted a wood and I wished the whole enterprise luck.

Looking at the map, I could see four large and some would say intrusive, urban settlements of doubtful provenance, immediately south of Gravesend. These new urban conglomerations would have skipped the London Green Belt and I guess would be inhabited largely by London commuters. They include Istead Rise, New Barn, Hartley and New Ash Green, which together with the older settlements of Longfield and Meopham, amounts to a substantial urban area on the long dip slope of the North Downs. One could also include here the similarly placed West Kingsdown, further south, Culveston Green and Vigo Village, up towards the scarp slope, and indeed the smaller places of Hook Green and Sole Street. The roads connecting these places were mainly coloured yellow on the map and, therefore, one would expect them to be quiet, but one instinctively knows that they would be full of traffic and unpleasant for walking. These settlements are not necessarily new, as I clearly remember being unimpressed with New Ash Green when I used to cycle out from the London suburbs as a lad. I remember clearly seeing Vigo Village on the map. I guess these places may have started fairly modestly but have swelled over time like a cancer in the countryside. This is an area I have avoided on my walks; although Longfield and Meopham may be worth a visit.

I made for Cobham, an attractive village steeped in history, and little changed because of its conservation area status. There was a fine prospect of attractively arranged buildings approaching the village. I passed the Owletts National Trust garden and the first village pub, The Leather Bottle, which I understand was a haunt of Dickens. The large and unusual church, much beloved of brass rubbers, is set back from 'The Street' in its historical precinct. I popped into the village store and bought a pasty and bottle of coke, which I consumed on a conveniently placed municipal seat. The pasty was very welcome and warming. Next to the village store was a perfectly nice bungalow, but it was set back from the road with a casual car parking area in front, which was out of keeping with the street scene. I would like to see the plot redeveloped in a more sympathetic manner. I was tempted to draw up a sketch scheme when I got back home to prove the point. As I sat on the seat devouring my food, a number of locals passed by, convivially bidding me good morning. Cobham seemed a very friendly little village.

At the end of the main street, by the ceremonial entrance to Cobham Hall, the ancestral home of the Earls of Darnley, I turned right down the Cobhambury Road and took the unfenced Batts Road, which descended to the dry valley, sweeping down from Luddesdown to Cuxton and the Medway Gorge. This impressively large, dry valley turned back on itself, past Meopham, and originated up near the scarp of the North Downs at Vigo Village.

Looking back to Cobham, I could see the distinctive church prominent on the skyline. I carried on down into the valley, over the railway line and took a footpath and lane under double pylons into the little village of Luddesdown, where I popped into the Golden Lion for a drink. The pub was set in an outsized car park which detracted from the appeal of the place, and I could imagine a more sympathetic and attractive arrangement of this space. I felt like offering my services to the landlady to redesign the pub surrounds, but thought better of it.

From there I walked up past the cricket ground, which is a curious, triangular-shaped field and one of the few relatively flat pieces of land in

Gravesend to Cobham

Cobham

Is an attractive, largely unspoilt village which is in a Conservation Area, lying adjacent to Cobham Park, the ancestral home of the Earls of Darnley, with gardens designed by Humphry Repton. The village has strong links with Charles Dickens who used to walk here from his base at nearby Gadshill, where he set part of *The Pickwick Papers*.

Cobham High Street

Green Belts

In the UK is a policy for controlling urban growth, by resisting urbanisation in a ring of countryside where agriculture, forestry and outdoor leisure pursuits are expected to prevail. The introduction of this policy was the culmination of over fifty years of environmental pressure with its roots in the garden city movement, to combat urban sprawl and ribbon development, from groups such as the Campaign to Protect Rural England. Implementation of the notion dated from Herbert Morrison's 1934 leadership of the London County Council, and was first proposed by the Greater London Regional Planning Committee in 1935, but it was not until 1947 that the Town and Country Planning Act of that year permitted Local Authorities to designate areas to be protected as part of the Green Belt within their development plans. The original Green Belt around London has been gradually extended as Local Authorities in Kent have tried to hold back the tide of urbanisation, and currently there are 72,240 hectares of such land covering the majority of Kent west of the Medway.

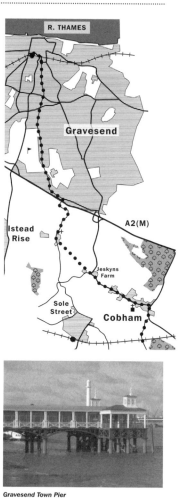

Gravesend Town Pier

Gravesend

New life entry point

From the old world

Old life exit point

For the new world

And the Sikh community still flourishes here.

16

40

the area. It was clear that there was a lot of local enthusiasm for this activity, with a nicely prepared pitch and a brand new shiny pavilion. I only wish, for the sake of the home team, that funds could be secured to acquire the other triangle of land over the fence, to make a decent square ground. As it is, a mishit pull to leg would clear the boundary for six. However, it must be said that in spite of the curious shape of the ground, it doesn't really matter because it is equal for both sides.

I made my way up to the upper village and observed the distinctive village sign on the small green by the church. Picking up the Wealdway, I made my way further up the charming side valley, all the way to the hamlet of Great Buckland. After Great Buckland, I passed through Greatpark Wood to Holly Hill, climbing up the dip slope of the North Downs to a high point of 196m. From there I had fabulous views down into the Medway Valley in the vicinity of Snodland. I could see the Thames Estuary hard to my left and the North Downs continuing on east across the Medway, and the vast chalk quarries in the vicinity of Upper Halling.

From the T-junction at the top of Holly Hill, I took the North Downs Way that ran diagonally down the scarp slope. It was frustrating, walking along this section, as there were no views out across the surrounding countryside. Until this point, I had largely been walking uphill and although my right knee was hurting, it was nothing compared with the pain of walking down the steep slope. When the traverse suddenly ended, I turned a right angle and emerged onto the lower slopes in the blazing sunshine. There was still a magnificent view out across the valley and I stood in awe for a time. I could see right round from the Medway gorge towards Rochester, right along the Greensand Ridge, and round to Wrotham, tucked back under the North Downs to the west. I even think I could see the purple outline of the Weald beyond the Greensand Ridge. I decided to kip down, head on rucksack, and have a rest for a few minutes. The air was buzzing with insects and many butterflies wafted around.

After a while, I forced my legs to respond to the challenge of walking on. I crossed the Pilgrim's Way, the route of a previous journey, and plodded on along a clearly evident promontory running out into the valley towards Birling Place Farm, affording spectacular views right and left. The track was bordered by a hedgerow on one side with a wide variety of plant species; I guess it was of some antiquity. Passing through

the farm, I followed a small stream down into the village of Birling. It was a pleasant enough village with a pub, church and some bucolic chocolate-box-looking cottages. The view of the church perched up on its mound was damaged by an unsightly, and unfortunately placed, telegraph pole with its attendant wires. It would be a good idea for the village inhabitants to club together and raise enough money to pay for the appropriate statutory undertaker to remove the poles and put the wires underground.

All that remained was to slog up the Birling Road towards the motorway. I crossed over the M20 and stumbled on beside the extra-vagant new A228 Tonbridge road, built to relieve Leybourne of traffic, and on to West Malling. I passed through Leybourne Wood, feeling very tired now, to the roundabout that gave access to the town. I then walked on up Town Hill and over the railway to the centre of West Malling, a quintessential small town. There were many old buildings in the town but what struck me most was the layout, which clearly reflected its medieval origins, with a wide main street that would have been the site of a market in times past. I had seen this pattern in many other towns and it was identical to the layout of Chipping Norton in the Cotswolds; I drew a sketch of the main features to illustrate the point. In the evening, I strolled around the town with an old friend with whom I was staying, and

Cobham to West Malling

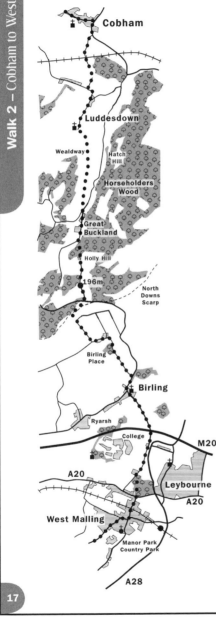

Dating Hedgerows

Is an inexact science. Other than the influence of man, the most powerful ecological factors influencing the rate of change in a hedge is the colonisation by outside species competing with those already present in the hedge. Thus the greater the age of the hedgerow the more varied the flora and fauna should become. Mature trees in the hedgerow can also be used as an indicator by tree ring dating. According to a hypothesis originally propounded by Dr Max Hooper in 1974, a rule of thumb method suggests that the age of a hedge is equal to the number of woody species counted in a 30-yard stretch of hedgerow multiplied by 110 years.

West Malling

Is an historic market town with an ancient street pattern, which has many fine buildings from the Norman, Medieval, Tudor and Georgian periods. St Leonard's Tower, a Norman keep and prominent landmark, built by Bishop Gundulf around 1080, lies to the west of the town. There is also a large Abbey precinct which is still used by Benedictine nuns today adjacent to Manor Park Country Park. This attractive small town of around 4,000 inhabitants lies immediately west of the urban sprawl to the west of Maidstone and maintains its separate identity by virtue of a narrow strip of undeveloped land. It is reputed to be the site of the first recorded cricket match in Kent in 1705, and one of the first grounds played on by Kent County Cricket Club.

The Farmhouse, High Street, West Malling

17

I think he was slightly disappointed that we only managed to consume six pints of proper beer.

In the morning, I went back into town to post my box, walked down the High Street and cut through the churchyard to the Offham road. From there I made my way past St Leonard's Tower, the ruined keep of a Norman castle, rising all the time. Picking up the Teston Road, I came to the attractive village of Offham. There was a pub and some pleasant houses grouped around an ample village green with a curious jousting device on it: a relic of medieval pastimes.

It was my intention to skirt around Mereworth Woods and go to West Peckham again on my way to Yalding. This loop in my route was primarily designed to avoid walking through the massive, sprawling settlement of Kings Hill, a modern development on the former West Malling airfield. It would appear that redundant airfields in particular, but also surplus mental hospitals I've noticed, are vulnerable to this type of opportunist, urban expansion.

From Offham I took the lower, so-called Quiet Lane, due west along the northern outskirts of Mereworth Woods. I understand that 'The Quiet Lane' is a scheme sponsored by the council to prohibit heavy traffic and encourage pedestrians. This lane soon turned into Comp Lane, which gave access to everything 'Comp' – Comp Farm, Comp cottages and Great Comp Garden. It was a pleasant walk along the lane in the morning sunshine and the hedgerows were strewn with blackberries in season. I feasted on the fruit as I went on my way, across the B2016, the Seven Mile Lane, to re-engage with the Wealdway to the south of Platt.

I then turned due south and walked the 2 miles up the gentle slope of the Greensand Ridge to Gover Hill. The route went through the edge of Mereworth Woods, one of the largest areas of wooded country in Kent. For the lower part, the path was open to the west and there were good views but very little shelter from the strong wind issuing from that direction. The upper slopes were through a dense, coppiced, chestnut wood. I had seen coppiced hazel on many occasions, particularly on the chalk of the North Downs, but on the Greensand hills the preference was for sweet chestnut. Eventually, I reached Gover Hill, at a height of around 135m, where the National Trust had thoughtfully provided a viewing point to the south-west. I could see Shipbourne Church spire in the distance and could trace the route that I had undertaken before, through the valley to Dunk's Green and West Peckham.

West Malling to West Peckham

Walk 2 – West Malling to West Peckham

Offham

Is a picturesque village with a large green on which stands its famed Medieval quintain, which is believed to be the last remaining example in the country. The quintain consists of a wooden post, about 8 feet in height, with a freely rotating arm on the top. One end of the arm is flat (the 'eye'), with the other end used to attach heavy objects such as a leather pack. In a sport dating back to Roman times, a horseman would ride at the quintain at full pace with his lance intending to strike the flat end. Should the horseman not be riding sufficiently quickly, the arm would swing round and the heavy object would knock him off his horse.

St Leonard's Tower in West Malling

A quintain on Offham Green

Common Blackberry
(Rubus fruticosus)

Is a widespread edible fruit and biennial plant, often called bramble, that grows wild in hedgerows and uncultivated places in the English countryside. There are many cultivars and this soft fruit is often used in desserts, jams and wines, and often mixed with apples in pies. The wild fruits are eaten by several mammals, such as deer, foxes and badgers, as well as man, and many small birds, who actively disperse its seeds.

Mereworth Woods

Are a large area of ancient semi-natural woodland and scrub lying on the Greensand Ridge, with an abundance of wildlife, including reptiles and small mammals. They are owned by the Ministry of Defence and have been used for training purposes since the Second World War, and this may help to explain their preservation. The straight 7-mile lane, the B2016, dissects the woods.

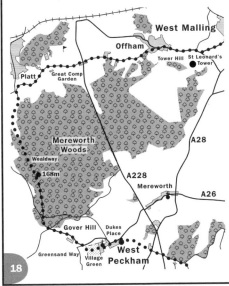

18

There was an uncomfortable stretch down Gover Hill before I picked up the Greensand Way, through orchards, to emerge triumphantly on the green at West Peckham. I crossed over the stile and caught my breath again at the quintessential village scene before me. I sat on the bench by the old horse chestnut tree in the corner and wondered how many walkers had done this before me. I crossed the green, taking photographs. The weather was a bit cold and blowy, much worse than the last time I was there, and I went inside the Swan again. The pub was under new management and had been 'poshed up'. The food was good but expensive, served up on one of those chopping boards, and the beer was made on the premises, although much of the fruit-flavoured brews were not to my taste. With the development of micro-breweries, it is now perfectly possible for each pub to brew its own beer in the back yard. I was a little disappointed after the immensely pleasurable visit last time, but I was philosophical, reasoning that places often disappoint on a second visit, being probably more to do with the state of my mind than the state of the pub.

I went outside to escape the cloying atmosphere inside and finish my last pint. I looked again at the village green, which had recently been registered as common land, and felt that it could be made even better if the far hedge was pushed back and planted up with a few large trees. This would also have the effect of creating a better cricket ground, giving more room in the outfield square of the wicket. After sheltering from a shower in the church door I pushed on down the lane, turning right at the Duke's Place, a historic building getting a new roof.

I continued to follow the Greensand Way out of West Peckham, down into a shallow valley and up again to Forge Farm. I crossed over two busy roads by means of a remaindered lane, whose hedgerow banks looked most unstable being riddled with rabbit burrows. I came up to the isolated and redundant East Peckham Church perched on its knoll with fine views from the churchyard, over the Vale of Kent, down towards Hadlow and the village of East Peckham, now located by the River Medway.

From the church I passed through orchards and parkland to Royden Hall and trudged on to Moat Wood, where I saw the familiar shape of a buzzard circling high up in the sky. Emerging from the wood, the sun was shining bright and I lay down for a rest. In front of me was a large, open, ploughed field carved out of the wood. The footpath ran right through the middle of this field, but I respectfully elected to walk around the edge.

West Peckham to Yalding

Yalding

Is a small village situated at a crossing point of the combined waters of the Rivers Beult and Teise, just before they join the Medway. Besides the three ancient Medieval stone bridges, there are many fine buildings in the village, including a row of Georgian buildings in the High Street. The area, being at the confluence of major rivers, has been prone to serious flooding on many occasions, including the winter of 2000/01. Alphabetically the village is the last in Kent.

Rabbit
(Oryctolagus cuniculus)

The European rabbit, the best known species, live in groups in underground burrows. They have a very rapid reproductive rate and can quickly increase in number although they are susceptible to numerous diseases which naturally limit their numbers. They are herbivores that can be farmed for food, and have been introduced into many parts of the world, often disrupting local ecologies and causing severe environmental problems.

Yalding

Damp lugubrious

Riverine place

Empty heart of Kent

A down turned face

Missing summer hoards of cockney visitors.

Yalding High Street

Buzzard
(Buteo buteo)

Is the commonest and most widespread bird of prey in the UK, and can be found soaring over woodlands in fine weather. It is quite a large bird, with broad, rounded wings, a short neck and tail, and when gliding will often hold its wings in a shallow 'v'. They eat small mammals, birds and carrion, and their plaintive mewing call could be mistaken for a domestic cat.

19

47

In time, I came to Nettlestead Green, where there were some pleasant old cottages, but the effect was spoilt by the busy B2015. To cap it all, the pub there was closed.

I continued on down into the valley of the River Medway and up the embankment to the railway, which I timidly crossed by a surface pedestrian crossing. I came out along a canal backwater of the big river dedicated to everything connected to boats and walked up to the road going to Yalding. The map showed a massive factory complex served by a canal from the main river, but the factories had been demolished; instead, there were fields of deep, pink-coloured rubble. It reminded me of Longbridge in Birmingham after the clearance of the car factories. I trudged along beside the canal to its junction with the main river and checked in to the Angel Inn, my berth for the night.

When I arrived at the pub, I was greeted with an amazing sight. It was full of old people in the late afternoon, many of whom were drinking tea inside, while those outside were drinking beer. It was clearly a coach outing and, judging by the accents, I guessed that they came from London. I went outside, joined the more hardy revellers with my pint of cider and leant on the railings overlooking the Medway. There was a vast weir holding back the waters and a lock to let boats through upstream. The canal that I had walked beside ran off to the left from behind the weir, giving a constant draught of water. The smaller branch of the River Teise joined at this point too, just above the weir. I spent a pleasant hour relaxing in this water world, soaking up the atmosphere and admiring the engineering marvels in harnessing the great river around me.

In the morning, at breakfast, I chatted to the landlord about the prevalence of flooding in this area. He said the last major flood they had was in the winter of 2000/01. After breakfast, I crossed the bridge across the canal that formed the main entrance to the pub and strolled up the Lees to the centre of Yalding. I dropped off my box in the post office adjacent to the ancient stone bridge across the River Beult. The effect was somewhat spoilt by a municipal dustcart disrupting traffic flow across the narrow bridge. I picked my way carefully through this pandemonium to Yalding High Street. The centre of Yalding has some quality buildings set around a widened High Street, creating a long, thin green which would once have no doubt been a market. Indeed, last time I passed through there was a fete utilising this space. The church at the bottom of the High Street was shielded from the road by buildings that had been built in the

Yalding to Linton

Damson
(Prunus domestica)

Is a small tree or large shrub, which is a sub-species of the plum tree, often found in hedgerows, which bears a blue-black edible fruit. They were first introduced by the Romans and are commonly used in the preparation of jams and jellies.

Linton

Is a well-preserved village on the southward facing slope of the Greensand Ridge on the busy A229 Maidstone to Hastings road. The village, although blighted by through traffic, is a Conservation Area with parts of the village having great views across to the Low Weald. Much of the history of the place is closely connected to the fortunes of the adjacent Linton Park.

Linton Park

Conservation Areas

Were first introduced by the Civic Amenities Act 1967 and subsequently consolidated in Section 69 of the Planning (listed buildings and conservation areas) Act 1990, which requires local planning authorities to define as conservation areas any 'areas of special architectural or historic interest, the character and appearance of which it is desirable to preserve or enhance'. Local authorities have some control over maintaining the area, including regulating the demolition of unlisted buildings and the erection of new buildings within the conservation area. The pruning or cutting down of any tree requires the council to be notified in advance in order that an assessment, about whether a Tree Preservation Order is appropriate, can be undertaken. There are now over 8,000 such designated areas in England of which the village of Linton is one.

Linton Park

Is a large eighteenth-century house associated with the village of Linton, built in 1730 and enlarged in 1825. It sits in a prominent location, part way down the south-facing slope of the Greensand Ridge, which provides excellent views of the grounds and the Low Weald beyond. The house is a grade I listed building and the park is grade II* listed, and contains specimen trees planted in 1825.

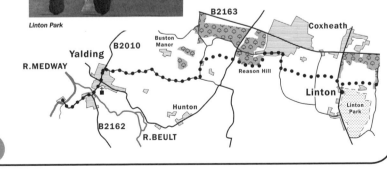

churchyard in the past. This arrangement, which I had seen many times before, creates a more secluded churchyard away from the main street and was the result of medieval churchman selling off plots of land on the road frontage for profit. A similar arrangement can be found in Moseley, in the Birmingham suburbs, close to where I have been living.

I carried on up the road until I turned right into Lughorse Lane, searching for a convenient point to pick up The Greensand Way. I passed a house with a 'Beware of the Dog' sign on the gate. I had almost put the property behind me when the dogs realised there was somebody going past. They made a belated effort at scaring me off, but you could almost hear the disappointment in their bark at missing the opportunity to confront me head on.

When I found the Greensand Way I set out in the direction of Sutton Valence, a lovely stretch of path overlooking the valley of the River Beult. Looking south, I could see the purple outline of the Weald rising up in the distance with Goudhurst Church clearly visible. The level path below the Greensand Ridge passed through orchards dripping with apples and pears ready for harvesting. As I walked along admiring the view, I helped myself to the produce of the hedgerows. There were blackberries, damsons and plums, as well as apples and pears for eating directly. There were also cobnuts, which I collected as I went along, as well as bird cherries and sweet chestnuts not quite ready for harvesting. I was amazed at all this fecundity and began to relax into my walk, trying to forget the pain in my right knee.

I reflected later that this stretch, to Sutton Valence and beyond, was one of the best walks I had experienced in the many long treks across Kent that I had undertaken in the last ten years. Unfortunately, and very irritatingly, I lost the way at Reason Hill and was diverted north to the bungalow outskirts of Coxheath. I was conscious of the distance I was trying to cover this day and any diversion was unwelcome and worrying. I regained the designated footpath and carried on to the pleasant hillside village of Linton, perched on the steep scarp slope of the Greensand Ridge, astride the busy A229, south from Maidstone.

I waited for The Bull in Linton to open for my first pint of the day. There was a notice on the door which asked walkers to take off their boots to avoid treading mud across the floor. As there was no mud on my boots, as conditions underfoot were bone dry, I risked the oppro-brium of the licensee and sheepishly kept them on. Looking at the map later at home, I wondered how it would be possible to by-pass Linton without damaging the environment even more. I concluded that the only way would be to tunnel the ridge, a somewhat ambitious proposal. I feared Linton would have to put up with the traffic thundering through.

After a short break, I pressed on towards Sutton Valence, leaving Linton by the back of the churchyard, and paced along above the village's big house situated in Linton Park. A little further on, lodged in the lower branches of a hedgerow tree, I saw a dead tawny owl. I stood and stared at the unfortunate creature, transfixed. Its unblinking eyes looked straight at me as I pondered its demise. It was a very sad sight and I hoped that this magnificent creature had met a natural death and simply fell off its perch. If I was at all superstitious I could have taken this encounter as a bad omen for the rest of my trip, but I did not allow such thoughts any credence.

I pressed on through Loddington Farm to Boughton Monchelsea parish church, with the main part of the village now lying half a mile to the north. Although settlements are capable of moving over time, and often do, churches rarely do, and remain rooted to the spot, sometimes isolated and remaindered. Before Wierton, I came across a field of goats, which were up for sponsored adoption. I cut down through the hamlet, tucked under the top of the scarp slope, and pressed on to Chart Sutton, trying to put the miles behind me. After Wierton, in a large orchard graced by an army of Eastern European pickers, I became distracted by their banter and lost the way again.

I took the wrong turning and ended up going north to Chart Corner. This was a serious mistake and by the time I regained the path at Chart Sutton church, I had added at least a mile to the walk. It did occur to me that the Greensand Way, although generally well-marked, was a very complicated path with many twists and turns between this hedgerow, that field and over that stile, making it quite difficult to follow on a Landranger Map. Although I knew there was no excuse for losing the way, I didn't think I was that bad a map reader and the nature of the path and the scale of the map may have contributed to the mistake. Anyway, it was a painful and irritating diversion, and to drown my sorrows I popped into the pub at Chart Corner for a drink. I regained the path and pressed on to Sutton Valence, the largest of the scarp settlements on the Greensand Ridge.

By early afternoon I reached Sutton Valence. I remembered this place

Linton to Sutton Valence

A229
B2163
A274
Chart Corner
Greensand Way
Linton
Boughton Monchelsea
Deer Park
Chart Sutton
Linton Park
Wierton
A274
Sutton Valence
A274

Tawny Owl
(Strix aluco)

The tawny owl is a stocky, medium-sized owl commonly found in woodlands in Britain. Its underparts are pale with dark streaks and the upperparts are either brown or grey. The bird typically nests in a hole in a tree, is strongly territorial, nocturnal in habit, and feeds mainly on rodents. It is a widespread breeding species in Britain, but is not found in Ireland.

Boughton Monchelsea

Is a parish situated astride the Greensand Ridge, with a small hamlet located around the church on the ridge, and the main settlement today having migrated to the north of the B 2163. The area is historically famous for the quarrying of ragstone, extensively worked in Roman times, and more recently used in the construction of Westminster Abbey, the houses of Parliament, and the repair of Rochester Castle. The quarries, which are located in the north of the parish, closed in 1960.

Sutton Valence

Is a picturesque village on the Greensand Ridge with panoramic views over the Vale of Kent. One of the main landmarks is Sutton Valence Castle of which only the ruins of the twelfth-century keep remain, which is looked after by English Heritage. The village has two parts: the principle and older part occupies the slope of the Greensand Ridge, with roads lined with attractive buildings running parallel to the slope. The newer part, known as The Harbour, is located at the bottom of the slope and comprised of a significant number of houses originally owned by the Local Authority. Many of the older buildings are constructed from ragstone mined locally at Broughton Monchelsea. The village has a long history, dating back at least to Saxon times, although Iron Age and Roman artifacts have been found. In 1265 Henry III granted the manor to his brother, William de Valence, from whom the village takes its current name.

Sutton Valence High Street

as a boy, travelling down to the coast in my grandparents' car, when the journey was part of the fun, and I had always wanted to return. I walked in past the church and came up onto the main road, the A274 Maidstone to Tenterden road. At first sight I was disappointed as there was much traffic, and noisy road works added to the confusion of the scene. I popped into the Kings Arms, on the corner, for a drink or two and a bite to eat. There was a newly refurbished bar billiards table in the pub and I just had to have a practise. It was a good, true table and I was able to play shots off the back cushion into the high value holes. I was delighted to find that there was no charge for these twelve minutes of self-indulgence. I spent a pleasant hour in the pub but, as a consequence, I didn't start out again until mid-afternoon and I doubted I could complete the day's planned itinerary.

After the pub, I walked through the centre of Sutton Valence and was rewarded with the spectacle of a fabulous Kentish village. There were many attractive houses and a number of delicious looking pubs, harmoniously strung out along the road on the side of the hill to a notable church at the end of the flower-decked High Street. The distinctive structure of the village, unlike any other I was familiar with, was a higher and lower road lying parallel to the slope, affording fine views to the south. I could have spent the rest of the day exploring this delightful village, but reluctantly I decided I had to push on.

It was clear by now that the Greensand Way went past many churches, all located in a similar position: facing south just under the highest point of the ridge at about 100m above sea level. These churches are at the centre of parishes which contain part of the gentle dip slope, and the steeper scarp slope of the Greensand Ridge, and are located on former drove roads running in a north-easterly to south-westerly direction. This pattern is explained by ancient farmers driving their livestock from the easily won open fields on the chalk of the North Downs to summer pastures in the heavily forested Weald. The settlements on the Greensand Ridge may well have been stopping off places on this migration. From west to east, the parishes and churches include Linton, Boughton Monchelsea, Chart Sutton, Sutton Valence, East Sutton, Ulcombe, Boughton Malherbe and Egerton. Any one of these settlements could no doubt have developed into a larger place like Sutton Valence if not but for an accident of history. The major settlements of Sutton Valence and Linton are located on main roads from Maidstone. Boughton

Sutton Valence to Liverton Street

Eight Parishes of the Greensand Ridge

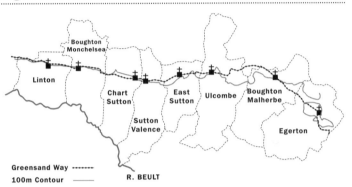

Greensand Way ·······
100m Contour ——
R. BEULT

The above map of parishes straddling the Greensand Ridge, in what are known as the Chart Hills, shows a remarkable consistency in the location of their parish churches, in the vicinity of the 100-metre contour. Thus, each parish has a similar arrangement of territory; namely a share of the ridge and slope, and lower land to the south in the clay vale occupied by the River Beult.

St Peter's Church, Boughton Monchelsea

St Nicholas Church, Boughton Malherbe

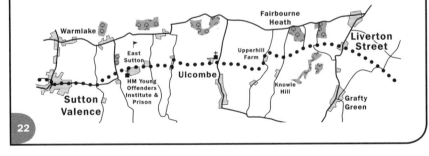

Monchelsea and Boughton Malherbe are no more than hamlets with large churches, a sure sign of shrinking fortunes. Chart Sutton is associated with a school and East Sutton with a prison. Ulcombe and Egerton amount to small villages off the beaten track. The only other settlements on the section of the path are Wierton, which is in the parish of Boughton Monchelsea, and Liverton Street. A place called 'street' usually indicates a more recent settlement without a parish church.

I continued along the Greensand Way towards Ulcombe. Amazingly, I managed to lose the way again, for a third time, and this may have been due to tiredness and the lack of concentration, related to the imbibing of several pints of beer. First I ended up in a small, rural, industrial complex at which I asked directions from a foreign-sounding gentleman and then, trying to follow his directions, took a wrong lane to the south. I realised this was wrong because I knew I shouldn't be going downhill. I guess these mistakes added a substantial part of another mile to the journey. I knew at this point that I would be unable to complete the ambitiously long day's walk and reach my intended destination at Charing, not least because I was struggling with my right knee. However, I did eventually regain the designated path and mused on the fact that most mistakes are made by not knowing exactly where one is on the Landranger Map.

I struggled on through East Sutton, between the church and Her Majesty's Young Offenders Institution and Prison, dedicated to female miscreants. Between East Sutton and Ulcombe there were still magnificent views southwards across the combined valley of the Rivers Beult and Teise, the major tributaries of the Medway. At Ulcombe the path comes in by the church and misses the village itself, which lies north to south down the slope. I plodded on in the late afternoon sunshine, probably a lot longer than I should have, not knowing when to stop. After Upperhill Farm I rested for a while on a wayside bench, considering my options. When I did eventually make Liverton Street I decided to cut my losses and headed north to Lenham Station. This was a painful walk with my knee seizing up as I hobbled through Platt's Heath, and across the motorway to Sandway. I caught a taxi to Charing from the station.

A few weeks later, I returned to Liverton Street to complete the walk to Charing. There were the same excellent views south across the valley all the way to Boughton Malherbe. This lovely hamlet has some old buildings suggesting antiquity, including an imposing manor house and a church, as well as stone-built barns. After Boughton Malherbe the

Greensand Way slips off the Greensand Ridge, crossing rough pasture to skirt Coldbridge Wood, which was unusually still being coppiced. The broken nature of the scarp thereabouts reminded me of the section, still on the Greensand, at Court-at-Street in the vicinity of Lympne, with that little lip of a cliff right at the top, no doubt provided by the same band of harder rock.

From there the path passes through heavily wooded, pheasant-occupied countryside with isolated fields, giving the strong impression of their origins as clearings in the original wild wood. Then there was a steep climb back up beside Foxden Wood of over 100m to the grade II listed, Georgian-styled Egerton House on the top of the hill. From there, again, there were splendid views southwards across the valley of the River Beult to the Weald. The approach to Egerton itself was through another apple orchard with the church looming large, by a path that was picked out by an avenue of larger plum trees. This was a well-established orchard of some age with the trees being heavily pollarded, restricting their eventual height to about 12 feet, making for greater ease of harvesting. I guess these were planted long before dwarfing rootstock was invented. The approach to the village was through the churchyard, which leads into a very pleasant hill-top village. The north-east/south-west orientation of the lanes, previously mentioned, is very apparent hereabouts. To the north-east of the village, the land plunges down into the valley of the burgeoning Great Stour River, and to the south-west down into the broad valley of the Rivers Beult and Teise.

After a short rest and a visit to the local village store to buy a drink and a lump of cheese, I set out north-eastwards towards Stonebridge Green, leaving the Greensand Way behind. I picked up the Stour Valley Walk to the lovingly cared for hamlet of Barnfield, where I had been before and where its opulent grouping of dwellings graced the valley. From Barnfield I took the narrow, twisting lane through pleasant countryside in the upper Stour Valley to the Newlands Bridge, over the railway and motorway. I did wonder whether this new single-track bridge was altogether necessary, given that there are other crossing points to both sides less than a mile away. Crossing over the bridge, I took the footpath behind Newlands Stud towards Coppins Corner. This well-used footpath was in urgent need of attention. The way across the back of the stud was unclear and confused, and the path across the fields to Coppins Corner was littered with broken stiles and damaged signposts. This, I thought, could only be

Liverton Street to Charing

Egerton

Is an attractive hilltop village surrounded by orchards on the Greensand Ridge, at the centre of a parish that includes Stonebridge Green, between the Great Stour River and the headwaters of the River Beult. Egerton House to the west of the village is an imposing listed building with stunning views over the valley of the River Beult.

Egerton House, Star and Garter Road, Egerton

Pheasant
(Phasianus colchicus)

A common naturalised game bird of the British countryside, typically found in woodland edges. The showy males have a barred, bright gold and brown plumage with green, purple and white markings, and a long black tail streaked with brown. The female bird is drab in comparison, with a mottled brown plumage.

Listed Buildings

Listing buildings status helps us acknowledge and understand our shared history. It marks and celebrates a building's special architectural and historic interest and also brings it under the consideration of the planning system, ensuring that some thought will be given to its future use. The older a building is, the more likely it is to be listed. All buildings before 1700 which survive in anything like their original condition are listed, as are most of those dating from between 1700 and 1840. The criteria become tighter with time, so that post-1945 buildings have to be exceptionally important to be listed, and normally a building has to be over 30 years old to be eligible for listing.

Grade I buildings are of exceptional interest, sometimes considered to be internationally important, and comprise only 2.5% of listed buildings.

Grade II* buildings are particularly important buildings of more than special interest, and comprise 5.5% of listed buildings.

Grade II buildings are nationally important and of special interest, and comprise 92% of listed buildings.

In England there are approximately:

374,081 listed buildings

19,717 scheduled ancient monuments

9,080 conservation areas

43 registered historic battlefield sites

46 designated wrecks

17 world heritage sites

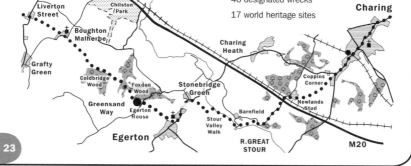

23

57

caused by the destructive effects of sheep grazing, since the little bullies have a habit of breaking through fences and knocking over stiles to create a distinctive, ravaged landscape. I thought I might write to the parish council and suggest they exercise their powers to maintain this clearly important footpath. On reaching Coppins Corner, all that remained of this fill-in leg was to pass up the lane, past modern houses, and cross over the railway and busy A20 to Charing.

I had been to Charing a number of times before on previous excursions and have come to know the place quite well. It is of course another beautiful Kentish village with an attractive High Street and an interesting abbey precinct. On this occasion, I managed to locate the old abbey fish ponds, which now form an area of open space to the east of the High Street. I had taken to staying in the Royal Oak, an excellent gastro-pub at the bottom of the High Street, and I noted this time that the other pub facing the main road had sadly closed.

In the morning, I set off up the High Street towards Charing Hill, a stiff climb at the start of the day. I soon realised that my knee was unlikely to last out for much longer and I seriously doubted at this point whether I would be able to complete the walk. I found this thought particularly lowering, but I struggled up Charing Hill to Stocker's Head and took the yellow road on the map alongside Longbeech Wood, up over the top to Shottenden. The first section to the junction with the A251 was surprisingly busy and more like a B-road, although it is not defined as such. As I breasted the hill on the top of the North Downs I could clearly see the Thames Estuary, Swale Bridge and Kingsnorth Power Station to the north.

I hobbled on as best I could, finding it harder to walk downhill than up. Just before the junction with the A251, the dramatic dry valley from Snoadstreet swept in from my right. At the junction, called Boundsgate Corner, opposite the horse rescue centre, I bought some Victoria plums from a roadside stall. I crossed over the main road and climbed up to Beacon Hill at 102m, a hill like many others with the same name, which was used to light warning beacons in times when this island had been threatened with invasion. After a shallow descent I continued climbing all the way to Shottenden where I peeled off through the village to slide down the lane to Chilham. There was nothing much in the hill-top village of Shottenden, except some pleasant houses and cottages, but it was obviously a good place to live. The unfenced lane snakes down into the

Charing to Shottenden

Beacon Hill, Shottenden

Beacon Hill is a name shared by many hills in the UK, and around the world, because they were historically the site of a warning beacon. In the UK most Beacon Hills take their name from their use as part of Britain's early warning system in Elizabethan times, when they were lit to warn of the coming of the Spanish Armada. However Shottenden Beacon, at a height of 102m, also played a part in the semaphore, optical or shutter telegraph, from Deal to London, built in 1795/96, to warn the Admiralty in London against invasion by Napoleon. Using a system of large wooden shutters, the telegraph passed a message along a long relay of stations between Deal and London: these were positioned at Deal, Betteshanger, Barham Downs, Shottenden, Faversham, Callum Hill, Gads Hill, Swanscombe, Shooters Hill, New Cross, Southwark and the Admiralty building in London. The message was supposed to take two minutes to reach London.

Kent's Changing Climate

The north Kent coast, in the rain shadow cast by the North Downs, is one of the warmest and driest parts of the country in summer, but can experience prolonged cold spells of weather with significant snowfall in winter. The following notable events have happened in recent years:

- The great storm of October 1987 recorded gusts of wind of 103mph in parts of the county.

- Extensive, repeated flooding in 2000.

- The heatwave of 2003 recorded temperatures of 38.5°C at Brogdale near Faversham – the highest UK temperature since records began.

- The heatwave of July 2006 broke records for the highest average temperature for the month of July.

Average annual temperatures in the UK between 1961 and 2006 rose between 1.0°C and 1.7°C, and this rise was particularly significant in south-east England. In addition to this, sea levels have risen recently by about 1mm per year and there has been a marked decline in summer rainfall.

This changing climate has had a severe effect on the amount of rainfall, the replenishment of groundwater acquifers and the water available for domestic, industrial and agricultural usage.

24

valley of the Great Stour River. Racked in pain, I really struggled to get down to the bottom of that hill.

I then crossed over the busy A252 and entered the village by the constricted rise at its western end. Nothing could have prepared me for the spectacle that opened up before me as I entered the square. I had never been to Chilham before and had no idea that it was such a lovely, chocolate-box vision of a place. I sat outside the White Horse pub for a while and soaked up the atmosphere. The buildings set around the square in front of the big house were Tudor in origin but have mostly received the Victorian, black and white treatment. I heard from the pub landlord that the village was often used as a film set for historical dramas.

At this point I think I had already decided to abandon the day's walk. My knee was hurting quite badly, despite the liberal application of painkilling gel, and I thought that if I rested it in the afternoon I might be able to complete the remaining two legs of my journey. I hobbled down the pleasant street to the bottom of the hill and popped into The Woolpack Inn for another pint and something to eat. I helped a bloke sitting at the bar with his *Telegraph* crossword then ambled on to a bus shelter and waited for a bus to take me to Canterbury. As I was not going to spend the afternoon walking, I was determined to relax and enjoy myself.

Arriving in Canterbury about mid-afternoon, I strolled through the city. Although I had been to Canterbury many times before, I did not think that I knew it very well. I asked directions to my place of rest for the evening and walked down past the famous cathedral. I decided to have another pint and sat outside in the sun, passing the time of day people-watching. What struck me was the multitude of young people of many nationalities milling about, attired for summer. The bronzed limbs attested to the fact that the weather in this corner of the country, unlike the rest, had been quite superb. This university city reminded me of Oxford, where I had spent four enjoyable and formative years. I checked into my accommodation in a pub called the Millers Arms, located, funnily enough, down by the River Stour; the mill had long since gone but the pub where the millers drank was still there. In the evening, I went for a modest stroll around the city before retiring back to my berth.

Some weeks later, I returned to Chilham to complete the leg from Chilham to Canterbury that I had missed out. I checked into the same Woolpack Inn and was shown into accommodation that consisted of cottages behind the pub. Outside my window was a huge sweet chestnut tree laden with nuts. Given that it was later in the year, the nuts were ripe and the strong winds of the day before had bought the nuts crashing to the ground. I spent some time methodically scouring the ground for nuts that had burst out of their spiky green outer cases, only picking up the largest ones. If the cases had not split open, a firm stamp with the foot was usually good enough to liberate the contents. I managed to collect a large bag full, which I triumphantly took home to Birmingham.

In the morning, I walked back up to the picturesque square and down past the church then crossed the main A252 and picked up the lane to Old Wives Lees. This was a steep climb out of the Great Stour Valley through orchards. Coming into Old Wives Lees there was a recreation ground, complete with a cricket square and some pleasant houses but little else. From the village centre I took Lower Lees Lane, following the North Downs Way, past a well-established fruit farm. At the end of the lane was a massive complex of oast house buildings that had been converted into residential properties full of character.

At the elbow of the lane I followed the footpath through an apple orchard. The path was picked out by a double line of pollarded lime trees about 2m apart, which had joined at the top to form a perfect green arch. After the orchard, I plunged into a dry valley running down to the great river and faced a sharp, steep climb up again to a height of 72m on the other side. I had to pause more than once on this ascent to get my breath. This was good walking in the morning sun along the side of the valley, affording spectacular views to the south-west. Then I came across another fruit farm and packing station whose orchards clothed the side of the valley. It occurred to me that fruit farmers did not seem to have the same antipathy towards walkers as other types of farmers, since generally the way always seemed clear and well respected.

I carried on to the railway line, but the crossing was closed. I was pushed down into the centre of the massive packing station before I could cross the line by means of a road tunnel. Down in this rather scruffy, working part of the farm there were lines of dilapidated caravans, presumably to house the army of seasonal workers needed to pick the fruit. Once under the railway I climbed back up again, cutting through the fruit laden trees to the skirts of Denstead Wood. Keeping high and following the track, I emerged at a charming group of dwellings in Hatch Lane under a radio mast.

Next, I picked up the lane to the undistinguished settlement of Chartham Hatch. It was a sure sign of the place's visual mediocrity that the North Downs Way didn't even bother to go through the centre of the village. At this point I elected to take Bigbury Road beside Howfield Wood to Harbledown rather than take the designated path through woods to the north. Once on the lane, I came across an enclosure containing a herd of red deer. Normally they are shy animals and hurry away, but today the deer were hard up against the fence, no more than a few yards away, and they made no attempt to flee. The keeper had laid out straw and a very young foal wobbled over and curled up on a patch of hay, while a large stag proudly looked on. I tried to blot out the thought that their tameness might indicate that they were destined to end up as venison.

The lane was quite congested with traffic and I thought I may have made a bad choice of route. I guess that the quantity of traffic could be explained by the fact that the lane crossed the busy A2 trunk road and formed a back entrance, much exploited by locals, to Canterbury. The lane passed through heavily wooded and hilly country and was lined with sweet chestnut trees. I took the opportunity to augment my store of nuts

Shottenden to Chartham Hatch

Chilham

Picturesque village

Film set square

Living the dream

Tourists beware

Preferring to walk out down the hill.

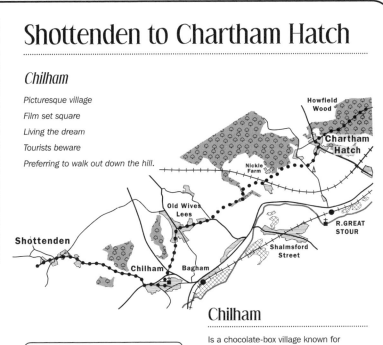

Lime Tree
(Tilia cordata)

Or Linden are large deciduous trees reaching up to 100 feet high which are widely found across the north temperate regions. The exact number of species is subject to debate since many will hybridise freely, both in the wild and in cultivation. The tree has a sturdy trunk and asymmetrical heart-shaped leaves, and the tiny fruit, looking like peas, hang in ribbons. Characteristically aphids are attracted by the rich supply of sap, and are themselves often 'farmed' by ants. Cars parked under these trees can quickly become coated with a film of syrup produced by the aphids. This complicated eco system does not appear to cause any damage to the trees.

Chilham

Is a chocolate-box village known for its charm and beauty, which has been the location for a number of films and television dramas. It is situated in the valley of the Great Stour River, and is centred around an erstwhile market square at the entrance to Chilham Castle. The Tudor buildings facing the square have been transformed by the Victorian 'black and white' treatment. On the north side of the square opposite to the entrance to Chilham Castle is the fifteenth-century church and the sixteenth-century White Horse public house. This arrangement of buildings creates a much admired quintessentially English village scene.

Chilham village square

25

63

already gathered in Chilham. As I was carrying little on my back, the extra weight in my rucksack was not a problem. The Iron Age hill fort and nature reserve of Bigbury Camp, situated in South Blean Woods, lay to the north. Hereabouts, the landscape changed markedly with the chalk bedrock being buried below younger sand and gravels. Erosion of these river terrace deposits of the last Ice Age has sculpted the terrain into sharper angles and steeper slopes. The change in the landscape was quite marked, moving away from the soft, rounded contours of the chalk after Chartham Hatch.

I pressed on to the growing crescendo of traffic noise and over the bridge spanning the A2 trunk road, effectively the Canterbury by-pass. From there I could have gone two ways: down the lane to the attractive village of Harbledown or keep to the North Downs Way. I chose the latter, which took me down a track adjacent to the trunk road through orchards, to a stream at the base of Golden Hill, which is owned by the National Trust. There was a steep climb up the hill, composed of the same dark sand and gravel deposits, thus the name of the hill, through groves of sweet chestnut trees, sharing their bounty. I came out in Mill Lane and made my way into the centre of Canterbury to complete this fill-in leg of the walk.

The following morning, after my original arrival in the city, I set off for the small village of Sarre on the Isle of Thanet. Sidling out of the city, my knee was hurting and I was in low spirits. I forced myself to move out through the outskirts and locate the Stour Valley Walk, which would take me to Fordwich. At first I trudged along a cycle path, which was easy, but after a while the footpath parted company with the cycle path and I struggled along a poorly made track through a growing wood. I crossed several golf course fairways carved out of the wood, a small stream and went straight across an arable field to Fordwich.

This attractive village, by the Great Stour River, used to be the river port for Canterbury. I noticed that there was an ancient building called the 'Town Hall', adjacent to the redundant church, so the place must have been important once. To the East of Fordwich are the Westbere Marshes, which used to be tidal-water accessible from the Wantsum Channel and the sea at Sandwich. I didn't have time to linger in this interesting village and I resolved to visit again as soon as possible.

Coming to the River Stour, I stood on the bridge for a while, observing a shoal of fish battling with the current, before passing over into the

Chartham Hatch to Sturry

Canterbury

Is an historic English cathedral city lying on the Great Stour River. It was colonised by the Romans before it became a Jutish settlement in the kingdom of Kent. After the kingdom's conversion to Christianity at the hands of St Augustine in 597, who became the first Archbishop of Canterbury, the city was established as a centre of religion. There are many historical remains including a city wall founded in Roman times, the ruins of St Augustine's Abbey and a Norman castle. Thomas Becket's murder in the cathedral in 1170 led to the venue becoming a place of pilgrimage for Christians. This pilgrimage provided the theme for Chaucer's fourteenth-century literary classic *The Canterbury Tales* and this literary heritage continued with the work of Christopher Marlowe, a contemporary of William Shakespeare, who was born in the city in the sixteenth century.

Until the Black Death ravaged the city in 1348, it had the tenth largest population, at around 10,000, of anywhere in England, but by the sixteenth century the population had declined to around 3,000. Between 1378 and 1402 the walls of the city were rebuilt and new wall towers were added. In 1381, during the Peasant's Revolt, the castle and archbishop's palace were sacked, and Archbishop Sudbury was beheaded in London.

In 1413 Henry IV became the only monarch to be buried at the cathedral. By the seventeenth century the city's population was growing again and had reached 5,000, with the influx of 2,000 Huguenots escaping religious persecution in the Spanish Netherlands. Canterbury, the only city in Kent, continues today as an important commercial, administrative and religious centre, dominating the east of the county.

Red Deer
(Phasianus colchicus)

The red deer is the largest species of deer and land mammal in Britain, and its meat is used in many parts of the world as a food source (venison).

In Britain, through reintroductions and conservation efforts, red deer populations have increased. It has a summer coat of reddish-brown and the stag has large branching antlers. Its natural habitat is woodlands and forests, but it can adapt to open moorland.

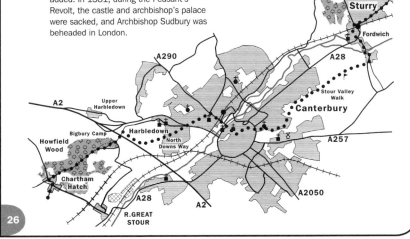

contiguous settlement of Sturry. In contrast to Fordwich, Sturry, located on the busy A28, was undistinguished. I carried on down the pleasant enough High Street, thankfully by-passed, to the railway crossing, where I had to wait for a number of speeding trains to pass through. Across the railway there was a scruffy corner with a ridiculously busy road junction and a derelict petrol station that desperately needed redevelopment. This has now become a common sight in the countryside, with local petrol stations being abandoned, largely, I suspect, due to the relentless competition from out-of-town supermarkets. I minced out along the busy A28 to pick up the road to Hoath. I thought that on another occasion it would be good to walk down through the village of Westbere to the south of the A28 and out across the marshes.

I found the road to Hoath and climbed up and hobbled down the ridge that separated the Great Stour Valley from that of the Sarre Penn. This watershed divides the catchment area of the Great Stour, which reaches the sea at Sandwich from the catchment area of the Wantsum River that flows north through the Chislet Marshes to the Thames Estuary. The Sarre Penn, although deeply cut, was no more than a small stream at this point, collecting headwaters from the north of Canterbury. After the stream, I climbed up again, past some lovely houses, along a Roman road that used to lead all the way to Reculver on the coast. At the Knave's Ash crossroads I turned right and walked on through the pleasant village of Hoath, which was again, unfortunately, devoid of any amenities. This village reminded me very much of Shottenden, a place I had passed through the previous day.

From there, it was all downhill to the marshes and I carried on along the unfenced lane to Chislet Forstal. I had passed through many places on my travels that were called something 'forstal' and I wondered what it meant. There was Chislet and Hicks Forstal locally, Painters Forstal, south of Faversham, and indeed Little Chart Forstal, west of Ashford. I found out later that the term 'forstal' literally means 'land in front of a farm and its farmyard', but that alone did not explain the prevalence of this place name in this part of Kent. The lane twisted around down to the hamlet of Hollow Street and then to the peaceful village of Chislet. I could have done with a rest here and something to eat and drink, but the pub had long since gone. I pressed on past Chitty and disgorged onto the level, parched and cracked plain of the Chislet Marshes. I ventured out into the reclaimed, ploughed fields south of the Gilling Drove, which was

Sturry to Chislet

Chislet Forstal

Hoath

Chislet

Roman Road

East Blean Wood

Rushbourne Manor

Buckwell

Upstreet

R. SARRE PENN

A28

Hersden

Westbere

R.GREAT STOUR

Sturry

A28

Fordwich

The Churches Conservation Trust

Is a charity whose purpose is to protect churches of historic and archaeological interest that are at risk and have been made redundant by the Church of England. The Trust's primary aim is to ensure that the buildings in its care are weatherproof and to prevent any deterioration in their condition. There are sixteen churches in Kent and two in East Sussex that are currently looked after by the trust:

Kent

Burham	St Mary
Capel	St Thomas a Becket
Capel-le-Fern	St Mary
Cooling	St James
East Peckham	St Michael
Fordwich	St Mary the Virgin
Goodnestone	St Bartholomew
Higham	St Mary
Kingsdown	St Catherine
Knowlton	St Clement
Luddenham	St Mary
Paddlesworth	St Benedict
Sandwich	St Mary
Sandwich	St Peter
Stourmouth	All Saints
Waldershare	All Saints

East Sussex

Hove	St Andrew
Preston Park	St Peter

Fordwich

Lying on the River Stour, Fordwich is the smallest place in Britain with a town council, having a population of 351 in the 2001 census. Although it now lies many miles inland, it was once the main port for Canterbury, before the Wantsum Channel silted up. The town grew in the Middle Ages as a port for boats on their way upriver to Canterbury. All of the Caen stone used by the Normans to rebuild Canterbury Cathedral in the twelfth and thirteenth centuries was landed here. It became a limb of the Cinque Ports, but finally lost its status as a town in 1880 when it ceased to have a mayor and corporation. The distinctive Town Hall, having been rebuilt in 1555, is supposedly the smallest in England. The ancient, now redundant, church, in the care of the Churches Conservation Trust, contains part of a carved sarcophagus reputed to have contained the remains of St Augustine.

Fordwich Town Hall

picked out by a line of trees to the north. As it was still relatively early and I only had a little further to go, I slumped down into a dry ditch and dozed off for a while.

Suitably refreshed, I plodded on along the raised track until it suddenly stopped in the middle of the marsh. I was pondering the way forward across the fields to Sarre when a fit-looking cyclist thundered up behind me. He said he knew the way and intended to cycle across the arable field to a point where a footbridge crossed the Sarre Penn. Luckily, I was able to follow in his tyre tracks across the field and successfully locate the bridge. From there, I walked along the southern bank of the Sarre Penn until its confluence with the Wantsum River, and then along the Wantsum to the village of Sarre. I came in by a back lane where there was an elaborate water installation to manage the flow of water between the two rivers, and a newer housing estate.

Sarre really is a settlement at the junction of two main roads, where the London Road to Ramsgate and Margate divides. It used to have two pubs, but only one survives, and there is only a windmill but no church.

Chislet to Birchington

Huguenots

Were members of the Protestant Reformed Church of France (or French Calvinists) from the sixteenth to the seventeenth centuries. These French Protestants were inspired by the writings of John Calvin, and by the end of the seventeenth century, around 200,000 had been driven from France during a series of religious persecutions, about 50,000 relocating in England. In relative terms this could be the largest immigration of a single community into Britain. Many of these refugees gravitated towards Canterbury, but there were also substantial communities in Sandwich, Faversham, Maidstone and London.

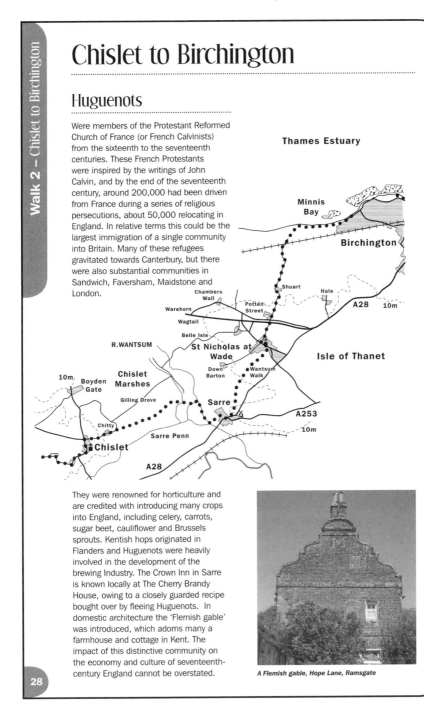

They were renowned for horticulture and are credited with introducing many crops into England, including celery, carrots, sugar beet, cauliflower and Brussels sprouts. Kentish hops originated in Flanders and Huguenots were heavily involved in the development of the brewing Industry. The Crown Inn in Sarre is known locally at The Cherry Brandy House, owing to a closely guarded recipe bought over by fleeing Huguenots. In domestic architecture the 'Flemish gable' was introduced, which adorns many a farmhouse and cottage in Kent. The impact of this distinctive community on the economy and culture of seventeenth-century England cannot be overstated.

A Flemish gable, Hope Lane, Ramsgate

28

Thus, if it has no church, I did wonder whether technically it qualifies to be a village. I sat outside the Crown Inn with a pint of beer and luxuriated in the afternoon sun for a while before booking in. This ancient, fifteenth-century building is also called the Cherry Brandy House. In the evening, the landlord explained that a special type of cherry brandy could be purchased which was based on a jealously guarded recipe brought over by the excellent Huguenots escaping the religious persecutions of Louis XIV. I spent most of the evening sitting at the bar talking to the landlord as there was nothing else to do in Sarre.

In the morning, I started out on the last leg of the walk to Broadstairs on Thanet. From Sarre I headed north on the Wantsum Walk towards St Nicholas at Wade. The path was paved as if encouraging the good citizens of Sarre to make their way to the parish church of St Nicholas. First the path skirted the marshes and then became a slow, gentle climb through arable fields to the village, which sits on the last low westerly manifestation of the Isle of Thanet. With the village at the centre there are roads radiating out to a series of hamlets which would have been on the water line when Thanet really was an island. They include, from west to east, Down Barton, Belle Isle, Wagtail, Warehorn, Chamber's Wall, Bartletts, Shuart and Hale.

I came into the village by way of a scruffy path past the recreation ground. St Nicholas at Wade itself is an undistinguished village with little to recommend it visually in my view, but it may well be a good place to live with an active community spirit. I walked on past the church and turned north in the centre of the village through fields full of horses. I crossed over the Thanet Way by an elaborate footbridge, past a small industrial estate and on to the dilapidated old hamlet of Shuart, to emerge onto Wade Marsh. Like the larger Chislet Marsh, Wade Marsh was reclaimed land and entirely given over to arable farming. Still following the Wantsum Walk, I crossed over the North Kent Railway and came up into Minnis Bay, my first sight of the sea.

I observed the flimsy embankment that ran from Birchington to Reculver, which held back the sea, preventing the marshes from flooding. Beyond, I could see the twin towers of the ruined church at Reculver and the new wind farm out in the estuary. Turning east towards Westgate-on-Sea, I followed an undercliff promenade around the coast, admiring the interesting geology hereabouts. The concrete rampart wound its way underneath the chalk cliffs and above a spectacular tide-deserted, wave-

Birchington to Margate

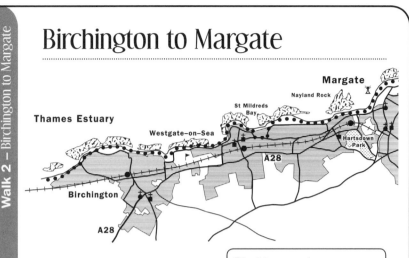

Wave-cut Platform

Is the narrow, flat area often found at the base of a cliff created by wave action, which is most obvious at low tide when they become visible as large areas of flat rock, often littered with rock pools and covered in seaweed. They are formed by destructive waves undercutting the cliff face between the high and low water marks, firstly causing a wave notch which is then enlarged into a cave, causing the cliff to collapse and retreat landward. The coast of Thanet, from Minnis Bay to Ramsgate, is surrounded by a splendid example of this formation, etched into the chalk bedrock, and the cliffs continue to retreat.

Westgate-on-Sea

Is a small seaside resort with a population of 6,600, comprising two sandy bays, Westgate Bay and St Mildred's Bay, separated by the rocky headland of Ledge Point. During the 1860s it was developed from a small hamlet as a more 'genteel' seaside resort, in contrast to the adjoining traditional working-class resort of Margate. Sir John Betjeman captured this atmosphere in his poem 'Westgate-on-Sea'. St Mildred's Bay is named after Mildrith, Thanet's patron saint and one-time abbess of nearby Minster.

Bladderwrack
(Fucus vesiculosus)

Is a type of brown seaweed commonly found on North Sea and Channel coasts with conspicuous air bladders. Three conditions are necessary for the growth of seaweed, namely the presence of  *seawater, sufficient light to drive photosynthesis, and a firm anchorage point. As a result seaweeds commonly occupy the littoral zone, typically on rocky shores.*

Bladderwrack was the original source of iodine, discovered in 1811, and used extensively as a medical preparation. It is also used as an additive and flavouring in various food products.

Westgate Bay, Westgate-on-Sea

cut platform. The cliffs showed clearly the discontinuity between the chalk laid down in the Cretaceous period and the wind-blown sands deposited after the last Ice Age. The indentations in the cliff were invariably paved or concreted over, presumably to help prevent erosion. However, I did feel this was a wasted opportunity; these alcoves, behind the concrete promenade, could be left to go natural, creating a series of habitats that could house interesting eco systems of flora and fauna. This would at least add interest to the promenade and create a reason for people to visit. As it is, I saw a few dog walkers and a few cyclists, but I could see little other reason to come down from the cliff above. There was certainly no beach to speak of. Although there were a number of unappealing access points to the promenade, the settlement of Birchington on top of the cliff seems to largely ignore the coast at this point. As a consequence, it felt neglected, threatening and graffiti ridden. Indeed, I noticed that the new houses on top of the cliff did not face the sea and instead, in a most curious arrangement, back gardens ran up to the cliff edge.

I pressed on to Westgate as the tide swept in, floating carpets of stinking, bladderwrack seaweed. Westgate-on-sea did come down to the shoreline and seemed pleasant enough, but seemingly with few amenities. I slogged on to Margate in the midday sun, rounding Ledge Point, past St Mildred's Bay, Westbrook Bay and Nayland Rock, a large lump of wave-cut platform exposed at low tide, which defines the bay in Margate. I looked for somewhere to lunch but saw only a couple of rundown pubs on the front. I opted to spend an hour resting in the sun and drinking lager in a Tardis-like construction down on the sandy beach. The lower deck contained a bar and bleached boards running over the sand high up on the strand; a most unusual and continental arrangement.

I may have caused raised eyebrows from fellow lunchers when I rolled up my trouser leg and applied lashings of painkilling gel to my knee, musing on the fact that T.S. Eliot, recovering from a mental breakdown, visited Margate sands where he could 'connect nothing with nothing', as recounted in *The Waste Land*. I think I was doing better than that, even though my right knee was killing me. I chatted to the Tardis doctor and barman, who talked me through the rest of my walk around North Foreland, and estimated I would have another 4 miles to go.

After a decent rest, I left Margate on the final leg of this walk. It was a scruffy exit in the vicinity of Margate Caves, up past the construction site

Margate to Broadstairs

Margate and J. M. W. Turner (1775-1851)

The town's history is intimately bound up with the sea, having a proud maritime tradition, being a 'limb' of Dover in the Cinque Ports Confederation, which it joined in the fifteenth century. Margate has been a premier seaside resort for at least 250 years, being a traditional holiday destination for Londoners, drawn to its sea air and sandy beaches. Its Victorian pier was largely destroyed by a storm in 1978. Despite its popularity as a resort in the first part of the twentieth century, with the advent of cheap foreign holidays and greater accessibility to the Continent, the holiday makers stopped coming, and the town was largely left to decay.

The current regeneration of the town is spearheaded by the construction of the Turner Contemporary Gallery, an iconic building situated on the harbourside. The association with Turner rests on the fact that he attended school in the town for a while, and that some of his most famous paintings depict scenes in the locality. Turner was an English romantic landscape painter, watercolourist and printmaker, and although he was a controversial figure in his day, he is now regarded as one of the greatest masters of British watercolour landscape painting. One of his most famous watercolours, *The Fighting Temeraire*, which hangs in the National Gallery, is thought to have been painted off Margate. It depicts one of the last ships of the line, which played a distinguished role in the Battle of Trafalgar in 1805, being towed by tugboats towards its final berth further up the Thames Estuary in 1838 to be broken up for scrap.

The Fighting Temeraire

Thanet

A long hump of chalk
Dry, bleached and harsh
Beached just like a whale
Abreast a marsh
Waiting for its time to swim again.

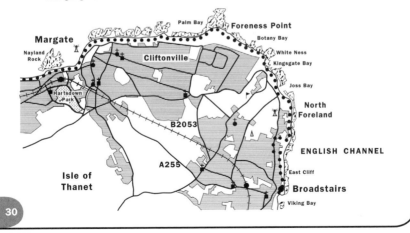

30

for the new Turner gallery, running down to the harbour side. Turner is said to have visited Margate frequently because of the quality of light, and painted perhaps his most famous painting *The Fighting Temeraire* in the town. I passed a derelict building to my right on the other side of the road, which needed redevelopment. In typical fashion, I imagined a scheme that would result in a great improvement in the public realm. I imagined the demolition of the warehouse-like building fronting the road, thereby liberating the houses behind to face onto a new, public, open space.

From then on it was an exhilarating cliff-top walk all the way to Broadstairs. I passed the elegant terraces and hotels of genteel Clifton-ville, by Palm Bay to Foreness Point. Above Kent's own Botany Bay I called into a hotel bar for a pint of cider and got talking to a group of jolly golfers extolling the virtues of this part of the country. Inevitably, the conversation came round to handicaps and I reluctantly admitted to playing off fifteen at one stage. I did not hesitate to mention that there was no way I could play at that level today. Before I had to leave they had convinced me of the merits of looking out for a property to buy in the locality so I could join their club.

I carried on further, past White Ness and on to Kingsgate Bay. Per-ched high above the cliffs it was not possible to appreciate the cliffs and shoreline, and I had no intention of descending for a closer inspection, given the pain in my knee. I popped into the Captain Digby, a cliff-top pub, for another pint of cider. At this point, at North Foreland, I had to walk along the coastal road around the dramatic castle hotel, as there was no cliff-top path. I struggled up past the North Foreland lighthouse before cutting back to the cliff-top at East Cliff, and all that now remained was to amble down into Broadstairs.

I felt elated that I had been able to complete the walk, in spite of problems with my right knee, and I rested on the broad quay overlooking Broadstairs Harbour, the official end of the walk. I stretched out on a bench and dozed off in the afternoon sun. When I was suitably refreshed, I walked slowly around Viking Bay and along the cliff-top to Dumpton Gap, to arrive at my brother's, and prepare for my return to Birmingham in the morning.

3

Dumpton Gap to Rochester (Summer 2010)

I left Dumpton Gap on a Sunday morning, starting another per-ambulation through Kent, my tenth long-distance walk in this part of the country. I walked down on the beach, underneath the crumbling chalk cliffs to Ramsgate, where I located the High Street for some cash. There were vacant shops in the High Street and I recalled a comment of my brother, who said that Ramsgate as a town is just surviving economically. Indeed, inland, at the back of the town towards the main station, in common with many seaside towns, is a most unattractive, rundown area of housing. I passed out of the town by The Grange, Pugin's masterpiece. I took time to appreciate the size of The Grange complex and thought I would have a look around one day.

Pressing on along the cliffs, above the ferry terminal towards Pegwell, I observed a dazzling display of wild flowers prospering on the steep white cliffs. Inland, behind a shaven green, ran the royal esplanade, which I expected to be Victorian or Edwardian, but it was of much more recent vintage. Pegwell itself is contiguous with Ramsgate and consists really of one street showing signs of antiquity, dominated by a large hotel and a pub hugging the cliff top, overlooking Pegwell Bay.

In the large expanse of the bay the tide was right out, and some intrepid people had walked out on the sand to commune with the retreating tide, just the sort of thing one has to do. In the shoreline park, by the mock-Viking ship I bought some water and chocolate to provide sustenance for the journey and strode on through the bungalows of Cliffs End. In time the bungalows gave way to smart new housing and I cut across St Mildreds Meadow to what passes for the centre of this unplanned settlement. To me it felt like a place needing a heart. The evidence of preparatory ground works for the new road, joining the A299 to the A256 to the west of Cliffs End, was all around me.

I carried on down the lane to St Augustine's Cross, erected by Lord

Dumpton Gap to Cliffs End

Augustus W. N. Pugin (1812-1852)

Was an English architect, designer and theorist, best remembered for his work in the Gothic Revival style, particularly churches and the palace of Westminster, (the Houses of Parliament), where he collaborated with Sir Charles Barry and was largely responsible for the interiors of the building. His association with Ramsgate stems from the building of his town house, 'The Grange', overlooking the sea, which has formed a template for domestic architecture. It was designed in a functional manner, from the inside out, the outward appearance being the result of the internal arrangement of functional spaces.

The Grange at Ramsgate

The Formation of the English Channel

Before the end of the last Ice Age, around 10,000 years ago, the British Isles were part of continental Europe, and the North Sea and almost all of the British Isles were covered in ice. The Weald and Artois anticline, that joined Britain and France, appears to have been breached on a number of occasions by catastrophic floods that emanated from large meltwater lakes, growing as the ice retreated in various glaciations, in the southern North Sea. At one time the River Thames was a tributary of the River Rhine, and during the last Ice Age, given that its normal course across the North Sea was blocked by ice, the water flowed through the Straits of Dover towards the Atlantic Ocean. The deep water channel through the straits follows the course of this ancient river today. Although Kent was never glaciated, in common with most of southern England south of the furthest extent of the ice, it has been fundamentally affected by the Ice Ages, including the deposit of wind-blown, rust-coloured brickearth overlying the chalk strata of Thanet.

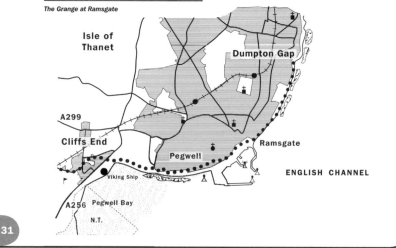

31

Granville, Lord Warden of the Cinque Ports in 1884, to mark the reputed landing place of the saint who reintroduced Christianity to England in 597 AD. I guess this saint has a lot to answer for in view of the atrocities carried out in the name of his captain over the centuries. But the thing that made me laugh was that it was made and sculpted in Birmingham no less, the industrial heartland of England, where every conceivable artefact has been made, and my adopted city.

Passing the golf club, I searched for the footpath alongside the railway that would have afforded me views over the marshes as I proceeded towards Minster; unfortunately, it was closed due to the aforesaid road works. Instead, I was forced to slog along the lane south of the main A229 road, called Cottington road, past Sevenscore and up Grinsell Hill, which was surprisingly busy with traffic on this Sunday morning. However, there were still splendid views out across Minster Marshes across the Stour Valley, with the redundant Richborough Power Station holding centre stage. I passed a farm growing asparagus in the light, friable, chalk-based soil, producing those dark-green, tumescent spears, still being picked after the plants on my own allotment had finished.

At the junction with the lane to the hamlet of Way, I took the footpath all the way into Minster, along a surfaced path, whose purpose, I guess, was to encourage the waverers to go to church. This was a similar arrangement that I had noted on a previous walk on the paved footpath from Sarre to St Nicholas-at-Wade in the neighbouring parish.

As I strolled down into Minster I observed two noisy parakeets in a large oak tree. These birds were first naturalised in England on Thanet and have now spread through much of the Thames Valley. There is much debate about the appropriateness of foreign species gaining a foothold in the country, and the effect on birds sharing the same habitat, but I think they add positively to the diversity of our fauna. I guess it is a question of how their populations are controlled in a highly managed natural environment.

Indeed, I sometimes think the vast number of excellent bodies and organisations operating in the field, within an impressive framework of legislation, are rapidly converting the United Kingdom into a wildlife paradise. I know from professional experience the hurdles one has to go through to achieve planning permission for major development projects and the cost that it adds to the project, sometimes making the scheme unviable. On the plus side, the protection and enhancement of our natural environment, whilst being an ethical position in itself, is greatly promoting our land as a wildlife tourist attraction with all the consequent economic benefits that follow from that: our own brand of eco-tourism if you like. I could envisage, as our traditional industries continue to decline, that in a post-industrial age, this will become a major industry, producing incalculable benefits to our wellbeing, lifestyle and the economy, if it doesn't already.

I came into Minster via Bedlam Court Lane and sat outside St Mildred's Priory for Benedictine nuns, better known as Minster Abbey. While I was sitting on a seat at the entrance, a party of nuns came out for a morning stroll and bade me good morning in a gentle sort of way. This was the second reference to St Mildred that I had come across, and I later found out that she was a Saxon abbess of Minster Abbey. Also, I found it curious that the abbey was located in Bedlam Court Lane, since bedlam is normally associated with a so-called lunatic asylum. I walked on through the pleasant streets of Minster, in the vicinity of the parish church, and turned south across the railway line, taking the long, straight Marsh Farm Road across the marshes to the massive sewage works. Looking back from the bank of the River Stour, I could see the panorama of the village laid out below the flat horizon of Thanet, with planes taxiing along the

Cliffs End to East Stourmouth

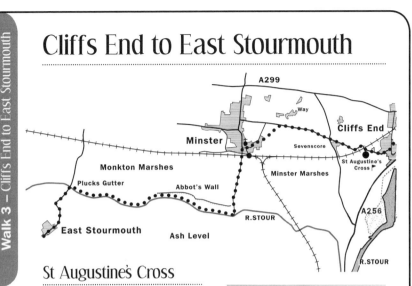

St Augustine's Cross

The cross was erected in 1884 by Lord Granville, Lord Warden of the Cinque Ports, to commemorate the site where St Augustine, the first person to bring Christianity to England, was said to have celebrated his first mass after landing near Ebbsfleet in AD 597. It is reputed that he met King Ethelbert here and converted him to Christianity.

St Augustine's Cross, near Ebbsfleet

Cuckoo
(Cuculus canorus)

The cuckoo is a dove-sized bird with blue-grey upper parts, head and chest, with dark-barred white under parts. With their sleek body, long tails and pointed wings, they are not unlike kestrels or sparrow hawks. They are summer visitors and well-known brood parasites, the females laying their eggs in the nests of other birds, especially reed and sedge warblers. Their range includes the whole of the UK, but they are more likely to be seen in the south and east of England, although a recent population decline makes them a red-list species. They migrate back to Africa in July or August with the young birds leaving a month or so later, having matured.

Sedge Warbler
(Acrocephalus schoenobaenus)

The sedge warbler is a small plump bird with a striking broad creamy stripe above its eye and greenish brown legs. It is brown above with blackish streaks, and creamy white underneath. It is a summer visitor, wintering in Africa, south of the Sahara Desert. Its song is a noisy rambling warble and the bird can be found in reedbeds and damp wetland across the UK.

32

79

runway of Kent International Airport above the village. I had often discussed the merits of developing the former Manston Airfield as a major international airport serving London with my brother. This scenario, however sensible it might seem, would require massive investment in the transport infrastructure, but is still a better option for a third London Airport than any other I have seen. Given that this would bring much needed employment, I can't see the citizens of Thanet objecting to this development as residents everywhere else seem to do.

I stumbled westward along the bank of the river, on an uneven footpath, through an inaccessible river frontage. The better footpath, the Saxon Shore Way, runs on the opposite bank, but there was no way of getting across without going for a swim. Between the Abbot's Wall and the river was an area of land no doubt prone to flooding, which was left to go wild. I saw sedge warblers acrobatically perching sideways on the top of the reeds. Then I also heard the distinctive, but now quite rare, call of its parasitic friend, the cuckoo, whose selfish life story is hard to accept, even in nature.

After a couple of miles along the riverbank, I crossed over the River Stour at Pluck's Gutter and popped into the Dog and Duck for lunch. It was here in the 1970s that four friends from Bexley came down for a weekend's camping. After imbibing at the pub I remember us playing cricket down the middle of the campsite as it was getting dark, much to the protests of the inmates of the other tents. One man came out and asked if he could have a bat and after a few balls, respectfully defending against my bowling, he hooked the ball into the River Stour, thus effectively ending our noisy and inconsiderate play, just as he had intended.

I walked on through winding lanes to East Stourmouth and stopped for another pint in The Rising Sun. The villages of East and West Stourmouth, lying on a promontory, reaching a height of 9m, would once have been at the mouth of the River Stour where it issued into the Wantsum Channel, which originally separated the Isle of Thanet from the mainland. Then, the villages would have been of more strategic importance, guarding the entrance to the River Stour, which was once navigable all the way up to Fordwich, Canterbury's port.

I took narrow back lanes to Preston to get away from the traffic. The hedgerows in Santon Lane were carefully tended to create tall windbreaks to keep the worst of the wind and frost off the fruit in the adjoining

East Stourmouth to Wingham

Ickham

The village is centred around a single, wide, unimproved road and has a thirteenth-century parish church plus many old and well-preserved houses. The street contains farm buildings, workshops and the pub, as well as cottages and the church, which gives it an evocative timeless quality. The church is perfectly set off by the village green in an exceptional, relatively unimproved Kentish village which harks back to former times.

Wingham

Is an attractive village with a distinctive tree-lined main street, with many fine old buildings dating from the thirteenth century. It is a surprising observation that the current twisting A257 from Richborough to Canterbury, which passes through the village, was once the ancient coastal road along the Saxon Shore, when Thanet was still an island.

Historic buildings, Wingham

Ickham Church and village green

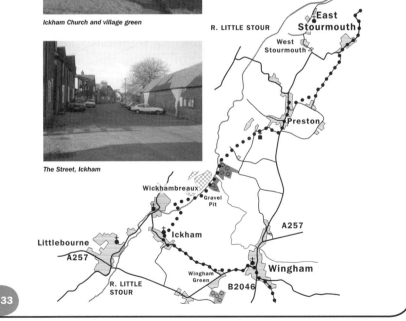

The Street, Ickham

81

orchards. Approaching Preston, I took a well-marked footpath to the pub on the main road, The Moon and Seven Stars, my third pit-stop in a relatively short distance. From there, I made my way to Preston church, by Preston Court, away from the centre of the village and through a small wood, to emerge on the soft low-lying fields of the Little Stour Valley. After crossing over a small bridge, marked as a weir on the map, although it now held back no water, I sauntered alongside the gurgling river, past its confluence with the Wingham river, between large sheets of water, the result of gravel extraction.

Picking up a pleasant lane at the back of Wickhambreaux, I made my final approach to Ickham across fields from the hamlet of Seaton, along a well-marked footpath lined with trees. I came into Ickham by its lovely church set back from the main street by a narrow green, flanked on one side by jet-black barns, no doubt of considerable antiquity. Finally, I arrived at the Duke William pub, the end of my first day's walk, holding centre stage in a strangely evocative English village street. I reflected that in this vicinity there were many attractive and well-maintained villages, including Stodmarsh, Wickhambreaux and Ickham itself, combined with the larger villages of Littlebourne and Wingham, set in a quiet, soft, well-watered landscape, intensively cultivated for peas, beans and potatoes. I spent a pleasant evening in the pub, eating, drinking and talking to the landlord and his bar staff, as there was nothing else to do.

In the morning, I walked down the unimproved village street, admiring for a moment the splendid prospect of the church. There were quaint cottages, farm buildings and workshops situated in the wide street without pavements, which created the impression of life in a previous time. I carried on towards Wingham through the rich farmlands of the Little Stour Valley. At Wingham Green, I joined the main A257 road for the stretch into Wingham Village, lying at the bottom of the North Downs. I paused for a while, appreciating the tree-lined High Street of this attractive village before heading south-west, taking a long lane beside a long, thin wood known as the Goodnestone Road. This wood was the home of Elvis the pig and his family, and I fed them fresh leaves from the trees bordering the lane, which they could not reach, before I came across a notice requesting me to desist from this activity.

Rising all the time, I picked up a well-marked footpath to Good-nestone, passing through a wood redolent with wild garlic. To my right I could hear the clamour of a rookery in a copse before the village.

Goodnestone was a pleasant, almost feudal village with a pub, church and large house, complete with parkland. I carried on through the park to Chillenden, an equally historic and attractive village on the gentle dip slope of the North Downs. Approaching the village, I could see an isolated windmill in a field to my left and indeed, the cooling towers of Richborough Power Station, some 6.5 miles away as the crow flies. Beyond that, a further 5 miles on, I could see the tall, distinctive block of flats on Thanet behind the town of Ramsgate, both very distinctive landmarks.

After Wingham, the landscape had changed with elevation to large, sweeping fields of wheat, or grass for grazing. These fields had probably always been larger than those down in the valley due to the different type of soil and climate, but it was quite clear from their shape that many hedgerows had been grubbed up in their development, making them suitable for mechanised forms of arable farming. The loss of hedgerows in the English countryside continues to be of considerable concern, but it attests to the fact that the landscape is always changing, responding to economic forces and new technology. Indeed, the typical hedgerow of the English countryside is itself a fairly recent event, dating from the field enclosures that took place in the 1800s as part of the agricultural revolution of that time. There are historical landscapes, which may well be worth preserving, and there are new, altered landscapes with distinctive character, which can hopefully be developed and improved, thus adding to the rich variety of the English landscape.

After Chillenden, from the splendidly named Cuckolds Corner, I took another long, winding lane all the way up to Elvington, a stiff climb on the best of days, past the sombre, derelict Kittingdon Farm, with its rusting wind pump and corrugated metal roofs, in the bottom of the dry valley. From this point on, looking north again, I could still see the landmarks of the power station and the block of flats on Thanet. From Elvington, I found a byway, now called the Miner's Way, and realised that I was slap bang in the middle of the Kent Coalfield. To my right, near the villages of Nonington and Aylesham, was the Snowdown Colliery; to my left, towards Deal, on the coast, were Betteshanger and Tilmanstone Collieries. The miners would have used these byways to get to and from work and this particular route, The Miners Way, led from Elvington to Sibertswold, both former mining communities.

I walked south-west along the Miner's Way for a mile or so before

Wingham to Elvington

The Kent Coalfield

Coal was discovered near Dover in 1890, which led to a rush to exploit this resource. Many coal mines were started, only to fail, and just four collieries survived: Snowdon, Tilmanstone, Betteshanger and Chislet. Most of the workers for these mines came from traditional mining areas such as South Wales, the Midlands, the North-East and Scotland, and to house them new villages were built, including Aylesham, Elvington and Hersden. Other villages such as Sibertswold were enlarged by the development of houses for miners. The last colliery, Betteshanger, closed in 1989.

In 2001 Dover District Council launched the Coalfields Heritage Initiative Kent project, led by Dover Museum and the White Cliffs Countryside Project, with the aim of recording and preserving East Kent's mining heritage.

The map below shows the surprising extent of the coalfield, from Folkestone in the south, to Canterbury and the Elham Valley in the east, to Pegwell Bay in the north, with coal bearing strata stretching out under the waters of the Channel.

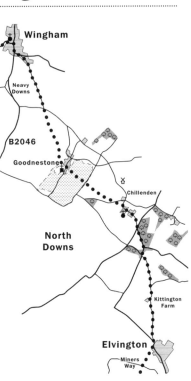

The Kent coalfield

Ramsons or Wild Garlic
(Allium ursinum)

The Latin name derives from the brown bear's taste for the bulbs, and they typically grow in deciduous woodlands with moist soils, preferring slightly acidic conditions. In early spring they show themselves as swathes of white flowering plants with a distinctive garlic smell. All parts of the plant are edible and have been used for food since ancient times. However, the leaves are very similar to that of lily of the valley and the autumn crocus, both of which are highly poisonous.

34

locating a footpath to take me down to Golgotha and over the East Kent Railway, another steam enthusiast's adventure running from Sibertswold to Eythorne, which used to be used for moving coal. Sibertswold is an ancient village, reputedly named after Sibert, a tribal king in these parts. It was expanded by providing housing for miners in the early twentieth century. Sibertswold is a curiosity in the sense that it is a village with two accepted names, the other being Shepherdswell. I came in to the village by the lower, south-eastern arm and climbed up to the pleasant green where I rested for a while. I lunched in the The Bell Inn on the green before forcing my legs to carry me on to Coldred, with the promise of another pint in the pub there. When I arrived in the pleasant, compact village of Coldred, with its large central village green and integral pond, I found that the pub, The Carpenters Arms, had clearly fallen upon hard times and closed down. Overcoming my disappointment, I could understand why a pub in such a small village would struggle to survive; after all, you can only have so many upmarket eating places, but I felt its loss at the centre of the village would be a devastating blow to village life.

I struggled on in sombre mood, passing another large rookery, up to the A2 and down the steep hill into the Lydden Valley, the first time I had descended significantly for many miles. My left hip was becoming painful and I minced down the hill into the village. Although my hip was hurting I was entirely pleased and grateful that my right knee, which had caused me so much trouble on my previous walk, was holding up well after an operation in the winter. The Lydden Downs lay to my left as I descended into the valley, a much-cherished stretch of chalk downland managed by the excellent Kent Wildlife Trust.

I passed by Lydden church, which was poorly set off by the adjoining scruffy complex of farm and industrial buildings strung out along the road. Down the bottom of the hill there was a bone dry hole in the ground, which used to be the village pond, or at least a pond when there was sufficient ground water to fill it, since such resources would be very scarce in a mainly dry valley. The pub at the bottom of the hill had closed for the day and I pressed on to the second village pub called Hope, where I managed another pint and a rest.

I couldn't help noticing how the atmosphere changed as I descended into the valley; Lydden was untidy and badly organised and perhaps owed more to the influence of Dover down the valley than to the high downs. The village consists of an unplanned triangle of roads lined with buildings with an open space in the centre. The future improvement of Lydden would require this central area to be integrated into the village structure, providing open spaces, pedestrian links, land for new housing and better access to and presentation of the church. In other words, the village needs a local plan and given its location in a dry valley in the North Downs, it could be a very attractive village, as it is now relieved of traffic by the A2 by-pass.

Finishing my pint, I braced myself for the hard climb up out of the valley on the road to Alkham. The road passed through an MOD training site and I read a notice which said its gate should be kept closed except when there was a sentry on guard. I wondered how often and for what this site was used, and whether this hillside was really required for military purposes. After the first steep slog out of the valley, on the broad top of the downs, I passed through the hamlets of Little London and Chalksole. I carried on climbing all the way to the final precipitous drop into the next dry valley, enfolding the picturesque village of Alkham. The houses in the village were piled up the sides of the valley, with the church looking over the shoulder of the Marquis Hotel, formerly the Marquis of Granby P.H., my billet for the night. Alkham reminded me of a village in the Yorkshire Dales, Swaledale or Wharfedale, and the only relatively flat piece of land right down in the valley bottom was given over to the cricket pitch, something every true Yorkshireman would understand perfectly well. The village is situated at the end of one arm of an extensive, mainly dry valley system, which also includes Lydden and the main valley that contains the fitful River Dour and Dover.

In the morning, I left the village, going south on the way to West Hougham, eventually making for the Folkestone Warren. I managed the first steep climb out of the Alkham valley with ease and felt that my body was getting used to the routine. It was a pleasant walk on a warm, damp morning on a day threatening serious rain; because of this, I wanted to make as much progress as quickly as possible. Soon, I came to West Hougham, a pleasant dormitory place without a parish church, and took a well-marked footpath to the A20, the extension to the M20 leading down to the docks at Dover, which appeared to allow me to cross the big road. However, when I arrived in the hollow of a truncated dry valley there was no such access across the road. After thrashing around for a while, searching for the way, I cut my losses and trudged west, beside the main road, back to the lane running from West Hougham to Satmar.

Elvington to Alkham

Alkham

Is an attractive, small village in a picturesque, extensive, dry valley in the North Downs. The valley stretches all the way to Dover and has a distinctive wind gap in the scarp slope in the country above Folkestone. According to the 2001 census, the parish population, which includes the settlements of Chalksole and Ewell Minnis as well as Alkham, was 691.

The Marquis of Granby, Alkham

Lydden Downs and The Kent Wildlife Trust

The Lydden and Temple Ewell Downs are a remarkable stretch of chalk downland owned and managed by the Kent Wildlife Trust. It is a National Nature Reserve, a Site of Special Scientific Interest and a Special Area of Conservation for its flora and fauna; notable for its range of orchids, insects and butterfies. The Kent Wildlife Trust, founded in 1958, is the leading conservation charity in the county, with the purpose of protecting wildlife, educating the public, influencing decision makers and restoring habitats. The Trust manages, with the aid of its 30,000 members, 60 nature reserves covering more than 3,000 hectares of land for wildlife. These endeavours aim to produce a high quality natural environment that contributes to people's health, well-being and quality of life, producing large wildlife-rich areas that can be of incalculable economic benefit through the development of tourism and ecosystem support, such as assisting crop pollination.

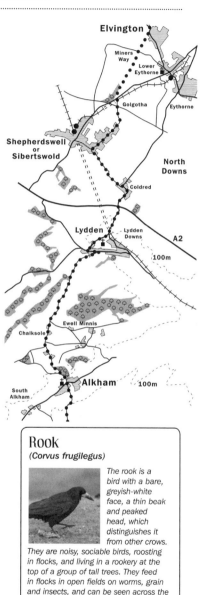

Rook
(*Corvus frugilegus*)

The rook is a bird with a bare, greyish-white face, a thin beak and peaked head, which distinguishes it from other crows. They are noisy, sociable birds, roosting in flocks, and living in a rookery at the top of a group of tall trees. They feed in flocks in open fields on worms, grain and insects, and can be seen across the whole of England.

35

From Satmar, by another well-marked footpath crossing the same dry valley, passing through Abbots Land Farm, I made for the B2011 coast road from Capel-le-Ferne.

I passed down the side of a mobile home park hugging the cliff-top and stood for a while where the footpath started to wind its way down the cliff into The Warren. There were stunning, dramatic views of the white cliffs, the undercliff, the railway and the sea beyond. I had always wanted to walk through this piece of country and now I was going to do it. The rain was just about holding off and it was time to commit to the journey. I clambered gingerly down the steep, winding path, pausing frequently to look back at the intimidating cliff and wonder at the breath-taking descent. Near the base of the cliff, the micro-climate seemed to change into warm, humid, jungle-like conditions and as a consequence, the vegetation became more luxuriant. This undercliff, the result of many landslips over the centuries, reminded me of the undercliff on the Jurassic Coast between Seaton and Lyme Regis, which I had walked recently with my partner. The Warren is renowned as a good place to find fossils and is the result of permeable chalk strata slipping over the impervious gault clay.

I came to a point down in The Warren where I had a choice of path: I could cross over the railway line by a little concrete bridge, hoping to cross the line again further on, or I could stay on the land side of the railway. I decided to cross over the railway, but was unable to re-cross the railway further down. I had to exit the undercliff by the Martello Tower on the outskirts of Folkestone, as the railway disappeared into a tunnel. No doubt, I managed to miss the wildest and most challenging walk to the landward side, underneath the cliffs, which I still might do on another occasion, but today I had a pleasant, almost-flat walk on tracks designed as vehicular access to the seafront. As I hiked along I was able to admire the magnificent sea cliffs towering above me, but I did not encounter the little creature whose husbandry would have given the place its name; namely, the humble rabbit. Maybe they had all been wiped out in the 1950s in the myxomatosis episode and had not yet made a recovery in this location.

From the entrance to The Warren, at the Folkestone end, I embarked on the lung-splitting climb up Dover Hill, to the Valiant Sailor pub at Capel-le-Ferne. I had done this climb once before on my second walk and, as then, needed frequent stops to catch my breath, allowing me time

Alkham to Capel-le-Ferne

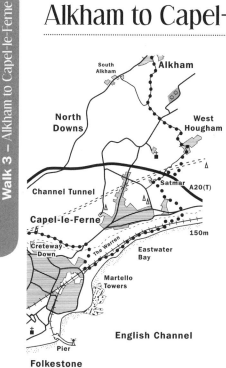

South Alkham · Alkham · North Downs · West Hougham · Channel Tunnel · Satmar · A20(T) · Capel-le-Ferne · 150m · Creteway Down · The Warren · Eastwater Bay · Martello Towers · English Channel · Pier · Folkestone

Orchids and Creteway Down

There are tremendous views across Folkestone from Creteway Down, which forms a wildlife corridor between The Warren and the Folkestone Downs further east. It is itself a Site of Special Scientific Interest of European importance, especially for the many types of orchid, including a colony of spider orchids, found growing on the down. The orchid family, believed to be the largest, is a diverse and widespread family of monocots, which includes the genus of the vanilla plant.

Kent is particularly blessed with a wonderful array of wild orchids which commonly grow in the many chalk grassland reserves in East Kent. The sheer elegance and beauty of these plants hold an enormous fascination for botanists, and many partake in an annual pilgrimage to photograph some of their favourite species. Some orchids are common and can be found throughout the UK, whilst others are rare and can be found in only one or two locations, such as the Monkey and Lizard orchids in Kent.

Besides the orchids there are many wild flowers of ancient chalk grassland to be found on Creteway Down, including quaking grass, salad burnet and rock rose, which can be seen best on the steep slopes leading down to Folkestone. On top of the down, which is covered with a mildly acidic clay-with-flint deposit, gorse and sheep's sorrel flourish.

The North Downs Way follows the crest of the hill on a route that has probably been a footpath for thousands of years, and it is thought that a Roman road from Lemanis, the ruined Roman port below Lympne, to Dover followed this path. Today, National Cycle Route No.2, which leads from Dover to Folkestone and on to the West Country, crosses the down.

Common Spotted Orchid
(Dactylorhiza fuchsii)

Is a commonly occurring species of European orchid which is widely variable in colour and height, ranging from 15 to 60 cm. The flower, which can be seen from June to August, can vary from white to pale purple with purple spots, and is highly perfumed, which attracts day flying moths. It is the most common orchid in Britain and can be found from alkaline marshes to chalk downland habitats.

36

to look over the vast, urban area that is Folkestone. As I reached the top at Capel, it started to rain and I went into the pub for lunch and a rest. With one eye on the lowering clouds and feeling damp and cold from my cooling, sweat-soaked clothes, my spirits plummeted. The weather continued to close in, so I decided to abandon the day's walk, and ordered a taxi to take me to Etchinghill.

A few weeks later, I returned to complete the missing leg and, starting from the Valiant Sailor public house on the top of the downs, I took the lane going west across Creteway Down. The lane was cut deeply into the hillside, worn down over the centuries by endless traffic, and lined with brambles in pink flower. Every so often, a gap would appear in the hedgerow, offering up fabulous views across Folkestone to the sea. Immediately, I noticed the great variety of plant species growing along the lane and gorse bushes cloaking the down. I passed a Second World War gun emplacement blockhouse in a strategic position with excellent views up and down the coast. I understand that some of these solid but less-than-attractive constructions, which are common on the Kent coast, are now listed buildings.

Passing behind the distinctive, conical mound of Sugarloaf Hill, I could see the extent of suburban Folkestone below me. Descending to cross the Canterbury Road to Hawkinge, I could see the whole sweep of St Marys Bay to Dungeness stretched out before me. I noticed the unusual, pale-blue, flowered, field scabious growing in the side of the lane. After crossing the road to Hawkinge and climbing again, I read some informative public notices which stated how the unimproved grassland of the Folkestone Downs were managed by grazing cattle to protect and promote the rich variety of plant species growing there. The boards described how field scabious had been reintroduced and that all seven species of native thistle, some distinctly rare, could be found growing on the downs.

I carried on, up and over Round Hill, where the A20 dramatically tunnels through the chalk escarpment, and then onto Castle Hill, which I circled by following the outer rampart of the ring and bailey earthwork chiselled out of the hill by our Iron Age ancestors. Making my way back to the lane, overlooking a peaceful reservoir in a severe indent into the scarp slope below, I observed how massive the ancient earthworks were, and thought that many people would have lived and worked in the extensive bailey. Indeed, archaeologists had discovered evidence of prehistoric settlement all around the area, and in particular at Holywell at the base of Sugarloaf Hill. I stood for a moment above the spot where the Channel Tunnel Railway made its clinical entrance underground, and observed the huge marshalling yards of the terminal complex.

I walked along the Pilgrim's Way through a tunnel of trees above the reservoir, before picking up the open downs again. There, I agreed with a public notice board which described the Folkestone Downs as a special place and of course, the habitat was internationally important for the rare plants found thereabouts. Below me, I observed the steady and orderly progress of a snaking line of cars being gobbled up by a hungry, interminable, double decker train, set to shoot off through the tunnel to France.

Above the village of Peene, I turned inland and dropped into a hollow bowl of chalk, which may have been a quarry at one time. To the west, I could see another conical hill in Summerhouse Hill, loosely attached to Tolsford Down, a twin to Sugarloaf. Both hills, in geomorphologic terms, were outliers, left high and dry by the retreating and eroding scarp face of the North Downs. A similar, albeit further developed example, occurs in the Cotswolds, east of Gloucester, with the free-standing hills of Churchdown and Robinswood.

Trekking north along the Pilgrim's Way, I stayed up high, picking up the lane that led me down into the village of Etchinghill. I noticed a large number of cyclists out for a ride on this pleasant Sunday morning, utilising National Cycle Path Number 2 out of Folkestone. Coming into the village, I made for the New Inn, where I had previously spent an evening and after consuming a pint of beer and some excellent crab cakes, I ordered a taxi to take me back to Capel-le-Ferne and my car, completing this missing part of the journey.

First time round, I had arrived in Etchinghill by mid-afternoon and sat in a bus shelter wasting time until I could get into my bed and breakfast accommodation. I felt a bit of a fraud really as the weather was still overcast but the rain was only light drizzle and I thought I could have completed this leg at a push. I was reminded of something that my brother said to me that now rang true, that the weather always looked worse over Capel, and that day proved to be the case. I spent the evening in the local pub, eating and talking to the landlord at the bar, before retiring to bed.

In the morning, I left the unremarkable village via a footpath opposite

Capel-le-Ferne to Etchinghill

Field Scabious
(Knautia arvensis)

Field scabious is a perennial herb, once used for treating scabies, occurring in grassland on well-drained soils. Locally, it is a common weed of cultivation, especially in field borders on chalk. It has an attractive light blue flower and established plants are drought resistant, with a deeply penetrating tap root. They are naturally found in open sunny situations, such as roadside verges.

Adonis Blue Butterfly
(Polyommatus bellargus)

Is a blue butterfly of chalk grasslands that has declined rapidly over recent decades due to the detioration of its habitat, by the absence of grazing. Great efforts have been made by conservation organisations and local Biodiversity Action Plans to stabilise and encourage the growth of populations of chalk grassland butterflies by managed grazing programmes.

The Folkestone Downs

Are an area of chalk downland above Folkestone, stretching from East Cliff to Peene Quarry, where the eastern end of the North Downs escarpment meets the English Channel, reaching heights of over 150 metres. Protected within the Folkestone to Etchinghill SSSI due to its geological and biological interest, it is one of the largest areas of unimproved chalk downland in Kent, with typically rare flora including horseshoe vetch, small scabious, bedstraw broomrape, orchids and lichens. It is also home to many birds, butterflies and moths, including the Adonis blue butterfly. Much of the downs are owned by Eurotunnel, whose massive installation lies below the downs, and are managed by the White Cliffs Countryside Project. The cessation of grazing, after the Second World War, encouraged the invasion of coarse grasses and scrub. This resulted in a reduction of the grassland flora, particularly after the rabbit population was devastated by myxomatosis in the 1950s. Cattle grazing was restored in 1990, and much of the downland is now open access land following the Countryside and Rights of Way Act 2000. The downs contain the distinctive Sugarloaf and Castle hills, the latter being the site of an extensive Iron Age fort. These features are known as outliers and are formed by erosion causing the scarp slope of the chalk to retreat, and eventually leaving free standing hills protected by a harder capping layer of rock.

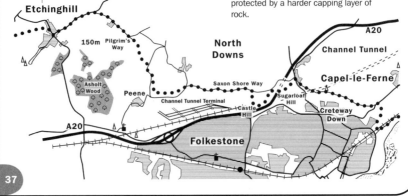

the pub and proceeded by a narrow path between properties to emerge in an area of paddocks and horse pastures. The footpath was badly maintained and uneven, and I managed to give myself an electric shock while holding onto a fence to keep my balance. It was a low-level, dull thud of a shock, as if someone had clapped me on the back too enthusiastically. Coming out of the village, I picked up a well-marked footpath that breasted the swelling down through fields of knee-high wheat. To my left was the Etchinghill beacon on the Tolsford Down, standing out like a steel sculpture on a high point of the North Downs at 180m. Such constructions are of course essential to modern communications, including radio, television and, not least, mobile phones, one modern invention that I would find it hard to do without.

I strode on, looking for the North Downs Way, and picked up a small lane, which I had walked before, down into the picturesque village of Postling, before clambering up to the top of the downs through a nature conservancy site. The site formed a delightful valley enclave into the downs, cropped by sheep, with those characteristic ridges of soil slipping down the slope. At this time of year it was smothered in buttercups, daisies and blue-flowered vetch. The view from the top was fabulous seeing the whole valley lying between the North Downs at 180m high to the Greensand Ridge at Lympne at 100m high spread out before me. I could clearly see Stone Street, Stanford and the Folkestone Races at Westenhanger, the motorway and railways, and Lympne Castle on the horizon.

After a lovely walk in the morning sunshine of maybe a mile or so along this high ridge, I came to Stone Street at Farthing Common, the Roman road from Lemanis near Lympne to Canterbury. The common was again managed by Natural England and it was also completely smothered in buttercups, the like of which I've not seen before anywhere. I carried on north along the edge of Stone Street and into a field graced by a herd of light-brown cattle, all looking very fetching with yellow tags for earrings. I guess the bull calves would not have been long for this world, so it was pleasing to see them enjoying their short lives in such pleasant surroundings.

At Cobbs Hill I plunged down into a significant recess of the North Downs Scarp, a so-called wind gap created by the novice stream that flows down to the East Stour River, which is occupied by the village of Stowting. I carried on along a twisting, undulating lane to the village of

Etchinghill to Brabourne

Creeping Buttercup
(Ranunculus repens)

Creeping buttercup is the common buttercup seen in the wild and as a garden weed. It is easily recognisable by its glossy yellow flowers and can grow practically anywhere, but it particularly likes poorly drained soil. ' It spreads by strong runners that root along the way, and if left undisturbed, in uncultivated ground, will form a dense mat, which can produce a spectacular display in summer.

Farthing Common and Postling Downs

Farthing Common forms an area of grassland that is common land on the North Downs at a height of 185 metres, at the junction of the ancient trackway along the downs from Folkestone and Stone Street, the Roman road running between Lympne and Canterbury. From the vantage of the common there are extensive views across Kent, and on a clear day it is possible to see as far as the cliffs at Fairlight in East Sussex, and even the South Downs. East of Farthing Common along the trackway on the ridge are the Postling Downs, a rich area of semi-improved chalk grassland with a wide variety of plant species including orchids. The sleepy village of Postling, which has a long history of occupation since before the Domesday Book, nestles below the downs.

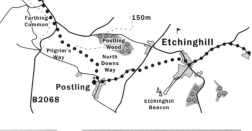

Five Bells Inn, Brabourne

The Postling Downs

38

94

Brabourne, where I had a lunch break in The Five Bells. The pub was under new management and I got talking to the new landlord who had incredibly ambitious plans for the place, including the provision of bed and breakfast accommodation to cater for walkers doing the North Downs Way, and an organic farm shop to sell locally produced food. I was impressed by his enthusiasm.

From this pleasant village on the Pilgrim's Way nestling under the downs, I continued west on an ancient track, long since lost under ploughed fields growing acres of wheat. Although the track was not discernible, there was a clearly managed path through the wheat, which had been created by the application of a systemic herbicide to clear the ground. This would no doubt have been the work of the local parish council after the farmer had sown right across the path. Last time I walked in this vicinity to the south of Wye, I had great trouble in picking out the footpaths, but this time, in keeping with the whole of this walk, the authorities appeared to have got their act together, and kept the footpaths clear. For me, this has made a huge difference to the enjoyment of this walk.

I cut back up to the Pilgrim's Way to strike diagonally up the scarp slope to join the North Downs Way towards Coldblow Farm, an area of outstanding natural beauty, farmed to enhance the chalk grassland, mainly by the grazing of sheep. Beyond Coldblow is the dramatic indentation in the line of the downs, locally named Devil's Kneading Trough, although it is not named on the Landranger Map. On this fine summer's afternoon there were many people who had made the trip out from Wye, or maybe even Ashford, to stroll around or sit on blankets on the ground, to admire the view over Brook below and the Great Stour Valley.

Further on, over the Wye Downs, the crowds disappeared and I made good progress towards Wye itself, which is situated in the throat of the Great Stour Valley. On the downs above Wye there was evidence of various earthworks associated with past memorials and statements of identity by the citizens of Wye, with the latest contribution being the Millennium Stone. I sat on a seat overlooking it and was amazed that the seat was dedicated to the memory of a namesake of mine, one Warwick Rance, a resident of nearby Wye. I was somewhat nonplussed by this curious coincidence. I cut down through a wood on a footpath called Wibberley Way and emerged in the fields above Wye where a number of overdressed souls had chosen to go for a walk in the heat of the early

Brabourne to Wye

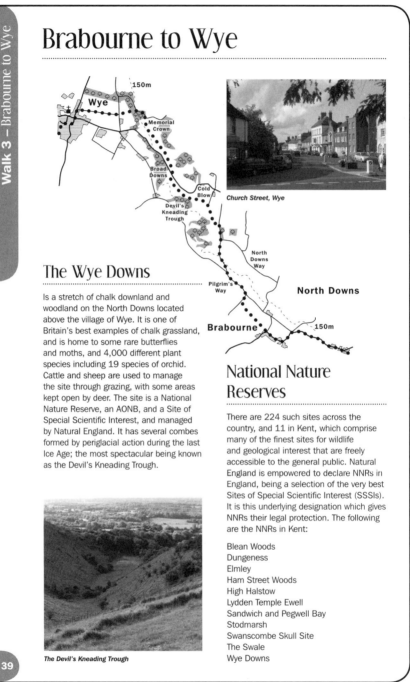

Church Street, Wye

The Wye Downs

Is a stretch of chalk downland and woodland on the North Downs located above the village of Wye. It is one of Britain's best examples of chalk grassland, and is home to some rare butterflies and moths, and 4,000 different plant species including 19 species of orchid. Cattle and sheep are used to manage the site through grazing, with some areas kept open by deer. The site is a National Nature Reserve, an AONB, and a Site of Special Scientific Interest, and managed by Natural England. It has several combes formed by periglacial action during the last Ice Age; the most spectacular being known as the Devil's Kneading Trough.

The Devil's Kneading Trough

39

National Nature Reserves

There are 224 such sites across the country, and 11 in Kent, which comprise many of the finest sites for wildlife and geological interest that are freely accessible to the general public. Natural England is empowered to declare NNRs in England, being a selection of the very best Sites of Special Scientific Interest (SSSIs). It is this underlying designation which gives NNRs their legal protection. The following are the NNRs in Kent:

Blean Woods
Dungeness
Elmley
Ham Street Woods
High Halstow
Lydden Temple Ewell
Sandwich and Pegwell Bay
Stodmarsh
Swanscombe Skull Site
The Swale
Wye Downs

afternoon. The famous line from Noel Coward's song '*Mad dogs and Englishmen go out in the midday sun*' sprang to mind.

I descended into Wye, past its famous horticultural college, which I was now led to believe had effectively closed for business after an unsuccessful takeover by Imperial College, London University. There were vast areas given over to greenhouses, which one can only assume are now redundant. There is little that depresses the spirit more than a redundant greenhouse, whose entire purpose is propagation and growth.

Once in Wye, my first port of call was the chemist to buy suntan and after-sun lotion, the latter to be administered to the burnt backs of my legs as soon as possible. It was not until recently, since we have become more conscious of the damaging effects of the sun, that I would have been aware of the difference between these two applications. It was still early and I decided to see if the attractive pub down by the river was open, but I was turned away by a rather officious barmaid who would not serve me one minute after closing time. I tried to suggest to her that I wouldn't be a problem, quietly sitting in the garden supping my pint, but my pleas fell on deaf ears. So, to waste some time, I retraced my steps up the High Street, sat in a park near the church and applied the after-sun lotion assiduously to my burnt legs, before retiring to my berth for the night, The New Flying Horse pub.

In the evening, sitting at the bar, I fell into conversation with a young woman propping up the corner. She was a local organic farm worker, working out of the greenhouses vacated by the college. While we were having an interesting conversation we were joined by the cook, her tattooed boyfriend. I felt slightly side-lined as the talk turned to motorbikes, guns and gigs, none of which is of any particular interest to me. I felt uncomfortable about the talk of guns on the same day as twelve people had been killed in a mass shooting in Cumbria by Derrick Bird.

The morning started bright and sunny, and the day promised wall to wall sunshine. I left Wye early in good spirits in order to make as much progress as possible before the day got too hot, and to keep out of the sun as much as possible to protect my burnt legs. I passed through Wye by the Stour Valley Walk and found the awkward corner where I had gone wrong the previous time. On this occasion, the path seemed better marked and I found the right path through featureless swathes of blue-green wheat. Looking east, I could see the Wye Downs and the Devil's Kneading Trough, where I had walked the day before, rising high above the valley floor. I made good progress to cross the River Stour by a rickety bridge with water lilies adorning the water, waiting expectantly to burst into flower. I crossed the main railway by one of those stop-look-listen signs, making straight for Kennington Church.

I came up to the main A28 by a pub with a sign asking travellers to consider what they had missed by passing it without stopping. I thought that good manners would surely require them to remove the sign now the pub was derelict. I walked up to Kennington Church, climbing out of the Stour Valley, through a settlement that had now been swamped by the growth of Ashford. Picking my way around the north-eastern outskirts of Ashford, I came to the grand entrance to Eastwell Park, marked by a large, ornate arch and gatehouse. Just past the entrance to the park, I took the winding lane to Westwell and wondered about the relationship, as there must be, between Eastwell and Westwell. I noted that the ruins of Eastwell Church lay further to the north, marooned in its park without any semblance of a settlement.

Leaving Ashford on the way to Westwell, walking under the North Downs, I had the strong impression that I had come out of the Stour Valley into another landscape zone. There were splendid views to Westwell up ahead, from the lane situated on the piedmont under the downs. Westwell was a quiet, dormitory village with some interesting and

Wye to Westwell

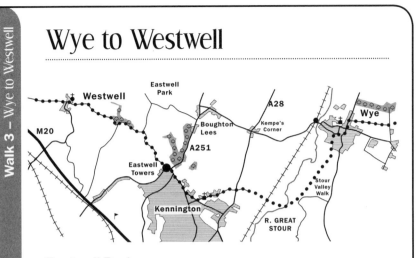

Walk 3 – Wye to Westwell

Eastwell Park

Is the extensive grounds of a stately home to the north of Ashford, which once served as a royal residence. It was built for Sir Thomas Moyle between 1540 and 1550, by Richard Plantagenet (Richard of Eastwell) who claimed to be a son of Richard III. Other residents of the estate included the ninth Earl of Winchelsea, and, from 1874 to 1893, the Duke and Duchess of Edinburgh; the Duke was the second son of Queen Victoria and the Duchess was originally a grand duchess of Russia. Their daughter, Princess Marie (who later became the Queen of Romania), was born on the estate in 1875. The family left the house upon the Duke's inheritance of the dukedom of Saxe-Coburg and Gotha in 1893.

Eastwell Park was demolished in 1926, and a large new house was built in the neo-Elizabethan style, called Eastwell Manor in the vicinity of the village of Boughton Lees, which is now a country house hotel. The Medieval church, marooned in the depths of Eastwell park high up on the Downs, has been a ruin since the 1950s, and is now cared for by the charity, The Friends of Friendless Churches. The original magnificent main gatehouse, known as Eastwell Towers, remains on the A251, at the very northern most extent of the urban area of Ashford in the suburb of Kennington.

Eastwell Towers

The ruins of St Mary's church, Eastwell

40

99

attractive buildings by the stream, running off the hills to join the Great Stour, west of Ashford. I sat on a bench under a tree on a small green opposite the pub and rested for a while.

By mid-morning, the day was beginning to heat up and I made a conscious decision to walk in the shade as much as I could through these quiet lanes beyond Westwell, even if it meant walking on the wrong side of the road. I wound my way down to Tutt Hill, no more than a trucking stop on the A20, although I may have missed part of the place in the process of crossing the modern traffic corridor containing the M20 and both main-line railways. From the new bridge over the railways, I took a local footpath that became obscured by an overgrown patch of waste ground at the back of a new road motel, and I was forced to take an illegal route to gain access to the main road. It was too early for a drink in the large roadside pub, so I crossed over the main road to the petrol station opposite and bought some chocolate and water, which I consumed in the shade of the building to the roar of traffic and the smell of petrol fumes.

I carried on down Ram Lane, past a derelict farm and an intensive horticultural business, whose plants were shaded by rows of polythene tunnels down by the Stour River. Crossing the river and following the winding lane, I came to Little Chart Forstal, the film set for the television programme and dramatization of H.E. Bates' novel, *The Darling Buds of May*. The setting of the film was inaccessible, located as it was in a farm complex behind a stone wall. However, the village itself was composed of an attractive group of buildings with some quintessential country cottages, set off by generous grass verges and around a large village green. All very English!

From Little Chart Forstal I followed the Greensand Way through fields of wheat to arrive at The Swan in Little Chart at midday, hoping to drink and rest. Unfortunately, this pub, the third on my route, was closed and did not open until the strange time of 1.00 p.m. Trying to be philosophical about this, I pressed on to the village of Pluckley, through the orchards of Surrenden and Sheerland Farms. I remembered passing this way before, through Surrenden, on a previous walk and noticing a group of massive sweet chestnut trees, which probably predated the establishment of the orchard, and I wondered whether the farm actually bothered to harvest the nuts commercially.

I arrived in Pluckley via the recreation ground, which gave access to an

Westwell to Pluckley

H. E. Bates (1905-1974)

Was a prolific author, born in Rushden, Northamptonshire, but he lived most of his life in Little Chart, Kent. His most famous work, *The Darling Buds of May*, was inspired by the Kent countryside in this vicinity, and by the 'local' characters he met. The book was made into a successful television programme after his death, starring David Jason, and filmed locally at Little Chart Forstal, Pluckley, and other spots in the area.

Sweet Chestnut
(Castanea sativa)

Sweet chestnut is a medium-sized to large deciduous tree which can reach a height of 35m with a trunk often 2m in diameter, and oblong, boldly toothed leaves. The tree, which originated in southern Europe, requires a mild climate and adequate moisture for good growth and a good nut harvest. The nuts can be cooked or eaten raw and the tree responds well to coppicing, producing a good supply of tannin-rich wood every twelve to thirty years. The tannin makes the wood durable and suitable for posts, fencing and stakes, and locally in Kent was used for hop poles. With modern production methods in hop-growing, the demand for hop poles has greatly diminished, and there are now vast areas of derelict chestnut coppice in Kent.

Market Gardening

During the medieval period there was little need for market gardening because towns were small and monasteries and large estates supplied their own needs. The growth of London stimulated market gardening in Kent and growers transported fruit and vegetables to the capital by cart, returning with night soil and manure on which productivity depended. Kent became known as the 'garden of England supplying large quantities of fruit, vegetables and flowers to London markets such as that at Covent Garden. With improved transport, and the development of the supermarket, production can now be undertaken on a much larger scale, and produce brought in from other parts of the country, and from overseas. Modern market gardening is epitomised by the massive installations under glass, and modern methods of cultivation, found at Thanet Earth, on the Isle of Thanet.

The Black Horse pub, Pluckley

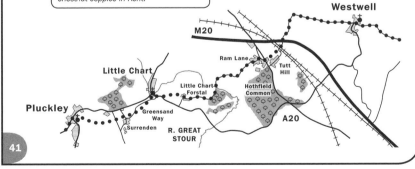

41

101

overgrown and neglected churchyard. This, in turn, fronted onto a scruffy main street with a pub and a few shops. I went in the old and imposing Black Horse pub in optimistic mood, which was immediately dampened by the failure of the bar staff to acknowledge my presence for a few minutes. They seemed more intent on serving and chatting to local ladies out for a lunchtime gossip, who simply pushed in ahead of me. When I did manage to get served, I could not believe that the pub had no beer or cider, so in extreme irritation I had to settle for lager, which I consumed outside in the garden, sitting in the shade, while the ladies exposed as much flesh as was decent, intent on sunning themselves.

I decided to press on to Pluckley Thorn and have a proper rest and lunch in the fifth pub on my route. I plunged down the hill on the Smarden road to Pluckley Thorn, off the Greensand Ridge into the clay vale of the River Beult, avoiding traffic on this busy stretch of road. When I reached The Carpenter's Arms at the bottom of the hill, I was dismayed to find that the pub was closed and derelict. I could not believe that I had now passed five pubs and managed only one measly pint of lager and no food. It was a good job I could see the funny side of this saga.

I struggled on along a very busy road to The Pinnock, where I managed to locate the footpath that led through Dering Wood. I mused on the fact that the roads in this vicinity were all marked yellow on the map, indicating a minor road, and yet the amount of traffic some were carrying warranted at least a B-road classification. This would provide the roads south of the M20 and west of Ashford with some hierarchy, making it easier to plan a safe and pleasant walking route. It was difficult to find the entrance to the wood on the one footpath running through it, and the uniformity and openness of the tree cover meant that it was very easy to lose the path and get lost in the wood, certainly adding to a sense of danger and foreboding. The village of Pluckley, and in particular Dering Wood, is supposed to be, according to locals, the most haunted place in Kent. I can understand how the propensity to get lost in the wood would make it quite a frightening place, but I can see no reason to invent the spectre of phantasms, unless it has more to do with engendering the tourist trade than anything else. I understand that the place crawls with so-called ghost hunters on Halloween, much to the annoyance of the local population.

Because I had not had a proper pit-stop during the day, I arrived in

Pluckley to Headcorn

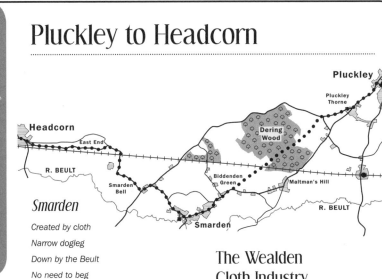

Smarden

Created by cloth

Narrow dogleg

Down by the Beult

No need to beg

Favours now of Flemish weavers.

Smarden

Is an attractive village on the upper reaches of the River Beult which prospered in the Middle Ages from the wool trade. Edward III, who bought weavers over from Flanders, granted the village a Royal Charter in 1333 permitting an annual fair and a weekly market to be held, thus elevating the village to the status of a town. As a consequence of this prosperity there are many fine buildings remaining in the village, including the Cloth Hall (1430), which is a fine example of a fifteenth-century yeoman's timber hall house.

Smarden Church and Cloth Hall

The Wealden Cloth Industry

Was, apart from iron-making, the other large-scale industry carried out in the Weald in medieval times. The availability of wool from local sheep, and the immigration from Flanders of cloth workers in the fourteenth century, ensured its place in Kentish industrial history. The development of this activity was greatly assisted by the fact that local deposits of Fuller's Earth existed between Boxley and Maidstone; it being an essential raw material for degreasing wool. Once the wool had been carded, to get rid of the tangles, and spun, both operations being undertaken in the worker's homes, it then required weaving. Purpose built, timber-framed cloth halls, such as those at Cranbrook, Biddenden and Smarden, were built to house the looms to facilitate this production process.

Dering Wood

Is an ancient woodland covering an area of 308 acres, lying between Pluckley and Smarden, and comprised mainly of oak and hornbeam coppice, managed by the excellent Woodlands Trust, for the benefit of its wide variety of plants and wildlife. It is renowned for its stunning display of spring bluebells and wood anemones.

42

103

Smarden via Biddenden Green early, and booked into the Chequers Inn in the heart of the village. I followed my normal routine of discarding sweaty clothes, jumping in the shower and having a rest. Re-emerging around 5.30 p.m., I retired to the pleasant pub garden, soaking up the evening sunshine and wrote up the day's journey. Afterwards, I had some food in the pub before visiting the other pub in the village, The Flying Horse, where I stayed drinking for most of the night.

Leaving Smarden, I took time to appreciate this attractive village, with its narrow dogleg of a main street, charming church precinct and the evocative group of buildings in Water Lane on the way out to Smarden Bell, which were built on the profits of the Wealden cloth-making industry. The roads towards Headcorn were busy and difficult, and related back to my previous thought about the lack of designated B-roads in this vicinity. After Smarden Bell, I was tempted to take a footpath to the left of Marley Farm but thought better of it since the way appeared to be poorly used and badly marked. I ploughed on into Headcorn, along the long straight road beside the railway, greeted by more and more traffic.

Headcorn itself is a place invigorated by a new shopping facility and an important commuter train station, but being on the main A274, it is desperately in need of a by-pass. There were buildings of real quality towards the church, which itself occupied a pivotal position on the bend of the road, only a stone's throw from the River Beult. I guess the natural route for a by-pass would be the west and south of the village, but this would take it perilously close to the capricious river, so I concluded that the route should go to the north of Headcorn, containing the growth of the village in that direction.

After a short rest, sitting on a wall in front of the church, I found a back road and picked up a lane going north towards Tilden, which disported some charming, opulent buildings. From Tilden, I took the footpath to Tong, crossing a tributary of the River Beult in the process. It was good to get away from the traffic and I relaxed into the day's agenda, crossing flat, productive fields. Before Tong, going north, I joined a 'byway open to all traffic' but met only one 4x4, who waved me effusively. The hamlet of Tong was graced by a string of ponds that provided home for a myriad variety of ducks. I admired a large family of geese ushering goslings out of the woods to the safety of the ponds. This was good walking north of Headcorn on the way to Sutton Valence, with the dramatic Greensand Ridge coming ever closer. Skirting Park Wood, I

Headcorn to Hollingbourne

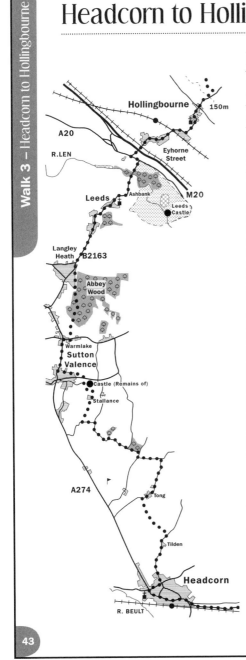

Headcorn

Is a busy village, strategically placed at a major crossing point of the River Beult, with a long history. Although today it has a pleasant high street, in the vicinity of the church, it is a busy centre, with an important commuter train station and new shopping complex. Today this large village is blighted by the heavy traffic passing through on the A274 Maidstone to Ashford and Tenterden roads, and is desperately in need of a by-pass. The development of the village follows the same pattern as many others in Kent, firstly as a 'den' or clearing in the Wealden Forest, and secondly from the period of the burgeoning wool trade in the fourteenth century, which has left the legacy of many fine buildings today, including the picturesque Grade II listed building in the High Street known as Shakespeare House.

Shakespeare House, Headcorn

Sutton Valence Castle

Is a ruined Norman stone keep and bailey fortress managed by English Heritage. Standing against the escarpment of the Greensand Ridge are the broken ragstone walls of a small two-storey keep, with a square forebuilding. The castle was abandoned in the fourteenth century, and now there are only glimpses of the bailey curtain wall along the ridge.

43

crossed over the little stream in Honiker Lane, that runs down from East Sutton Park and I could see the village of Sutton Valence up ahead, strung out along the ridge.

I approached the village through an orchard and braced myself for a stiff climb through the delightful hamlet of Stallance, a fine grouping of buildings in oast-house character. Looking back, there were spectacular views over the valley of the River Beult, across which I had been picking my way over the last couple of days. The weather over the last few days was greatly improved and today was very hot, almost too hot for walking. I passed the remains of Sutton Valence castle, and emerged in the perfect High Street, taking note once again of its attractive hillside location. I dived into The Swan for a much-deserved drink and rest, but also to get out of the sun. I resolved to have a good, long rest and sit out the heat of midday and of course, this entailed eating a meat salad and consuming three pints of real ale. I climbed up to the back of the pub garden to appreciate the fine view out across the rooftops to the valley beyond.

After an indecent interval, I found the footpath by the side of the pub, climbed to the top of the ridge through wooded slopes and emerged in a wide open field, searching for the footpath continuing to Warmlake. I ended up trudging through Sutton Valence School and was politely, but insistently, shown off the premises by a schoolmaster who insisted there were no footpaths through the school grounds, even though my map proved him wrong. I was forced back onto the main road but it was comfortable going for the most part, along a generous tree-lined footpath all the way to the crossroads at Warmlake. There was more evidence of the paternalistic dominance of the private school in this locality, in a well-tended sports ground at a high point of 123m above sea level. I turned right at the crossroads and found the footpath that took me north through Abbey Wood, skirting the back of Langley Heath. In the refreshing cool of the wood, I sat on a mossy bank under mature pine trees and reflected on the journey. Towards Langley Heath the wood consisted primarily of coppiced, sweet chestnut trees, which I have found to be typical of the Greensand Ridge.

I strolled along the B2163 on a Friday afternoon, down the hill into Leeds, where I popped into the Ten Bells: the first friendly pub in the village. The locals remarked on the state of my sunburned legs, and compared my plight to that of a young lady sitting at the bar with a low-cut top, low enough to avoid the sore bits of an ample sunburnt chest. In

the older part of the village, I popped into The George and sat outside, consuming a pint of cider. Leeds is basically a village strung out along the noisy busy road and could also benefit from a by-pass. However, the relationship between the village and the park that is Leeds Castle is important, and any new road should not sever that relationship. Thus, any new road should pass to the west of the village, and there is an obvious route, linking up to the second roundabout on the A20 by the large new motel where I was staying that night.

I carried on down the hill and crossed the River Len, whose head-waters gathered in the vicinity of Lenham, upstream, and which flows through Leeds Castle grounds and Mote Park in Maidstone before joining the Medway. I finally made it to the A20 and walked along to the large motel situated there. This would not have been my first choice of berth but I could find no other accommodation locally. The motel was perfectly comfortable, as one would expect from the price, but it was not geared up to cater for scruffy walkers. It was full of coach party hoards, no doubt visiting nearby Leeds Castle, and it was difficult to get anything to eat in the evening. The staff did not understand the significance of the box I had left, and some kind soul had ripped it open to check its contents, making it impossible to post back the next day. In the morning, I came down too early for breakfast and when checking out, attired in boots and with my rucksack on my back, the receptionist asked me if I would like a taxi. I did try to comment sarcastically, inviting her to regard my garb, but the significance of this gesture completely passed her by. The look of puzzlement on her face demonstrated to me that the activity I was engaged in was entirely beyond her comprehension, so I sidled out into the sanity of the morning air, somewhat abashed.

I located the road to Hollingbourne, crossed over the motorway and the high-speed rail link, and passed into Eyhorne Street in the parish of Hollingbourne. The entrance to the village was carefully tended and the twisting High Street seemed to be the centre of a lively community on this Saturday morning. I crossed under the second railway and approached Hollingbourne village by a footpath across the fields. This is an exceedingly attractive village seen from this angle, against the backdrop of the North Downs.

I carried on, up and over the Pilgrim's Way, onto the top of the North Downs, and followed the designated footpath towards Thurnham and Detling. As expected, the view from the top was stunning and the hillside was smothered with the little, deep-blue, Chalkhill Blue butterflies. I startled a small, brown game bird down the slope, which I thought might be a woodcock, and it quickly disappeared in the natural camouflage of the longer grass. Below the downs were vast sweeping fields of yellow wheat, interrupted only by the green, intimate oasis of Broad Street, containing houses, farms and paddocks, and looking like an intricate postage stamp on the bland expanse of an arable letter.

After crossing the lane from Hucking to Broad Street, I passed gratefully into cool woods and enjoyed the shade they provided. I passed two fellow travellers going the other way: the first was running and looked immensely fit and the second, a great big bloke, was walking with a full rucksack on his back. I wished the runner a fleeting good morning as he sped past me, but stopped and talked to the hiker. He had come out from Chatham that morning and was aiming for Canterbury, but admitted he might have to break his journey and camp for the night. I enquired about the runner I had passed earlier, and he evidently was running to Dover, with his backup cycling down below on the Pilgrim's Way. After overcoming my amazement at the herculean feat in which each was engaged, I bid him good morning and moved on, slightly overawed by the comparison with my own pathetic efforts.

With 2 miles to go to Detling, I came across a clump of Japanese knotweed, my first sighting on this trip, an invasive and pernicious weed that has escaped from botanical gardens and is now wreaking havoc in the countryside. Luckily for Kent, the dreadful weed prefers acid soils, more common in the west of the country rather than the alkaline soils found around here. As I came level with Thurnham, the path started to veer crazily up and down the slope and became really hard going, so I cut my losses and plunged down, past the ruined Thurnham Castle, into the village to walk the remaining mile or so to Detling along the Pilgrim's Way.

In the Cock Horse at Detling, I rested to an accompaniment of traffic noise from the A249, which was clearly better than the traffic thundering through the village, but still unpleasant. I wanted to go down into the village and cross over the main road by the church but realised there was no crossing there. So, after my second visit to Detling, I had no option but to cross the road by means of Jade's Memorial Bridge, missing out on the village and not being able to walk, church to church, from Detling to Boxley as I would have preferred.

I proceeded along the Pilgrim's Way, through shady woods, and picked up a footpath down into the village of Boxley, being welcomed by a peel of church bells ringing in celebration of a wedding about to take place. I was drawn cheerfully down into the village by the exuberance of the bells, passing an archery competition in progress on the recreation ground; all very English. It was still very hot, so hot that the sheep hunkered down in the grass could easily be mistaken for lumps of stone. The picturesque village with its distinctive village green, running from the entrance to the churchyard to the doors of the pub, sweltered in the heat. The cool of the pub was a relief for a while before I continued on along an ancient track out of the village.

Taking advantage of the natural slope of a grassy bank, I lay down for a while, looking over the massive urban sprawl of the county town. I was struck by the notion that in times past, the Pilgrim's Way, lying just to the north under the downs, would have been the main highway and this track connecting church to church would have been the local road. The track ended short of Boarley Farm, and taking a right-angled turn I eased my way back up to the Pilgrim's Way. I continued along a wooded, rutted track to the big road, the A229, plunging down the North Downs Scarp

Hollingbourne to Boxley

Hollingbourne

Is an attractive village nestling under the North Downs, located on the Pilgrim's Way, whose parish includes the contiguous settlement of Eyehorne Street, and Broad Street further west. It has a number of fine buildings including Hollingbourne Manor, a Grade I listed Elizabethan manor house, a former house of members of the notable Culpeper family, who had many houses in this part of Kent.

Hollingbourne church

Japanese Knotweed
(Fallopia japonica)

Is a large herbaceous perennial native to eastern Asia in Japan, China and Korea. Escaping from botanical gardens, where it was prized for its racemes of attractive flowers, it has successfully established itself in this country, where it is classed as an invasive species. It prefers acidic soils and is less commonly found in the alkaline soils in the south east based on chalk and limestone. It is a frequent coloniser of roadsides and waste places where it forms thick, dense colonies that crowd out any other herbaceous species. The invasive root system and strong growth can damage building foundations, roads and paved areas, retaining walls and architectural sites. It commonly grows in watercourses and can damage flood defences and reduce the capacity of water channels to carry away flood waters. The eradication of the plant is extremely difficult due to its deep rampant root system and its ability to sprout again from roots when cut down. The most effective method of control is the continual application of herbicides in the flowering stage in late summer or autumn.

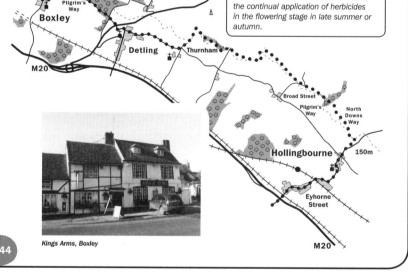

Kings Arms, Boxley

at Bluebell Hill. Boxley Warren, an AONB, nature reserve and SSSI, loomed over me as I approached the road. I had passed so many sites of the same ilk along the North Downs scarp that I thought it would be a good idea to map them as they don't all appear on the Landranger series of Ordnance Survey Maps. Boxley Warren was proclaimed by a helpful notice, to be one of the most important sites of this nature in Kent and in Europe; I thought Europe might be a bit farfetched.

Just before the big road, I came across the White Horse Stone, one of three ancient monuments in this locality. I looked at it quite carefully and any resemblance to a white horse was long removed by erosion and vandalism. Then, just across the railway, as the track became diminished, the Pilgrim's Way seemed to come to a brutal lesion up against the big road. If I had followed the North Downs Way I would have come across a scruffy tunnel under the main road, but I elected to risk life and limb, jaywalking and hopping over the central barrier of this fast road. I did feel that when the road was built, the authorities could have shown more respect to the ancient track by providing a footbridge over the road at this point.

To the south, the old Chatham Road, giving access to the village of Sandling, was extensively used as a lorry park. Down this ugly road was also the Tyland Barn, headquarters of the excellent Kent Wildlife Trust. I did manage to scramble over the road with trepidation, only to resume my route on the other side. The only trouble is that a main road like this one does not only cut the passage but disrupts the footpaths on either side, creating a zone of footpath and access blight. Once over the road, I missed the splendours of Little Kit's Coty House and picked up the Pilgrim's Way, heading in the direction of Burham. At the next junction, I made a detour and found the footpath up the slope to Kit's Coty House, the most distinctive, ancient monument of the group in this location, being the entrance stones to a long-gone, Bronze Age, long barrow. I marvelled at how the large slabs of stone had remained upright and in place after all the years since its construction. I walked around the monument, encased in wrought-iron railings, and would have tarried longer, except that I came across two scantily clad lovers taking a breather, soaking up the sun behind the monument. I wondered whether they were seeking mystical inspiration in their love life, being set down behind such a well-known, but I guess, infrequently visited public monument.

Not wishing to climb up Bluebell Hill, on the North Downs Way, I elected instead to stay down on the lower ground. I returned to the road

Boxley to Burham

Burham

Village was originally sited around the redundant St Mary's Church at Burham Court on the banks of the River Medway. There was a famous battle here in AD 43 when the invading Roman army were confronted by the massed army of the ancient British tribes at this crossing point. Latterly, the village was relocated away from the river, because of continual problems of flooding, under the chalk escarpment, and in about 1830 it became an important 'cement village'.

North Downs

Burham

Little Culand

Kit's Coty

Kit's Coty House

Eccles

White Horse Stone

Pilgrims Way

Boxley

Detling

Kit's Coty House

Kit's Coty House is the name of the remains of a Neolithic cambered long barrow on the side of Blue Bell Hill in the Medway Valley. Although badly damaged by ploughing and later vandalism, the impressive entrance to the tomb still survives. It consists of three sarsen stones supporting a horizontal capstone with a height of nearly 3m. In 1885 the monument was one of the first sites in Britain to become a Scheduled Ancient Monument and it is now in the care of English Heritage. The site is traditionally known as the burial place of Catigern, brother of Vortimer and son of Vortigern, following a battle with the Saxon Horsa in the mid-fifth century AD.

Chalk Quarrying

Was once a commonplace activity in the North Downs, which has been undertaken since Roman times. The lower Medway Valley had particular advantages which encouraged the development of quarrying for chalk: easily accessible chalk strata on the valley sides and cheap bulk transport by barge along the river Medway. As early as the 13th century farmers were using chalk, in a process called marling, to improve the fertility of acidic sandy soils, creating many deneholes and chalkwells in the area. The main impetus for the expansion of quarrying was the emergence of brick, cement and paper-making industries in the valley for which chalk was an essential ingredient. Burham Court Farm in 1828 was described as containing 'an inexhaustible mine of chalk', and this open cast quarry is one of the few active today, although the area is littered with disused pits which now form valuable wildlife sanctuaries.

Kit's Coty House

45

junction and had no choice, risking life and limb, but to pass along the crazy section of dual carriageway in the middle of nowhere, on the way to Burham. The road, naturally, was not intended for pedestrians but I could see no other way of getting towards Burham. I noticed that a new vineyard had been planted beside the road on the slope leading down to the River Medway. Before the village I was able to take the lower road to Burham Court. I rested for a while at a point where I could see down to the river and Snodland on the opposite bank. Behind me, towards Burham, was a vast, open-cast chalk extraction operation in full swing, eating back into the hillside. The original village used to be based at Burham Court where the church still is, but it migrated up the slope underneath the downs because of constant flooding problems with the river. From Burham Court, I walked along the lower road to Wouldham, no more than a dusty track in parts, alongside the Medway, through a post-industrial landscape of disused riverside wharfs.

After a quick drink in the first friendly pub, The Waterman's Arms, I strolled through the prosaic village of Wouldham. The village had a distinctive row of small terraced cottages along the main street and seemed to shun its river. Although access could be gained to the river, there were no public spaces facing it. Eventually, I arrived at Wouldham Court Farm, opposite the parish church, my billet for the night. The premises were sixteenth century in origin and still retained large oak beams and wide, wooden planks for floorboards that one might expect to find on a wooden ship. The amply proportioned rooms of a house dated from the time of Lord Nelson. The landlady, who had delved into the history of the place, told me the house was owned by the purser on Nelson's ship who was buried in the churchyard opposite. Evidently, the purser used to row Nelson up the river from Rochester to the Manor House further upstream for secret assignations with Lady Hamilton.

I spent a pleasant evening in the Medway Inn, under new management, and observed a picture hanging on the wall. It showed a public park next to the pub, a pleasure ground really, stretching down to the river. I thought it was a great shame that this facility had been lost and built on with new, nondescript houses.

In the morning, I had a look around the churchyard and regarded the river flowing strong and deep on its way to the Thames Estuary, before setting out on the last leg of my journey, towards Rochester. Along the undulating road, I saw glimpses of the river but the main feature was the

Burham to Rochester

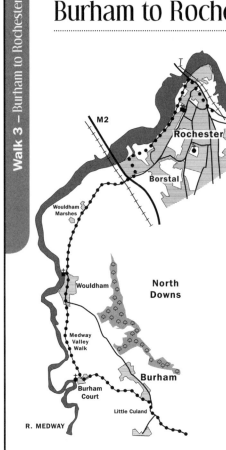

Rochester's Lost City Status

Rochester was recognised as a city from 1211 to 1998. On 1 April 1974, the city council was abolished, becoming part of the Borough of Medway, a new local government district. However, under letters patent, the former city council area was to continue to be styled the 'City of Rochester' to 'perpetuate the ancient name' and to recall 'the long history and proud heritage of the said city'. The city was unique, as it had no council or charter trustees, and no mayor or civic head. In 1979 the Borough of Medway was renamed Rochester-upon-Medway, and in 1982 further letters patent transferred the city status to the whole borough. On 1 April 1998, the existing local government districts of Rochester-upon-Medway and Gillingham were abolished and became the new unitary authority of Medway. Since it was the local government district that officially held city status under the 1982 letters patent, when it was abolished, it also ceased to be a city.

Thus, by an administrative mistake and repeated local government reorganisation, Rochester now unbelievably is not a city, although a current campaign is seeking to reverse this situation. Consequentluy, Kent now only has one city, Canterbury, and even Maidstone is merely a county town, not to mention the burgeoning settlement of Ashford.

Borstal

Is a type of youth prison run by the Prison Service for the reform of seriously delinquent young people. The term is sometimes used loosely to apply to other kinds of youth institutions and detention centres. The name derives from the first prison of its kind established in the village of Borstal, on the outskirts of Rochester, in 1902. The film, *The Loneliness of the Long Distance Runner* (1962), was set in a borstal, and based on the book of the same name by Allan Sillitoe.

Rochester High Street

46

Medway Bridges coming ever closer. Looking across the river, I could clearly see Cuxton with its church, ringing the bells on this Sunday morning. Just before the bridges was the Borstal cricket ground with boys getting ready for a game. The sports club also curiously had a Pétanque section, a French game similar to boules, where metal balls are thrown towards a jack: a sort of aerial bowls.

Passing under the Medway Bridges, past the lane that runs down to Nashenden Farm, a route that I had taken previously, I entered the village of Borstal, now contiguous with Rochester. This was the site of Borstal Prison, a corrective institution for young offenders set up in 1902. The term 'borstal' is now used widely and loosely to describe other kinds of youth institutions, such as approved schools and detention centres. I walked into Rochester alongside the river and as I approached the original Medway Bridge, always appearing to be in a state of repair, I observed a party of folk dressed up in Dickensian costumes disembarking from a paddle steamer moored up against a pier. I passed down the High Street in front of this Dickensian pageant to the cheers and applause of the crowds lining the street. I thought that was a very appropriate way for me to finish my walk.

I made my way to Rochester Station, from whose platform there is a great view of Limehouse Reach on the river, to catch a train back to Dumpton Gap, near Broadstairs.

4

Gravesend to Romney Marsh (Autumn 2010/Spring 2011)

By the time I arrived at Gravesend it was late morning and for the start of this adventure, I had a stinking cold. I moved out of the grand station and down the busy High Street, just as I had on a previous walk. I bought some provisions and carried on down to the river through the newly designated heritage quarter. The properties lining the High Street were in much better condition than when I had walked this way last time, but there was still no evidence that the initiative was pulling pedestrians down from the High Street to the waterfront. I came up to the River Thames by the historic pier, which had been converted into a restaurant, and observed the scene. The tide was out, exposing sandy coloured banks of mud, which attracted a grey heron to feed by the water's edge. Opposite, across the river in Essex, was Tilbury Fort where Queen Elizabeth I rallied the troops before the Spanish Armada threat in her famous, rousing speech.

I passed on along the river, eastwards through intermittent gardens, following the Saxon Shore Way, until I reached the dark, threatening canyon created by a derelict factory site. For some unfathomable reason, I lost the designated footpath at this point, even though I had been this way before, and got pushed inland though interminable factories and depots along a long curving road beside the railway. In time, I came to the start of the disused Thames and Medway Canal as I had intended and strode out on the towpath. To my right was the canal, with a little brackish water in the bottom, and the railway, on which a new Javelin train powered past in its blue livery with a yellow nose. To my left, eventually, the factories suddenly stopped and across the police firing range, I could see the disembodied upper parts of ships, eerily sliding by on top of the river embankment.

Up ahead, on the long, straight track, I could see a group of people, looking almost official in yellow 'vissey' jackets. I thought they might be trainspotters. I wasn't far wrong in fact; they were concerned with a campaign to bring the canal back to a useable, navigable waterway. As I approached, I was abducted by two ladies proffering leaflets. As I showed mild interest, and having explained my mission, they introduced me to their Chairman named Brian. I joked that that made two of us, where-upon and rather disconcertingly, he volunteered the information that most of the men out today were also called Brian. I guess it was an age thing. He explained that the original route of the canal, the one they were trying to reinstate, did not go through the Higham Tunnel with the railway, but to the north of the higher ground to join the Medway in the vicinity of Frindsbury.

I told him I was headed for Shorne and he advised taking the footpath across Shorne Marshes, since the road I had intended to pick up further on was closed. I thanked him for this information and bid the assembled company good day. I thought that the aims of the group were all very laudable, but their plans would bring them into conflict with an equally, if not more laudable cause, championed by the Environment Agency, who

Gravesend to Shorne

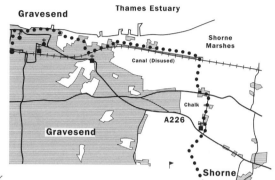

Chalk

Is the charming name for a former village that is now part of the urban area of Gravesend. The church and some attractive houses are detatched from the built-up area to the east. The settlement dates back to Saxon times and was mentioned in the Domesday Book, and a large Roman villa was discovered here in 1961. However, its main claim to fame, in common with many places hereabouts, is the Dickens connection. He spent his honeymoon here with his new bride, Catherine Hogarth, and wrote early instalments of *The Pickwick Papers*. The old forge in the village was used as a model for Joe Gargery's cottage in *Great Expectations*, and still stands as a historically listed building.

Crane Fly
(Tipula paludosa)

Is a harmless type of fly with very long legs (hence their common name Daddy Long Legs), a long thin abdomen and two lacy wings. They hatch out and swarm when conditions are right, living for a short time and dying after mating. Crane fly larvae are called leatherjackets and live in the soil and eat the roots of grass and other vegetation.

The Javelin Train

On 12 December 2008 the first Javelin Train raced into London on its inaugural journey. These dark-blue liveried trains offer the fastest domestic rail service in the UK, and went into full passenger service in December 2009. There are now around 29 such trains in service with Southeastern rail on the Kent to London (St Pancras to Ebbsfleet/Ashford) domestic rail service and High Speed 1 Channel Tunnel rail link, reducing previous journey times from around 83 minutes to 37 minutes. In 2012 the Javelin Train regularly used its 340 seat capacity to ferry spectators from St Pancras to the main Olympic Games site in Stratford East London in 7 minutes.

The Javelin Train

47

had set aside a section of the canal further on for habitat conservation. This is a good example of the conflicts of interest that beset the effective planning of the countryside.

I crossed over the canal by the suggested footpath and stood on the bridge for a moment, admiring the scene. I could hear rifles popping off from the firing range and, to the south, I could see a distinctive church, unnamed on my map, which I was making for. I crossed over the railway and plunged down into the marshes. It became deathly quiet and I was assailed by clouds of daddy long legs, the common name for the crane fly. Coming up to the road by an attractive group of buildings, I doglegged into the lane to East Court Manor. There was a steep climb up the lane, past extremely pleasant dwellings on the outskirts of the massive settlement of Gravesend, to the distinctive church, which, on closer inspection, was the parish church of Chalk. With further research I discovered that the main part of the evocatively named village of Chalk lies on the edge of the urban area that is Gravesend, further to the west. I skirted the church precinct on a green lane to the east and came up to the main A226 road.

Then, by well-marked footpaths, climbing all the time, I cut across the fields to Upper Ifield below Shorne. Stopping from time to time to look north from whence I had come, I could see over the top of Chalk Church to the panoramic spectacle of the River Thames. From this point, it was obvious why a church would have been built there, on a bluff, overlooking the river, giving commanding views of the traffic going up and down the great waterway. There was another stiff climb up along the lane to Shorne from Upper Ifield and I came into the village by a footpath across the front of the church. Being lunchtime, I popped into the excellent Rose and Crown pub for sustenance and recuperation.

Leaving Shorne later than I had envisaged, I made my way up to Shorne Ridgeway, a settlement consisting largely of modern houses strung out along the road, up the hill and along the ridgeway. At its centre is a small, triangular green adorned by a collection of six heavily pollarded, sweet chestnut trees. Passing through, initially I took the lane truncated by the massive road junction to the south where the A2, M2 and A289, the new northern Rochester by-pass giving direct access to the Isle of Grain, join together. Then I located the footpath that took me through a wood and across the fields to Park Pale, where I was able to cross over the A2 into Cobham Park. Once over the main road, I picked up the Darnley trail, a circular path through the extensive park.

In the pub earlier, talking to some old boys at the bar, they confirmed my suggestion that the Darnley in question was Lord Darnley, one of Queen Elizabeth I's favourites at court. Also, intriguingly, they volunteered the information that another more recent Lord Darnley was captain of the English cricket team that lost in Australia in 1882, and who reputedly burnt the bails, thus creating the Ashes trophy. Cobham Hall, one of the most notable estates in Kent, was, until recently, the ancestral home of the Earls of Darnley. Today, it is an independent girls' school.

I pressed on through the trees to the top of Great Wood at a height of 130m and, at this point, I had been climbing continuously since I walked off the Shorne Marshes. All that remained now was to trek down through woods to Lower Bush in the dry Cuxton Valley that stretched all the way back to Luddesdown, and on which I have remarked before. I squatted on the brow of the hill and admired the sweeping contours of the North Downs leading down into the valley, the light-brown soil showing that iridescent, white sheen derived from the underlying chalk. I tunnelled under the railway, the London line, and on to the hamlet of Lower Bush. Here I met two lady walkers who enquired after my exploits, explaining where I had come from and what my plan was. Their exploits matched my own that day, since they had walked from Wrotham. I enquired where they were bound, but they said they had arrived at their home, in Lower Bush. I did wonder whether I could charm a cup of tea out of them but lacked the temerity to try.

Striding down the lane to Cuxton, I noted how wonderfully quiet the valley was. I passed some pleasant, newer houses with fabulous views across the valley on the way down, but as I approached the older centre any visual quality evaporated. The centre of the village is quite disappointing with no real focus, the majority of the housing perched up the hill below the railway line. I came down to the incredibly busy main road, the A228, which runs through the centre of the village. At this point, as it was quite late and I was still suffering from a bad cold, I gave up and caught a train to Maidstone.

From there, I caught a bus, using my newly acquired bus pass, to West Malling where I was staying the night with friends. On the way, the bus passed through Ditton, Larkfield and East Malling, which, together with Leybourne, form a large urban area in its own right, spilling out along the

Shorne to Halling

The Medway Valley Line

Is a north/south railway line linking Strood and the Medway towns to Maidstone and on to Paddock Wood, passing through some of Kent's most picturesque countryside alongside sections of the River Medway. There are stations at Strood, Cuxton, Halling, Snodland, New Hythe, Aylesford, Maidstone Barracks, Maidstone West, East Farleigh, Wateringbury, Yalding, Beltring and Paddock Wood. The original two-tone brown livery can still be seen in the station at Cuxton.

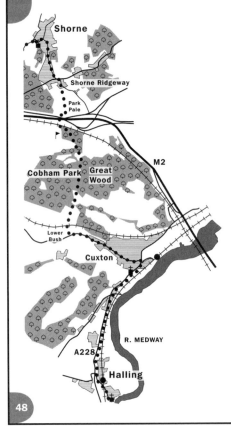

Lord Darnley and the 'Ashes'

The term the 'Ashes' was first used after England lost a cricket match to Australia, for the first time on home soil, at The Oval on 29 August 1882. A day later, *The Sporting Times* carried a mock obituary to English cricket which concluded that 'the body will be cremated and the ashes taken to Australia', and the concept caught the imagination of the sporting public. A few weeks later, an English team, captained by the Hon. Ivo Bligh, the future Lord Darnley of Cobham Hall, set off to tour Australia, vowing to return with the 'ashes'. During the tour Bligh was given a small terracotta urn as a symbol of the ashes that he had travelled to Australia to regain. Bligh regarded this as a personal gift, and it remained at the family home at Cobham Hall until his death as Lord Darnley, when his wife donated it to the MCC. Today, over 75 years later, the tiny, delicate and irreplaceable artefact resides in the MCC museum at Lord's, where each year thousands of visitors, from all parts of the world, come to see it. In the 1990s, recognising the desire for the two teams to compete for an actual trophy, rather than an idea, MCC commissioned an urn-shaped crystal glass.

The Ashes urn

48

A20 to the west of Maidstone. Maybe in time this urban area will come together and acquire one prominent collective name; my betting is on Larkfield as the one, obviously, older place.

A few days later, with my cold having somewhat abated, I returned to Cuxton to complete the Cuxton to West Malling section of the walk. From the White Swan in Cuxton, I tried to gain access to the riverside across the quaint level crossing on the Mid Kent Railway. Although there appeared to be a track on the map, my way was soon barred by for-bidding metal gates, disporting elaborate security devices, and I was forced to retrace my steps back to the station. Thus, there was plenty of opportunity for boating enthusiasts to enjoy the river since there were numerous marinas, but no public access where one could sit down and indulge that more instinctive pleasure of watching the river. I was reminded of the folly of ignoring the river by the opening passage in T.S. Eliot's third quartet, 'The Dry Salvages', about the river being 'a strong brown god...unhonoured...by worshipers of the machine...but waiting, watching and waiting'.

I sidled back up to the main road and set off in the direction of Halling, deafened by the noise of passing traffic. I passed underneath Cuxton Church, a view of which from the main road was blocked by two ugly, three-storey houses. I slogged along the main road, crossing a number of newly established roundabouts. At North Halling the river was close but I could see no way of getting to it. Eventually, I got off the main road and walked through Halling New Town.

The upper Medway Valley is an entirely industrialised landscape where the historic industries of cement and paper-making have resulted in the creation of massive chalk quarries, which provided one of the key ingredients of these enterprises. Large factory complexes grew up, some now largely derelict with the decline in these industries, and settlements like New Halling appeared to house the workers. In its industrial heyday, the valley was a very unhealthy place to live with the omnipotent chalk dust and smoke from numerous chimneys polluting the air. Now things are very different and the pleasant, well-maintained terraced houses in Halling new town are no longer stained white with the chalk dust.

As Andrew Hann recounts in his excellent book, *The Medway Valley: A Kent Landscape Transformed*, in 1750, the lower Medway Valley, the area between Maidstone and Rochester, was firmly part of Kent's 'Garden of England'. A century later, this tranquil, agrarian landscape had been transformed into a hive of industry and commerce, through the emergence of paper-making, cement manufacture, brick-making, brewing, ship and barge building, seed-crushing and engineering. By the end of the Second World War, much of this industry had disappeared and the valley has returned to a rural state, albeit scared by chalk pits and derelict factory sites.

I crossed over the railway and by the church in Halling, I was at last able to gain access to the river. There was a new riverside promenade on a raised levee associated with a modern housing estate nearby, giving it a sense of place, greatly facilitated by the route of the by-pass, which did not cut off the settlement from its river. There was a ruined bishop's palace by an ancient crossing point on the river, adjacent to the church, which appeared to be totally unregarded. I'm sure this notable site would benefit from some care and attention.

My spirits were raised by my passage through Halling, but soon dampened again by coming up to the busy main road to the Holborough roundabout. Here I thought I might gain access to the river and come into Snodland that way, but instead I was pushed inland on the other side of the main road, passing a curious clock tower dedicated to the memory of a local industrialist. When I reached the lively shopping centre I decided to make a detour down to the river. I cut through a municipal park with a cleverly designed surface car park, to bridges over the main by-pass road and railway, the only access I could see to the lower church by the river. The riverside at Snodland is an entirely depressing spectacle. Once this was an important crossing point on the River Medway, but now the ferry house is a private dwelling, blocking any natural access to the river. The lower church shuns its position by the river adjacent to a massive industrial site. The whole area is cut off from the rest of the town by the by-pass.

I crossed back over the bridges and found a dank footpath that led to the bottom of the dismembered High Street. The once-thriving Red Lion pub next to the higher church was derelict. I understand that the pub had been subject to a compulsory purchase order by the Local Authority, but in the event the land was not required for the construction of the by-pass. I could not believe that in planning the by-pass an attempt was not made to preserve the main axis of the High Street, if only by a pedestrian bridge across the big road, giving access to the lower church, thus giving people a reason to pass through this now-derelict location. If this had been the case the pub may have stood a chance of reincarnation. Opposite the derelict pub and church there were some old buildings of note, and I drew a little diagram to explain my dismay at the shoddy treatment of old Snodland. I walked back up the High Street, back into the main centre, and on up through the residential penumbra of Snodland on the way to Birling.

Along the lane to Birling I thought about my impressions of the three riverside settlements I had just visited. I thought that in the construction of the new A228 road, a major north/south road link in Kent, Halling had fared better than Snodland, and Cuxton was still unrelieved. In terms of riverside access, both Cuxton and Snodland have repudiated their riverside inheritance, whilst Halling had re-engaged with the river. Halling should be congratulated, although one could not but also applaud the town of Snodland, which has reinvented itself to the west of the intrusive main road. As for Cuxton, I can only say that it needs some attention.

I carried on along the lane to Birling where I popped into the pub, the Nevill Bull, for lunch, which was this lunchtime, a meeting place for people dressed up for a posh wedding in the nearby church. The men wore morning suits, a design that seems to me uncomfortably similar to the dress that funeral directors wear. As I have mentioned before, last time I passed through the village, the bold prospect of the church was diminished by an intrusive telegraph pole and myriad wires, which I thought should be removed and put underground in this sensitive location, but I somehow doubt whether the assembled company would have noticed such matters.

Further down the lane, I came to Ryarsh, another pleasant village under the shadow of the North Downs. Heading due south from the distinctive village pub, I took the footpath, which would have been a lane in its own right before the construction of the motorway. I crossed the big road and headed for the detached parish church, half a mile from the village. Passing through the churchyard, I picked up the well-surfaced footpath that ran alongside a small stream, whose headwaters stretched back to Addington and Trottiscliffe and which eventually helps to fill the ample lakes around New Hythe. I came up onto the A20, carried on across fields to the railway and limped into West Malling alongside the cricket ground, which reputedly was the ground first used by Kent County Cricket Club.

When I left my friend's house the next morning, I passed back through

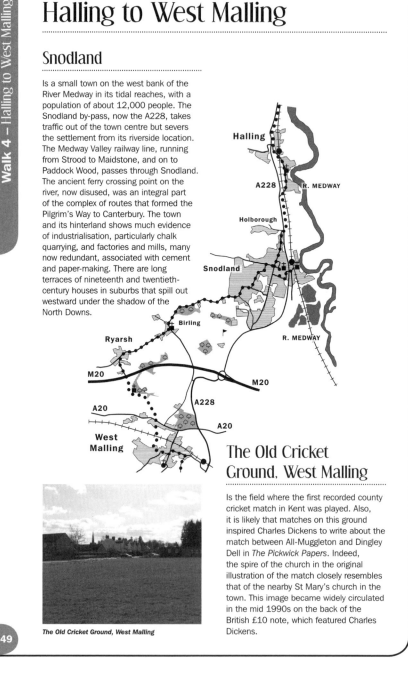

Halling to West Malling

Snodland

Is a small town on the west bank of the River Medway in its tidal reaches, with a population of about 12,000 people. The Snodland by-pass, now the A228, takes traffic out of the town centre but severs the settlement from its riverside location. The Medway Valley railway line, running from Strood to Maidstone, and on to Paddock Wood, passes through Snodland. The ancient ferry crossing point on the river, now disused, was an integral part of the complex of routes that formed the Pilgrim's Way to Canterbury. The town and its hinterland shows much evidence of industrialisation, particularly chalk quarrying, and factories and mills, many now redundant, associated with cement and paper-making. There are long terraces of nineteenth and twentieth-century houses in suburbs that spill out westward under the shadow of the North Downs.

The Old Cricket Ground, West Malling

The Old Cricket Ground, West Malling

Is the field where the first recorded county cricket match in Kent was played. Also, it is likely that matches on this ground inspired Charles Dickens to write about the match between All-Muggleton and Dingley Dell in *The Pickwick Papers*. Indeed, the spire of the church in the original illustration of the match closely resembles that of the nearby St Mary's church in the town. This image became widely circulated in the mid 1990s on the back of the British £10 note, which featured Charles Dickens.

49

the town and out on the road to East Malling. West Malling is a fine, small town with an ancient street pattern and some notable buildings, thankfully separated from the urban sprawl emanating westwards from Maidstone by the horrible, badly designed, highly intrusive, new Tonbridge Road, the A228. I strolled past the waterfall spilling out of the abbey grounds and turned south through Manor Country Park by the narrow lane called Lavender Road. This took me up to and over the horrible road, called the Ashton Way. I wondered whether a Mr Ashton could be held responsible for the planning or construction of this road, which, for all its faults, does relieve West Malling of through traffic.

Across the A228, I passed into orchard country, where the dwarf apple trees were dripping with fruit in this late September season, and I could have helped myself to armfuls by just stretching out my hand. Passing a group of indolent apple pickers, sitting around, smoking and talking, I couldn't imagine how such a small workforce could pick so many apples in what was this year's bumper harvest, and of course they couldn't possibly. Many countless millions of apples would remain unpicked, simply to fall on the floor and rot. If you have ever observed a modern apple orchard closely you will have noticed that the strip of land under the trees is always bare and often covered in fallen apples. It is a sobering thought that the absence of any grass or weeds under the trees can only be due to the liberal application of herbicides.

Passing Broadwater and Springhead Farms, I came up to the crossroads with the East Malling to Teston road, and took a footpath through a chestnut wood around the back of East Malling Heath. Entering the gloomy wood, it started to drizzle as I passed a chap over in the far corner, coppicing the trees. His efforts, no doubt over many months, would have cleared this very small corner of Oaken Wood, a more modest version of Mereworth Woods to the west. The reason for the large acreage given over to chestnut coppice in this area was to supply poles for the hop-growing industry, but since the introduction of the American post and wire system, and the decline of hop-growing, the demand for this product has evaporated. Thus, many areas of chestnut coppice now remain unworked and have become derelict. I carried on down the cobbled footway into the Medway Valley, through Livesey Street and down to Teston. Looking at the map, this was the straightest route, as the crow flies, and would have been more important in times gone by, before the lane over East Malling Heath gained pre-eminence.

Coming down into Teston, I passed the quaint-looking cricket and hockey ball factory of Alfred Reader & Co., established in 1808, central to the development of the game of cricket and evidently still churning out balls. It started to rain properly in the pleasant village, so I called into the local shop to buy water and chocolate, and struggled into wet gear in the lych gate of the parish church. I cut down beside the small village green to the A26 and on down to the historic Medway Bridge. This is one of a number of significant, medieval stone bridges across the Medway, which also includes one at East Farleigh, down river, and those up river at Yalding. I took the Medway Valley Path westwards on the north bank of the river to Wateringbury. Himalayan balsam had invaded the river bank below Teston Bridge.

I passed timidly through a field of bulls engaged in 'conservation grazing', and I thought this gave a whole new meaning to the phrase 'put out to grass'. I rather liked the idea of these old chaps, after a lifetime of breeding and being too tough for eating, being allowed to live out their days together in this lush riverside pasture, while altruistically helping to preserve the open riverside habitat. Further along, I came face to face with a big, belligerent bull that wouldn't budge from the path, fixing me in a defiant stare and forcing me to walk round him. I did think about waving my arms around to scare him off, but I was doubtful about picking a fight I probably couldn't win.

The Medway is a tamed river with large lock installations at regular intervals, making it navigable all the way to Tonbridge. Also, it is a very accessible river with the path often hugging the river bank and much coveted by fishermen, the collective organisations of which own large stretches of the river bank. Along this picturesque river, I saw a sign which said 'No camping, no barbecues, no fishing, no mooring and no picnicking'; I wondered whether breathing was allowed. As I came into Wateringbury, the bank was lined with pleasure craft and I wondered what would happen to these boats, moored tightly to the bank as they were, when the river flooded, as it does from time to time. Reaching the combined river and railway crossing at Wateringbury, I returned a waved greeting from two men precariously perched on a signal box, engaged in mending its roof, and I speculated that they were not greatly constrained by modern health and safety regulations. On this well-used river there were numerous groups of people playing boats.

Strolling over the tracks to the Railway Inn, I sat outside for a while until it opened. A sign outside said the kitchen, which had been closed for refurbishment, was to open this very day and I was hopeful that I could get lunch. When I did gain access, I was informed that the kitchen was still closed, the barman being totally unconcerned that the notice outside was incorrect. Resigned, I settled for a pint and a packet of crisps. Leaving the pub and carrying on up river on the north bank, I passed another line of pleasure craft, but this time with an interesting variant; they had accompanying, touring caravans parking behind at the back of the towpath. I don't think I had seen that combination of leisure-time innovation anywhere before.

Two swans landed on the river with some aplomb, pushing out their splayed, yellow feet in front to act as brakes. They then proceeded to let every creature in the vicinity know of their arrival by issuing a triumphant, raucous chorus. I observed Nettlestead Church across the railway, somewhat detached from the main village, and of course severed from the river, which it once would have gracefully presided over. Between the ever-narrowing river and the railway was a large, inaccessible, unim-proved area of land, no doubt liable to flood from time to time, that had been allowed to remain gloriously wild. Then I came to another large field that was the playground of a substantial population of pheasant.

I reached the massive lock installation before Yalding that gave access to a marina, and the canal that runs alongside the B2162. I came up to

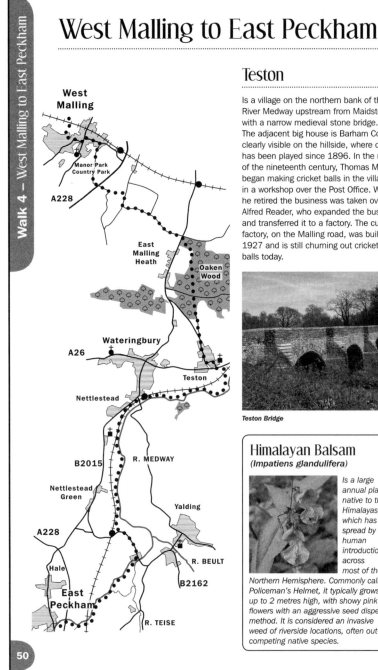

West Malling to East Peckham

West Malling

Manor Park
Country Park

A228

East
Malling
Heath

Oaken
Wood

Wateringbury

A26

Teston

Nettlestead

B2015 R. MEDWAY

Nettlestead
Green

Yalding

A228

Hale

R. BEULT

B2162

East
Peckham

R. TEISE

Teston

Is a village on the northern bank of the River Medway upstream from Maidstone, with a narrow medieval stone bridge. The adjacent big house is Barham Court, clearly visible on the hillside, where cricket has been played since 1896. In the middle of the nineteenth century, Thomas Martin began making cricket balls in the village, in a workshop over the Post Office. When he retired the business was taken over by Alfred Reader, who expanded the business and transferred it to a factory. The current factory, on the Malling road, was built in 1927 and is still churning out cricket balls today.

Teston Bridge

Himalayan Balsam
(Impatiens glandulifera)

Is a large annual plant native to the Himalayas, which has spread by human introduction across most of the Northern Hemisphere. Commonly called Policeman's Helmet, it typically grows up to 2 metres high, with showy pink flowers with an aggressive seed dispersal method. It is considered an invasive weed of riverside locations, often out-competing native species.

50

130

the road by the station and observed the massive brownfield factory site, that I have remarked on before, now completely cleared; I wondered what possible use this area could be put to. I traipsed along beside the canal, much loved by canoeists, to the Anchor Inn, my berth for the night. I had stayed at the Anchor Inn once before, while passing along the Greensand Way to Sutton Valence, feeling a bit cold and reduced, but this time I had a proper cold and did not feel much better. After resting up for a while in the rundown hotel adjacent to the historic, low-level inn, I decided to walk across the Lees to Yalding Village. Crossing over the distinctive, metal footbridge in front of the pub, and the ancient stone bridge over the Medway, I took the well-marked footpath across the field, known as The Lees. I read a notice that warned of the dangers of Weil's disease, caught from rats, and advising anyone in contact with the waters to wash their hands before eating.

The village of Yalding proper forms a settlement at a crossing point on the River Beult, just above its confluence with the Medway, with another ancient stone bridge. In the steeply rising High Street across the river, I was struck by the amount of traffic using this road, the B2010, whose time had come, given the date it now was. I decided to turn tail and return across the river to visit The George on the main B2162, also extremely busy in this rush hour, and whose time would have to wait for another fifty-two years. I couldn't settle there so I returned across the Lees to the Anchor Inn, where I spent the evening. However, as there was a complete lack of company, I had no choice but to watch a football match on the television.

If anywhere in Kent could claim to be at its very centre then I think Yalding has a good case, situated in the Medway Valley where major rivers come together. It is, curiously, also the last town or village alphabetically in Kent. However, the main impression of Yalding is that it is largely devoid of activity, being empty and riverine, in what I have previously referred to as 'the empty heart of Kent'. It is a wet, lugubrious place, afflicted by a rat-borne disease. In years gone by, Yalding attracted crowds of summer visitors from London and even before that, Londoners taking working holidays in the hop fields. Now, it appears to be much reduced, while the traffic thunders through, testing its medieval bridges to destruction, waiting for the next flood.

In the morning sun, I set off upstream, via Teapot Island, created where the minor arm of the River Teise joins the Medway, and on along the south side of the river towards East Peckham. It was pleasant walking in the morning sun, the best day so far that week. Before I reached the A228, I came across an ugly conveyer-belt system, carrying gravel across the river from a pit on one side to a storage mound on the other. I passed under the railway and the new section of the A228 Tunbridge Wells road, which forms a by-pass to East Peckham and Hale, and approached the village full of anticipation. I had imagined an old settlement of quality based around an ancient river crossing; I was sorely disappointed. In the vicinity of the river crossings, there was nothing of any antiquity, surrounded as they were by derelict warehouses and car showrooms. I decided to walk up into East Peckham to find a shop to buy some provisions. I found a shop but nothing of any merit in the lower part of the village. Thinking about it later, the absence of a parish church in this settlement indicated its relatively recent development. Indeed, the original parish church, now disused, that I had passed on a previous journey lay 2 miles to the north.

Disappointed with East Peckham, I pressed on towards Tonbridge. It was about a 5-mile walk along the river with no intervening farms, hamlets or settlements of any kind, presumably because of the propensity of the valley to flood in this section. After about a mile or so, having negotiated a number of riverside woods and passed by the confluence with the River Bourne on the opposite bank, I decided to have a rest, leaning against a large trunk of a fallen tree, soaking up the warmth of the sun. Halfway along this stretch, I had to cross over the river by sluices and locks at a place where the river divided around an island in the stream, where an important-looking footpath from Golden Green to Five Oak Green crosses the river and brings the Wealdway to join the Medway Valley Path. I passed groups of fishermen along the north bank, as the sun became progressively obscured by clouds, resulting in an abrupt drop in temperature.

Staggering into Tonbridge, I had to put up with the distraction of a badly behaved dog disobeying its irate lady owner, running ahead and round my legs. He was very fond of disturbing the concentration of the fishermen and consumed large quantities of one chap's bait. As I approached Tonbridge, I walked through the scruffy outskirts of the town, either side of the A26 ring-road, before reaching the smart, new, riverside apartment blocks in the centre. The river was navigable up to this point and the old quays and warehouses, many having been

East Peckham to Tonbridge

The Wealdway

Is an 82-mile public footpath from
Gravesend to Eastbourne, conceived
in 1970 by members of the Rambler's
Association. It passes through the
Kent and Sussex Weald, crossing chalk
downland, river valleys and wooded
farmland, and affording a full traverse of
Ashdown Forest. Motorway construction
and the building of the Tonbridge Flood
Relief Barrier at Leigh, forced changes to
the original route. On the section leading
into Tonbridge, the Wealdway and the
Medway Valley Walk follow the same route
for about 4 miles alongside the River
Medway.

The Medway Bridge, Tonbridge

The River Bourne

Is a small but significant tributary of the
River Medway of approximately 10 miles
in length, originating in the Greensand
Ridge in the vicinity of Ightham. It flows
generally in a south-east direction through
the parishes of Plaxtol, Hadlow and East
Peckham through the Vale of Kent. The
area around the confluence, near East
Peckham, is prone to flooding, in part
due to the significant volume of water
entering the River Medway at this point
downstream from Tonbridge. The stretch
of the river from Ightham, through Hadlow
to Golden Green, has powered numerous
watermills, whose principal products were
flour and paper.

The Ramblers

Formerly known as The Ramblers'
Association, The Ramblers is the largest
walkers' rights association in Great Britain,
which aims to look after the interests of
walkers. It is a charity which was formally
created on 1 January 1935, after years
of radical protest and trespass, typified
by the mass trespass of Kinder Scout in
the Peak District on 24 April 1932. After
the Second World War the association
was active in campaigning for access to
the open countryside and for the creation
of long distance footpaths, the first being
the Pennine Way. Eventually, after years of
campaigning for access to open land, this
was achieved by the provisions contained
in the Countryside and Rights of Way Act
2000. In Kent, the fourth largest Ramblers
area, there are 13 groups which promote
the aims of the organisation. These groups
were instrumental in the creation of The
Wealdway.

51

converted to residences, were clearly evident. The navigation stopped at the main bridge across the river in Tonbridge and I sojourned for a while outside the riverside bar in the fitful sunshine with a pint of cider, soaking up the atmosphere of the place. Later, I crossed over the bridge and sat in a warmer place, on a bench by the river under the castle ramparts, before retiring to the Rose and Crown Hotel.

In the evening, after a very satisfactory meal and several glasses of red wine in a pizza restaurant, I found a delightful pub called the Man of Kent in an unspoilt terrace, in a street off the High Street. This was a slightly inappropriate name for the pub, given that it was only a few yards north of the Medway. It had a bar billiards table on which I indulgently practised for a while, before joining a group of olds boys for a quiz. In common with the last time I was in Tonbridge, I had a very pleasant evening and returned to my hotel quite merry.

In the morning when I tried to continue with my planned journey, I was assailed by appalling weather and was forced to give it up. When I resumed the walk the following spring, I proceeded down Tonbridge High Street and picked up the Eden Valley Walk, westwards, along the bank of the River Medway. I passed in front of the famous medieval castle and around the castle mound, the original Norman castle. Looking north across the well-manicured grounds of Tonbridge school, I could see the Greensand Ridge in the distance. Four lady canoeists paddled sedately down the river towards Tonbridge in perfect formation. At this time of the year, the grass verge by the side of the path was smothered with cow parsley and ragged robin. It was a splendid walk out along the river, the whole area before the railway being prone to flooding and left to nature. The river bank was clothed with dog rose and other small shrubs and trees. Crossing under the railway through cool woods, I was pleased to see a song thrush scampering through the undergrowth. However, all the while, the noise from the A21 was becoming more insistent.

Further on, I climbed up the bank that formed the Leigh flood barrier, constructed in 1981 to hold back the waters of the Wealden rivers, thus helping to protect Tonbridge and the settlements downstream from the excess rush of water in times of flood. This massive construction, which is the largest flood barrier of its type in the country and capable of storing 1,230 million gallons of water, can be clearly seen from the A21 flyover across the valley. The ample bowl created to house the flood waters when needed is now a nature reserve and I can't imagine any other useful purpose that it could be put to. There were people with cameras on tripods busily recording the wildlife and numerous gentlemen with binoculars, observing the multitude of butterflies around. However, I had a strong impression that some gentlemen were busy observing other gentlemen observing butterflies. It was a pleasant prospect but I did wonder how this valued ecosystem would survive in times of flood. In the damp recesses of the reserve yellow flag irises were flourishing.

Crossing under the main road, majestically roaring overhead, I came to a huge lake known as Haysden Water. Along the shore, by a boatyard, were numerous yachts, and the wind oscillating the rigging made that distinctive hollow clanking sound on the aluminium masts. This was, for me, a very evocative sound, which reminded me of the time I nearly drowned in Chichester Harbour. On that occasion, with my best friend from school, we, as novice sailors, had got caught in a force 6 squall which severely tested our sailing skills. In fact we capsized twice and bravely swam under the boat to right it on both occasions. Exhausted and still struggling with the conditions, we were given a tow by a friendly motor boat and beached by West Wittering. Here we rested and licked our wounds.

Foolishly, when all the boats had gone home, we tried once more to make it back into port at Bosham, but succeeded only in capsizing again. As the boat filled up with water, we got out and hung onto the sides. The natural buoyancy of the craft gradually lifted it out of the stream and my friend climbed back in, but I was left, holding on for dear life, strung out in the fierce ebb tide. The force of the current meant that I could not hold on and just as I lost my grip, my friend grabbed my hand and pulled me aboard. Although I have heard it said that one's life passes before one's eyes during near-death experiences, believe me, it is true. In that moment, my life passed before me as a kaleidoscope of images in a matter of seconds. We managed to get the boat back to the beach where numerous yachts were moored and as I recovered my land legs, I vividly remember that same sound of metallic clanking rigging on masts. Every time I hear the sound, as at Haysden Water, the memory of the near-fatal accident comes back to me in all its stark horror. The long walk back to civilisation from the deserted beach where we left the boat, in the gathering gloom, was an absolute pleasure. Needless to say, I have found it difficult to venture out on the open water in small boats ever since.

Dog roses with their pale-pink flowers were very much in evidence

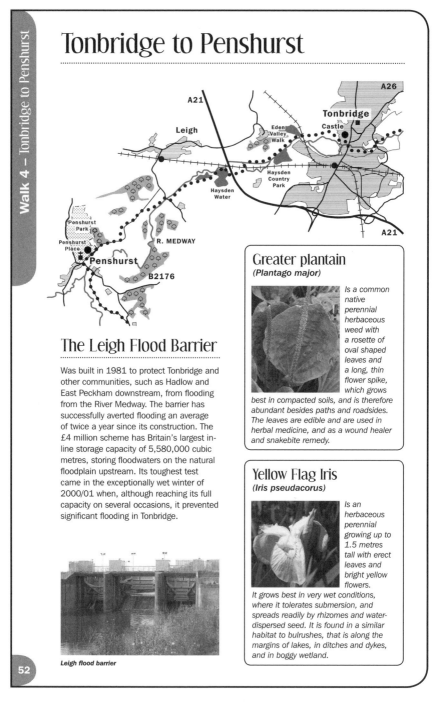

Tonbridge to Penshurst

The Leigh Flood Barrier

Was built in 1981 to protect Tonbridge and other communities, such as Hadlow and East Peckham downstream, from flooding from the River Medway. The barrier has successfully averted flooding an average of twice a year since its construction. The £4 million scheme has Britain's largest in-line storage capacity of 5,580,000 cubic metres, storing floodwaters on the natural floodplain upstream. Its toughest test came in the exceptionally wet winter of 2000/01 when, although reaching its full capacity on several occasions, it prevented significant flooding in Tonbridge.

Leigh flood barrier

Greater plantain
(Plantago major)

Is a common native perennial herbaceous weed with a rosette of oval shaped leaves and a long, thin flower spike, which grows best in compacted soils, and is therefore abundant besides paths and roadsides. The leaves are edible and are used in herbal medicine, and as a wound healer and snakebite remedy.

Yellow Flag Iris
(Iris pseudacorus)

Is an herbaceous perennial growing up to 1.5 metres tall with erect leaves and bright yellow flowers. It grows best in very wet conditions, where it tolerates submersion, and spreads readily by rhizomes and water-dispersed seed. It is found in a similar habitat to bulrushes, that is along the margins of lakes, in ditches and dykes, and in boggy wetland.

under the A21 flyover, with bulrushes clothing the side of the lake. Then, amazingly, I saw a pair of great crested grebes gracing the lake. The cracked, yellow, mud-baked path around the margin of the lake had patches of hardy plantain weeds, which were tough enough to withstand the constant trampling of feet. Further on, I crossed over the river and entered a field containing perfectly white cattle with delightfully ebullient calves. Further on still, the Eden Valley Walk departs from the river to scale a 60m bluff in a bend of the river, passing behind Well Place Farm. From the top of the rise there are panoramic views all around, back towards Tonbridge, Sevenoaks and Maidstone on the Greensand Ridge, and the blue line of the North Downs beyond, and the other way, down to the stately splendour of Penshurst Place, nestling in the valley to the west.

I came down across the bottom of Penshurst Place, past ponds bedecked with glorious clumps of yellow flag irises, underneath an imposing brick wall enclosing a walled garden, and through a grand arch, to emerge into the village of Penshurst. A signpost told me I had walked more than 5 miles from Tonbridge. Along this stretch, below Penshurst Place, I passed a fellow walker who I thought I recognised from his picture on his book cover as Kev Reynolds, the doyen of walking guide book writers. I nearly summoned up the courage to accost this walker and test out my theory, but not being quick-witted enough, the moment of opportunity passed.

The old village centre in Penshurst has that harmonious integrity in red-brick style that results from its creation by a single land owner, as an extension to the adjacent stately home. It reminded me very much of the village of Waddesden, north of Aylesbury, in this respect. In this case, it was the creation of the Earls of Leicester, and the name of the historic inn in the village eponymously celebrated this fact, as the Leicester Arms. It occurred to me that Penshurst is where the Medway, joined by the River Eden and all its other headwater tributaries, emerges from the Weald to flow down into the Vale of Kent. This juxtaposition of land-scape zones creates a wonderful scenic landscape quality in this locality.

I popped into the pub for lunch. In this up-market establishment I searched for something simple to order. The barman, taking pity on my plight, recommended a croque monsieur and, feigning ignorance, I was informed that it was a posh toasted ham sandwich with chips and salad. Although it was perfectly splendid and expensive, I was unable to finish

Penshurst to Groombridge

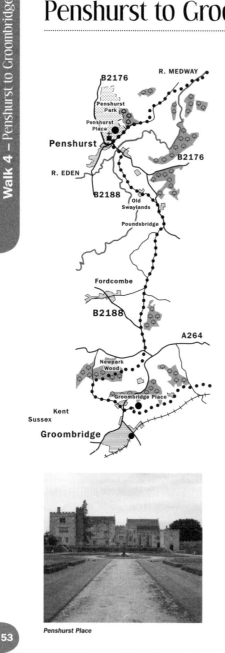

Groombridge

Is a village that straddles the border between Kent and East Sussex. The main part of the village (new Groombridge) lies in East Sussex, but the smaller and older part (old Groombridge) lies in Kent. Old Groombridge has a pub, the Crown Inn, and some attractive cottages surrounding a small sloping green, a church and Groombridge Place, an ancient, privately owned moated manor house dating from 1239. The village is on the Spa Valley line, a standard gauge heritage railway that runs from Tunbridge Wells to Eridge Station, providing access to the tourist attractions of High Rocks and Groombridge Place.

Groombridge Place

Penshurst Place

Is the ancestral home of the Sidney family and birthplace of the great Elizabethan poet, courtier and soldier, Sir Philip Sidney. The original medieval house is one of the most complete examples of fourteenth-century domestic architecture in England surviving in its original location. Philip Sidney (1554–86) died after a fatal wounding at the battle of Zutphen, and was buried in the old St Paul's in London, but his tomb was destroyed in the great fire of 1666. His brother, Robert Sidney, inherited the estate and also the Earldom of Leicester. The village pub is today called The Leicester Arms. After a period of neglect during the First World War, the house has been restored, and house and gardens are open to the public today.

Penshurst Place

53

the meal, since when walking, really, all that is required is a light snack. And I paid £3.70 for a pint of beer, surely a record. I have never discovered a satisfactory explanation of why the price of beer varies so much from pub to pub and in different parts of the country, except perhaps that it relates to what people are prepared to pay.

From Penshurst, I crossed over the Medway again and found the pleasant lower footpath to Old Swaylands, which I had missed last time I passed this way, down in the luxuriant broad valley of the big river. And then from Old Swaylands, I carried on to Poundsbridge, along a quiet lane, across a flat-bottomed valley formed by a tributary of the Medway. Approaching Poundsbridge, I came again to that most distinctive house at the junction, with black beams and yellow plasterwork dating from 1593. After this relaxing walk down in the valley came the hard miles: a long, good hour's slog due south to a height of 129m at the junction with the B2188 and beyond to the A264. I was tempted to go down into Fordcombe and take a right-handed detour to Groombridge, my day's destination, but decided to keep on going straight. The stretch along the B2188 was most uncomfortable in that I had to flinch from fast-moving, sporadic traffic, but thankfully at the junction with the A264, at Crockers Hatch Corner, I was able to pick up the Weald Way going south.

Unfortunately, I lost the way almost immediately, probably due to a combination of tiredness and complacency, thinking it was only a stone's throw from Groombridge. I made the basic mistake again of not being accurate about my place on the map, thinking I was further advanced than I actually was and as a consequence, took the wrong footpath. I became diverted through Newpark Wood, much frequented by horse riders, rather than proceeding to Top Hill Farm. Realising my mistake, I elected to continue on the lane to the north of Burrswood, kicking myself because of the realisation that I could have taken the detour to Fordcombe and Stone Cross after all.

Slipping off the edge of the hill down a winding lane from Burrswood, past a fabulous manor house, I came into Groombridge. The triangular, sloping green is surrounded by an attractive collection of buildings, including the Crown Inn, my berth for the night. There, the Kent/Sussex border runs along the stream down the so-called Spa Valley, a tributary of the Medway, and the Kentish side of Groombridge has a lot more to offer in terms of historical importance and visual appeal than the Sussex side. Adjacent to the pub, on the other side of the green, is a curious church and the historic, privately owned Groombridge Place. I sat for a while in front of the pub, under a carefully pollarded row of lime trees, soaking up the atmosphere. It was slightly spoilt by the thunderous traffic tearing down the hill from Tunbridge Wells on its way back home to the many housing estates of Crowborough.

The Crown Inn at Groombridge was an ancient building, seemingly incapable of improvement. The landlord complained bitterly that the cost of improvement, bearing in mind the army of professional consultants that would need to be employed because of its listed status, was prohibitive. The view from my room was spectacular, with a clear view of the bridge crossing the stream that formed the Kent/Sussex border. I spent a pleasant evening in the bar, eating, writing up the day's events and chatting to the landlord. Looking at the map, I noticed that the area around Groombridge, west of Tunbridge Wells, is smothered in long-distance footpaths, including the Wealdway, The High Weald Landscape Trail, The Sussex Border Path and The Tunbridge Wells Circular Walk.

In the morning, after posting my box on the Sussex side, I strode out eastwards through the grounds of Groombridge Place. The path passed round the moat, right in front of this privately owned stately home, by the lake created by the damming of the stream. I carried on through pleasant fields in the timid sunshine beside the small stream, with the Spa Valley Railway occupying the other side of the valley. I kept on the Tunbridge Wells Circular Walk until I reached the massive sewage works, which I had to pass around. Inside the forbidding fence, the grounds consisted of acres of dutifully mown grass. I thought about this and could not see the point of the water company being so fastidious, obviously talking a pride in the grounds' appearance. Why not let the grounds go wild and let nature in, since it would hardly interfere with the primary function of the works in processing human waste from Tunbridge Wells.

As I approached High Rocks, the valley narrowed and steepened as I passed through a cool glade, before arriving at High Rocks Halt. After a quick look around the massive sandstone outcrop, I proceeded eastwards through the adjoining car park to pass under Ramslye Wood, where the bluebells in the bank had gone over, walking in East Sussex now. There, the landscape was markedly different from down in the valley, from the sewage works really, with massive woods, conifer plantations and bare, rock-laden fields carved out of the high sandstone forest. I pressed on to the A26 out of Tunbridge Wells at Strawberry Hill, along a drive which

Groombridge to Frant

Frant

Is an ancient hilltop village in East Sussex on the northern edge of the Weald on a ridge of hard sandstone, that was heavily involved in the Wealden iron Industry. It is believed that King John once owned a hunting lodge in the village, and during the reign of Edward I in 1296 the village was granted a market and fair at the beginning of November. The sixteenth century brought the manufacture of cannons to the village, much of which was owned by the local iron masters. This delightful village, with its main street lined with cottages leading to the church, is set off by large areas of open ground, one part of which is used as the village cricket ground.

Bluebells
(Hyacinthoides non-scripta)

Is a spring blue flowering bulbous perennial woodland plant that occurs massed together, carpeting the ground in bluebell woods. The English bluebell should not be confused with the Scottish bluebell or harebell (Campanula rotundifolia). Although endemic to much of Europe, it is estimated that over 70% of all common bluebells are found in Great Britain, and it is a protected species under the Wildlife and Countryside Act 1981.

High Rocks

The George Inn and church, Frant

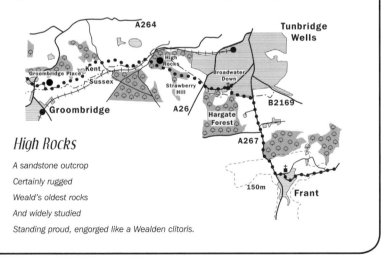

High Rocks

A sandstone outcrop

Certainly rugged

Weald's oldest rocks

And widely studied

Standing proud, engorged like a Wealden clitoris.

54

was flanked by a large patch of invasive Japanese knotweed, and passed on into the affluent suburbs on Broadwater Down, on the outskirts of Tunbridge Wells, and back into Kent.

After a steep little rise into Broadwater Down, I passed an entrance to the Hargate Forest, managed by the Woodlands Trust. I wanted to cut down through the forest but elected to proceed to the church on the down and take the second footpath shown on the map down through the forest. I passed by opulent dwelling houses on the way to the church, where I turned south and found the second entrance to the forest locked and barred. I cursed my luck and thought this policy may have had something to do with the fact that this entrance lay exactly on the border. My strong recommendation if anyone should be foolish enough to try and copy my journey, is to make sure you take the first footpath through Hargate Forest. As a consequence, I was forced out onto the main A267 road, proceeding southwards on a roadside path to the village of Frant. After a descent into a shallow valley, I climbed up to the hill village of Frant at 179m. Exhausted by the climb, I took the back lane past the new school to the church and sought out The George Inn for a lunchtime break.

I sat outside the pub for a while, on its scruffy forecourt, which doubled up as a car park, waiting for the pub to open. I regarded the street scene with interest; there was a mixture of types of buildings leading down to the church in what must be the main street. I was cold and damp after the climb up to the village and the sun had disappeared, which took the edge off the experience. I went inside the old pub, which was full of character with many original features, but cold and gloomy because of a power cut. I ordered a pint of cider and sat at the bar, while the harassed landlord was busy trying to trace the source of the problem. I observed a mass of wires running all around the bar, having proliferated as more and more bar equipment had been installed. Clearly a circuit had become overloaded and blown, and I did wonder whether the premises were entirely safe.

When I came out of the pub, the gloom had lifted to some degree and Frant demonstrated that it was, as anticipated, a very attractive village. There were many fine, typical, Wealden buildings, some timber-framed, having received the normal black and white treatment, and some tile-hung or white, weather-boarded, ragstone cottages, all arranged in a harmonious grouping along the main street and around large areas of common, interlaced with small sunken lanes. The footpaths in the main street were made of distinctive red brick, which reminded me very much of Winchelsea. All in all, Frant was a beautiful hilltop village with incredible views out all around.

Striding out eastwards from Frant, there were stunning views down into the valley to the south, whose stream formed one of the headwaters of the River Teise, which, in common with other major Kentish rivers, has its origins in the Sussex Weald. The grass verge was covered in the sprawling, yellow and orange, pea-like flowers of bird's-foot trefoil, commonly known as eggs and bacon, the purple spikes of bugle together with buttercups and ferns. I noticed this time, when walking in mid-May, the verges and hedges were full of flowering plants which are not always so evident later on in the season.

On the way to Bells Yew Green, by Frant Station, I located another pub, the Brecknock Arms. This pub was a railway pub in its arrangement and design, and elsewhere could have been called The Station or Railway Hotel. I wondered if there was a Welsh connection in this vicinity, given that there was also a pub called the Abergavenny Arms on the main A267. After admiring the pictures of railway memorabilia on the walls, I sat outside and consumed my pint, observing the lunchtime scene. After further research, I found that the Welsh connection did exist, in that much of the land thereabouts belonged to Lord Abergavenny of the nearby Eridge Park. The family originally came from Abergavenny in Monmouthshire.

Negotiating a short, uncomfortable stretch of the B2169 before turning south into Higham Lane, I passed down to the same small stream that had gathered pace since its inception in the valley below Frant. Looking at the map, it was as if the headwaters of the River Teise were clutching at the hill village with long sinuous fingers. I stood for a while at a field gate and was assailed by the bleating of sheep. It seemed as though they were collectively complaining about the lack of grass in their field, a consequence of the complete absence of any rain to sustain its growth. I thought that the farmers must be getting pretty desperate by now at the lack of rain in this part of the country so early in the season. I'm sure the sheep were talking to me because as I passed down the lane, I could hear that they had stopped their plaintiff protests.

Further down the lane, I took a steep footpath down into a dell in another valley to cut off an extravagant kink in the lane, and had another ovine adventure. I came across a nearly fully grown lamb with its head stuck in a wire fence of about 5-inch mesh. No doubt the poor creature had been desperately searching for longer grass on the other side of the fence and had probably been stuck for some time because its back legs had created a muddy depression in an attempt to exert sufficient force to extricate itself from the wire. Its mother and sibling looked on helplessly in close attendance. I decided that I had to try and help the creature get out of its predicament. Once I held the animal firmly by the scruff of the neck with it trapped between my legs, it stopped struggling and I was able to carefully bend the wire, flatten out its fleece and release it. I pulled it out backwards and it rolled over onto its feet in an undignified manner. It stared at me for a few seconds, before running off to join its family, lurking in the background. It was the first time I had ever felt a fleece and I was amazed at how soft, fine and moist it was, suffused with lanolin. I wondered in that moment what thoughts were going through the sheep's head and whether any of them amounted to gratitude. I felt rather pleased with myself for being able to execute this good deed, but when I recounted this tale to friends at work it evoked many ribald laughs and knowing winks, which rather disconcerted me.

I plodded on, through a wood in the depths of the dell and along the lane past Whitegates Farm towards Turners Green, to a high point of 150m, and admired the panoramic view to the north and east, with the

Frant to Wadhurst

Wadhurst

Is a market town in the East Sussex Weald on a high sandstone ridge. The name is Anglo Saxon and thought to derive from Wada, the name of the tribe which is believed to have inhabited the area. Henry III granted the town a charter to hold a weekly Saturday market, and during the sixteenth to eighteenth centuries, as with many other places in the Weald, it had a thriving iron industry. Two of the large Georgian buildings in the High Sreet, Hill House and the Old Vicarage, were iron master's houses.

On 20 January 1958 an RAF Gloster Meteor night fighter jet crashed into the High Street, destroying the Old Queens Head Hotel and shops, killing the crew and two people on the ground. The town has a variety of vernacular building styles, dating from the fifteenth century, though little in the town centre is very modern except the buildings replacing the bombed hotel. The Victorian era saw expansion towards the railway station, which is on the Charing Cross to Hastings line, resulting in the growth of the hamlets of Sparrow's Green and Turner's Green to the west.

Bugle
(Ajuga reptans)

Is a creeping perennial with erect stems, square in section, bearing whorls of deep purplish flowers in the axils of leaves. It is a spreading ground cover plant that can grow into a dense mat. It is a food plant for fritillary butterflies.

Bird's-foot Trefoil
(Lotus corniculatus)

Is a common perennial herbaceous flowering plant native to the temperate grasslands of Eurasia and North America. The orange and yellow flowers develop into pea-like pods or legumes, and the name bird's foot refers to the appearance of the seed pods. Its common name is bacon and eggs, and it is often used in wild flower seed mixes and is poisonous to humans.

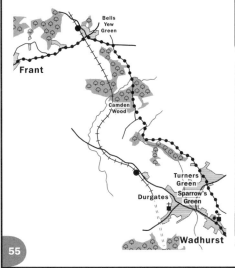

St Peter and St Paul's Church, Wadhurst

North Downs clearly visible in the distance. Turners Green itself is a very nondescript place, with an ugly crescent of a car park in front of the recreation ground and a hideous village hall fronting the small green. The settlements of Turners Green, Sparrows Green and Durgates, forming an urban sprawl contiguous with Wadhurst, amount to a significant urban area. I hoped that Wadhurst itself would have more to recommend it.

I carried on along a lane to the north of Wadhurst and came into the village by the church after a steep climb out of another Wealden Valley, whose stream fed the nearby Bewl Water. I booked into my accommodation for the night, at the Greyhound Inn, and rested before exploring the village. The High Street seemed to be quite knocked about and standing outside the other pub in the village, I imagined I was in the Wild West, fully expecting some gun-slinging local to fall out of the pub and challenge me to a duel. This reverie may have been triggered by the fact that when dropping off my boxes, I had inadvertently called in at this other pub and been told rather rudely to sod off by the landlord. Two hombres drinking at the bar had kindly explained that the Greyhound Inn was further down the road.

Wadhurst would no doubt once have been an attractive village with a harmonious High Street containing buildings of merit. Now, unfortunately, due to the ravages of time, unsympathetic development and an unforced jet plane crash that destroyed the old Queens Head Hotel in the middle of the High Street, it is only good in parts. The buildings that have replaced the hotel could visually be a lot worse. At least the height and rhythm of the buildings and the materials used in the construction are broadly in keeping, but not the long, curving sweep of the road frontage. But even worse, next to this redeveloped site is an incredible ugly, and now disused, warehouse which desperately needs pulling down. Thus, the centre of Wadhurst has a hole in it and together with the heavy traffic pounding through, it is difficult to claim that the village really has any visual quality.

I left Wadhurst the following morning in overcast conditions, producing light rain and walked down to Stone Cross, presumably named after the war memorial at the junction, and planned a shorter walk to Burwash. I set off down the ivy-strangled, oak tree-shuttered lane, keeping high all the time, to the railway line. The railway was hidden away in a deep cutting, and I paused for a while on the bridge, whose crumbling brick parapet was festooned with lichen and wild strawberries. Further on there was a pleasant grouping of dwellings at a hamlet called Buttons. At Flattenden Farm, at the end of the road, I carried on through the edge of a wood and came down to a delightful grove by a stream that was part of the headwaters of the River Rother. I sat on a stile with the smell of wild garlic and birdsong all around, and started thinking about those lines from Ezra Pound's poem, '*The Tree*': 'Nathless I have been a tree amid the wood, and many a new thing understood.' I thought I could corrupt his verse and say in that moment, 'I stood still in the wood, and all things understood'.

This lovely interlude was spoilt by me losing the way through Batts Wood, another wood managed by the Woodlands Trust. I ended up going west along the stream, by a large lake in the grounds of Wadhurst Park. Pleasant as the wood was, I was slightly irritated at this diversion and I climbed up out of the wood on a path strewn with tiny yellow butterflies, no more than 1cm wide. At the summit I could see Brightling Beacon in the direction I was travelling tomorrow. It occurred to me that in managing a wood for visitors, by providing carefully signposted, circular walks, as was the case in Batts Wood, it was easy to neglect the requirements of hikers who were simply intent on passing through, failing to indicate clearly the main through route.

Eventually, I emerged into the Sussex countryside and took the undulating footpath that led to the small lane below Bivelham Farm. Along the lower track from Hawksden Park Wood I saw evidence of badger setts in the hedgerow bank. Once in the winding lane, I made for the bridge over the River Rother in its broad, fertile, upper valley. The river was deeply cut and its headwaters stretched back westward as far as Mayfield and Rotherfield. Across the river there was a gorgeous meadow beside the lane with an exuberant display of ox-eye daisies, bird's-foot trefoil and clover. This was a lovely valley, with gracious cottages, and if the sun could have been shining, it would have been idyllic: a perfect English scene.

I struggled on up to the top of Witherden Hill at about 95m, from where I could see the spire of Burwash Church where I was headed, and took the track to Woodknowle Farm, where I came across a field of hops and saw a fox slinking away into the trees. Sometimes, when taking such a path, one ends up in difficulties, but on this occasion the path through the farm was clear and unadulterated. Before coming back to the lane, I passed into another wood redolent at this time of year with wild garlic

Wadhurst to Burwash

Wild Strawberry
(Fragaria vesca)

Also known as the Alpine Strawberry, this plant is native to Europe and grows happily in a variety of habitats, including unusually the brick parapet of railway bridges. It propagates primarily by runners, although viable seeds, eaten and spread by mammals and birds, can also germinate when the soil is disturbed away from existing populations. Evidence from archaeological excavations suggests that the wild strawberry has been eaten by humans since the Stone Age.

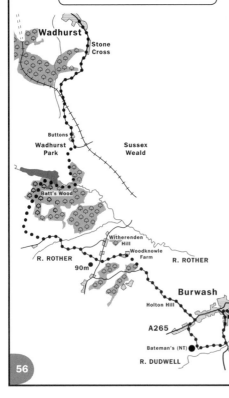

Burwash and Kipling

Burwash is a rural village situated on a ridge between the valley of the River Rother and its tributary the River Dudwell. The High Street has many splendid buildings, and has been designated as a conservation area, and the buildings have been listed by English Heritage. The village, like many others in The Weald was an important centre of iron making, and in the eighteenth and nineteenth centuries was involved in smuggling. The toll road, which passes through Burwash, was a notorious spot for highwaymen.

The village's main claim to fame is the connection with Rudyard Kipling who lived at Bateman's for half his life (1865-1936). This magnificent Jacobean mansion is now owned by the National Trust and lies just outside the village in the valley of the River Dudwell, where delightful gardens run down to a working water mill. He used the house's setting, and the wider local area, for many of his stories in *Puck of Pook's Hill* (1906) and the sequel *Rewards and Fairies* (1910). Kipling was awarded the Nobel Prize for Literature in 1907 and a copy of the citation can still be seen in the house today.

There is a Kipling room in The Bear public house in the High Street. A complete collection of Kipling's works, including the *Just So* stories, was published as the 'Burwash Edition' in 1941.

Bateman's, Burwash

56

down by another stream. It occurred to me, walking through this terrain, that I was traversing a series of ridges created by the headwaters of the Rivers Teise, Medway and Rother, so I had no problems imagining more ups and downs before I reached Burwash. Indeed, this was the case in having to pass over Holton Hill and then face the 100m cliff that formed the last ridge on which Burwash was perched.

I reached the top of the ridge in the early afternoon and decided to pay a visit to Bateman's, the National Trust property that was the home of Rudyard Kipling, which involved vicariously descending again off the ridge. The signpost from the main road indicated that it was a further 150 yards to Batemans and if this was true, it was the longest 150 yards I've ever experienced. I reasoned, as a member of the National Trust, that I could gain access without paying and then eat and rest for a few hours before walking back up to Burwash.

The chap on the entrance booth eyed me with great suspicion, doubting my credentials, before permitting entry. I then drank a lot of tea and organic ginger beer, but little food as it was inordinately expensive. After resting for a while I did have a look around the house. However, my rucksack and my inability to abide by the one-way circulation system caused a minor diplomatic incident. I did have the pleasure of lurking for a while, in relative isolation, in the great man's study, where he wrote so much of his splendid verse. Departing, I had a look around the walled garden and got into conversation with a lady tour guide who took an encouraging interest in my exploits.

Leaving Batemans, along the lane opposite, I came to a farm with a notice in the lane saying, 'SLOW – young children and young animals.' I thought that the sign would be more effective if it read, 'SLOW – young children and *other* young animals.' All that remained now was to slog back up the ridge to my berth for the night, the Rose and Crown pub, just off Burwash High Street. I recuperated for a while, had a satisfactory repast in the pub, had a look around the village and spent a pleasant evening talking to locals back at the bar. Burwash is indeed an attractive village, with a complete set of period buildings lining the High Street and an active community spirit. I noticed that parts of the pavement along the High Street were paved with bricks, just as I had observed in Frant, adorned by pollarded lime trees, just as I had observed in Groombridge. The village seems to have escaped that tatty discontinuity that attends Wadhurst, even though the traffic still thunders through, this time on the busy A265. The main visual aberration is caused by the motel car park in the main street, which could be less ostentatious and more sympathetically enclosed on its car park frontage.

The main conversation in the evening at the bar was in saving another pub in the village, The Bell, from a fate worse than death – closure. I did suggest that a village the size of Burwash could perhaps not support three pubs, but I was quickly contradicted. Evidently, the pub had been purchased by interests who were not concerned to run it as a pub, but were just living there. My companions were intent on invoking planning law, claiming this constituted a change of use, but I felt it incumbent on me to explain that arguably no development had taken place, and therefore planning law would not apply. All in all, I had a very pleasant stay in the Rose and Crown at Burwash.

Leaving Burwash in the morning, I sat for a while in the churchyard, looking south over the valley of the River Dudwell, soaking up the warmth from the morning sun. The landscape before me was laid out in a series of ridges formed by the streams that constituted the headwaters of the River Rother and I could see that my intended route to Battle would be undulating. I located the desired footpath from the back of the churchyard and descended into the lovely valley of the River Dudwell, on which Batemans was located a little further upstream, aiming all the time for Old Brick Farm across the valley. I disturbed some pigeons resting in a hedgerow tree who took off with an enormous commotion, crashing through the branches; it always amazes me how they don't break their wings doing this.

I then crossed over the deeply incised River Dudwell, caused by erosion in times of flood, but now the river was a trickle at the bottom of its trench. I carried on through Old Brick Farm to a plaintive symphony of bleating, with the distinctive, meaty, chewed grass smell of sheep all around. I then passed the farm pond and walked out along the drive through fields that appeared to be laid out as a park. To my left was a classical, white, cupula-like, stone folly, possibly associated with the nearby Glydwish Hall. Up again on the next ridge and looking north from the lane, I could see Burwash picked out elegantly across the valley. A pair of pied flycatchers flitted about along the lane; I have noticed that these birds prefer to feed on open, bare patches of terrain, including tarmac. The silence all around sang to me through the tinnitus in my right ear.

Trekking south past Brown's Oak Farm, I could see Darwell Wood looming up in front of me, with Rounden Wood to my right. I was entering a heavily wooded, relatively sparsely populated part of East Sussex around the village of Brightling. I came down to another stream and climbed again to Oxley's Green. Between this pleasant hamlet and the next at Hollingrove, I passed under an active conveyor belt, enclosed like a train carriage overhead, on its way to Brightling Mine in Rounden Wood. To come across a mine in the East Sussex countryside is perhaps somewhat surprising, but even more surprising is the commodity that is being mined; namely, gypsum: an important mineral resource typically used to manufacture that ubiquitous building material, plaster board. The gypsum deposits occur in the upper Jurassic strata that underlies the primarily cretaceous rock of the Weald, but because of the creation of the Wealden Dome, now heavily eroded, the Jurassic strata come closer to the surface, and are indeed exposed in a few places in river valleys, on the spine of the original dome from Burwash, all the way to Hastings. Thus, the area I was trekking through is riddled with underground tunnels, since gypsum is mined much like coal. The conveyor belt under which I had passed takes the gypsum rock to nearby Mountfield, past abandoned mines in Darwell Wood, where it is processed in the factory there. In the pub the previous night, the chaps at the bar suggested the underground tunnels may even stretch as far as Hastings on the coast.

Coming up to the hamlet of Hollingrove, I had my third sighting of a grass snake, this time about 1-foot long and squashed by passing traffic. With the aid of a hedgerow stick, I returned the unfortunate snake to the verge, hoping it would survive, but the most likely outcome I feared was that it would become food for some other creature. I pressed on southwards, admiring swallows on the wire and was reminded of those lines by Leonard Cohen in his song, '*Bird on the wire*', which goes, 'Like a bird on the wire, like a drunk in a midnight choir, I have tried in my way to be free.' I thought my perverse rambles, sometimes drunken, were my version of these same sentiments.

After Hollingrove, I reached a high point of 123m, walking on a lane with newly laid tarmac, which was soft and easy to walk on, providing an extra spring to my step. I carried on down through Twelve Oaks and Cackle Street but saw no witches, past the vast expanse of Darwell Wood to my left, passing a field with brown bulls and bull calves marching off somewhere, as if on a mission, in a purposeful line. The edges of the pleasant lane were bedecked by ox-eye daisies, buttercups, cow parsley and ferns. I slipped down and down into Darwell Hole at 61m, formed by the incipient rust-coloured stream that feeds Darwell Reservoir, one of the many headwaters of the River Rother. Looking back north-westwards, I could see the ornamental temple folly standing up prominently on its mound in Brightling Park. As I rested by the stream at the bottom of the hill, feeling the presence of the brooding woodland piling up all around, I observed a chaffinch bouncing from tree to tree, catching insects.

From Darwell Hole, I was faced with a difficult and quite dangerous slog up the hill to Netherfield on the B2096. Halfway up the hill on the right, I came across an inaccessible war memorial in a small, untidy garden dedicated to Polish airmen of 304 Squadron in the Second World War, who crashed in their Wellington Bomber, returning from France in May 1941. After a hard half-mile up the hill into Netherfield at about 130m, I was pleased to find a pub in the right place, just when I needed it, at the top of the hill, and I popped into the White Hart for a couple of pints and something to eat. Although the exterior of the pub from the main road was scruffy and unprepossessing, inside was comfortable and the garden at the back boasted fabulous views of the Sussex countryside to the south. A flock of house martins were performing their aerial acrobatics for my delight as I tucked into a massive ploughman's lunch. I could clearly see the sea at Pevensey Bay and the outer rim of the Wealden dome, picked out clearly in the South Downs, reaching the coast at Beachy Head. Sitting in this pub garden and going back in earth's history, it was easy to imagine the much-vaulted Wealden Dome towering above me on its way north to join up to its northern rim in the North Downs.

Resisting the temptation to imbibe in a second pub in Netherfield, I passed on into the centre of the village, towards the church, which was in the care of English Heritage. A flock of thuggish, noisy starlings clamoured in to take over a tree on the edge of Netherfield Wood, situated in the heart of the village on Netherfield Down. All that remained to do that day was walk down the lane, past the entrance to Battle Golf Course, where a sign proclaimed a 'special OAP roast'; I couldn't help but wonder how tender and appetising this could really be, or whether indeed it was entirely legal. Walking on, there were stunning views to the north-east before the lane into Battle became lined with dwellings. This is normal for

Burwash to Battle

Mining Gypsum in the Sussex Weald

Gypsum (calcium sulphate) is a naturally occurring mineral that is extensively used in the building industry, especially for the production of plaster board. The mineral occurs in several seams in the Jurassic Purbeck beds that underlie the eroded Wealden anticline. First discovered in the 1870s while searching for coal deposits, and mined in a similar way to coal, two seams were discovered which were substantial enough to merit extraction. The original mine was located at Mountfield, but in the 1950s a second larger mine opened at Brightling, the raw material being taken back to Mountfield for processing by means of an aerial conveyor belt, which is a conspicuous feature running across the Sussex countryside. The Mountfield–Brightling reserves, mined by British Gypsum, are the largest in the UK, and are estimated to be sufficient for another 20 years of extraction.

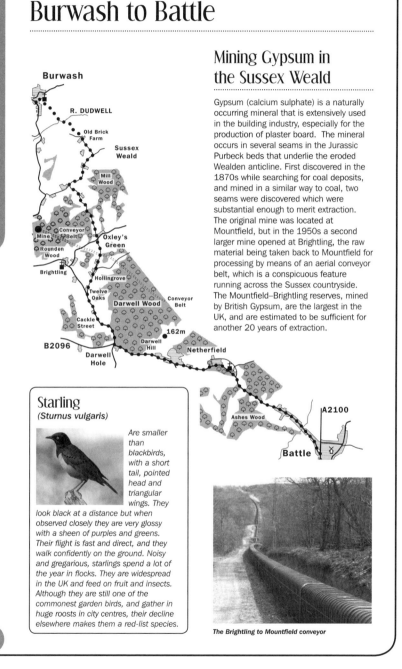

Starling
(Sturnus vulgaris)

Are smaller than blackbirds, with a short tail, pointed head and triangular wings. They look black at a distance but when observed closely they are very glossy with a sheen of purples and greens. Their flight is fast and direct, and they walk confidently on the ground. Noisy and gregarious, starlings spend a lot of the year in flocks. They are widespread in the UK and feed on fruit and insects. Although they are still one of the commonest garden birds, and gather in huge roosts in city centres, their decline elsewhere makes them a red-list species.

The Brightling to Mountfield conveyor

57

the roads radiating out of Battle in a spider pattern of ribbon development.

At the low point of 38m, by another stream, this time a headwater of the River Brede, I paused and contemplated a final climb up into Battle on its own ridge. There was a sharp little climb from the stream through the confluence with the main A2100 road, effectively scaling the heights of Caldbec Hill. Coming down into Battle by the roundabout in the early afternoon, I sauntered along the High Street. I decided to have a quick look in the abbey grounds and selected a vantage point overlooking the famous historic battlefield; I guess I was standing on Senlac Hill where Harold's housecarls, his professional Anglo-Saxon soldiers, tried to beat off waves of attacks from the Conqueror's knights. Later, I retired to a pub on the High Street and sat outside drinking beer in the hot sun, people-watching, to waste an hour or so.

The morphology of Battle is striking, with the roads and ribbon settlement following the ridges etched out by the work of the headwaters of the River Brede to the east, and the smaller Powder Mill Stream, originating in the battlefield, running into the Combe Haven River, reaching the coast between Hastings and Bexhill. The town has two hills: Caldbec Hill to the north at a height of 107m, and the lower Senlac Hill to the south at 86m. The High Street occupies the narrow ridge between these two hills, caressed by small streams, less than a quarter of a mile apart. It is as though a giant fist has grabbed the town by the High Street's throat, squeezing all communication, movement and connection into this congested conduit. It is easy to understand why Harold chose this spot to make his last stand.

Sitting in the High Street, I was struck by the continual, intrusive stream of traffic pouring through this conduit, and felt exceedingly embattled in Battle. If there was ever a place desperately in need of a by-pass, Battle would be top of the list. The High Street not only accommodates through traffic, but also takes local traffic from north to south, and this particular configuration, with its peculiar geography, makes it difficult to by-pass the town. Given that the main A21 Hastings road passes the town to the east, the obvious place for a by-pass road would be well to the south from Blackhorse Hill on the A271 to the junction of the A271 with the B2096, skirting the National Trust owned battlefield grounds. Purists might argue that it would be wrong to separate these grounds from the open countryside to the south, traipsed over by

Battle to Westfield

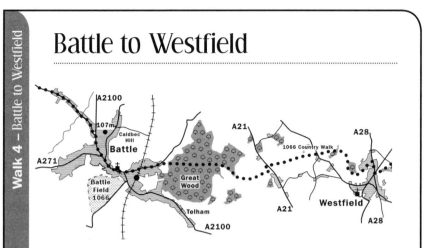

Battle

Is a small town largely concerned with tourism because it is the site of the decisive and important Battle of Hastings, where William, Duke of Normandy, defeated the Anglo-Saxon King Harold II, thus becoming William I in 1066, and ushering in years of Norman rule. The most significant building is Battle Abbey, which was dedicated in 1095 to commemorate the battle. The high alter of the Abbey church was reputedly built on the spot where Harold died on Senlac Hill and the grounds that overlook the battlefield. The abbey gateway is still the dominant feature of the south end of the main street, although little remains of the rest of the Abbey buildings. The remaining cloisters, part of the west range, were leased to Battle Abbey school shortly after the First World War, and the school is still there today.

The town gradually built up around the Abbey, and later developed a reputation for the quality of the gunpowder produced in the area. Although the A21 by-passes the town to the east, the main street suffers from severe traffic congestion due to circulation of local traffic, and its popularity as a tourist destination. The map (right) shows the striking nature of Battle's position on a pronounced north-west/south-east ridge.

Battle

Astride Senlac hill

Battlefield renown

Historic Hastings

Embattled town

Desperately in need of a by-pass.

Battle Abbey Gatehouse

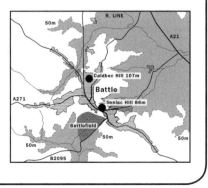

58

William, but I consider on balance the removal of some through traffic from Battle High Street would constitute an overall environmental benefit. I wondered whether this debate had already raged in some forum. I soon made my way to The George Hotel, where I was staying and since there was no bar on the premises, I was forced to inflict myself on the town in the evening.

I left Battle in the morning to the roar of traffic, by the road going eastwards, giving a splendid view of Caldbec Hill. I passed through Great Wood on a straight, wide, undulating, sandy bridleway that was designated as the 1066 walk, in a wood dominated by conifer trees, that reminded me of Cannock Chase in the Midlands. Crossing into Sedlescombe Golf Course, I was pleased to be of service to three lady golfers in tracking an errant drive, which squirted out of the heel of the club into the rough. After the golf course I crossed the dreaded A21. It was my intention to follow the 1066 walk all the way to Winchelsea, since it happened to be going where I wanted to go. The walk was so well signposted that I hardly needed my map, which made an agreeable change. I noted that the small streams were still stained red with iron from the Wealden hills.

As I walked along I was conscious of succumbing to a terrible habit of putting words and phrases in my head to the melodious blackbird's song; for some reason it only seemed to work with this thankfully common bird. I was reminded of those lines by W.H. Auden, in his poem 'Rimbaud', which describes verse as 'a special illness of the ear', and I thought I might have it.

I passed through a lovely part of the country with rolling downs, woods and pastures, dotted with charming dwellings, on the way to Westfield. After Battle, the landscape had softened, being distinctly different from the valleys and ridges of the Weald I had been walking over during the previous days. Before Westfield, I passed through a delightful glade where the willow trees were shedding their seeds like snow, beside a pond fringed by bulrushes and teasel, in an inspiring, uncultivated corner of a farm.

It was a stiff climb up to the large dormitory village of Westfield on the main A28 Tenterden to Hastings road. In the centre of the village, away from the church, there was a corner plot consisting of a derelict garage and an adjoining house for sale, which was desperately in need of redevelopment. After buying some bottled water and chocolate from the

Walk 4 – Westfield to Icklesham

Westfield to Icklesham

Teasel
(Dipsacus fullonum)

Are characterised by a prickly stem and leaves, and the purple, dark pink or lavender coloured flowers, that form a distinct head on the end of tall stems. They are herbaceous biennial plants, and the dried seed heads are a popular architectural element in floristry. The seeds are an important winter food source for birds, especially goldfinches, and are often grown in nature reserves to help sustain bird populations.

1066 Country Walk

Is a 31-mile circular, waymarked, long-distance walk in East Sussex which commemorates 1066, the year of the Battle of Hastings. It follows the route taken by William the Conqueror, and honours the people and places of that seminal year in English history. It runs from Pevensey, where William gathered his army of Normans, to Battle, where he defeated King Harold II in the so-called Battle of Hastings. The walk passes through mainly low-level rolling countryside and parts of the South Downs.

The Effects of the Ice Age on Southern Britain

The furthest extent of the ice did not reach Kent or East Sussex, and thus the landscape does not bare the scars of glaciated areas: typically U-shaped valleys, terminal moraines and drumlins. However this frozen, largely lifeless tundra was subject to erosion through frost action, and the extensive re-shaping of the landscape by glacial melt water, which established the current pattern of river drainage, including the current course of the River Thames. It is thought that the pattern of dry valleys on the dip slope of the North Downs were formed in this way. Also, the rock pulverised by the action of the glaciers and frost, blown away by the wind, formed fertile layers of loess across Europe, which occurs locally on the Isle of Thanet as brickearth.

During the Ice Ages sea levels were lower than today, because vast quantities of water were locked up in the ice caps, and there was dry land between Britain and France. As the ice melted, and the southern edge of the ice moved north, the land thawed and life recovered. Vegetation took hold and animals from Europe moved in to exploit this new food resource. Man slowly followed, returning to areas that had been occupied in warmer inter-glacial periods. Trees such as birch and pine began to establish themselves, and animals such as horse, reindeer, wolf and bear moved in. Eventually, melt water gathering in a vast lake in the southern North Sea broke through the land bridge with the continent, and the English Channel was created, and further migration of species from the south was halted.

59

local store, I regained the path going eastwards out of Westfield. After passing through a number of farm complexes and under a railway, through quiet rolling countryside, I came up to the lane that led down to Lidham Hill Farm, where I was savaged by a young terrier dog.

Leaving this unwelcome commotion behind, I descended to a small stream before Lower Snailham Farm. While searching for a way to cross the stream, a fellow walker came up behind me. I knew he was coming because I heard the same commotion behind me as he passed through the farm with the dog. While locating the crossing we disturbed some pretty goats which scampered off across the field at our approach. I offered to walk on with him, but he graciously declined, saying he was sure I would prefer to walk alone. He was younger than me and his legs were longer and fresher, not having been walking all week, and he soon left me behind. He did however ask me whether the rolling hills we were walking on were drumlins, and I had to inform him they were not, since drumlins are features of glaciated landscapes, and East Sussex completely escaped this fate.

After Lower Snailham Farm, I crossed over a down of 60m in height, which afforded marvellous views north across the valley of the River Brede. After Brook Farm I descended again into the Brede Level. This undulating path from Westfield, through a series of farm complexes, had one final sting in its tail, in a stiff climb through sheep-inhabited fields to Icklesham. Following the path around the back of the overblown village, there were fabulous views out across Walland Marsh where I was headed.

I called in the popular Robin Hood pub at Icklesham, displaying union jacks outside, for a few pints, where there were many animated diners in a warm, claustrophobic, dusty space, bedecked with memorabilia. I felt it would be churlish to ask for a sandwich, so I sat outside in the scruffy garden with a pint, admiring the view southwards towards Fairlight. I have always found it rather curious that the pub name 'Robin Hood' occurs in many places, often miles away from his stamping ground in Sherwood Forest. Maybe, unwittingly, I have answered my own question, in that he was a folk hero and thus celebrated throughout the land.

Leaving Icklesham by the church and manor farm, in orchard country, I passed through an attractive grouping of buildings, before reaching a windmill on the last hill at 47m. Walking down the rabbit-strewn hill behind the windmill there were absolutely amazing panoramic views out to the east and south, across Pett Level to the sea, Winchelsea and Rye to

Walland Marsh, with the new wind farm showing up clearly in the distance. Still following the 1066 Walk, I made my way by a pleasant, winding lower lane into Winchelsea.

In time, I came to a stone arch, the so-called new gate of the old town of Winchelsea, with the massive encircling ramparts and town ditch clearly evident. I passed on, up into the much-reduced town to seek out my berth for the night. Winchelsea was once, in the Middle Ages, a thriving town and eventually a Cinque Port in its own right, famous for the import of wine. The town then was much larger, with buildings stretching down to the New Gate down by Pett Level, and across on the other side of the main A259 through the town. The historic importance of the town can be judged by the size and grandeur of its church, and the huge precinct surrounding it, occupying a central position in the settlement. Winchelsea is an attractive, atmospheric place with many beautiful, flower-decked houses, a village shop and post office and a pub, the New Inn, where I was staying. One feature that sets it off are the brick-clad footpaths, the same I had already seen in Burwash and Frant, two of the other most visually attractive places I had visited on this incredible walk.

After a slow start on the breakfast front, I posted my box and passed out of Winchelsea northwards, down the hill to the precarious hairpin bend by the Pipewell Gate, then located the lane to the railway station and passed out across Brede Levels. Reaching the other side of the valley, I turned east towards Rye. The sun was shining bright and strong as I made my way along the back of the floodplain of the river, by the old sea cliffs, called Cadborough Cliff, still following the 1066 walk. The heat in my sunburnt right arm was being reignited and I resolved to buy some sun cream in Rye.

While I was trudging along this cycle path, I heard a cuckoo in the distance and happily saw a song thrush singing its heart out in the top a small tree, a bird that is now becoming distinctly rare. Unlike the blackbird's song I have already remarked upon, which is a free melody, the thrush repeats its mellifluous song. I was reminded of those lines from Browning's poem, '*Home Thoughts from Abroad*,' which says, 'That's the wise thrush; he sings each song twice over, lest you should think he never could recapture the first fine careless rapture.' The wild tumbling aspect of the old sea cliffs was clothed with bushes and small trees, forming a valuable wildlife habitat.

I came to elegant Rye again, by the landward side, searching for a

Icklesham to Rye

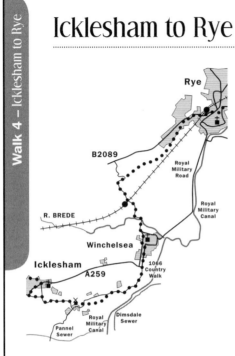

Rye

B2089

R. BREDE

Winchelsea

Icklesham
A259

1066
Country
Walk

Royal
Military
Road

Royal
Military
Canal

Royal
Military
Canal

Pannel
Sewer

Dimsdale
Sewer

Winchelsea

Is a small village which stands on the site of a Medieval new town, founded in 1288, which itself replaced an older town of the same name, lost to the sea. After the Norman Conquest, the old town was of great importance in cross-channel trade and as a naval base, and became famous in the wine trade from Gascony. There were, in the 1260s, over 700 houses, two churches, and over 50 taverns, thus implying a population of around several thousand people at the time. During the middle of the thirteenth century, incursions by the sea destroyed much of the old town, until it was completely destroyed by the famous flood of 1287. The original site of the old town is thought to be in Rye Bay.

The current settlement on its hill location was the result of the old town's population moving to the new site, when in 1281 King Edward I ordered a planned town to be built, based on a grid pattern.

The new town inherited the name Winchelsea and retained its affiliation to the Cinque Ports confederation.

The town had a tidal harbour on the River Brede, and flourished until the middle of the fourteenth century. It then suffered French and Spanish raids in the Hundred Years War until the fifteenth century, when it was hit heavily by the Black Death. The town remained prosperous, although reduced in size, to the 1520s, when the silting up of its harbour ultimately consigned it to its present state, as a peaceful, elegant backwater village, still retaining its Medieval setting on a hill surrounded by empty marsh. The original layout of the planned town, with its substantial church precinct and the largest collection of Medieval wine cellars in the country, with the possible exception of Norwich and Southampton, still remains. It also retains three of the original town gates, from which can be gauged the extensive size of the original settlement. The Royal Military Canal was built below the hill and connects to the River Brede, as a defensive measure against invasion by Napoleon in the early nineteenth century. The village now stands on the main south coast road, the A259.

Song Thrush
(Turdus philomelos)

Is a widespread and popular garden songbird whose numbers are declining seriously, especially on farmland, making it a red-list species. It has spotted breast feathers and a brown back, and has the habit of repeating song phrases, which distinguishes it from the ubiquitous blackbird. It is a ground feeder and likes to eat snails, which it breaks into by smashing them against a stone with a flick of the head.

chemist's shop, which I eventually found in the High Street. As I emerged from the shop after purchasing the efficacious sun cream, almost immediately a sea mist rolled in, obscuring the rotating sails of the wind farm down on the marsh. I applied some of the cream just for the hell of it. I felt rather disrespectful in passing through Rye so swiftly, not observing the wonderful townscape more fully, but I had reported on this aspect on previous journeys. However, I did leave through the splendid land gate, built in 1329, and the only surviving gate of the original medieval town on the way out onto the marsh.

From Rye, I headed out eastwards along the A259, just as before, to the hamlet of East Guldeford. Then I turned into the lane going to Camber Sands for a few hundred yards, before picking up the bridleway across Walland Marsh. I did wonder whether I would be able to see where I was going and pick out my intended route across Walland Marsh to Lydd, with the lowering mist all around, obscuring the turbines in the nearby wind farm. I took the lower path that runs along the Wainway Wall, past the back of Camber to the lonely, derelict Chillenden's Cottages out on the marsh. The Wainway Wall is an ancient bank that was constructed to contain the waters of the Wainway Channel, which conveyed the waters of the River Rother in the Middle Ages, through its wide estuary, to the mouth of the river at the former port of New Romney. As explained elsewhere, the River Rother was then diverted, presumably as the result of violent storms that hit this coast during the thirteenth century, to its outlet at Rye, and the marshes were systematically reclaimed. However, the Wainway Wall still remains as the only significant landscape feature in this stretch of flat marshland.

Trekking from East Guldeford to Lydd, across Walland Marsh, skirting the wind farm to the south, is about 7 miles across an empty landscape lacking any signs of habitation, except the odd derelict building or sheep pen. I had always wanted to complete this path and today I was going to attempt it, but I could have done without the mist, which gave the whole enterprise a sense of cold foreboding. Ploughing on across the marsh, I was thrown on my own resources of stamina and map-reading skills to keep going and not lose the way in the relatively featureless landscape. To start with, I could track the billowing sand dunes of Rye Bay and Camber Sands to my right, and although the bridleway was marked from time to time, at certain critical times the signage seemed to evaporate. I was forced to take account of local features, such as the

Rye to Camber

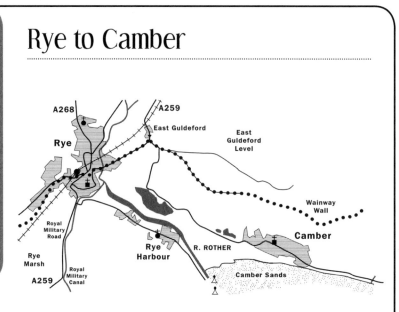

Wainway

From the thirteenth century the Wainway Channel was a tidal creek off the Appledore Channel which flowed into Rye Bay, approximately the current course of the River Rother. It was a sheltered anchorage until about 1550 that ran eastwards towards Lydd, but it was continually reduced by silting. Between 1600 and 1700 a succession of walls, some of which can clearly be seen on the ground today, were built across the tidal inlet, progressively reclaiming the land.

East Guldeford

Is a hamlet located on the A259, on the Guldeford level on Walland Marsh, which was reclaimed from the sea by Sir Richard Guldeford to create rich farmland during the late 1400s. Before reclamation, the area was mostly salt marsh, and had a thriving salt production industry, which operated by evaporating sea water in shallow pools. The unusual barn-like church is one of the churches supported by the Romney Marsh Historic Churches Trust.

Land Reclamation by Inning

This process involves the reclamation of land from the sea. The East Guldeford Level, and much of Walland Marsh, was created in this way, by enclosing salt marsh which was accessible to the tides, by constructing an earth bank around a certain area. By controlling flooding within the earth bank, and progressively allowing sediment to be deposited, fertile enclosures have been created. Many of these innings have an irregular shape, reflecting the pattern of the original salt marsh creeks.

The Landgate, Rye

61

pattern of small streams, derelict buildings and electricity pylons. After all, the easiest way not to lose the way is to always know exactly where one is.

I followed the Wainway Wall for a long way, but eventually lost the path and got too close to the wind farm, but by now the mist was lifting and I could see the closest turbine columns looming large. Interestingly, the wind farm is located below Little Cheney Court to the very southerly edge of Kent, across the border, since I was still walking in East Sussex. I worked out my mistake by walking along the edge of dykes, through sheep-festooned fields, and relocated the bridleway. Towards the Red House, swathes of corn and then potatoes replaced the sheep pasture. The farmers were engaged in pumping water out of the dykes to irrigate their parched fields, which unfortunately had caused some dykes to go completely dry. While I don't blame the farmers for trying to save their crops, the destruction of the eco system in these dry dykes would have been catastrophic for the flora and fauna living there.

From the Red House, I plodded along a long, straight drive towards Scotney Court, with the tower of Lydd Church getting reassuringly closer all the time. Before Scotney Court, I lent on a field gate and observed sheep in the process of being sheared. When relieved of the weight of all that wool, the sheep seemed to be much lighter on their hooves, bouncing around ecstatically like new-born lambs. The young lady helping with the shearing even offered to give me a haircut and even though this could have been an interesting experience, I felt I had to decline her kind offer.

I carried on towards Lydd, along another significant bank called the Tore Wall, and by a well-marked footpath across a field of corn, to the crossing point over Jury's Gut Sewer. There, I was forced to detour around the edge of a vast potato field, because the farmer had not respected the footpath. I could have aimed for a pylon across the middle of the field, but slithering over the ridges of potatoes in newly watered ground would have been impossible, so the farmer got away with it. Thus, coming into Lydd, I walked alongside a series of large lakes, the result of past gravel extraction, picking up the bridle path to the inland lane to Lydd, and sauntered into the pleasant town by the church. In spite of the fact that I was pretty much exhausted by my hike across the marsh, I had another look around Lydd, at the church precinct and town square, and out to The Dolphin pub beside The Rype. The pub was very busy and I couldn't get served, so I gave up and retired to The George Hotel for the rest of the day.

Camber to Lydd

Little Cheyne Court Wind Farm

Sits on Walland Marsh, in the southern most part of Kent, near the East Sussex border. Each of the 26 Nordex N90 wind turbines at the site is 115m high and weighs over 275 tonnes. The site was built by Npower at a cost of £50 million, and was opened in 2009, when it was the biggest onshore wind farm in England, though larger wind farms opened soon after. The wind farm is capable of providing electricity for up to 33,000 homes.

At the beginning of March 2012, the installed capacity of wind power in the UK was 6,580 megawatts, with 333 operational wind farms containing 3,506 wind turbines. Wind power in the UK is the second largest source of renewable energy after biomass. It is projected that by 2020 the UK could have more than 28,000 MW of wind generated capacity.

Little Cheyne Court Wind Farm

Dungeness

A sea of pebbles

Assails the eye

Wooden fishing shacks

Lighthouses high

In this curious deadening retreat.

Potato
(Solanum Tuberosum)

Is a starchy tuberous crop from a perennial plant in the nightshade family. After flowering, the culms die back, and some varieties produce small green fruits resembling small green tomatoes, to which they are closely related. New varieties are grown from seed but existing varieties are grown from tuber pieces known as seed potatoes. All parts of the plant except the tubers are poisonous. First introduced into Europe from South America following the Spanish conquest of the Inca Empire in the second half of the sixteenth century, there are now about 5,000 varieties worldwide. It is the world's fourth largest food crop, following rice, wheat and maize.

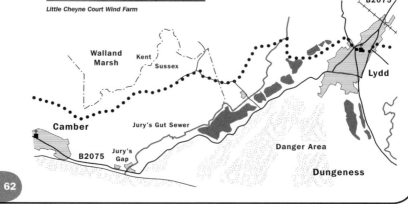

In the morning, I set off on the final leg of my journey, to St Mary in the Marsh, a somewhat shorter walk. However, it was my intention to hike across the pebbles of Dungeness to Lydd-on-Sea. I left Lydd by a footpath opposite the town cemetery and proceeded across a surprisingly well-marked footpath through a field of corn, to the seldom-used railway that only gives access to the Dungeness Power Stations. I guess since these power stations are now redundant, the railway may come in handy in the lengthy decommissioning process, dictated by the rate of decay of uranium, its half-life being 112 years, before the element succumbs to a new, less-dangerously radioactive incarnation, lead.

Picking my way alongside the railway for a while, across the back of the airport, with light planes taking off over my head, I found the route of the disused railway that used to swing round to New Romney and link up with the narrow gauge track of the Romney, Hythe and Dymchurch Light Railway. From there, through an area of rough grassland, scrub and pebbles, I embarked on a trek of about 1 mile, across the shingle to Lydd-on-Sea. There was no footpath marked across the pebbles, so I fixed my sights on a distinctive building on the shoreline and made for it. This cuspate foreland, which is a National Nature Reserve, consists of parallel ridges of shingle, which represent former beach lines. There was the odd oasis of larger trees and shrubs, which helped with navigation, but mostly it was a pebble desert interspersed with the occasional patch of course grass, and a lichen-type plant, all of which must be extremely drought tolerant. A helpful notice explained that Dungeness is home to a unique group of plants and insects, including some very unusual spiders. As I crunched my way across to Lade, the closer I got to the sea, the greater number of prostrate flowering plants became evident, including the dazzling yellow blooms of broom.

To my left, I could see the listening ears, a pre-Second World War experimental sound detection system for picking up planes crossing the Channel. They consisted of three different-shaped concrete mirrors, whose purpose was to gather and amplify the sound of approaching plane engines. Although they worked perfectly well, they were never used in combat due to the development of the superior radar system. I was surprised at how insignificant these structures were in the vastness of the Dungeness foreland. Instead of passing directly into Lade, I turned north along the dismantled railway that used to serve the listening ears for a closer look at these technological relics. They could not be approached directly as they were surrounded by water, situated in the middle of a bird reserve, no doubt fortuitously protecting their tempting concrete faces from the ravages of graffiti.

Before a massive caravan site, I finally gained access to the coast road and carried on the road to Greatstone-on-Sea, a nondescript bungalow resort behind soft sand dunes. I went down to the sea, washed my boots and could have walked on the beach all the way to Greatstone's smaller relative, Littlestone-on-Sea, but chose to cut back to the road, just to make sure I didn't miss the place. I popped into the pub, The Seahorse, for a pint of cider. As a building, the pub had no provenance and the name appeared to me to have no particular relevance. I suggested to the landlady that it might be more appropriate to call the pub the 'Sunburnt Arms', but I wasn't sure she got the joke. The names of Greatstone and Littlestone derive from actual stones placed in the ground, which used to mark the estuary of the River Rother as it flowed into the sea before it was diverted to Rye bay.

I was getting close to journey's end and was beginning to feel nostalgic as I approached the Victorian splendour of the terraced, residential blocks facing the sea in Littlestone. This was a place, in spite of the

Lydd to St Mary in the Marsh

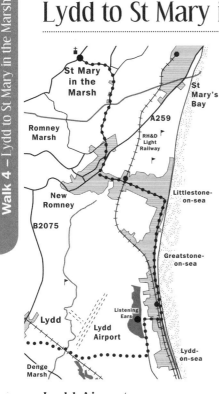

Listening Ears

Is the colloquial term for three experimental acoustic mirrors located in the midst of a disused gravel pit between Greatstone-on-Sea and Lydd Airport. They were built in the late 1920s and early 1930s as an early warning system for incoming aircraft, developed by Dr W. S. Tucker. Several were built along the south and east coasts but the complex on the Dungeness foreland is the best preserved. Acoustic mirrors did work and could effectively detect slow-moving enemy aircraft before they came into sight. They worked by concentrating sound waves towards a focal point, where a microphone would have been located. Their use, however, was limited as aircraft became faster, and they quickly became obsolete due to the invention of radar in 1932.

Listening Ears

Lydd Airport

Was the first airport built in the UK after the Second World War in 1956. Known originally as Lydd Ferryfield, it was used initially for air freight services. From the 1980s the airport benefitted from the boom in cheap overseas package holidays, being used for flights to Spain, Italy and Austria. Currently there are plans to expand the facility, and on 3 March 2010 Shepway District Council voted in favour of these plans, which involve an extended runway towards Greatstone, and a new terminal to cater for an anticipated 2 million passengers per year. Objections to the development relate to the possible damage to the local RSPB bird reserve and unique European ecological sites. A public inquiry has been held to consider the issues and conflicting interests and a decision is expected during 2013.

Littlestone

A group of jackdaws

Graced the scene

White painted cannon

On sandy green

Evoke a colonial past.

Star Inn, St Mary in-the-Marsh

aspiration of some splendid Victorian entrepreneur, that didn't quite make it as a successful seaside resort. I turned into The Avenue, past the little parched green sporting patriotic canons and flagpole, and strode on all the way to New Romney town. I passed by the Captain Howey pub by the light railway and museum, the builder and promoter of which the pub was named after. In New Romney, I turned right towards Dymchurch and tarried for a while in the Plough, whose primary purpose on this Sunday lunchtime was to provide carvery meals. The young lady haunting the door, hoping to trap hungry punters, had great trouble understanding that I didn't want to eat a Sunday lunch, only wanting to drink beer supported by the bar. After a difficult passage of negotiation, I did triumphantly get my way, but was made to feel like an eccentric curiosity, parked in a corner for the amusement of the smartly attired diners.

All that was left was to walk through the back lanes of my beloved Romney Marsh, to where I was staying for the night and where I had left my car, at the wonderful Star Inn at St Mary in the Marsh. I passed through familiar lanes, past Brodynex Farm and the Slinches, and over the much-reduced waters of the New Sewer, where I fished for eels with my granddad. Arriving at the beautiful old pub, I remade the acquaintance of the landlord, who was also called Brian, and found out that he had known my dad, sharing a pint or two with him when he was alive. In the evening I drove to New Romney in search of food and, on the way back, I called in to the Bailiffs Sergeant in St Marys Bay, after driving down Beechwood Close to see if my rented bungalow, formerly belonging to my parents, was still there. I chatted to the landlady and some regulars, before making my way back into the marsh and turning in for the night.

5

Dartford to Rye (Summer 2011)

I arrived at Dartford Station about mid-morning and changed into wet gear in the station, much to the amusement of the people sheltering in the concourse from the deluge outside. I made my way, with some disquiet, to the mundane High Street, through unappealing service yards, and looked for a hole in the wall to get some cash for the journey. I stammered out of the town, down Lowfield Street, searching for a way up onto the heath. After a climb of about 1 mile past a bright new college, I issued onto the heath in a brief, delightfully warm, sunny interlude between the heavy showers. I located the footpath I was looking for across the heath and strode on with the drone of traffic all around. The sandy topsoil of the heath had rapidly soaked up the morning's rain, making it feel like walking on a sodden carpet.

This lowland heath, a distinctly uncommon type of habitat in south-east England, is covered with open grassland and woodland in equal measure, but certainly it was more heavily wooded than I remember as a boy, when cycling around it. I recall that once, when attempting to plunge down a particularly steep slope, I came off my bike and grazed my cheek; although the contusion has long since healed, I still bear the scar. Moving ever forward, I read a noticeboard that described how, as always, the conservators of the heath were endeavouring to hold back the growth of woods in order to preserve the rich variety of landscape and habitats to promote the local flora and fauna. The Dartford warbler was first identified on the heath, but is no longer present, being largely confined to the lowland heaths of Dorset and Suffolk. Although I did not see the rare warbler, I saw many, much more common, magpies and pigeons, and swathes of the yellow ragwort reaching their mid-summer prime.

As I approached the main A2018, joining Dartford to the A2, the woods became dense and gloomy. I crossed over the road and found the old remaindered Rochester Way, the first Dartford by-pass, the very same as that on which I grew up further west, and carried on towards Old Bexley. I passed a perfectly splendid public recycling centre, but as I proceeded westward the road deteriorated into a lorry park, largely associated with a private recycling depot, containing all the vehicles and equipment, including numerous cranes, hoists and skips, required by such an operation. As is often the case, remaindered roads become very scruffy and uncared for places as they approach their truncation up against a new fast road.

I passed on down a muddy path, beside the A2, towards the railway. To my right was a large tract of wild, uncultivated land laced with ponds, to the south of Crayford, known as Bowmans, which really was an extension of Dartford Heath. To pass over the railway, I had to come up and cross over the bridge afforded by the main road before I could go down into the serene grounds of Hall Place. This greatly restored and carefully tended historical house and garden owned by Bexley Borough Council, lies in the valley of the River Cray. It was on these playing fields associated with Hall Place that I used to play cricket every summer weekend for a local club after I left school.

From Hall Place, I made my way into Old Bexley, past the Black Prince Roadhouse, where we used to break our car journeys back from the coast, which is now a Holiday Inn. At this point, the little River Shuttle, draining the Sidcup suburbs, joins the River Cray. In Old Bexley I bought some provisions before locating the Cray Valley Walk adjacent to Old Bexley station. As I pushed out into the valley besides the railway I was hit by a heavy downpour and got exceedingly damp. I passed by lovingly maintained cricket grounds and came to a wide open, convex, unculti- vated down of a place, which I assumed to be a reclaimed landfill site, unnaturally prominent in the landscape of the valley. By large, fenced utilities premises, with acres of mown grass, I saw a young fox and noisy parakeets in the trees, the latter having colonised most of the Thames Valley and the former ubiquitous in suburban London.

Making my way down to the crystal-clear river I crossed over to the eastern bank and proceeded upstream. I trudged on, below Loring Hall, past another immaculate cricket ground, beside the multi-coloured, pebble-dressed river, to the elegant Five Arches Bridge. Evidently, the former owner of North Cray Place had laid this part of the valley out as a park, of which the Five Arches Bridge was a feature, designed no less by the famous landscape architect 'Capability' Brown. Below the bridge is a broad weir which holds back the waters to create a large feature lake upstream, and an attractive cascade of water.

This part of the Cray valley, on the very edge of suburban London, has been left to return to nature and as a consequence, it supports a sur- prising variety of wildlife. Across the valley, I could see the field where we used to camp when I was a scout, which like other places I have revisited many years later, had become overgrown with trees and shrubs. As I climbed up to Foots Cray Church, after crossing back over the river, I disturbed a group of about four or five green woodpeckers who were foraging for ants in the lea of a large clump of shrubs. I read an infor- mation board by the church that described how Foots Cray Meadows, the area through which I had just passed, had been created out of the former grounds of two eighteenth-century stately homes, Foots Cray Place and North Cray place, and that the Cray Valley Walk was a 10-mile footpath from Foots Cray Meadows through Old Bexley and Hall Place to Erith on the bank of the River Thames.

I carried on into the ancient village of Foots Cray which is now a mess of a place, consisting as it does of a busy crossroads and a High Street with shops and houses, and large factories and warehouses all mixed together. I recall Schweppes, famous for their soft drinks, before many takeovers, and Crittalls, who made those distinctive metal windows which

Dartford to Foots Cray

Dartford Heath

This area to the south-west of Dartford covers some 314 acres of open space, an example of the fast disappearing lowland heath habitat. Historically it has always been of importance since prehistoric barrows and Bronze Age artefacts have been found here. The first recorded cricket match took place here in 1723. The heath is an AONB and contains three ponds, and a variety of habitats, including acid grassland, broadleaved semi-natural woodland, and heather and gorse scrub. It is common land and therefore escaped being enclosed during the late eighteenth and early nineteenth centuries. The Dartford Warbler once graced the heath but is now largely confined to the heathlands of Dorset and Suffolk.

Foots Cray Meadows

This 250-acre area of parkland and woodland was created out of two historical estates, namely Foots Cray Place and North Cray Place, and is managed by Bexley Borough Council. The meadows are a local nature reserve, listed by English Heritage as a Grade II historic park, and notable features include the river bridges, the Five Arches bridge and the Penny Farthing bridge. This extensive informal area down by the River Cray, provides a wealth of diverse habitats for flora and fauna, as well as providing recreational facilities for the nearby London suburbs.

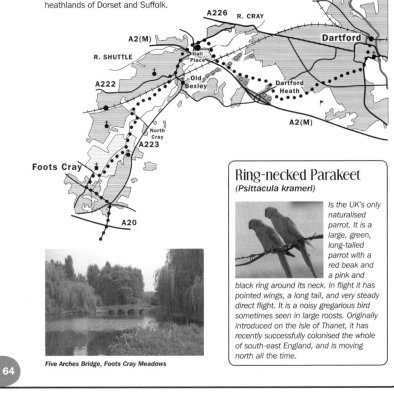

Five Arches Bridge, Foots Cray Meadows

Ring-necked Parakeet
(Psittacula krameri)

Is the UK's only naturalised parrot. It is a large, green, long-tailed parrot with a red beak and a pink and black ring around its neck. In flight it has pointed wings, a long tail, and very steady direct flight. It is a noisy gregarious bird sometimes seen in large roosts. Originally introduced on the Isle of Thanet, it has recently successfully colonised the whole of south-east England, and is moving north all the time.

64

adorn many 1930s, Art Deco buildings, being located in Foots Cray. But if you look closely, especially down by the river crossing, the original reason for the settlement, mentioned as far back as the Domesday Book, one can still see some dilapidated older buildings. Across the river bridge I popped into a café for a late lunch, a rest and a chance to dry off a little. I thought I had been quite courageous in persevering with the walk in the face of the unseasonably inclement weather.

Refreshed and fortified, I traipsed up to Ruxley Corner and on down the busy lane, under the new A20 by-pass towards St Paul's Cray. Although the scruffy lane was traffic calmed it still took a lot of cars and was uncomfortable walking. To my right was a large stretch of open countryside stretching down to the river. Further on, I came to St Paul's Cray. Although the main part of this suburb lay to the west of the main A224 road, there were some pleasant buildings and an attractive row of cottages hard up against the river, with its willow-haunted, riverside garden. It did occur to me that if a footpath could be created down by the river between Foots Cray and St Paul's Cray, it would be possible to extend the Cray Valley Walk southwards into the London Borough of Bromley.

At St Mary's Cray, past the old church, there was a pleasant group of buildings nestling under the shadow of the railway viaduct. There was a square composed of an old pub and some newer buildings, carefully designed to recreate an historical atmosphere: a reminder of what the village may have looked like a few hundred years ago. I clearly remember cycling out through the village to reach the open countryside beyond while I was still at school in Bexley, and I thought this village was the natural starting point of the Cray Valley Walk.

From St Mary's Cray I had a long slog out of the valley, up to the village of Chelsfield by nondescript housing estates, spilling out from Orpington. As the lane became very narrow, and it was carrying a lot of traffic this Friday afternoon, I took a footpath to the east and came into Chelsfield from the north by Squibbs Lane. It seemed to be a well-preserved, unspoilt village, only a stone's throw from the urban sprawl of Orpington, consisting of a group of older buildings unadorned by modern development. I crossed over the ample recreation ground on the way to Maypole, but got tangled up in an orchard and came up to a lane that led me to the mega roundabout on the A21, which gives access to the motorway. I literally took my life in my hands by crossing this

Foots Cray to Halstead

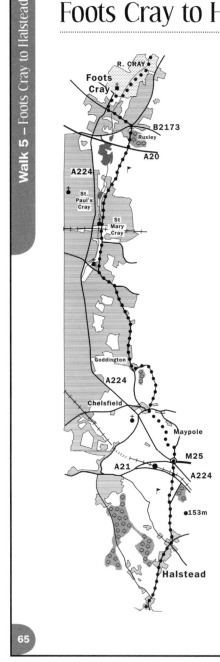

Foots Cray

Is an ancient settlement that takes its name from Godwin Fot, a local Saxon landowner recorded in the Domesday Book, and from the River Cray that passes through the village. It originally lay on the old Maidstone road, until it was by-passed by the A20, and once dominated the nearby hilltop hamlet of Sidcup. In the twentieth century the fortunes of the two settlements were reversed as the traditional industries of Foots Cray declined, and Sidcup grew rapidly as a commuter town after the railway was built linking it to Central London. The nearby Foots Cray Place was an elegant Palladian-style house which burnt down in 1949, leaving only a stable block and an adjoining walled garden. These remains of the old estate were placed on English Heritage's 'at risk' register, and rescued recently by a private development company. Today the area consists of an inharmonious mixture of shops, houses and factories.

Chelsfield

Is an attractive, carefully preserved village with weather-boarded cottages and mellow brick buildings, within a stone's throw of the burgeoning suburbs of Orpington. It is a commuter village in the Green Belt and a Conservation Area on the dip slope of the North Downs. The quaint village hall lies on the edge of an extensive, carefully tended recreation ground.

Chelsfield Village Hall

65

exceptionally busy junction, and my advice to anyone who may be tempted to copy my exploits, is to make an exception and not go this way. Instead, I would recommend finding the path that crosses the A21 by a bridge on the way to Knockholt Station, as I would hate to think that I might have contributed to any fellow rambler's demise on the big roundabout.

Somewhat abashed at my temerity at crossing the A21, at this point I dropped down over the railway to the original route of the A21 with its own string of ribbon development buildings. I proceeded up Cadlocks Hill on the way to Halstead, all the time walking up the dip slope of the North Downs. The road into Halstead was also uncomfortably busy, but soon I reached my bed and breakfast for the night at the centre of the village. I was struck by the fact that the buses from Orpington seemed to terminate here, placing it clearly within the catchment area of that most southerly of London suburbs. Although the weather had brightened up in the afternoon, I was pleased to finish the first leg of this walk because of pretty bad weather.

In the morning, I took the road to Knockholt Pound, climbing all the time, passing through the straggly village, eventually to reach Knockholt Church at a height of 220m, with one of the highest points in Kent on the North Downs at 237m being nearby. Although there has been a church on the site for over 700 years, the present church looked incongruous in that it has a square flint and brick-built tower with what looks like a modern, church-like building attached. I turned south at Knockholt, down Sundridge Lane, a quiet, deeply sunken lane affording little in the way of views out. To my left was a heavily wooded landscape associated with the historic Chevening Park. It wasn't until I had descended to the junction with Pilgrim's Way that the view opened up. Careering down the long, winding lane, I had the very strong impression that I was passing into another world, or landscape zone, with Knockholt on top of the downs, like Halstead, being part of the world under the influence of Orpington.

As the lane approached the motorway it turned through a right angle, shooting off to the east, leaving only a puddle-strewn track to cross over the road on the way to Sundridge. Unfortunately, across the motorway, the track, no longer used as a thoroughfare, became unkempt and scruffy. Since there were no accesses off this track, I wondered why it could not be closed to traffic, thereby preventing the track being used for various nefarious purposes, such as the dumping of waste, and allowed to revert to a narrower, tree-lined footpath.

I passed an exclusive private school on the way into Sundridge, on the headwaters of the River Darent, and rested for a while by the central crossroads. As I sat there, on the council's seat by the War Memorial, I observed a cyclist in all his slick, Lycra gear, trying to mend a puncture. He explained that his tyres were also slick, like those used in Formula 1 racing, and the rain of the last few days had washed gravel onto the road surfaces, which caused havoc with them. I must say that when I used to cycle around Kent I had one set of tyres for all weathers, wore ordinary clothes and had no streamlined helmet, and when I ventured this information to the exasperated cyclist he gave me a rather pitying look. I did get the impression that dressing up like a diver was part of the fun, showing off well-developed muscles in the process.

After a short rest in Sundridge, I carried on due south, hurrying along, climbing up onto the Greensand Ridge. It was one of those stretches that even a walking enthusiast like me could not call enjoyable, and I wanted to get it over as soon as possible, but when I reached Penn Lane, at least I was able to get off the main road up the hill and take my time with the

Halstead to Ide Hill

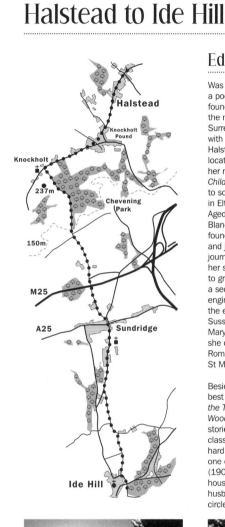

Edith Nesbit

Was a prolific author of children's books, a poet and a political activist, who co-founded the Fabian Society, a precursor to the modern Labour Party. She was born in Surrey in 1858, and lived for many years with her family in Europe, before moving to Halstead Hall in the village of Halstead, a location that supposedly inspired perhaps her most famous work, *The Railway Children*. At the age of 17 she moved to south-east London, living variously in Eltham, Lewisham and Lee Green. Aged 19 she met and married Hubert Bland, and together they were among the founding members of the Fabian Society, and jointly edited the society's radical journal. Eventually settling down in Eltham, her success as a chilldren's author began to grow. After Bland died she married for a second time to Thomas Tucker, a ship's engineer on the Woolwich Ferry. Towards the end of her life she lived in Friston, East Sussex, before moving to the coast at St Mary's Bay. Suffering from lung cancer, she died in 1924 at the age of 65 at New Romney, and is buried in the churchyard of St Mary in–the–Marsh.

Besides *The Railway Children* her other best known books include *The Story of the Treasure Seekers* (1898) and *The Woodbegoods* (1899), which both recount stories about the Bastables, a middle-class family that has fallen on relatively hard times. The Bastables also appear in one of her adult novels, *The Red House* (1902), which is based on the grand house she shared in Eltham with her first husband, where they entertained a large circle of friends and admirers.

St Katharine's Church, Knockholt

The Cock Inn, Halstead

66

climb. Entering Penn Lane, I could see Ide Hill Church up ahead, the highest point, at over 200m, on the Greensand Ridge. I had to descend to cross a small stream before rising again, taking a final steep climb across a field and through a small council estate, before arriving at the wonderful Cock Inn, nestling below the green at Ide Hill. I stayed in the pub for the best part of an hour before continuing my journey.

I careered down the lane called Hanging Bank, where the cottages perched precariously on the side of the hill, with breath-taking views to the south and west. The lane wound its way down the hill, giving a panoramic view of Bough Beech Reservoir where I was headed, before ending up in a footpath, running alongside a long, narrow wood. During this descent, I could see the high ridge of the Weald up ahead with High Rocks to the left and Ashdown Forest to the right, with the blue line of the South Downs showing over the top, giving an amazing insight into the underlying structure of the landscape.

Coming down into Winkhurst Green, I resisted the temptation to call into the Bough Beech Visitor Centre and crossed the northern extremity of the reservoir by a causeway. There, I met a birdwatcher who commented on the number of common terns flying around; I had seen common terns before by the coast, but evidently they had successfully bred around the shores of the reservoir, which to the birds must look, sound and smell like a beach. As I was strolling alongside the reservoir, a heavy shower swept in. I took the liberty of sheltering under the tailgate of a car, whose owner was doing voluntary work in the reserve on behalf of the Kent Wildlife Trust. I got talking to this chap and we discovered that we had many interests in common, and mutually applauded the splendid deeds done by the trust. When the rain abated, I bid him good day so that he could continue with his good work of mending a fence and erecting a signpost.

I carried on along an easy, flat road alongside the reservoir, making good distance, up to the junction with the B2027, where I took the footpath past Somerden Farm, down to the railway and on to the River Eden. The path down to the pleasant hamlet of Somerden Green was once a lane in its own right, but being no longer maintained it is gradually returning to a more natural state. There were many fields around this area which had been left to grow clover as a soil conditioner. Mixed with mayweed, flax and other wild flowers, it formed a most pleasing sight.

Approaching the River Eden, I could clearly see the elegant spire of

Ide Hill to Chiddingstone

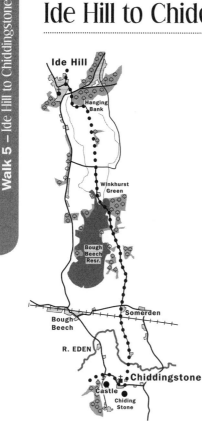

Chiddingstone

Is a village by the River Eden, a major tributary of the River Medway, which reputedly takes its name from the large sandstone rock formation to the south of the High Street, called the Chiding Stone. Tradition asserts that the stone was used as a seat of judgement, mainly to remonstrate with overbearing local wives. The village is unique, since apart from the church and the castle, the entire place is owned by the National Trust, thus preserving arguably the most perfect surviving example of a Tudor village in Kent. Consequently the village has become a tourist attraction, and the parking of cars in the High Street detracts from its visual merit.

Chiddingstone High Street

The Chiding Stone

Chiddingstone

Single street village

Frozen in time

Local brewery

So very fine

Patronised by the National Trust.

The River Eden

Is a 22-mile long tributary of the River Medway, rising from a source in Titsey, Surrey, just north of Clacket Lane Motorway Services on the M25, under the shadow of the North Downs. From here, in its upper reaches, it flows west and south through the Surrey town of Limpsfield, and south and east to Edenbridge. Thence it continues eastwards through its delightful valley to its confluence with the River Medway at Penshurst, passing the historic Hever Castle and the village of Chiddingstone. Water from the river is pumped out to fill up Bough Beech Reservoir when the water level is low.

67

Chiddingstone Church and the square proportions of Chiddingstone Castle occupying higher ground on the other side of the river. It was a very satisfying trek through the verdant vale of Kent. In time, I came to the bridge over the river, whose source lay far away to the west near Titsey in Surrey, and stood looking downstream, admiring the scene. There was a splendid oak tree by a bend in the river, bedecked with bulrushes and yellow water lilies about to burst into bloom. Climbing out of the valley on the other side, I was passed by a young man wearing walking boots and carrying a rucksack; I thought how grand it was that someone forty years younger than me was engaged in the same sort of activity. He did, however, manage the short rise into Chiddingstone with much greater alacrity than I was able to muster, but I didn't resent his youthful energy.

Soon, I reached the village of Chiddingstone and paid an obligatory visit to the Chiding Stone, a large outcrop of sandstone rock, which was evidently used as a place where wrongdoers were reprimanded in times past. Seeing this stone brought back the memory of cycling here from south-east London probably forty-five years ago with my best friend from school. The entire one-street village was bought in 1939 by the National Trust to ensure its preservation, and this jewel of a village, which has often been used for film sets, has remaining unaltered since then. For me, the effect was spoilt by parked cars lining the main street, and I did think the Trust should consider investing some money in the village to create an unobtrusive car park to get the cars out of the main street.

When I arrived at my bed and breakfast, there was a note addressed to me, pinned to the door, inviting me to go inside and make myself at home, which I did. After cleaning up and a rest, I retired to the Castle Inn next door. Imbibing at the bar of a pint of locally brewed Larkins bitter, I remarked to a chap next to me that it was a fine pint of ale. He turned out to be the brewer operating from Larkins Farm just up the road, and insisted that I have a pint on him. We got talking and he inquired about what brought me to the village and my week's walking. On this Saturday night there was a succession of local groups frequenting the unimproved bar, including the victorious cricket team, all-night fishermen and bell-ringers. After many pints of his fine beer and a very convivial evening, I retired next door, unconcerned about the prospect of a hangover, since the brewer had assured me that he had taken the headache out of his beer, and indeed he was right; I didn't suffer from a hangover next morning.

In the morning, I left Chiddingstone on the road to Markbeech, passing under the church, past the lake in the grounds of Chiddingstone Castle, still encamped by fishermen. I saw one chap baiting his hook with a large ball of bread, presumably to catch a large fish like carp, skilfully casting under trees at the far side of the lake. I noticed that the surface of the lake was covered with many large lumps of bread from previous casts; I thought there was probably enough food on the surface to last the entire fishy population of the lake for many months. I carried on along the lane, perched on the bluff above the River Eden, admiring the views northwards to the Greensand Ridge. I put my head down and started pacing the lane to Lockskinners Farm and beyond, strafed by cyclists out for a bit of gentle exercise on this Sunday morning.

Markbeech seemed a pleasant little village, centred around the pub and church, and I passed on through the churchyard to the sound of a Sunday service, to pick up a footpath that would take me up to the B2026 by Pyle Gate Farm. I reflected on the fact that the map nearly always represented the shape of woods accurately, thereby making it easy to navigate through the countryside by these references, and this was the case in passing out of Markbeech. This footpath plunged into a deep, wooded valley beside an adolescent stream feeding the Kent Water, a tributary of the River Medway, but was well-marked and easy to follow. I climbed up to, and crossed over, the busy road from Edenbridge to Hartfield by Pyle Gate Farm and proceeded across fields to Cowden, another beautiful Kentish village.

On the way down into the village I was struck by the incidence of many different types of butterfly in the meadowland; and one brown butterfly with a large eye on its wing in particular, which I later identified as the common meadow brown butterfly. It was a very pleasing hike from Markbeech and particularly down from Pyle Gate Farm into Cowden. I came up into the village, as one would expect, by the church and rested for a while on a seat in the churchyard. I was desperate for a drink of water, but after enquiring after an emporium which might sell such a commodity, I was told by a local, 'Not in Cowden.' There was nothing except a pub and a church. Unfortunately, if one doesn't want to go to church and the pub is closed, as it was, there is no incentive to linger in Cowden, pretty as it might be.

Chiddingstone to Cowden

Common Carp
(Cyprinus carpio)

Or European carp is a widespread fish of lakes and large rivers. The wild populations are considered vulnerable to extinction, but the species has also been domesticated and introduced into many environments as a sport and food fish. It is related to the common goldfish with which it is capable of interbreeding. It is considered in many parts of the world to be an invasive species and is the most intensively farmed fish exceeding the weight of all other fish, including trout and salmon.

Holy Trinity Church, Markbeech

Meadow Brown Butterfly
(Maniola jurtina)

Is one of our commonest and most widespread butterflies, and a familiar sight throughout the summer months. This highly variable species, with respect to the amount of orange on the forewings and the number of black spots on the underside of its hind wings, can typically be found in grasslands, and the field margins of heavily grazed meadows.

Cowden

Is a small, unspoilt village in the very south-west corner of Kent, with its old High Street having many Grade II listed cottages, a church and a pub. This is old Wealden iron country, commemorated by the cast iron slab in the church to John Bottinge, dated 1622. This was a time when the area was producing guns for the army and navy, as well as domestic and agricultural ware, and the village had its own blast furnace, sited in Furnace Lane, from 1573 until the eighteenth century.

Cowden High Street

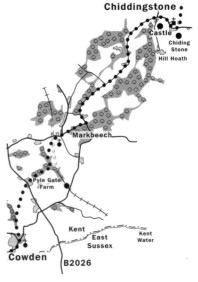

In Cowden I was in the most south-westerly corner of Kent, and soon I was to pass into East Sussex. I descended to a small stream, the Kent Water, which forms the artificial boundary between Kent and East Sussex, on my way to Holtye Common. I passed Furnace Lane, which led to Furnace Farm, which tells its own story. I understand that the last working blast furnace in Kent was located there. It was a stiff climb into East Sussex, but my reward was a rest, food and drink in the pub at the top, the White Horse, on the main A264 East Grinstead to Tunbridge Wells road. Holtye Common was smothered by a golf course astride the main road, which like so many east/west routes in this part of the country follows one of the ridges of the Weald. From the back of the pub, I had a splendid view of the wild, broken, northern slopes of Ashdown Forest, the source of Kent's major river.

After a short rest, I took the track going due south by the side of the clubhouse, which was bedecked with ferns; the common king fern I believe. Strolling down the quiet lane, I thought I had made a good choice of route and the sun was showing itself more and more from behind summer clouds. I fashioned a walking stick from a hazel stem discarded by the side of the lane. I observed it closely and put my foot on it to break it in the right position, and it turned out just right. This was the first time I had resorted to making a stick and it seemed to aid my walking, putting an extra spring in my step.

Further down the lane, after a sharp bend, I took a footpath across a field of corn, growing more freely now after recent rain in a very dry spring. As the authorities were about to declare drought conditions across most of eastern England and the Midlands, the weather turned wetter, just in time. I came up to another small lane before Beeches Farm and proceeded happily towards Hartfield, negotiating steep little undulations in the terrain. Getting nearer to my destination, I took a bridleway to Chartners Farm, alongside a wood, to cross over the River Medway. Even these headwaters made a powerful small river, gathering the waters from further west, running off the slopes of Ashdown Forest. Just over the river was a disused railway to Groombridge, which now accommodated the Sussex Border Path and a cycleway. Climbing up to Hartfield through a field of scented mayweed, I passed some smart, newly turned out dwellings in a small close at the bottom of the High Street, coming to the junction of the B2110 and the Edenbridge Road.

The strategically important field in Hartfield, on the corner below the

Cowden to Hartfield

Hartfield and A. A. Milne

Hartfield is a small, attractive, ancient village on the northern margin of Ashdown Forest. The River Medway issuing from the forest flows through a shallow valley to the north of the village, which grew from its agricultural roots until it became a centre for iron and timber production.

In 1924 the village saw its main claim to fame arrive in the guise of the Milne family, who bought the nearby Cotchford Farm, where the author A. A. Milne wrote the Winnie-the-Pooh stories. The area around the village is included in his books, with the bridge over a stream on the farm being the place where Poohsticks were invented. This bridge was restored by East Sussex County Council in 1979, and there is a shop in the village that sells everything related to Winnie-the-Pooh.

St Mary's Church, Hartfield

Scented Mayweed
(*Matricaria recutita*)

Is a common annual plant of the daisy family, which is one of the many plants that are sometimes referred to as camomile, growing on road verges and in cultivated fields as an invasive weed. It has been commonly used in herbal medicine and can be used to make a herbal tea.

Male Fern
(*Dryopteris filix-mas*)

Is one of the most common UK ferns, favouring damp shady conditions, as an understory in woodland and in hedge banks. The half-evergreen leaves have an upright habit and reach a maximum length of 1.5 metres, with a single crown on each rootstock. The spores are released from August to November, and thereafter the foliage dies back to reappear in the next spring.

Pooh Corner Shop , Hartfield

church, protected as common land, was graced by two big, black bulls that were helping to keep the field in a manageable state. I walked through the village and booked into the Anchor Inn. I was shown to a splendid, recently refurbished room and settled in. Later, exploring the village, I called into the second pub, The Hay Wagon, and was persuaded to enter into a quiz. Sitting at the bar, playing on my own, I managed to become somewhat of a celebrity by winning the quiz, much to my amazement.

Apart from being an attractive little village with an active community spirit, its main claim to fame is that A.A. Milne, the author of *Winnie the Pooh*, lived nearby at Cotchford Farm, while writing his books for his son, Christopher Robin. In spite of the tourism generated by this association, I was to find out that there was no post office in the village, so I had to rely on my host to post my parcel back. Later I found out that it was in this same farm where Brian Jones of the original Rolling Stones line-up, and one of my boyhood heroes, was found dead floating in the swimming pool.

In the morning, I left Hartfield by the church and followed the Sussex Border Path to Withyham, which is dominated by one large estate. It was pleasant walking in the early morning sunshine before the serious walking started. Looking at the map, I was slightly abashed by the extent of the ground I was trying to cover in walking to Wadhurst. The Sussex Border Path, which I vaguely intended to follow, veered back and forth all over the place and by the time I had reached Withyham, I had decided to depart from the designated route, hoping to cut off a large detour. I ploughed on up the B2110, even though I knew it would be an uncomfortable stretch up the hill, to pick up a smaller high road to the south-east, to the B2188. It was indeed an uncomfortable stretch and even the smaller road joining the two B-roads was quite busy. However, as recompense for the hard climb, I was rewarded with fabulous views from this lane, which reached a height of 113m, of the country laying before Ashdown Forest on the horizon. I crossed over the B2188 with the intention of re-joining the long-distance footpath in the vicinity of Leyswood.

For some unfathomable reason, I failed to pick up the footpath along the edge of Leyswood and after unintentionally exploring the hamlet nestling by the stream under the wood, I found myself climbing into the middle of the gloomy wood, where I lost the way and ended up back on

Hartfield to Stonewall

B2026
B2188
Batts Green
B2110
Hartfield
113m
Withyham
Harrison's Rocks
Leyswood
Eridge Station
Forge Wood
A26
Stonewall
141m

Ashdown Forest

Is an ancient area of open heathland and forest in East Sussex occupying the highest ridge top of the High Weald A.O.N.B., rising to 223 metres (732 ft), and the source of Kent's premier river, the Medway. The forest has a rich archaeological heritage, containing much evidence of prehistoric human occupation, including Bronze Age, Iron Age and Romano-British remains. It is composed of a sandstone formation of the Lower Cretaceous period, and as such forms some of the oldest rocks of the Weald. Its origins are as a Medieval hunting forest, carved out of the original vast Forest of Anderida, and created soon after the Norman Conquest. The forest continued to be used by royalty for hunting into the Tudor period, graced notably by Henry VIII, who courted Anne Boleyn at the nearby Hever Castle. In the seventeenth century 9.5 sq. miles (2,500 ha) was set aside as common land, and today this forms the largest area of open access land in south-east England.

The Ashdown Forest

Hartfield

In the shadow of

Ashdown Forest

Slumbering gently

Outcomes modest

A real village with community spirit.

Harrison's Rocks

Fans of mountaineering and climbing list these rocks among the best climbing training areas in the whole of south-east England. The sandstone rock formations, the same as those at nearby High Rocks, were carved out of the hillside by the small river in the valley at the bottom of the cliffs, which is a tributary of the River Medway. These rocks offer climbers a wide variety of easy and difficult climbs.

Harrison's Rocks

70

the lane further on. When I had worked out where I was, I decided to cut my losses and stick to the lane, which doubled up as a cycleway, and walk down by the significant stream that flows down to Groombridge. I passed beneath the dramatic slopes of Harrison's Rocks, just across the railway and the stream, another rugged outcrop of the Ardingly sandstone formation that forms the nearby High Rocks. It was here, on a school expedition, that my nerve as a rock climber was tested and found wanting, but I enjoyed the trip into the Sussex countryside all the same. This fine, winding lane took me to Eridge Station where I was looking forward to a rest and a few pints in the pub marked on the map.

When I arrived at midday, the pub was closed and my patient attendance seemed to make no difference to the prospect of it ever opening, so I gave up and passed on. I have remarked on this before, but the liberalisation of opening hours and the economics of rural pubs have made the availability of pubs at lunchtimes very much a lottery. My disappointment was compounded by the fact that the small road shown white on the map, which I could have reasonably expected to be a right of way through the grounds of Hamsell Manor, was in fact prohibited. Thus, by a series of decisions, which each seemed logical, as far back as Withyham, I had now got myself in a bit of a fix and was faced with an unappealing hike up a steep rise, back along the A26, towards Tunbridge Wells, as there was no other way to go.

From this low point, being tired and thirsty, facing a long slog up the A26 and having only covered half the day's allotted journey, I had to dig deep. But then things started to improve, since I found a pleasantly shaded bridleway adjacent to the main road and made good progress up the hill. I guess at one time it could have been the original route of the road before the A26 was improved. At the top of the hill in a layby, I came across a mobile café shop and purchased two cans of cold drinks, one of which I gratefully consumed on the spot and the other I stuffed into my rucksack. A little further on, I picked up the long lane going south and after a brief descent to a small stream, I laboriously climbed up to Stonewall, where I hoped to locate the Sussex Border Path again.

Towards the top of this climb to 141m, I came across a camp site with a shop open for the campers at Danegate and I indulged myself in buying two cans of cider, one of which I consumed on the premises. I rested for a while in the scruffy campsite, talking to a friendly, elderly couple who enquired after my exploits. Even after Stonewall, I struggled to find the

path, but I located it at Great Danegate, even though it was not signed, and carried on hopefully. I careered down the hill after consuming my second can of cider, seeing a mangy fox cross the path in broad daylight. I turned east through a cool wood and across a small stream before climbing again, below the wood containing Saxonbury Hill at 202m, the site of an Iron Age hill fort. I climbed up onto the down at a similar height before the main A267 and looked around. There was an amazing panoramic view across the High Weald from this point and I could clearly see the hilltop village of Frant to the north.

Crossing over the main road, I came to Pococksgate Farm on an infrequently used path, but the views to the north were absolutely stunning. Alongside Nap Wood, I could clearly see Wadhurst up ahead in the distance. I passed on through Lightlands, Earlye Farm and Buckhurst Place on the way to Wadhurst, following mainly local footpaths, which, strung together, constituted the poorly signed Sussex Border Path. On the final stiff climb up into Durgates, the day became hot and still, as if everything had gone to sleep in the late afternoon. I crossed over the railway and passed beside a wild garlic wood on the way into Wadhurst. Strolling down the busy Wadhurst High Street, I felt I may have been overly critical on my last visit; clearly, there were the same ugly buildings, but the overall effect was not unpleasing to the eye.

Stonewall to Wadhurst

Silver Birch
(Betula pendula)

Is a medium-sized deciduous tree with a slender trunk and a crown of arched branches with drooping branchlets. The bark is white, often with black diamond-shaped marks, or larger patches, particularly at the base. The flowers are wind-pollinated catkins, produced before the leaves in early spring, the small winged seeds ripening in late summer. It tends to favour dry sandy soils, and is widely planted as an ornamental tree.

Red Fox
(Vulpes vulpes)

Is a shy, mainly nocturnal, dog-like mammal, which is widespread in the countryside, and in towns and cities, where it is sometimes regarded as a pest. They are opportunist feeders; typically rural foxes eat voles, rats, squirrels, rabbits and fruit, while urban foxes will eat pigeons, scavenge in dustbins, and even raid bird tables. Currently in the UK the fox has no natural predator, and thus their numbers can be considerable.

Saxonbury Hill and Nap Wood

Saxonbury Hill, at 202m metres, has an iron age hill fort at its summit, with a 19th century folly, in the style of a gothic tower, built by the Abergavenny family who own much of the land in the vicinity. The Lords Nevill of Abergavenny can trace their lineage from the Norman Conquest, and they retained possession of their Monmouthshire Estate until it was disposed of in the 20th century. The family owns land in Sussex, Kent and the Midlands but their principle residence is at the nearby Eridge Park in Kent. The Welsh connection is reflected in the name of one of the pubs in Frant, the Abergavenny Arms on the main Tunbridge Wells road.

Nap Wood, owned by the National Trust, is a Site of Special Scientific Interest, consisting of 107 acres of semi-natural oak and birch woodland. Variety is provided by some impressive old beech trees, and some fine ageing scots pines.

Scots Pine
(Inus Sylvestris)

Is the only native species of pine identified by its combination of fairly short, blue-green leaves and orange-red bark. This tall evergreen coniferous tree, growing to 35 metres or more, has the habit of producing a long, bare and straight trunk, topped by a rounded or flat-topped mass of foliage. The tree was one of the first to spread across the British Isles after the last Ice Age, and now occurs naturally only in Scotland. Elsewhere it has been reintroduced as forestry and ornamental planting.

In the evening, in the bar of the Greyhound Inn, I got talking to a professional weatherman, whose job it was to advise the Ministry of Defence; strangely, he was a climate change sceptic. The simple fact of global warming seemed lost on him due to his superior knowledge of the subject; one might say that I felt he couldn't see the wood for the trees. Given the facts of global warming; namely that average temperatures are rising, ice caps are melting and sea levels rising, it is only possible to hide the significance of these events by claiming they are a blip within longer weather cycles. It is more difficult to demonstrate that these climatic changes are the result of human activity, but personally I would prefer us to change our behaviour and take sensible precautions now, rather than bury our heads in the sand.

In the morning, I left Wadhurst in good spirits and walked past Little Pelt Farm, where hops were being grown, on the way to Bewl Water. I found the Sussex Border Path, which skirted round the northern shores of the reservoir along a gently undulating track. Water levels in the reservoir were very low and the gentle slopes below the high watermark were clothed in a verdant green sward. The interesting organic shape of the lake, caused by the natural contours of the valleys converging at this point, reminded me of the manicured splendours of Stourhead, but without the Italianate follies and rhododendrons. I passed through lakeside woods and broad, open bluffs sweeping down to the tranquil lake, passing numerous walkers, cyclists and dog walkers taking the air. After Hook Farm, by the shores of the lake, before the causeway dam, the emphasis changed to more energetic pursuits, that is, boating and camping for the young, fit and adventurous.

I carried on across the reservoir's dam, which formed a causeway across the valley of the River Bewl, a major tributary of the river Teise. Looking down the Bewl valley from this windy ridge, I could clearly see Scotney Castle, a splendid National Trust property on the outskirts of Lamberhurst. Although fishing was not allowed from the causeway dam, there were many small, two-man boats out on the lake engaged in this activity. The reservoir dam was less than halfway round the northern shores of the lake so I plodded relentlessly on. The southern shores of the lake consist of finger-like tentacles of water reaching out for Ticehurst and Wadhurst. At the eastern end of the lake, I severed the last tentacle and made my way up through woods to Union Street on the B2087, and then on to the hamlet of Quedley, still following the Sussex Border Path.

Walk 5 – Wadhurst to Union Street

Wadhurst to Union Street

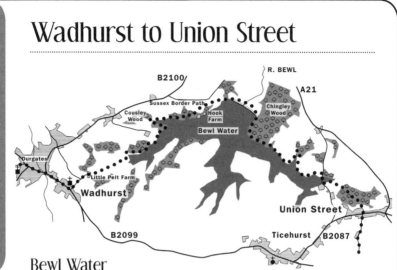

Bewl Water

Is a reservoir in the valley of the River Bewl, which is itself a tributary of the River Teise, straddling the Kent/East Sussex border. Construction of the dam across the valley, completed in 1975, created a reservoir capable of holding 31,300 million litres of water, the largest inland body of water in south-east England. In common with most large, clean water lakes, the reservoir is host to a multitude of wildlife, and many recreational activities, such as sailing and fishing. From the dam it is possible to see the historic Scotney Castle downstream.

Scotney Castle

Is an English country house with formal gardens in the valley of the River Bewl, a major tributary of the River Teise, owned by the National Trust. The gardens are a celebrated example of the picturesque style, the central feature of which is the ruins of a Medieval, moated manor house on a small island, known as Scotney Old Castle. The lake is surrounded by sloping wooded gardens with fine collections of rhododendrons, azaleas and kalmia for spring colour, summer wisteria and roses, and spectacular autumn colour. At the top of the garden is Scotney New Castle, built in the Tudor revival style between 1835 and 1843 to replace the Old Castle.

Wadhurst and Ticehurst

Suckling on Bewl Water

Identical twins

Nursed in the Weald

Where one twin wins

More sense of place than the other.

Wadhurst High Street

Scotney Castle

72

I crossed a golf course and descended into a rugged valley which formed the headwaters of the Kent Ditch, itself a tributary of the River Rother.

There, I hit rock bottom, being tired and fed up with struggling to find the way and suffering one of those spasms of not feeling too well, when the heart begins to race. I was in the middle of nowhere, so I pressed on slowly, hoping that the turn would pass. Changing direction from south to east and by punishing little climbs, I made my way towards the dreaded A21. Again, the footpath was poorly marked in the vicinity of Mumpum, and I was nearly seduced by a path that would have led me miles out of my way into Boarzell Wood. Feeling better, I carried on to make the big road by Ringden Farm, where I opportunistically visited the farm shop and consumed two bottles of their famous apple-based drinks, endorsed by a celebrity chef.

Picking my way south for a short distance along the A21, I regained the designated path, and passed on to Brookgate farm. There, the path was impossible to follow, made more difficult I suspect by the owners not encouraging people to pass through, and I felt like giving up on the border path. I ended up illegally scrambling through fields and over fences, only to emerge at a recognisable place at Seacox Heath on the main A268. Thereafter, not wishing to slog along the main road into Hawkhurst, I dropped down into a lane and picked up the footpath again, through an extensive orchard and on to The Moor. This immensely attractive settlement to the south of Hawkhurst, grouped around its sloping green, is certainly worth a visit. This time I took the lower road, past extremely pleasant cottages, over a small stream, one of the head-waters of the Kent Ditch, and hobbled wearily up into the current centre of the village, where I was stabled for the night.

That evening, in the pub, I got talking to two chaps. One was a former shepherd who subsequently worked in an abattoir and was now selling sheepskin. He explained that sheepskin makes high quality leather, used for gloves and jackets, something I never really considered before, thinking that all leather came from cows. The other local was a jack of all trades, an admirable type often found in rural communities. He organised clay pigeon shoots, but our conversation soon turned to keeping down species that were regarded as pests in the countryside, including pigeons, foxes, mink and deer, all of whom have no natural predators except man. He would have included badgers in this category if they were not protected; not because of bovine tuberculosis, but because of their rapid

Union Street to Hawkhurst

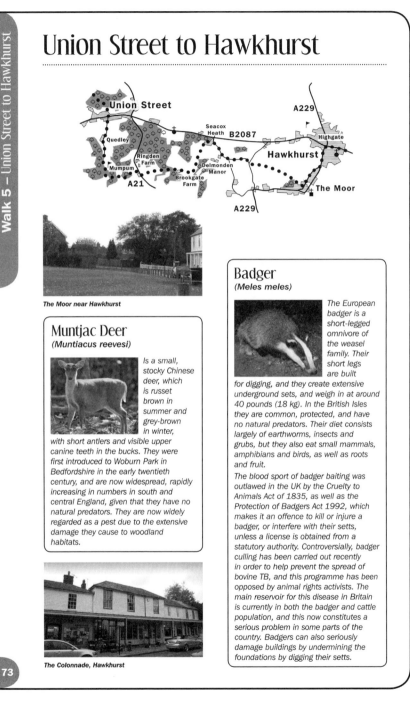

The Moor near Hawkhurst

Muntjac Deer
(Muntiacus reevesi)

Is a small, stocky Chinese deer, which is russet brown in summer and grey-brown in winter, with short antlers and visible upper canine teeth in the bucks. They were first introduced to Woburn Park in Bedfordshire in the early twentieth century, and are now widespread, rapidly increasing in numbers in south and central England, given that they have no natural predators. They are now widely regarded as a pest due to the extensive damage they cause to woodland habitats.

The Colonnade, Hawkhurst

Badger
(Meles meles)

The European badger is a short-legged omnivore of the weasel family. Their short legs are built for digging, and they create extensive underground sets, and weigh in at around 40 pounds (18 kg). In the British Isles they are common, protected, and have no natural predators. Their diet consists largely of earthworms, insects and grubs, but they also eat small mammals, amphibians and birds, as well as roots and fruit.

The blood sport of badger baiting was outlawed in the UK by the Cruelty to Animals Act of 1835, as well as the Protection of Badgers Act 1992, which makes it an offence to kill or injure a badger, or interfere with their setts, unless a license is obtained from a statutory authority. Controversially, badger culling has been carried out recently in order to help prevent the spread of bovine TB, and this programme has been opposed by animal rights activists. The main reservoir for this disease in Britain is currently in both the badger and cattle population, and this now constitutes a serious problem in some parts of the country. Badgers can also seriously damage buildings by undermining the foundations by digging their setts.

73

expansion in numbers and the damage caused to buildings by their setts. He was particularly concerned about the massive increase in Chinese deer in the area and the devastating damage caused to plantations by their activities. He also made walking sticks and I couldn't resist showing him mine, the one I had fashioned from a hazel pole discarded in the lane below Holtye Common. He was quite complimentary and advised me about how I could look after it, including fitting a copper ring over the base to stop it fraying.

Next day I passed out of Hawkhurst, along the main road, until I reached the small lane that took me off the ridge towards Gun Green. There were some lovely cottages strung out along the lane and wonderful views down to the significant Hexden Channel, which eventually joined the Rother in a confusion of waterways by Maytham Wharf. Dropping off the ridge with its busy main road, the sound of traffic disappearing, I warmed to the morning's escapade. I took the footpath skirting the grounds of St Ronan's School, on the way to The Paper Mill naturally located on the stream; an establishment whose name is a reminder that paper-making has been an important local industry for many centuries in this part of Kent. I passed by the side of a wood swamped with rampant, dull laurel and horse chestnut trees afflicted by that virulent disease that streaks the leaves with brown in summer. Before the working mill, I passed a splendid, timber-framed, small manor house, which would have graced the landscape for a few hundred years.

After The Paper Mill, I turned north, climbed up the hill to Diprose and found a footpath across the fields to Sarnden. From this path on the side of the hill, I could see clearly down the Hexden Valley to the plains beyond and over the ridge petering out east of Sandhurst, to Hastings on the coast. After the hamlet of Sarnden, I plunged down into a deeply cut valley before climbing up again to the village of Iden Green at about 60m. I observed a grand display of wild honeysuckle growing in the hedges as I struggled up the narrow lane. I passed across the northern edge of Iden Green and picked up a footpath through Moor Wood, which had been heavily harvested, leaving the occasional mature tree. The patchwork of cleared ground was covered with young trees and swathes of ferns.

Coming out of the wood and crossing a small stream, I came to a scruffy lane junction, sporting a signpost, which was a damaged, rutted triangle, being more mud than grass, caused by wayward vehicles skewing off the road. I have encountered this situation on numerous occasions. It

Hawkhurst to Rolvenden

Wooden-fronted houses in Rolvenden

Rolvenden

Is a village that dates at least from Saxon times and is mentioned in the Domesday Book. Rolvenden village originally consisted of the Street, located along what is now the A28 Ashford to Hastings road, which was almost entirely burned down in 1665 during the Great Plague. This caused the villagers to abandon the Street to move a mile down the hill to the common land at Rolvenden Layne during the 1660s. Later, they returned and rebuilt the main village by the church, resulting in the two distinct settlements of today.

Wild Honeysuckle
(Lonicera periclymenum)

The common or European honeysuckle is a vigorous, deciduous, native, climbing hedgerow plant also known as woodbine. It produces clusters of sweet-smelling, yellow tubular flowers, flushed with purple and red in summer, much loved by birds and insects. It grows in most soils and prefers full sun, but tolerates partial shade. The plant is usually pollinated by moths or long-tongued bees and produces bright red berries. It is commonly grown as a garden plant and numerous varieties have been developed for this purpose.

Paper-making in the Weald of Kent

There is a long history of paper-making in the Weald of Kent. The earliest mills, situated on the headwaters of the major rivers, particularly the River Teise, were at Benenden and Goudhurst, in the seventeenth century. At this time paper was made from rags which were beaten in water to make a fine pulp. In the eighteenth century there was a paper mill at Ockley, on the headwaters of the Hexden Channel, north of Hawkhurst. Today, further downstream, in Foxhole Lane, there is a working paper mill. During the eighteenth century, paper-making was a profitable business in The Weald of Kent, but the last historical mill at Benenden closed in the mid-nineteenth century, and production moved to the increasingly mechanised mills in Maidstone and Dartford.

© *Paper Making in the Weald of Kent* by Tony Singleton

seems to me that more care should be taken in looking after these significant landmarks in order to protect the visual appeal of country lanes. Maybe these junctions, much like roundabouts in towns and cities, could be looked after by volunteers in some adoption scheme.

Shortly after this junction, I joined the High Weald Landscape Trail, in which I had more confidence that the Sussex Border Path, to enable me to get to Rolvenden. I passed through the pleasant hamlet of Dingleden, boasting some cosy cottages, and through a field with young rams, who are more inclined to stand and stare one out than yews, who tend to shy away. It was a pleasure to walk the High Weald Landscape Trail on this section, and I made good progress through fields of sheep, coming into Rolvenden by the church. I made a short detour north along the village main street, the busy A28, to sojourn in The Star Inn for lunch.

After a well-earned break, I proceeded east and picked up the small lane to Upper Woolwich: a carefully tended hamlet with expensive barn conversions. When I noted the hamlets of Upper and Lower Woolwich on the map, I knew I had to pass through, as I was born in Woolwich proper. Slipping down the track to Lower Woolwich, another gorgeous hamlet where I could imagine living, there were satisfying views out across the flat landscape of the plain that carries the Newmill Channel, a smaller version of Shirley Moor further to the east. There is a big difference between walking down into a river valley and walking down into a flat plain that used to be an inlet of the sea; the shape of the valley is flat-bottomed and entirely different from a typically V-shaped valley. For me, the most evocative place to live would be in a situation that overlooked a flat-bottomed valley like the plain occupied by the Newmill Channel. From the sloping track I could clearly see the original course and valley of the River Rother, to the north of the Isle of Oxney, now occupied by the Reading Sewer.

Passing by the lovely spot that is Lower Woolwich, on a bluff which would once have overlooked the sea, I observed herds of gaily coloured cattle grazing on the bottom fields. I came down past a glowing field of corn and a hedgerow filled with birds, dunnocks mainly. As I descended on to the atmospheric marsh, peace descended on my mind, and I felt comfortable, in tune with my surroundings, feeling no need to charge on, maybe for the first time on this walk. I lost the footpath and strolled alongside the Newmill Channel, graced by four swans parting the surface algae, while a steam train powered its way along the line to Tenterden. I

Rolvenden to Tenterden

Dunnock
(Prunella modularis)

Or hedge sparrow is a relatively common, small, brown and grey bird, which is resident throughout the UK. It typically inhabits field hedges and deciduous woodlands, keeping close to the ground and cover. It feeds on insects, spiders, worms and seeds.

White Willow
(Salix alba)

Is a medium-sized deciduous tree growing up to 30 metres tall with a trunk up to 1 metre in diameter and an irregular, often leaning crown. The grey-brown bark is deeply fissured in older trees. The leaves are paler than most other willows due to a covering of silky white hairs on the underside, giving the trees a shimmering white appearance. The wood is tough and light in weight, and the stems or withies are coppiced from pollarded plants to be used in basket-making. Charcoal made from the wood was once important for gunpowder manufacture, and the bark was used for tanning leather.

William Caxton
(c.1422-1492)

Was the first English printer. He was also a translator and importer of books into England. He was supposedly born in Tenterden around 1422, but went to London at the age of 16 to become an apprentice to a merchant. He later moved to Bruges, the centre of the wool trade at the time, where he became a successful and important member of the merchant community. From 1462–1470 he served as governor of the 'English Nation of Merchant Adventurers', which allowed him to act as a diplomat for the king.

Caxton affiliated himself with the household of Margaret, the duchess of Burgundy, sister of the English King Edward IV. She became one of his most important patrons and encouraged him with his translation of *The Recuyell of the Histories of Troye* from French to English. In the early 1470s he spent time in Cologne learning the art of printing. He returned to Bruges in 1472 where he and Colard Mansion, a Flemish calligrapher, set up a printing press. Caxton's own translation of *The Recuyell of the Histories of Troye* was the first book printed in English.

In 1476 Caxton returned to London and established a printing press at Westminster. Amongst the books he printed were Chaucer's *Canterbury Tales* and Mallory's *Le Morte d'Arthur*. He printed more than one hundred books in his lifetime, books which were known for their craftsmanship, careful editing and translation. He died in 1492.

75

noted that the crayfish lagoons shown on the map were no more; they had been abandoned and reverted to scrub. I thought I might enquire into the history of crayfish farming in this location. By not picking up the High Weald Landscape Trail after Lower Woolwich, I guess, technically, I was lost, but it made no difference as I could see exactly where I was going in the flat landscape and felt no stress.

I found a crossing point over the stream and railway track and headed for a place called Cold Harbour, just before the town of Tenterden, and mused on the fact that this seemed a common name in the countryside, and that I had never come across a warm harbour. From there, I continued on into Tenterden, skirting the grounds of Heronden Hall, locating The William Caxton pub on the junction of the A28 and B2082, my berth for the night. When inquiring why the pub was so-called, I found out that the great man evidently did some of his earliest printing in the town.

I had a very pleasant evening, eating and drinking at the bar, and talking to the barman who was preparing to study law after a period of backpacking around the world. We had a very interesting discussion about the rights of bereaved parents, complaining at their treatment by lawyers seeking to defend the accused murderer, but we both agreed that this was the price we paid for a just and robust judicial system, in spite of current public opinion siding strongly with the unfortunate parents. I am pleased to report here that, under new management, I had a very pleasant stay in The William Caxton and would thoroughly recommend it to other walkers.

I left Tenterden next morning by a footpath directly opposite the church, which I think would have been a more important route into the town in times past. I came out beside an allotment garden, still following the High Weald Landscape Trail, towards Belcot Manor Farm. There, I cut across a field to a low corner, to descend through a wooded valley created by the deeply incised stream flowing south to join the Reading Sewer. Halfway down, the stream was dammed to form a long, thin lake in a delightful, wooded glade. Crossing a small pasture, I saw a large, white butterfly up ahead, so large that it looked like a small, white bird. When I was able to get closer, I noticed the butterfly had black shading on its wing tips, which identified it as the large white. The fields became more extensive around Dumbourne, and I passed through a charming herd of remarkably tame cattle; there were bulls, cows and heifers all living happily together. I reflected on the fact that I had never seen such a variety of butterflies away from the chalk hills as I had done on this perambulation, due no doubt to the time of year.

Coming to Small Hythe, a place strung out along the B2082, I bought a bottle of water from a farm shop. Passing down through the settlement, being wary of traffic needlessly speeding down the hill, I observed the historic Smallhythe Place, owned by the National Trust. This small hamlet was the site of an investigation by Channel 4's archaeological programme *Time Team*, when they were searching for evidence of Tudor shipbuilding activities. As Tenterden's port, Small Hythe, formerly on the navigable River Rother, had good deep water access to the sea, and shipbuilding was a major industry here, producing ships for Henry VIII's navy.

I paused for a while on the bridge across the Reading Sewer, admiring its peaceful, life-giving waters, judging by the symphony of birdsong filling the air. Standing there, looking eastwards towards Appledore and the marshes, I was following the former course of the river. I crossed over the stream and by a right-angled bend in the road, took a causeway grazed by sheep, due south through flat fields towards the Isle of Oxney. The mature sheep had been sheared, but the nearly fully grown lambs had not and I guess this did not bode well for their future longevity. To my right was a field full of beautiful cattle of all shades: black, brown, white, brown and white and black and white; the same coloured cattle that I had observed sweeping down into the flat fields by the Newmill Channel. Again, I would guess that this broad causeway would once have been the main track up on to the Isle of Oxney, avoiding the huge detour off the road via Peening Quarter.

After a sharp climb on to the Isle of Oxney at about 40m, I looked back north across the Rother levels and could clearly see the old, rolling, now heavily wooded former seashore, that I had just passed through. Looking north-east across Shirley Moor, I could see the blue line of the North Downs, probably in the vicinity of Wye, prefaced by the Greensand Ridge running down to Ham Street. I had noticed on this walk that it was normally possible to see the North or South Downs from any vantage point as an unbroken line on the horizon, which gave the sense of identity and closure, allowing a greater awareness of the complex structure of the Weald, of this 'miracle of rare devise' that I have elsewhere compared to Coleridge's '*Xanadu*'.

When I reached the main road, I elected to take a footpath through swathes of golden corn, to Swan Street. From there, I made the short detour up to The Swan Inn at Wittersham for a lunch break. When I reached the pub, just after it opened, I had to compete with a group of indecisive women, taking their time to order, before I could get served. They seemed to have no concept of the fact that I was thirsty and pining for a drink. When I did get served, I went outside and sat in a scruffy garden in the sun, being assailed by an inordinate amount of noise made by the same women and their offspring. On this occasion, I didn't particularly enjoy my visit, so after a couple of pints I drank up and left, keen to move on and complete my journey.

I strode back down the lane and picked up the footpath headed for the church, through the meadow where I had previously met the vicar that Sunday morning, and this time enjoying the evocative smell of newly cut hay. I crossed over the little gorge taking a stream off the isle and through the well-established orchards to the towered church. I noticed a lovely group of cottages gathered around the church, which would have been the original centre of the village. I carried on down the lane, through Ham Green to the broad, flat-bottomed valley of the River Rother. It occurred to me that, in landscape terms, one would expect flat-bottomed valleys in glaciated landscapes, but Kent and East Sussex were never covered in ice; these flat-bottomed valleys were silted up inlets of the sea.

Approaching the big river, I nearly had my nose taken off by a sparrow hawk that darted into the hedges in front, which were refreshingly not scalped, although I imagine their turn would come later in the season. Then I came down to the River Rother and saw a mink scamper across the road ahead of me. I stood on the bridge and observed the passage of the river across the empty Rother Levels towards Iden Lock. Last time I was here, I struggled along the north bank of the river through long grass, in the wake of the foot and mouth outbreak of the winter of 2000-2001. Further on, I passed an untidy farm, as one does from time to time in the countryside, with a mass of discarded metal machinery and equipment rusting away in the fields. When I see this sight, I can never understand why the farmer doesn't recycle this metal – it must be worth a fortune – or why some enterprising scrap dealer doesn't pay a call. In the warm, still afternoon, the air was filled with butterflies. Slogging up the lane to Peasmarsh, I paused, leaning on a field gate and looking east,

Tenterden to Peasmarsh

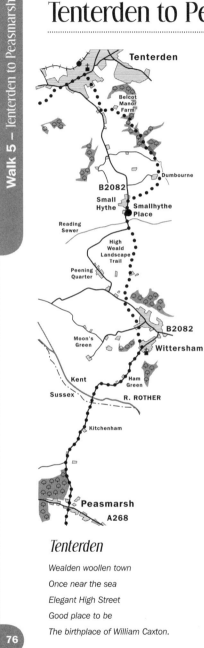

Tenterden

Belcot Manor Farm

Dumbourne

B2082

Small Hythe

Smallhythe Place

Reading Sewer

High Weald Landscape Trail

Peening Quarter

B2082

Moon's Green

Wittersham

Kent

Ham Green

Sussex

R. ROTHER

Kitchenham

Peasmarsh

A268

Tenterden

Wealden woollen town

Once near the sea

Elegant High Street

Good place to be

The birthplace of William Caxton.

Smallhythe Place

Is a half-timbered house built in the late fifteenth or early sixteenth century in the hamlet of Smallhythe, looked after by the National Trust. The house was once called Port House, reflecting the history of the place as a port of Tenterden on the seashore, where it served as an important ship building centre in Tudor times. It was the home of the Victorian actress Ellen Terry from 1899 to her death in the house in 1928. The popular TV programme *Time Team* excavated areas around the hamlet, along the original sea shore, hoping to find evidence of ship-building activity.

Smallhythe Place

Mink
(Mustela vison)

Is a species introduced from the United States as long ago as 1929, primarily bred for their fur. Large numbers of these captive animals quickly escaped and adapted to living in the British countryside, and are now well established. They are generally dark brown to black in colour, resembling a large weasel or stoat. Mink will devastate wildlife in their territory, having no natural predators, and preying on anything they can kill, including ducks. They are now regarded as a pest and are regularly trapped to keep their numbers under control.

76

where the fields were dotted with ancient oak trees, an iconic symbol of the English countryside.

After a steep climb up onto the ridge on which Peasmarsh is situated, at about 50m, between the Rivers Rother and Tillingham, I decided to keep straight on and take the lane to Peasmarsh Place rather than pass through the village on the main A268 road. Down the lane, I observed a field sown with flax in copious white flower, for ploughing in, and a field of barley with bearded stalks swaying in the breeze, the main ingredient in brewing beer. I passed by the track leading to Sir Paul McCartney's place, and imagined meeting him, jogging in the lane. Just after the small church, undergoing extensive renovation, I found the unmade road that re-joined the High Weald Landscape Trail and took me all the way to Rye.

Passing by Clayton Farm, through a large orchard and coming out under a large oak tree, I stood still and admired the stunning view down to Rye and the sea at Winchelsea Beach. I was surprised by how big the settlement of Rye looked from this angle, with all its inland housing estates billowing out like a hernia on the floodplain. I carried on down to the River Tillingham, through fields of smelly sheep, around the large loop of the river, under cliffs to the north-western outskirts of Rye, where there was a new sound in the air, the screeching of seagulls. I walked in by the river, past allotment gardens, and gradually the town devoured me.

Savouring a bag of cherries, I headed for the bus station, and caught

Peasmarsh to Rye

Rye

Is a small historic town, which exists in its present form primarily due to its failure as a Medieval port, when the harbour silted up and the sea retreated. Smuggling was an important activity, and the imposition of taxes on the export of wool from 1275 saw its rapid growth. By the end of the seventeenth century, owling, the smuggling of wool, had become widespread throughout Kent and Sussex. When luxury goods were also added, smuggling became a criminal pursuit, and groups like the Hawkhurst Gang resorted to murder and were subsequently hanged. The population of the town has changed little over the past sixty years and stands at about 4,500 inhabitants. In 1971 the historic core was designated a Conservation Area, and tourism now forms a significant source of employment. Rye continues to operate as a fishing port with some fish landed daily and sold directly from the quayside below the town.

The town has attracted many famous writers, such as Henry James and E. F. Benson, who lived at Lamb House, now owned by the National Trust, and visitors such as H. G. Wells and Rudyard Kipling to mention a few. G. K. Chesterton referred to Rye in the first line of his famous poem 'The Rolling English Road', and more recently Patric Dickinson based many of his poems on the town.

Barley
(Hordeum vulgare)

The domesticated plant is a major cereal grain, a member of the grass family. It serves as an important animal fodder, a source of fermentable material for beer and distilled spirits, and as a component of health foods. This grass can be distinguished from the more common wheat by the bearded nature of its seed heads. This versatile grain was ranked fourth in 2007 amongst cereal crops in the world in terms of the quantity produced and area cultivated.

Flax
(Linum usitatissimum)

Also known as linseed is an erect annual plant with glaucous, green leaves and pale blue flowers. It is grown for its seeds, which are the source of the edible linseed oil, and for its fibres which have been used to make fabric and paper. It is commonly ploughed in as a soil conditioner.

The River Tillingham

Is a 10-mile major tributary of the River Rother, which rises in the Sussex Weald near the village of Staplecross, to the south of Bodium, and flows eastward parallel to the River Brede, to their confluence with the River Rother in the town of Rye. At one time the river valley was tidal, before it was reclaimed from the sea, and the town of Rye would have been an island on the highest tides, Mount St Mary's, much like St Michael's Mount in Cornwall today.

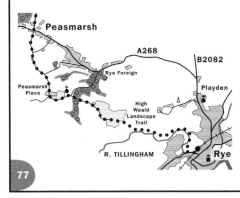

the bus to St Mary's Bay. Relaxing on the top deck of the bus, working my way back up the coast, I admired the familiar passing scenery. I disembarked at Jefferstone Lane and walked down to the pub, the Bailiff's Sergeant, to have a celebratory pint of beer before catching a taxi to St Mary in the Marsh, where I had left my car. I had a pleasant evening in The Star Inn, where I was staying before returning home in the morning, having successfully completed another ridiculous ramble through Kent and parts of East Sussex.

6

Bromley to Deal (Autumn 2011)

Disembarking from Bromley South Station, I set out southwards along massive busy roads. Generally, I felt dreadful, having a hangover from the folk evening the night before at The Star Inn on Romney Marsh, where I had left my car. Also, I was nursing a painful left knee. In fact, I was finding it difficult to walk at all, on what was an encouraging, bright, sunny morning. I passed the two distinctive churches on the main A21, turned right by Bromley College and cut up across Bromley Common. It was there, in this college, that I studied A-level sociology at evening classes, and succeeded in gaining a grade B in the late sixties, before returning to resume my studies in Oxford.

In Hayes, I bought a bottle of water for the sole purpose of washing down a painkilling tablet, something I had never resorted to before. I strode out south past affluent houses on the way to Hayes Common: a pleasant walk in the morning sunshine. Hayes Common was delightful, but heavily wooded, and I crossed over the A232 with some difficulty, pressing on to Keston. I came up to a pretty little green at the northern edge of Keston facing the common.

I was following the London Loop, a long-distance walk around Greater London. I passed by Keston into Ravensbourne Meadows, and along by a series of attractive lakes hard up against the A233 by Caesar's Camp. These were known as Keston Ponds and formed the source of the River Ravensbourne, which flows northward to the Thames at Greenwich. Resting for a while beside the last lake, I saw a shoal of fish swimming in the shallow, reedy water, as if mocking the anglers on the other side of the lake that were trying to catch them.

I hurried across the main road, still following the London Loop, through a wood to the Wilberforce Oak, now only a desiccated trunk in a clearing of the wood. From this spot there are fabulous views to the south into the Vale of Keston. When William Wilberforce, that splendid

Victorian, met Prime Minister Pitt in 1788 underneath the oak tree there, which would have been in its full glory then, he announced his intention to bring forward a bill in Parliament to abolish the slave trade.

As I followed the path, limping along as best I could, small planes were flying overhead on their way to and from Biggin Hill Airport. I passed around the back of Holwood Farm and saw the stately pile of Holwood House, which used to be William Pitt the Younger's abode, on the top of the hill. Hiking at this time of year, the hedgerows are full of seasonal berries, including blackberries, damsons and sloes. There was the sound of horses all around, making the noise that was onomatopoeically described by Swift in *Gulliver's Travels* as 'houinnyms'. In case you haven't got it, try saying the word out loud and I bet it sounds like a horse making its presence felt.

I pressed on, across the contours to High Elms Golf Course, the first proper public golf course I had ever played on, where I thought I might locate the clubhouse and have a rest. The London Loop passed by the clubhouse, but my route departed, striking up and down into Cuckoo Wood, where I disturbed a noisy, green woodpecker. I struggled on up to the settlement of Hazlewood and on across undulating terrain to Norstead Manor Farm and beyond. It was a passage that consisted of ups and downs across the dip slope of the North Downs, through leafy woods and across dry valleys, occasionally affording views back north towards Orpington and Green Street Green. I came up to Rushmore Hill and beat myself up over a growing desire to throw in the towel and relieve the agony in my left knee. I stumbled on further for the best part of a mile, coming into Halstead by the soft, tree-lined Church Lane.

Halstead is a pleasant village, in the form of a five-legged spider, strung out along the contiguous lanes, but firmly centred around the main crossroads, where there are two pubs, a school and a shop. There is, between the Cock Inn and the main crossroads, a substantial horse paddock, which would make a commodious village green if acquired by the community and would greatly add to the visual quality of the village. In the evening I ate and drank in the Cock Inn before wearily returning to my bed and breakfast accommodation and turning in.

Next day, I strode out up the Otford Road, past a second pub, the Rose and Crown, in the morning sunshine. It was a long slog up the road and my left knee reminded me again that it was not too keen on this adventure. As I approached Polhill, the traffic noise from the A21

Bromley to Halstead

The River Ravensbourne

Rises at Keston ponds and flows northwards through Catford, where it is joined by the River Pool, in Lewisham, eventually to enter the Thames at Greenwich. It is about 11 miles long. There are three picturesque ponds at its source, beside the A223, the main road to Biggin Hill. For much of its length, through the London Boroughs of Bromley, Lewisham and Greenwich, due to its propensity to flood, it forms an open space corridor.

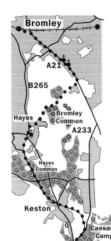

Keston

Lies on the southern edge of Hayes Common, and still forms a separate village on the outskirts of suburban London. Flint implements and pit dwellings on the common show occupation of the area dating back at least to 3000 BC. There are Iron Age encampments on Keston Common and Roman remains in the valley below the village, and at Caesar's Camp.

William Wilberforce, famous for promoting the abolition of slavery, was a frequent visitor to the area, as his close friend, William Pitt the younger, lived nearby at Holwood House. It was on top of the vale of Keston, near a distinctive oak tree, that he discussed the abolition of slavery with his friend. Only the partial dead remains of the 'Wilberforce Oak' are left, but a new oak tree has been planted in its place. A stone bench, the 'Wilberforce Seat', commemorating the discussion between the two men, now marks the spot and bears the inscription from Wilberforce's diary, 'Just above a steep descent into the vale of Keston, I resolved to give notice … in the House of Commons of my intention to bring forward the abolition of the Slave Trade.'

The London Loop

The London Outer Orbital Walk, usually called the London Loop, is a 150-mile long distance footpath, from Erith on the south side of the River Thames to Kingston–upon–Thames in the west, and back to Purfleet on the north bank of the river, almost directly opposite across the river from its starting point. It passes through parks, woods and fields around outer London, and has been described as the 'M25 for walkers'. It was conceived at a meeting between ramblers and the Countryside Commission in 1990 and fully opened in 2001.

Keston Ponds

became intrusive. I passed by the discreet entrance to the massive Fort Halstead, a Ministry of Defence research site on the crest of the North Downs. By the Polhill Arms, which appeared to be undergoing a complete refurbishment, I found the footpath that took me over the M25 at the very brow of the hill. I passed through woods to emerge at the Polhill Bank, overlooking the valley of the River Darent, the very same place where I camped with my cousin. The site is now a nature reserve and registered access land managed by the Kent Wildlife Trust. I sat down on the steep bank for a while and admired the prospect, maybe on the same spot upon which I had camped all those years ago. Further along the track there was a patch of mauve scabious-like flowers clothing the bank, with basal plates of leaves and long, thin stems topped with small flowers. They were very popular with the bees and I later identified them as the small scabious.

Sliding down into the Darenth Valley, I hit the lane to Shoreham at Filston Farm and sauntered along into the lovely village, thankfully not swamped by weekend visitors from the suburbs. I ambled past cottages full of character to the river and wondered where the artist, Samuel Palmer, had stayed when he lived in the village and painted the landscape around here. I leant on the bridge parapet over the river for a while and observed a large, brown dog paddling in the river, snuffling around the edges of the bank while his mistress sat on a seat and busied herself with some sort of electronic book. There were water boatman insects sculling around on the surface of the river: accurately named, oblong creatures with oars at each corner, suspended by the surface tension of the water. One could see their efforts bending the surface of the water but not breaking it. After the bridge, the river ran beside the High Street for a while, creating a satisfying arrangement at the heart of the village.

I passed on by the church and walked up to the railway, reflecting on the fact that the last time I had walked this stretch was during walk three in my first book, and that time I was struggling too, with a painful right ankle, so what was new? I crossed over the main A225 road and straight into a steep climb out of the valley, up White Hill. Pausing on the climb, I looked back across the valley and observed a white cross etched into the hillside, which presumably was the site of an air crash. Once up on top of the downs, I walked through a wood strewn with fallen trees and along Fackenden Lane southwards, getting into the rhythm of walking maybe for the first time this trip, as the painkillers began to bite.

At the fork in the lane in Doctor's Wood I ignored the route to Magpie Bottom and proceeded over the brow of the hill at 200m to join the North Downs Way. I passed a lovely group of brown cows with their calves hard up against the hedged fence, whose resident population of flies decided to hitch a ride on me. It was many yards down the lane before I managed to shake them off. At the junction of the lane, by the high point above Otford Mount, I located the North Downs Way by Rowdow Wood on a glorious, late-September day.

I walked on through Shorehill Farm to Shore Hill and paused for a while above Kemsing Down Nature Reserve to appreciate the spectacular view down into the valley and the Greensand Ridge beyond. Again, the reserve was managed by the Kent Wildlife Trust and owned by the parish council, and was notable for its butterflies, orchids and bluebells in spring, in beech and oak woodlands, with ancient yew trees. At this time of year, in late summer, the small scabious was also much in evidence. I walked down a well-organised path into Kemsing, through a former field returning to woodland but currently containing a wide variety of species, including apple and cherry trees, hawthorn, sloe and rowan to name a few. It is a sobering thought that fifty years ago this would have been a

Halstead to Kemsing

Samuel Palmer (1805-1881)

Was a British landscape painter, etcher, and printmaker who lived for much of his early life in Shoreham. He was a key figure in the Romantic Movement, produced richly coloured, visionary pastoral paintings, and was greatly influenced by William Blake. His generally regarded best work is based upon the rural landscapes around Shoreham, of which the following are notable and attributed locally: *Oak Trees Lullingstone Park*, *In a Shoreham Garden*, *Scene at Underriver Kent* or *The Hop Garden*, *Farmyard and Shaded Stream Shoreham*, *View from Rooks's Hill Kent*. He was largely forgotten after his death and his son burnt much of his father's handiwork. His reputation did not recover until the 1950s, when his Shoreham work began to receive the acclaim it deserved.

Shoreham

Is a delightful village in the fertile valley of the River Darent, and mentioned in the Domesday Book. The valley was a major centre of Stone Age settlement and paper-making was once a local industry. The village stood on the turnpike which ran from Dartford to Sevenoaks, opened between 1750 and 1780, now the route of the A225. London-born artist Samuel Palmer lived in the village for most of his life.

Shoreham Bridge over the River Darent

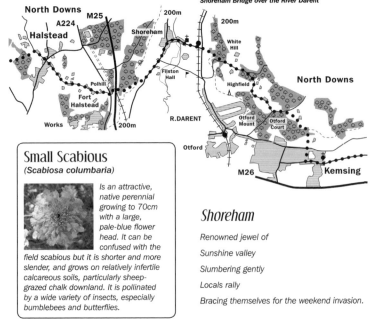

Small Scabious
(Scabiosa columbaria)

Is an attractive, native perennial growing to 70cm with a large, pale-blue flower head. It can be confused with the field scabious but it is shorter and more slender, and grows on relatively infertile calcareous soils, particularly sheep-grazed chalk downland. It is pollinated by a wide variety of insects, especially bumblebees and butterflies.

Shoreham

Renowned jewel of

Sunshine valley

Slumbering gently

Locals rally

Bracing themselves for the weekend invasion.

heavily grazed or cultivated open field and in fifty years' time, if left unmanaged, it would be a mature wood achieving its climax vegetation of beech or oak wood, with a reduced number of species.

In the centre of Kemsing, now a much-expanded village which is virtually continuous with Otford further west, is a small, triangular, carefully tended public garden adjacent to an impressive war memorial. Unfortunately, the little decorative stream that winds its way through the garden was dry. I popped into The Bell Inn for lunch and a rest, observing that the other pub in the village opposite had burnt down, creating an eyesore and completely spoiling what little of the historic heart of Kemsing remained. I got talking to a chap at the bar who, in recounting the events of that day, expressed panic on seeing the smoke, thinking that it might be The Bell, his local. I felt the least I could do was share my bowl of chips with him, understanding the trauma he must have felt.

After a decent rest, I carried on eastwards on the way to the hamlet of Crowdelham, past the distinctive St Edith Hall, with a prophetic message under its clock, which read, 'Tis mine each passing hour to tell. Tis thine to use it ill or well.' Further on, the attractive parish church in its quiet precinct was set back from the road, with an adjoining heritage centre. Next, along the lane, under the brooding presence of the downs, was an over-sized recreation ground. I cannot believe there could be a demand for such a large area of mown grass in Kemsing and I wondered whether it would be preferable not to take the easy option of mass mowing, and plump for less intensively managed solutions, allowing the margins to revert to natural grassland. I walked on along a pleasant lane to Hea-verham where I imbibed in The Chequers Inn, in the delightful vale between the chalk hills and the Greensand Ridge.

After Heaverham, I strolled along a footpath below the stately pile of St Clere with its redundant, walled garden, passing by a line of twelve evergreen oaks, no doubt planted as a windbreak. I had seen these trees before, growing in places in East Kent, but this was the furthest north and west I had seen this Mediterranean species. It occurred to me that the valley at this point was quite elevated, the lane dancing with the 120m contour, effectively forming a col between the waters flowing west to the River Darent and the waters flowing east towards the River Medway. The radio mast above Wrotham was now clearly visible on top of the downs. As I proceeded eastwards into the narrow neck of countryside between

Kemsing to Wrotham

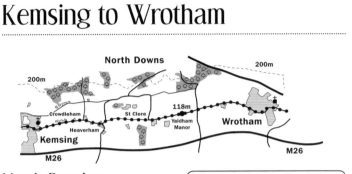

Morris Dancing

Is a form of English folk dance, usually accompanied by music. It is based on the rhythmic stepping and execution of choreographed figures by a group of dancers, usually wearing bell pads on their shins. Implements such as sticks, swords and handkerchiefs may also be wielded by the dancers. The origins of the Morris Dance are lost in history, and there appears to be no mention of it before the late fifteenth century. There is no evidence of the dance being a pre-Christian ritual, as is often claimed. Today, it is commonly thought of as a quintessentially English activity, although morris dancing has spread, mainly by British expatriates, around the world.

Mountain Ash
(Sorbus aucuparia)

Or rowan is a small to medium-sized deciduous tree with a number of sub-species, native to the UK. It is unrelated to the true ash though the leaves are superficially similar. It has a smooth bark, silvery grey in young trees, turning grey-brown and occasionally fissured in old trees. The creamy coloured flowers are produced in terminal corymbs, and are insect pollinated. The bright red berries appearing in late summer are eaten by birds, particularly winter visitors, such as fieldfare and redwing.

Evergreen Oak
(Quercus ilex)

Or holm oak is a medium-sized tree with a fissured black bark and leathery evergreen leaves. It is native to the Mediterranean region, thriving in relatively arid climates at low or moderate elevations, and thus was successfully introduced into southern England. Normally the tree is unable to withstand frost, which would normally prevent it from spreading north, but with climate change its range is expanding. Its wood is tough, used since ancient times for general construction purposes as pillars, tools, wagons, vessels and wine casks. Leaf shape is variable, and the leaves on the lower branches of young trees are often larger and spiny, possibly as a protection against grazing animals. A resemblance to the European Holly (Ilex aquifolium) has led to its botanic and common names.

Wrotham High Street

80

the converging M20 and M26 motorways, the background hum of traffic noise reasserted itself.

Past Yaldham Manor, the hedgerows were brutally massacred, with no tree being allowed to get established, thus, unfortunately, creating a featureless stretch of lane into Wrotham. This practice of mechanised hedge-cutting is something I detest and although I appreciate the economic efficiency of the activity, I don't see why some hedgerow saplings can't be identified, or planted, protected and allowed to grow into mature trees. If the practice continues unabated, the hedgerow trees will disappear in time and this would be a tragedy. The irony is that where the hedgerow is punctuated by, say, a telegraph pole, the mechanised cutting device cannot get close and often one finds hedgerow growth hugging the vertical element, just where it is not wanted. The bucolic lane with its flanking hedgerows are very much part of the highly valued, rural English landscape and I have often thought that the prospect could be improved, made more picturesque, by the judicious planting of new hedgerow trees.

Coming into Wrotham, I observed many discarded tyres in the hedgerow, and I could see the large 1960s council estate below the church, perched above Blacksole Field. This was the site of the famous battle where Sir Thomas Wyatt of Allington Castle and his supporters, who opposed the proposed marriage of Queen Mary and Philip of Spain, were defeated by the Queen's army. Sir Thomas paid the ultimate price for leading this rebellion. Also, across the field, the white scar slashing across the chalk escarpment carrying the M20 away to the north, could clearly be seen. The combined effect of all these factors created a rather scruffy landscape to the west of Wrotham. The village itself, with many fine houses, particularly along the historic High Street leading down to a distinctive church, lifted my spirits. The dead tree in the central space, which I referred to last time I passed through, had been removed and replaced with a mountain ash; I wished it luck.

I checked into The Bull Inn and recuperated. After a satisfactory meal, I went for a walk along the High Street and ended up in the Rose and Crown. There, I got talking to the landlord and joined him at the bar for a general knowledge quiz, in which we came a creditable second. A troop of morris dancers were engaged in their annual meeting and the political tension in the air could be cut with a knife. It appeared that the assembled ladies drinking in the bar were not allowed to take part in these proceedings. Later, I returned to The Bull Inn, hoping to get another drink but all was dark, locked and barred before closing time, so I turned in. I felt a bit like the highwayman may have felt in the poem of that name by Alfred Noyes when 'he tapped with his whip on the shutters, but all was locked and barred'. Indeed, the poem could well have been set in an old coaching inn, such as The Bull at Wrotham, twice by-passed by modern roads.

In the morning, I left Wrotham and headed east, up to the main roundabout on the A20. I crossed over the main road and stumbled along an old roadside path, which was badly overgrown in places and clearly barely used now. After a few hundred yards, I found a footpath that took me alongside the motorway, where I found a large, deserted area of fields returning to teasel-dominated wasteland. I saw a charm of goldfinches flitting between the teasels, feeding on their many seeds. Such a strip of land as this, between two main roads, is clearly unsuitable for a living place, and what dwellings there were seemed to have reverted to commercial premises of various descriptions. Places like this should formally be set aside for nature to return, since nature doesn't seem to mind the roar of traffic, or used as industrial or other commercial sites.

I found a lane going under the motorway and passed on to Little Wrotham, leaving the dreadful noise, untidiness, litter and mayhem behind. I emerged on an unfenced road onto the light-reflecting soil on the arable slopes below the downs. I located the straight footpath to Wrotham Water and picked up the lane to Trottiscliffe. As I had previously suspected, Trottiscliffe was a pleasant little village, once the home of the famous painter, Graham Sutherland, but some of his most famous landscapes are not of Kent but of the Pembrokeshire coast in Wales. I took the bridleway to Troseley Court, presumably the site of the original settlement given that the church was situated there, and cut diagonally across fields to join the Wealdway, affording panoramic views all round.

When I reached the road to Addington, I kept to the Wealdway going west and passed into a massive area devoted to the extraction of sand in extensive open cast pits, either side of the motorway. I stood for a while by a redundant travelator contraption and mused on the thought that these great holes in the ground, hidden in the midst of pleasant countryside, could only be used for accommodating society's waste or used as nature reserves, when extraction had stopped. There was little evidence of water in the pits, but this is not surprising since I guess the greensand would not hold the water, so I'm not sure what value they would have for wildlife habitats. I did notice, however, that there was a massive mound of blue-grey gault clay, which had clearly been scraped off and put to one side for reuse, allowing access to the vast depth of greensand strata below. There, one could see the layered geology of the Weald exposed for all to see.

I passed a sign which said, 'Slow Pedestrians Crossing' and I thought they had better hurry up a bit in case they got run over. As if to admonish me for this unkindly thought, the next moment, a massive earth-moving truck thundered around the bend and nearly knocked me down. The driver of the monster vehicle didn't even see me as I was no more significant in the scheme of things around there than a pedestrian ant. I crossed under the motorway and came across another sandpit, also disused, which had been allowed to revert to nature.

At this point, I left the Wealdway and made my way by footpaths to Addington Church, hoping to come across the long barrow marked on the map, but managing to miss it. At the end of the church drive, amidst a religious settlement by a wood, there was a notice proclaiming the presence of adders, since evidently one had bitten a local dog. From Addington Green I carried on south, across Plowenders Bridge and up to

Wrotham to West Malling

Adder
(Vipera berus)

Or common European viper is a widespread venomous snake, which has been the subject of much folklore in Britain and other European countries. The snake is not aggressive and usually only bites when alarmed or disturbed. Bites can be painful but are seldom fatal. It feeds on small mammals, birds, lizards, spiders, worms and insects. It can grow to a length of 90cm, has a large distinctive head and typically a zigzag pattern along its body. In the UK it is illegal to kill, injure, harm or sell adders under the 1981 Wildlife and Countryside Act.

Graham Sutherland
(1903-1980)

Was an English artist who was born in South London and lived for much of his life in Trottiscliffe. His early work was influenced by Samuel Palmer and his landscape paintings show an affinity with the work of Paul Nash. Like Nash, he was an official war artist during the Second World War, working mainly on the home front. He focussed on the inherent strangeness of natural forms, and abstracting them, sometimes giving his work a surreal appearance. Much of his work was inspired by the landscape of Pembrokeshire in South Wales. He famously painted a portrait of Winston Churchill in 1954, which was apparently destroyed on the orders of Lady Churchill, and designed the tapestry for Basil Spence's new Coventry Cathedral. Works such as *Oast House* and *Cray Fields* demonstrate his Kentish connection.

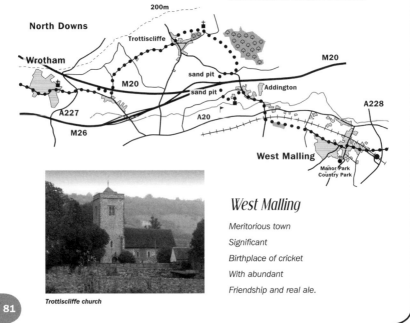

Trottiscliffe church

West Malling

Meritorious town

Significant

Birthplace of cricket

With abundant

Friendship and real ale.

81

the busy A20. Then I plunged down again, under the railway, to pick up a long straight footpath towards West Malling. At this point, I was beginning to struggle a bit with the journey, as my left knee was very painful, and decided to curtail this day's walk at West Malling.

I climbed up a steep rise onto a bluff by the heavily coppiced Stubbersdown Wood, besides horse-dominated fields, and stood for a while looking north, taking in the view. From this splendid vantage point, the whole valley beneath the North Downs was laid out before me. The regular line of the downs, from Bluebell Hill in the west to the Medway Gap, was peppered with white scars, the evidence of chalk quarrying in the past. Immediately below the downs there was the strip of rolling, translucent fields on the chalk, showing light green for pasture and pale brown for ploughed arable. Below that again is the greensand strata, which, west of Addington, has been heavily exploited and is pock-marked with massive sand pits. Down in the valley, the communications corridor rumbles on and the urban growth spills out west from Maidstone to the conglomerate settlements of New Hythe, Leybourne, Larkfield and Ditton.

At the end of the wood, another evocative vista opened up, this time down to the classic small Kentish town of West Malling, set among rolling slopes, dominated by a slender church spire. On the way down I passed beside an area of land given over to market gardening. The brown soil was intensively prepared, heavily watered and thrown up in precise, mechanically-cut ridges to receive crops to be grown in a strip arrangement, not dissimilar, I imagine, from the open field system employed in medieval times before the fields were enclosed. Hobbling down into West Malling, there were stunning views north across the valley to Ryarsh, Birling and the Medway Gap. This footpath, up past Stubbersdown Wood, is a splendid track offering wonderful views north and east, across the high vale between the chalk and the greensand. It is of a quality that would merit its inclusion in a more formalised, long-distance footpath, of which there are none in the vicinity of West Malling.

I struggled down the lane, past redundant orchards now looked after by the community, by the area called New Town, past the historic cricket ground and into the centre of West Malling. I kept my resolve and abandoned the day's walk, which should have terminated in Aylesford because of the condition of my left knee. I was hoping that if I rested the aforesaid joint that afternoon I might be able to travel on hopefully. A couple of days later, flushed with the success of making it to Deal, I completed the rest of this leg to Aylesford with some ease.

When I returned I bought a new map in West Malling, because my old Landranger Map had disintegrated, so I threw it away. The only map in the shop that covered the area I wanted to walk was an Explorer Map of Maidstone and The Medway towns, at a larger scale. I did feel somewhat disloyal, but soon found it much easier to work with. Thus, an accident of purchase introduced me to this new map and I did wonder if I could have avoided the many wrong turns of the past if I had been equipped with the excellent Explorer Maps.

I strode out of West Malling, past the Abbey, in the pleasant morning sunshine, passed under the railway and the massive A228, and found a well-organised footpath to Mill Street. There were some pleasant cottages interspersed with modern development hard up against the road, and the original mill building had been converted to an upmarket residential block. The old mill stands on a small stream that originates up on the Greensand Ridge flowing north to Ditton and eventually to the River Medway. Moving on east to the adjoining settlement of East Malling, I could see the church straight ahead. There was a pleasant grouping of buildings at the junction, including the church and pub, the original centre of the village. Unfortunately, on the corner opposite the pub, there were vacant retail premises, suggesting that these older buildings were struggling to find an economic use.

Passing out of the village past the church, I observed a massive yew tree in the churchyard and stunning views of the North Downs. I turned north towards Ditton and crossed over the access road to East Malling Horticultural Research Station. This famous research establishment has made an enormous contribution to agricultural progress, producing various varieties of raspberry and dwarfing root stock, to name but a few of its many achievements. I understand that the invention of dwarfing rootstock was never patented; thus, the public-serving research station never benefitted from the vast fortune that would have been generated by the use of this technology throughout the world. On the way to Ditton, I passed alongside the extensive orchards where much of the research was carried out.

Approaching Ditton, I got waylaid in a new housing estate, whose development had contrived to totally obliterate the footpath. I passed on into the centre of Ditton, lying well off the main A20 road, past the parish church set off behind a pleasant green, and a small parade of local shops and a pub. Carrying on up to the A20 I took the lane opposite, past a recreation ground, and crossed over the motorway and railway to emerge in a scruffy, haphazard industrial area by the River Medway in the vicinity of Aylesford Station, known as Millhall. There were actually some pleasant old cottages mixed in with all this mayhem and I did think this was a terrible waste of a superb riverside location. If the depots and factories could be relocated and a green park established, these dwellings would be in a great location and maybe the settlement could reinvent itself. However, unfortunately, the noisy, untidy industrial uses have to go somewhere. I passed a scrap metal processing yard, where squares of compressed metal were being dropped by a massive contraption into what was presumably a furnace, with the aim of melting the scrap into a more usable commodity.

I made it to the banks of the Medway as the tide was going out and walked the remaining half mile into the ancient riverside settlement of Aylesford. Strolling beside a small wood between the river and the railway, I looked across the river to The Friars, a modern working monastery. If Henry VIII were alive today I'm sure he would have something to say about this prosperous religious establishment.

As I approached the many-arched stone bridge there was a magnificent prospect of Aylesford with its church hanging over the village on the north bank of the river. I triumphantly strode over the bridge and repaired to the Chequers Inn in the narrow, traffic-calmed, High Street. I ordered a pint, went outside and sat in the pub garden, just as I had done a few days before when I first arrived there, and marvelled at the incredible view. This was a special spot: one of the few where one can get close to the river in its lower reaches, with a fabulous, mesmerising view of the river by the ancient bridge, whose importance lies in the fact that it was historically the lowest crossing point of the River Medway upstream from Rochester.

When I first arrived in Aylesford, I searched out my berth for the night, which was a large house down by the river on what would have been the river quay at one time. It was a splendid house with a lovely terraced, award-winning garden stretching back to the road. My hosts made me very comfortable and volunteered the information that Aylesford, although very close to Maidstone and the urban sprawl around Ditton, remained a separate entity by virtue of the river and a large industrial estate north of the river at Forstal. This seemed a curious virtue to attach to one of several massive industrial estates in this part of Kent.

Leaving Aylesford to the sound of church bells peeling to the count of nine, I cut down through riverside gardens. Finding my way barred along the footpath on the north bank of the river, I crossed back over by the new road bridge. I scrambled alongside the river, between it and the railway, along the Medway Valley Walk, until I came to the curious little hamlet of Little Preston, whose sole access appeared to be directly from the motorway, junction 5 to the south. I pressed on, along the other side of the railway, mounting a small river bluff, to cross back over the motorway and railway, before descending to Allington Lock.

Coming down to the river at the highest point of its tidal reach, I was astonished at how shallow the river became at low tide and realised why boats could only pass to and fro at high tide. At the cleanly presented Allington Lock, I crossed over the river again and sheltered from a heavy shower under the dense foliage of a weeping willow tree. I marvelled at this clinical installation, made massive by the size of the river it was attempting to control, with its lock, weirs and ringing metal footways. Crossing over lock gates gives that same frisson of fear as crossing a railway line.

From Allington Lock, I plodded on along the riverside into Maidstone, initially using the trees as shelter while it was still raining, taking on the big bend in the river. At the apex of the bend I glimpsed Allington Castle through a gap in the trees by its water gate. I was surprised how close this authentic-looking, privately owned castle was to the river, secluded in its enclave in a bend of the river, separated from the urban area of Maidstone by a railway line. This castle was the ancestral home of Thomas Wyatt, referred to earlier, regarding his revolt in the Blacksole Field by Wrotham. Carrying on into Maidstone, the rain eased up, but then it was a disadvantage to be under trees as the wind blew the residual moisture out of the branches to drip down my neck.

Approaching Maidstone town centre, past the rowing club, I walked along a concrete riverside promenade before cutting up into the centre of the county town. The central spine of the town, which used to be along the old A20, is a former wide market street with a narrow strip of buildings, including the town hall, built down the middle. From the town hall, the southern part of the High Street is pedestrianised and lined with notable medieval buildings. However, this obvious, rich heritage seemed

West Malling to Maidstone

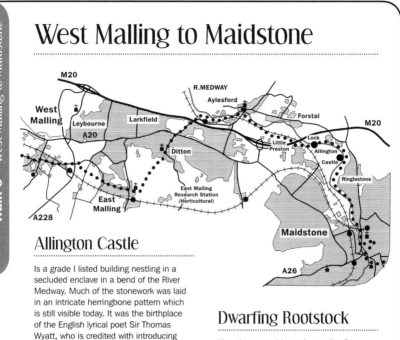

Allington Castle

Is a grade I listed building nestling in a secluded enclave in a bend of the River Medway. Much of the stonework was laid in an intricate herringbone pattern which is still visible today. It was the birthplace of the English lyrical poet Sir Thomas Wyatt, who is credited with introducing the sonnet into the English language. His son, the rebel leader Thomas Wyatt, was born in 1521. Towards the end of the sixteenth century, while under the ownership of the Wyatt family, the castle was badly damaged by fire. It was largely derelict until 1905, when it was restored, remaining in private ownership today.

Allington Castle

Aylesford

Perched prominent on

The river's bend

Flushed out twice daily

A tidal trend

For this historic Medway crossing.

Dwarfing Rootstock

Have been used in apple growing for over 2,000 years, and were probably discovered by chance in China. From 1912, research workers at the East Malling Research Station began to collect existing rootstock, and systematically test and classify material, resulting in a standardisation of apple tree rootstocks. The original classification is no longer used and only two of the original selections, M7 and M9, are still used commercially. In collaboration with other research stations, and extensive breeding programmes involving the cloning of vegetative material, there are five commonly used rootstocks in the Malling–Merton series: M25 (very vigorous), M26 (moderately dwarfing), M27(very dwarfing), MM106 (moderately vigorous) and MM111 (vigorous).

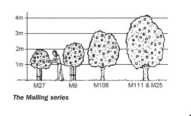

The Malling series

82

221

to be somewhat neglected in the hustle and bustle of the big town, with many of the retail premises being empty. It does occur to me, with the changing patterns of retail provision epitomised by out-of-town shopping centres, that there is bound to be less demand for marginally placed retail outlets in towns and cities; thus, the solution, surely, especially in the case of buildings of merit, is to allow them to revert to other uses, such as offices, if the demand exists, or even better housing, if the money required for expensive conversions could be found. In this way, the historical nature and appeal of such places can be preserved.

Making my way back to the river and past old, riverside, religious buildings by the ring-road, following my nose, through another heavy shower, I found the entrance to Mote Park. I followed the cycle route through the park, below the cricket ground that used to be a venue for Kent County Cricket Club. I wondered what the official explanation was for abandoning this venue, since it could not make economic sense, given the population of the Maidstone area. I came down to a large lake, created in the valley of the River Len, and observed an imposing white house on the other side, an arrangement that reminded me of Danson Park in Bexley. Down by the boathouse there was an area of the lake roped off for model speedboat enthusiasts to put their toys through their paces, making an incredible din in the process. While not wishing to cast aspersions on anybody obsessed with an anorak hobby, because I've probably got a few myself, I did think this particular one was pretty mindless.

I passed right in front of the white mansion over the lake, the so-called Mote House, which was boarded off, preparing itself for a new rein-carnation in a perfect setting as a retirement home. In front of the building were many splendid, mature oak and sweet chestnut trees, looking very stately, having had the room to spread their branches in a parkland setting. Further on, as is the modern trend, the interminable acres of mown grass were softened by unmown strips allowed to revert to a more natural habitat. The eastern end of the park was deserted and less manicured, allowing wildlife to return and probably to save the council money.

At the end of the path through the park, I emerged by a busy local road, which I crossed with some difficulty to find a signpost indicating a Len Valley Walk. There, I had a choice to make; I could follow the Len Valley Walk, hoping to emerge eventually below Penfold Hill on the

Leeds road, or I could strike up to Otham and across to Leeds Village, as I had planned. I chose the former and for a while it seemed to be a good choice. I passed on through a well-used suburban park with an attractive, crowded lake graced by a variety of ducks, Canada Geese and young swans noisily exercising their wings.

Carrying on with the river on one side and the burgeoning estates of Bearsted on the other, I came to a point where the footpath dramatically petered out. It should have carried on along the river, but it was quite obvious that somebody didn't want this to happen, as it was clearly blocked. I had no choice but to strike up through the modern estates, asking directions a couple of times to the main A20 and the centre of Bearsted. Cutting my loses, I found a lively pub, The Lion of Kent: a splendid name for a pub. Sitting at the bar, drying off and smelling a bit high, I studied the menu. I went for a starter as I didn't think I could manage a full meal from the carvery and ordered crab fish cakes and guacamole. They were absolutely lovely, washed down by tied house beer.

I started to enjoy myself watching a football match on the big screen and talking to locals, so, indulgently, I had a few more pints on this Saturday lunchtime. I was informed that the real centre of Bearsted lay north of the A20 at Bearsted Green, by the church, and I resolved to visit one day. I got talking to the barmaid who was studying at my old university in Oxford and this lifted my spirits enormously. After self-indulgently consuming probably five pints, and not wishing to walk down the busy A20 to my berth for the night, I ordered a taxi to take me down the road.

After a satisfactory meal in the expensive motel, I spent most of the evening sitting at the bar, drinking double gin and tonics, entertaining the many foreign guests with pidgin English. I did feel that the management should have paid me a retainer to sit there entertaining their guests. I was certainly just as deserving of this remuneration as the terrible piano player who was just pleased if he hit the right notes.

I left the hotel early on a bright sunny morning, with the mist still swirling around on top of the downs. Coming out on the main A20, I proceeded to the nearby roundabout and took the road leading to the village of Leeds. I crossed over the River Len and proceeded up Penfold Hill to Burberry Lane, and from the back of the curiously shaped church I picked up the footpath through the grounds of Leeds Castle. There were a number of elegant lakes fashioned out of the waters of the River

223

Maidstone to Leeds

Leeds Castle

Is a picturesque castle built on islands in a lake formed from the waters of the River Len, with a long history of royal patronage. Built in 1119 as a Norman stronghold, it came into the ownership of Edward I and his queen, Eleanor of Castile, in 1278, was substantially redeveloped and became a favourite royal residence throughout the Middle Ages. It was later transformed by Henry VIII in 1519 for his first wife, Catherine of Aragon. The castle escaped destruction during the English Civil War, because its owner, Sir Cheney Culpeper, sided with the Parliamentarians. Other members of this notable Kentish family sided with the Royalists, and John, first Lord Culpepper, was rewarded with land in Virginia for assisting the escape of the Prince of Wales.

The River Len

Is a 10-mile tributary of the River Medway, rising in Affer's Wood on the Greensand Ridge, south-east of the village of Lenham, just over half a mile from the source of the Great Stour River. It runs in a generally westerly direction, running parallel to the M20 motorway for the first part of its journey, before forming the lake in Leeds Castle. It then flows through Mote Park, forming the large picturesque lake in Maidstone, after which it enters the River Medway. The river powered many water mills on its course and its tributaries in the parishes of Ulcombe, Leeds, Hollingbourne, Boxley and Maidstone. Many of these mills were concerned with fulling, the cleansing of wool in the cloth-making process, by the use of fullers earth dug up locally.

This American connection was to prove vital for the castle's fortunes, and Thomas Fairfax, sixth Lord of Cameron, the great grandson of Thomas Fairfax who led the parliamentarian attack at the Battle of Maidstone in 1648, was born at the castle in 1693. He settled permanently in America to oversee the Culpeper estates, and cement the relationship with America.

In 1793 the castle was sold by Robert Fairfax to the Wykeham Martins, and sale of the family estate in Virginia released large sums of money to allow the castle to be extensively remodelled in a more appropriate Tudor style, completed in 1823, which resulted in the appearance seen today.

The last private ownership of the castle ended in 1974, with the estate being left to the Leeds Castle Foundation, a private charitable trust whose aim was to preserve the castle and its grounds for the benefit of the public. The castle was opened to the public in 1974 and hosted the Northern Ireland peace talks held in September 2004 and led by the Prime Minister at the time, Tony Blair. The castle and its grounds are now a major international tourist attraction, which attracted over half a million visitors in 2010.

83

Len, right in front of the famous, moated castle: an impressive pile indeed. I skirted a lovely lake, glistening in the early morning sun, whose banks were the subject of a habitat conservation scheme to benefit the future viability of the water vole. Talking to a lady attendant, I found out that the castle was closed to the public that day, so I had the place delightfully to myself as walking on the public footpath through the grounds was free. As I strolled through the park, a whole gaggle of Canada Geese decided to emerge from the lake and cross the path right in front of me, blocking my passage, making a huge indignant racket in the process.

To the east of the castle, the path passed through a golf course before emerging again on the busy A20 trunk road. I passed under the motorway and the new railway, and hiked up the lane, under the old railway, towards Greenway Court. There were donkeys in a field opposite a scruffy complex of farm buildings hard up against the lane. There were also some pleasant cottages there but the prospect was spoilt by the disrespectful farm. On my travels, I have found that it is not uncommon for some farms to show a total disrespect for the care of the countryside and its appearance, not realising, or even caring, that this is one of the greatest assets of the English countryside. Thankfully this occurrence is fairly unusual and generally speaking farmers take their role as custodians of the countryside seriously.

I took the footpath across wide, undulating fields, beneath the scarp slope of the North Downs, on the way up into Salisbury Wood. In the lower field below the Pilgrim's Way, there was a pile of recently cut logs smelling very fragrant. The hedgerows surrounding this large field were peppered with brown trees, which were unfortunately horse chestnut trees afflicted with the blight caused by a virulent leaf minor, which turns the leaves brown and causes them to drop way before their time, thus weakening the trees. This is an epidemic that appears to be as serious as that which befell our native elm trees during the 1970s. Crossing over the Pilgrim's Way, I proceeded up the slope, across the arable, chalk-based fields that can be seen along the whole length of the North Downs from Westerham to Dover. This effectively consists of a piedmont, admittedly not as vast as the geological formation in Italy below the Alps from which it is named, as the scarp has retreated over time due to erosion.

Looking back down into the valley, I was struck by the rush of traffic in what is, and always has been, a communications corridor. The whole valley, from the Greensand Ridge to the Chalk Downs was filled with noise, especially from the motorway. At the very highest edge of the fields there was a narrow strip of land that could only be 'set aside', which gave a wonderful display of wild flowers, including purple poppies (the red ones having gone over), sorrel, ragwort, thistles and the yellow flower of a plant from the dandelion family. It was an amazing, spirit-lifting show at the field's edge, underneath the wood. The cut logs I had smelt down in the valley were cut out of Salisbury Wood; they were Corsican Pine, which were evidently struggling to survive on the thin chalk soils. Consequently, the Woodlands Trust were removing them with the objective of opening up the woodland canopy to let in light and encourage the growth of broadleaved trees and diversity of species.

I carried on across fields on top of the downs to Ringlestone Road, converging on a route previously taken up through High Wood, across the field to my left. Even there, on top of the downs, I could still hear the noise of the motorway, much more intrusive than any railway could be. And so, after walking down the lane towards Ringlestone, I came again to the Black Post at the top of Stede Hill, a spot I had been through on two previous occasions. My intention was to walk down to Ringlestone Hamlet and take a footpath north to the village of Frinsted. On the way

Leeds to Frinsted

Horse Chestnut
(Aesculus hippocastanum)

Is a large deciduous tree growing up to 30 metres, introduced into Britain in the late sixteenth century. It has become the typical tree of village greens and city parks.

Distinctive white flowers are produced in the spring in erect panicles. Normally five leaflets comprise a compound leaf, and the fruit - shiny brown nut-like seeds known as conkers - develop within a spiky green capsule.

The common name horse chestnut is reported as having originated from the erroneous belief that the tree was a kind of chestnut, together with the observation that when eaten by horses, despite being poisonous, they cured equine chest complaints.

The tree has suffered increased levels of attack from the horse chestnut leaf miner, a moth which was first observed in Macedonia in 1984, being described soon after as a new species. Severely damaged leaves shrivel and turn brown by late summer and fall early, well before normal leaf fall in the autumn. Despite the unsightly appearance of infested trees, there is no evidence that damage by the insect leads to tree death. Trees survive repeated infestations and re-flush normally and it would appear that the damage caused occurs too late in the growing season to significantly affect tree performance.

Leeds Castle

Water Vole
(Arvicola amphibius)

This small mammal is widespread around Europe, living in the banks of slow-moving rivers, streams and other waterways. The waterside burrows of these strong swimmers have many floor levels that protect against flooding, as well as nesting chambers and a food store for the long winter months. Although they are a quick meal for predators, the UK population has suffered a catastrophic decline after the naturalisation of the American mink. They are often mistaken for rats. Ratty, a character in Kenneth Grahame's The Wind in The Willows was actually a water vole.

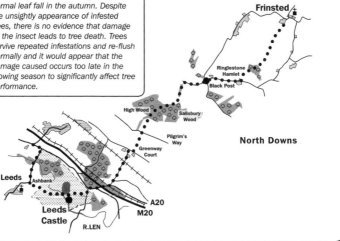

to Ringlestone I got caught up in the slipstream of many cyclists out for a glorious ride that Sunday morning. From the lane I could clearly see Kingsnorth Power Station and across the Thames to the extremely foreign county of Essex. I think the only time the inhabitants of these two most south-easterly counties have cooperated with one another was in the Peasants' Revolt, and that was unsuccessful.

I rested outside the Ringlestone Inn for a while, taking the opportunity to apply lashings of painkilling gel to my left knee. I then headed north along a well-appointed footpath, resisting the temptation to plunge down into the dry valley that swept all the way down to Sittingbourne, keeping high to the pleasant village of Frinsted. The next village on my gradual descent down the dip slope of the North Downs was the linear village of Milstead. In the centre of the village, I passed the church and a spectacular cedar tree on a small, triangular green outside the prosaic village hall. Thereafter, the M2 severs the village along Rawling Street, visually and psychologically, if not actually, from the houses and pub at its northern extremities.

Further down the lane, on the way to Rodmersham Green, I passed an orchard of mature cherry trees. This is a sight that has become increasingly rare recently, since cherry cultivation today, in this area of North Kent which is famous for them, is now largely managed on dwarfing root stock, many of the old orchards having been grubbed up. Coming into Rodmersham Green by Bottles Lane, I passed the cricket ground that was hosting a lively village fete or the like. Across a massive, ploughed field that reminded me of an open field in medieval times, before an extensive orchard, I could see across the top of Rodmersham Church to the Isle of Sheppey. There was a satisfying group of buildings around the dissected green at Rodmersham Green and I popped into the Fruiterers Arms for something to eat and drink.

Leaving the village, past some lovely cottages overlooking the green, I took a footpath through productive orchards towards Rodmersham Church. As I plodded on, I was more and more conscious of how much this area, as was indicated by the name of the pub, was dedicated to fruit-growing. On that Sunday afternoon the countryside was empty of people. Not for the first time, I passed a complex of farm buildings that exuded age, as if these fruit-growing activities had remained unchanged for many centuries, and this is probably not far from the truth. The yard was stacked full of fruit cages, which would very soon be brought into action,

Frinsted to Bapchild

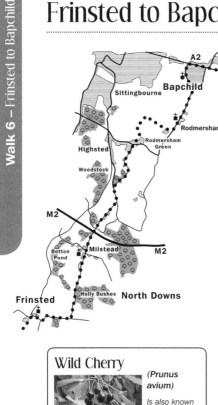

Cherry Cultivation

There are two species of native wild cherry in the Kent countryside: the gean (Prunus avium) and the dwarf or wild cherry (Prunus cerasus). It is thought that cultivated cherries were first introduced by the Romans, but cherry orchards first became common in the sixteenth century during the reign of King Henry VIII, at the hands of Richard Harris, fruiterer to the King. During the seventeenth century there was a massive expansion in cherry cultivation in North Kent, from Thanet and Sandwich in the East to Dartford, Erith and Woolwich in the west, which helped to create the idea of Kent as 'the garden of England'.

Cultivation has declined in recent years, with many old orchards being grubbed up, so that the evocative sight of traditional cherry blossom in spring in orchards undergrazed by sheep has become rare. There are many factors leading to this decline. Cherries are difficult to pick, requiring long ladders and an army of seasonal labour. In recent years many mature trees have succumbed to disease, and cheaper foreign imports have made cherry cultivation uneconomic.

Following a campaign to promote Kentish cherries, the acreage of production is increasing, but modern cultivation is on dwarfing rootstock which makes the management and harvesting of the crop much easier. Brogdale National Fruit Collection, near Faversham, holds many old varieties of the fruit. Traditional cherry orchards are now valued and conserved in certain locations.

Wild Cherry

(Prunus avium)

Is also known as the sweet cherry, bird cherry or gean and is a deciduous tree native to Europe, including the UK. It occurs in woods and hedgerows, reaching a height of 25 metres in favourable conditions. The bark is smooth purplish-brown and peels off in horizontal strips with age. It typically exhibits copious blossom in spring and produces a stone fruit which is readily eaten by numerous birds and animals. Wild cherries have been an item of human food for several thousands of years. The stones have been found in deposits at Bronze Age settlements throughout Europe, including Britain. It is often grown as a flowering ornamental tree and planted in parkland, along city streets and in gardens.

The Fruiterers Arms, Rodmersham Green

groaning with apples and pears picked from the surrounding fields. The unimproved nature of the brick buildings on that warm, sunny afternoon gave a timeless quality to the locality. In the hamlet of Rodmersham I came across another orchard of mature cherry trees, just where they should have been, opposite the church. In the churchyard, on the frontage to the lane, there was a row of eight ancient yew trees in the original pleasant settlement before the centre of population moved up the hill to the green.

Entering the compact settlement of Bapchild, I passed St Laurence church with a spire that reminded me of those common on Romney Marsh. I reached the main A2 opposite the Fox and Goose pub, and proceeded eastwards along the main road to my hotel. Whilst I'm sure there are some pleasant streets in Bapchild, away from the main road, this stretch was pretty desperate. In the evening, as I had no desire to slog back up the road, I stayed in the expensive hotel. At dinner, in this rather august, upmarket establishment, one was served by waiters with one arm tucked behind their back and one arm draped with a white cloth. I amused myself in engaging the poor fellows in rather common conversation while slurping pints of lager at the table, much to the disapproval of fellow diners on nearby tables drinking wine.

In the morning, for a mile or so, I struggled along the A2 to Teynham, carrying my box, because the hotel was unwilling to post it for me, until I could find a post office. I passed a number of old properties full of character, totally ruined by their location, hard up against the busy trunk road. In Teynham also, the cottages often fronted directly onto the busy main road, seriously detracting from the appeal of the place. I posted my box and proceeded north towards the station, where there were some more pleasant if unremarkable streets. Once over the railway, however, in the relatively inaccessible hamlet of Barrow Green, there were some charming cottages in a scruffy, quirky, rural-type setting amid horse pastures and allotments. The area around Teynham is reputed to be the location of the first orchards planted by Richard Harris, fruiterer to King Henry VIII and this gives rise eventually to Kent being regarded as the Garden of England. From Barrow Green I took the footpath across flat, sheep-infested fields to Conyer.

There were some interesting modern dwellings in Conyer, taking advantage of the riverside location, amidst a confusion of maritime activities. I walked in beside the creek, which formed a haven for many types of boats and equipment connected to the sea. Every small part of river frontage was occupied with this paraphernalia and jealously guarded, with many 'Private: Keep Out' signs. As a consequence, there was nowhere for the public to view the scene and appreciate the creek, apart from the garden of the large pub, The Ship, before the wharf. Conyer seemed a chaotic, totally unplanned settlement and I mused on the proposition that public spaces define the quality of places, but were greatly lacking in Conyer.

I picked up the Saxon Shore Way, which was channelled out of Conyer behind high fences, and strolled out onto the marshes, helping myself to blackberries from the hedgerows. I have observed that the biggest, cleanest and most tasty blackberry normally resides at the very tip of the fruiting spur. All of a sudden, I emerged onto a marsh-side bank, leading down to the Swale Estuary, giving splendid atmospheric views out over Teynham Level. The day was heating up as I reached the Swale, with the sun shining in a cloudless sky, and the tide was out. I slipped down the inland side of the bank, out of the cold northerly breeze, looking out over the peaceful marsh, and rested for a while.

Looking out over Fowley Island in the Swale Estuary, it was possible to imagine how once, before the River Thames settled in its current position, that the Swale was a mighty river in its own right, flowing eastwards into the North Sea to join the River Rhine, before the southern North Sea was flooded at the end of the last Ice Ages. As I proceeded eastwards, around countless sinuous bends on the bank of the Swale, I could see the Isle of Harty up ahead getting closer all the time. It looked higher than its 27m above sea level, but that may have been accounted for by the fact that it was low tide, probably adding many metres above the water level. Pacing along the bank, I disturbed a common newt as it was sunning itself, which scampered off into the long grass for protection. I passed piles of concrete blocks and disused bases, the remnants of long-abandoned buildings and fortifications, which I thought could be broken up and used to supplement and extend the protective boulders in the sea wall. There were boats moored out in the Swale and I did wonder how anybody could get out to them in the first place, except by using another boat.

Below the hamlet of Uplees, I came across a substantial, disused dry dock, evidence of former industry. Looking along the coast, I could clearly see Whitstable dominating the estuary across Faversham Creek and the Graveney Marshes. In time, I came to the Oare Nature Reserve with a kestrel hovering expectantly above the reeds. I passed the jetty where the ferry used to ply back and forth to the Isle of Harty, and looked longingly across the water, hoping one day to make a crossing. Striding on to the point, I observed a wide variety of birds dotted around in the complex network of islands, lagoons and marsh. I spoke to a birdwatcher who explained that the main event, the autumn migration, had not yet got into gear; thus, there wasn't anything special to see. If I had had more time to linger I would have been perfectly happy to shack up in one of the many observation points and take a rest, and to see what I could see.

Making my way down Faversham Creek, there were rotting hulks of barges marooned on muddy banks. The opposite bank was lined with boats and I did wonder how often they were allowed an outing into the waters of the Swale and beyond to fulfil their purpose in life. The rigging striking the aluminium masts made that distinctive clanking sound that I have remarked on before, but because some masts were bigger than others, and the oscillating ropes were therefore of a different length, the noise made varied in rhythm and pitch, creating a subtle musical percussion symphony, not unlike repetitive electronic music.

Ahead of me was the village of Oare, occupying the higher ground beside the creek, which at this point was reduced to a soodling thread of water. There was a church up on the ridge, with a graveyard tumbling down to the flat fields beside the creek, but there was curiously no footpath across to the church. The dissected banks of mud across the creek looked like a row of massive crocodiles sliding into the water, their nostrils flared at the water line and their eyebrows, marked green with high water patches of vegetation above clearly discernible eye sockets.

Reaching the first road, I was able to gain access to the former coastal village. There were two pubs there and I was determined to try both. Access to the village is by a steep little rise above the flat land bordering the creek, where the road narrows, passing between sheer walls of buildings: a space that could easily be blocked in times of invasion or flood. It reminded very much of the arrangement at Appledore facing on to Romney Marsh. I had a pint in the higher pub, The Three Mariners, which seemed to be mainly geared up to lunchtime meals, before retiring to the lower pub, The Castle, facing the flat plain bordering the creek, for a few more pints and something to eat.

I sat in the small garden, somewhat spoilt by parked cars, looking across to a strip of grassland, grazed by cattle, on the valley side below the main residential part of Oare, managed by the Kent Wildlife Trust. The landlady come out of the pub and tipped a bucket of vegetable remains over the gate to feed the expectant group of cows gathered there. Oare, I felt, was an interesting, unmanicured sort of place, rather neglected at the sea end of Faversham, with a distinctive structure that would benefit from a local village plan proposing a few careful improvements in traffic and pedestrian circulation. There was a large patch of fenced-off land opposite the pub, below the slope, which looked as though it may have once had a building on it and was waiting for redevelopment. If this was the case, it would be a disaster since this area should be incorporated into the area managed for wildlife by the Trust, and used to improve pedestrian access along the road. I reflected on the idea that Oare, along with many other spots in the North Kent Marshes, like Cliffe and Queenborough, now much reduced in importance, would once have been thriving places in their own right before the various estuaries silted up.

I slogged on through the northern outskirts of Faversham, past Davington, once a distinctive settlement with its own parish church on its

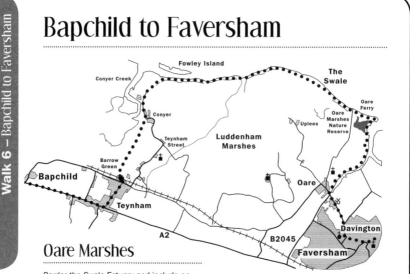

Bapchild to Faversham

Oare Marshes

Border the Swale Estuary and include an internationally important nature reserve known especially as a site for migrating birds. The reserve consists of 81 hectares of grazing marsh with freshwater dykes, open water 'scrapes', seawall and saltmarsh, on the mainland opposite the Isle of Sheppey. Suitable habitat is achieved through the manipulation of water levels and livestock grazing. Among the breeding species found here are pied avocet, common redshank, common snipe, northern lapwing, water rail, bearded reedling, common tern and garganey. Migrating species include black-tailed godwit, ruff, little stint, curlew, sandpiper and whimbrel. Overwintering species include brent goose, dunlin, Eurasian curlew, Eurasian wigeon, merlin, hen harrier, short-eared owl, Eurasian bittern and twite.

The land, which is known for its tranquil remoteness, was used from 1787 until 1916 for the manufacture of gunpowder. The Harty Ferry to the Isle of Sheppey used to operate from the jetty at the north of the reserve. The muddy Oare creek forms the eastern edge of the reserve, leading inland to the village of the same name. There is a history of boat building, and the repair of historic boats and Thames sailing barges in the creek. Below the village is Oare Meadow, also operated, like the Oare Marshes, by the Kent Wildlife Trust.

Faversham

Medieval streets

So well preserved

On a muddy creek

Nicely conserved

Endorsed by King Stephen and his consort.

Common Newt
(Lissotriton vulgaris)

Also known as the smooth newt, is the most common species of amphibian in Britain. It is about 10 cm in length and both sexes are of a similar size and colour, pale brown to yellow, except in the breeding season, when the male develops a wavy crest along the spine. They emerge from hibernation on land from February and head to fresh water to breed, favouring ponds and shallow lakesides by running water. Tadpoles emerge in spring and typically leave water after ten weeks. While the species is by no means endangered, in the UK the common newt is protected under schedule 5 of the Wildlife and Countryside Act (1981) with respect to sale only.

86

own little hill. Then I trundled on past the lake that forms the source of Faversham Creek to locate the fabulous West Street, which took me into the centre of the town. I have rarely seen such a long, perfectly preserved and intact medieval street anywhere in Britain. The pedestrianised street contained buildings with that typical, first-floor overhang, and my accommodation for the night, The Sun Inn, was one of them. In the evening I had a walk around Faversham, as I had promised myself last time I was there, to take in the full splendour of the old town centre.

In the evening, leaning on the bar of The Sun Inn, I got talking to a group of chaps who were keen on walking and compared notes. Three of the chaps were firemen who had completed many long and arduous charity walks in their time. The last fireman standing, as we approached last orders, having been born in Sheerness on the Isle of Sheppey, was interested in my previously reported unquenched ambition to cross the Swale, at the old Harty Ferry. He boldly proposed that we should paddle across the water in a canoe and was keen to organise it straight away. I sheepishly agreed to think about it and get back to him, if I could work it into my next walk.

After a faltering start in the morning, due to the fact that the post office decided not to open until 9.30 a.m., I made my way past the town hall down Abbey Street, to find the parish church. I passed by the abbey, whose most famous guests are King Stephen and his consort Matilda, to pick up the Swale Heritage Trail from the side of the church by the grammar school. I walked out past recreation grounds across the backs of houses to emerge into the sunlit fields by an exotic-looking tree with large oval leaves, which I thought might be an Indian Bean Tree. I pressed on through a low, water-logged hollow and across a railway line to pass through a hop field that was already harvested bare. I came across another Indian Bean Tree and a field of strawberries being picked by a gang of migrant workers. In the middle of the fruit farm I reached Goodnestone Church, in the care of the Churches Conservation Trust, and rested for a while, sitting on the graveyard wall opposite a massive old yew tree.

Across the lane to Graveney, I timidly walked through an aggressive fruit farm, down into a shallow valley littered with fruit-picking detritus. I crossed a small stream feeding the Graveney Marshes and thrust on towards Wey Street Farm, where I got waylaid in a dense wood. Initially, I lost the way before finding the infrequently used path up the bluff on

Faversham to Dargate

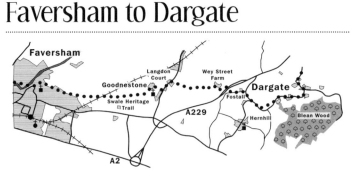

King Stephen and Matilda

King Stephen was a grandson of William the Conqueror and reigned from 1135 to his death in Dover in 1154. His reign was marked by the Anarchy, a civil war with his cousin and rival to the throne, the Empress Matilda, who was the daughter of Henry I. Henry's son, William, the rightful heir to the throne, was drowned in the sinking of the White Ship in 1120. Stephen was also aboard and narrowly escaped drowning. He married Matilda of Boulogne, inheriting additional estates in Kent and Boulogne that made the couple one of the wealthiest in England. When Henry I died in 1135 Stephen quickly crossed the Channel and took the throne, reneging on his earlier oaths to support the claim of Henry I's daughter, the Empress Matilda.

The early years of his reign were largely successful, despite attacks on his territories by David I of Scotland, Welsh rebels and Empress Matilda's husband, Geoffrey of Anjou. The civil war was ushered in by the invasion of Robert of Gloucester, Empress Matilda's half-brother, in 1139, who took control of the south-west of England. Stephen was captured in the battle of Lincoln in 1141, and was abandoned by many of his followers, losing control of Normandy in the process. He was only freed after his wife and William of Ypres, one of his military commanders, captured Robert at the Rout of Winchester. The civil war dragged on for many years with neither side able to gain the advantage.

Stephen became increasingly concerned that his son, Eustace, should inherit the throne. In 1153 Henry FitzEmpress, son of Empress Matilda, invaded England and built an alliance with powerful regional barons to support his claim to the throne. The two armies squared up to each other at Wallingford, but neither side were keen to engage in another pitched battle, and Stephen, after the sudden death of Eustace, began to examine a negotiated peace. Stephen and Henry agreed the treaty of Winchester later in the year, in which Stephen recognised Henry as his heir in exchange for peace, passing over William, his second son.

Stephen died the following year and is buried with his wife, Matilda, in the ruins of Faversham Abbey, and Henry became Henry II, Empress Matilda's son, the first Angevin king.

The Swale Heritage Trail

Is a relatively short footpath of 11 miles from Murston, north-east of Sittingbourne, to Goodnestone, near the village of Graveney, inland from the Saxon Shore Way. It passes through Conyer, situated on a creek off the Swale, and skirts the back of Luddenham Marshes to Oare, also situated on a distinctive creek. The trail then passes through the historic centre of Faversham to end at the redundant church in Goodnestone, under the care of the Churches Conservation Trust. This trail, promoted by Swale District Council, which ends abruptly at Goodnestone, would lend itself to an extension to Herne Hill and The Blean NNR.

which the farm was located, passing again through orchards to come up against the A229 Thanet Way. Crossing over the main road I reached the pleasant hamlet of Fostall, attached to the village of Hernhill further south. The sandy hills thereabouts, under the shadow of Blean Wood, were riddled with disused sandpits.

This was the westernmost extension of The Blean, a vast area of ancient woodland stretching for 11 miles from Hernhill to Maypole between Canterbury and the North Kent towns of Whitstable and Herne Bay. The woods, which are situated on the more recent tertiary sand and gravel deposits, were laid down over the eroded lower cretaceous surface of the chalk strata, and this discontinuity robs Kent of evidence in the rocks of the K2 boundary: the geological division between the Cretaceous and Tertiary periods when the dinosaurs were wiped out. Thus, there is very little point in trying to find the fossil evidence of dinosaurs in the rocks of Kent.

I took lunch in the Dove Inn at Dargate, not wishing to test its excellent reputation for food, but happy to sit at the bar drinking a couple of pints of the local brew, which in this part of the world is inevitably from the Faversham Brewery. I amused an elderly couple out for a lunchtime drink by rolling up my trouser leg and applying painkilling gel while sitting on a bar stool. Waking out of Dargate, I was surrounded by a flock of swallows taking advantage of the late summer insects on offer. The noise of traffic from the Thanet Way became more evident as I approached Yorkletts, which consisted merely of a string of modern bungalows and a few older houses: not a proper place in my under-standing of the word. I passed the entrance to Victory Wood, an extension of Blean Wood, an open-access area looked after, like so many woods in Kent, by the excellent Woodlands Trust.

When I pass through a place like Yorkletts, my natural instinct is to think of ways in which it could be improved. In this case, there is the desperate need for a focal point, maybe with a shop, pub and some public space. Also, it would be desirable to plant a wood hard up against the Thanet Way to shield the village from the worst effects of noise and pollution from the road. Between the newly planted wood and the existing road through Yorkletts would be the natural place for further development.

I dived down under the Thanet Way and emerged on Seasalter Level, picking blackberries from the side of the lane. It never ceases to amaze

Dargate to Whitstable

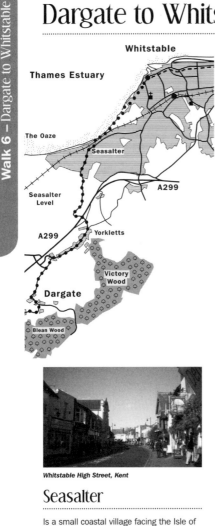

The Blean

Is the largest area of ancient, broadleaved woodland in southern Britain at about 11 square miles. Lying between Canterbury and the coastal towns of Faversham, Whitstable and Herne Bay, it is now divided into separate woods. It stretches from Hernhill and Boughton Street in the west to Maypole and Hoath in the east. The village of Blean itself, on the A290 Canterbury to Whitstable road, lies in the middle of what once was the Medieval Forest of Blean. Today, part of the area, Blean Woods, is a National Nature Reserve managed by the RSPB. And Clowes Wood is a large, open-access area.

Trees found here include hornbeam, hazel, beech, oak, birch and sweet chestnut. Brambles, bracken and bluebells are dominant on the woodland floor, but plants such as common spotted orchid, common centaury and St John's wort are found in woodland rides. The Blean is home to many forest birds such as woodpeckers, tree creepers and nuthatch, spotted flycatcher, nightjar, bullfinch and hawfinch. There is also an important population of nightingales. The woods are one of the few places in Britain that supports the heath fritillary butterfly and the scarce seven spotted ladybird.

Whitstable High Street, Kent

Seasalter

Is a small coastal village facing the Isle of Sheppey across the Swale Estuary, that is contiguous with Whitstable. Historically, the settlement came to prominence as a centre for salt production in the Iron Age and on into Roman times, and the resulting prosperity gave rise to Viking raids on the area. In the eighteenth century the marshes were drained to create the Seasalter levels, and in the great flood of 1953, the area was severely inundated.

Toadflax
(Linaria vulgaris)

The common or yellow toadflax is a perennial plant native to the UK. It is an erect plant with fine, threadlike, glaucous, blue-green leaves and short spreading roots. The yellow flowers are similar to those of the snapdragon borne in dense terminal racemes from mid-summer. It is an important food plant for a large number of insects, including moths and butterflies.

88

me how, just like strawberries, every fruit tastes subtly different. The damp fields on the marshes were covered with yellow toadflax amid grazing cattle. In time, I arrived at Seasalter Cross, which evidently was inundated in the Great Flood of 1953. Also, way before this in Roman times, as the area's name suggests, Seasalter was an important centre of the vital activity of salt production.

In the centre of Seasalter, I crossed over the railway by a splendid, brick-built, humpbacked bridge and walked along the beach for a while, before coming to a charming row of well-maintained, gaily painted beach huts. Last time I was there, walking the other way, I was forced inland behind the golf course for some unfathomable reason, but today I kept on, straight into the centre of Whitstable. I located the Duke of Cumberland Hotel, strategically placed at the end of the High Street and checked in. It was a building of some provenance, and built in the round with a dance floor surrounded by 1950s memorabilia. No doubt, after a period of neglect, the current management were trying to revive its fortunes. Before settling down in the hotel, I was determined to buy some oysters, as I am generally keen on seafood. In a friendly High Street oyster bar I achieved this ambition and was pleasantly satisfied with the outcome.

Coming back to my room after an evening's drinking at the bar I spent some time leaning out of an upstairs window, observing the street below,

Whitstable to Herne

The Thanet Way

Otherwise known as the A229 is a major trunk road which runs from Brenley Corner near Faversham (where it merges into the M2) to Ramsgate via Whitstable and Herne Bay, serving the North Kent coast. Most of the road was constructed in the 1930s as an employment relief project, but prior to this all traffic from the west to the Isle of Thanet had to go through Canterbury. The road was upgraded in the 1990s to dual carriageway for most of its length. Whitstable and Herne Bay were by-passed, with the old coast road being downgraded to the A2990. The road leads to Kent International Airport and Ramsgate Harbour on the Isle of Thanet. The section from the Minster roundabout to the Lord of the Manor roundabout, by the recently demolished Richborough Power Station, has been diverted on to a new dual carriageway, to the west of the village of Cliffe, as part of the East Kent Access Phase 2 works.

Whitstable

Refined seaside town

Slurping oysters

In a High Street bar

Roof top cloisters

Observing the street as it hardly understands.

Herne

Is an ancient village that is separated from Herne Bay, its more recent satellite, by the Thanet Way, with a population of over 7,000. The village incorporates the former hamlet of Hunters Forstal, and the built-up area stretches all the way to Broomfield. Herne Common lies to the south, bordering East Blean Wood, the most easterly manifestation of the former Forest of Blean. The A291, Herne Bay to Sturry and Canterbury, passes through the village, forming a distinctive curving section of road in the centre, around the church precinct. Adjacent to the church is the Upper Red Lion public house, which is now, unfortunately, disused, detracting from the visual appearance of the village.

Upper Red Lion Pub, Herne

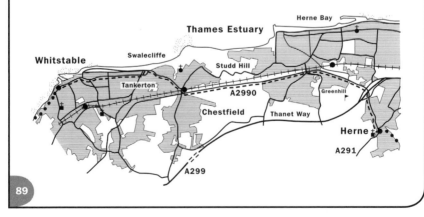

where the street cannot see you. I thought of the lines by T.S. Eliot, from the third of his '*Preludes*', which suggests, 'You had such a vision of the street as the street hardly understands', as economic chaos was descending on the Eurozone. Late into the night, the lights kept blazing out and careless conversations rattling around the street drifted up to me in my lofty perch.

In the morning, having a long way to go to Sandwich, I decided to take a taxi to Herne as I had no desire to walk through the outskirts of Whitstable. I was dropped by the church, in front of a derelict pub, the Upper Red Lion, which seriously detracted from the visual quality of this very distinctive village. I searched for the footpath to Maypole, which again would take me along the backs of houses, to Ridgeway Farm. Beyond the farm, I passed down into a shallow valley with a stream that is a tributary of the north stream that feeds the Chislet Marshes. Rain showers blew in from the west over East Blean Wood and I put on wet gear. I passed through a copse and climbed the slope to emerge on a flat plain in front of Maypole, which was used as an airstrip. A notice advised me to look both ways when crossing the strip. The church spire I had seen crossing the valley was that of Hoath, really part of the same settlement as Maypole.

Passing through the pleasant hamlet of Maypole to Old Tree, an even smaller hamlet, I emerged at the wide open fields stretching down to Chislet. This was the sort of place where I had gone badly wrong in the past, so I took some time to properly appraise the arable landscape. The lanes in this vicinity are unfenced and I was trying to make for Hollow Street, so, from the map, I could see I needed to stay south of an imaginary line to Chislet Church and north of Chislet Forstal. Initially, I could see the path marked out by the residual unploughed trail of stalks of a previous crop, so I set off with my eyes raised to distant landmarks. Soon the trail dried up and I was forced to stumble across ploughed fields full of potatoes. I think they had already been harvested, but I couldn't work out why so many potatoes were left to rot in the soil. Maybe they were rejects, not being the exact size required by supermarkets, and had failed some sort of test. But one thing was for sure, if they were finished with, and judging by the way missed potatoes on my allotment grew back the next season, the field would be covered with another crop in the following year.

Re-joining the lane at Hollow Street, I carried on to the Sarre Penn, the major tributary of the River Wantsum, separated from the Great Stour River by the ancient Sarre Wall, along the ridge between Upstreet and Sarre, on the current route of the A28. Climbing out of the shallow valley up to Upstreet, I looked west over the fields to see if I could see any signs of the disused Chislet Colliery, which would have been located near to the former mining village of Hersden. I slogged up the lane past Nethergong Farm to the main road, just as it began to rain again. I turned right towards Canterbury and located the village shop, where I bought some provisions and rested, pulling on wet gear and sheltering against the persistent shower.

I descended off the ridge and under the railway to the wet banks of the Great Stour River, along the Wantsum Walk. Views of the torpid river were restricted to the holes punched through the riverside vegetation by fishing stations. I plodded along the banks of the big river for a quarter of a mile to Grove Ferry where I crossed over, past the back side of the Stodmarsh Nature Reserve, and strolled through a public, grassy area down by the river where people could park and walk their dogs. Across the flat fields between the Little Stour and Great Stour Rivers, I passed through fields that were evidently the site of salt-making activities in Roman times, an activity which occupied a large acreage of coastal land in historical times.

Crossing the Little Stour, I made my way to West Stourmouth, which, with its twin, East Stourmouth, sits on a promontory of a maximum height of 9m. In historical times it would have stuck out into the Wantsum Channel before it silted up. This strategic location would once have been so much more important than it is now, and one can't help thinking that some archaeological excavation in the vicinity might be fruitful, perhaps uncovering the remains of a much larger settlement. Now, the agreeable pair of villages are strung out along the lane that encircles the higher ground. I kept going on, through West Stourmouth, past the redundant church and crossed over the centre of the ridge to the Rising Sun in East Stourmouth, where I repaired.

From the highest point on the promontory I could see north to the line of the Sarre Wall and eastwards to Richborough Power Station, the direction in which I was headed. Leaving the pub in East Stourmouth after a couple of pints, I pressed on eastwards into another serious patch of orchard country. I followed the Stour Valley Walk through many orchards to Westmarsh, with the cooling towers of the disused power

Herne to East Stourmouth

Stourmouth

This relatively isolated settlement, formerly at the mouth of the River Stour before the Wantsum marshes were reclaimed, consists of two villages, East and West Stourmouth. West Stourmouth has an ancient church, originating in Saxon times, an imposing vicarage and a few scattered farms. The church is surrounded by trees and has a small spire and bell tower, with a body made of flint, ragstone and brick. It is looked after by the Churches Conservation Trust. The main population centre is in East Stourmouth, strung out along the B2048 road that bridges the River Stour at Pluck's Gutter.

West Stourmouth church

Colonel Mudge's Map of Kent

William Mudge (1762–1820) was an English artillery officer and surveyor, an important figure in the work of the Ordnance Survey. His survey of Kent, published in 1801, the so-called Mudge's map of Kent, was the very first 1-inch-to-the-mile Ordnance Survey map, and one of the finest maps ever produced.

Colonel Mudge's map of Stodmarsh

Sarre Penn

Is an 8-mile long tributary of the River Wantsum, running from its source near Dunkirk at the edge of The Blean, and flowing north of Canterbury, below Tyler's Hill. It joins the River Wantsum near Sarre, where it is known locally as the Fishbourne Stream, running parallel to The Great Stour River from which it is separated by the Sarre Wall.

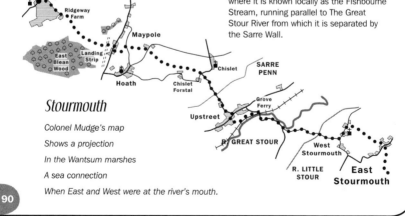

Stourmouth

Colonel Mudge's map

Shows a projection

In the Wantsum marshes

A sea connection

When East and West were at the river's mouth.

station bobbing above cordoned apple trees grown on dwarfing root-stock, as the weather began to lift. In Westmarsh, the hoped-for pub had succumbed to its inevitable fate in a small village. There was a satisfying collection of houses in the village and a large warehouse-type building, which would formerly have stored apples, converted to residential dwellings. In historical times, Westmarsh would have been a coastal village and again, probably more significant than it now is.

I pressed on to the charmingly named Paramour Street, through many orchards dripping with fruit, to lower Goldstone and on to the next lane, before taking the small, winding lane to Richborough hamlet. After an unpromising start, the weather had settled down with sunshine and a light breeze. This lane past Guston Farm would have, in times past, been right on the edge of the sea, but now it borders Ash Level, a large reclaimed marsh of the Great Stour River, devoid of human habitation, probably because it is still prone to flooding.

I paced along the winding lane, past Richborough Farm and a scattering of dwellings, searching for a glimpse of the ruins of the famous Roman fort called Rutupiae. I located a track to the north of the lane, and proceeded across a shallow bluff, and the Roman walls, remarkably intact, appeared before me. Taking the footpath around the back of this spectacular ruin, I followed the conglomerate red walls and intimidating dry ditch, and linked up with Saxon Shore Way. Staying west of the railway, I climbed up a slope to re-join the lane to Sandwich and on past the Roman amphitheatre at a height of 18m above sea level. This area of higher land would once have been, in Roman times, a promontory, surrounded on three sides by water; a strategic location indeed, with a commanding view over the Wantsum Channel and the generally agreed landing point in Britain of the Roman invasion of AD 43. These impressive, ancient monuments, which are under the care of English Heritage, appeared to me to rival the much-vaunted Roman remains in other parts of the country, such as those at Wroxeter for example.

All that remained was to stroll down the lane beside the Great Stour River, through the flat river plain, into the western outskirts of Sandwich and on into the historic town. It is not hard to imagine how impressive and important this town would have been in medieval times, from the many well-preserved buildings in a carefully conserved urban fabric. I reached my resting place in the late afternoon sun and sat outside in the

---

East Stourmouth to Sandwich

Sandwich

Round and round about
Medieval
Patterns of the past
Speak to us all
Grateful for the toil of Huguenots.

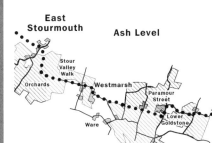

Richborough Castle

Situated in the East Kent marshes, Richborough Castle is perhaps the most symbolically important of Roman sites in Britain, seeing both the beginning and end of Roman rule. Rutupiae was founded by the Romans when they landed in AD 43, and was a major port and a starting point for Watling Street, the road to Canterbury and London. As conquest moved north it became an increasingly large civilian settlement with temples, an amphitheatre, a bath house and a mansio, for visiting officials.

During the late third century this large civilian town was remilitarised by its conversion to a Saxon Shore fort. These were a series of forts built by the Romans on the Channel to guard against invading Saxon pirates. The fort was 5 acres in area and was surrounded by massive walls, some of which still stand today, forming an almost perfect square. During the decline of the Roman Empire, Richborough was eventually abandoned by the Romans and was occupied by a Saxon religious settlement. Recent excavations of the Roman wall uncovered the original coastline along with the remains of a medieval dock. The site is now 2.5 miles inland from the current coastline in an area of reclaimed marshes of the River Great Stour.

Richborough Castle with the soon to be demolished towers of Richborough Power Station in the distance

Barbican Gate, Sandwich

91

garden of the King's Arms, recuperating for a while after a long trek, before checking in.

The next morning, I passed through the town, past the parish church at its centre, with more Georgian-style buildings in evidence: testimony to the fact that the town continued to develop and reinvent itself after its medieval heyday. The centre of the town in Market Street reminded me of Southam in Warwickshire in this respect. I pressed on to the Bulwark, the old town walls, to pick up the footpath leading east along the Great Stour River. Along the banks of the river I could see the vast, industrial, chemical complex of Pfizers gleaming white in the distance. I strode out on a causeway called the Green Wall, beside a waterway curiously called the Vigo Sprong that presumably once fed the moat by the bulwark, which defined the southern extent of Sandwich.

Crossing over the North Stream, just before it joined the Great Stour River, I entered the Royal St George's Golf Links, famous for its periodic hosting of the British Open Golf Championship, most recently last year. I felt distinctly nervous about crossing this hallowed turf, but there was nobody around to appreciate my discomfort. I passed some charming little thatched, octagonal huts, whose sole purpose was to shelter golfers from the rain while waiting to tee off. Within the manicured acres of the undulating golf course there were untamed pockets, presumably way out of the reach of any wayward drive, sporting carmine patches of rose bay willow herb and other wild plants.

As I approached the coast, I had a dramatic view of Pegwell Bay and the Isle of Thanet to the north. I came up on the road that gives access to the Princes Golf Course and proceeded south to Deal. The strand was littered with patches of sea holly, cineraria maritima with its yellow flowers and wild brassicas. I was struck by the observation that this shingle spit, running north to Pegwell Bay, was of a similar construction to that of the largest and most famous example of Chesil Beach in Dorset.

In time, I reached the affluent Sandwich Bay Estate, with substantial dwellings dotted around the grounds, seemingly in a random manner. I had passed by this estate on the inland lane on a previous walk, but today I was to walk across its front by the sea. There was a very old-looking, thatched house, an unusual dwelling right on the coast, and some substantial mansion buildings set off by a manicured grass verge. However, inland, there were wild, untamed paddocks, sometimes within warm brick

Walk 6 – Sandwich to Deal

Sandwich to Deal

Royal St George's Golf Club

Founded in 1887, is one of the premier golf clubs in the UK, and one of the courses on the Open Championship rotation. It has hosted thirteen Open Championships since 1894, when it became the first club outside Scotland to host the event. This links course is located on the coast in a setting of wild duneland, with many holes featuring blind or partially blind shots and deep bunkers. The perceived unfairness of some of the holes has been reduced somewhat by twentieth-century modifications. The course is located on the same stretch of coastline as the Royal Cinque Ports Club and the Prince's Club, both former Open Championship venues. The last time the course hosted the Open event was in 2011, when it was won by Darren Clarke.

Starters hut, 1st hole on Royal St George's Golf Club

Deal Pier

Is the sole surviving complete pleasure pier in Kent, and the last to be constructed in the UK, having opened in 1957, after the previous pier was thought not worth repairing following the Second World War. It is a relatively short, 311-metre long, reinforced concrete pier, primarily used by sea fishermen. Also in Kent, Herne Bay pier survives, but in a much truncated form.

Deal Pier

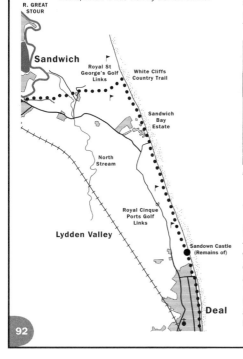

The White Cliffs Country Trail

Was created in 1987 by Dover District Council, linking the towns of Dover, Deal and Sandwich, going along the famous 'White Cliffs' east of Dover, with several inland routes to Deal and Sandwich. It is approximately 28 miles in length with a highest point of 124 metres.

92

walls, in which it would be a nightmare to grow anything but grass, based on underlying sand and pebbles. I passed a complex that looked like a ruined military fortification graced by a family of jackdaws.

After the estate, the road passed inland and I walked on along the sea wall to Deal. I observed the range of coloured pebbles making up the shingle bar, each being derived from a particular type of rock, washed out of cliffs further down the coast. I pressed on, looking across the Royal Cinque Ports Golf Course into the low-lying Lydden Valley, drained by the North Stream. I dropped down out of the breeze and trudged along the sandy path into Deal. At the northernmost point of Deal I read a notice that described how the ruined Sandown Castle had been incorporated into the sea defences at this point.

I carried on to the Deal Pier, the official end of this journey, observing stately, black-backed seagulls perching on tall breakwaters down on the shelving beach. I passed Deal Rowing Club and thought it quite curious that such an enterprise should be located on the wild coast rather than on a tamed river. I strolled along the elegant seafront parade called Beach Street, with its multi-coloured, multi-storied houses facing the sea, laid out on top of the very same shingle bank on which I had been walking earlier that morning. Deal Pier itself was relatively undeveloped as a tourist facility, but rather harked back to its original purpose with its T-piece jetty at the end for ships to moor up against. Today, the unattractive, concrete pier construction seemed to be mainly used by fishermen.

At exactly midday, I reached the pier, set among copious flower beds at the centre of the town, and sojourned for a while in a sea-front pub, the Port Arms. The name of this pub gives a good idea how Deal has seen itself through history, as a port without a harbour. Finally I caught a bus back down the coast to Romney Marsh. I was, rather guiltily, able to use my recently acquired bus pass for this substantial journey.

7

Deal to Winchelsea (Summer 2012)

Starting another walk at Deal, I passed by the timeball tower on the seafront, which had now been converted into a museum. Although it was just short of mid-summer, the weather promised to be awful. I set off, along the main street, through the substantial outskirts of the comfortable seaside town. I carried on up to Mill Hill where I intended to take a footpath to a back lane to the south of Great Mongeham. However, the footpath was overgrown with wet grass, the result no doubt of a very wet May and June, and this was to prove a recurring theme in this walk. Instead, I took a dogleg through a part of the village that was securely anchored to the urban fabric of Deal, flaring away into the countryside like a sunspot. I climbed up through the pleasant village past some attractive, thatched cottages and a church set back off the road. Entering Northbourne Lane, I paused for a while and admired the view to the north. I could clearly see the large block of flats at the back of Ramsgate on the Isle of Thanet, but the iconic cooling towers of the redundant Richborough Power Station, which had been a feature of many previous rambles, were no more; they had been demolished recently in spite of a campaign to keep them as a distinctive landmark.

Getting stuck into the journey, striding down to Northbourne, I was serenaded by a robin perching on the wire, urging me off his patch, heading for base camp 1 at Ratling. Then I peered at the remains of Northbourne Abbey through its ancient gateway and passed into the agreeable village on the dip slope of the North Downs. I plodded on through swathes of growing wheat in the centre of the Kent coalfield, to the hamlet of Little Betteshanger. To the north, I could see the massive greenhouses of Thanet Earth glinting on the skyline. I reflected on the fact that after the judicious scraping of both knees during consecutive winters, I might now have the platform to carry on walking for a few more years.

Deal to Tilmanstone

Deal

Is a Channel coast and former garrison town, which used to be engaged in fishing and mining activities. Once a busy port, today it enjoys the reputation of being a quiet seaside resort with its quaint streets and houses. Middle Street was the first conservation area in Kent to be designated and since that time the boundary has been extended three times. The coast of France is approximately 25 miles from the town, and is visible on a clear day. Its finest building is Deal Castle, commissioned by King Henry VIII and designed on an attractive rose floor plan.

The proximity of Deal to the notorious Goodwin Sands has made its coastal waters both a source of shelter and danger. 'The Downs', the water between the coast and the sands, provided a naturally sheltered anchorage, which allowed the town to become a significant shipping and military port in past centuries despite the absence of a harbour. Deal once had a naval shipyard, which provided much of the town's trade. On the site of this yard stands a building originally used as a semaphore tower, and then a coastguard house, and now as the timeball tower which has been converted into a museum.

Deal

Elegant parade

Facing the sea

Timeball charade

No longer needed

To send messages to Greenwich.

English Yew
(Taxus baccata)

Is a native, small to medium-sized evergreen conifer tree with dark green leaves, and the seeds are contained in bright red, berry-like structures. It is a slow growing tree, and can survive for many years, the longest living plant in Europe. Most parts of the tree are highly poisonous, particularly to horses, cattle, pigs and other livestock. The yew is often found in churchyards in England, where the danger to animals is reduced, and it famously provided the wood for the English Longbow.

Robin
(Erithacus rubecula)

Is a widespread, familiar bird with a bright red breast in both sexes, that is happy to live in close association with man. Young birds have no red breast, being spotted with golden brown. They sing most of the year, and despite their cute appearance, they are aggressively territorial and quick to drive away intruders. They are omnivorous, feeding on worms, seeds, fruits and insects, living in a wide range of habitat including woodland, hedgerows, parks and gardens.

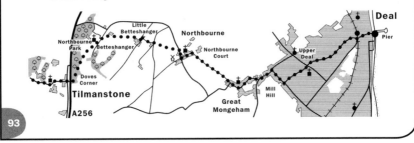

93

Coming into Betteshanger, I took a wrong turning and gained the church through a field of broad beans. There was nothing there to suggest that this sleepy, ancient village would give its name to one of the four major collieries in the Kent coalfield. After the historic village, by a well-marked footpath, I crossed the route of a Roman road that stretched on to Eastry and Woodnesborough in the direction of Richborough Castle. I passed on through wet woods and crossed the busy A259 by a bridge to Doves Corner. Next I arrived at Tilmanstone, the name of another colliery, also an attractive village, with thatched cottages, seemingly unaffected by the mining of coal. In the churchyard there was an ancient yew tree reputedly 1,600 years old, which would have been around when the Roman legions were withdrawing from Britain. Curiously, the church was dedicated to the Knights Templar, whose organisation and mission I have commented on before. The actual pit head was located close to the mining village of Elvington, which was plonked unceremoniously down, in isolated splendour, in the Kent countryside to house the miners.

From Tilmanstone, I pressed on along footpaths and winding lanes, past Thornton and Shingleton Farms, through the edge of a wood, to the Sandwich Road. On the way into Nonington, across the front of Nonington Court, a footpath had been created off the road in the field's edge, allowing safe passage. The village of Nonington was strung out along the Sandwich Road and I popped into the Royal Oak for lunch, but unfortunately there was no food, so I consoled myself with four pints of beer. The rather lugubrious host was an ex-rugby playing miner who had experienced some matrimonial difficulties. He was leasing the pub from the local landowner and bemoaned the fact that nobody from the village used the pub; his main customers came from the nearby mining village of Aylesham, serving the former Snowden Colliery. He explained that the layout of the village of Aylesham was in the form of the distinctive pit head winding gear, and I thanked him for that knowledge. There were only two other people in the pub and I did wonder how such places could possibly survive. Indeed, I got the very strong impression that the pub was half dead and soon to be added to the litany of closures that is now blighting the countryside.

Leaving the pub, I strode down the lane to the church, where there was an evocative grouping of old buildings, which demonstrated the antiquity of the village. The lane beyond the church was bedecked by oxeye daisies.

Tilmanstone to Ratling

Ratling
Knowlton Park
Nonington Court
Shingleton Farm
Aylesham
Nonington
The Downs
Tilmanstone

Oxeye Daisy
(Leucanthemum vulgare)

Is a typical grassland perennial wildflower, growing in a variety of plant communities, including meadows and fields, under scrub and open forest canopies, and on disturbed ground. It has a long flowering season from late spring to autumn, and consists of white florets surrounding a distinctive yellow eye.

Working Men's Clubs

Are a type of private social club which were first created in the nineteenth century in industrial areas, particularly in the north of England, the Midlands and south Wales, to provide recreation and education for working class men and their families. A working men's club is a non-profit making organisation run by members through an elected committee. Most clubs affiliate to the Working Men's Club and Institute Union (commonly known as the CIU), where a member of one affiliated club is entitled to use the facilities of other clubs. There are around 2,200 affiliated clubs in the UK. Many clubs, with declining membership, are now struggling to survive, and the club in Aylesham, reflecting the roots of many of the former miners, may well be a case in point.

Aylesham

Was established in 1926 as a planned settlement in order to provide housing for miners working at the newly sunk Snowdown Colliery. The layout of the village is based on the shape of pit head winding gear. Miners from all parts of the UK (notably South Wales, Scotland and the Northeast) seeking better wages and safer working conditions were drawn to the area.

This large village, and other mining settlements in the Kent coalfield set down in the countryside, are relatively isolated and typically accessed by narrow, winding lanes. The coal won from this pit was taken out by railway, now disused, except the lower section to its junction with the main line at Sibertswold, which has been restored as the East Kent Railway by steam train enthusiasts. The population of the village today is relatively static, at around 4,000 people, still housing the families of former miners.

Snowdown Colliery, looking towards Aylesham, 1986

94

As I walked up the slope, I could see the largest mining village of Aylesham to my left, marooned beyond an interminable field of wheat on the windswept downs, even now, after many years, looking alien in the landscape. Climbing to a height of 70m, I could see the blue line of the North Downs to the north-west, in the direction I was headed over the next few days.

Around this side of Aylesham there were a number of scruffy enclaves containing various nefarious enterprises and pieces of land with dilapidated shacks, derelict cars and storage yards. It was as if the citizens of Aylesham were trying to break out of the confines of their regimented community into the fresh air, spreading contagion into the countryside. Whilst I find it perfectly admirable that the citizens of Aylesham should want to get out of the village and do their own thing in the countryside, I did form the impression that little respect was paid to the visual appearance of the area in the process. The lane from Aylesham to Ratling was particularly tainted in this way and reminded me of the area west of Wrotham, with an uncared for appearance. At Ratling I reached my goal for the first day's walking and sat out the onset of inclement weather. In the evening, in a clear slot, I went out, seeking a pint of beer in the nearby Working Men's club, but unfortunately this rundown establishment was closed, so I had no choice but to return to my excellent digs in Ratling Farmhouse.

In the morning, I set out in the rain walking towards Adisham. I crossed under the railway line and arrived at a large triangular green set off by an imposing church, but down the High Street there is the unfortunate prospect of the derelict Bulls Head pub. There were some pleasant cottages in the main street interspersed with nondescript modern houses and bungalows. I traipsed down Woodlands Road in the pouring rain, climbing all the time to Oxenden Shaw, an area of woodland at 80m. There was a water tower with an inscription on it proclaiming the ownership of the Margate Water Board and presumably from here, somehow, water was, and maybe still is, piped to Margate.

Coming out of the wood, there were impressive views down towards Bridge and Canterbury, over extensive fields of green wheat and peas. Passing the orchards of Highland Court Farm, I came up to the A2 road on the ridge. I crossed under the by-pass and strolled into Bridge along the original old straight road. To the left was the valley of the Nail Bourne and I could look down from the ridge into Bourne Park, where I had trod

Ratling to Bridge

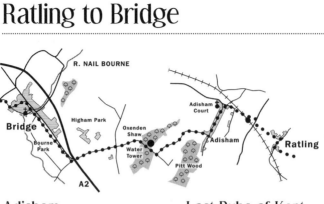

Adisham

Is an ancient village on the B2046 between Wingham and Barham, which has a large, impressive church adjacent to a commodious village green. However, the village's only shop closed in 2004 and the public house, The Bull's Head, is now closed and derelict. It is a commuter village on the main Chatham to Dover line.

Church of the Holy Innocents, Adisham

The derelict Bull's Head, Adisham

Lost Pubs of Kent and East Sussex

The following list represents some of the lost pubs passed in this book:

- The Bull's Head, Adisham
- The Carpenter's Arms, Coldred
- The Wheatsheaf, Kemsing
- The Kings Arms, Headcorn
- The Upper Red Lion, Herne
- The Blacksmith's Arms, Pluckley Thorn
- The Smeaton Stores, Rye
- The Kings Head, Sarre
- The Bull, Sissinghurst
- The Red Lion, Snodland

The above list is merely a small sample of the rash of pub closures currently underway in the Kent and Sussex countryside.

The Water Tower in Woodlands Wood

before. I passed the grand entrance to Higham Park before issuing into the pleasant village of Bridge.

After a quick pit-stop in the corner shop, run by a lively Sikh gentleman, I proceeded west out of Bridge through a housing estate graced by a massive evergreen oak. I passed under an impressive brick arch, supporting a disused railway, on the way to Lower Hardres. Initially, I strolled down a dry valley but opposite Middle Pelt Farm, I climbed out of the valley to skirt the south western edge of Whitehill Wood. Thereabouts, the valley sides, but not the valley bottom, were clothed with orchards. I believe the absence of trees on the valley bottom is due to the ruinous effects of frost, and its tendency to sink and gather to the lowest level.

Whitehill Wood was composed of a redundant coppice of beech trees, with a holly understory guarding the woodland edge, where there was sufficient sun to allow it to thrive. There were stunning views from this wood, into the dry valley sweeping down to Pett Bottom. The bridleway was well signposted through the wood and at the south-western end, it had been heavily harvested. The occasional, misshapen tree was left standing, grown unnaturally tall due to competition for light in a crowded wood, but providing the necessary seeds for future growth and regeneration.

I came up to a small lane that wound its way down into the delightful small village of Lower Hardres in the next dry valley. Leaving the village, I found a farm shop in the middle of nowhere and opportunistically bought some provisions. Taking another bridleway, I passed through orchards and fields with horses to skirt the edge of Cobsdane Wood. There were spectacular views to the north-west, over rolling downland dotted with clumps of woodland, towards the Stour Valley. After an arduous slog up the hill beside Shoot Wood to a height of 117m, I crossed the long straight Roman road from Lemanis to Durovernum Cantiacorum, now known as Stone Street, which runs between Lympne and Canterbury.

Standing for a while above the next dry valley, I admired the scene. The very English village of Petham nestled in the bottom, having the dual advantages of rural isolation and proximity to a city, namely Canterbury. I slithered down the steep slope into the village, kicking up dust in a field with grey-white soil, the colour reflecting its origins as chalk. Climbing out of Petham, in the lane to Chapel Farm, I came across a swathe of

Bridge to Petham

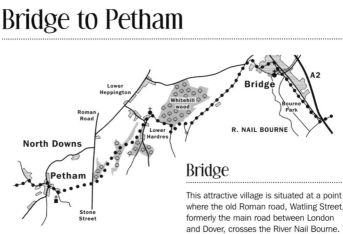

Stone Street

Is a perfectly straight, 12-mile, archetypal Roman Road, from Watling Street at Canterbury (Durovernum) to Lympne (Lemanis). Today it is occupied for most of its length by the B2068. Starting on the old greensand sea cliffs above Romney Marsh, it passes through Lympne, New Inn Green, Westenhanger and Stanford, before climbing up the scarp slope of the North Downs. Descending to Canterbury, the road is completely devoid of settlement for many miles, joining the City as a minor road in the vicinity of Wincheap.

Bridge

This attractive village is situated at a point where the old Roman road, Watling Street, formerly the main road between London and Dover, crosses the River Nail Bourne. Thankfully, the main A2 now by-passes the village. On its edge are two large country estates. Bourne Park, with its Queen Anne mansion dating from 1702, and Higham Park, with its neoclassical mansion, once the home of the eccentric racing driver Count Louis Zborowski.

Bridge High Street

Holly
(Ilex aquifolium)

Or English Holly is an evergreen tree usually found as a shrub less than 10 metres in height, with dark green leaves sporting sharp spines. It is a pioneering tree and has a great capacity to adapt to different conditions, often repopulating the margins of woods and forest clearings. The fruit is a red or yellow drupe, maturing in the autumn, and eaten by rodents, birds and larger herbivores.

St Mary's church, Lower Hardres

wild cyclamen growing on a shady bank at a corner in the lane. Before Chapel Farm, I picked up another long, straight bridleway through Chapel Wood to the lane beyond Buckholt Farm. This bridleway, with its tarmac surface, would once have been a lane in its own right. Halfway along, I sat down on a tree stump for a rest, becoming covered in wood ants, which on closer inspection covered the woodland floor. Although I managed to shake most of them off in a wild dance, a few got through to bite me on exposed arms.

At the end of the bridleway, I changed direction, striking out north along the lane between Eggringe Wood and Denge Wood. At the side of the lane, I was enchanted by a host of white butterflies feasting on the nectar provided by the thistle-like flowers of burdock. On the summit, at 141m, I read an information board about Denge Wood. This large area of ancient, semi-natural, mixed woodland, within the Kent Downs AONB, was home to a rich variety of flora and fauna, including orchids and the very rare Duke of Burgundy butterfly. I noticed from the map the large number of tumuli within the wood, marking out this area, and the Stour valley below, as a centre of Bronze Age settlement.

Emerging from the wood, I breasted a large, high wheat field, whose short plants were being unceremoniously gathered in by a massive combine harvester. This monstrous machine gobbled up the field at an

Petham to Chilham

Julliberrie's Grave

Is an unchambered, earthen, Neolithic long barrow on the Julliberrie Downs overlooking the village of Chilham in the Great Stour valley. It is currently 44 metres in length and 15 metres wide, the northern end being destroyed by chalk extraction. It is one of a number of prehistoric barrows overlooking the Stour valley, and the name is likely to derive from antiquarian speculation, although folk etymology is that it was the burial site of a giant named Julaber. A popular early explanation was that it was the grave of a Roman tribune, Quintus Laberius Durus, mentioned in Julius Ceasar's Gallic Wars as being slain by the Britons, *Jul Laber* therefore being a corruption of '(the grave of) Julius (tribune) Laberius'. Later assessments of the importance of the site have emphasised the strategic location of the barrow rather than its significance as a funerary monument.

Chilham village square

Burdock
(Arctium minus)

Known as common or Lesser burdock, is a biennial thistle native to the UK. It is a large, bushy plant with pink to lavender flowers from July to October, with large leaves and burrs with hooked bracts. These hooked bracts attach easily to the fur of animals and human clothing to aid seed dispersal, and is said to be the inspiration behind the design of Velcro, the fastening.

Hairy Wood Ant
(Formica lugubris)

Is a common species of ant in woods and forests in the UK, living in massive colonies. They are carnivorous, feeding on pestiferous insects and forest defoliators, but they rarely form prey themselves. Nests are visible above ground and can reach a metre in height. They thrive in open, sunny areas of woods and forests, a decreasing habitat due to modern forestry practice.

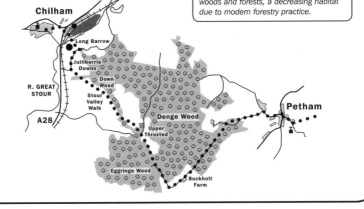

alarming rate, throwing up clouds of choking black dust in the process. I hurried on, timing my passage to miss the return traverse of this giant vehicle. From this high field, I cut down diagonally through a wood, past a tree with gigantic bracket fungus, a layered cantilevered construction, to pick up the Stour Valley Walk. Descending gradually into the Stour valley, I managed to locate Juliberries Grave, a Neolithic long barrow on the eponymously named downs outside Chilham. This impressive antiquity would be easily missed if one wasn't looking carefully for it, because it is largely hidden, covered by trees and unmarked. Indeed, the footpath down into the valley disrespectfully passes over the burial mound.

Coming into Chilham, I passed through an area of private lakes festooned with prohibitive notices saying, 'Private Fishing', 'Poachers will be Prosecuted', 'No Boating or Canoes', 'Deep Water – No Bathing'. I thought that just about covered everything. I crossed over the railway by Chilham Mill and across the busy Ashford road into the pleasant enclave on the Bagham Road. I strode triumphantly into the particularly special village and hobbled up the hill into the square for a celebratory pint in the historic White Lion pub. I mentioned the antiquities outside the village to the landlord who admitted that he hadn't known anybody find them. Leaving the pub to retire down the hill to the Woolpack Inn, I noticed two boys playing football in the churchyard, ingeniously using gravestones as goalposts. I thought the sitting tenants could only applaud such inventiveness.

I left Chilham on a very windy day, threatening rain, travelling north up the Great Stour Valley. I paced along the main road for a while, past motor car sales, garden centres and small industrial units, to pick up Pickelden Lane in the bottom of the valley. This sodden lane took me down to the bridge over the swollen river and past private fishing lakes, proclaiming again that poachers would be prosecuted. Then I took a well-prepared footpath through a field of wheat to join the lane into Shalmsford Street, a curious, linear settlement with a housing estate at the end, like a heavy-headed bulrush waving around in the Chartham Downs.

Crossing Shalmsford Street, I carried on along the lane beside the railway to Chartham. As I approached the village I could see the large paper mill down by the river, which, I guess, was historically the main industry there. I understand that the estates in Shalmsford Street were built to house the workers. The main product now emanating from this industry is the vitally important, but probably increasingly redundant,

Chilham to Harbledown

Chartham

Is located on the Great Stour River and lies within the Kent Downs Area of Outstanding Natural Beauty. The church is located next to a triangular village green surrounded by cottages, and contains the oldest peel of bells in Kent. The river provided the power for paper mills until some point before 1955. Paper-making has been a major occupation in the village for the last 625 years, and the current mill dates back to the late eighteenth century, and now specialises in the production of tracing paper. The village is contiguous with the smaller settlement of Shalmsford Street, with a large housing estate extending up the valley into the Chartham Downs.

Tonford Manor

Is a privately owned, grade II listed building, and crenelated manor house, in Thanington Without. It lies on the western bank of the Great Stour River, and on the route of the Stour Valley Walk, and was the home of Thomas Browne. He was MP for Dover 1439-44, High Sheriff of Kent 1443-44, and held the post of Chancellor of the Exchequer 1440-50 during the reign of King Henry VI. He was executed for treason on the gallows at Tyburn on 29 July 1460.

Tonford Manor viewed from the Stour Valley Walk

Chartham church and green

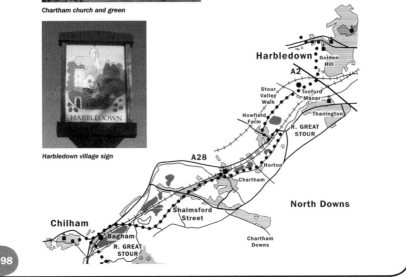

Harbledown village sign

tracing paper. Crossing the river led me directly into the centre of the village, attractively draped around a central, triangular green with the church at one corner, sporting the obligatory yew tree in the churchyard. I passed through all too quickly, needing to make progress, following the Stour Valley Walk. Beyond Chartham, the walk doubled up as a cycle path, so I was able to make good progress along the winding, carefully prepared surface, along the willow-haunted bank of the river.

I followed the awkward dogleg of the official path along the A28 and up into Howfield Lane and through the scruffy Howfield Farm. The path was difficult to follow through this agro-industrial complex and the work personnel scurrying around couldn't have cared less about my predicament. Struggling to find the right path out, I passed a substantial area of tatty, static caravans, no doubt used to house the army of migrant workers required to pick the fruit from the massive acreage of orchards adorning the northern slope of the valley. Some of the caravans displayed Polish flags in the windows. There were rows of neatly stacked wooden crates impatiently waiting for their time to come again, to receive the fecund autumn fruit. Proceeding along a concrete road, I had a splendid, inspiring view of the magnificent Canterbury Cathedral dominating the valley downstream. It is impossible to underestimate the importance of this religious institution on the landscape of Kent and indeed, on the social history of Britain, if not the world. Well done, St Augustine!

There was a vineyard hard up against the path in front of the ancient, moated ruins of Tonford Manor. Just past the manor, the rain set in with a vengeance and I hurriedly pulled on wet gear. The Stour Valley Walk passes over the busy A2 where I parted company with the approved way and passed under the London railway line to skirt the bottom of Golden Hill, the slopes of which were also covered in apple orchards. I came into Harbledown along the small stream running at the base of Golden Hill down to the Great Stour. The church on the hill presided over an attractive grouping of buildings, on Watling Street, once the main road into Canterbury.

I crossed over the A2050 and struggled up a very steep rise into the linear and undistinguished settlement of Rough Common, where I broke my journey in The Dog for lunch. Just up from the pub was one of the main entrances to Church Wood, contiguous with the Blean Woods National Nature Reserve further west, which together form the heart of the ancient area of woodland known as The Blean. I resisted the

Harbledown to Boughton Street

Victory Wood

Consists of 140 hectares, purchased in 2004 by The Woodland Trust, lying east of the Thanet Way, between the villages of Dargate and Yorkletts. It is part of the continuous arc of ancient woodland, lying to the north of Canterbury, known as 'The Blean'. At the time of purchase the Victory Wood consisted of 133 hectares of grade 3 agricultural land and 7 hectares of existing woodland. From 2005 to 2008 the wood became a major woodland creation project when 80 hectares along its southern boundary were planted up by community effort, linking once again Blean Wood to the west and Ellenden Wood to the east. These two woods had been connected up until the early to mid-twentieth century, when the ancient woodland was cut down in a piecemeal way and converted to agriculture when it was part of Lamberhurst farm.

The wood is so named because it is the flagship site for the Trafalgar Woods Project of 2005 to commemorate the bicentenary of the Battle of Trafalgar, organised by the Woodland Trust and the Society for Nautical Research. The Trafalgar Woods Project established 27 new woods, one wood for every boat which took part in the British fleet at this battle. At Victory Wood there are a number of interpretative structures which are themed around the Battle of Trafalgar but which are linked to the importance of trees and woodlands, and how different tree species were traditionally used.

Boughton-under-Blean

Is a large village on Watling Street, the historic route between London and Canterbury, which remained the main road until the completion of the Boughton A2 by-pass in 1976. The main part of the village, containing the oldest buildings on this route, is referred to as Boughton Street, but the parish church is isolated from the village, about a mile away to the south across the by-pass. There are other places in Kent with the name Boughton, including Boughton Malherbe and Boughton Monchelsea, which is Anglo-Saxon in origin, and refers to an enclosure where beech trees grew.

White Horse Inn, Boughton Street

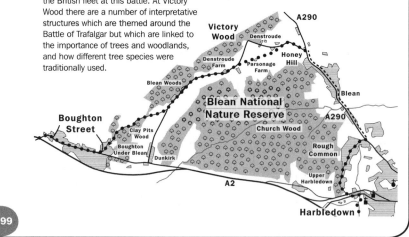

262

temptation to walk through the woods due to the severe winds that assailed me, and elected instead to catch a bus through Blean village itself to Honey Hill, where I located Denstroude Lane and took a northern route through The Blean. This route would take me through a shallow valley between Victory Wood and The National Nature Reserve and the two halves of Blean Wood.

Descending Denstroude Lane, I took the footpath to Parsonage Farm, struggling all the time into the teeth of this unseasonal wind. Coming back to the lane before Denstroude Farm, Victory Wood, a recently planted-up area on the southern slopes of Clay Hill and an open-access area, dominated the scene. In the tranquil, pastoral valley between the woods, there were fields with horses and one containing llamas, running around excitedly, making high-pitched chirping noises like birds. At the junction with the road from Dargate, looking north I could clearly see the Thames Estuary. I struggled against the wind up Courtenay Road and then, turning into Dawes Road, in a less sheltered spot, I found it difficult to make headway. I was toying with the magical woodland edge all the way along Dawes Road to a high point of 90m, with the wind testing my resolve. On a col between Blean Wood and Clay Pits Wood, there were spectacular views of the Swale Estuary and Sheppey beyond, which seemed to make the effort of slogging up the lane worthwhile.

I came into Boughton under Blean, nestling at the foot of Clay Pit Wood, and stumbled down the main street. Continuing westward along the once-significant main road, passing a milestone which said, 'London: 50 miles', I entered the older part of the village, known as Boughton Street. There were attractive cottages strung out along the street on a generous, raised walkway each side of the sunken road, worn down by countless traffic over the ages, from Roman legions to horse-drawn coaches. There were many timber-framed buildings lining the street in the vicinity of The White Horse Hotel, my berth for the night. Curiously, the thirteenth-century parish church of St Peter and St Paul lies about a mile to the south of the village.

Next morning, at the end of the street, I crossed over the main road, now thankfully by-passing the village, and made my way down Nine Ash Lane. Although I didn't see any ash trees, I did see a field of hops with the vines climbing up wires at this mid-summer time of year. I have sometimes wondered, given the complexity of the post and wire system that supports the hops and the fact that they are clearly permanent, intending that a crop be grown every year, why the soil does not get exhausted. It seems to fly in the face of the normal rules of horticulture, encouraging the rotation of crops. Perhaps the farmers rest and fertilise the hop fields in order to maintain the quality of the harvest, or maybe hops can put up with impoverished soil.

In this fruit- and hop-growing area, as in others I had passed through, the farmers pay particular attention to the hedges to produce carefully sculpted and manicured windbreaks. I carried on down the twisting lane just south of the motorway roaring away over the fields. I passed over the railway by a level crossing at the Clock House Crossing and passed through the pleasant hamlet of Colkins. The road displayed a faded, white line down the centre and the repair marks where cat's eyes had been extracted, demonstrating that this quiet lane was once a more important road. After the hamlet, I took the long, straight bridleway beside the motorway, past a field growing blackcurrant bushes. A chaffinch was singing his heart out in the top of a small tree, seemingly unaffected by the roar of the motorway.

Walking past Westwood Court, there was further evidence that this bridleway was once an important road leading down to the Clock House Crossing, with the tarmac surface now breaking up, creating the conditions for large, deep puddles to develop. At the end of the bridleway I picked up Salter's Lane, climbed up towards the hamlet of Copton and crossed diagonally across a field of wheat by a well-used path to the A251, the Ashford Road. I pressed on southwards along this road for a short section before picking up Porter's Lane. As I walked, I observed a group of crows, not quite a murder, mobbing a buzzard, which was trying to get on with his business, I guess purely for the fun of it. In the lane, with damaged edges, passing behind the National Fruit Collection Farm at Brogdale, the distinctive purple and yellow flowers of woody night-shade adorned the hedgerow; not related or to be confused with deadly nightshade, but closely related to potatoes and tomatoes.

Coming up to the Brogdale Road by Lorendon Park Nature Reserve, I observed a couple out running, who understandably declined to say hello, since all their effort was directed towards keeping going. After a stiff climb up to Painter's Forstal, I rested a while by the small green opposite The Alma pub. This was the second time I had passed through this village, south of Faversham, and both times it was too early to have a drink. I wondered about the origin of the pub's name and found out later

Boughton Street to Painter's Forstal

Brogdale National Fruit Collection

Is one of the largest fruit collections in the world, located at Brogdale Farm, south of Faversham, and looked after by the University of Reading, in 150 acres of orchards. The collection includes over 3,500 named apple, pear, plum, cherry, bush fruit, vine and cob nut cultivars. The collection is owned by the Department of Environment, Food and Rural Affairs (Defra) and is part of the international programme to protect plant genetic resources for the future. Public access is organised by the Brogdale Collections who are developing the site as a visitor attraction. On 10 August 2003 the temperature reached 38.5°C here, a record for the United Kingdom.

Woody Nightshade
(Solanum dulcamara)

Also known as bittersweet, is a native species of vine in the potato family, which occurs in a wide range of habitats, including woodland, scrubland, hedges and marshes. It is a semi-woody perennial vine, which scrambles over other plants, capable of reaching a height of 4 metres where suitable support is available. The purple and yellow flowers are in loose clusters and the red fruit is poisonous to humans and livestock, but widely eaten and dispersed by birds.

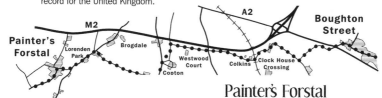

Blackcurrant
(Ribes Nigrum)

Is a temperate, medium-sized shrub which produces a soft fruit crop cultivated both commercially and domestically for its abundant small black berries. When not in fruit, all parts of the plant are strongly aromatic. An established bush can produce up to 5kg of fruit, and the currants are an important source of vitamin C. During the Second World War it was made into a syrup and fed extensively to children as a health drink.

Painter's Forstal

Is a village in the parish of Ospringe from which it is now separated by the M2 motorway. It takes its name from a local farm, 'forstal' being the land before such a farm. It is centred on a small green and a pub, The Alma, which dates back to the sixteenth century, and straddles an ancient drover's road. The name of the pub derives from the Battle of Alma, an engagement in the Crimean War. It lies with the Kent Downs AONB and has a nearby nature reserve in Lorenden Park, with a dry water course which used to feed Faversham Creek.

The Alma Public House, Painter's Forstal

100

265

that the Alma is a river in the Ukraine, and the site of an 1854 battle in the Crimean War. Striding out of Painter's Forstal there was a large area of derelict orchard tumbling down into the dry valley, part of a massive system stretching from Faversham all the way up to, but not quite breaking, the scarp ridge, which I had toyed with on a previous walk.

I took the Elverland Lane up and over into the next and equally massive, dry Syndale Valley, containing the villages of Newnham and Doddington. At a high point in this lane, at about 85m, looking north, I could see the River Thames shining in the distance like a silver thread. Near the junction with the main Faversham Road, I came across a field with carthorses, clearly relishing the freedom from not having to pull heavy loads. There were a couple of incredibly fetching foals, exhibiting that cute and cuddly attraction of young mammals that ensures that older mammals, such as ourselves, want to look after them. These young horses would never have to endure the imagined labours of their parents; instead, they would be admired as a fine example of selective breeding, and preserved for our delight.

Newnham is an attractive village grouped around the church and pub, The George, with a pleasing arrangement of old and new buildings, demonstrating that, with a little bit of care in respecting the scale and layout of the village, it is perfectly possible to mix the two. In this tied pub I got chatting to a retired biology teacher who did not disagree with me when I recounted the suggestion made in other pubs run by the same local brewer based in the nearby town, that they were known as the 'Kentish mafia'. I wish I could have tarried longer in the pub but felt I had to pass on to Doddington. On the way out of the village, I passed a charming cottage with distinctive pargetting on the front wall, a traditional, decorative plastering technique producing elaborate patterns on the exterior walls of buildings, more commonly seen in East Anglia. Between Newnham and Doddington, I walked on a weed-strewn pavement, skirting the grounds of Doddington Place, which housed English Heritage gardens, beside a row of mature lime trees under-grazed by sheep. Many new trees had been responsibly planted in the margin of this estate, protected against numerous nibblers by metal guards.

Coming into the village, I noticed that the church was detached, lying to the north of the main street, up the slope out of the dry valley. Compared with Newnham, the village was prosaic, not being blessed with a particularly pleasing arrangement of buildings. This is not particularly

Painter's Forstal to Doddington

Pargetting

Is the ornamentation of plastered and rendered building facades that would otherwise be smooth or roughcast. It ranges from simple geometric surface patterning to exuberant sculptural reliefs of figures, flowers and sea monsters, but it is only skin deep, applied onto masonry or a lathed, timber-framed wall. English plasterwork became increasingly elaborate in the sixteenth century, and some of the most opulent examples of pargetting were produced over 150 years up to a high point in 1660. East Anglia is the traditional home of pargetting, but it can also be seen in Kent, and before the fire of London in 1666, it was common in London too. Neglect, redevelopment, fire and changing tastes are the main enemies of this form of external decoration, which may simply more commonly survive in East Anglia due to the slower rate of change and less industrialisation.

© Tim Bauxham

Battle of Alma

Took place on 20 September 1854, and is usually considered to be the first battle of the Crimean War (1853–1856), a conflict between the Russian Empire and an alliance of the French Empire, the British Empire, the Ottoman Empire and the Kingdom of Sardinia. The war was part of a long-running contest between the major European powers for influence over territories of the declining Ottoman Empire. The Crimean War is known for the logistical and tactical errors during the land campaign, including the disastrous 'Charge of the Light Brigade' in the battle of Balaclava. Also the war is remembered for the terrible devastation caused by disease, mostly cholera and dysentery. The battle of Alma took place just south of a river of that name in the Crimea peninsula, and was commanded by Lord Raglan, and regarded as an allied victory. The Alma is the name of a public house in the village of Painter's Forstal

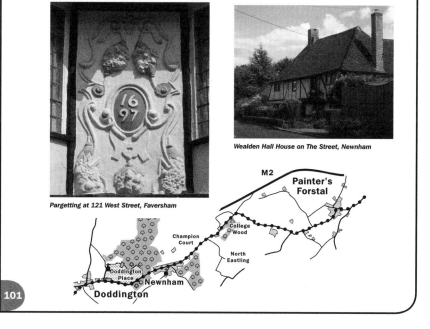

Pargetting at 121 West Street, Faversham

Wealden Hall House on The Street, Newnham

uncommon, as not every village can be a gem. Unlike the pub in
Newnham, I had no desire to linger in The Chequers Inn, since the
clientele was somewhat boorish, in spite of being made welcome by the
long-suffering barman. This pub, in the centre of the village, would have
been a coaching inn on the road between Maidstone and Faversham, and
was clearly quite ancient, with a priest hole beside the bar.

Coming out of Doddington, I peeled off down the Old Lenham Road
and passed below the hamlet of Wichling. Climbing all the time, I put my
head down and paced along the Faversham Road for a couple of miles.
After Woodside Green, I found a well-prepared footpath through
swathes of green wheat to the top of the North Downs scarp at about
200m, where I paused for a while, adjacent to Tophill Farm, and admired
the prospect. I passed through a cool wood and slipped down into an
indent in the scarp slope. In this peaceful enclave, in a short interlude of
sunshine, I slumped down, still carrying my rucksack, against a wooden
signpost, gratefully enjoying the moment of rest. After crossing the Pilgrim's Way, I carried on down the lane to come up to the main A20 trunk
road and walked triumphantly into Lenham in blazing sunshine.

Doddington to Lenham

Red Lion

Is the most common pub name with about 600 examples in the UK. The lion is one of the most common charges in coats of arms and thus the red lion pub sign probably has multiple origins. It is thought to originate from a decree by James I of England, to assert his authority over his new kingdom, saying that all public buildings must display, in prominent places, a heraldic red lion. It is also very common in Kent, and the fourteenth century Red Lion in the square at Lenham is a good example, with the building predating James I's edict. Alternatively, the sign may have originated from the heraldic emblem of John of Gaunt, the first Duke of Lancaster, third son of Edward III and brother to the Black Prince, who died in 1399. In this book, as well as Lenham, Red Lion pubs passed include those at: Farningham, Bridge, Milstead, Herne, Biddenden and Snodland, to name but a few. A pub called the Red Lion appeared in the sitcom *Dad's Army*.

Red Lion, Lenham

Lenham

A picturesque square

Sunday Market

Communal clamour

Bustling racket

Searching for the way to leave.

Doddington

Is a small linear village lying in the Syndale Valley, on the dip slope of the North Downs, in the Kent Downs AONB. The church is located out of the valley, north of the Faversham road, near the entrance to Doddington Place, with its famous listed gardens, comprising 10 acres of a beautiful landscape set in the grounds of a Victorian mansion. At the junction with the Teynham road is the historic twelfth-century Chequers Inn, complete with priesthole. The pub was used by pilgrims on the journey to Canterbury and later, as a coaching inn on the Maidstone to Faversham road.

The Chequers Inn, Doddington

After cleaning up, resting and eating in the Dog and Bear Hotel, I spent most of the evening drinking in The Red Lion, the historic pub on the corner. I was able to talk about my exploits to locals at the bar and tell them about my recently published book, the precursor to this volume.

In the morning, for some unfathomable reason, I woke up with a pain in my right foot that made walking difficult. I hoped it would wear off when I started walking. There was an enthusiastic Sunday market in full swing in the village square, although there was nothing square about it. I have always found the configuration of Lenham confusing and I had to take particular care in choosing which direction to take out. After thrashing around for a while and an abortive visit to the church, I found the right road and tentatively started on my way.

Coming out of Lenham I crossed the railway on the way to Leadingcross Green, crossing over the new railway and up to the Sandway junction. There the White Horse pub appeared to be redundant. It did occur to me that the name Sandway could be derived, in a similar manner to that of Sandling just north of Maidstone, from the underlying greensand strata and the propensity to quarry this raw material in the strip of country north of the Greensand Ridge. I carried on climbing, across the motorway and up past the entrance to Chilston Park Hotel. It was a stiff climb up to the top of the Greensand Ridge at about 135m and the stubborn pain in my foot refused to wear off. From this high point I could see back to the chalk scarp of the North Downs across the intervening valley and forward to the foothills of the Weald across the Vale of Kent. From the top of the Greensand Ridge it is possible to appreciate the grain of the land, the parallel ridges that give Kent its unparalleled landscape appeal.

Crossing the Greensand Way, I came again to the charming hamlet of Boughton Malherbe, with spectacular views southwards towards the River Beult. As before, I sat on the seat below the church and admired the scene, realising that all the hard miles of slogging along roads in less-attractive quarters were vindicated in these moments of delight. I slid off the ridge by a long, curving lane down to Grafty Green, passing a newly planted orchard and a newly constructed reservoir, gathering the waters flowing off the ridge for irrigation purposes. All was quiet in Grafty Green on this Sunday morning and the local shop was naturally closed, but Sunday papers were available outside on an honesty system. Further on, out of the village, was a pub-cum-hotel called the Who'd A Thought

It, and I decided to stop and have the luxury of a cup of coffee, allowing me to take some painkillers in an attempt to ease the discomfort in my foot.

After a short rest, I carried on to Headcorn and happily the painkillers did the trick of masking the pain in my foot. This road, carrying considerable traffic, reminded me of the road I took previously into Marden, in that houses, businesses, paddocks and nefarious yards were strung out along the lane. On the way into Headcorn, I passed by a large cricket ground but saw no indication that a match was to be played that Sunday afternoon. A chaffinch on the wire ushered me into Headcorn. I sat down on a seat in the understated, rectangular green outside the village school and consumed some energy boosting chocolate. I popped into The White Horse for a pint, only to be kept waiting and unwelcomed for an inexcusable amount of time. This caused me to reflect on the original purpose of inns; that is, to welcome strangers and travellers, rather than providing a private club for locals.

After a short break, I pressed on into the centre of the village and observed that the iconic Kings Arms pub on the corner opposite the church had been converted into an Italian restaurant. Certainly, given that I have Italian antecedents, and being not unsurprisingly partial to the food, I have nothing against Italian restaurants or the reuse of important, listed buildings in historic villages. I did, however, feel that it was wrong that the pub in this critical location should be lost. It just didn't seem right and I began to wonder whether there should be a scheme designed to conserve historic pubs in such critical locations, even if their economic viability was in doubt. After all, special, redundant churches are conserved by The Churches Conservation Trust, so why not pubs, which are just as important to the life of their communities? I have observed on my travels that nothing detracts from the visual quality of villages than a disused or derelict pub, as in Adisham, and if we are serious about protecting this very English village scene to enhance tourism, could not a case be made for historic pub subsidisation and preservation? If public money is spent on the conservation of redundant churches, why could it not also be spent on saving valued pubs?

Headcorn is a village with an attractive, historic heart in the vicinity of the church by the River Beult, which is, as I have remarked before, desperately in need of a by-pass to take out through traffic using the busy A274 road. From the shady churchyard, I followed a path paved with

Lenham to Headcorn

Headcorn

Is an ancient village on the north bank of the River Beult on the busy A274 Maidstone to Tenterden road in the centre of the County of Kent. The prosperity brought to the village by the weaving industry, established in the reign of King Edward III, is reflected in the fine houses built in the High Street and the enlargement of the parish church, set in its verdant precinct. With the railway connecting Headcorn to London and Ashford, it is an important commuter station for the village and surrounding area. Originally, the Kent and East Sussex railway connected the village to Tenterden via Biddenden. This busy, large village, with its commuter station and large supermarket complex suffers from traffic congestion and would greatly benefit from a by-pass. To the south of the village is an aerodrome, which was used extensively by American and Canadian troops during the Second World War, and is now a private civil airfield. The historic and pivotal pub, The Kings Arms, opposite the church precinct, has been lost to become an Italian restaurant.

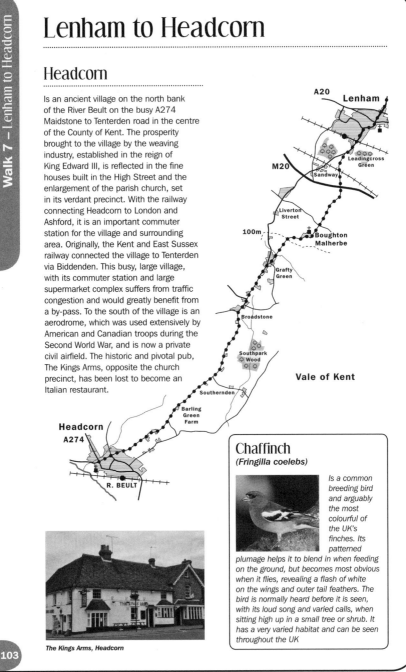

The Kings Arms, Headcorn

Chaffinch
(*Fringilla coelebs*)

Is a common breeding bird and arguably the most colourful of the UK's finches. Its patterned plumage helps it to blend in when feeding on the ground, but becomes most obvious when it flies, revealing a flash of white on the wings and outer tail feathers. The bird is normally heard before it is seen, with its loud song and varied calls, when sitting high up in a small tree or shrub. It has a very varied habitat and can be seen throughout the UK

103

stone flags, south out of the village. I skipped across a railway line by pedestrian crossing in front of an oncoming train that greeted me with a loud blast on its horn. Next, I crossed the lovely River Beult, cloudy and swollen with the heavy recent rains to afflict southern England. I trudged on along the long, straight track, past a pretty meadow in flower, with light aircraft from the nearby Headcorn Airfield circling overhead. The antiquity of this footpath was demonstrated by a row of fabulous, mature oak trees: a lovely sight indeed. I crossed over the significant Hammer Stream, which has its headwaters on the skirts of Hemsted Forest, joining the River Beult just upstream from Headcorn. I trudged along the edge of a wood to Little Brockwood, where I joined the lane to Frittenden, walking through the low, wide pastoral valley that is the Vale of Kent.

Reaching the village of Frittenden, I popped into the pub, unusually called the Bell and Jorrocks. I sat outside and got talking to a local handyman reading the Sunday papers, somewhat down on his marital luck, who explained the pub's name. Evidently, there were once two pubs in this small village, one called The Bell and the other called Jorrocks, the later closing and joining forces with the former. Frittenden was an agreeable if unremarkable village, a bit off the beaten track. As I strode out past the church with an elegant slender spire, the weather started

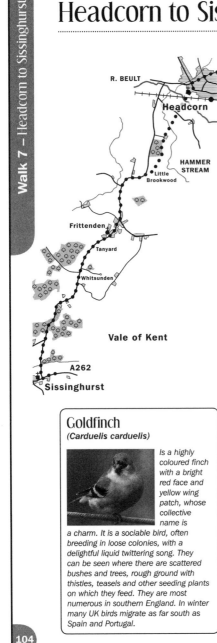

Headcorn to Sissinghurst

Walk 7 – Headcorn to Sissinghurst

R. BEULT

Headcorn

HAMMER
STREAM

Little
Brookwood

Frittenden

Tanyard

Whitsunden

Vale of Kent

A262

Sissinghurst

Sissinghurst

Is a small village situated on a ridge in the Weald of Kent, and located on the A262, a major east/west route from Tenterden to Goudhurst, north of Cranbrook. The village is virtually joined to the settlement of Wisley Pound on the A229 to the west. Its busy main street is lined with many attractive buildings but suffers severe traffic congestion. The main buildings of note are the nearby Sissinghurst Castle and Gardens owned by the National Trust. The Bull Inn, in the heart of the village, is now deserted, boarded up and facing an uncertain future.

Bull Inn, Sissinghurst

Sissinghurst

Village in crisis

Derelict pub

Appalling traffic

Redundant hub

Losing the fight to stay alive.

Hammer Stream

Is a many branched tributary, of around 10 miles in length, of the River Beult, which it joins at Headcorn. It flows north, across the Vale of Kent from the Hammer Mill Farm located on the main A262. Upstream it divides into several branches, wrapping around Hemsted Forest, and draining the foothills of the Weald as far south as the B2086 west of Benenden. The B2086 forms a watershed between waters flowing north to the Medway and south to the Rother. A significant tributary runs through Cranbrook, the capital of the Weald.

Goldfinch
(Carduelis carduelis)

Is a highly coloured finch with a bright red face and yellow wing patch, whose collective name is *a charm. It is a sociable bird, often breeding in loose colonies, with a delightful liquid twittering song. They can be seen where there are scattered bushes and trees, rough ground with thistles, teasels and other seeding plants on which they feed. They are most numerous in southern England. In winter many UK birds migrate as far south as Spain and Portugal.*

104

closing in. I reflected on my masterstroke of taking painkillers earlier on, which had allowed me to get this far. At a bend in the lane, I took a footpath through an orchard to come up into Sissinghurst on the A262, to the east of the church.

That was the planned end of the day's walk and I had hoped to get accommodation in The Bull in Sissinghurst, but the pub was closed and looking extremely shabby. I cannot overemphasise, how much of a disaster this is for the village, in social and visual terms, as well as having to struggle with horrendous traffic congestion. Thus, what potentially could be a vibrant, attractive village with many buildings of quality is struggling to survive, and in the pouring rain its prospects looked even dimmer. I had arranged to stay in The George Hotel in nearby Cranbrook and I rang the hotel to organise a taxi for me. To my amazement, the landlord's son came out and picked me up: excellent service indeed. I spent the evening in Cranbrook, relaxing and resting in the very commodious and friendly hotel. This was the fourth mafia-run establishment I had graced on this trip and I was very impressed by the organisation and friendly service ethic of the management and bar staff, which almost made up for the lack of choice in beer.

In the morning, I caught a bus back to Sissinghurst and set out past the church, along the main road towards Sissinghurst Castle. I fell in with a lady who was also going my way. As I knew the way to the gardens, she fell in behind me along the busy road. Passing the church, she drew my attention to two goldfinches in the churchyard, not quite a charm. Turning into the lane that led to the castle, we were able to talk. She was born and raised in Surrey and loved the English countryside, but married a Swedish man and lived there with her family, only rarely visiting her homeland. Her husband had returned to Sweden and she had a glorious week when she could explore the gardens of Kent. She complained bitterly that the landscape in Sweden was monotonous: all dark conifers and cold, lugubrious lakes. I found her enthusiasm for her adventure infectious, but kept apologising for the lowering, dispiriting weather. She showed considerable interest in my first book and insisted on taking a photograph of me in front of the castle. I explained that I did not intend to visit the excellent, atmospheric gardens, but had to press on. We parted company and I passed through the manicured complex to the estate fields beyond.

The fields were farmed with wildlife in mind, with a generous area

Sissinghurst to Biddenden

Sissinghurst Castle

Consists of the remains of an Elizabethan mansion associated with a beautiful garden laid out by the novelist Vita Sackville-West and her diplomat husband, Harold Nicholson, in the 1930s, now owned and managed by the National Trust. It is one of the most famous gardens in England. The garden is designed as a series of 'rooms', each with a different character of colour and/or theme, the walls being high, clipped hedges and brick walls.

A manor house with a three-armed moat was built here in the Middle Ages. By 1305 it was impressive enough for King Edward I to spend the night. In 1490, Thomas Baker purchased Sissinghurst. The house was given a new brick gatehouse in the 1530s by Sir John Baker, one of Henry VIII's Privy Councillors, which still stands today. The house was greatly enlarged by his son, Sir Richard Baker, when it became the centre of a 700-acre deer park.

The Elizabethan tower at Sissinghurst

In 1573 Queen Elizabeth I spent three nights at Sissinghurst. After the collapse of the Baker family in the late seventeenth century, the building was used for many purposes, including a prisoner–of–war camp during the Seven Years War, as the workhouse for the Cranbrook Union, and homes for farm labourers. Sackville–West and Nicholson bought the derelict castle in 1930 and creating the gardens we see today, which were greatly influenced by Gertrude Jekyll and Edward Lutyens. The National Trust took over the whole of Sissinghurst, its garden, farm and buildings, in 1967. The garden epitomises the English garden of the mid-twentieth century, and is now a popular tourist attraction.

Yellowhammer
(Emberiza citrinella)

Is a passerine, ground-nesting bird in the bunting family, which is most commonly found on lowland arable and mixed farmland. It is a robust bird with a strong seed eater's bill which forms small flocks in winter. The male has a bright yellow head and yellow underparts, and a heavily streaked brown back. The female is much less distinctive. Their natural diet consists of insects when feeding young, but otherwise seeds. Recently their numbers have plummeted in the UK.

105

276

around the field margins being set aside. The benefits were immediately obvious with the appearance of many yellow hammers performing their aerial acrobatics. I crossed over the Hammer Stream again and proceeded to Bettenham Manor in the lane. Instead of making for Three Chimneys on the main road, I carried on along a little-used lane to the hamlet of Hareplain. I saw four Canada Geese feeding in the adjacent field. Taking a footpath opposite Brookwood Farm, I came across a number of delightful ponds. In fact, looking at the map, the whole area around Biddenden was littered with this feature, no doubt due to the impervious nature of the underlying clay. I also noticed a massive acreage of ungrazed, uncultivated land put aside for wildlife in these parts, under the Countryside Stewardship Scheme. One cannot but applaud the good intentions behind the scheme, in paying farmers taxpayers' money to leave land uncultivated, for the benefit of wildlife, but I did wonder about the long-term management arrangements for this land.

I came into the back of Biddenden through a housing area, showing that typical transition from newer, well-designed enclaves of recent times on the outskirts, through the more uniform and regimented houses of the post-war period towards the centre. I made for the church set in its attractive precinct that causes the main road to violently dogleg around it. I sat outside the Red Lion pub for a while, divesting myself of very wet gear, and observed the heavy traffic ploughing through this distinctive old main street. The village was suffering from the same problem as Sissinghurst, with heavy cross-country traffic on the A262, but at least it had retained one of its pubs, the other succumbing to a new life as a Chinese restaurant. Inside the old atmospheric pub I was slightly disappointed that the landlord would not let me eat at the bar, my favourite place, because it offended house rules, so I sulked in a secluded corner instead.

I trekked out east of Biddenden by well-marked, but rarely walked footpaths, the grass having grown long in a wet summer, one of the wettest on record. Also, the grass was soaking wet after a rain shower while I was in the pub and because I foolishly didn't pull on waterproof trousers, I quickly got soaking wet from brushing through. I went through another large area of fields looked after under the Countryside Stewardship Scheme, and passed alongside Hook Wood. I crossed a disused railway line, an extension of the line brought back into service by steam train enthusiasts operating out of Tenterden, which used to run all the way to Headcorn. Eventually, I came up to the A262 again after a

Biddenden to Tenterden

Biddenden

Is a large village, at the junction of the A274 and A262 roads, with an attractive High Street and large parish church. The place name is derived from Old English, meaning Bidda's woodland, probably named after a family who would have used a clearing for grazing. It was once the centre of the Wealden iron industry and clothmaking, after Flemish weavers settled in the area in the reign of Edward III. In 1100, Mary and Eliza Chulkhurst, a pair of conjoined twins, were born in the village. The Biddenden Maids, as they became known, are celebrated in the village sign. The village was once served by a railway station on the Kent and East Sussex line, but this closed in 1954.

Biddenden High Street

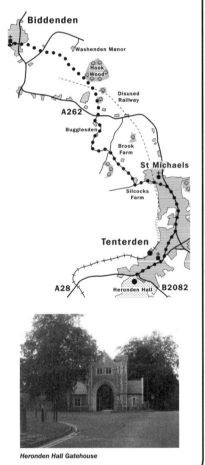

Countryside Stewardship Scheme

Was introduced as a pilot scheme in England in 1991 and operates outside Environmentally Sensitive Areas. Payments are made to farmers and other land managers to enhance and conserve English landscapes, their wildlife and history, and to improve opportunities for public access. The scheme has now closed and has been superseded by the Environmental Stewardship Scheme. Some existing agreements will, however, continue until 2014. Farmers with an existing agreement, which lasts for ten years, receive an annual payment on each hectare of land entered into the scheme. Grants are also available towards capital works, such as hedge-laying and planting. The Environmental Stewardship Scheme is an agri-environmental scheme with similar objectives, managed by Natural England, superseding the Environmentally Sensitive Areas Scheme and the Countryside Stewardship scheme. The scheme aims to improve the natural beauty and diversity of the countryside, enhance, restore and re-create targeted landscapes, their wildlife habitats and historical features, and to improve public access.

Heronden Hall Gatehouse

pleasant walk, if hard slog, through wet grass from Biddenden. One could imagine on a bright sunny day it would be a very rewarding trek.

Picking up Norton's Lane, heading south towards Tenterden, I came across many more fields set aside for wildlife. In fact, the whole area between Biddenden and Tenterden was in danger of becoming one vast nature reserve. I slogged up Readers Bridge Road, past Bugglesden, to a height of 66m by Silcocks Farm and realised that Tenterden and its northerly suburb, St Michaels, was in fact a hilltop town. From this point, on the high ridge, it was easy to appreciate how the land fell away on all sides, giving spectacular views across the Sussex countryside towards Hastings. In times past, Tenterden would have been on the last piece of high ground before the marshes associated with the Rother Estuary. I could have taken the footpath due south, down off the ridge and back up to Tenterden by the station, but I had run out of map. I was tired, so I decided to take the easy option of keeping high and limping into St Michaels and along the uninspiring main road into the delightful small town of Tenterden.

After sitting for a while with a pint outside The White Lion in the centre of the High Street, as had become my normal practice, I made my way to West Cross, the end of the town by the grand entrance to Heronden Hall. I booked into the splendid William Caxton pub, my billet for the night, and rested. The following morning, the weather was simply awful and I decided not to walk on, and so I stayed in the pub for another enjoyable night, being made extremely welcome by the landlady and her regulars. On the second night, I was even required to perform on the darts board as the team were short of players. I explained that I hadn't played for about twenty years, but that didn't seem to matter, since the players were not that confident of their abilities. As it turned out, I was one of only two players on our side to fluke a game.

The next morning, I set out again for Rye with the weather at last set to be fine. I strolled down the attractive High Street again, unfortunately beset with traffic, and left by the B2080 towards Reading Street, along wide grass verges. At a bend in the road, after Leigh Green, I took a mowed footpath through unused fields to Kench Hill and on to Frenchay Farm. The footpath was in good condition to Frenchay Farm and beyond, but as I descended off the ridge down to Reading Street, I was forced to slither along the edge of corn fields, teetering on the edge of an unstable, deeply-cut stream, before regaining the road. However, the one bonus of walking off the ridge was the fabulous views across the flat plain of Shirley Moor to the east. Also, looking south-east, I could see right out across Walland Marsh to Dungeness. I paused frequently to admire the scene.

Coming up to the main road by The Century Farm, I paused again and looked down on Shirley Moor with its large, flat fields dominated by swathes of wheat, creating almost prairie-like conditions. The roadside verges at this time of year showed the rampant growth of cow parsley, with its white to pink compact heads, competing with the dense, dark-green patches of stinging nettles. Down the road in Reading Street there was a curious roadside church, no more than a chapel really, called the Ebony Church.

I found the small lane going south, passing through the charming hamlet of Reading Street, with some extremely desirable cottage dwellings on the very last projection of the ridge stretching down from Tenterden. At the bottom of the slope, by the Reading Sewer, I stood still and looked around. In times gone by, I would have been standing on the edge of the sea, no doubt with a quay where boats could tie up in the estuary of the River Rother, which has now been diverted to the southern side of the Isle of Oxney due to subsequent land reclamation.

Ahead of me was the distinctive hill known as Chapel Bank, which I approached by footpaths across the flat-bottomed, grain-dominated former river valley floor. I climbed up the slope to Chapel Bank, looked west across the Rother Levels and observed a classic, winding lane through Stone Corner dotted with a string of farms, like beads on a necklace. I stood still and was overwhelmed by a sense of wonder: one of those moments that make the journey worthwhile. Standing there transfixed, with birdsong ravishing the silence and the sun warming the air through dappled, white clouds, my spirits were lifted.

On the top of Chapel Bank, I came across an overgrown graveyard but no chapel, and this got me thinking about what had happened there. In medieval times, before the valley below was reclaimed from the sea, there was a church on this site, on what was known as Ebony Island. In 1858, after the settlement on the island had ceased to serve any purpose, the church was moved stone by stone by an enterprising community, to Reading Street, where it became the previously mentioned Ebony Church. I waded through the graveyard at the top of the hill and was serenaded by another chaffinch with its characteristic descending song.

Coming out the other side, an equally amazing view opened up: northwards across Shirley Moor, eastwards to the Appledore salient and the Greensand Ridge, and southwards across the current valley of the River Rother to the Isle of Oxney. I could clearly see the wind farm down on Walland Marsh, forming a distinctive feature in the landscape. I pondered on its visual effect and concluded that it was generally benign, forming a distinctive landscape feature, not unlike the power station at Dungeness or the recently demolished cooling towers at Richborough. I felt this walk across Chapel Bank was so spectacular that it should feature in every good walking guide book in this part of the country.

I dropped down off the bank by a long, straight footpath through fields of wheat and up to the lane by Luckhurst, passing through a scruffy farm where a massive store of putrefying silage was leaking effluent into a corner of a wheat field, killing the crop in the process. At the pretty hamlet of Luckhurst, I picked up the Saxon Shore Way and proceeded south onto the Isle of Oxney. After Luckhurst, I lost the path across a ploughed field and reached the Appledore Road below the village of Stone-in-Oxney. I walked up the hill, past a large, well-maintained cricket ground into the centre of the village, with bullfinches flitting along the hedge in front of me. The village sign says Stone-cum-Ebony, reflecting

Tenterden to Stone in Oxney

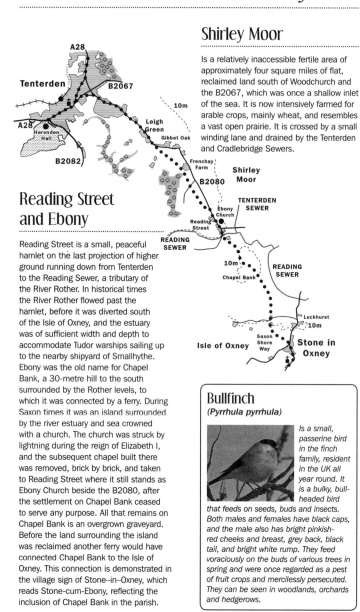

Shirley Moor

Is a relatively inaccessible fertile area of approximately four square miles of flat, reclaimed land south of Woodchurch and the B2067, which was once a shallow inlet of the sea. It is now intensively farmed for arable crops, mainly wheat, and resembles a vast open prairie. It is crossed by a small winding lane and drained by the Tenterden and Cradlebridge Sewers.

Reading Street and Ebony

Reading Street is a small, peaceful hamlet on the last projection of higher ground running down from Tenterden to the Reading Sewer, a tributary of the River Rother. In historical times the River Rother flowed past the hamlet, before it was diverted south of the Isle of Oxney, and the estuary was of sufficient width and depth to accommodate Tudor warships sailing up to the nearby shipyard of Smallhythe. Ebony was the old name for Chapel Bank, a 30-metre hill to the south surrounded by the Rother levels, to which it was connected by a ferry. During Saxon times it was an island surrounded by the river estuary and sea crowned with a church. The church was struck by lightning during the reign of Elizabeth I, and the subsequent chapel built there was removed, brick by brick, and taken to Reading Street where it still stands as Ebony Church beside the B2080, after the settlement on Chapel Bank ceased to serve any purpose. All that remains on Chapel Bank is an overgrown graveyard. Before the land surrounding the island was reclaimed another ferry would have connected Chapel Bank to the Isle of Oxney. This connection is demonstrated in the village sign of Stone–in–Oxney, which reads Stone-cum-Ebony, reflecting the inclusion of Chapel Bank in the parish.

Bullfinch
(Pyrrhula pyrrhula)

Is a small, passerine bird in the finch family, resident in the UK all year round. It is a bulky, bull-headed bird that feeds on seeds, buds and insects. Both males and females have black caps, and the male also has bright pinkish-red cheeks and breast, grey back, black tail, and bright white rump. They feed voraciously on the buds of various trees in spring and were once regarded as a pest of fruit crops and mercilessly persecuted. They can be seen in woodlands, orchards and hedgerows.

107

inclusion in the parish of the northern area around Chapel Bank, formerly called the Isle of Ebony. I called in to the much-improved, back-to-front, Crown Inn for lunch, rest and recuperation.

Before setting off again, still following the Saxon Shore Way, I saw a signpost indicating that it was 6 miles to Rye. It was a hard slog up Church Hill on the first sunny day on this walk, up to Stone Cliff. From the top of Stone Cliff, which was once part of sea cliffs along the southern edge of the island, I could see down across the extensive Rother Levels, which presented an unbroken sea of green wheat. In the distance, the flat lands stretched away to Rye and down to the coast. After lingering over the stunning views for a while, I came down off the steepest part of the cliff by a diagonal belay across a field of sheep and then through a field covered in ant hills. Above the Rother Levels, I disturbed a flock of crows, which created a murderous din in this delightful spot. Further round the cliff, the steep slope was clothed with bushes forming, no doubt, a fine wild nature area. I reflected on the fact that wildlife does not necessarily need pretty countryside, but that wildlife makes the countryside interesting.

I exploded out onto the featureless Rother Levels, past a low electric fence designed to keep the rabbits out of the growing corn, along a poorly marked section of the Saxon Shore Way, which meandered along the field edges by reed-festooned dykes. I looked back several times to appreciate the dramatic cliffs, presided over by an acrobatic kestrel quartering the ground, stretching along the southern edge of the Isle of Oxney. This watery world provided a suitable habitat for a myriad of iridescent blue mayflies. It was difficult going on little-used footpaths and it did occur to me that to make this part of the Saxon Shore Way viable, the authorities would need to create a better-articulated path, maybe by buying a strip of land and creating a new direct bridleway.

After half a mile or so, the footpath crosses the long, straight lane that is the Military Road, and up onto the bank of the Royal Military Canal. Again, the path was overgrown with excessive growth of grass in a very wet year, and the banks of the tranquil canal were bedecked by a line of self-seeded cherry trees. The thirty-five wind turbines on Walland Marsh were looming closer all the time. I came down to the disused Iden Lock, crossed over the wide River Rother and proceeded to walk back westwards along the river bank, searching for a footpath that would take me up to the village of Iden. I left the river by a pumping station and walked along a damp field edge planted with struggling sweet corn but invaded by pernicious horsetail.

I soon reached the break in the slope and clambered up another distinctive fossil sea cliff on the way to Bosney Farm, through a verdant gulley with more uncultivated land, naturally affording spectacular views of the surrounding countryside. There, the farmer had deliberately blocked the footpath, giving me no choice but to walk out to the lane east of the hamlet called The Elms. Looking north, I was struck by the observation that I was at exactly the same height as on the Isle of Oxney; the level plain that would have been raised out of the sea many millions of years ago had subsequently been eroded by rivers to create today's undulating landscape. I strolled along the pleasant lane into Iden.

I sojourned for a while in The Bell at Iden, opposite the village bowling green, presided over by the church, before walking the final leg, along bigger roads into Rye. Here I had the weird experience of the lady attending the bar lecturing me on the correct procedure for walking down country lanes, as if I needed instruction. I was tempted to explain where I had walked from that day, how far I had come on this walk and what my project was, but I couldn't summon up the energy. In disgust I sat outside and finished my pint before setting off again.

Further on, a sign proclaimed Playden to be an ancient village, but walking down the wide main road, with a path along generous tree-lined verges, much of the village, including the church, lay back from the road and was obscured from view. At the bottom of Rye Hill, I passed an elegant terrace of houses striking off down the lower road beside the river. I crossed over the railway and passed through some interesting streets below the land gate, a side of Rye I was unfamiliar with. I passed up through the town and down to the Strand, where I booked into the excellent Ship Hotel. As before, the landlady made me very welcome and I spent a pleasant evening in the pub talking to the bar staff and other guests about my first, recently published book.

In the morning, on my last day of walking, I set out from Rye, intending to walk to Winchelsea via Rye Harbour. I crossed the bridge over the River Tillingham, with its complicated set of water gates, and walked along the opposite bank on the New Winchelsea Road. I hiked past the Smeaton Stores, a building which looked like a former pub, named, no doubt, after the famous builder of lighthouses. The wharf below the Strand on the Tillingham is navigable by small boats from the

Stone in Oxney to Rye

Field Horsetail
(Equisetum arvense)

Is widely distributed in the UK in meadows, gardens and wasteland, flourishing on damp soil. It is poisonous to livestock and reproduces by means of spores rather than seeds, and spreads via underground rhizomes and tubers. It is, curiously, a 'living fossil', as it is the only living plant genus in its entire class, which for over one hundred million years was much more diverse and dominated the understory of late Paleozoic forests. Some species in the class were large trees reaching to 30 metres tall, and plants formed the basis of coal deposits in the Carboniferous period. Today it is simply an invasive weed that is very difficult to eradicate. The plant has the ability to accumulate metals, including gold, in its tissues, and extracts have been successfully used as a fungicide.

Kestrel
(Falco tinnunculus)

This bird is a familiar sight, with its pointed wings and long tail, hovering, with a motionless head, beside a roadside verge. They are found in a wide variety of habitats, from moor to heath, to farmland and urban areas, but do not favour dense forests, wetlands and mountains. Although they have adapted well to man-made environments, and their numbers are recovering from the sharp decline experienced in the 1970s, they are still included on the amber list. As is usual with monogamous raptors, the female bird is slightly larger, allowing the pair to fill different feeding niches over their home range. They are resident all year round and feed on small mammals, insects and birds.

Stone in Oxney

Is a small, scattered village which occupies a commanding position on the east end of the Isle of Oxney, affording spectacular views out across Romney Marsh. The parish boundary runs along the Reading Sewer to the north and the Kent ditch to the south and includes Chapel Bank. The stone that gives the village its name is a Mithraic alter stone in the church. It is possible to make out the outline of a bull, an important emblem of the Mithraic cult practised by many Roman soldiers, which may have been brought from nearby Stutfall Castle, a Roman garrison below Lympne, also known as Lemanis.

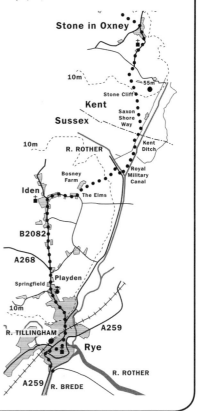

108

River Rother by using a short section of the River Brede. The town of Rye is surrounded by these three rivers on three sides. The quayside displayed many new, shiny boats but older boats, never to return to the water, were left to rot. By a Martello Tower I turned east across the River Brede and strode off down the straight lane to Rye Harbour.

The first part of the Harbour Road was on a causeway through fields, and in one field I saw ostriches strutting their stuff and glimpses of Camber Castle out in the marsh to my right. Soon, I passed through an industrial area and noted a small church with a stone spire, which looked completely different to the way I had described it in my very first walk, from the other side of the river. This was a rather sobering experience, having to question that which I had reported previously in good faith, but inaccurately.

Having reached the atmospheric village of Rye Harbour, I passed by the first pub, called the Inkerman Arms. In common with The Alma in Painter's Forstal, the pub was named after a battle in the Crimean War. The second pub was down by the harbour, a working harbour with the sounds of engines driving machinery counterpointed against the cries of seagulls. There were attractive houses in a somewhat scruffy, pebble-strewn enclave with considerable charm, much like Dungeness. It was possible to get right up to the river and observe the scene from a viewing platform. The appeal of the place was demonstrated by the posse of amateur painters out for the day. The small settlement at the mouth of the river Rother is graced by another Martello tower and a large holiday park sporting numerous caravans.

Coming back towards the church, I took a long gravel path across the back of the Rye Bay Nature Reserve, between a system of extensive lakes and the sea wall, past The Nook and the Watch House. I was slightly perturbed about the lack of access from this path to the nature reserve and indeed, there were frequent 'Keep Out' and 'Private Property' signs. I must say I had never thought of a nature reserve as private property. After The Nook, I sat down on a grassy bank and looked out over the lacustrine scene towards Winchelsea, perched on its wooded hill. The telegraph wires in this vicinity were adorned with bits of coloured plastic, no doubt to warn weary incoming birds of the hazard when coming in to land after a marathon flight from Africa.

At the furthest extent of a large body of water, I turned through 90 degrees and made my way up to the Morlais Ridge, sounding like the site

Rye to Winchelsea

Battle of Inkerman

Was another battle fought during the Crimean War, on 5 November 1854, between the allied armies of Britain and France against the Russian Imperial Army. The battle broke the will of the Russian Army to defeat the allies in the field, and was followed by the siege of Sevastopol. The role of troops fighting mostly on their own initiative, due to the foggy conditions prevailing during the battle, has earned the engagement the name of 'The Soldier's Battle'. The Inkerman Arms is the name of a public house in the village of Rye Harbour.

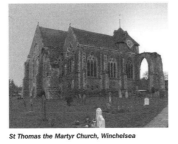

St Thomas the Martyr Church, Winchelsea

John Smeaton
(1724-1792)

Was an English civil engineer and eminent physicist, responsible for the design of bridges, canals, harbours and lighthouses, who is often regarded as the father of civil engineering. He is best known for the construction of an Eddystone lighthouse off the coast of Cornwall, using a technique involving dovetailed granite blocks. He was also involved in harbour works at Ramsgate, and acted as a consultant on the disastrous 63-year-long project to build the New Harbour at Rye, designed to combat the silting up of the port of Winchelsea.

The project is now known informally as 'Smeaton's Harbour', even though his advice was sought 39 years after construction had commenced. The retreat of the sea, and the process of silting up, made the harbours of Winchelsea and Rye redundant, and Camber Castle, which commanded the entranced to both harbours, was abandoned In the 1640s as it had ceased to serve any useful purpose. The Smeaton Stores, a lost pub on the Winchelsea Road, having been converted to residential use, is named after these historical events.

Merlin
(Falco columbarius)

Is the UK's smallest bird of prey. This compact, dashing falcon has a relatively long, square-cut tail, and broad-based pointed wings. Its small size enables it to hover and hang in the breeze as it pursues its prey. They can be seen in almost any open country but often near the coast. They feed mainly on small birds and, although recovering from a population crash in the twentieth century, are still on the amber list.

109

of a First World War battle, emanating from the back of Winchelsea Beach. I passed through horse pastures and met an avid birdwatcher who pointed out a merlin, a small grey hawk, quartering the field hedgerows: a bird I had never seen before. I joined the Sea Road from Winchelsea Beach at its ridiculously acute bend and proceeded along it to Winchelsea, observing the Strand Gate across the fields. I disturbed a grey heron feeding from a front garden pond in a house backing onto the river Brede. I then crossed over the Royal Military Canal, departed from the Saxon Shore Way and clambered up into the sedate, ordered town, the end of my perambulation through Kent and East Sussex: journey's end!

In the town, I enquired after a bus that would take me up the coast, eventually to return to my brother's house in Dumpton Gap on Thanet, where I had left my car. This interesting journey took me the rest of the day and even included a tour of the mining villages behind Deal, through which I had walked on the first day. I was struck by the narrowness of the lanes serving these former mining communities and the problems it caused for the bus driver trying to negotiate this route. I mused on the fact that this walk, starting in Deal and ending in Winchelsea, mirrored the patriotic sentiments expressed in the poem, 'The Other Little Boats,' by Edward Shanks, about the Dunkirk evacuation, when they were crewed by men from Deal and Winchelsea.

This Land is Your Land

This land is your land, this land is my land,
From the city suburbs to the Channel waters,
From the Wealden forest to the reclaimed marshland,
This land was made for you and me.
As I went walking along your highways
Your sylvan byways that are my ways,
I saw below me a pleasant valley,
This land was meant for you and me.

I've roamed and rambled, I've followed my footsteps
Through dripping orchards and verdant pastures,
And all around me a voice was sounding,
This land belongs to you and me.
The sun came shining as I was strolling,
The wheat fields waving and the west wind blowing
As the rain was lifting a voice came chanting,
This land was made for you and me.

Long-distance Walks Logos in Kent and East Sussex

References

Buxbaum, Tim, 'Pargetting' in *The Building Conservation Directory* (2001).

Green, Brynmor, H., *Natural Kent* (S.B. Publications, 2008)

Hann, Andrew, *The Medway Valley: A Kent Landscape Transformed* (Phillimore, 2009).

Major, Alan, *Cherries in the Rise: Their Cultivation in Kent Through the Centuries* (S.B. Publications, 1997).

Shaw, George, *Graham Sutherland: An Unfinished World* (Modern Art Oxford 2012)

Wilcox, Timothy, *Samuel Palmer* (Tate Publishing, 2005).

Image Copyright Acknowledgements

In general, all images used in this book are subject to the generic licence obtained by Wikipedia. The following images are taken from the Geograph Project, and are covered by the Creative Commons Attribution Share-alike license 2.0 .

Plate 3. Quebec House. Image copyright Oxyman.
Plate 8. Goudhurst. Image copyright Ron Strutt.
Plate 9. Cranbrook High Street. Image copyright Colin Smith.
Plate 12. Henden Place. Image copyright Oast House Archive.
Plate 13. Warehorne Church. Image copyright Iain Macauley.
Plate 17. The Farmhouse, West Malling. Image copyright Nigel Chadwick.
Plate 21. Sutton Valence. Image copyright John Brown.
Plate 39. Church Street, Wye. Image copyright Chris Downer.
Plate 41. The Black Horse, Pluckley. Image copyright Nigel Chadwick.
Plate 42. Smarden Church. Image copyright John Brown.
Plate 44. Kings Arms, Boxley. Image copyright Chris Whippet.
Plate 50. Teston Bridge. Image copyright Colin Smith.
Plate 51. Medway Bridge. Image copyright Pete Chapman.
Plate 52. Leigh Flood Barrier. Image copyright Nigel Chadwick.
Plate 54. The George Inn, Frant. Image copyright Andrew Hill.
Plate 56. Bateman's. Image copyright Linda Spashett.
Plate 58. Battle Abbey. Image copyright Simon Carey.
Plate 66. St. Katharine's and the Cock Inn. Image copyright Nigel Chadwick.
Plate 67. The Chiding Stone. Image copyright Nikki Mahadevan.
Plate 68. Holy Trinity Church. Image copyright Dr. Neil Clifton.
Plate 72. Wadhurst High Street. Image copyright Julian P. Guffogg
Plate 73. The Moor. Image copyright Nick Macneil.

Plate 76. Smallhythe Place. Image copyright David Ansley.

Plate 81. Trottiscliffe Church. Image copyright Robert Edwards.

Plate 85. Fruiterers Arms, Rodmersham Green. Image copyright Terry S. Blackman.

Plate 88. Whitstable High Street. Image copyright Martyn Ayre.

Plate 89. Upper Red Lion. Image copyright Nigel Chadwick.

Plate 90. West Stourmouth Church. Image copyright Oast House Archive.

Plate 91. Richborough Castle/Power Station. Image copyright Oast House Archive.

Plate 91. Barbican Gate, Sandwich. Image copyright Penny Mayes.

Plate 92. Starters hut at 1st hole on Royal St George's Golf Club. Image copyright Ken Duff.

Plate 95. The derelict Bull's Head, Adisham. Image copyright Oast House Archive.

Plate 95. The Water Tower in Woodlands Wood. Image copyright Nick Smith.

Plate 96. Bridge Village. Image copyright Roger Smith.

Plate 96. St Mary's Church Lower Hardres. Image copyright Roger Smith.

Plate 97. Chilham Village Square. Image copyright Jonathan Billinger.

Plate 98. Tonford Manor. Image copyright Nick Smith.

Plate 98. Harbledown Village Sign. Image copyright Oast House Archive.

Plate 99. White Horse Inn, Boughton Street. Image copyright Oast House Archive.

Plate 100. The Alma Public House, Painter's Forstal. Image copyright Pam Fray.

Plate 101. Pargetting at 121 West Street, Faversham. Image copyright Oast House Archive.

Plate 102. Red Lion Pub. Image copyright Oast House Archive.

Plate 102. The Chequers Inn. Image copyright Penny Mayes.

Plate 103. Kings Arms. Image copyright Brian Chadwick.

Plate 104. Bull Inn, Sissinghurst. Image copyright Oast House Archive.

Plate 109. St Thomas the Martyr Church, Winchelsea. Image copyright Paul Russon.

NOUVELLES PRATIQUES SOCIALES

**Volume 10, numéro 1
Printemps 1997**

Dossier
10e anniversaire

Sous la direction de
Lucie Fréchette

1997

Presses de l'Université du Québec
2875, boul. Laurier, Sainte-Foy (Québec) G1V 2M3

La publication de ce numéro a été rendue possible grâce au soutien
de l'Université du Québec à Montréal,
de l'Université du Québec à Hull,
de l'Université du Québec à Chicoutimi,
de l'Université du Québec en Abitibi-Témiscamingue,
de l'Université du Québec à Rimouski,
du siège social de l'Université du Québec
et de l'Université de Sherbrooke.

Cette revue est publiée grâce, entre autres, à une subvention du FCAR
pour la formation de chercheurs et l'aide à la recherche.

La revue *Nouvelles pratiques sociales* est indexée dans *Repère, Science
et technologie au Québec,* et *Médias et communications au Québec* et
dans l'*Index de la santé et des services sociaux.*

Révision linguistique : Gislaine Barrette

ISSN 0843-4468
ISBN 2-7605-0974-5

Dépôt légal – 4ᵉ trimestre 1997
Bibliothèque nationale du Québec
Bibliothèque nationale du Canada
Envoi de Poste – publications – Enregistrement n° 07591

Nouvelles pratiques sociales est une revue avec comités de lecture.

Pour toute correspondance concernant la direction et la rédaction de la revue, s'adresser à :

Nouvelles pratiques sociales
Département de travail social
Université du Québec à Montréal
C.P. 8888, succ. Centre-ville
Montréal (Québec), Canada H3C 3P8
• Tél.: (514) 987-3000, poste 4721 • Téléc.: (514) 987-4494
• Courrier électronique : nps@uqam.ca

Pour toute correspondance concernant les abonnements, les autorisations de droits d'auteur et la publicité, s'adresser à :

Presses de l'Université du Québec
2875, boul. Laurier
Sainte-Foy (Québec)
Canada G1V 2M3

Comité de consultation international

Ricardo Hill Acosta y Lara, *Catédratico investigator, Ciudad universitaria, Mexique;*

Harry C. Boyte, *Humphrey Institute of Public Affairs, University of Minnesota, États-Unis;*

Samira Kria Chaker, *Maître de conférences en sciences économiques, Institut des hautes études commerciales, Université de Tunis, et Directrice générale, ministère des Affaires de la femme et de la famille, Tunis, Tunisie;*

Yves Chaloult, *Département de sociologie, Université de Brasilia, Brésil;*

Marie-Josèphe Doublier, *École normale de l'Ouest, France;*

Aimé Gogué, *Directeur du programme de 3e cycle interuniversitaire, Ouagadougou, Burkina Faso;*

Jean-Claude Jean, *Directeur, Institut culturel Karl-Lévêque, Pétion-Ville, Haïti;*

Jeremy Kendall, *Personal Social Services Research Unit, London School of Economics, Londres et University de Kent, Canterbury;*

Jean-Louis Laville, *Laboratoire de sociologie du changement des institutions, Centre national de la recherche scientifique, Paris, France;*

Kenneth I. Millar, *Recteur de l'école de service social, Louisiana State University, États-Unis;*

Sœur Arnalfy Ortega, *Cooperazione internationale (COOPI), Guatemala;*

Enrique E. Raya Lozano, *Faculté d'anthropologie et de travail social, Université de Grenade, Espagne;*

Maryse Tripier, *Unité de recherche migrations et sociétés (URMIS), Université de Paris VII, Paris, France;*

Monica Viana, *Département de travail social, Université de Sherbrooke, Québec, Canada.*

Sommaire

Tendances sociales et renouvellement des pratiques. Rétrospectives sur 10 ans à *Nouvelles pratiques sociales*

Lucie FRÉCHETTE
Département de travail social, UQAH
Rédactrice en chef de Nouvelles pratiques sociales

À l'automne 1988, dans l'éditorial du premier numéro de la revue *Nouvelles pratiques sociales*, Yves Vaillancourt indiquait qu'il fallait une bonne dose de témérité pour lancer une nouvelle revue spécialisée dans le domaine de l'intervention sociale au Québec pour offrir un peu d'oxygène intellectuel à ceux et à celles qui tentent de mieux cerner et travailler la spécificité sociale dans le Québec d'aujourd'hui. *Nouvelles pratiques sociales* a aujourd'hui dix ans. Nous sommes fiers de constater que le défi a été relevé avec succès. Le dixième anniversaire de la revue méritait d'être souligné et nous avons choisi de le faire en portant un regard rétrospectif sur les tendances sociales et le renouvellement des pratiques qui ont marqué ces dix ans.

RELEVER LE DÉFI D'UNE TRIBUNE
SUR LA QUESTION SOCIALE QUÉBÉCOISE
ET LE RENOUVELLEMENT DES PRATIQUES SOCIALES

Nouvelles pratiques sociales a été conçue comme une revue axée sur les pratiques sociales et leur renouvellement. Elle a voulu alimenter l'analyse des gens de terrain et soutenir la créativité dans l'intervention. Elle a offert une tribune aux chercheurs et aux intervenants pour rendre compte de l'intervention soutenue par la recherche scientifique et pour stimuler la réflexion critique sur l'actualité. Les dossiers thématiques abordés se sont situés dans la foulée des objectifs de départ de la revue : ils ont permis d'examiner de plus près certaines pratiques sociales (Pratiques féministes, Prévention sociale, Coopération internationale, Relations interethniques et pratiques sociales, etc.), d'approfondir de nouvelles problématiques (Chômage et travail, Santé mentale, Jeunes et enjeux sociaux, etc.), d'analyser une tendance ou un mouvement social ou, encore, de scruter un projet politique (Mouvements sociaux, Quinze mois après le Rapport Rochon, La réforme vingt ans après, etc.). En 1994, la revue ose faire un autre pas en avant en organisant son premier colloque sur « L'arrimage entre le communautaire et le secteur public » qui sera, dans les années subséquentes, suivi par deux autres, l'un sur l'appauvrissement des communautés locales et l'autre sur l'économie sociale et les services sociaux et de santé. Intervenants, chercheurs, étudiants et militants trouvent dans ces rassemblements un nouvel espace pour s'exprimer et échanger.

Un bilan sommaire de ces dix dernières années révèle que les dossiers thématiques et les colloques de NPS ont contribué de façon significative à la construction d'un climat collectif dynamique dans les milieux institutionnels et communautaires préoccupés par le renouvellement des pratiques sociales. La parole et l'écrit, la réflexion, la recherche et le débat nous ont semblé constituer des moyens complémentaires qu'il fallait exploiter pour que NPS stimule l'émergence de nouveaux partenariats et revitalise les solidarités dans le vaste champ des pratiques sociales.

Comme chacun le sait, une revue tire sa vitalité non seulement des gens qui s'y expriment, mais aussi des gens qui en tissent la toile de fond et en assurent la publication. Sous l'impulsion de professeurs du Département de travail social de l'UQAM, rapidement rejoints par d'autres de l'UQAH, l'UQAC et l'UQAT, un comité de pionniers a mis en branle le projet initial de revue et formé le premier comité de rédaction en s'adjoignant des collaborateurs du secteur communautaire et du milieu institutionnel des affaires sociales. Aujourd'hui, une vingtaine de personnes sont membres du comité de rédaction et six d'entre elles siègent au comité exécutif. Depuis les débuts de la revue, une quarantaine de personnes (voir la liste à la fin) en tout ont consacré des énergies à bâtir *Nouvelles pratiques sociales* et à en faire ce qu'elle est aujourd'hui. L'amalgame de chercheurs et d'intervenants s'est avéré des plus heureux, et la synergie créée assure la pertinence sociale et scientifique de la revue. Ils ont impulsé à *Nouvelles pratiques sociales* un processus collectif où la question sociale et sa mouvance sont sans cesse remises à l'ordre du jour. À l'occasion du dixième anniversaire de la revue, ce sont ces artisans, membres des comités de rédaction d'hier ou d'aujourd'hui, qui reprennent la plume pour offrir un tour d'horizon de ces derniers dix ans.

DES CHOIX PARMI UN LARGE ÉVENTAIL DE SITUATIONS SOCIALES ET DE PRATIQUES EN RENOUVELLEMENT

Dans son introduction au *Traité des problèmes sociaux,* Fernand Dumont (1994) soutient que l'appréhension des problèmes sociaux dépend des représentations collectives et qu'il faut un travail militant considérable pour éveiller l'attention publique aux inégalités sociales et lui faire adopter des causes pour lesquelles elle engagera la bataille. Une revue comme la nôtre participe à cet effort de mise en lumière des inégalités sociales et de soutien à l'émergence de pratiques sociales constructives. Jeter un regard rétrospectif sur les dix dernières années permet de dégager des éléments de l'éventail des situations fort diversifiées composant la réalité sociale québécoise, d'analyser leur évolution et d'en discerner les pratiques novatrices.

La question sociale étant large et complexe, il a fallu faire des choix. Nous aurions pu parler de la pauvreté et de ses divers visages, de la famille et de ses nombreuses mutations, de la précarité du travail, de la citoyenneté et de la participation sociale, de l'itinérance ou de la maltraitance, des pratiques territoriales ou de la prévention et de la promotion sociale, bref, de bien d'autres pratiques ou problématiques qu'englobe l'univers de la question sociale au Québec. Nous avons choisi de donner la parole à des artisans de la revue et de profiter de leur expertise dans des domaines au demeurant fort pertinents au regard du renouvellement des pratiques sociales.

Deux grands champs de pratiques et d'évolution des conditions sociales ont donc retenu notre attention en ce dixième anniversaire : les pratiques du mouvement des femmes et la question des dynamiques ethnoculturelles. Francine Descarries et Christine Corbeil retracent les phases du développement et les formes d'expression de la pensée et l'activité du mouvement des femmes au Québec. De son côté, André Jacob, qui sans cesse, ces derniers dix ans, a posé et reposé sous de multiples formes la question des rapports à l'ethnicité et à la culture, brosse le portrait des tendances qui ont structuré l'immigration et la dynamique d'intégration des immigrants au Québec.

Par ailleurs, en ce qui concerne les pratiques sociales traitant plus particulièrement des inégalités sociales, un retour sur le champ de la santé mentale s'imposait. Les dix premières années de NPS coïncident avec celles de la gestation et de la mise en place de la « nouvelle politique de santé mentale au Québec » font observer Jean Gagné et Henri Dorvil qui en retracent l'itinéraire assorti d'un bilan où les tendances contradictoires jalonnent la trajectoire des services en santé mentale. La question des inégalités sociales et de la recomposition du tissu social dans les communautés locales met en relief non seulement la vulnérabilité des personnes, mais aussi celle des communautés locales. Les CLSC y sont particulièrement sensibles et en font une priorité en agissant par l'intermédiaire de l'organisation communautaire. Au moment où les fusions administratives érodent la marge de manœuvre des CLSC menaçant leur caractère social, il a paru essentiel, avec le concours de Denis Bourque, de résumer l'évolution de l'action communautaire dans ces établissements. Finalement, tant en milieu institutionnel que dans le secteur communautaire, les questions relatives à l'économie sociale font surface. Même si elles ne datent pas d'hier, il importe aujourd'hui de distinguer le projet des pouvoirs publics du projet communautaire et du potentiel qu'il recèle en matière d'économie sociale. Rétrospectives et prospectives en matière d'économie sociale forment la trame du texte de Louis Favreau et de Benoît Lévesque.

L'édition savante, tout comme la presse en général, joue un rôle important dans la définition des problèmes sociaux. La recherche scientifique et la diffusion des expertises font ressortir des situations qui sont ensuite confirmées en tant que problématiques sociales. NPS s'inscrit dans ce mouvement en veillant à renouveler sans cesse la pertinence sociale de son contenu. Forte de son expérience des dix dernières années et soutenue par près de 1 200 lecteurs, elle se propose de jouer un rôle tant dans l'analyse des problématiques sociales, que dans la prospection et le soutien de pistes d'intervention novatrices, et ce pour les dix prochaines années !

NOUVELLES PRATIQUES SOCIALES
DÉSIRE REMERCIER CEUX ET CELLES
QUI ONT CONTRIBUÉ ACTIVEMENT
À SON DÉVELOPPEMENT
EN SOULIGNANT LEUR PARTICIPATION

La protection
de la jeunesse :
à l'heure de la réforme

*Entrevue avec **Suzanne Lemire***
Directrice de la protection de la jeunesse
Les Centres jeunesse de Montréal

Paul LANGLOIS
Centre jeunesse de Québec

Jean-Marc MEUNIER
Département de travail social
Université du Québec à Hull

Née à Chicoutimi, Suzanne Lemire fait partie de la génération à cheval entre le cours classique et le cégep. Après des études de baccalauréat en service social à l'Université Laval (1971), elle fait ses premières armes au sein du ministère des Affaires indiennes, sur la Côte-Nord puis à Québec. Ensuite, elle passe au ministère de la Justice, service de détention et de probation (Sept-Îles et Baie Comeau). À la fin des années 1970, elle s'inscrit à la maîtrise en service social (Laval), dans la perspective de systématiser sa pratique. Son intérêt se centre alors sur la jonction des fonctions d'intervention et de formation en service social. Depuis, elle caresse un projet d'études supérieures en bioéthique.

En 1980, elle entre au Centre de services sociaux de Québec à titre de responsable du point de service Loretteville (équipe famille). Elle se frotte alors aux premières tensions engendrées par l'entrée en vigueur de la *Loi sur la protection de la jeunesse* (LPJ) : dur apprentissage du domaine famille-enfance. En marge, elle enseigne à l'Université Laval, s'implique dans l'Association des grands frères et grandes sœurs et effectue diverses réflexions sur la trajectoire des services dans le cadre de l'application de la *Loi sur la protection de la jeunesse* (parcours des clients à travers les diverses étapes d'intervention de la DPJ). Puis, en 1985, elle accepte de devenir chef du service de protection à la DPJ de Québec.

Après une étroite collaboration au Rapport Harvey (partie I) et en pleine participation au Groupe de travail pour les jeunes (Rapport Bouchard, *Un Québec fou de ses enfants*) en 1990, elle relève le défi que représente le poste de DPJ à Trois-Rivières. La conjoncture l'amène, en 1993, à accepter le poste de DPJ à Montréal.

Son arrivée à la table des DPJ lui permet d'apporter une vision différente, car elle considère que le complément féminin à cette table ne peut qu'enrichir les discussions et les décisions. De plus, elle sent qu'elle revitalise la DPJ de Montréal en raison de ses diverses réflexions et de ses expériences de la protection de la jeunesse «en région». Femme centrée sur la tâche, formée en service social de groupe, elle conçoit sa gestion comme une implication professionnelle permettant d'animer le milieu, d'identifier les forces des acteurs et de les mettre en interaction, de les harmoniser et de les multiplier si possible. Elle nomme les enjeux, recherche les consensus puis décide en fonction des priorités établies et des résultats visés. Attentive aux personnes qui l'entourent, elle rappelle sans cesse la cause qui justifie son action.

SYSTÉMATISATION DE LA PRATIQUE

Après plusieurs années d'expérimentation dans l'application de la *Loi sur la protection de la jeunesse* (LPJ), et suite à d'importantes difficultés d'harmonisation des pratiques, d'allocation des ressources, de gestion des listes d'attente, un effort soutenu de systématisation des pratiques voit le jour. Outre les réflexions de Bouchard et de Jasmin inscrites au cœur des orientations du MSSS en matière de services à la jeunesse, les rapports Harvey (I et II) contribuent à préciser notamment les dimensions de la pratique touchant les modalités d'intervention (protocoles), le recours au placement et à la judiciarisation, la productivité des intervenants, etc. Les nombreux moyens privilégiés par Harvey, en ce qui a trait aux aspects administratifs et cliniques du mandat de protection des jeunes, se trouvent ensuite, aux côtés des volets préventifs et légaux, résolument intégrés dans le Plan d'action-jeunesse du MSSS (1992) et orientent désormais le domaine.

NPS – *Quels gains et quelles difficultés a engendrés l'effort de systématisation de la pratique en protection de la jeunesse faisant suite aux conclusions des rapports Harvey?*

SL – À l'époque où Harvey a commencé à examiner l'intervention en protection de la jeunesse, il y avait un besoin d'harmonisation et un besoin de développer des façons de faire. Il y avait aussi toute cette nouvelle approche en contexte d'autorité qu'il fallait qualifier davantage et intégrer. En fait, Harvey a décrit le processus méthodologique du signalement à la prise en charge. Évidemment, l'objectif était aussi d'éliminer les listes d'attente ; le gouvernement n'avait pas vraiment donné tout ce qu'il fallait pour appliquer la Loi et les Centres de services sociaux (CSS) ont dû revoir leurs priorités à l'interne pour faire face aux exigences de l'application de la *Loi sur la protection de la jeunesse*. On a balisé le concept de protection par l'analyse et l'interaction entre trois notions : les faits, la vulnérabilité de l'enfant, la capacité des parents et des autres ressources du milieu. On a donné du contenu à ces notions qui, à l'époque, commençaient seulement à poindre. On a démontré le besoin en ressources humaines. Une fois le Ministère satisfait de la démonstration des changements qu'on avait faits dans nos pratiques, et de la rigueur qu'on y avait mise, le Conseil du Trésor était plus à l'aise pour accorder des budgets plus substantiels et récurrents.

De fait, la diminution des listes d'attente passait par l'application des protocoles lesquels exigeaient une systématisation de la pratique. C'est dans les protocoles qu'on aborde notamment les délais d'exécution des actes et des décisions. Ce fut un gain lorsqu'on a qualifié les urgences en code 1, 2 et 3 (évaluation immédiate, dans les 24 heures, dans les 36 heures). On a réussi à mieux encadrer la gestion du risque. Un autre élément qu'on a documenté dans Harvey, c'est la charge de cas pour les intervenants. On reconnaissait qu'au-delà de 10-12 situations à l'évaluation, il est dangereux de devenir inefficace. L'orientation retenue qui m'apparaît la plus importante aujourd'hui, c'est la décision sur la compromission qu'il faut prendre rapidement. La *Loi sur la protection de la jeunesse* permet une intrusion de l'État dans la vie privée des familles et nous avons le devoir de décider rapidement si cette intrusion est justifiée. À l'époque, c'était nouveau de parler en termes de quantité. Dans notre domaine, qualité et quantité étaient comme opposées dans la tête des gens.

NPS – *Les intervenants ont-ils accepté cela sans protester ? Souvent, la systématisation est perçue comme du contrôle !*

SL – Cela n'a pas été facile, en effet. Au début, justement, les intervenants le recevaient comme si on voulait les contrôler davantage. Avec Harvey I, les intervenants à l'évaluation-orientation étaient beaucoup ciblés. On avait constaté que certains d'entre eux gardaient des situations en évaluation pendant des mois. L'intervention, particulièrement à l'étape évaluation-orientation dans le cadre de la *Loi sur la protection de la* *jeunesse*, comporte des différences majeures par rapport à celle dans le cadre de la *Loi sur les services de santé et les services sociaux*. En réalité, ils ne saisissaient pas que le cadre légal de leur intervention et, conséquemment, leurs mandats et fonctions étaient par le fait même modifiés. Les intervenants se sentaient heurtés dans leurs fibres de cliniciens. Ils avaient tendance à glisser très vite vers de l'intervention de prise en charge ; ces intervenants étaient beaucoup plus préoccupés de donner des services aux enfants et aux familles dont ils avaient évalué la situation qu'aux enfants en attente d'une évaluation. On venait baliser la pratique avec des contrats, identifier ce qu'on veut faire et parler de résultats, etc.

NPS – *Avec l'informatique, certains irritants étaient aussi présents. On pouvait remettre en question la productivité. Tout était mesuré, n'est-ce pas ?*

SL – Oui, parce qu'on avait un souci de productivité. On avait le souci d'augmenter notre capacité de répondre à la demande. Là-dessus, j'ai toujours été intraitable. N'oublions pas qu'il s'agissait d'enfants pour lesquels on avait des inquiétudes quant à la sécurité et au développement. Avec le recul, on peut dire que c'était le début d'une volonté de quantifier les choses. En somme, on était un groupe de personnes qui avaient été à l'abri de bien des comptes à rendre. Avec Harvey, on a été mis dans une position – et on est encore dans cette position actuellement – où l'on avait des comptes à rendre, des obligations, à cause notamment de la conjoncture économique. Je pense toutefois que lorsque les gens ont commencé à voir un profit personnel dans ces nouvelles façons de faire, les changements ont été facilités. La pratique s'est également enrichie ; pensons à la mise sur pied des transferts personnalisés, à l'identification de principes cliniques, à l'intervention en contexte d'autorité, au développement d'expertise dans des problématiques telles que l'abus sexuel, l'abandon, etc. Enfin, reconnaissons les gains pour la clientèle en termes d'équité d'une région à l'autre et de qualité dans le cas à cas.

Harvey a réussi à nous amener à l'ère des communications modernes (informatique, télématique, etc.). L'application des protocoles a permis d'encadrer la pratique. Encadrer, faire des normes, être plus transparent, clarifier des attentes... ce n'est pas cela qui va porter atteinte à la qualité de l'intervention, bien au contraire. Il y a une différence entre rigueur et rigidité ; le jugement professionnel doit s'exercer avec rigueur. Il ne s'agit pas d'appliquer bêtement un protocole, ce serait même plutôt inquiétant.

INTÉGRATION DES MISSIONS PSYCHOSOCIALE ET DE RÉADAPTATION

Avec le démantèlement des Centres de services sociaux en 1993, une vaste entreprise de restructuration s'amorce dans l'environnement organisationnel des DPJ : création d'un seul conseil d'administration pour gérer à la fois les nouveaux centres de protection à l'enfance et à la jeunesse (CPEJ) et les centres de réadaptation pour jeunes en difficulté d'adaptation (CRJDA), et ensuite fusion de ces établissements en une seule entité régionale, les Centres jeunesse. Deux groupes de professionnels, les intervenants du psychosocial et ceux de la réadaptation, font l'expérience d'une cohabitation pour le moins difficile, les premiers éprouvant un malaise d'autant plus accentué que les effectifs rattachés au mandat psychosocial se retrouvent maintenant en nombre nettement minoritaire.

NPS – *Afin de surmonter cette importante crise d'identité profession- nelle engendrée par l'intégration des organismes de protection et de réadaptation, quels rôles divergents et complémentaires chacun des groupes de professionnels impliqués est-il en mesure d'assumer dans l'avenir ? Quelle zone commune d'intervention peut être aménagée ?*

SL – D'abord, je veux être claire là-dessus, je suis très contente des orien- tations de la réforme en matière jeunesse et je trouve qu'il y a là une valeur ajoutée pour la clientèle et même pour les intervenants. Je suis contente de la fusion des établissements qui travaillent auprès de la jeunesse ; cela a permis de multiplier les forces et de diminuer le cloison- nement entre les établissements. Quand je dis que cela multiplie les forces, il s'agit non seulement des ressources humaines et financières, mais aussi d'expertises. Je reconnais cependant que c'est un chambardement pro- fond pour tout le monde : les travailleurs, la direction générale, le service d'accueil, la téléphoniste, etc. C'est une transformation qui implique des modifications profondes au niveau des cultures, des façons de faire, des valeurs. Évidemment, j'ai de la difficulté à en évaluer pleinement l'impact actuellement, puisque ces transformations sont en cours et se font sur une arrière-scène de compressions budgétaires qui pourrait fausser le sens premier des modifications de pratiques par ailleurs nécessaires.

Il y a plusieurs enjeux, notamment d'ordre corporatiste et d'ordre syndical. On ne peut pas le nier. Il y a des enjeux pour la formation aussi. La formation va évoluer vers l'idée d'avoir un corpus unique dans le domaine des sciences humaines, dans ce qu'on nomme la relation d'aide. On reconnaît enfin que l'être humain est en contact avec un environ- nement, que cet environnement est politique, économique, social. Il me semble qu'on adopte une approche globale, au même sens que la *Politique de santé et bien-être*. Je pense qu'une approche se développera où il y aura une grande zone commune et quelques zones complémentaires, plus spécifiques, en fonction des besoins de la clientèle et non plus en fonction d'une profession. On parle d'identification d'actes partagés et d'actes réservés. Tout est à définir présentement, et le meilleur endroit pour que cela se fasse, c'est à la base. On a eu le sens du service pendant plusieurs années, développons le sens du client. Les Centres jeunesse doivent identifier les grandes orientations et permettre aux personnes qui travaillent sur le terrain d'inventer de nouvelles façons de faire en impliquant véritablement les enfants et leur famille et en acceptant de plus de travailler plus en complémentarité avec les autres réseaux. C'est tout un changement ! On n'a pas le choix, c'est la clef de l'amélioration des conditions de vie des enfants les plus vulnérables de notre société.

NPS – *On a souvent reproché à la DPJ d'avoir trop de monde impliqué dans les situations. Ces nouvelles façons de faire poseront-elles toujours cette difficulté ?*

SL – C'est une question qui est entière sur la table actuellement. La multiplicité des intervenants dans un dossier, c'est compliqué, surtout quand ils ne se parlent pas. Il est donc nécessaire d'assurer d'abord une compréhension commune des besoins des jeunes et des familles, ensuite de développer une approche complémentaire. Prenons l'exemple récent de cette discussion de cas entre psychiatre, psychologue, praticien des ressources, éducateur, personne autorisée par la DPJ. La discussion peut être longue et épique quand des valeurs différentes sont en jeu, quand des écoles de pensée s'affrontent. La façon de s'en sortir, c'est d'impliquer l'enfant et les parents et de bien identifier le but de l'intervention dans le cadre de cette loi générale mais d'application restreinte, c'est-à-dire pour une clientèle d'exception. Les amendements de 1994 ont d'ailleurs réaffirmé ces deux éléments. La nature des services à donner pour atteindre les résultats souhaités déterminera le nombre d'intervenants impliqués et la nature de l'expertise nécessaire.

NOUVEL EXERCICE DU RÔLE DE DPJ
ET STATUT DE PERSONNE AUTORISÉE

De l'avis même des rapports Harvey, un des principaux défis qui se posent en protection de la jeunesse, pour la décennie 1990, c'est de décloisonner les services donnés dans le cadre de la LPJ pour en faire une responsabilité élargie qui viserait notamment les partenaires du réseau. Dans cette lancée, la table provinciale des DPJ convient aujourd'hui de modifier substantiellement la façon d'exercer le rôle de DPJ, en assurant une présence plus active au sein de la communauté et en se libérant de la gestion des opérations, à l'exception des responsabilités exclusives énumérées à l'article 32 de la LPJ (décisions de recevabilité du signalement, de compromission de la sécurité ou du développement, de judiciarisation, de révision, de fermeture de dossier, de tutelle, d'adoption). Les responsabilités restantes pourraient alors être exercées par toute personne autorisée à cet effet par le DPJ (article 33). Quoique, la plupart du temps, les personnes autorisées proviennent des services d'application des mesures du CPEJ, on n'exclut pas la possibilité qu'il puisse s'agir du personnel des centres de réadaptation ou d'intervenants d'autres milieux (milieu hospitalier, scolaire, CLSC, etc.).

NPS – *De quelle manière cette nouvelle façon d'exercer le rôle de DPJ contribue-t-elle à impliquer davantage les éléments du milieu à l'égard du mandat de protection des jeunes ? Par ailleurs, quels enjeux l'appropriation de la fonction de personne autorisée par un grand nombre d'intervenants soulève-t-elle ?*

SL – La nouvelle façon d'exercer le rôle de DPJ oblige d'abord à clarifier le régime d'imputabilité dans lequel tous les acteurs impliqués exercent leurs responsabilités. Je pense ici aux établissements et organismes, mais aussi aux personnes, gestionnaires ou intervenants. Les articles 32 et 33 de la Loi donnent au DPJ des responsabilités exclusives. Par ailleurs, plusieurs autres articles reconnaissent aux établissements et organismes des responsabilités au regard de leurs interventions dans le cadre de l'application de cette loi. Les enjeux à ce moment-ci se résument à bien cerner qui est responsable, de quoi, et à qui il doit rendre des comptes. Prenons, par exemple, les régimes dans le cadre desquels des mesures de protection sont identifiées, soit le régime volontaire ou le régime judiciaire. Cette responsabilité est exclusive au DPJ. C'est donc mon personnel qui est responsable de décider et il doit m'en rendre compte. Je suis donc à ce moment tout à fait justifiée de critiquer le taux élevé de judiciarisation puisque je favorise l'entente sur des mesures volontaires.

En ce qui a trait à la question de la personne autorisée en vertu de l'article 33, je dirais que, historiquement, elle joue trois rôles : elle a un mandat légal (pour lequel elle a des comptes à rendre au DPJ), elle donne des services et, parfois, elle coordonne un plan de services. Ma réflexion actuelle m'amène à vouloir préciser les mandats des personnes autorisées. La redéfinition des mandats spécifiques, essentielle dans un régime d'imputabilité, devra se faire dans le but premier de bien distinguer le rôle de la personne autorisée du rôle de celle qui dispense des services, et il s'agira donc de distinguer l'imputabilité du DPJ de celle des gestionnaires de services-clientèles. Deuxièmement, cette redéfinition devra aplanir certaines difficultés actuelles, reliées au nombre de personnes autorisées, à l'expertise requise, au temps requis pour assumer cette fonction, etc.

J'ai traité du mandat légal, mais je ne voudrais pas minimiser l'importance de la responsabilité collective en matière de protection de nos jeunes. Tous nos réseaux de services tant institutionnels que communautaires y jouent un rôle important. Bien que le DPJ soit à l'intérieur des Centres jeunesse, je considère que notre rôle transcende les Centres jeunesse et que nous sommes «le DPJ d'une région». Notre position nous amène à porter un regard critique sur l'ensemble des services disponibles aux jeunes dans une région et à cerner les facteurs qui font que des jeunes ont besoin de «l'intervention extraordinaire» de l'État. C'est pourquoi nous avons un rôle important à jouer dans le virage-prévention, dans le virage-milieu, dans la création d'un véritable réseau interactif de services. Et dans ce réseau interactif de services, le DPJ agira comme soutien quand ce sera nécessaire.

Quand les gens des Centres jeunesse, des CLSC, des organismes communautaires auront une lecture commune et quand ils auront mieux cerné les clientèles à risque, ensemble ils vont planifier une intervention dirigée vers cette clientèle. Il reste encore beaucoup de chemin pour faire une intervention de prévention auprès des clientèles qui sont à risque d'aggravation. Au-delà du cas à cas, c'est un milieu, un territoire qui prend en charge ses enfants.

NPS – *Qu'en est-il de la troisième fonction de la personne autorisée, la coordination des services?*

SL – Cela va être traité en même temps que le reste, dans chacun des Centres jeunesse. Par exemple, nous avons, à l'interne, pour la réadaptation et le psychosocial, un plan d'intervention interdisciplinaire (PII). Je veux essayer de mettre l'expertise professionnelle de chacun dans une nouvelle configuration, dans un nouveau partage des rôles. Comme pour la personne autorisée, la coordination du plan de services ne correspond pas à une profession. L'identité professionnelle, au sens d'expertise clinique, de compétence développée, ne doit pas être perdue. Au contraire, on doit la mettre à profit dans une nouvelle façon de jouer les rôles, de partager les rôles. L'identité professionnelle est reliée à autre chose qu'à une appartenance corporative; elle est liée à une formation, d'une part, et surtout à un service à donner à un client. Si l'on se définit de cette façon-là, on se définit en fonction de la tâche à accomplir.

DISTRIBUTION DES SERVICES
SUR UNE BASE TERRITORIALE (SOUS-RÉGIONALISATION)

Le virage donné par la réforme de la santé et des services sociaux constitue le point de départ d'une vision nouvelle en matière de distribution de services. On cherche désormais à mieux adapter ces services aux régions et aux sous-régions ; on veut un rapprochement du milieu de vie des clientèles en s'appuyant sur le potentiel de l'environnement social et du réseau de support. On compte sur la concertation des partenaires du réseau et des autres organismes à l'égard de la population d'un territoire donné. Ces orientations s'accordent en tout point avec le désir souventes fois formulé de faire en sorte que la protection de la jeunesse devienne enfin un projet collectif. Pour ce faire, les Centres jeunesse miseront sur l'intensification des rapports interétablissements, sur des modalités d'intervention de type « approche milieu », etc.

NPS – *Dans le cadre des aménagements propres à la distribution des services sur une base territoriale pour les Centres jeunesse de Montréal, de quelle manière les usagers, les membres des populations concernées peuvent avoir voix au chapitre, interagir dans un contexte de protection, voire influencer les services de protection ?*

SL – Le simple fait qu'on soit en territoire implique une dynamique avec beaucoup moins de personnes que lorsque c'était régional. La majorité des gens des Centres jeunesse sont regroupés dans les mêmes bureaux ; en outre, ils sont en interface avec le personnel des CLSC. Déjà, c'est ramené à une dimension plus humaine ; cela permet de prendre davantage en compte la réalité de chaque territoire (plus multi-ethnique, plus pauvre, avec enfants plus âgés, etc.). On veut faire un réseau de services intégré, interactif ; les gens ont le mandat d'établir des interfaces avec les CLSC, les écoles, les organismes communautaires. Ils travaillent en partenariat, et ce n'est pas juste en théorie : il existe un véritable partenariat où le client est placé au centre. C'est une force plus grande : il y a plus de monde concerté.

NPS – *Qu'en est-il justement des relations avec le milieu communautaire ?*

SL – La réforme donne une place particulière aux organismes communautaires et il y a de la réallocation de ressources au profit de ce secteur. Actuellement, entre les organismes communautaires et le réseau professionnel, il y a de grosses discussions ; le communautaire ne veut pas être assimilé au réseau. Moi, ce que je dis depuis longtemps, c'est que les organismes communautaires sont complémentaires à l'approche professionnelle. Il y a des clientèles qu'on ne peut pas rejoindre, mais qu'eux sont en mesure de rejoindre à cause de leur approche. Par ailleurs, on observe parfois certains dédoublements; pensons au rôle joué par les maisons pour femmes violentées et celui d'un centre pour mères en difficulté; il y a des choses à revoir pour éviter ces dédoublements et instaurer une véritable concertation. Il n'y a pas une seule solution; il y a plusieurs solutions et il faut qu'elles soient trouvées sur le terrain avec les gens qui sont là.

NPS – *Peut-on penser que l'organisation des services sur une base territoriale ira jusqu'à permettre aux communautés locales de venir elles-mêmes influencer la manière d'intervenir du DPJ?*

SL – Oui, en termes d'ouverture et de volonté de notre part de faire avec et de faire ensemble. On a actuellement un projet avec les communautés haïtiennes qui constitue un bel exemple de cette volonté de tenir compte des besoins particuliers d'une communauté locale. On a réalisé, il y a trois ans, qu'il y avait un taux de judiciarisation et de placement élevé chez ce groupe. Pourquoi? Les Haïtiens ont de la difficulté à bien saisir le sens de notre intervention. Alors, avec cette communauté, on a bâti une trousse à l'usage de nos intervenants en protection, une trousse qui comprend une cassette d'explication en créole sur la *Loi sur la protection de la jeunesse* et un petit document qui vient préciser le sens de certains termes. Parallèlement, on a identifié des gens d'organismes communautaires haïtiens qui agissent comme répondants susceptibles de venir soutenir une intervention mieux adaptée de notre part. C'est maintenant démontré, on a de fait diminué notre taux de placement et de judiciarisation à cause de ces moyens-là. On l'a fait pour et avec la communauté haïtienne. Il va falloir le faire pour et avec d'autres.

RENOUVELLEMENT DES PRATIQUES EN PROTECTION DE LA JEUNESSE

NPS – *Dans la conjoncture actuelle, à quelles conditions le renouvellement des pratiques pourra véritablement s'actualiser au sein des Centres jeunesse?*

SL – Il importe de rappeler qu'il y a encore, dans notre société, des enfants qui sont l'objet de violence sous toutes ses formes, que ce soit de la négligence, de l'abandon, etc., j'associe toujours cela à de la violence. La société doit le reconnaître et se donner les moyens d'intervenir d'autorité dans les familles où les enfants vivent ces situations. On a beau vouloir transformer les choses, faire autrement, prévenir, je ne voudrais pas qu'on évacue l'idée qu'il y a des enfants qui sont en besoin de protection dans notre société. Qu'on le fasse de façon différente, qu'on dise qu'il faut mettre à contribution plus de monde, qu'il faut être plus ouvert et mettre le jeune et le parent au centre des décisions, le DPJ a toujours un rôle à jouer.

Quand on parle de conditions pour le renouvellement des pratiques, je pense d'abord à la recherche. Depuis quelques années, la recherche dans le domaine social est en développement et elle s'est beaucoup rapprochée des milieux de pratique. C'est une des forces qui peut alimenter les nouvelles pratiques ; on a enfin compris la nécessité de favoriser les échanges et le transfert des connaissances. Les instituts universitaires de recherche sociale vont aider dans ce sens. Une autre condition, c'est d'établir une nette différence entre l'articulation du mandat légal, donné sous la *Loi sur la protection de la jeunesse*, et la dispensation des services. Il y a là une confusion et, d'après moi, il y a un espace clinique qui a été perdu inutilement, qui a été évacué et qu'il faut retrouver. Je suis très inquiète de la forte coloration légale qu'a prise la pratique sociale. En fait, je ne sais plus si on fait vraiment de la pratique psychosociale, et l'intervention en protection, à cet égard, m'inquiète. On a beaucoup plus développé l'approche légale, le mandat de surveillance et de contrôle que le mandat d'aide. Jusqu'à un certain point, c'est une pratique confortable aussi. Il faudrait la réviser. L'approche légale amène une judiciarisation alors que la Loi, dans son esprit fondamental, prône la déjudiciarisation des problèmes familiaux. Or, partout la judiciarisation est à la hausse.

Pour assurer un renouvellement, il importe aussi que notre fonctionnement s'ouvre encore plus à la multidisciplinarité, autant en réadaptation qu'en psychosocial. Nous pouvons ainsi mieux nous préparer à faire face à certaines situations, par exemple, à celles des gens qui éprouvent des problèmes de santé mentale. On a besoin d'éclairages nouveaux relativement à la détérioration du tissu social, à la désinstitutionnalisation, à la réalité des familles monoparentales, etc. La formation est une autre condition importante du renouvellement des pratiques. Comme dans le monde de la santé, il faut que les gens améliorent constamment leur pratique et soient au courant des récentes découvertes pour offrir les meilleurs services possible. Dans notre domaine, on doit aller voir ailleurs comment on a résolu les problèmes ; on doit accepter d'être alimenté et de se tenir à jour. Il faudrait qu'on se donne les moyens de faire de la formation continue comme cela se fait dans d'autres disciplines.

Enfin, il ne faut pas avoir peur de s'interroger sur les résultats, au-delà du cas à cas, puisque nous avons une responsabilité à l'égard des clientèles vulnérables dont la situation est parfois chronique. Et cette chronicité est souvent fort reliée aux conditions socio-économiques dans lesquelles elles vivent. Au-delà de la concertation, il doit donc y avoir une cohérence des politiques, des orientations et des approches, afin que la protection, au sens large du terme, soit véritablement une responsabilité collective.

Égalité, solidarité et survie : les pratiques du mouvement des femmes au Québec

Francine DESCARRIES
Département de sociologie
Université du Québec à Montréal

Christine CORBEIL
Département de travail social
Université du Québec à Montréal

Les pratiques féministes logent à plusieurs enseignes, écrivions-nous à l'automne 1990 en introduction au dossier présenté sur cette question dans la revue *Nouvelles pratiques sociales*[1]. Aujourd'hui, un tel diagnostic est encore plus d'actualité que jamais. En effet, réalité aux multiples visages, le féminisme québécois se présente tantôt sous les traits d'un ensemble de discours et de théories pour dire et penser les femmes et leur expérience, tantôt sous ceux des nombreux services et organismes qui œuvrent à l'amélioration de leurs conditions de vie. Tantôt encore, il prend la forme d'un mouvement social engagé dans la quête de l'égalité entre les sexes et, plus récemment, celle d'un mouvement populaire au cœur d'une lutte collective pour améliorer la situation des plus défavorisés, hommes et femmes réunis.

---

1. « Pratiques féministes », *Nouvelles pratiques sociales*, vol. 3, nº 2, automne 1990.

Féminisme *en acte,* le mouvement des femmes québécois a cherché, dès le début des années 1980, à redéfinir la façon de produire et d'agir le *Nous femmes* des années 1960-1970 en vue de développer un réseau élargi de soutien et d'entraide apte à répondre aux besoins les plus urgents et aux multiples intérêts des femmes[2]. Sans pour autant abandonner l'idée d'instaurer un discours et des savoirs qui rendent compte des conditions de production et de reproduction des rapports sociaux sexués, il opte à cette époque pour une militance plus concrète et sociale. Il revêt dès lors essentiellement la forme d'un réseau de services et d'entraide communautaire, notamment dans les domaines de la santé, de l'avortement, de l'éducation populaire, de la lutte contre la violence et l'isolement des femmes, et de leur insertion en emploi.

Si le type d'interventions privilégié implique une mise en veilleuse des luttes collectives et des idéaux politiques du féminisme radical[3], cette impulsion pragmatique donne lieu, au fil des ans, à l'implantation de plus de 2 000 groupes ou associations locales, régionales et nationales (Secrétariat à la condition féminine, 1997 : 22). Des grandes associations ou fédérations nationales aux centres de femmes, des associations de femmes d'affaires aux Comités-femmes des syndicats, des maisons d'hébergement pour femmes victimes de violence conjugale aux centres de santé, des groupes d'entraide aux comités d'action des femmes dans les partis politiques, des comités-étudiantes dans les institutions d'enseignement au réseau des chercheuses féministes, des travailleuses au bas de l'échelle aux femmes autochtones du Québec en passant par les collectifs de femmes immigrantes, au sein de chacun de ces regroupements et de centaines d'autres, des militantes, des bénévoles ou des permanentes œuvrent sur l'ensemble du territoire québécois à l'amélioration des conditions de vie et de travail des femmes.

L'engagement intensif sur le terrain qui en résulte amènera plusieurs analystes à désigner cette phase comme étant celle d'un *féminisme de services* (Lamoureux, 1990), largement induit et consolidé par l'apport financier de l'État. Et si cette appellation évoque une réduction des visées

---

2. Sous le terme du mouvement des femmes, nous désignons les discours et les pratiques qui remettent en question les rapports sociaux sexués, dénoncent les conditions discriminatoires subies par les femmes et préconisent des modalités de transformation de ces conditions, quels que soient leurs fondements politiques, idéologiques et théoriques. (Descarries et Roy, 1988)

3. Au risque de trop simplifier une réalité sociopolitique et théorique fort complexe, on mentionnera tout de même que sous le vocable de féminisme radical sont désignées les diverses tendances du mouvement des femmes qui convergent dans leur dénonciation de la société patriarcale et le rejet de ses institutions ; dans leur refus d'expliquer l'infériorisation des femmes par des arguments d'ordre naturel ou biologique et dans la primauté qu'elles accordent à la lutte contre l'oppression des femmes.

politiques et idéologiques formulées aux premières heures du féminisme contemporain, de même que les risques d'assujettissement des groupes et des associations à des règles de définition, de composition et d'efficience régies par les bailleurs de fonds (Couillard, 1994), la priorité donnée à l'intervention directe permettra au mouvement des femmes non seulement d'ouvrir un nouveau champ d'expérimentation, d'expertise et de pratiques féministes, mais encore de favoriser la démocratisation de son action et la diversification de ses assises. Encore aujourd'hui, ces centaines de groupes dispersés à travers le Québec représentent la véritable base du mouvement et confirment son inscription comme fait social incontournable.

En cette fin de millénaire, peut-être un peu essoufflé, mais certainement ni ringard, ni moribond, le mouvement des femmes québécois semble donc vouloir résister à l'usure du temps et se redéployer à contre-courant du raz de marée néolibéral qui a envahi toutes les dimensions de la vie sociétale. En dépit d'un ressac antiféministe qui tend à banaliser toutes références aux effets pervers des rapports inégalitaires de sexe (Fournier et Guberman, 1988), notamment dans les domaines de la violence, de l'exclusion, de l'emploi, de la sécurité du revenu et des responsabilités parentales, il s'est en effet (ré)imposé au cours des dernières années comme lieu de résistance et comme force sociale de premier plan, en raison du poids de sa présence sur le terrain et de la portée de ses pratiques.

Ainsi, au cours de la dernière décennie, bien que les grandes manifestations féministes en Occident se soient faites de plus en plus rares et que prime un individualisme revanchard, plusieurs événements sont venus concrétiser la force de ralliement du mouvement au Québec. Le premier, « Femmes en tête », immense rassemblement féministe de trois jours organisé à l'orée de la décennie pour souligner le 50e anniversaire de l'obtention du droit de vote des femmes, a permis de renouer avec les grands ralliements populaires et de renouveler les liens de solidarité entre plus de cinq mille femmes venues de tous les milieux du Québec. En 1992, plus de mille femmes se sont réunies à l'invitation de la Fédération des femmes du Québec (FFQ) pour discuter d'un projet féministe de société sous le thème « Un Québec féminin pluriel » plus attentif à la diversité des communautés culturelles.

Plus près de nous, le troisième événement a monopolisé, du 20 mai au 4 juin 1995, des milliers de Québécoises à l'occasion d'une marche contre la pauvreté. Mieux connue sous le nom de la « Marche du pain et des roses », cette manifestation sans précédent, organisée par la FFQ visait à obtenir l'engagement du gouvernement du Québec en faveur d'une lutte commune pour l'éradication de la pauvreté des femmes et des familles. Un an plus tard, jour pour jour, insatisfaites des gains obtenus, dix mille femmes, regroupées au sein de la Coalition nationale des femmes contre la pauvreté, participent à Québec à une vigile sur la colline parlementaire. Elles disent haut et fort que les femmes refusent de se contenter «de pain sec et de fleurs fanées» (Giroux, 1996), voire de «miettes et d'épines» (Rhéault, 1996). Elles exigent à nouveau l'engagement gouvernemental face aux mesures prioritaires revendiquées par la «Marche du pain et des roses»: hausse du salaire minimum, adoption rapide de la loi sur l'équité salariale et abolition des coupures à l'aide sociale.

Le 12 mars 1997, un autre rassemblement a lieu devant la Bourse de Montréal pour exprimer une chaîne de solidarité provinciale. Cette mobilisation, organisée sous le thème «Coude à coude, sans relâche», veut réitérer publiquement le mécontentement des femmes devant la tiédeur du gouvernement dans sa lutte à la pauvreté. Mais cette fois, la contestation, dont l'emplacement a été stratégiquement choisi, vise également le pouvoir occulte de la droite économique et le contrôle exercé par ce «pouvoir non élu.» L'ambition de voir s'instaurer un projet de société féministe basé sur «une culture publique commune» dans un «Québec solidaire, équitable, inclusif et ouvert sur le monde» (FFQ, 1997a: 1) y est réitérée. D'ores et déjà, «Une marche internationale des femmes de l'an 2000» pour l'égalité, le développement et la paix s'organise sous le leadership du mouvement des femmes québécois. Cet événement, comme les précédents, est prévu comme un moment charnière dans la lutte des femmes contre la pauvreté et l'établissement d'assises de solidarité et d'entraide avec les femmes d'autres pays.

Sans l'ombre d'un doute, ces grands ralliements témoignent de l'ancrage social des luttes et des stratégies du mouvement des femmes et constituent, à notre avis, des temps forts de ce que nous qualifions de troisième vague du féminisme québécois. L'exploit que représente l'organisation de ces manifestations, dans un contexte politique par ailleurs passablement léthargique, donne un message clair et précis: les Québécoises refusent collectivement et solidairement que la lutte au déficit se fasse sur leur dos et sur celui des personnes âgées ou des jeunes, des travailleurs et des travailleuses à statut précaire ou celui de tout autre groupe menacé d'exclusion.

Aussi, face à la crise socio-économique que provoquent tant les actuelles stratégies gouvernementales de désétatisation et de désinstitutionnalisation que la restructuration accélérée du marché du travail télécommandée par les changements technologiques et l'attrition des emplois, le mouvement des femmes représente au Québec l'une des rares voix qui formule une critique sociale concertée contre la marchandisation des personnes et des rapports sociaux. Il continue non seulement de maintenir son appel en faveur d'une transformation des pratiques sociales, mais encore il se révèle «le chien de garde» d'une certaine conception de l'État-providence et de son rôle, conception qui est loin d'être celle préconisée par l'idéologie néolibérale. Les avis récents émanant des grandes organisations féministes relatifs à la nouvelle politique familiale et au projet de réforme de la sécurité du revenu proposés par le gouvernement du Québec sont des exemples probants de cette orientation.

D'ailleurs, l'engagement du mouvement des femmes dans la lutte contre la pauvreté a pris une telle envergure au cours des dernières années que certains iront même jusqu'à se demander si cette lutte n'est pas en train de devenir un combat exclusivement féminin (Navarro, 1996) ou encore d'envahir l'agenda féministe au détriment des revendications pour l'égalité. Certes, il est encore trop tôt pour évaluer l'impact de l'implication du mouvement des femmes dans cette lutte. Il est néanmoins possible d'affirmer que sa mobilisation politique au cours de la présente décennie aura permis de confirmer le mouvement des femmes en tant qu'interlocuteur incontournable sur la scène politique, et de susciter un capital de sympathie qui lui faisait défaut depuis quelques années.

À L'AUBE DU PROCHAIN MILLÉNAIRE

Après l'éclipse plus ou moins réelle d'un discours ouvertement contestataire, le mouvement des femmes a donc ressenti, au cours de la présente décennie, l'urgence de renouer avec un militantisme politique plus visible et rassembleur pour dénoncer le désengagement de l'État, l'omniprésence des marchés financiers et l'appauvrissement alarmant des femmes et des familles. Et ceci, au moment même où la crise des finances publiques oblige les groupes et les associations à faire des acrobaties pour survivre à la réduction de leur budget et à la déstabilisation continuelle de leur programmation, de leur capacité d'embauche et de leurs priorités. Au moment même, également, où les groupes de la base sont submergés et voient leur efficacité réduite en raison de la multiplication et de la «complexification des dossiers politiques due, entre autres, à la régionalisation et à la diversification des façons de faire et de s'organiser» (Guberman, Fournier et al., 1997 : 63). Enfin, au moment où les demandes des usagères sont de plus en plus nombreuses et pressantes, où les organismes se font concurrence entre eux pour les minces subventions encore disponibles et où les risques de se voir transformés «en simples sous-traitants de l'État» (CSF, 1996 : 37) constituent une menace réelle. Face à ces contraintes, les groupes de la base réussissent difficilement à défendre la marge de manœuvre qui était la leur et à maintenir des activités de réflexion et de contestation politique. (Couillard, 1994)

Dans une telle conjoncture, il est pour le moins impressionnant de voir que par le biais de ses associations régionales et nationales, le mouvement des femmes a été en mesure, au fil de la décennie 1990, de maintenir envers et contre tous une présence politique, un leadership indéniable et de s'engager dans une multitude de lieux d'intervention gouvernementaux, institutionnels et communautaires pour y défendre les intérêts et les droits des femmes[4]. En fait, comme le souligne la FFQ dans son *Rapport d'activités 1994-1995*, l'intérêt des groupes de femmes pour les questions économiques et politiques s'est renouvelé et renforcé à partir du moment où les positions des États canadiens et québécois remettaient en cause l'assistance financière accordée aux femmes les plus démunies. Reprenant son statut de groupe de pression national, le mouvement des femmes revendique depuis une meilleure justice redistributive et réclame des mesures concrètes pour arrêter l'appauvrissement des plus démunis et assurer un minimum de dignité aux personnes les plus vulnérables. Se voit ainsi réintroduite une approche critique à l'égard des politiques gouvernementales et ramenée une problématique du social fondée sur un principe de solidarité. Pour accroître l'efficacité politique, une plus grande importance est dorénavant accordée au développement de nouveaux modes de concertation avec les autres groupes sociaux et communautaires et à l'établissement d'une collaboration plus soutenue, mais également à un partage des dossiers, entre les groupes de femmes, tout en respectant la diversité des expériences organisationnelles, sociales et régionales.

Ainsi, la «Marche du pain et des roses», en plus de constituer un démenti formel à toute mise à mort anticipée du féminisme québécois, concrétisa l'actualisation de cette volonté renouvelée de faire front commun et de donner voix au mouvement de solidarité engendré par certaines revendications fondamentales pour un projet de société non sexiste et démocratique. Le féminisme, en tant que nouvel humanisme, apparaît en conséquence comme un projet plus global, plus rassembleur, moins sectoriel et plus ouvert aux diversités. Il s'impose comme mode d'observation critique des changements sociaux préconisés et s'ouvre à tous les

---

4. La présence assurée depuis plus de dix ans par les groupes réunis au sein d'une table de concertation, mieux connue sous le nom de Groupe des Treize, est exemplaire à cet égard.

champs du social, même ceux où les femmes ne sont pas nécessairement les premières concernées. La diversité de ses orientations idéologiques et de ses pratiques se voit ainsi confirmée. L'accent est dorénavant mis sur le développement de solidarités avec les femmes d'ici et d'ailleurs plutôt que sur l'obtention d'un consensus. Sous ce rapport, les années 1990 marquent une rupture définitive avec cette fausse conception, entretenue de l'extérieur, du féminisme comme doctrine monolithique. Le mouvement des femmes a abandonné l'idée de rallier ses membres autour d'une seule bannière. Il a plutôt réorienté son action avec l'intention de rejoindre les femmes là où elles sont, à travers la multiplicité de leurs expériences, en portant une attention plus consciente et directe aux problèmes des femmes doublement discriminées.

Depuis toujours, le recours à la notion de *condition féminine* posait problème à sa dynamique, tant sur le plan de l'élaboration du discours et le recrutement des membres que dans l'application des stratégies, compte tenu de l'hétérogénéité des situations et des rapports sociaux englobés sous le concept de condition féminine ou encore sous celui de *femme*. Aussi, au fur et à mesure que la recherche d'homogénéité a été abandonnée comme priorité politique, les leaders du mouvement ont réalisé que la consolidation de celui-ci passait nécessairement par sa capacité à répondre à la diversité des besoins quotidiens des femmes, par le développement d'une perspective plus inclusive que ne le permet la seule prise en considération des rapports de sexe ou du *féminin* et par l'établissement de nouvelles formes d'alliance ne se limitant pas aux seuls intérêts des femmes.

Bref, un nouveau canevas de pensée et d'action est dorénavant déployé. Dans son engagement dans la lutte contre la pauvreté, pour la reconnaissance sociale du travail non rémunéré des femmes, comme dans sa récente interrogation critique de la problématique de l'économie sociale, le mouvement des femmes est sans conteste l'un des acteurs les plus présents au sein d'une coalition vouée à faire échec aux contre-réformes imposées dans les secteurs de l'éducation, de la santé et des services sociaux. C'est dans cette optique que les groupes de femmes étudient actuellement les potentiels et les risques du projet d'économie sociale dont l'État fait la promotion et exigent d'y être activement associés. Du *côté espoir*[5], le projet est dit porteur de valeurs de solidarité, d'entraide et de justice sociale et représenterait, de ce fait même, une voie de compromis acceptable. Il est alors interprété comme offrant la

---

5. Nous empruntons cette métaphore au titre du document publié par le Comité d'orientation et de concertation sur l'économie sociale (1996).

possibilité «de réconcilier l'économique et le social» (Lemieux et Vaillancourt, 1997 : 3), de développer des emplois durables et de relative qualité (FFQ, 1997b : 9) et d'assurer l'implantation de divers services complémentaires aux services sociaux et de santé.

Enfin, dans la mesure où «l'économie sociale est avant tout basée sur la richesse que les personnes produisent en dehors du marché» (Belleau, 1996 :21), son développement est envisagé comme susceptible de permettre une meilleure accessibilité de l'emploi aux femmes et, en même temps, une certaine forme de reconnaissance pour le travail qu'elles effectuent hors de l'univers marchand. Du *côté doute*, le projet est perçu comme une stratégie gouvernementale qui balaie vers le milieu et à des coûts moindres une part des responsabilités de l'État envers les personnes les plus vulnérables et qui risque d'entraîner, contre leur gré, un nombre considérable de femmes vers des emplois de services aux personnes et aux communautés, secteurs d'emplois qui demeurent socialement et économiquement sous-évalués (Belleau, 1996). En outre, dans les circonstances, plusieurs craignent que les femmes ne reçoivent pas leur juste part des initiatives que le gouvernement entend soutenir dans le virage vers l'économie sociale. La réflexion sur cette question est donc présentement au cœur des préoccupations des principaux regroupements provinciaux et des groupes nationaux de femmes.

Pour conclure, nous constatons que la fin des années 1980 a ramené une certaine radicalisation d'une portion non négligeable du mouvement des femmes, radicalisation alimentée à la fois par le dernier échec référendaire et par la mise en place accélérée de politiques de sortie de crise d'orientations néolibérales au fédéral comme au provincial. En effet, si l'agenda référendaire avait, d'une certaine façon, contribué à la mise en veilleuse des différends entre l'État québécois et les groupes de femmes au nom de l'intérêt supérieur de la nation, une fois la fièvre référendaire retombée, non seulement le couvercle sur les désaccords n'est plus stratégiquement rentable, mais les sources de conflits sont devenues de plus en plus manifestes, compte tenu des conséquences désastreuses qui découlent de l'orientation «déficit zéro» sur la vie des femmes. Mais, de toute évidence, le dynamisme même du mouvement est encore une fois mis en péril par les contradictions que sous-tendent son désir d'assurer son indépendance politique et sa volonté d'accéder à un maximum de ressources financières pour renforcer sa vie associative et améliorer la qualité des services que ses groupes assurent.

De même, la radicalisation des luttes du mouvement ainsi que la quête de solidarité entre les femmes, à l'origine du renouveau politique dont il a été ici question, sont mises à rude épreuve par les situations de plus en plus intenables que connaissent celles-ci et leurs familles. Plusieurs en viennent même à remettre en question les stratégies féministes qui ont été déployées jusqu'ici pour permettre aux femmes d'atteindre l'autonomie, face au déclin inexorable de l'emploi et aux nouvelles contradictions engendrées par le succès de certaines revendications du féminisme. Si plusieurs groupes de femmes, dans une saine contestation de l'économisation à outrance des rapports sociaux, proposent de cesser de voir le monde du travail comme la seule voie vers l'insertion sociale, d'autres, par ailleurs, se replient sur des positions plus ambiguës lorsqu'il s'agit de lutter pour la reconnaissance du travail non rémunéré effectué par les femmes ou les hommes qui décideraient de demeurer au foyer pour prendre soin de jeunes enfants[6]. Certes, il ne viendrait à personne l'idée de préconiser un retour en arrière ou d'abandonner les revendications traditionnelles du mouvement des femmes en faveur de l'égalité. Mais, de toute évidence, pour conserver son rôle d'agent de changement, le mouvement des femmes devra se prémunir contre les attraits de solutions ponctuelles et individuelles, ou de compromis consentis au nom des « sacrifices » exigés par l'actuel contexte de crise : de tels replis stratégiques ne permettent nullement de remettre en cause ni les tendances conservatrices à l'œuvre ni les fondements à la fois matériels et idéels de pratiques sociales et de projets sociopolitiques qui portent en eux-mêmes la marque d'une référence à une réalité sexuée[7].

Bibliographie

BELLEAU, Josée (1996). « Exposé de Josée Belleau de l'R des Centres de femmes du Québec », *Actes du Séminaire international sur l'économie sociale*, Montréal, 20-24.

COMITÉ D'ORIENTATION ET DE CONCERTATION SUR L'ÉCONOMIE SOCIALE (1996). *Entre le doute et l'espoir*, Montréal, mai, 87 pages.

COUILLARD, Marie-Andrée (1994). « Le pouvoir dans les groupes de femmes de la région de Québec », *Recherches sociographiques*, vol. XXXV, n° 1, 39-65.

DESCARRIES, Francine et Shirley ROY (1988). *Le mouvement des femmes et ses courants de pensée : essai de typologie*, Ottawa, Documents de l'ICREF, n° 19.

FÉDÉRATION DES FEMMES DU QUÉBEC (1997a). *Le féminisme en bref*, vol. 7, n° 3.

FÉDÉRATION DES FEMMES DU QUÉBEC (1997b). *Rapport d'activités. 1996-1997.*

FOURNIER, D. et N. GUBERMAN (1988). « Quelques défis pour le mouvement des femmes au Québec », *RIAC,* vol. 20, n° 60, 183-188.

---

6. F. DESCARRIES et C. CORBEIL, *Le Devoir*.

7. Nos remerciements à Lyne Kurtzman pour ses judicieux commentaires et à Céline Séguin pour sa participation à la démarche d'analyse.

GIROUX, Raymond (1996). « Pain sec et roses fanées », *Le Soleil*, 4 juin, Cahier B-6.

GUBERMAN, N., FOURNIER, D. *et al.* (1997). *Innovations et contraintes. Des pratiques organisationnelles féministes,* CFP / Relais-femmes, Rapport de recherche.

LAMOUREUX, Diane (1990). « Les services féministes : De l'autonomie à l'extension de l'État-providence », *Nouvelles pratiques sociales,* vol. 3, nº 2, 33-43.

LEMIEUX, Diane et Yves VAILLANCOURT (1997). « L'économie sociale et la transformation du réseau des services sociaux et de santé : définitions, état de la situation et enjeux », UQAM, LAREPPS, Colloque NPS, 32 pages.

NAVARRO, Pascale (1996). « Marche ou crève », *Voir,* 30 mai, 8.

RHÉAULT, Ghislaine (1996). « Des miettes et des épines », *Le Soleil*, 4 juin, Cahier A-5.

SECRÉTARIAT À LA CONDITION FÉMININE (1997). *La place des femmes dans le développement des régions,* 5ᵉ orientation, Québec, Gouvernement du Québec.

❖ Grandes tendances
et renouvellement
des pratiques en santé
mentale (1988-1997) :
pour une mise à jour
de la politique de santé
mentale du Québec

Jean Gagné
*Regroupement des ressources alternatives
en santé mentale du Québec*

Henri Dorvil
*Groupe de recherche sur les aspects sociaux
de la santé et de la prévention
Université de Montréal*

De sa naissance en 1988 à aujourd'hui, *Nouvelles pratiques sociales* a régulièrement ouvert ses pages aux chercheurs et praticiens sociaux du domaine de la santé mentale. En conformité avec son objectif, la revue ne pouvait d'ailleurs faire autrement. Les dix premières années de vie de NPS coïncident en effet avec celles de la gestation, de l'implantation et de l'évaluation de la «nouvelle Politique de santé mentale du

Québec ». De plus, cette politique, adoptée en 1989, s'implantait comme le prototype de la Réforme globale des services sociaux et de santé du Québec. C'est d'ailleurs ce que nous confirmait en entrevue le ministre en poste en décembre 1991. (M.-Y. Côté, 1992).

La Politique de santé mentale et l'esprit général de la Réforme appartiennent à un nouveau modèle de gestion étatique qui consiste en une déconcentration administrative du sommet vers les régions et, arrivé à ce palier, à la promotion d'un partenariat multipartite, c'est-à-dire impliquant les établissements, les organismes communautaires et les ressources privées. Il s'agit de répondre aux impasses du dispositif ultracentralisé hérité de la période de l'État-providence et dont la remise en question s'alimente à deux sources principales : le néolibéralisme et la social-démocratie. Les perspectives de développement du champ social de la santé mentale sont donc soumises à des forces complexes et contradictoires qui peuvent lui impulser au moins trois directions : une privatisation des services gérés à distance par l'État, le maintien d'un statu quo appauvri ou l'élaboration d'un modèle public mixte où le secteur communautaire occuperait une place significative et jouerait un rôle de vigilance et d'innovation par rapport à un réseau public qui, lui, assurerait toujours une distribution universelle des services requis pour l'ensemble de la population.

Récemment, le ministère de la Santé et des Services sociaux (MSSS) publiait un document de consultation *Orientations pour les services de santé mentale au Québec* (MSSS, avril, 1997, ci-après : *Orientations*). Ce document a surtout retenu l'attention parce qu'il affirmait la détermination du ministère à fermer 3 000 lits de soins psychiatriques et à en réallouer les ressources vers la communauté d'ici l'an 2002. Précisons d'emblée que cette prise de position spectaculaire au premier abord ne ferait, si elle se réalisait, qu'aligner le Québec sur des normes courantes dans nombre de provinces canadiennes, d'États américains, en Grande-Bretagne et dans d'autres pays du monde anglo-saxon. Mais, outre cette annonce, le document entreprend la mise à jour de la Politique de santé mentale de 1989.

RÉTROSPECTIVE DES TRAVAUX DE MISE À JOUR DE LA POLITIQUE DE SANTÉ MENTALE

Le but avoué de la Politique de santé mentale était précisément de renouveler les pratiques en ce domaine à partir de cinq orientations principales : assurer la primauté de la personne ; accroître la qualité des services ; favoriser l'équité ; rechercher des solutions dans le milieu de vie et consolider le partenariat. Le bilan d'implantation du MSSS s'est intéressé à la réalisation effective de ces orientations. Pour y arriver, il a procédé à une enquête, sous forme d'entrevues de groupe, auprès des différents « partenaires » impliqués : les associations d'établissements, les regroupements régionaux et nationaux d'organismes communautaires, la CSN, des corporations professionnelles et des associations d'usagers. Toutefois, la définition des objectifs de l'enquête, la méthode de collecte de données et leur analyse sont demeurées aux mains d'un comité formé exclusivement de professionnels du ministère et des régies régionales.

Mentionnons, pour mémoire, la publication des *Recommandations pour développer et enrichir la Politique de santé mentale* du Comité de la santé mentale du Québec en 1994 et une consultation postale menée par le ministère à propos de ce même avis, en juin 1995 (résultats non publiés). La Direction de la planification et de l'évaluation du MSSS a aussi créé un Comité de travail sur les services de santé mentale offerts aux femmes dont les travaux sont terminés mais non publiés en avril 1997. En août 1996, le MSSS a formé un Comité de mise à jour de la Politique de santé mentale dont les travaux n'étaient pas terminés au moment d'écrire ces lignes. Par contre, un document de consultation sur la prévention du suicide était publié depuis février 1997 tandis que la Commission des affaires sociales du Québec avait terminé ses audiences de consultation à propos de la *Loi sur la protection des personnes atteintes de maladie mentale.*

Le problème ici n'est pas tant la multiplication des consultations que la manière dont elles sont menées. La problématique générale est segmentée en plusieurs éléments et les différents groupes concernés n'ont jamais l'occasion de débattre ensemble de leur compréhension respective des enjeux. Ce qui rend difficile une perspective globale. C'est d'ailleurs pour cette raison que le RRASMQ, l'AGIDD-SMQ, la CSN et la coalition Solidarité Santé réclamaient un débat public sur tous les enjeux de la mise à jour de la Politique de santé mentale. La Fédération des infirmières et infirmiers du Québec a, pour sa part, aussi déploré que cette consultation ne se mène que sur une base privée évitant ainsi la tenue d'un débat public des plus importants (FIIQ, 1997).

Première orientation : assurer la primauté de la personne

Le Bilan d'implantation souligne l'échec de plusieurs mesures prévues comme celle concernant la « primauté de la personne ».

En premier lieu, le Plan de services individualisé (PSI), bien que rendu obligatoire par la Loi, n'a guère été adopté par le milieu. En fait, il est presque unanimement rejeté par les usagers, par les organismes communautaires, par les groupes de défense de droits, par les associations de familles et par les intervenants (Potvin, 1997 : 17-24). Calqué sur un modèle emprunté à ce qui se faisait déjà dans le secteur de la déficience intellectuelle, le PSI voulait coordonner autour de la personne l'ensemble des interventions de manière à éviter les doubles messages, les doublements ou les ruptures de services. En réduisant les difficultés des personnes à un problème d'habileté ou de « savoir-faire », le PSI devient, selon ses détracteurs, un système envahissant. La multiplication des conseillers menace les droits à la confidentialité, à la liberté de choix et, de là, à la reconquête de l'autonomie citoyenne des usagers. On laisse néanmoins la porte ouverte à sa relance : « [...] on doit reconnaître aujourd'hui les limites de cet instrument ainsi que la nécessité de diversifier et d'intensifier l'action à cet égard. » (MSSS, 1997 : 9) On ne répond pas à la demande des groupes alternatifs et de défense de droits, à savoir le retrait pur et simple de ces plans de la Loi 120.

Par ailleurs, en même temps que le ministère commence à reviser son enthousiasme pour l'implantation des PSI, il manifeste un engouement pour les « programmes de suivi intensif dans la communauté ». Il s'agit de programmes déjà adoptés dans une trentaine d'États américains et connus sous l'acronyme de PACT pour Program for Assertive Community Treatment. Le PACT, à l'instar du PSI, vise à coordonner l'ensemble des services destinés aux personnes. Il s'agit d'organiser une intervention concertée impliquant les établissements, les organismes, la famille, le voisinage, l'employeur et les institutions en général. Le document précise : « Le suivi est assuré régulièrement sans qu'une demande expresse soit formulée, le retrait social étant considéré comme un symptôme précurseur d'une crise. » (MSSS, 1997 : 15) Comme on le voit, cette nouvelle formule soulève encore les problèmes éthiques du respect de la confidentialité et du consentement aux soins. Il faudra prendre garde à cette nouvelle recette miracle qui, comme les PSI ou encore le *case management*, pourrait très vite se révéler un mirage. La littérature (Goering *et al.*, 1988) indique déjà que les programmes de type PACT ne s'avèrent efficaces que pour des personnes souffrant de schizophrénie, soit 25 % de la clientèle. Selon le plan de transformation de l'Hôpital Louis-H.-Lafontaine (version du 11 février 1997), il y aurait plutôt 10 à 20 % de personnes atteintes de troubles mentaux graves qui pourraient bénéficier du Suivi intensif en milieu naturel (SIMN). D'où la nécessité d'utiliser ces trois formules à leur juste mesure en les adaptant aux situations particulières des usagers.

Le deuxième moyen, l'information, parce que réduit à des campagnes médiatiques d'envergure nationale avec des slogans tels que «comprendre, c'est fondamental» et «accepter, c'est fondamental», n'aura pas eu les impacts attendus. On a reproché à ces «*spots*» publicitaires de présenter un aspect trop général pour toucher les gens tout en reproduisant une image de la santé mentale réduite à la maladie. Dans une nouvelle stratégie de sensibilisation du public, le MSSS devrait capitaliser sur l'évolution lente, mais positive des perceptions et des attitudes des Québécois à l'égard des personnes ayant des troubles mentaux (Dorvil, 1988; Lamontagne, 1993; St-Laurent et Clarkson, 1989).

Enfin, la mesure promotion du respect et de la défense des droits semble avoir été implantée avec plus de succès. On note, cependant, que s'il existe désormais des comités régionaux et indépendants de défense de droits partout au Québec, leur financement demeure encore parfois trop réduit pour répondre à l'ampleur de leur mandat. Les groupes concernés déplorent aussi le peu de collaboration qu'ils obtiennent des institutions : «Encore aujourd'hui, dans plusieurs centres hospitaliers, on refuse à la personne l'accès à un conseiller en défense de droits en santé mentale des départements et hôpitaux psychiatriques.» (AGIDD-SMQ, 1997 : 18)

On se surprend, par ailleurs, que les *Orientations* tout en prévoyant une bascule importante des services d'hospitalisation vers la communauté (60 % / 40 %), n'insistent pas pour autant sur la consolidation des groupes d'accompagnement et de défense des droits.

Deuxième orientation : l'amélioration des services

En ce qui concerne la seconde orientation, «l'amélioration des services» par un investissement accru dans la recherche, la formation et l'évaluation, on constate aussi de nombreux ratés. Le ministère ne serait même pas en mesure de vérifier si l'objectif d'affecter 15 % des fonds de recherche en santé à la santé mentale est atteint. Il y aurait tout de même eu augmentation. Un fonds spécial FRSQ-CQRS a été créé et a permis de distribuer 1 million de dollars pour 25 nouvelles recherches qui, cependant, ne répondent pas nécessairement aux problématiques prioritaires soulevées par la Politique de santé mentale. L'arrimage entre les universités, le MSSS et l'enseignement supérieur reste toujours à faire. (Potvin, 1997 ; 47-48)

Par ailleurs, dans le document *Orientations*, on nous annonce la création d'un Institut universitaire de recherche en santé mentale sans nous dire ce qui en a empêché la mise sur pied, dès lors que le MSSS en avait la possibilité légale depuis 1991 (en vertu de l'article 89 de la LSSSS). On sait qu'en 1996, au moment où le ministère mettait sur pied un comité de réflexion à ce sujet, qui n'a d'ailleurs jamais siégé, les grands centres hospitaliers psychiatriques tentent de s'associer aux universités pour obtenir la gouverne de cet éventuel institut. De plus, et pour peu que la santé mentale soit un phénomène bio-psycho-social, l'institut de recherche qu'on lui dédie devra refléter ce nouveau consensus scientifique dans sa structure même et ne pas être confiné à un seul site traditionnellement voué à la bio-psychiatrie. Il faudra plaider résolument pour un institut multiparadigmatique et multisite.

En ce qui a trait à l'évaluation, le MSSS a publié une proposition de cadre général en 1990 ainsi qu'un guide particulier pour les organismes communautaires en 1994, le *Cadre de référence concernant une évaluation respectueuse des organismes communautaires et bénévoles financés par le MSSS*, rédigé en collaboration avec des représentantes du milieu communautaire et de la Conférence des régies de la santé et des services sociaux du Québec. Le 16 juillet 1996, le ministre le recommandait à toutes les régies du Québec en tant que document de référence pour expérimenter les évaluations des ressources communautaires. À notre connaissance, ni l'un ni l'autre de ces guides n'a encore été testé sur le terrain. Les *Orientations* relancent cet objectif sans faire l'analyse de sa faible implantation, ni même mentionner les deux publications issues du ministère.

Le dossier est éminemment politique. Ainsi, les communiqués de l'Association des psychiatres du Québec (*TELBEC*, 6 février 1997) et de l'Association des hôpitaux du Québec (*Le Devoir*, 24 janvier 1997) réclament en chœur l'évaluation de l'efficacité et de la pertinence des objectifs des organismes communautaires. Les *Orientations*, quant à elles, prévoient de confier le mandat de développer des outils d'analyse et de vérification de la qualité des services offerts dans le cadre du virage communautaire au Comité de la santé mentale du Québec. Il est clair que toute l'opération menée par le ministère depuis 1989 vise à corriger une situation héritée des trente années où ce sont précisément les centres hospitaliers et les psychiatres qui ont tenu le haut du pavé. Selon les chiffres du MSSS, 84 % de ses ressources financières allouées à la santé mentale sont dépensées pour les services hospitaliers (Breton, 1995) alors que 3 % seulement le sont pour les organismes communautaires (*Orientations*). Toutes les dépenses publiques méritent d'être évaluées au nom du principe de l'imputabilité.

Troisième orientation : assurer une meilleure équité

La troisième grande orientation visait à assurer une « meilleure équité » des services intra- et suprarégionaux. Ainsi, on prévoyait d'abord favoriser l'accès de tous les citoyens à une gamme complète de services : l'information, la prévention et la promotion, la défense de droit, le traitement spécialisé, le soutien aux familles et des services de réadaptation et de réintégration. On observe que les deux premiers éléments de la gamme – information, prévention et promotion – sont plutôt négligés et inégalement disponibles selon les régions.

Le traitement spécialisé est, quant à lui, demeuré l'apanage quasi exclusif des établissements psychiatriques. Très peu de nouveaux projets alternatifs ont fait leur apparition sur ce terrain, bien qu'il existe une expertise réelle mais non publicisée faute de financement. On constate, par contre, que dans certaines régions les départements psychiatriques des hôpitaux ont débordé leur mandat pour investir, d'une part, dans certaines régions, les services de première ligne en lieu et place des CLSC ou des organismes communautaires et, d'autre part, en recevant des clientèles à long terme. Enfin, les mandats de réadaptation et de réintégration sociale seraient surtout confiés aux organismes communautaires. On déplore cependant la trop faible disponibilité d'hébergements communautaires ainsi que de services de formation et de placement à l'emploi. La situation s'avère d'autant plus inquiétante aujourd'hui puisque les résidences d'accueil (anciennement famille d'accueil) et les pavillons, deux entités sous contrôle hospitalier, occupent en moyenne 75 % du parc d'hébergement (Morin, 1993). Plus encore, cette tendance s'accentue depuis la disparition des centres de services sociaux (CSS) qui contrebalançaient autrefois le pouvoir psychiatrique. En confiant ainsi un pan entier du processus désinstitutionnel aux tenants traditionnels et « modernistes » du monopole hospitalier, ne risque-t-on pas de recréer sciemment l'asile ? La désinstitutionnalisation a été créée, faut-il le rappeler, en réaction aux effets dépersonnalisants et aliénants produits par le monde asilaire. Ainsi, la désinstitutionnalisation ne saurait se faire sur les mêmes prémisses que l'institutionnalisation déjà tant décriée.

Dans plusieurs régions, la gamme prévue, bien qu'existante formellement, n'est pas accessible à toute la population pour des raisons de sous-financement. On peut évidemment à cet égard s'inquiéter de la priorisation exclusive des catégories de clientèles dites « sévères et persistantes » dans les *Orientations* au détriment de celles plus jeunes dans le réseau qui, si elles ne sont pas aidées rapidement, risquent à leur tour la chronicisation.

Quatrième orientation :
rechercher des solutions dans le milieu de vie

La quatrième grande orientation de la Politique est celle de « rechercher des solutions dans le milieu de vie ». Il s'agit sans contredit de l'objectif qui a fait le plus illusion depuis 1989. Il visait à mieux reconnaître les organismes communautaires et à compléter la désinstitutionnalisation. La publication du tome II du Rapport du vérificateur général pour l'année 1995-1996 (Breton, 1996) a porté un dur coup à l'image du MSSS. Le vérificateur a en effet démontré que le Québec subventionnait encore le double du nombre de lits affectés aux soins psychiatriques que lui permettaient théoriquement ses propres normes adoptées depuis 1976. Qui plus est, les quelques réductions de lits intervenues de 1991 à 1996 n'avaient nullement donné lieu à des transferts dans la communauté mais plutôt à un enrichissement des centres hospitaliers. Le vérificateur conclut : « Six ans après l'élaboration de la Politique de santé mentale, on ne peut que constater un échec quant au réaménagement souhaité des ressources en santé mentale. »

Quant à la reconnaissance des ressources communautaires, il est certain qu'elles ont reçu un coup de pouce appréciable depuis 1989. Cependant, ce qui est le plus marquant, c'est la reconduction constante du déséquilibre du système en faveur des ressources d'institution-nalisation : 64 % du budget global est consacré aux hospitalisations alors que tous les services et activités dispensés par les organismes commun-autaires et le CLSC n'en grèvent que 6 % (*Orientations*). Le Bilan d'implantation recommande de viser une augmentation des subsides aux organismes communautaires (rien n'est dit des CLSC) pour atteindre un minimum de 10 % du budget global. Dans les *Orientations*, le ministère adopte cependant une perspective qui ne prend en compte que la réduction des dépenses attribuables aux « lits » de soins psychiatriques. Toutes les autres formes de services sont désormais considérées comme des mesures alternatives ou communautaires. Ainsi, dans son Plan de transformation (1997 : 8), l'Hôpital Louis-H.-Lafontaine définit les ressources alternatives vers lesquelles il entend réaffecter ses ressources : « Il faut comprendre ici des ressources ou services de l'hôpital utilisant du personnel formé et expérimenté avec l'approche préconisée. » Dès lors, on risque fort de se retrouver dans la situation déjà dénoncée par le vérificateur général.

Cinquième orientation : consolider le partenariat

Enfin, la cinquième grande orientation concernait la « consolidation du partenariat ». Maintes critiques furent adressées au partenariat tel qu'il est pratiqué par les régies au moment de rédiger les fameux Plans régionaux d'organisation des services (PROS). Les participants des tiers «hors réseau» ne bénéficiaient pas d'un soutien logistique et pédagogique suffisant. Le rythme des travaux ne permettait pas des débats de fond. Les règles du jeu n'étaient pas clairement établies, entre autres, les rôles des fonctionnaires des régies régionales par rapport à celui de leur conseil d'administration ainsi que les modalités et conséquences de l'approbation des PROS par Québec (deux seulement l'ont été à ce jour!). Malgré ces difficultés, le milieu communautaire en santé mentale a constamment soutenu la formule des comités tripartites qui permettait au moins de créer un espace public favorisant l'ouverture du système (Guay, 1991; Lamoureux 1994; Gagné, 1997). Depuis, la formule s'est transformée en faveur de la multiplication des lieux de concertation sur des bases variées (sous-région, MRC, regroupement de problématiques ou de services), mais sans reconduire un Comité régional exerçant une vigilance sur la planification ou l'implantation de tous les services en santé mentale sur son territoire. Encore une fois, du Bilan d'implantation aux *Orientations*, on constate une dilution de la détermination du ministère à «communautariser» le système. Le Bilan d'implantation recommande la reconduction de la formule des Comités tripartites pour entreprendre la seconde phase d'implantation de la Politique alors que dans les *Orientations*, le ministre se contente de parler d'un vague «[...] lieu d'échange et de concertation pour favoriser le partage des expériences, soutenir les nouvelles solidarités et proposer les ajustements requis en cours de route» (*Orientations*, 1997 : 37).

Un dernier moyen prévu par la politique initiale au chapitre du partenariat concernait celui d'établir, au niveau du gouvernement lui-même, un système d'harmonisation des politiques, comme celles du logement, de la sécurité du revenu, de la jeunesse, de la sécurité publique, etc., à celle adoptée en santé mentale. On appelait donc à l'adoption d'une politique d'ensemble. Le Bilan d'implantation récidive en réduisant ce moyen à un Comité interministériel devant favoriser l'intersectorialité. Enfin, les *Orientations* parlent plutôt d'un «mécanisme» interministériel.

Les tensions

Selon le document de consultation du MSSS, les ratés de la politique seraient attribuables à «Des conflits dans les approches, les juridictions et le contrôle des ressources [qui] ont accentué dans certaines régions la difficulté de fournir des services continus» (MSSS, 1997 : 9). Une telle formulation a le défaut de mettre à plat une problématique qui dépasse de beaucoup les «chicanes de clocher». En fait, ces «tensions» expriment un état de crise équivalent à celui auquel faisait face le champ québécois de la santé mentale, au début des années 1960, sous la houlette des religieuses hospitalières. Encore une fois, tout le système des services de santé mentale est pratiquement dominé par une seule approche, l'approche biomédicale et par un club limité d'orthodoxes, celui des psychiatres et des administrateurs hospitalocentristes. L'État voudrait bien que les différents groupes d'intérêt s'entendent pour une meilleure harmonisation du système de santé mentale. Les groupes communautaires veulent une reconnaissance de leur action thérapeutique non explicitement statuée, par ailleurs, dans la Politique de santé mentale. Les professionnels, voulant protéger leur territoire, s'opposent à cette reconnaissance et remettent en question les compétence thérapeutiques des groupes communautaires. Plus encore, le président de l'Association des médecins-psychiatres va même jusqu'à tracer leur champ d'action : soutien aux familles et aide aux changements des mentalités à l'égard des patients psychiatriques (Boudreau, 1991 ; Gagné, 1996). Pour les psychologues, ils sont par la voix de leur corporation professionnelle, les seuls avec les psychiatres habilités « *in the treatment of mental health problems* » (Boudreau, 1991). Quant à l'Ordre professionnel des travailleurs sociaux ainsi que l'Association des infirmières et infirmiers, ils contestent tous deux la hiérarchie de pouvoir régissant le système des services sociaux et de santé mentale et plaident pour une union des acteurs à l'horizontale (Boudreau, 1991).

Pourtant, le partenariat suppose des partenaires égaux. Le sont-ils réellement ? Non, répond la sociologue Françoise Boudreau (1991). Un autre auteur (Domergues, 1988) précise les conditions de réalisation du partenariat :

> [...] dans la société partenariale, les acteurs doivent avoir des droits et des devoirs réciproques. Ils doivent avoir un pouvoir et des responsabilités comparables. Ils doivent retirer des avantages tangibles ou intangibles de même importance. Bref, ils doivent être égaux dans la coopération. Cette équité – les Américains disent fairness – est essentielle [...] sans équité, il n'y a pas de partenariat.

QUE CONCLURE ?

Deux faits sont à inscrire dans la mémoire du temps. Tout d'abord, en dépit de quelques ratés inhérents à toute expérience humaine, la désinstitutionnalisation a des effets positifs. Les psychiatrisés ont pu retrouver leur liberté hors des murs asilaires, ont réappris des habiletés sociales. Il y a eu également démystification de la notion de « maladie mentale », acceptation par la communauté des personnes manifestant des troubles mentaux, pressions de la part des associations de bénéficiaires, de parents, d'amis pour l'allocation de ressources nécessaires à l'intégration sociale, programme répit dépannage pour les familles, renforcement des droits des usagers à l'échelle nationale. Ensuite, ce qui est décevant, c'est le manque de courage politique des gouvernements successifs du Québec et le machiavélisme des pouvoirs professionnels inféodé au conservatisme des administrations en place qui n'ont pas voulu porter remède à trois problèmes cruciaux pourtant diagnostiqués par deux commissions d'enquête, le Rapport Harnois (1987) et le Rapport Rochon (1988) :

- la compétition des services entre eux et la discontinuité des soins ;
- la prise en otage des services de santé mentale par les groupes d'intérêt ;
- la reconnaissance de l'importance des ressources communautaires et leur sous-financement.

Faire le bilan des dix années de la Politique en santé mentale, c'est en fin de compte faire le bilan de plus de trente ans de tamponnage. Puisque, à chaque décennie, on préconise des choses qu'on n'a pas réalisées la décennie précédente. Bref, en santé mentale et en psychiatrie, on dit avec un vocabulaire différent à peu près les mêmes choses depuis le Rapport Bédard, Lazure, Roberts du début des années 1960. Pour le dixième anniversaire de la revue NPS, la santé mentale n'a que quelques biscuits à la mélasse à lui offrir en lieu et place d'un vrai beau gâteau.

Bibliographie

Association des groupes d'intervention en défense des droits en santé mentale du Québec (1997). *Réactions de l'association des groupes d'intervention en défense des droits en santé mentale du Québec aux orientations pour la transformation des services de santé mentale,* Document photocopié, Montréal.

Boudreau, Françoise (1991). « Stakeholders as Partners : The Challenges of Partnership in Quebec Mental Health Policy », *Canadian Journal of Community Mental Health,* vol. 10, nº 1, 7-28.

Breton, Guy *(1996). Rapport du vérificateur général à l'assemblée nationale pour l'année 1995-1996,* Tome II, Le vérificateur général du Québec, Québec.

Breton, Madeleine (1995). *Salles d'urgence situation en santé mentale : questionnements et pistes d'action,* Québec, Gouvernement du Québec, MSSS.

Comité de la santé mentale du Québec (1994). *Recommandations pour développer et enrichir la politique de santé mentale,* Québec, Les Publications du Québec.

Comité de travail sur les services de santé mentale offerts aux femmes (1997). *Écoute-moi quand je parle...,* Rapport du Comité de travail sur les services de santé mentale offerts aux femmes, Document de travail inédit.

CÔTÉ, Marc-Yvan (1992). «La délicate cohabitation du communautaire et de l'institutionnel en santé mentale», Entrevue avec le ministre Marc-Yvan Côté réalisée par Henri Dorvil et Jean Gagné, *Nouvelles pratiques sociales*, vol. 5, n° 1, 7-23.

DOMMERGUES, P. (1988). *La société de partenariat – économie, territoire et revitalisation régionale aux États-Unis et en France*, Paris, AFNOR, Anthropos.

DORVIL, Henri (1988). *Histoire de la folie dans la communauté 1962-1987*, Montréal, Éditions Émile-Nelligan.

FÉDÉRATION DES INFIRMIÈRES ET INFIRMIERS DU QUÉBEC (1997). *Un virage vers l'autonomie en santé mentale et en psychiatrie*, Mémoire présenté au ministre de la Santé et des Services sociaux dans le cadre de la consultation privée portant sur les Orientations pour la transformation des services de santé mentale, FIIQ, 41 pages.

GAGNÉ, Jean (1996). «Le virage ambulatoire en santé mentale: un détour qui évite l'alternative», *Santé mentale au Québec*, vol. XXI, n° I, 15-26.

GAGNÉ, Jean (1997). «Le partenariat dans le champ de la santé mentale à la période post pros», tiré de *Au-delà de la tourmente, de nouvelles alliances à bâtir*, Actes du colloque des intervenants et intervenantes en action communautaire en CLSC et en centre de santé, Chicoutimi, GRIR, Université du Québec à Chicoutimi, p. 67-80.

GOERING, P.N., WASYLENKI, D.A., FARKAS, M., LANCEE, N.J. et R. BALLANTYNE (1988). «What Difference Does Case Management Make?», *Hospital and Community Psychiatry*, vol. 39, n° 3, 272-276.

GUAY, Lorraine (1991*).* «Le choc des cultures: bilan de l'expérience de participation des ressources alternatives à l'élaboration des plans régionaux d'organisation de services en santé mentale», *Nouvelles pratiques sociales*, vol. 4, n° 2, 43-58.

HARNOIS, Gaston et COMITÉ DE LA POLITIQUE DE SANTÉ MENTALE DU QUÉBEC (1987). *Pour un partenariat élargi*, Projet de Politique de santé mentale pour le Québec, Québec, Les Publications du Québec.

HÔPITAL LOUIS-H.-LAFONTAINE (1997). *Plan de transformation, les orientations et le modèle d'organisation des services en psychiatrie*, Montréal, 44 pages.

LAMONTAGNE, Yves (1993). «Perceptions des Québécois à l'égard de la maladie mentale», *L'Union médicale du Canada*, vol. 122, n° 5, 334-343.

LAMOUREUX, Jocelyne (1994*). Le partenariat à l'épreu*ve, Montréal, Éditions St-Martin.

MINISTÈRE DE LA SANTÉ ET DES SERVICES SOCIAUX (1989). *La Politique de santé mentale du Québec*, Québec, Gouvernement du Québec.

MINISTÈRE DE LA SANTÉ ET DES SERVICES SOCIAUX (1996). *La transformation des services de santé mentale: orientations jusqu'en 2002*, Document de consultation, 27 pages.

MINISTÈRE DE LA SANTÉ ET DES SERVICES SOCIAUX (1997). *Orientations pour la transformation des services de santé mentale*, Document de consultation, Québec, Gouvernement du Québec.

MORIN, Paul (1993). *Espace urbain montréalais et processus de ghettoïsation de populations marginalisées*, Thèse de doctorat en sociologie, Montréal, Université du Québec à Montréal.

POTVIN, Nelson (1997). *Bilan d'implantation de la politique de santé mentale*, Québec, Gouvernement du Québec, Ministère de la Santé et des Services sociaux.

ROCHON, Jean et COMMISSION D'ENQUÊTE SUR LES SERVICES DE SANTÉ ET LES SERVICES SOCIAUX (1988). *Rapport*, Québec, Les Publications du Québec.

ST-LAURENT, D. et M. CLARKSON (*1989*). « Intégration, les barrières s'estompent », *Santé et Société*, vol. 11, n° 2, 23-25.

❖ Dix ans sur la scène du multiculturalisme

André JACOB
Département de travail social
Université du Québec à Montréal

Dans le grand théâtre du monde, le lieu commun le plus répandu consiste à rappeler que nous vivons à l'ère de la mondialisation ou de la globalisation de l'économie. Évidemment, on sous-entend que les lois du marché, c'est-à dire l'accumulation et la consommation, déterminent les rapports entre les êtres humains sur les plans social, culturel et politique. Cette vision romantique du capitalisme triomphant ne devrait-elle pas suffire à souligner les conditions de l'avènement d'un univers unifié, sans frontières ni conflits ethniques ? L'idéal n'est-il pas de voir le monde entier se ressembler dans le paradis de la consommation sous les mêmes bannières commerciales, par exemple, Coca-Cola, McDonald, Ford, etc.

L'histoire récente démontre d'une façon brutale que cette utopie « mondialiste » ne réussit pas à tuer les références identitaires fondées sur les particularismes ethniques et culturels. À cet égard, la dernière décennie marque une nouvelle étape dans le questionnement et la redéfinition des rapports entre les nations et les individus de diverses origines ethniques, nationales et culturelles. Depuis la fin de la Seconde Guerre mondiale, en 1945, la plupart des pays anglo-saxons se sont autoproclamés champions de la promotion du multiculturalisme au nom du respect des différences individuelles fondées sur l'origine ethnique ou nationale, les références culturelles, la couleur de la peau, les caractéristiques phénotypiques, la langue, la religion, les coutumes, les valeurs, etc. En somme, le paradigme « différence ethnoculturelle » a orienté les perceptions et la gestion « quotidienne » des rapports entre les individus et entre ces derniers et les institutions. Stack (1986) parle d'une conception romantique de l'identité qui conduit à une sorte de déterminisme culturel servant de pierre d'assise à la construction de stéréotypes au sujet du caractère spécifique de l'ethnicité. Par ailleurs, dira Kitano, l'identité ethnique peut aussi être utilisée pour la promotion d'intérêts particuliers de groupes ou d'individus. Le fait que la référence ethnique a été catapultée à l'avant-plan de la redéfinition des rapports civils et politiques des sociétés développées a fait en sorte que l'ethnicité est maintenant un levier social important. Ce phénomène n'enlève rien aux paradoxes profonds qui en découlent.

Bien sûr, il faudrait expliquer plus en détail la portée historique de la dynamique sociale et politique créée par l'adoption de ce paradigme. Retenons seulement le fait que les années 1990 se caractérisent par un questionnement en profondeur du multiculturalisme. Au Canada, les débats sur le sujet ne manquent pas ; à titre d'exemples, le livre de Neil Bissoondath, publié en 1995, jetait un pavé dans la grande mare de ce qui semblait un consensus sur la survalorisation de la culture comme référence obligée dans les rapports entre les citoyens et les citoyennes, tout particulièrement ceux et celles nés en dehors du Canada. Le fait que Neil Bissoondath soit né dans les Caraïbes ajoutait du piquant à sa dénonciation du multiculturalisme outrancier qui finit par camper tout le monde dans des rapports entre minorités et majorité et, par voie de conséquence, à engendrer diverses formes d'exclusion maquillées de bonnes intentions crasses, naïves ou sciemment conçues. L'exacerbation des tensions « ethniques » a amené d'autres immigrants ou descendants d'immigrants à dénoncer aussi les effets pervers et contradictoires de l'utilisation des références ethnoculturelles à des fins politiques ; que l'on songe à Marco Nicone et à Claude Larbo, par exemple. Évidemment, une analyse plus poussée nous entraînerait dans des considérations plus vives de tous les méandres d'un tel débat.

Le cheminement critique des dernières années ne remet pas en question la reconnaissance des droits de tous les citoyens et de toutes les citoyennes, peu importe leur origine. Bien au contraire. Au cours de la dernière décennie, toutes les institutions (services de santé et services sociaux, écoles, universités, services de police, ministères, etc.), les entreprises privées tout autant que nombre d'organismes non gouvernementaux ont consolidé la reconnaissance de ce fait par diverses mesures (politiques d'embauche, programmes de formation du personnel, politiques d'accès, etc.). En somme, les acquis ne sont pas menacés. Le questionnement qui a cours porte essentiellement sur une redéfinition des rapports civils sans risques de dérapages où les stéréotypes et les différences à caractère ethnoculturel marqueraient davantage les relations entre les citoyens et les citoyennes que l'égalité des droits.

❖ L'accueil : une pratique en mouvance[1]

André JACOB
Département de travail social
Université du Québec à Montréal

L'accueil des immigrants et des réfugiés est forcément influencé par la conjoncture sociale politique dans laquelle il s'inscrit. En ce sens, l'accueil n'est pas qu'une attitude propre à des individus mais aussi une pratique sociale collective, même si on l'a trop peu souvent envisagé sous cet angle. L'accueil est à la fois un objectif social et collectif à atteindre et une stratégie de soutien concret aux individus.

Malgré une immigration massive dans les années 1950, l'accueil relevait d'abord à l'époque de la responsabilité privée (Églises, syndicats, conseils des œuvres, entreprises privées, etc.). C'est surtout dans les années 1960 que la perception du phénomène de l'immigration allait évoluer rapidement, tant au Canada qu'au Québec. Au fédéral, le gouvernement lance la politique du multiculturalisme où la société canadienne se définit comme une mosaïque culturelle. Du côté québécois, on assiste à une montée du nationalisme, à la recherche d'une identité nationale distincte pour cet îlot francophone d'Amérique. Dans les deux cas, cette «reconceptualisation» de l'immigration va marquer profondément le rapport à l'autre.

---

1. Ce texte a été publié dans *Vivre ensemble*, Bulletin de liaison en pastorale interculturelle, Centre Justice et Foi, hiver-printemps 1997.

LES PRATIQUES D'ACCUEIL

L'immigration étant un phénomène continu, les efforts pour en saisir le sens et l'impact mais surtout pour agir concrètement devraient être constants. Si les gouvernements se préoccupent des mécanismes nécessaires pour favoriser l'établissement, l'accueil, lui, se vit dans le quotidien de tous les jours. L'accueil comme pratique sociale fait donc étroitement partie du processus d'adaptation et d'intégration de l'immigrant à la société.

L'évolution politique mentionnée plus haut va donc rapidement influencer les pratiques d'accueil. D'un côté, fortes des orientations données par la politique du multiculturalisme du gouvernement fédéral et par l'affirmation culturelle du gouvernement québécois, deux politiques qui prônaient l'affirmation des identités ethniques et culturelles, les organisations mises sur pied sur une base monoethnique se multiplièrent rapidement (l'Association des Chiliens, l'Association des Vietnamiens, etc.). Par contre, dans les années 1970, de même qu'au début des années 1980, un certain nombre d'organisations naquirent, préoccupées autant de promotion et de défense des droits que d'affirmation culturelle et de distribution de services, soit sur une base monoethnique (Association des travailleurs grecs, Fédération italienne des travailleurs immigrants et de leur famille, Mouvement démocratique portugais, Association des Ukrainiens, Maison d'Haïti, Bureau de la communauté chrétienne des Haïtiens de Montréal, etc.) ou sur une base pluriethnique (Union des travailleurs immigrants, Association des travailleurs immigrants, Centre des femmes immigrantes, Association du personnel domestique, Au bas de l'échelle, Association multiethnique pour l'intégration des personnes handicapées du Québec, Table de concertation des organismes de Montréal pour les réfugiés, Alliance des communautés culturelles pour l'accessibilité aux services sociaux de la santé, etc.).

Ce mouvement d'affirmation de l'identité immigrante créait une sorte de pression constante sur diverses organisations civiles. Plusieurs grandes centrales syndicales, de même que des syndicats locaux prirent le virage de l'intégration, se mirent à analyser le phénomène dans des colloques et des recherches et adoptèrent des mesures, dont la création de comités immigration, pour faciliter la participation des travailleurs de diverses origines à la vie syndicale. De même, de nombreuses organisations sans but lucratif engagées dans la promotion des droits ou la distribution de services sociaux (santé mentale, toxicomanies, aînés, jeunes femmes victimes de violence, etc.) ont aussi cherché à modifier et à adapter leur intervention et leurs services en tenant compte des exigences nouvelles d'une société devenue cosmopolite.

On doit souligner aussi le rôle déterminant des Églises chrétiennes dans leurs efforts pour amener leurs croyants à s'impliquer dans l'accueil et le soutien des immigrants et des réfugiés. Depuis une vingtaine d'années, on ne compte plus les initiatives en ce sens. De même, d'autres secteurs comme le monde artistique et le monde des affaires, surtout depuis que les gouvernements favorisent l'arrivée d'immigrants investisseurs, ont commencé à faire une place grandissante aux nouveaux arrivants. Cette participation active, dans leurs milieux respectifs, d'artistes fort divers, de même que d'entrepreneurs et de travailleurs venus de partout, illustre bien les progrès accomplis depuis quelques décennies. Ce qui ne signifie pas, pour autant, que tout aille pour le mieux, comme le montre bien le phénomène de l'exploitation de la main-d'œuvre immigrante, souvent corvéable à merci et prête à accepter tous les types d'emploi.

Ces pratiques d'accueil, de même que les exigences et les pressions de la réalité plurielle de notre société, ont peu à peu provoqué des changements dans toutes sortes de domaines de notre vie collective. Les médias de communication, par exemple, comptent de plus en plus de journalistes de diverses origines et commencent à offrir des contenus qui reflètent la diversité culturelle. De même, le rapport aux institutions étant fondamental pour l'intégration des nouveaux arrivants, plusieurs d'entre elles, comme les municipalités, les services policiers des grands centres, les universités et les hôpitaux, se sont dotées de politiques de gestion de la diversité et de programmes de sensibilisation et de formation de leur personnel aux exigences du travail dans une société cosmopolite.

Enfin, il faut souligner le fait que de plus en plus de citoyens et de citoyennes «accueillent» directement, à travers des rapports interpersonnels, des immigrants ou des réfugiés avec qui ils sont jumelés par l'intermédiaire de divers organismes communautaires (comme l'Hirondelle, par exemple) qui coordonnent de tels programmes. Ainsi, dans plusieurs villes et villages, on voit des regroupements d'individus et de familles s'organiser pour accueillir des familles ou des individus dans leur communauté. En somme, la liste des initiatives est longue et elle parle d'elle-même.

Divers autres programmes visent également, à des degrés divers, à faciliter l'accueil et l'intégration: les programmes d'apprentissage linguistique bien sûr, mais aussi les programmes de régionalisation (implantation des immigrants dans les régions), les programmes d'échanges culturels, les programmes de coopération internationale, etc. Ainsi, au moment d'écrire ces lignes, un programme d'accueil de réfugiés bosniaques par des familles rimouskoises est en voie d'implantation, un autre à Joliette pour accueillir des familles chiliennes, etc.

UN BILAN POSITIF

En terminant, j'ai la conviction que la compréhension du phénomène de l'immigration a changé profondément et d'une façon positive, au cours des dernières années, et c'est sans doute là un levier significatif pour favoriser l'accueil. À mon humble avis, le climat général, les attitudes des gens et les pratiques ont évolué en profondeur. Contrairement à ce que serinent sur tous les tons les alarmistes qui crient haut et fort que l'affirmation nationale du Québec est un blocage majeur à l'accueil et à l'intégration, je réaffirme que les changements me semblent plutôt positifs. Paradoxalement, le nationalisme québécois contemporain, malgré quelques dérapages, rappelle à tous les citoyens et à toutes les citoyennes l'importance de l'affirmation identitaire, peu importe l'origine ou la culture. Tous les Québécois et toutes les Québécoises, au sens de tous les individus qui habitent le territoire québécois, sont appelés à s'affirmer et à négocier leur participation à un projet de société, dans le respect des droits de chacun et des particularités identitaires.

En ce sens, l'adoption de la Loi 101, pierre d'assise d'un projet de société québécois, a certainement marqué un point tournant au niveau de l'accueil : en rendant l'apprentissage du français obligatoire pour la plupart des immigrants et des réfugiés, elle plaçait la capacité de participer activement à la vie sociale, économique, culturelle et politique au cœur de l'accueil. L'apprentissage de la langue d'usage dans une société est partout une clé essentielle dans le processus d'accueil et d'intégration. Peu à peu, depuis une vingtaine d'années, divers ministères ont adopté d'autres politiques de soutien à l'accueil, mises en œuvre soit par des organismes communautaires ou sans but lucratif, soit par des services publics. Des programmes de subventions équivalant à des millions de dollars ont permis la mise en place de tout un réseau d'organismes, qui visent d'une façon plus ou moins directe à faciliter l'accueil, l'adaptation et la participation à la société.

Bien sûr, tout n'est pas parfait et il reste encore beaucoup à faire. Il se trouve encore des gens qui adoptent des positions racistes et prétendent que ces milliers de nouveaux citoyens «viennent voler nos emplois», ou pour voir l'accueil comme un «problème» strictement culturel où les différences sont souvent insurmontables. Mais il me semble qu'un courant de fond parallèle et dominant existe, qui perçoit davantage l'arrivée des immigrants ou des réfugiés comme une force nouvelle et comme une richesse culturelle, économique, politique et sociale.

Bibliographie

BISSOONDATH, Neil (1995). *Le marché aux illusions : la méprise du multiculturalisme*, Montréal, Boréal-Liber.

KITANO, Harry H.L. (1997). *Race Relations*, Upper Saddle River, N.J., Prentice-Hall.

LARBO, Claude (1996). *Lettre fraternelle, raisonnée et urgente à mes concitoyens immigrants*, Outremont, Lanctôt éditeur.

NICONE, Marco (1995). « Un rempart contre le déferlement de la droite canadienne. Les allophones, un poids politique sans précédent », *Le Devoir*, 19 octobre.

STACK, J.F. (1986). « Ethnic Mobilization in World Politics : The Primordial Perspective », dans STACK, J.F. Jr. (dir.), *The Primordial Challenge*, New York, Greenwood Press, 1-9.

❖ L'immigration et l'intégration des immigrants au Québec au cours des quinze dernières années[1]

Yvan TURCOTTE
Directeur des politiques et des programmes d'immigration
Ministère des Relations avec les citoyens et de l'Immigration

Trois tendances de fond, au cours des deux dernières décennies, ont particulièrement concouru à structurer l'immigration et la dynamique d'intégration des immigrants au Québec.

La mutation qu'a connue le Québec sur le plan démographique est l'une de ces tendances. Naguère caractérisée par un taux de natalité comptant parmi les plus élevés du monde occidental, la société québécoise n'assure plus, depuis la fin des années 1960, le renouvellement des générations. L'indice de fécondité, qui devrait se situer à environ 2,1

---

1. Ce texte a été publié dans *Vivre ensemble*, Bulletin de liaison en pastorale interculturelle, Centre Justice et Foi, hiver-printemps, 1997.

pour assurer ce renouvellement, a oscillé entre 1,35 et 1,65 depuis 15 ans. La prise de conscience grandissante de ce phénomène et de ses consé-quences prévisibles (vieillissement de la population et, à plus long terme, diminution nette de la taille de celle-ci ; diminution du poids du Québec au sein de l'ensemble canadien) ont largement déterminé, surtout à partir du milieu des années 1980, les politiques d'immigration du Québec.

La volonté du Québec d'acquérir un contrôle accru de son immi-gration représente une autre de ces tendances fondamentales. La collectivité québécoise entend déterminer elle-même, dans la plus large mesure possible, et en fonction de ses besoins et de ses valeurs, tant les volumes et la composition de son immigration que les différents aspects de l'intégration de ses immigrants. Cette volonté s'était notamment manifestée par la conclusion de l'Entente Couture-Cullen, en 1978, qui reconnaissait au Québec ses premiers pouvoirs significatifs d'intervention en matière de sélection. Elle s'est aussi traduite par l'inscription de l'immigration au cœur des revendications constitutionnelles du Québec, tant par le gouvernement Lévesque dans le cadre du «Beau risque», que par le gouvernement Bourassa dans la liste des cinq demandes qui devaient mener aux accords du lac Meech. Et elle a entraîné l'Accord Canada-Québec de 1991 qui consolide et élargit les pouvoirs québécois d'intervention en particulier au chapitre de l'accueil et de l'intégration des immigrants.

Sans pour autant – beaucoup s'en faut – avoir atteint la pleine maîtrise de son immigration, le Québec a depuis une quinzaine d'années acquis et exercé des pouvoirs significatifs. Cette période a ainsi vu la mise en place des instruments d'intervention du Québec. Celui-ci a notamment développé des instruments de planification des niveaux d'im-migration et de consultation sur ceux-ci ; il a adopté, puis fait évoluer, ses propres politiques et programmes de recrutement de sélection ou de parrainage visant les composantes humanitaires, économiques et familiales du mouvement d'immigration ; il a, de même, structuré des interventions originales en matière d'accueil, de francisation et d'aide à l'intégration des nouveaux venus. Enfin, l'Énoncé de politique de 1990, qui a fait l'objet d'une large adhésion, est venu cristalliser les acquis des années précédentes et tracer les grands axes de l'action du Québec pour l'avenir.

S'inscrivant dans un contexte d'affirmation nationale et de progres-sion socio-économique des Québécois francophones, l'adoption de la Loi 22 puis de la *Charte de la langue française* est venue clarifier les conditions dans lesquelles doit se réaliser la démarche d'intégration des immigrants à la société québécoise. *L'affirmation du statut de la langue française comme seule langue officielle au Québec et les mesures visant à en assurer la protection et l'usage auront ainsi induit une troisième tendance fondamentale.* Selon les termes mêmes de la Charte, «...langue distinctive d'un peuple majoritairement francophone, la langue française permet au peuple québécois d'exprimer son identité...». Le français apparaît donc dès lors, de façon non équivoque, comme la langue commune de la vie publique pour les Québécois de toutes origines.

Ces trois grandes tendances conjuguées ont en quelque sorte constitué la trame et les ferments de l'évolution des problématiques touchant l'immigration et l'intégration des immigrants au Québec depuis 15 ans. C'est ainsi, par exemple, que depuis plusieurs années, les sondages d'opinion témoignent de *l'ouverture significative de la population québécoise face à l'immigration*, le niveau de cet appui dépassant régulièrement celui qui se manifeste ailleurs au Canada. Or, cette ouverture a été grandement déterminée par la prise de conscience de l'actuelle dynamique démographique, celle-ci devenant un des enjeux centraux associés à l'immigration, pour une collectivité qui avait longtemps été en situation d'autarcie démographique du fait de sa forte natalité. Mais cette ouverture a sans doute aussi été facilitée par la confiance et le sentiment de contrôle qui ont découlé au sein de la population québécoise, du rôle accru qu'a joué le gouvernement québécois dans l'élaboration et la mise en œuvre de politiques d'immigration et d'intégration qui lui soient propres, et de l'imposition claire du français comme langue de l'intégration.

La progression du français au sein de la population immigrée représente du reste une caractéristique marquante de la période en cause. Signalons, par exemple, que, selon les données du recensement de 1991, 71 % de cette population résidant alors au Québec déclarait pouvoir converser en français. Pour mémoire, rappelons que cette proportion était d'à peine 50 % en 1971. La tendance observée, chez les cohortes d'arrivées plus récentes, quant aux transferts linguistiques (abandon de la langue maternelle au profit d'une nouvelle langue, comme langue d'usage à la maison) est également significative. Chez les personnes immigrées depuis 1976 et ayant effectué un tel transfert, on constatait en 1991 que celui-ci s'était effectué dans une proportion de 67 % vers le français, comparativement à 33 % vers l'anglais. Et cette tendance devrait se renforcer considérablement au cours des prochaines décennies, la Loi 101 commençant à peine à produire son plein effet à cet égard. Les transferts linguistiques se réalisent en effet généralement à l'âge adulte, au moment où les écoliers d'hier fondent leur propre foyer. Or, seule une faible proportion des «enfants de la Loi 101» avaient atteint cet âge en 1991.

Les dispositions de la *Charte de la langue française* relatives à la langue de la scolarisation au primaire et au secondaire auront par ailleurs contribué à une transformation radicale de la dynamique d'intégration des nouveaux arrivants. En entraînant la présence massive des enfants immigrants à l'école française, elles auront bien sûr permis un apprentissage rapide du français chez ces enfants et favorisé cet apprentissage chez leurs parents ; mais elles auront aussi contribué à créer les conditions d'une mise en relation quotidienne largement accrue des immigrants et de la communauté québécoise francophone. *Cette mise en relation élargie des Québécois francophones et des immigrants* s'est vécue non seulement à l'école mais aussi, à des degrés divers, au travail, dans les commerces, dans les loisirs, dans les milieux culturels et, au premier chef, dans la vie de quartier. Et la nature et le sens de cette mise en relation ont aussi été modelés par les *modifications profondes qu'ont connues les flux migratoires accueillis au Québec.* Très largement composés de candidats originaires d'Europe ou des États-Unis jusqu'aux années 1990, ces flux se sont par la suite rapidement diversifiés, les ressortissants de pays d'Asie, du Moyen-Orient, des Antilles, de l'Amérique latine et d'Afrique en venant à constituer une nette majorité des admissions.

Désormais caractérisée par cette diversité d'origine ethnique et culturelle et par l'absence, en son sein, de groupes nationaux particuliers pouvant prétendre à une quelconque hégémonie du fait de leur poids numérique, la nouvelle immigration vit son parcours d'intégration dans un contexte où des attentes précises ont été clairement exprimées par la majorité francophone, et où celle-ci contribue elle-même à la réalisation de ces attentes par l'intensité des rapports qu'elle établit avec les nouveaux arrivants. *Cette nouvelle donnée de l'intégration s'incarne en particulier dans le milieu montréalais.* Près de 85 % des immigrants continuent d'avoir pour destination l'Île-de-Montréal où, par ailleurs, le poids relatif des francophones se trouve en diminution, en conséquence de l'étalement urbain et de la faible natalité des récentes décennies. Il faut toutefois signaler, à ce chapitre, l'émergence d'une tendance, chez les immigrants d'arrivée récente, à une dissémination plus large au sein de la grande région de Montréal, Laval et la Montérégie bénéficiant principalement de ce nouveau modèle d'établissement des immigrants.

On ne saurait terminer cette trop brève description de l'évolution de l'immigration et de l'intégration au Québec au cours des quinze dernières années sans faire état de trois autres phénomènes ayant marqué cette époque. Il s'agit, d'abord, de *l'importance accrue qu'a revêtue l'accueil humanitaire,* celui-ci ayant constitué un volet permanent des politiques québécoises d'immigration et les admissions à ce titre ayant représenté, année après année, une proportion importante du flux migratoire. Amorcé au tournant des années 1980 par le parrainage des réfugiés de la mer et par le programme visant les ressortissants haïtiens en situation irrégulière, cet accueil s'est par la suite poursuivi au profit des Libanais notamment, et, plus récemment, des ressortissants de l'ex-Yougoslavie. Et il a en outre été alimenté par le mouvement des revendicateurs du statut de réfugié, le Québec ayant reçu près de 130 000 demandes d'asile depuis 1982.

La progression du taux de rétention des immigrants admis au Québec est un autre de ces phénomènes. Alors que la capacité du Québec à retenir ses immigrants a longtemps été moindre que celle du reste du Canada et qu'elle est encore aujourd'hui souvent mise en doute, le taux de présence de la population immigrée au Québec dépasse désormais 80 %, et est donc tout à fait comparable à celui observé pour l'ensemble du Canada. Le rôle accru que joue désormais la collectivité québécoise dans la sélection et l'intégration de son immigration n'est certainement pas étranger à cette évolution.

Notons enfin, en guise de conclusion, *la création récente du ministère des Relations avec les citoyens et de l'Immigration*, dont la Loi constitutive confie notamment au ministère titulaire les fonctions de favoriser «[...] l'exercice pour les citoyens de leurs responsabilités civiques et sociales [...]» et de «[...] promouvoir la solidarité [...], l'ouverture au pluralisme et le rapprochement interculturel, favorisant l'appartenance au peuple québécois».

❖ Trajectoire de l'organisation communautaire professionnelle

Denis BOURQUE
CLSC Jean-Olivier-Chénier

Même si l'organisation communautaire apparaît comme une constituante du service social, elle a connu une trajectoire qui lui est propre et qui est largement tributaire de son insertion institutionnelle, de l'évolution des mouvements sociaux et des communautés, et de celle des politiques sociales. Elle est née au Québec au cours des années 1960 en prônant l'action collective comme stratégie de modification des conditions de vie, se démarquant ainsi du modèle traditionnel en service social, soit le service individualisé visant l'adaptation sociale.

L'histoire de l'organisation communautaire peut se subdiviser en plusieurs périodes[1]. Nous suggérons les périodes suivantes : l'animation sociale (1961-1971) ; l'institutionnalisation (1972-1980) ; la crise identitaire (1981-1987) et la consolidation de la profession (1988-1995).

---

1. DOUCET, L. et L. FAVREAU (1991) en identifient trois : avant 1960, de 1960 à 1975 et de 1975 à nos jours ; DORÉ, G. (1992) identifie les périodes de 1961 à 1970, de 1971 à 1980 et de 1980 à 1990.

L'organisation communautaire dont il est question ici est celle qui se pratique en milieu institutionnel, essentiellement en CLSC. Même si l'organisation communautaire en tant que profession est présente sur d'autres terrains (organismes communautaires, coopératives, syndicats), il nous semble que les conditions d'exercice sont fort différentes. Nous concentrerons donc notre analyse sur l'un des lieux spécifiques de l'organisation communautaire, soit le milieu institutionnel.

L'ANIMATION SOCIALE (1961-1971)

L'animation sociale est née en 1963 au Conseil des œuvres de Montréal, lieu de stage des animateurs formés aux écoles de service social et qui sont à l'origine des premiers comités de citoyens (Doucet et Favreau, 1991 : 37). En 1969, plus de cinquante comités de citoyens sont actifs à Montréal et adressent aux pouvoirs publics leurs revendications concernant la justice sociale, la participation à la vie politique et la mise en place de services collectifs publics. Comme le soulignent Bélanger et Lévesque (1992 : 718), le mouvement social que constituent les comités de citoyens s'insère rapidement parmi les forces sociales qui contribuent (volontairement ou non) à construire l'État-providence. L'animation sociale se développa un peu partout au Québec, particulièrement avec la Compagnie des Jeunes Canadiens en 1966 et l'Action sociale jeunesse par la suite, qui existeront jusqu'au début des années 1970.

Au Bureau d'aménagement de l'Est du Québec (BAEQ), mis sur pied en 1963, on recruta des jeunes diplômés en service social chargés de mener une vaste opération d'animation sociale autour de l'aménagement du territoire de l'Est du Québec. Pour Doucet et Favreau (1991 : 37), le BAEQ était le premier projet de développement communautaire au Québec, alors que le Conseil des œuvres a donné naissance aux premières interventions de type action sociale. BAEQ et Conseil des œuvres ont été des lieux d'expérimentation sociale qui ont marqué le début de la professionnalisation de l'organisation communautaire au Québec. Il nous apparaît que la professionnalisation se caractérise au point de départ par le fait que des personnes font de l'organisation communautaire l'activité principale dont ils tirent leurs moyens d'existence. De plus, la professionnalisation renvoie à l'acquisition graduelle par l'organisation communautaire d'un domaine propre d'intervention, d'un corpus de connaissances, de modèles d'intervention et de méthodes de travail cohérents et, enfin, d'une identité et d'une éthique partagées (Favreau et Hurtubise, 1993 : 134).

LA PÉRIODE DE L'INSTITUTIONNALISATION (1972-1980)

Cette période débute avec la réforme de la santé et des services sociaux ainsi que par la création des premiers CLSC en 1972 où l'organisation communautaire en milieu institutionnel, celle qui nous intéresse, se concentrera. Les demandes de participation et de services collectifs soumises par les comités de citoyens issus de l'animation sociale seront insérées dans le compromis que sera l'État-providence, mais sous forme de participation formelle à la gestion étatique et centralisée des services publics (Bélanger et Lévesque, 1992 : 718).

L'organisation communautaire s'inscrit alors dans la dynamique d'implantation des premiers CLSC en favorisant la participation des milieux à l'orientation des services. Elle centre par la suite son action sur la mobilisation autour des conditions de vie dont les questions de logement, d'aménagement du territoire, de garderies, etc. Comme le soulignent Doucet et Favreau (1991 : 51), les CLSC étaient pourvus d'équipe d'organisation communautaire dont les pratiques s'inspiraient de différents courants dont la négociation conflictuelle (Alinsky et le *grassroots democracy*), la lutte des classes (Marx et les groupes de gauche) et la conscientisation (Freire et les progressistes chrétiens). L'action sociale est le modèle principal de pratique qui se heurte souvent aux élites locales qui font pression sur les CLSC afin de contenir l'action des intervenants communautaires.

Avec les négociations provinciales du début des années 1970, les organisateurs communautaires se verront reconnaître la protection de leur titre d'emploi et leur statut de professionnel. Depuis cette époque, les conventions collectives décrivent ainsi les fonctions de l'organisateur communautaire en CLSC :

> Personne qui fait l'identification et l'analyse des besoins de la population avec des groupes concernés. Conçoit, coordonne et actualise des programmes d'organisation communautaire afin de répondre aux besoins du milieu et de promouvoir son développement. Agit comme personne ressource auprès des groupes[2].

Or, l'attribution d'un statut professionnel à cette pratique par les conventions collectives ne lui confère pas automatiquement une dimension professionnelle plutôt qu'une dimension militante ou encore technocratique. Ainsi, même avec son propre domaine d'intervention,

---

2. Les titres d'emploi de travailleur communautaire et de quartier existent aussi mais n'exigent pas de formation universitaire. Leurs fonctions sont la participation à l'identification des besoins du milieu et l'application des programmes d'organisation communautaire.

l'organisation communautaire en CLSC avait encore un certain chemin à parcourir pour développer un corpus de connaissances, de modèles d'intervention et de méthodes de travail cohérents, et pour acquérir une identité et une éthique partagées.

LA PÉRIODE DE LA CRISE IDENTITAIRE (1981-1987)

Doucet et Favreau (1991 : 22-25) signalent que les années 1980 correspondent à une période de bouleversements dont le repli des mouvements sociaux de type revendicatif, la transformation des communautés locales, la crise de l'État-providence et la remise en question de l'organisation communautaire à la faveur de « l'approche communautaire » et d'une étude sur les CLSC, intitulée le Rapport Brunet, particulièrement critique envers l'organisation communautaire. On y propose que l'organisation communautaire abandonne le champ des conditions de vie (emploi, logement, environnement, etc.) pour se concentrer sur le support aux réseaux d'entraide auprès de clientèles à risques prioritaires (Brunet, 1987 : 65). Il nous apparaît toujours qu'il s'agit ici d'une orientation technocratique de l'organisation communautaire (Bourque, 1989).

Comme le démontrent Favreau et Hurtubise (1993 : 81), le Rapport Brunet n'a pas réussi à standardiser l'organisation communautaire, car ces auteurs ont relevé une diversité d'orientations et de pratiques entre deux pôles opposés, soit celui de l'animation neutre des groupes et celui de la politisation. On note, cependant, une certaine diminution (et non leur disparition) des pratiques axées sur les conditions de vie au profit du champ sociosanitaire, comme le maintien à domicile et l'organisation de groupes de services (Favreau et Hurtubise, 1993 : 76).

LA CONSOLIDATION DE LA PROFESSION (1988-1995)

La fondation en 1988 du Regroupement québécois des intervenants et intervenantes en action communautaire en CLSC (RQIIAC) marque le passage d'une position défensive de l'organisation communautaire à une position d'affirmation d'une identité redéfinie. Ainsi, ce qui est apparu comme un repli dans les années 1980 est vu avec le recul, par Doucet et Favreau (1991 : 25), comme une période de transformation, prélude à un renouvellement de la pratique et faite de ruptures mais aussi de continuités. De nouveaux mouvements sociaux sont apparus et de nouveaux enjeux sont à l'ordre du jour dont ceux du développement local et du développement économique communautaire qui touchent non seulement le milieu rural, mais aussi les centres urbains.

Pour Favreau et Hurtubise (1993 : 78-88), la nécessité d'une consi-dération globale des problèmes, du lien entre la santé et les déterminants socio-économiques, ainsi que le développement de la concertation comme nouvelle stratégie d'action, sont à l'origine d'un renouvellement des pratiques d'organisation communautaire. L'organisation communau-taire des années 1990 se caractérise par une pluralité de modèles et de champs d'intervention. Elle se caractérise aussi par la reconnaissance par les intervenants communautaires que leur pratique fait partie inté-grante du réseau institutionnel et public de santé et de services sociaux, comme le notent Favreau et Hurtubise (1993 : 134) :

> Notre enquête a également permis de confirmer la fin d'une conception unique de l'intervenant perçu comme un militant engagé socialement et conscientisateur, redevable qu'à sa communauté. Cependant, cela ne laisse pas un vide, mais fait place peu à peu à un projet professionnel, à une conception de l'organisation communautaire qui est une pratique profes-sionnelle avec son autonomie, c'est-à-dire sa marge de manœuvre, son domaine propre d'intervention, ses méthodes de travail, son « know how », son savoir-faire particulier et ses stratégies ou « modèles » d'intervention. Une éthique est aussi en train de se construire qui en est une à la fois de solida-rité et de responsabilité à l'égard des citoyens d'une communauté desservie par le CLSC et à l'endroit de l'institution d'appartenance, le CLSC.

La réforme de la santé et des services sociaux de 1991 fut un moment fort de cette période. Les CLSC s'en trouvèrent renforcés puisque leur légitimité y était reconnue, ainsi que l'organisation commu-nautaire avec l'adoption en 1991 par la Fédération des CLSC d'un document d'orientation dont nous reparlerons plus loin. Or, depuis 1995, nous entrons probablement dans une nouvelle période aux contours mal définis, mais caractérisée par le mouvement de fusion des CLSC avec d'autres types d'établissement et par une série interminable de compressions budgétaires. Les fusions et les compressions, dont les limites sont loin d'être atteintes encore aujourd'hui, auront des consé-quences sur l'organisation communautaire qui restent à mesurer, mais dont nous pouvons déjà estimer qu'elles nous feront entrer dans une période inédite de la trajectoire de l'organisation communautaire professionnelle.

LES GRANDS COURANTS DE L'ORGANISATION COMMUNAUTAIRE PROFESSIONNELLE

Nous avons eu recours à différents auteurs (Doré, 1985 et 1992 ; Doucet et Favreau, 1991 ; Favreau et Hurtubise, 1993 ; FCLSCQ, 1991) pour cerner les grands courants qui traversent aujourd'hui l'organisation communautaire. Nous suggérons trois courants : péri-institutionnel, professionnel et stratégique.

Le courant péri-institutionnel

Selon Doré (1992), les organisateurs communautaires de CLSC seraient appelés, depuis le début des années 1980, à agir comme gestionnaires de nouveaux services sociaux privés de type communautaire et bénévole dans un rapport de sous-traitance avec l'État. L'auteur inclut dans cette catégorie les 33 % d'organisateurs communautaires qui, dans une enquête de 1988, déclarent appuyer ou offrir *des services qui visent l'amélioration des conditions de vie d'une population ; travaillant parfois en collaboration avec d'autres institutions ou des groupes bénévoles ; si nécessaire, contribuent à la mise sur pied du groupe bénévole* (Doré, 1992 : 142). De ce point de vue, l'organisation de services n'est pas de l'organisation communautaire mais de la gestion des services sociaux ou de l'administration sociale. Pourtant, nombre de groupes bénévoles ou communautaires qui offrent des services ont été mis sur pied grâce au travail d'un intervenant communautaire qui cherchait à aider des personnes à s'organiser pour agir collectivement sur les situations-problèmes auxquelles elles devraient faire face et cela, sur la base de la participation active des intéressées.

De plus, la thèse de l'auteur est que l'organisation communautaire produit en bout de piste inévitablement de l'institution et qu'elle risque de s'y perdre. Elle doit pour se retrouver, se réactiver à la marge des institutions qu'elle a contribué à créer, *là où l'attend son prochain rendez-vous avec le mouvement* (Doré, 1992 : 132). Elle doit renouer avec l'expérience fondatrice et réaffirmer son identité par le *déplacement focal du centre de l'institution vers sa marge, de sa rationalité vers la réalité existentielle des collectivités aux prises avec des problèmes sociaux [...]* (Doré, 1992 : 151). Ainsi, l'organisation communautaire rencontrerait un obstacle majeur du fait d'être pratiquée en milieu institutionnel. Il s'agit d'un courant de l'organisation communautaire que nous qualifions de péri-institutionnel.

Le courant professionnel

Pour Doucet et Favreau (1991 : 6), l'organisation communautaire est une pratique sociale qui est devenue une profession et qui tire son fondement premier de l'affirmation selon laquelle les problèmes sociaux sont de nature collective et doivent faire l'objet de solutions collectives. Pour ces auteurs, l'organisation communautaire se caractérise par les éléments suivants : elle agit surtout au niveau des communautés locales et mise sur le changement social à partir des problèmes causant des tensions dans ces communautés ; elle possède une visée de démocratisation permanente et elle vise l'organisation de nouveaux pouvoirs et services. Ces auteurs reprennent la typologie de l'organisation communautaire de Rothman (1979) selon trois modèles types : l'action sociale, le développement local et le planning social.

L'action sociale vise des changements institutionnels fondamentaux ainsi que la redistribution du pouvoir et des ressources au profit des classes populaires. Ses moyens d'action sont la création de groupes de pressions et de défense des droits, l'éducation populaire et la conscientisation, ainsi que l'action politique.

Le développement local vise à contrer la désintégration des communautés en renforçant leur capacité d'auto-organisation et d'auto-développement. La stratégie se caractérise par la concertation et le partenariat entre les acteurs et la mise sur pied d'organisations agissant au niveau socio-économique.

Le planning social vise la résolution de problèmes communautaires prioritaires. On parle alors de la démarche scientifique fondée sur le recours aux experts en vue de la mise sur pied de services de premières lignes (publics ou communautaires) s'adressant à des populations cibles.

Ces trois modèles types ne sont pas mutuellement exclusifs et se mélangent plutôt dans la pratique sous forme *d'approches multimodales* en fonction de facteurs comme l'échelonnement dans le temps d'une intervention communautaire, le contexte conjoncturel entourant cette intervention et les valeurs et préférences des intervenants impliqués (Doucet, 1997 : 13). Or, comme Doucet et Favreau (1991) le notent, le planning social peut appartenir à l'organisation communautaire ou à l'administration sociale. Il y a sans doute une certaine difficulté conceptuelle à inclure dans les modèles de base de l'organisation communautaire un modèle qui renvoie aussi à l'administration sociale. La mise sur pied de services de premières lignes s'adressant à des populations cibles constitue difficilement en soi une pratique d'organisation communautaire. Pour ce faire, il faut que ces services s'appuient sur la participation des populations concernées et favorisent l'*empowerment* des collectivités.

Favreau et Hurtubise (1993 : 168) évaluent que, depuis 20 ans, l'organisation communautaire en CLSC, tout comme le mouvement communautaire, a connu une évolution caractérisée par la professionnalisation, la diminution du modèle de l'action sociale, la stabilisation du modèle de planning social, ainsi que la remontée du développement local et du partenariat. De ce point de vue, que nous qualifions de professionnel, l'organisation communautaire est déterminée par la conjoncture des orientations normatives des intervenants, de son insertion institutionnelle, de l'évolution des communautés et de celle des politiques sociales.

Le courant stratégique

En 1991, la Fédération des CLSC du Québec (FCLSCQ) publiait un document d'orientation sur l'organisation communautaire qui la définit ainsi :

> Une forme de support organisationnel ou professionnel qui consiste à sensibiliser, à structurer et à organiser un milieu pour que celui-ci apporte une solution collective à un problème perçu lui-même comme collectif. Elle mise sur la capacité des collectivités à se prendre en charge et repose sur le principe que des solutions collectives doivent être apportées aux problèmes dans leurs dimensions sociale et collective. (FCLSCQ, 1991 : 3)

L'organisation communautaire comprend ici six types d'intervention, soit l'identification des problématiques, la sensibilisation et la conscientisation du milieu, le support aux ressources existantes, la création de nouvelles ressources, la mobilisation et la concertation des ressources, et finalement l'action politique.

Doré (1992 : 147) estime que ce document contient des références permettant aux intervenants de défendre leur pratique, mais qu'il entretient une confusion avec l'approche communautaire et l'administration sociale et il en conclut que l'institutionnalisation de l'organisation communautaire se traduit ici par un déplacement de son identité première reliée à l'expérience fondatrice de l'animation sociale *vers les compromis de l'identité institutionnalisée.*

Or, c'est peut-être la caractéristique de ce document et du courant qu'il représente : un compromis stratégique entre la conception technocratique de l'organisation communautaire du Rapport Brunet (toujours vivante chez plusieurs gestionnaires et planificateurs) et celle de l'organisation communautaire péri-institutionnelle. Les six types d'intervention identifiés font de la place à une pratique qui respecte l'identité de l'organisation communautaire comme pratique sociale et comme mode d'intervention professionnelle en service social *qui a pour finalité le travail sur les problèmes sociaux des communautés* (Favreau et Hurtubise, 1993 : 1) [en visant] *l'organisation et la mobilisation des populations ou de parties des populations de ces communautés locales en vue de leur assurer plus de force et de pouvoir local* (Doucet et Favreau, 1991 : 12).

Ce document représente l'expression d'un courant de l'organisation communautaire que l'on peut qualifier de stratégique. Ce courant fait de la place à une pluralité de modes d'intervention en organisation communautaire dont la plupart respectent sa spécificité comme pratique sociale et comme mode d'intervention professionnelle en service social.

LE DEVENIR DE L'ORGANISATION COMMUNAUTAIRE

L'organisation communautaire professionnelle est en constante adaptation aux changements qui surgissent dans ses conditions et déterminants comme en témoignent, entre autres, le développement économique communautaire et les pratiques de concertation. Elle a su s'attaquer aux enjeux de l'appauvrissement, de l'exclusion sociale et de la désintégration socio-économique des communautés locales. Au-delà de ce diagnostic plutôt optimiste, il existe des facteurs qui remettent en question le devenir de l'organisation communautaire. Ces facteurs sont de deux ordres : les conditions organisationnelles et les déterminants sociopolitiques de la pratique.

Parmi les conditions organisationnelles qui auront une influence sur la pratique, il faut noter la transformation du réseau sociosanitaire et les fusions d'établissements qui menacent de fragiliser l'intervention communautaire, et même le service social, dans ces nouveaux méga-établissements très sensibles au modèle médical et aux approches curatives. Les compressions budgétaires représentent également une menace concrète à l'organisation communautaire. Ces risques et menaces prennent différentes formes dont celle carrément de l'abolition des postes en organisation communautaire, mais aussi la forme de pressions institutionnelles en faveur d'une pratique technocratique.

Parmi les déterminants sociopolitiques reliés au devenir de la pratique, mentionnons la transformation du rôle de l'État qui passe par une redéfinition des rapports entre les services publics, le communautaire et le privé, redéfinition qui s'opère au creuset de la régionalisation et de la décentralisation vers le palier local.

Cette régionalisation-décentralisation ouvre de grandes possibilités, au moins théoriques, de démocratisation sociale, mais comporte à court terme une tendance à intégrer le mouvement communautaire et l'intervention communautaire à une logique technocratique de planification de services par programme-clientèle. Elle comporte aussi une tendance à mettre en compétition les acteurs pour les développements budgétaires quand ce n'est pas pour leur propre survie avec l'imposition des compressions. Les intervenants communautaires se retrouvent alors souvent en porte-à-faux entre leur engagement professionnel auprès de groupes communautaires qui revendiquent des enveloppes budgétaires elles-mêmes revendiquées par le CLSC avec lequel l'intervenant est aussi solidaire. En fait, une partie importante du mouvement communautaire est en voie de passer en « mode entrepreneurial », soutenue en cela par les régies régionales.

Il existe également une tendance de fond, au Québec comme un peu partout dans le monde, en faveur des espaces locaux comme lieux de définition et d'action sur les problèmes sociaux. Cette tendance lourde s'appuie sur la décentralisation et représente un terrain fertile pour l'organisation communautaire parce qu'elle fait appel à la mobilisation des communautés locales. Les CLSC seront d'ailleurs interpellés par la création imminente des centres locaux de développement (CLD). Le développement local et le soutien à l'économie sociale amèneront les organisateurs communautaires à travailler à la jonction de secteurs aussi diversifiés que le communautaire, le municipal et les MRC, le scolaire, le sociosanitaire, les syndicats et le monde des affaires. Cela exigera de développer une connaissance de ces acteurs, de leur culture et des rapports dynamiques entre eux.

La concertation et le partenariat occuperont une place importante dans l'organisation communautaire des années à venir. D'ailleurs, ces pratiques font partie des nouvelles pratiques de l'organisation communautaire depuis le début des années 1980 (Favreau et Hurtubise, 1993 : 80). Dans une recherche sur la concertation et le partenariat sur le plan local, Panet-Raymond et Bourque (1991) soutiennent que les organisateurs communautaires de CLSC y jouent un rôle très important même s'il existe des variantes importantes dans les pratiques. Ces auteurs relèvent que dans les situations de partenariat réussi, le rôle de l'organisateur communautaire est celui d'un formateur et d'un expert-conseil visant l'*empowerment* des personnes et des groupes engagés dans la relation partenariale. Toutefois, lorsqu'il s'agit d'un partenariat qualifié de *pater-nariat,* ce rôle en devient presque un de gestionnaire mandaté par l'institution pour orienter la relation partenariale dans une direction prédéterminée en fonction des intérêts du CLSC. Serions-nous en présence d'une orientation technocratique versus une orientation professionnelle telle qu'elle est décrite dans les situations de partenariat réussi ? Ou bien, les pratiques communautaires observées dans les situations de *pater-nariat* relèvent-elles du modèle de planning social, et si oui, peut-il exister une orientation normative plus démocratique et participative de ce modèle ? Ces questions mériteraient sûrement réponse, si tant il est vrai que l'organisation communautaire en CLSC se situe à l'intersection de la relation État-société civile comme l'affirment Favreau et Hurtubise (1993 : 47).

Les changements en cours exigent que les organisateurs communautaires possèdent une forte identité professionnelle pour réussir à maintenir le cap sur le renforcement des communautés dans la tourmente des mutations sociales présentes et à venir.

Bibliographie

BÉLANGER, P.-R. et B. LÉVESQUE (1992). « Le mouvement populaire et communautaire : de la revendication au partenariat (1963-1992) » dans DAIGLE, Gérard et Guy ROCHER, *Le Québec en jeu*, Montréal, PUM, 713-747.

BOUCHER, J. et L. FAVREAU. (1997). « L'action communautaire à l'épreuve du développement local et de l'économie sociale », *Intervention,* Ordre professionnel des travailleurs sociaux du Québec, n° 104, 40-51.

BOURQUE, D. (1989). « La mise au pas tranquille des CLSC », *Nouvelles pratiques sociales*, vol. 1, n° 1, 43-58.

BRUNET, J. *et al.* (1987). *Rapport du Comité de réflexion et d'analyse des services dispensés par les CLSC*, MSSS, Québec.

DORÉ, G. (1985). « L'organisation communautaire : définition et paradigme », *Service social*, vol. 34, n°ˢ 2-3, 210-230.

DORÉ, G. (1992). « L'organisation communautaire et les mutations dans les services sociaux au Québec, 1961-1991. La marge et le mouvement comme lieux d'identité », *Service Social,* vol. 41, n° 2, 131-161.

DOUCET, L. (1997). « Les modèles de Rothman : "blue chips" de l'organisation communautaire », *Intervention,* Ordre professionnel des travailleurs sociaux du Québec, n° 104, 7-15.

DOUCET, L. et L. FAVREAU (1991). *Théories et pratiques en organisation communautaire,* Sainte-Foy, Presses de l'Université du Québec, 462 pages.

FAVREAU, L. (1989). *Mouvement populaire et intervention communautaire de 1960 à nos jours. Continuités et Ruptures,* Montréal, Le Centre de formation populaire / les Éditions du fleuve, 314 pages.

FAVREAU, L. et Y. HURTUBISE (1993). *CLSC et communautés locales. La contribution de l'organisation communautaire,* Sainte-Foy, Presses de l'Université du Québec, 221 pages.

FCLSCQ (1991). *Document de réflexion numéro 3. L'action communautaire*, Montréal, Fédération des CLSC du Québec, 46 pages.

PANET-RAYMOND, J. et D. BOURQUE (1991). *Partenariat ou pater-nariat ? La colla-boration entre établissements publics et organismes œuvrant auprès des personnes âgées à domicile*, Groupe de recherche en développement communautaire, Montréal, École de service social, Université de Montréal, 175 pages.

ROTHMAN, J. (1979). « Three Models of Community Organization Practice, Their Mixing and Phasing », dans COX, F., ERLICH, J. *et al., Strategies of Community Organization,* Itasca, Illinois, Peacok Publishers, 387-397.

L'économie sociale et les pouvoirs publics : banalisation du « social » ou tremplin pour une transformation sociale ?

Louis FAVREAU
Chaire de recherche en développement communautaire
Université du Québec à Hull

Benoît LÉVESQUE
Collectif de recherche sur les innovations sociales
dans les entreprises et les syndicats (CRISES)
Université du Québec à Montréal

Depuis un peu plus d'une année, la notion d'**économie sociale**, y compris dans sa version **économie solidaire**, est devenue objet de débat, voire de controverses, en raison entre autres de la très grande diversité des acteurs qui l'utilisent. Désormais, cette notion n'appartient plus à la seule communauté des chercheurs[1]. L'ensemble des mouvements

---

1. Jusqu'au début des années 1990, la plupart des organisations du mouvement coopératif, syndical et communautaire ignoraient ou refusaient cette appellation (LÉVESQUE ET CÔTÉ, 1991). Seuls ou presque, des chercheurs liés à la revue *Coopératives et Développement*, devenue depuis peu la revue *Économie et Solidarités*, travaillaient à partir de cette notion inspirée de travaux européens du CIRIEC (DEFOURNY et MONZON CAMPOS, 1992). Le collectif CRISES (1989) participait également à cette dynamique de recherche (FAVREAU et LÉVESQUE, 1996).

sociaux et des pouvoirs publics l'ont reprise à leur manière, lui donnant ainsi des significations diverses[2]. Avec le **Chantier d'économie sociale** initié par le gouvernement Bouchard en 1996 et avec les projets gouvernementaux des Centres locaux d'emploi (CLE) pour l'insertion des prestataires de la sécurité du revenu et des sans-emploi (la réforme Harel) et des Centres locaux de développement (CLD) en matière de développement local (la réforme Chevrette), l'économie sociale occupe plus que jamais l'espace public. Il devient donc impératif de fournir quelques points de repère pour mener une réflexion qui permette non seulement de dissoudre la présente confusion, mais également de distinguer plus clairement les enjeux en cause.

LA QUESTION DE LA DÉFINITION

Si l'on s'inspire de travaux qui se sont imposés à l'échelle internationale (Defourny et Monzon Campos, 1992 ; Laville, 1994), l'économie sociale désigne un ensemble relativement bien défini, soit des entreprises et des organisations qui utilisent pour la plupart les statuts juridiques de coopératives, de mutuelles ou encore d'organisations sans but lucratif. Dans un cas comme dans l'autre, ces entreprises et organisations sont caractérisées par **une structure associative** donnant la priorité aux personnes sur le capital (par conséquent, un fonctionnement démocratique) et par une finalité de services aux membres de sorte qu'on y retrouve habituellement une « construction conjointe de l'offre et de la demande » par les usagers et les professionnels (Laville, 1994). Ce faisant, ces entreprises et organisations sont généralement créées par des acteurs relativements dominés (classes populaires, femmes, jeunes, etc.) en alliance avec des groupes promoteurs appartenant à la classe moyenne (par exemple, organisateurs communautaires). Ces expérimentations, qui contribuent à l'*empowerment* des groupes impliqués, supposent une **mobilisation volontaire** combinant l'initiative et la solidarité. De ce point de vue, les entreprises d'économie sociale se distinguent clairement des entreprises capitalistes et des entreprises d'État.

Cependant, lorsqu'il est question d'économie sociale, on peut faire référence aussi bien aux entreprises et organisations prises une à une (**niveau micro**) qu'aux problèmes de la régulation sociale et économique

---

2. Voir à ce propos trois exemples récents : la définition du Chantier Économie sociale du gouvernement du Québec, celle du Comité d'orientation et de concertation sur l'économie sociale (dans la foulée de la Marche des femmes du printemps 1995), celle de la CSN (AUBRY et CHAREST, 1995).

(**niveau macro**). Le débat sur l'économie sociale touche tout autant sinon plus la place et le rôle de celle-ci dans le refaçonnage de l'État-providence et dans la modernisation de l'économie que les expériences prises une à une. En effet, par leurs finalités, leurs structures et règles et par les acteurs impliqués, les entreprises d'économie sociale prises individuellement offrent des possibilités nouvelles pour la création d'emplois (et notamment dans le cas des exclus) et pour l'organisation de services dans les communautés où l'on insiste sur la proximité et la participation des usagers[3].

En revanche, à un niveau plus général, il faut affirmer que l'économie sociale n'est pas pour autant une réponse globale et ne constitue pas en elle-même un contre-projet de société. Cependant, elle peut contribuer à la mise en œuvre d'un autre contrat de société, lequel suppose à la fois le renouvellement de l'État-providence et la modernisation du système de production (Lévesque, 1997). Dans cette visée, on ne peut faire l'économie d'une analyse de la société actuelle qui, en vingt ans, s'est transformée au point où la seule revendication du maintien des acquis sociaux conduit aussi bien à l'isolement qu'à l'impuissance.

ÉCONOMIE SOCIALE ET CRISE DE SOCIÉTÉ

La crise économique dont nous parlons beaucoup depuis quelques années représente plus qu'une récession longue, plus qu'une crise des finances publiques, plus qu'une crise de gestion du service public, plus qu'une crise économique. Il s'agit d'une crise de société qui remet en cause les fondements mêmes sur lesquels reposait son organisation depuis plusieurs décennies.

Quelques tendances clés traduisent l'ampleur et la densité de cette crise. En premier lieu, la fin de la montée en puissance du salariat comme mode principal de régulation économique et sociale, tendance bien analysée par Castel (1995). La fin de la montée du travail à temps plein, régulier, à contrat indéterminé de même que la montée de la sous-traitance et des travailleurs dits indépendants constituent les principales coordonnées de la crise de l'emploi et donc du salariat qui en est son corrollaire obligé.

En second lieu, cette crise du monde du travail s'est répercutée directement sur l'État-providence dont le travail salarié forme l'assise principale des prélèvements fiscaux pour la redistribution et le financement

---

3. Pour la démonstration de cette hypothèse autour de la nouvelle économie sociale, voir notre dernier livre (FAVREAU et LÉVESQUE, 1996) et la revue *Économie et Solidarités*.

des services collectifs. De plus, la rigidité de la définition des services collectifs dispensés par l'État et la rigidité de l'organisation du travail dans ce secteur remettent en question le monopole public dans la production de ces services.

Si la crise de la « société salariale et providentialiste » est tout à la fois une crise du travail et une crise du « vivre ensemble » sur un territoire donné, il faut dès lors examiner de plus près les solutions possibles qui prennent en compte ces deux dimensions, le travail et le territoire : quelles sont les expériences en cours les plus pertinentes ? Où puiser pour généraliser ces expériences ? Ici, nous faisons l'hypothèse que l'économie sociale et le développement économique communautaire (DEC) constituent des leviers pertinents si l'État, au lieu de s'engager dans l'avenue néolibérale, en devient le partenaire dans une perspective de démocratisation (Noël, 1996).

ÉCONOMIE SOCIALE ET ÉTAT

Dans les champs de la santé et des services sociaux, de l'aide sociale, de l'assurance-chômage et de la formation professionnelle, le problème central auquel se butent les pouvoirs publics est celui d'une crise persistante de l'emploi. Le chômage s'est aggravé en se massifiant. Il s'est aussi durci, car les chômeurs le sont de plus en plus longtemps. L'ampleur du chômage, sa durée prolongée, sa diffusion dans tout le corps social introduit progressivement une « déchirure sociale » (Lipietz, 1996). La perte prolongée d'un emploi a désormais un **effet cumulatif** : baisse de revenu mais aussi et surtout isolement social, perte d'estime de soi et immense difficulté à demeurer actif. Sensibles aux problèmes sociaux et plus attentifs que d'autres à la demande sociale, certains secteurs de l'État vont alors reprendre à leur compte la nécessité d'une redéfinition au sein même de l'État de certaines politiques publiques[4].

Certains secteurs de l'État perçoivent les limites d'une logique principalement d'urgence qui risque de s'installer à demeure. Cette logique qui pare au plus pressé mais ne prépare pas l'avenir a provoqué un **empilement de mesures destinées à réparer les dégâts du « progrès »** et dont la cohérence est absente. Au cours de la période 1980-1995, l'État s'est confiné à un rôle de simple accompagnateur qui

---

4. Le Sommet de l'économie et de l'emploi, en dépit de toutes les controverses suscitées, et en partie grâce à ces dernières et aux solutions qui s'en sont dégagées, en fait foi.

pallie, supplée, **gère – ou cherche à faire gérer par des associations – l'exclusion** à partir de mesures d'assistance.

Dans cette visée, il serait dangereux de donner *à l'économie
sociale, à l'insertion et au développement local* toutes les vertus. Au
lieu d'être un laboratoire d'expérimentations inspirant la transformation
de la société et de l'économie dans leur ensemble, l'économie sociale,
comme d'ailleurs l'insertion et le développement local, pourrait être un
obstacle au changement social si elle en venait à cautionner le statu quo.
Il faut plutôt promouvoir la reconnaissance étatique de l'économie
sociale comme occasion d'un renouvellement de l'État-providence. D'un
côté, le service public se renouvellerait et, de l'autre, le secteur communautaire y trouverait une nouvelle place. De ce point de vue, tous les
acteurs seraient touchés d'une façon ou d'une autre. Ce qui suppose
évidemment **un débat dont le contenu ne saurait se limiter à être
« pour ou contre l'économie sociale ».**

LA NAISSANCE
D'UNE NOUVELLE ÉCONOMIE SOCIALE (NÉS)

La mobilisation d'acteurs locaux pour faire émerger de nouvelles entreprises d'économie sociale a été forte dans plusieurs pays durant la
dernière décennie. Au Québec, elle semble s'être réalisée autour de
trois types d'initiatives : 1) d'abord par des **initiatives de formation
à l'emploi** ; 2) ensuite, par des **initiatives sectorielles** d'insertion
sociale par l'activité économique (entreprises d'insertion) ; 3) enfin, par
des initiatives territorialisées de revitalisation économique et sociale
qui travaillent en partenariat avec les divers acteurs sur un territoire
pour y favoriser une intervention multiactivité, ce qui suppose une
gouvernance locale (CDÉC ou CDC, par exemple).

Sur une période de quelques décennies, les nombreuses initiatives
de la NÉS ont fini par constituer un réseau socio-économique combinant
des dimensions marchandes et non marchandes au sein d'activités pro-
ductives traversées par une perspective d'économie solidaire dont la
démocratisation et l'*empowerment* des collectivités constituent les visées.
En effet, ces initiatives ont pour objectif non seulement la création
d'emplois mais également et simultanément le renforcement de l'appartenance sociale à une communauté et une régulation socio-économique
qui remet en cause la compétitivité sans limite et la seule logique d'adaptation au marché (IFDEC, 1996).

En d'autres termes, tout en assumant une partie des contraintes liées à l'économie de marché, ces activités économiques (d'animation de projets, de formation au travail, de production ou de revitalisation de quartiers en difficulté) cherchent à se distinguer qualitativement : 1) en regroupant des personnes exclues du marché du travail ; 2) en poursuivant des objectifs sociaux et économiques tout à la fois ; 3) en misant principalement sur un mode de gestion associatif ; 4) en utilisant le capital disponible dans une perspective d'entrepreneuriat collectif et social (Comeau, 1997). L'histoire des mouvements sociaux et de l'économie sociale vient fournir la confirmation de la pertinence de cette problématique d'intervention, y compris dans le social.

ÉCONOMIE SOCIALE ET HISTOIRE DES MOUVEMENTS SOCIAUX

La première leçon que l'on peut tirer d'un siècle et demi d'histoire de l'économie sociale est sans doute la suivante : l'économie sociale, notamment la coopération, s'est développée parmi des classes laborieuses exploitées luttant pour améliorer des conditions de vie très précaires. En d'autres termes, la coopération a d'abord été «fille de la nécessité», réponse à des besoins sociaux non pris en charge selon les modalités dominantes de l'économie et d'intervention de l'État. L'économie sociale sert non seulement de dispositif «alternatif» aux défaillances du marché (*market failure*) ou des pouvoirs publics (*State failure*) mais contribue également au renouvellement de l'un et de l'autre, y compris de leurs rapports réciproques.

Mais la nécessité ou l'intérêt ne suffit pas à expliquer la mobilisation issue de nombreuses initiatives de l'économie sociale. Cette mobilisation s'explique aussi par le besoin d'appartenir à un collectif de travail et / ou à une communauté (un quartier, un territoire à pertinence sociale), bref par le **besoin d'identité** et par le **besoin d'un projet** qui donne sens au vivre ensemble.

Le dynamisme de l'économie sociale au XIXᵉ siècle et au début du XXᵉ siècle a été l'expression d'une culture de classe très forte, d'une identité collective, d'une classe certes exploitée mais largement solidaire, au travail et dans les quartiers ouvriers. Le mouvement ouvrier s'est en effet donné un ensemble d'institutions propres : des syndicats, des partis ouvriers mais aussi des mutuelles, des coopératives et des associations (Dubet et Lapeyronnie, 1992). C'est une communauté de destin qui a été en partie génératrice d'institutions nouvelles dont plusieurs appartenaient à l'économie sociale. Enfin, l'économie sociale s'est toujours inscrite dans un projet social qui dépassait la somme des initiatives prises. On retrouve ici les diverses dimensions du **mouvement** social entendu dans le sens tourainien[5]. Dans le meilleur des cas, l'économie sociale ne se réduit pas au développement de réponses là où l'État et le marché ont laissé des espaces vides, elle est une **fonction d'anticipation** de la demande sociale qui concerne l'ensemble des institutions.

ÉCONOMIE SOCIALE :
SA DIMENSION INTERNATIONALE

L'internationalisation des marchés prend aujourd'hui une ampleur et une signification nouvelles : elle s'accompagne de la constitution de blocs économiques de grandes régions (Europe, Amériques, Asie du Sud-Est) ; elle est également stimulée par la globalisation financière qu'a permise la levée généralisée des contrôles de mouvements de capitaux (Aglietta, 1995) ; elle est soutenue par la déréglementation et la libéralisation des échanges qui sont à leur tour multipliés par les possibilités qu'offrent les nouvelles technologies des communications. Les résultats de cette mondialisation sont ambigus.

D'une part, les entreprises se focalisent beaucoup plus sur les débouchés extérieurs que sur leur marché intérieur : leur extraversion croissante les incite à une réorganisation qui mise sur la sous-traitance, sur le travail à temps partiel, sur l'intensification des changements technologiques. D'autre part, les États nations perdent une partie de leur souveraineté au profit d'une adaptation à la contrainte dite « externe ». C'est de cet ensemble de tendances liées à l'internationalisation des marchés que résultent la montée actuelle de la précarité pour une partie de plus en plus importante de la population active et le recul du champ de la démocratie. D'un côté, la crise a produit au Nord un accroissement des écarts entre le travail qualifié et le travail non qualifié, de l'autre, elle a provoqué au Sud une nouvelle polarisation où la situation des perdants se détériore. Pour ces derniers, l'économie informelle, soit la version grise, voire noire, de l'économie sociale, est devenue le seul pare-choc pour absorber la secousse sociale[6].

---

5. Même si avec le temps ces dimensions d'identité et de projet ont pu s'affaiblir dans les principales institutions de l'économie sociale que sont, par exemple, les coopératives financières.

6. L'économie informelle occupe plus ou moins 50 % de la population dans les villes du tiers monde (LAUTIER, 1994).

Mais la mondialisation telle que proposée par le néolibéralisme est-elle la seule possible ? Si la Banque mondiale et le FMI encouragent systématiquement la régulation quasi exclusive par le marché, il existe toutefois des contre-tendances, telles celles-ci : 1) la montée d'une société civile mondiale et la multiplication des ONG ; 2) les courants politiques nouveaux (valorisant le partage du travail, le développement d'une économie solidaire, de nouvelles formes de coopération internationale, etc.) ; 3) les demandes de démocratisation de la part des divers mouvements sociaux (participation des travailleurs à la gestion des entreprises, participation des usagers dans les services collectifs, exigence de contrôle des populations locales sur leur territoire, mobilisation pour la protection de l'environnement, etc.). Dans cette foulée, des travaux de plus en plus nombreux mettent en lumière la **face cachée de la mondialisation** que constituent la revalorisation du local, les solidarités territoriales et les entreprises d'économie sociale. Bien que toujours menacées de repli identitaire, ces contre-tendances sont également porteuses d'une nouvelle universalité[7].

Bien que timidement pour le moment, un nouveau contrat social mondial émerge (Groupe de Lisbonne, 1995). Dans cette visée, il faut tenir compte de l'existence de près de 500 000 organisations non gouvernementales (ONG) dans le monde dont plus de 50 000 sont déjà reliées entre elles par Internet (le réseau APC)[8], ce qui leur permet d'avoir à leur disposition des banques de données, les « infos » d'une agence de presse alternative et des forums thématiques de discussion. Face à l'offensive néolibérale, il existe donc une perspective de travail et de nouveaux dispositifs dont **le défi est de multiplier les échelles d'intervention** (locale, régionale et fédérative, nationale et internationale) **et d'en tenir compte** pour passer du micro, des organisations prises une à une et du local, au macro qui permet d'agir sur les pouvoirs à l'échelle nationale et internationale. Plus largement, la réussite de l'économie sociale dépend, en amont, de la force propulsive que lui fournissent les mouvements sociaux (associatif, de femmes, syndical) et, en aval, de la perspective que lui procure un projet de société (Lévesque, 1997).

---

7. « Pas de marin sans port d'attache » (ROUSTANG, LAVILLE et al. 1996). Ces auteurs plaident avec raison pour la reconnaissance du caractère pluriel de l'économie. Ils plaident également pour une économie non seulement plus ouverte sur le monde mais pour une économie des territoires. Voir aussi DEMAZIÈRE (1997) et FAVREAU (1997).

8. Pour en savoir plus long, voir leur site Internet à l'adresse suivante : http://www.apc.org

POUR CONCLURE

Tout bon stratège affirmera qu'il faut «profiter de l'état d'incertitude institutionnelle créée par l'arrivée de nouveaux dispositifs» de développement local, d'insertion et de soutien à des projets d'économie sociale «pour faire passer des ambitions réformatrices [...]» (Ion, 1990 : 136). Il faut ajouter qu'une bonne stratégie concernant l'économie sociale se doit de bien distinguer le niveau micro du niveau macro.

Au Québec, l'articulation entre les initiatives de la NÉS et les pouvoirs publics est aujourd'hui au centre du débat social. Si ces initiatives sont considérablement soutenues par les pouvoirs publics, elles feront émerger de **nouvelles instances d'accompagnement** du développement pour **l'ensemble** des quartiers et des régions en difficulté. Nous pensons ici, entre autres, au modèle de développement local des CDEC (Favreau et Lévesque, 1996). La question de l'articulation de ces instances communautaires de gouvernance locale avec les CLE et les CLD, instances étatiques, devrait faire partie du débat puisque les enjeux sont majeurs.

Les pouvoirs publics doivent se débarrasser de leur attitude de détenteur du monopole du service d'intérêt collectif pour favoriser une institutionnalisation de la NÉS sans pour autant l'assimiler, ce qui ne pourrait que la banaliser, la rendant ainsi non seulement inoffensive mais également inefficace. Nous faisons l'hypothèse que **ces expériences, en devenant plus fortement organisées** de manière autonome et sans exclure le partenariat, pourraient engendrer des solutions inédites aux crises de l'emploi et de l'État-providence. La NÉS ne constituerait alors pas un secteur séparé mais occuperait **un espace intermédiaire** à l'intersection de la relation entre l'État et la société civile, de l'économique et du social, du local et du national, sans exclure une ouverture sur le monde. Ce faisant, les entreprises de la NÉS représenteraient une sorte de tremplin pour la transformation de l'économie et du social à l'échelle de la société et dans le sens d'un élargissement de la démocratie. Il serait alors possible de parler de l'économie sociale comme d'une économie solidaire.

Bibliographie

AGLIETTA, M. (1995). *Macro-économie financière*, Paris, La Découverte, « Repères ».

AUBRY F. et J. CHAREST *(1995)*. *Développer l'économie solidaire*, Montréal, Service de recherche, CSN.

CASTEL, R. (1995). *Les métamorphoses de la question sociale*, Paris, Fayard.

COMEAU, Y. (dir.) [1997]. «L'insertion sociale par l'économique», *Économie et Solidarités*, vol. 28, n° 2, 11-22 et 33-94.

DEFOURNY, J. et J.L. MONZON CAMPOS (1992). *L'économie sociale entre l'économie capitaliste et l'économie publique*, Bruxelles, CIRIEC/De Boeck Université.

DEMAZIÈRE, C. (dir.) [1997]. *Du local au global : les initiatives locales pour le développement économique en Europe et en Amérique*, Paris, L'Harmattan.

DUBET, F. et D. LAPEYRONNIE (1992). *Les quartiers d'exil*, Paris, Seuil.

FAVREAU, L. (1997). *L'économie sociale mise en perspective : renouvellement au Nord, émergence au Sud*, Cahier de la Chaire de recherche en développement communautaire, Hull, UQAH.

FAVREAU, L. et B. LÉVESQUE (1996). *Développement économique communautaire, économie sociale et intervention*, Sainte-Foy, Presses de l'Université du Québec.

GROUPE DE LISBONNE (1995). *Limites à la compétitivité*, Montréal, Boréal.

IFDEC (1996). *Les pratiques de DÉC au Québec : conjoncture et convergences*. Actes de colloque, Université de Montréal, juin.

ION, J. (1990). *Le travail social à l'épreuve du territoire*, Toulouse, Privat.

LAUTIER, B. (1994). *L'économie informelle dans le tiers monde*, Paris, La Découverte, «Repères».

LAVILLE, J.-L. (dir.) [1994]. *L'économie solidaire, une perspective internationale*, Paris, Desclée de Brouwer.

LÉVESQUE, B. et D. CÔTÉ (1990-1991). «L'état du mouvement coopératif au Québec : rétrospectives et perspectives», *Coopératives et Développement*, vol. 22, n° 2, 123-158.

LÉVESQUE, B. (1997). *Démocratie et économie sociale : un scénario pour contrer le chômage et l'exclusion*, Montréal, Cahier du CRISES, UQAM.

LIPIETZ, A. (1996). *La société en sablier (le partage du travail contre la déchirure sociale)*, Paris, La Découverte.

NOËL, A. (1996). «Vers un nouvel État-providence ? Enjeux démocratiques», *Politique et Sociétés*, n° 30, 3-27.

ROUSTANG, G., LAVILLE, J.-L., EME, B., MOTHÉ, D. et B. PERRET (1996). *Vers un nouveau contrat social*, Paris, Desclée de Brouwer.

La recherche collaborative : essai de définition[1]

Richard LEFRANÇOIS
Institut universitaire de gériatrie de Sherbrooke

Cet article présente une argumentation à l'appui de la recherche collaborative et une analyse des conditions de réalisation de ce modèle de partenariat en gérontologie. La praticabilité (pertinence, excellence, intégration des savoirs et réflexivité) et les composantes structurelles (organisationnelles, instrumentales, valorielles) sont examinées sur la base d'une recension des écrits et d'une expérience concrète de recherche collaborative (projet GRAPPA). La recherche collaborative est définie comme une stratégie planifiée d'investigation scientifique et d'intervention et une stratégie d'intégration des connaissances visant à accroître le niveau de compétence des participants en vue d'apporter des solutions novatrices, efficaces et efficientes aux problèmes émanant de la pratique professionnelle.

Cette présentation se propose de dégager quelques principes clés de la recherche collaborative à partir d'une analyse des conditions de réalisation de ce modèle de partenariat en gérontologie. L'essentiel de la réflexion repose sur l'expérience accumulée dans le cadre d'un projet

---

1. Sujet de la conférence de clôture prononcée par l'auteur lors d'un colloque régional en gérontologie tenu à Hull en juin 1994.

de recherche de partenariat, soit le Groupe de recherche sur l'actualisation du potentiel des personnes âgées (GRAPPA). Ce projet regroupe des personnes-ressources de l'Institut universitaire de gériatrie de Sherbrooke, dont l'auteur, et des praticiennes œuvrant dans divers établissements régionaux de santé et de services sociaux. Une recension des écrits sur cette thématique a ensuite permis de mieux structurer cette réflexion. Dans un premier volet, nous présentons les éléments de définition de la recherche collaborative pour ensuite aborder les principaux arguments à l'appui de ce modèle de partenariat. Dans un second volet, nous exposons ses conditions de réalisation pour enfin déboucher, en conclusion, sur un essai de définition.

LA RECHERCHE COLLABORATIVE : ÉLÉMENTS DE DÉFINITION

Deux interrogations principales ont guidé notre réflexion. Premièrement, à quelles conditions la recherche collaborative peut-elle s'avérer une stratégie de recherche à la fois rigoureuse, productive et utile ? Et deuxièmement, dans quelle mesure la recherche collaborative peut-elle contribuer à l'intégration des connaissances ?

Dans la documentation, la recherche collaborative n'est pas présentée comme une méthode de recherche, ni comme une nouvelle approche scientifique. Ce terme est plutôt utilisé pour désigner les différentes formes de partenariat impliquant la coopération entre des acteurs sociaux, intervenants et chercheurs principalement. Le souci de l'interdisciplinarité et du travail en équipe expliquerait, en grande partie, l'intérêt pour la recherche collaborative (Dussault, 1990).

Essentiellement, la recherche collaborative est une *démarche d'investigation scientifique multifinalisée* impliquant une coopération étroite entre des personnes œuvrant dans le domaine de la recherche et de l'intervention, et, éventuellement, entre des gestionnaires et des bénéficiaires. Ce mode de partenariat vise à atteindre les objectifs qui suivent :

- **dans le champ de la pragmatique** : *développer une expertise sur des problématiques* concrètes qui intéressent les intervenantes et les intervenants (prévention, adaptation psychosociale, autonomie fonctionnelle) et les populations cibles (bien-être physique et psychologique, autonomie, santé, sécurité). Elle s'appuiera sur des descriptions globales (situationnelles et contextuelles) et sur des lectures interdisciplinaires des situations telles que vécues et appréhendées par les participantes et les participants.

- **dans le champ de l'heuristique** : *développer un savoir gérontologique global* (holistique) intégrant dans un même corpus les connaissances théoriques (découvertes) et pratiques (innovations) construites autour des problématiques retenues.

- **dans le champ de l'innovation** : *expérimenter et évaluer de nouveaux modes d'intervention* dans le but d'améliorer la compréhension des problématiques et d'accroître l'efficacité et l'efficience des programmes d'aide ou de soutien aux personnes âgées.

- **dans le champ de l'expérienciel** : *enrichir le champ de compétence des participantes et des participants* grâce à la réflexivité[2] et à une mise en commun structurée des expériences de recherche et d'intervention de chacun.

LES ARGUMENTS EN FAVEUR DE LA RECHERCHE COLLABORATIVE

La plupart des disciplines scientifiques (ou des champs interdisciplinaires) comportant un volet « clinique » (comme la psychologie, la gérontologie, la criminologie) se sont profondément transformées au cours des 20 dernières années, notamment dans leurs rapports avec l'État, la communauté et les professionnels de l'intervention psychosociale (Lefrançois et Soulet, 1983). Nous nous référons ici aux axes prioritaires de la recherche subventionnée, aux commandites, aux expériences de solidarités avec le milieu, aux efforts pour enrayer les problèmes sociaux. Ainsi, ces mêmes disciplines scientifiques sont de plus en plus sollicitées pour éclairer des problématiques ou des enjeux sociaux complexes, servir d'appui (et parfois de caution) aux actions et décisions touchant les bénéficiaires des réseaux de distribution de services et, enfin, évaluer les programmes s'adressant aux clientèles visées.

À ces mutations et extensions de rôles disciplinaires s'ajoutent les contraintes qui frappent les milieux de la pratique professionnelle. Elles ont esssentiellement pour sources des réaménagements institutionnels et des compressions dans les dépenses publiques qui continuent de frapper tout le réseau de la santé et de services sociaux. Les restrictions

---

2. La notion de réflexivité est surtout employée en ethnométhodologie pour montrer comment les activités de la vie quotidienne interviennent dans la description, l'interprétation et la constitution d'un cadre social.

sont manifestement amplifiées par le vieillissement accéléré de la
population, phénomène qui se traduit par un accroissement sensible de
la demande de prestation de services, par des requêtes pour que soit mieux
précisé le partage des responsabilités entre les intervenantes et les intervenants et par des pressions visant à corriger le tir des politiques sociales.

Parallèlement, la prévention des problèmes sociaux et de santé, le
maintien de l'autonomie fonctionnelle, la promotion ou l'amélioration
de la qualité de vie, l'adaptation psychosociale et le soutien aux aidantes
et aux aidants naturels sont devenus les nouveaux credos de l'intervention. Ces finalités, imposées en partie par le recadrement des politiques
sociales, s'étendent jusqu'aux modèles de pratique jusque-là dominants,
c'est-à-dire ceux axés sur le curatif ou la réadaptation. Avec l'introduction
de nouvelles philosophies en matière d'assistance aux personnes âgées
(tels que les plans de soins individualisés, les nouvelles thérapies, les
approches intégrées), nous assistons en fait à des efforts d'ajustements
de la part des spécialistes de l'aide sociale. Ces déploiements visent
précisément une meilleure coordination des interventions à la faveur
d'une mise en commun de l'expérience acquise.

En gérontologie, la coordination des ressources est devenue une
nécessité d'autant plus grande que le fardeau des prestations s'alourdit
année après année, d'où le besoin d'offrir des services professionnels
spécialisés, diversifiés et complémentaires. En effet, le phénomène de
l'hypervieillissement tend à infléchir la trajectoire des soins gériatriques
qui doivent désormais s'orienter vers des modes d'assistance à plus long
terme (Clark, 1994 ; Chafetz, West et Ebbs, 1987).

Enfin, considérant les coûts afférents à la prise en charge des
personnes âgées (hébergement collectif, soins à domicile), une plus
grande coordination est requise entre les milieux de vie ou d'assistance
(centres hospitaliers de soins de longue durée, maisons d'accueil, centre
de jour, famille des bénéficiaires). Le travail en équipe pluridisciplinaire
et son complément, la recherche collaborative, sont devenus en quelque
sorte de nouvelles stratégies d'unification des énergies et des expertises.

Les conditions sont donc réunies pour que l'exercice des rôles
traditionnels, l'application d'une réglementation bureaucratique rigide
ou les querelles territoriales (Dussault, 1990) soient remis en question :
le travail professionnel cloisonné doit faire place à la collégialité, aux
équipes multi- et interdisciplinaires. L'idée de la *concertation ou du
partenariat* est ainsi devenue, dans plusieurs milieux, une formule à privi-
légier pour 1) faire face à des réalités sociales de plus en plus complexes
(surcharge de travail, épuisement professionnel, considérations éthiques),
2) remédier à la pénurie des ressources, 3) analyser les implications et

les conséquences de l'alourdissement des clientèles (pluripathologie) et enfin, 4) répondre à des demandes de visibilité et d'efficacité émanant de la population (Gitlin, Lyons et Kolodner, 1994 ; DePoy et Gallagher, 1990 ; Pranger et Brown, 1990 ; Bennett et Miller, 1987).

Malgré ces transformations sociales, disciplinaires et professionnelles, le milieu de la recherche n'a pas toujours prêté une oreille attentive aux nouveaux défis que pose l'intervention, notamment dans le contexte des réformes sociales et bureaucratiques et des changements de parcours dans l'offre de services destinés aux personnes âgées. En outre, les retombées pratiques des études scientifiques sont soit insuffisamment développées, soit mal évaluées, soit mal exploitées. Parallèlement, le personnel œuvrant auprès des personnes âgées est ou bien peu préparé à participer à des travaux de recherche, ou ignore l'existence d'importantes études et des possibilités qu'elles offrent, ou encore n'est pas encouragé à évaluer ses propres interventions. L'écart qui les sépare des milieux de la recherche paraît donc, à première vue, considérable.

Par ailleurs, il faut reconnaître que les méthodologies de recherche traditionnelles paraissent parfois inaptes à favoriser un rapprochement entre les différents partenaires de l'aide sociale. Elles ont un effet de repoussoir. Le cadre positiviste, fort de ses principes sacrés (la distanciation observateur-sujet, l'objectivité et la neutralité) et de ses protocoles rigides (le schéma expérimental), est la plupart du temps privilégié au détriment d'approches plus souples (la recherche qualitative, la triangulation des méthodes), souvent plus aptes à tenir compte des particularités de chaque milieu d'intervention.

En dépit de ces difficultés, on assiste présentement à des tentatives pour combler ce fossé. La littérature scientifique ou professionnelle fait de plus en plus état de la nécessité de concevoir et d'expérimenter des modèles de recherches alternatifs capables de mieux conjuguer les expertises et de relever les défis relevés plus haut (Hoshmand, 1989). Cette préoccupation, voire ce retournement de l'activité scientifique, s'observe depuis plusieurs années à travers des entreprises de recherche-action, de recherche participative, de science fondamentale orientée, de technoscience (Fourez, 1988). Concrètement, des critères tels que la *pertinence*, la *transférabilité des connaissances* ou *l'applicabilité des produits scientifiques, l'utilité sociale* et *l'efficacité* sont devenus les canons de légitimité, presque incontournables, de ces nouvelles pratiques scientifiques. À cet égard, la *recherche collaborative* représente une voie de solution ingénieuse et féconde pouvant informer des questions de recherche plus pertinentes et significatives (Hoshmand, 1989).

LES CONDITIONS DE RÉALISATION
DE LA RECHERCHE COLLABORATIVE

Examinons maintenant les conditions qui, sur la base de l'expérience GRAPPA et d'après une recension des écrits, représentent des facteurs clés de réussite de l'approche collaborative. Il s'agit en fait d'insister sur les *critères de praticabilité* de la recherche collaborative (la pertinence, l'excellence, l'intégration et la réflexivité) et de tenir compte des principaux *aspects structurels* (l'organisationnel, l'instrumental et le valoriel) en vue d'implanter avec succès un programme de recherche collaborative.

Les critères de praticabilité

La pertinence

Pour qu'un programme de recherche collaborative voie le jour, donc reçoive un soutien financier, il importe qu'il prenne racine dans un ou des milieux bien identifiés et qu'il s'inscrive dans le cadre d'une politique d'intervention ciblée (p. ex., le maintien à domicile, le soutien aux aidantes et aux aidants naturels) ou, encore, dans un secteur jugé névralgique (p. ex., la démence, l'ostéoporose, la surmédicamentation). Le caractère spécifique (par opposition à *diffus*), prioritaire, novateur, opportun et pragmatique d'un projet offre plus de garanties de mobiliser des ressources (humaine, financière, technique).

Par exemple, GRAPPA s'est donné, dès le départ, une vocation régionale sur le thème rassembleur de l'actualisation du potentiel des personnes âgées (conception positive du vieillissement). Il réunit présentement cinq universitaires de diverses disciplines (santé, psychologie, sociologie, andragogie) et cinq intervenantes professionnelles dont la formation est variée (service social, ergothérapie, sciences infirmières) œuvrant dans différents milieux de pratique dans la région de Sherbrooke (CHSLD, CLSC). Les partenaires sociaux engagés dans ce programme sont les plaques tournantes de l'enseignement, de la recherche et de l'intervention en gérontologie dans la région : 1) sept CLSC de l'Estrie à travers la table de concertation regroupant les coordonnateurs des services de maintien à domicile ; 2) l'Hôpital d'Youville (maintenant l'Institut universitaire de gériatrie de Sherbrooke) et son centre de recherche en gérontologie et gériatrie où loge GRAPPA ; 3) le centre d'hébergement Foyer Saint-Joseph ; 4) l'Université de Sherbrooke (Faculté des lettres et sciences humaines et Faculté de médecine) ; et 5) l'Université du Québec à Trois-Rivières (la collaboration revêt ici un caractère interuniversitaire puisqu'une chercheuse du Laboratoire de gérontologie est membre de l'équipe GRAPPA). Le programme de recherche correspond au principe directeur qu'a adopté le comité d'experts mandaté par la Régie régionale de la santé et des services sociaux pour développer un programme régional d'organisation des services (PROS) pour la région de l'Estrie.

Le critère de la *pertinence* mentionné plus haut touche non seulement à l'objet d'investigation en tant que tel, mais également à l'utilité sociale des connaissances produites. Il s'agit en l'occurrence de la *transférabilité des connaissances dans l'action*. Sur ce point, un projet de recherche collaborative sera jugé pertinent, d'une part, *s'il est porteur d'espoir tout en demeurant réaliste* et, d'autre part, *s'il est susceptible d'introduire des changements significatifs*, à court ou à moyen terme, dans le milieu de l'intervention ou dans celui de la gestion des problèmes liés au vieillissement. Une telle conception n'exclut évidemment pas l'idée de revoir les pratiques existantes : cette définition est délibérément élastique, allouant l'espace nécessaire à des analyses critiques sur les pratiques et, corollairement, à des projets de démonstration capables de réorienter les interventions.

Remarquons que la notion de pertinence est associée, à tort, uniquement à l'objet de l'intervention ; il faudrait aussi l'étendre à l'objet scientifique comme tel. Ainsi, le choix de l'objet de recherche tiendra avantageusement compte de sa portée heuristique, c'est-à-dire de sa capacité à faire évoluer les connaissances théoriques tout en offrant des possibilités concrètes pour l'action.

En résumé, les promoteurs d'un projet de collaboration auront intérêt à démontrer que leur orientation et leur investissement (comme, par exemple, le dégrèvement du personnel) se justifient aussi bien sur le plan des préoccupations des milieux d'intervention que sur celui de la communauté scientifique. Bref, ils veilleront à mettre en évidence les retombées scientifiques et pratiques de leurs activités. Dans le cas de GRAPPA, la stratégie de concertation a surtout consisté à associer la démarche de recherche à un plan d'action régional visant à promouvoir l'actualisation du potentiel des personnes âgées, spécialement les groupes à risque, en misant sur les conditions de leur pleine insertion et reconnaissance.

L'excellence

Les organismes subventionnaires associent d'emblée l'excellence à la qualité et à la rigueur scientifiques ou méthodologiques d'un devis de recherche. Or, s'agissant de la recherche collaborative, le critère de l'excellence devrait en principe s'appliquer à toutes les instances qui participent au processus d'élaboration, d'implantation et d'évaluation des activités. L'excellence vise donc tout autant les spécialistes de l'intervention, les bénéficiaires que les gestionnaires du projet qui, collectivement, devront rendre compte des vertus de leur action et de leur capacité à transposer de façon satisfaisante les résultats de la recherche et de la réflexion dans leur milieu de pratique. L'expérience collaborative constituant en quelque sorte un mode collectif d'apprentissage, Clark (1994) a énuméré les conditions à réunir pour améliorer la performance de l'équipe de partenariat :

- une interdépendance constructive entre les membres ;

- une communication soutenue impliquant des interactions ou des échanges en face à face ;

- un sens des responsabilités individuelles ;

- des aptitudes à la coopération ;

- des mécanismes clairs de fonctionnement du groupe (*group processing*).

Quant au volet scientifique, deux conditions essentielles ressortent. D'une part, il importe d'inculquer des réflexes et une conduite méthodologiques afin que la recherche produise des résultats de haut calibre scientifique, obtenus donc suivant les règles de l'art : 1) recension systématique des écrits ; 2) développement d'un système conceptuel clair s'articulant autour d'un modèle ou d'un cadre théorique ; 3) élaboration des hypothèses et leur mise à l'épreuve à partir d'un matériau empirique sûr ; 4) rigueur du plan d'observation et de mesure ; 5) validation des instruments. Ainsi, GRAPPA a créé un foyer de convergence des énergies autour du développement de deux instruments de mesure complémentaires ; le premier, intéressant surtout la recherche (instrument de mesure de l'actualisation du potentiel global) et le second, l'intervention (instrument de mesure de l'actualisation du potentiel spécifique).

D'autre part, afin d'assurer le maximum de crédibilité à la démarche scientifique, l'équipe interdisciplinaire recrutera des individus aguerris en recherche (compétence), experts dans leur secteur respectif (qualification), notamment pour la qualité de leurs travaux scientifiques (réputation). Le choix de la coordonnatrice ou du coordonnateur est capital à cet égard (crédibilité, leadership, dynamisme, disponibilité et accessibilité)[3].

---

3. Le coordonnateur de GRAPPA est Gilbert Leclerc, Ph.D., andragogue et responsable du programme de la maîtrise en gérontologie de l'Université de Sherbrooke.

L'intégration

Par intégration, il faut ici entendre l'aboutissement du processus de synthèse et de mise en réciprocité des composantes multiples d'un projet de collaboration (institutionnelle, scientifique, professionnelle et expériencielle). L'intégration permet d'obtenir un résultat cohérent, harmonieux et de niveau plus élaboré. Il ne s'agit pas d'une composante abstraite de la recherche collaborative, mais bien d'une nécessité liée aux exigences du travail à accomplir. Il y a lieu de distinguer entre l'intégration verticale et horizontale.

L'intégration verticale s'adresse à l'objet même de l'activité de partenariat : elle n'a donc pas une connotation hiérarchique. Elle se reflétera, par exemple, dans l'enrichissement des contenus théoriques et dans l'affinement des modèles et des stratégies d'intervention. Concrètement, les partenaires auront pour tâche d'alimenter une réflexion et de produire des connaissances qui aideront à dégager une compréhension élargie du problème à l'étude. Il s'agit donc d'un transfert des connaissances à l'interne, d'une synergie impliquant un nouveau savoir élaboré à partir des expertises de chacun (passage d'une compréhension de spécialiste à une compréhension de généraliste).

Dans le cadre du projet GRAPPA, l'intégration vise d'une part à augmenter notre connaissance de la trajectoire développementale du vieillissement (entropie, néguentropie), sa composante dynamique (cycles, états transitoires, défis majeurs) et de potentialisation (stratégies d'adaptation, actualisation du potentiel résiduel, mobilisation des ressources environnementales) en vue de mieux comprendre comment sélectionner et enchaîner les meilleures actions pouvant contribuer à actualiser le potentiel des personnes âgées.

L'intégration horizontale, de son côté, renvoie aux processus facilitants et à l'appropriation par le groupe des contenus de réflexion et d'intervention en vue d'augmenter l'efficacité et l'efficience de l'équipe. Il s'agit donc essentiellement d'évoluer vers une forme de collaboration plus structurée, solidaire, continue et productive (Toner, Miller et Gurland, 1994). Concrètement, il conviendra de sélectionner un *modus operandi* pouvant satisfaire tous les membres de l'équipe (rythmes et séquences des ateliers de travail, mécanismes de liaison et d'échange avec le milieu, soutien technique). La rotation des rôles pour certaines tâches (telles que l'animation des séances de rencontre, la production des compte rendus) peut aussi favoriser l'intégration horizontale en donnant l'occasion à chaque partenaire de se familiariser avec plusieurs rôles (Lipson, 1984). Enfin, l'intégration horizontale touche aux mécanismes facilitant l'incorporation de nouveaux membres dans l'équipe (développement d'un guide de gestion).

La réflexivité

La réflexivité est du ressort des attitudes et de l'expérience. Ainsi, la personne réflexive accordera plus d'importance aux règles établies démocratiquement par le groupe qu'à celles régissant sa conduite professionnelle (Clark, 1994). Dans la même veine, elle ne placera pas ses intérêts personnels au-dessus de ceux de l'équipe. Enfin, elle demeurera ouverte à son expérience et à celle des autres membres du groupe.

Hoshmand (1989) distingue deux modalités de la réflexivité : celle du « bracketing » qui consiste à aborder ouvertement la réalité (sans discrimination), par une prise de conscience de ses préjugés ou de ses biais et celle de « l'horizontalisation » qui part de l'idée qu'il existe plusieurs solutions au problème étudié, et que les données et les perspectives d'analyse doivent au départ se voir attribuer une valeur équivalente.

Par ailleurs, le projet de partenariat s'attachera à créer les conditions pour que l'expérience serve de révélateur des forces et des faiblesses de chacun, pour ensuite rejaillir dans l'univers de compétence des membres. Par exemple, une situation de conflit entre les membres, même si elle représente une source potentielle de tension, sera idéalement vécue comme une occasion de créativité et de dépassement (Toner, Miller et Gurland, 1994).

Le projet de collaboration n'est donc pas une activité désincarnée ; il répond à des besoins à la fois humain (croissance personnelle, communication), scientifique (créativité, connaissances) et pratique (utilité, efficacité).

Les aspects structurels

L'organisationnel

Dans l'implantation et le fonctionnement d'une recherche collaborative, *le critère organisationnel* recouvre plusieurs volets. Faut-il rappeler que les liens de collaboration constituent l'essence même de ce type de partenariat, d'où l'importance de planifier soigneusement les mécanismes de liaison à l'externe comme à l'interne ? À défaut d'un tel souci, le groupe s'expose à se replier sur lui-même, à se comporter comme une petite clique, bref, à se couper du monde extérieur, ce qui le condamnerait à plus ou moins longue échéance.

La principale difficulté à laquelle se heurtent les promoteurs d'une activité de partenariat tient aux résistances institutionnelles (pénurie de ressources, méfiance, manque d'expertise) et à l'absence de modèles éprouvés (validés) de collaboration susceptibles d'en indiquer les avantages et les inconvénients (Chafetz, West et Ebbs, 1987). En conséquence, les projets de collaboration sont souvent approuvés sur une base expérimentale. En effet, tant dans les milieux universitaires que professionnels, il existe peu de structures aptes à faciliter l'émergence et le soutien de telles activités. L'organisation qui embauche les professionnelles et les professionnels se montrera souvent réticente à consentir des dégrèvements, tandis que dans les milieux universitaires on hésitera à libérer des ressources humaines ou financières, ce genre d'activité étant peu valorisé ou perçu comme étant improductif. C'est pourquoi, estime Satin (1987), maintes expériences ne parviennent pas à atteindre l'objectif d'interdisciplinarité ; elles finissent par adopter un mode de fonctionnement multidisciplinaire (comportant des mécanismes de coordination), voire monodisciplinaire (comportant des suivis sporadiques).

Pour espérer atteindre un niveau de fonctionnalité et de succès acceptables, une recherche de partenariat reposera sur deux niveaux de collaboration : interne et externe (Crow, Levine et Nager, 1992). En termes de *collaboration externe* (interorganisationnelles), on veillera à nouer des liens harmonieux et efficaces entre les principaux partenaires, soit les milieux cliniques ou professionnels, d'une part, et l'université ou le centre de recherche, d'autre part. La collaboration externe concerne aussi les liens que tissera l'équipe de travail avec la communauté, c'est-à-dire les associations de personnes âgées ou de personnes retraitées, les médias et les établissements d'hébergement, notamment. Par exemple, GRAPPA organise régulièrement des activités de sensibilisation et d'information dans le milieu, soit par le biais de rencontres, de participation à des colloques régionaux, d'articles de journaux et d'un bulletin de liaison.

Selon Mergendoller (1980), les intérêts de chaque partenaire doivent faire l'objet d'une négociation guidée par les principes suivants : la parité, la réciprocité et le langage commun. On fera donc en sorte que chacune et chacun ait la conviction de contribuer significativement à l'avancement des travaux et que des consensus puissent se dégager lors des échanges (Chafetz, West et Ebbs, 1987).

Sur le plan de la *collaboration interne*, la littérature fournit plusieurs modèles pouvant servir de guide dans la constitution d'une équipe interdisciplinaire et intersectorielle (Drinka, 1991 ; French et Bell, 1984). Deux points essentiels ressortent : créer un climat de travail agréable, stimulant et coopératif entre les partenaires et bien différencier les rôles.

S'appuyant sur la théorie de l'échange, Gitlin, Lyons et Kolodner (1994) ont énuméré les conditions nécessaires à la création d'une équipe de collaboration efficace :

- développer une atmosphère de confiance réciproque ;
- susciter des mécanismes de soutien et d'échange durables ;
- permettre aux individus d'exprimer librement leurs idées et de résoudre les conflits ;
- négocier les niveaux de contribution, en s'appuyant sur le principe des coûts-bénéfices.

Sur ce dernier point, l'équipe sera consciente que chaque membre est porté à évaluer sa participation suivant le modèle de l'échange. Le bilan de cette évaluation modulera en quelque sorte l'intensité et la durée de son engagement : 1) les avantages (avancement professionnel, terminer un diplôme, établir des contacts, acquérir des connaissances, prendre de l'expérience) et 2) les inconvénients (représailles de la part des collègues de travail non engagés dans le projet, les heures consacrées au projet entraînant une surcharge de travail auprès de la clientèle régulière, retombées immédiates moins visibles).

L'instrumental

Le volet instrumental concerne essentiellement l'orientation méthodologique des activités de recherche. Étant donné les objectifs visés et la nature collaborative du projet, les partenaires-chercheurs ne contrôlent plus de manière unilatérale le processus de recherche. Le modèle « expert vs non-expert » caractérisant l'approche positiviste classique n'est plus approprié et il est remplacé par un modèle plus participatif, interactif et ouvert, trouvant, pour l'essentiel, ses racines dans l'épistémologie subjectiviste, celle du sens et de l'historicité (par exemple, l'enquête ethnographique, la phénoménologie). Les vertus du pluralisme méthodologique (Lefrançois, 1995, Patton, 1988 ; Schensul, 1985 ; Price et Barrel, 1980), c'est-à-dire l'hybridation des méthodes et l'adoption de normes de recherche en rupture avec la tradition objectiviste, sont ici à l'honneur.

En ce qui a trait aux méthodes de recherche, le recours à une stratégie flexible autorisant le mixage des procédés de collecte et d'analyse des données (syncrétisme et éclectisme) paraît le plus indiqué. En effet, l'intégration des savoirs théorique et pratique commande un élargissement du faisceau d'observation et en même temps une confrontation de plusieurs modes de collecte de données. Seront privilégiées l'observation en milieu naturel et une démarche cyclique ou en spirale favorisant des retours sur le terrain (*unplanned backlooping*). La procédure d'évaluation des résultats s'appuiera donc sur d'autres principes méthodologiques tels que la validité pragmatique et la congruence écologique.

Concernant les normes ou attitudes méthodologiques, la littérature souligne l'importance d'appliquer une transférabilité des rôles chez les membres, de favoriser l'immersion dans le milieu et de concevoir les personnes-ressources en recherche elles-mêmes en tant qu'instrument (intersubjectivité) [Lipson, 1984]. Finalement, dans l'hypothèse où un projet de démonstration serait mis à l'essai, on s'assurera qu'il soit conçu pour devenir un modèle pouvant permettre la réplicabilité.

Le valoriel

Toute initiative de recherche collaborative, c'est-à-dire axée sur l'interdisciplinarité et l'intersectorialité, doit composer avec un système de valeurs dominantes (chasse gardée) caractérisé par l'individualisme, la compétitivité et la pensée monodisciplinaire (Clark, 1994). Ces valeurs peuvent devenir des obstacles importants au bon fonctionnement de l'équipe. La prégnance de ces valeurs est telle que celles-ci moduleront éventuellement les relations de pouvoir, l'identification des rôles et la communication entre les partenaires. Ce problème existe tant dans les secteurs insitutionnels que cliniques. Côté institutionnel, l'université est construite sur le modèle des départements uniques. Les mécanismes de promotion reposent sur la productivité individuelle et celui des nominations, sur le prestige individuel. En fait, il existe peu de mécanismes de soutien aux activités collaboratives, même si certaines percées s'observent sur le plan de la recherche industrielle. En ce concerne l'enseignement, le travail en équipe existe certes, mais seuls les individus sont récompensés en bout de ligne. Côté clinique, les conduites monodisciplinaires exercent une forte attraction malgré l'existence des équipes «multidisciplinaires». Le problème est d'autant plus aigu que persiste, dans de nombreux milieux de l'intervention, une propension vers les droits et valeurs individuelles : par exemple, l'autonomie de la personne âgée, le droit de refuser des traitements, l'éthique du mourant.

CONCLUSION

L'objectif visé dans cet article était en premier lieu de souligner les transformations sociales, institutionnelles et socio-économiques qui militent en faveur d'un décloisonnement de l'intervention et de la recherche.

En second lieu, nous avons présenté les avantages de la recherche collaborative comme mode de partenariat, tant du point de vue du développement de l'intervention que de celui des connaissances. Ayant effectué une recension des écrits sur le sujet, nous nous sommes ensuite inspirés d'une expérience concrète, soit le projet GRAPPA, pour mettre en relief les conditions de succès de ce modèle de partenariat. Au terme de cette analyse des conditions d'implantation et de réalisation d'un projet de concertation comportant un volet « recherche » et un volet « intervention », nous nous limiterons à proposer la définition suivante :

> La recherche collaborative est (1) une stratégie planifiée d'investigation scientifique et d'intervention, structurée autour du modèle de la concertation interdisciplinaire et intersectorielle, et (2) une stratégie d'intégration des connaissances théoriques et pratiques dont le but est d'accroître le niveau de compétence des partenaires et de compréhension d'une problématique multiple et complexe en vue d'y apporter des solutions novatrices, efficaces et efficientes.

Ainsi formulée, cette définition générale de la recherche collaborative recouvre les principaux éléments relevés dans la documentation et traduit l'essentiel des préoccupations concrètes observées sur le terrain.

Plusieurs approches de recherche ont été proposées pour conjuguer les finalités de l'activité scientifique et celles de l'intervention (telle que la recherche-action). La recherche collaborative, sans être une méthode ou une approche de recherche en soi, constitue plutôt un principe d'action reposant sur le partenariat.

Bibliographie

BENNETT, R. et P. MILLER (1987). « Interdisciplinary Approach to Graduate Health Sciences Education in Geriatrics and Gerontology », dans LESNOFF-CARAVAGLIA, G. (sous la direction de), *Handbook of Applied Gerontology,* New York, Human Sciences Press, 155-170.

CHAFETZ, P., WEST, H. et E. EBBS (1987). « Overcoming Obstacles to Cooperation in Interdisciplinary Long Term Care Teams », *Journal of Gerontological Social Work,* vol. 11, nos 3-4, 131-140.

CLARK, G.P. (1994). « Social, Professional, and Educational Values on the Interdisciplinary Team : Implications for Gerontological and Geriatric Education », *Educational Gerontology,* vol. 20, 35-51.

CROW, M.G., LEVINE, L. et N. NAGER (1992). « Are Three Heads Better Than One ? Reflections on Doing Collaborative Interdisciplinary Research », *American Educational Research Journal,* vol. 29, no 4, 737-753.

DEPOY, E. et C. GALLAGHER (1990). « Steps in Collaborative Research Between Clinicians and Faculty », *American Journal of Occupational Therapy,* vol. 44, 55-59.

DRINKA, T.J.K. (1991). «Development and Maintenance of an Interdisciplinary Health Care Team : A Case Study», *Gerontology & Geriatrics Education*, vol. 12, 111-125.

DUSSAULT, G. (1990). «Impact de la pratique interdisciplinaire sur la gestion», dans HÉBERT, R. (sous la direction de), *Interdisciplinarité en gérontologie,* Actes du Vᵉ Congrès international francophone de gérontologie, Saint-Hyacinthe, Maloine/Edisem, 41-45.

FOUREZ, G. (1988). *La construction des sciences (les logiques des inventions scientifiques. Introduction à la philosophie et à l'éthique des sciences,* 2ᵉ éd., Montréal, Erpi.

FRENCH, W. et C.H. Jr. BELL (1984). *Organizational Development : Behavioral Science Interventions for Organization Improvement,* 3ᵉ éd., Englewood Cliffs, NJ, Prentice-Hall.

GITLIN, N.L., LYONS, J.K. et E. KOLODNER (1994). «A Model to Build Collaborative Research or Educational Teams of Health Professionals in Gerontology», *Educational Gerontology*, vol. 20, 15-34.

HOSHMAND, L.T. (1989). «Alternate Research Paradigms : A Review and Teaching Proposal», *The Counseling Psychologist*, vol. 17, nᵒ 1, 3-79.

LEFRANÇOIS, R. et M.H. SOULET (1983). *Le système de la recherche sociale (tome 1, la recherche sociale dans l'État),* Université de Sherbrooke, Collection «Recherche sociale», nᵒˢ 3-4.

LEFRANÇOIS, R. (1995). «Pluralisme méthodologique et stratégies multi-méthodes en gérontologie», *Canadian Journal on Aging,* vol. 14, hors série 1, 52-68.

LIPSON, J.G. (1984). «Combining Researcher, Clinical and Personal Roles : Enrichment or Confusion», *Human Organization*, vol. 43, nᵒ 4, 348-352.

MERGENDOLLER, J. (1980). *Mutual Inquiry : The Role of Collaborative Research on Teaching in School-based Staff Development,* San Francisco, Far West Laboratory for Educational Research and Development.

PATTON, Q.M. (1988). *Qualitative Evaluation Methods,* Beverly Hills, CA, Sage Pub., chap. 5.

PRANGER, T. et T.G. BROWN (1990). «Collaborative Research : Campus and Clinic Working Together», *Canadian Journal of Occupational Therapy*, vol. 57, 268-272.

PRICE, D. et J. BARRELL (1980). «An Experiential Approach with Quantitative Methods : A Research Paradigm», *Journal of Humanistic Psychology*, vol. 20, nᵒ 3, 75-95.

SATIN, D.G. (1987). «The Difficulties of Interdisciplinary Education : Lessons from Three Failures and a Success», *Educational Gerontology*, vol. 13, 53-69.

SCHENSUL, J.J. (1985). «Systems Consistency in Field Research, Dissemination, and Social Change», *American Behavioral Scientist*, vol. 29, nᵒ 2, 186-204.

TONER, J.A., MILLER, P. et B.J. GURLAND (1994). «Conceptual, Theoretical, and Practical Approaches to the Development of Interdisciplinary Teams : A Transactional Model», *Educational Gerontology*, vol. 20, 53-69.

❖ # Le mouvement des centres de santé : grandeur et misère de la participation et stratégies politiques de transformation du discours de l'État

Jacinthe MICHAUD
Programme d'Études des femmes
Université York

Cet article met en lumière les terrains discursifs de la participation à l'intérieur desquels les groupes de femmes sont appelés à développer leurs stratégies d'action dans le contexte de la régionalisation du système de santé et des services sociaux au Québec. L'évolution discursive propre au mouvement des Centres de santé des femmes implique tout autant une stratégie d'apprentissage du fonctionnement administratif et bureaucratique des structures gouvernementales qu'une stratégie de transformation idéologique et politique du discours de l'État envers les femmes. La possibilité pour les groupes de femmes d'opérer des changements qualitatifs dans le discours de l'État reste liée au potentiel de renouvellement du discours féministe à partir de l'expression des identités collectives au sein du mouvement des femmes.

INTRODUCTION :
LES TERRAINS DISCURSIFS DE LA PARTICIPATION

Avec la réforme du système de santé surgissent de nouvelles appréhensions concernant une participation renouvelée des groupes de femmes aux structures régionalisées de l'État. L'orientation politique de non-participation, quel que soit le niveau de gouvernement concerné, s'est principalement justifiée dans le passé par la crainte de la récupération des services et du recul de l'autonomie organisationnelle. Dans le contexte de la présente restructuration du système de santé et de la reconnaissance du communautaire par certaines instances gouvernementales, cette position se maintient avec davantage de précarité au sein des groupes de femmes. De plus, l'argument dominant voulant que l'État représente désormais une réalité incontournable dans la vie des femmes et des groupes semble avoir triomphé des dernières réticences (Lamoureux, 1994 ; Franzway, Court et Connell, 1989 ; Regroupement provincial des maisons d'hébergement et de transition pour femmes victimes de violence conjugale, 1989).

Cependant, le processus de participation oblige à considérer deux terrains discursifs à l'intérieur desquels les groupes de femmes ont intérêt à clarifier leurs stratégies d'action (Michaud,1995). Le premier concerne la maîtrise du langage administratif et du modèle de gestion bureaucratique à l'intérieur duquel les groupes de femmes doivent approfondir leurs connaissances du fonctionnement étatique structurant le modèle de participation s'ils veulent être efficaces dans la gestion des prises de décision. Le deuxième terrain, obscurci par la foisonnante activité du premier, est celui des idéologies et de la recomposition de l'hégémonie. Lorsque les groupes de femmes émergent comme acteurs collectifs dans un espace de visibilité politique, ils véhiculent un contre-discours qui s'oppose à une représentation traditionnelle du rôle des femmes. Et ils ne sont pas les seuls à le faire. Plusieurs autres acteurs collectifs sont particulièrement soucieux d'intervenir dans la définition de « nouveaux paradigmes sociétaux » (Jenson,1991, 1989 et 1986) pouvant aller jusqu'à englober des questions aussi diversifiées que les unités familiales et parentales, la sexualité, la reproduction des diverses catégories sociales de femmes, la sécurité du revenu, la santé mentale, les droits des individus au logement, au travail et autres enjeux sociaux.

Dans l'article qui suit, il sera question de l'expérience des Centres de santé des femmes, de leur émergence et de leur place au sein du système de santé québécois. Nous verrons, dans un premier temps, l'évolution des rapports du réseau féministe et alternatif de la santé des femmes avec le réseau institutionnel. J'aimerais également examiner le sens que prennent les concepts de « partenariat » et de « complémentarité » largement retrouvés dans l'approche et les textes ministériels (Boivin, 1996 ; Valois, 1995 ; Lamoureux,1994 ; Lamoureux et Lesemann,1987). Suivant le sens donné au processus de participation, des terrains discursifs se dessinent à l'intérieur desquels les acteurs doivent tout autant apporter un sens politique et idéologique à la participation elle-même qu'un sens politique et idéologique à l'application des objectifs et des politiques à laquelle ils sont censés participer. La dernière partie de l'article reviendra sur les éléments structurant le renouvellement du potentiel contre-discursif des groupes de femmes[1].

LE CONTEXTE D'ÉMERGENCE DES CENTRES DE SANTÉ DES FEMMES ET LEUR POSITION SPÉCIFIQUE À L'INTÉRIEUR DU SYSTÈME

Au Québec, six Centres de santé des femmes ont été créés entre 1975 et 1982. Le premier, celui de Montréal, a remplacé le service de référence en avortement mis sur pied d'abord par le Front de libération des femmes du Québec (1969-1971) ensuite par le Centre des femmes (1972-1974) [O'Leary et Toupin,1982]. Le Centre de santé des femmes de Québec a été, par ailleurs, le premier centre à offrir un service complet d'avortement dès sa fondation en 1978. Au cours de la même année, le Centre de santé des femmes de Sherbrooke a ouvert ses portes. En 1981, c'est au tour des Centres de santé de Trois-Rivières et de Hull de voir le jour, suivi de celui de Lanaudière l'année suivante. En 1985, les Centres de santé procèdent à la fondation officielle du Regroupement des Centres de santé des femmes du Québec. Aujourd'hui, après vingt ans d'histoire marquée par deux fermetures et un départ, seuls les centres de Montréal, de Sherbrooke et de Trois-Rivières demeurent membres de ce regroupement.

L'absence de contrôle des femmes sur leur vie reproductive, principalement la difficulté d'accès à des services d'avortement dans les hôpitaux francophones du Québec[2], a constitué le contexte, en même

---

1. Les données de base de cet article font partie d'une recherche entreprise sur le mouvement des Centres de santé des femmes du Québec. L'information provient pour l'essentiel de documents produits par les Centres de santé et d'autres groupes de femmes, ainsi que d'une série d'entrevues réalisées entre 1991 et 1992 auprès d'informatrices de ces groupes ainsi qu'auprès d'intervenantes de certains regroupements provinciaux des groupes de services.

2. Le Comité de lutte pour l'avortement libre et gratuit révèle qu'en 1975, sur 5 657 avortements, 5 418 ont eu lieu dans les hôpitaux anglophones ! (Comité pour l'avortement libre et gratuit, 1978 : 21-22)

temps que le prétexte de leur émergence. En offrant, en premier lieu, un service de référence pour avortements illégaux quoique non clandestins, les premières militantes féministes en santé en sont venues à développer une critique radicale de la médecine scientifique. Elles tirèrent aussi avantage du nouveau système de santé, partiellement sous contrôle étatique, pour rendre visible la réalité des femmes (Comité pour l'avortement libre et gratuit,1978).

Dans ce contexte, on peut dire que les Centres de santé se sont positionnés comme agents de transformation idéologique et politique de la médecine scientifique et de l'ensemble du système de santé. Ils ont développé leur approche discursive liant étroitement la dénonciation de l'oppression des femmes à celle de la quête de leur autonomie. Cette étroite relation entre oppression et autonomie posée comme base du discours contre-hégémonique des centres de santé (Michaud,1995) est inscrite dans les principes fondamentaux retrouvés dans l'énoncé des trois « D » : « démédicalisation », « déprofessionalisation » et « désexisation ». Les trois « D » représentent non seulement la critique féministe de la médecine scientifique mais créent également un lieu où s'élabore un corpus de connaissances sur la santé, où se pratique une autre manière d'intervenir sur le corps des femmes, où se développent des pratiques alternatives et féministes impliquant une approche collective, l'abandon des structures hiérarchiques et l'adoption d'un statut égalitaire pour toutes les femmes.

La position des Centres de santé à l'égard de la participation a été marquée du sceau de l'ambiguïté tout au cours des années 1980 (Michaud,1992,1995 ; Relais-femmes,1985). Par la suite, les centres se retrouvent dans l'obligation de clarifier leur position à différents niveaux du système de santé. Néanmoins, il faut sans doute remonter aux débuts des Centres de santé pour retrouver l'origine de la relation complexe qui les lie au réseau institutionnel de santé. Les premières militantes féministes venaient d'horizons divers, et un nombre suffisamment important d'entre elles travaillaient déjà dans les institutions médicales. Elles étaient infirmières, travailleuses sociales, parfois même médecins. Leurs pratiques au sein du réseau institutionnel leur permettaient d'en constater les lacunes. Avec d'autres militantes, elles ont collaboré à la formation d'une critique radicale de la médecine scientifique et de son discours sur le corps des femmes. De la même manière, elles ont participé à l'élaboration d'un nouveau savoir et d'une expertise féministe inspiré de la publication, *Our Bodies Ourselves* (Boston Women's Health Collective, 1971) qui a marqué le « *self-help* » américain.

Nous parlons ici de la circulation de connaissances entre deux réseaux fort différents quant à leur mode d'intervention. Dans le cas du réseau institutionnel, ce type de circulation s'est traduit par une lente et indéniable infiltration de l'expérience des Centres de santé. Ainsi, l'approche collective si chère aux Centres de santé a pu, d'une certaine manière, être reprise par quelques centres locaux de services communautaires (CLSC) avec l'organisation de sessions de formation ou de groupes de rencontres sur des sujets concernant la santé des femmes.

> Les travailleuses qui étaient dans les CLSC, c'étaient des féministes, aussi féministes que les militantes du centre de santé. C'étaient des femmes qui ont mené des batailles terribles [...] Il y en avait qui se battaient dans leur CLSC pour qu'il y ait des pratiques collectives aussi et elles en ont fait d'ailleurs des pratiques collectives. (Informatrice du Centre de santé des femmes du Quartier de Montréal)

Plusieurs se plaindront toutefois qu'en agissant de la sorte, le réseau institutionnel ne reconnaissait que peu ou prou l'expertise féministe si patiemment élaborée dans les Centres de santé, qu'il ne faisait que récupérer et remodeler à son image une façon de faire des Centres de santé répondant à une demande de plus en plus pressante des femmes. Quoi qu'il en soit, la tendance chez les intervenantes des Centres de santé a bel et bien été de faire valoir leur expertise féministe à divers niveaux du système particulièrement dans les CLSC, mais aussi dans certains hôpitaux. Les objectifs étaient fort simples : changer les pratiques médicales traditionnelles, faire valoir l'analyse féministe, se poser comme une ressource alternative incontournable en lien avec la communauté des femmes estimée la seule à être capable de répondre de façon satisfaisante à leurs besoins propres.

L'impact de la circulation des services, des intervenantes et des connaissances venant du réseau alternatif, même s'il demeure difficilement mesurable, n'en demeure pas moins indéniable. À partir du moment où les Centres de santé ont commencé à faire valoir la qualité de leurs services, de leur expertise féministe et forts de la demande des femmes en provenance des milieux où ils se sont implantés, ils ont recherché une reconnaissance formelle. Et la matérialité de cette reconnaissance passait par un financement suffisant.

> Contrairement aux années soixante-dix où on considérait que le financement de l'État c'était de la récupération, dans les années quatre-vingt [...], nous pensons répondre aux besoins des femmes et nous développons des pratiques féministes en santé [...] C'est une alternative, ça remet en question le système médical, le système de santé, ça donne du pouvoir aux femmes et il faut que l'État le reconnaisse parce que les femmes nous appuient. C'est un peu comme développer un réseau parallèle que l'État doit reconnaître

et financer comme tel. C'est un peu le requestionnement du rôle de l'État. Je trouve, avec le recul, on peut le voir comme de la récupération, mais moi je pense que c'est la réalisation que le système de santé au Québec, comme bien d'autres systèmes, n'arrive pas à répondre à tout. (Informatrice du Regroupement des Centres de santé)

L'ÉVOLUTION DU DISCOURS ET DES PRATIQUES DE PARTICIPATION

Les Centres de santé se sont donc attardés, dans un premier temps, à la formation interne d'un contre-discours féministe. De manière concomitante, cependant, des relations d'échange s'élaborent entre les réseaux institutionnel et féministe. C'est donc auprès de certaines instances administratives du ministère de la Santé et des Services sociaux que les Centres de santé tentent alors de faire valoir les lacunes du système et leur présence indispensable auprès de la communauté des femmes. Tout au cours des années 1980, jusqu'à la création des Régies régionales en 1992, les rapports administratifs et bureaucratiques entre l'État et les groupes de femmes se sont considérablement modifiés. Au milieu des années 1980, par exemple, le gouvernement du Québec reconnaît clairement, dans son plan d'action, les groupes de femmes en tant que « partenaires essentiels » (Gouvernement du Québec, 1987b). À cette époque, les groupes de femmes, en particulier les groupes de services, avaient l'habitude de faire une demande annuelle de financement directement au bureau de la ou du ministre. Cette présentation était généralement suivie d'une réunion qui se voulait informelle et amicale, quoique significative politiquement, avec de hauts responsables du ministère. Chaque demande présentée était ensuite étudiée par le programme « Soutien aux organismes communautaires » (SOC) [Gouvernement du Québec, 1992b]. Par un tel procédé, les représentantes des groupes de femmes avaient la chance de s'asseoir avec les acteurs politiques et parfois même avec la ou le ministre, ne manquant jamais une occasion de souligner leur importance dans leur milieu de même que la qualité de leur expertise.

Il est nécessaire de se rappeler ici que le discours de l'État sur la participation s'inscrit à l'intérieur du contexte décrit par Lamoureux et Lesemann dans leur rapport soumis à la Commission Rochon en 1987. La crise de l'État-providence, écrivent-ils alors, fait appel à la responsabilité communautaire, à la solidarité des citoyens, au développement du bénévolat et au partenariat. Toujours selon les auteurs, l'appel du gouvernement à la responsabilité communautaire s'est fait de façon plutôt ambiguë au début, mais la logique qui soutient cette approche met toutefois en lumière la base d'un nouveau modèle de services qui s'adapte aux exigences gouvernementales de rationalisation économique et administrative.

Depuis la publication du rapport de la Commission Rochon en 1988 et l'instauration des régies régionales, la pratique du partenariat prend une configuration beaucoup plus contraignante pour les groupes. Les représentantes féministes, pour ne parler que de celles-ci, doivent maintenant négocier leur financement au niveau régional. Les régies régionales sont devenues les maîtresses d'œuvre de la redistribution des budgets alloués par le ministère, et par là, de la reconnaissance officielle des groupes (Pineault, 1992). Il est à noter, cependant, que les régies demeurent liées aux priorités établies par ce même ministère, ce qui maintient le caractère centralisé de l'État ; du moins quant à l'identification des problèmes et des groupes sociaux cibles, objets de l'attention ministérielle. Avec ces nouvelles règles du jeu, la possibilité d'obtenir une rencontre au plus haut niveau du ministère devient limitée. La reconnaissance procédera du niveau régional et se matérialisera de façon inégale d'un endroit à un autre.

> Des fois, c'est important que ça soit centralisé pour éviter [d]es jeux de pouvoir. On est pas toujours d'accord avec les décisions mais il reste [que] quand il y en a une qui est prise et qu'elle est en notre [faveur], qu'elle s'impose partout. C'est quand même un avantage [...] (Informatrice du Centre de santé du Québec)

On pourrait objecter qu'un pas vers la reconnaissance formelle a été franchi avec la création de ces régies régionales. Les groupes communautaires ont vu leur importance confirmée et leur représentation reconnue. La représentation allouée aux organismes communautaires est de 20 %, laquelle doit inclure un 5 % de représentation des groupes de femmes. Ce dernier pourcentage demeure contesté puisque aucune documentation écrite ne fait état, à ce jour, d'une telle proportion pour les groupes travaillant sur la question des femmes[3].

Outre le 20 % alloué aux organismes communautaires, la composition des régies régionales est la suivante : 20 % de représentants et représentantes des municipalités, 20 % élus par les organismes que les régies régionales auront désigné comme étant les plus représentatifs des groupes socio-économiques de la région et 40 % de membres des conseils d'administration des établissements médicaux privés et publics (Pineault, 1992 : 83).

---

3. Propos recueillis auprès d'une ancienne agente gouvernementale du Comité de la condition féminine du MSSS. Le pourcentage de 5 % a été suggéré lors d'une entrevue informelle avec deux agentes du SOC.

À partir de cette distribution, nous pouvons constater que les groupes de femmes doivent entrer en action à deux niveaux. En premier lieu, ils doivent exercer des pressions au sein des groupes communautaires eux-mêmes, leurs plus proches alliés dans cette nouvelle donnée politique ; ils doivent assurer une représentation juste et équitable de leurs préoccupations. En deuxième lieu, les groupes de services doivent mobiliser leurs énergies pour les élections à différents niveaux des institutions locales, tels les hôpitaux et les CLSC, là où la participation des citoyens et citoyennes est sollicitée, afin de s'assurer une représentation sympathique à leur cause.

La nouvelle régionalisation élimine le genre de centralisation de la période précédente mieux adaptée aux Centres de santé et aux groupes de femmes en général. Par exemple, les nouvelles régies régionales peuvent se montrer favorables à quelques Centres de santé seulement, ceux qui auront argumenté avec succès leur pertinence au sein de leur communauté ou qui auront démontré leur capacité de prendre en compte les priorités politiques du gouvernement. Il y a aussi, bien sûr, tout l'aspect financier qui emprisonne les Centres de santé à l'intérieur de cette nouvelle structure de participation. Mais plusieurs sont déjà déterminés à y faire face et à continuer de faire pression pour l'instauration de politiques et de réformes qui répondent aux besoins des femmes. Après tout, les intervenantes des Centres de santé maintiennent que le gouvernement n'a pas d'autre choix que de leur prêter une oreille attentive.

> Le partenariat, ce n'est pas un hasard que le gouvernement fonctionne de cette manière-là. Ils sont obligés de tenir compte d'une force qu'ils ont méconnue ou ignorée pendant des années. Parce que nous sommes très critiques par rapport à ce partenariat-là. [...] On le sait qu'on est partenaire à parts inégales, c'est bien clair. C'en est plein maintenant dans le nouveau discours du gouvernement, le partenariat, la complémentarité, alouette, y en mettent [...] Mais ça dit aussi d'une certaine façon la reconnaissance forcée qu'ils font du communautaire, des mouvements de femmes... Ils sont poignés avec ça. (Informatrice du Regroupement des Centres de santé)

LA COMPLÉMENTARITÉ CONTRE LE PARTENARIAT

Une question demeure pourtant. Quel sens faut-il attribuer au concept de partenariat ? Recouvre-t-il les mêmes réalités selon que l'on se place du côté des groupes de femmes ou du côté de l'État ? Parmi les concepts utilisés pour définir les relations de participation entre l'État et les organismes communautaires, Lamoureux et Lesemann attiraient déjà notre attention en 1987 sur ceux de « partenariat » et de « complémentarité », lesquels caractérisent la nouvelle configuration des rapports qui se nouent. Partenariat et complémentarité, disent-ils, ne sont pas interchangeables mais doivent être placés en compétition l'un par rapport à l'autre. Ces deux concepts ont connu une évolution de sens. La complémentarité, plus que le partenariat, peut être comprise en tant que pratique de régulation étatique, en tant que domination et récupération de certaines forces vitales de la communauté, alors que d'autres sont évincées (Lamoureux et Lesemann,1987).

Dans *Partenariat à l'épreuve*, Lamoureux parle peu de la complémentarité mais soutient que ce concept représente une caractéristique négative de la participation. La complémentarité fait référence à une pratique et à un type de relation que les groupes refusent. Avec la complémentarité, les services rendus par les groupes ne sont reconnus que partiellement, sélectionnés sans égard à l'ensemble de l'expertise alternative patiemment développée dans le communautaire au fil des années (Lamoureux,1994).

Cet aspect négatif de la complémentarité jette également une ombre sur le sens que le terme de partenariat peut adopter suivant le contexte. Selon Gary Kinsman (1992), dans la mesure où la négociation se déroule entre partenaires aux intérêts divers et où l'État se réserve le rôle de médiateur, l'utilisation du terme de partenariat exige la neutralisation du rapport inégal de pouvoir et élimine la possibilité de transformer le sens hégémonique attribué au processus lui-même.

> *Partnership has a nice neutral ring to it. It is difficult to question or oppose because it draws us into constructing a consensus. Partnership sounds consensual, it implies that everyone is being an equal voice, that all partners are equal. It is therefore a useful conceptualization for the construction of hegemonic relations. [...] As problems emerge, the terrain of struggle becomes framed by the terms of partnership but not the concept of partnership itself. The struggle takes place within the shared discursive framework of partnership and does not burst its hegemonic boundaries.* (Kinsman,1992 : 223)

En dépit des recommandations de la Commission Rochon, les documents gouvernementaux ne sont pas toujours aussi clairs. Par exemple, certains textes décrivant la réforme et la nouvelle politique de la santé et du bien-être (Gouvernement du Québec, 1992, 1990) semblent mystérieusement discrets quant à l'engagement envers un partenariat véritable au sens où les groupes le souhaiteraient. Par contre, le concept de complémentarité y est utilisé, signifiant l'instauration d'un processus sélectif par lequel une partie seulement des activités sont reconnues.

En raison du type de complémentarité refusé, le Regroupement provincial des maisons d'hébergement et de transition pour femmes victimes de violence conjugale avait déjà, en 1987, particulièrement critiqué la récupération de certains de leurs services au sein des structures administratives du réseau institutionnel (Godbout *et al.*,1987). Il n'est donc pas étonnant de constater que ce même regroupement continue de lutter contre la récupération d'un problème social qu'il a patiemment travaillé à rendre visible.

La complémentarité est loin d'être disparue avec la publication de la *Politique de la santé et du bien-être* (1992a) qui décrit les orientations du gouvernement sur la violence à la suite de la restructuration du système de santé et des services sociaux. On pourrait se demander si la régionalisation du système ne viendra pas institutionnaliser cette complémentarité tant décriée par les groupes, une complémentarité avec les établissements de santé qui viendra renforcer l'inégalité des statuts non seulement avec ces établissements mais aussi avec d'autres groupes d'intérêt se réclamant de quelque expertise dans le domaine.

Dans un tel cas, on pourrait craindre que l'intégration officielle et administrative des organismes communautaires conduise à accroître l'invisibilité et l'exclusion, et pour finir, à éteindre les voix qui furent, à une certaine période, les plus importantes critiques des politiques et de l'action gouvernementales dans la société civile. La pertinence des Centres de santé des femmes se trouve aussi affaiblie depuis que certains établissements de santé, en particulier les CLSC, ont intégré lentement une certaine manière de faire empruntée au réseau alternatif, prétendant maintenant offrir les mêmes services que les Centres de santé.

Les militantes féministes de la santé parviendront-elles à contrer cet apparent dédoublement des services entre les deux réseaux et à faire valoir ce qui leur reste en propre et qui ne se retrouve nulle part ailleurs, c'est-à-dire leurs pratiques alternatives, l'approche collective et l'expertise féministe qu'elles ont su développer en lien avec la communauté des femmes? Autrement dit, est-il possible de poursuivre la dynamique du renouvellement du contre-discours féministe dans le champ politique et idéologique où se forment et se transforment les discours sur la santé et sur le corps des femmes?

DISCUSSION: À PROPOS DU RENOUVELLEMENT DU CONTRE-DISCOURS FÉMINISTE

On pourrait penser que l'effort du mouvement des Centres de santé et des groupes de femmes s'arrête là. Ils ont obtenu une reconnaissance comme organisme communautaire et même si le financement demeure aléatoire, cette reconnaissance leur confère un atout dans la répartition des budgets. Ils ont aussi obtenu la possibilité de jouer un rôle, même si la portée de leur influence s'exerce au niveau régional.

Pour restreint qu'il soit, l'espace régional représente en soi un espace de visibilité politique où le jeu des alliances, de même que les rapports de confrontation entre les nouveaux «partenaires», nécessite bien plus qu'une parfaite maîtrise des dossiers gouvernementaux et que l'apprentissage du langage bureaucratique et administratif. Malgré les apparences, les régies régionales ne font pas qu'assurer le bon fonctionnement des services suivant les priorités et les budgets préétablis par le ministère. Les régies régionales constituent également un espace politique discursif où circulent plusieurs visions du monde et des visions idéologiques et politiques diverses concernant la santé des citoyennes et des citoyens.

Ainsi, les groupes communautaires, dont les groupes de femmes, suivant le pourcentage de représentation qui leur est assuré, doivent s'asseoir avec les représentants municipaux, les groupes socio-économiques et surtout les professionnels de la santé. En plus de s'initier aux jeux des négociations, ils doivent créer des alliances avec les forces qui se rapprochent le plus de leur plate-forme politique.

L'enjeu est d'une importance réelle. Déjà, certains groupes de femmes et communautaires ont fait savoir que refuser ces espaces de participation et de visibilité politique était laisser le champ libre à d'autres forces sociales qui n'ont pas nécessairement à cœur la défense d'un modèle alternatif en santé ni l'expertise féministe (Lamoureux, 1994 ; Regroupement provincial..., 1989). C'est de cette façon que déjà, en 1989, le Regroupement provincial des maisons d'hébergement comprenait son rôle, se donnant l'obligation d'intervenir contre l'idéologie «familialiste» du réseau institutionnel et l'approche «psychologisante» adoptée par certaines composantes du milieu (Regroupement provincial..., 1989). Nous avons vu également que c'est en ces termes que les intervenantes des Centres de santé ont disséminé leur expertise au sein de certains milieux du réseau et ont tenté de changer les attitudes envers les femmes, voire la représentation traditionnelle du corps des femmes véhiculée par la médecine scientifique.

On objectera toujours, cependant, qu'une telle participation demeure fondamentalement inégale (Boivin, 1996 ; Lamoureux et Lesemann, 1987) et que la voie d'une institutionnalisation aussi contraignante ne peut qu'influencer négativement le potentiel de formation d'un contre-discours au sein des groupes de femmes (Relais-femmes, 1985). Et pourtant, il en va ainsi de l'ensemble des espaces de visibilité au sein desquels les groupes de femmes choisissent d'intervenir pour transformer les discours dominants. Au-delà de le stabilité financière et de la reconnaissance institutionnelle, à partir du moment où les groupes acceptent le jeu de la participation, l'objectif de contrer les modèles discursifs dominants prend une importance considérable dans les stratégies d'action. Dès lors, l'enjeu n'est pas de refuser ou d'accepter la participation, mais de reconnaître que l'ultime priorité réside dans la dynamique qui préside à la formation d'un discours féministe qui sache mettre en lumière toute la diversité et la multiplicité des expériences de la vie des femmes.

Cela signifie que le potentiel contre-discursif du mouvement féministe doit s'appuyer encore et toujours sur la communauté des femmes. C'est avec la communauté des femmes que le projet féministe sur la santé a vu le jour, c'est à partir de leurs besoins de «démédicalisation», de «désexisation» et de «déprofessionalisation» que ces mêmes Centres ont ensuite senti le besoin de créer leurs propres espaces alternatifs de santé. Des lieux d'élaboration d'une critique radicale de la médecine scientifique ont aussi été créés et un discours féministe de dénonciation de l'oppression des femmes et de leur quête d'autonomie sous toutes ses facettes (personnelle, politique, économique et sociale) a été élaboré.

Cependant, la manière de définir la communauté des femmes sur les plans politique, idéologique, social, culturel, s'est largement modifiée depuis que de multiples voix collectives se sont faites entendre et ont réclamé la visibilité et l'inclusion de leur réalité à l'intérieur du mouvement féministe. Les militantes de la santé, quel que soit leur lieu collectif d'intervention, doivent reconnaître dans une perspective de transformation interne du contre-discours féministe la centralité d'un tel enjeu dans l'expression des besoins des femmes. Les revendications venant de femmes de différentes classes sociales, d'orientations sexuelles diverses, d'origine ethnique multiple ou vivant avec un handicap, même si elles émergent en marge du contre-discours féministe, doivent agir de manière à en transformer la plate-forme politique principale. Les questions de race, de classe, d'orientation sexuelle, de handicap, ne deviennent pas seulement de nouvelles revendications qu'il suffit d'ajouter à une liste d'épicerie déjà longue, mais leur inclusion à la plate-forme politique principale doit pouvoir se faire de manière à y opérer une transformation qualitative. Ce contre-discours féministe, ainsi renouvelé de manière constante, agira comme élément déterminant dans l'élaboration d'une nouvelle manière de définir et de voir les besoins des femmes au sein d'un nouvel espace de visibilité politique (Michaud, 1997,1995,1992).

C'est donc dire que la dynamique interne de la formation du contre-discours féministe doit être reconnue dans toutes ses composantes. Cela d'autant plus que les groupes de femmes sont constamment engagés dans bon nombre de coalitions de solidarité où le processus de mise ensemble des intérêts et des préoccupations nécessite une négociation continuelle (Michaud,1992,1995). Ce qui est essentiel alors dans le phénomène d'inclusion des identités collectives concerne non seulement le résultat final en termes de contenu, mais le processus par lequel se sont négociées la formation discursive centrale et l'action de l'ensemble des parties.

L'analyse féministe, lorsqu'elle évolue à l'intérieur du champ de la politique institutionnelle, doit renouveler son potentiel discursif, non seulement pour exiger et obtenir des réformes ou s'opposer au recul des acquis sociaux, ou encore exiger et obtenir de la reconnaissance et du financement, mais surtout pour mettre de l'avant un discours capable de transformer le discours hégémonique sur le corps et la santé des femmes.

Bibliographie

BOIVIN, Louise (1995-1996). « L'économie sociale : ou comment faire passer en douceur la réduction des dépenses sociales de l'État », *Temps fou*, nᵒˢ 8-9, 10-11.

BOSTON WOMEN'S HEALTH COLLECTIVE (1971). *Our Bodies Ourselves*, Boston, Boston Women's Health Course Collective (1973) [1976], New York, Simon and Shuster.

COMITÉ DE LUTTE POUR L'AVORTEMENT LIBRE ET GRATUIT (1978). *C'est à nous de décider*, Montréal, Éditions du Remue-ménage.

FRANZWAY, Suzanne, COURT, Diane et R.W. CONNELL (1989). *Staking a Claim : Feminism, Bureaucracy and the State*, Polity Press.

GODBOUT, Jacques, LEDUC, Murielle et Jean-Pierre COLLIN (1987). *La face cachée du système*, présenté à la Commission d'enquête sur les services de santé et les services sociaux, Québec, Publications du Québec, 161 pages.

GOUVERNEMENT DU QUÉBEC (1987a). *Une politique d'aide aux femmes violentées*, Québec, Ministère de la Santé et des Services sociaux, 51 pages.

GOUVERNEMENT DU QUÉBEC (1987b). *Vers l'égalité : orientations triennales en matière de condition féminine 1987-1990*, Québec, Secrétariat à la condition féminine, 42 pages.

GOUVERNEMENT DU QUÉBEC (1988). *Rapport de la Commission d'enquête sur les services de santé et les services sociaux*, Québec, Publications du Québec.

GOUVERNEMENT DU QUÉBEC (1990). *A Reform Centred on the Citizen : Health Social Services Reform*, Québec, Ministère de la Santé et des Services sociaux, 83 pages.

GOUVERNEMENT DU QUÉBEC (1992a). *La politique de la santé et du bien-être*, Québec, Ministère de la Santé et des Services sociaux, 187 pages.

GOUVERNEMENT DU QUÉBEC (1992b). *Programme de soutien aux organismes communautaires 1993-1994*, Québec, Ministère de la Santé et Services sociaux, 24 pages.

JENSON, Jane (1986). « Gender and Reproduction : Or, Babies and the State », *Studies in Political Economy*, vol. 20, 9-46.

JENSON, Jane (1989). « Paradigms and Political Discourse : Protective Legislation in France and the United States Before 1914 », *Canadian Journal of Political Science*, vol. 2, 235-258.

JENSON, Jane (1991). « All the World's a Stage : Ideas, Space and Times in Canadian Political Economy », *Studies in Political Economy*, vol. 36, 43-72.

KINSMAN, Gary (1992). « Managing AIDS Organizing : "Consultation", "Partnership", and the National AIDS Strategy », CARROLL, William K. (dir.), *Organizing Dissent : Contemporary Social Movements* dans *Theory and in Practice*, Garamond Press, 215-231.

LAMOUREUX, Jocelyne (1994). *Le partenariat à l'épreuve*, Montréal, Éditions Saint-Martin.

LAMOUREUX, Jocelyne et Frédéric LESEMANN (1987). *Les filières d'action sociale : les rapports entre les services sociaux publics et les pratiques communautaires*, présenté à la Commission d'enquête sur les services de santé et les services sociaux, Québec, Publications du Québec, 246 pages.

MICHAUD, Jacinthe (1992). « The Welfare State and the Problem of Counter-Hegemonic Responses Within the Women's Movement », dans CAROLL, William K. (dir.), *Organizing Dissent : Contemporary Social Movements in Theory and in Practice*, Garamond Press, 200-214.

MICHAUD, Jacinthe (1995). *Angel Makers or Trouble Makers ? The Health Centres Movement in Québec and the Conditions of Formation of a Counter-Hegemony on Health*, Thèse de doctorat, University of Toronto, 349 pages.

MICHAUD, Jacinthe (1997). « On Counter-Hegemonic Formation Within the Women's Movement and the Difficult Integration of Collective Identities », dans CAROLL, William K. (dir.), *Organizing Dissent : Contemporary Social Movements in Theory and in Practice*, 2ᶜ éd., Garamond Press.

O'LEARY, Véronique et Louise TOUPIN (1982). « Nous sommes le produit d'un contexte », *Québécoises debouttes !*, Montréal, Éditions du Remue-ménage, tome 1, 21-50.

PINEAULT, Raynald (1992). « The Reform of the Quebec Health-Care System : Potential for Innovation ? », dans DAVIS, Mathwin (dir.), *Health Care : Innovation, Impact and Challenge*, Kingston, School of Policy Studies / School of Public Administration, Queen's University, 73-94.

REGROUPEMENT PROVINCIAL DES MAISONS D'HÉBERGEMENT ET DE TRANSITION POUR FEMMES VICTIMES DE VIOLENCE CONJUGALE (1989). « Au grand jour », Madeleine LACOMBE (rédigé par), Montréal, Éditions du Remue-ménage.

RELAIS-FEMMES (1985). *Le Regroupement des centres de santé pour les femmes et la non-participation*, Josée Belleau (rédigé par), Les rapports des groupes de femmes avec l'État, Compte rendu de la journée de réflexion organisée par Relais-femmes, 15-20.

VALOIS, Pierre (1995). « Désengagement ou "des engagements" ? », *Virtualités*, vol. 3, nᵒ 1, novembre-décembre, 9-14.

❖ La réticence familiale à recourir au soutien formel : un obstacle à la prévention de l'épuisement des personnes-soutien de personnes âgées dépendantes

Mario PAQUET
Direction de la santé publique
Régie régionale de la santé et des services sociaux de Lanaudière

INTRODUCTION

L'intervention auprès des personnes-soutien de personnes âgées dépendantes visant à les soutenir pour maintenir à domicile l'aidé et à les soulager, un tant soit peu, des tâches qu'elles ont à réaliser de façon quotidienne pose un grand défi. D'une part, les besoins des personnes-soutien sont complexes : en plus d'être nombreux et diversifiés, ils sont singuliers. D'autre part, même si le soutien aux familles constitue une priorité de toutes les politiques sociales, le milieu d'intervention doit composer avec le retrait de l'État-providence qui impose, pour des raisons entre autres économiques, une nouvelle règle : faire plus et mieux avec moins. Or, le défi se confirme lorsque l'on constate que le milieu d'intervention doit composer en plus, semble-t-il, avec la réticence des personnes-soutien[1] à l'égard de l'utilisation des services de soutien formels[2]. Ce phénomène de réticence est retracé dans la littérature scientifique et préoccupe nombre de chercheurs (Paquet, 1995a). Selon Garant et Bolduc (1990 : 116) : «[...] on observe dans plusieurs projets des difficultés à rejoindre les aidants et des réticences à utiliser les services offerts» .

Les intervenants sont parfois désarmés devant la réticence des personnes-soutien, et ce, même quand les services sont disponibles et accessibles (Paquet, 1995b). En effet, les professionnels réalisent que souvent, malgré l'ampleur du fardeau des personnes-soutien, il ne suffit pas de mettre sur pied des services pour qu'on soit assuré de leur utilisation. En fait, on comprend mal ce phénomène de réticence et aucune étude n'a été conduite pour améliorer véritablement la compréhension. Actuellement, la connaissance sur ce phénomène se limite à des éléments d'explication à caractère essentiellement anecdotique. Il apparaît donc primordial d'étudier cette réticence. En effet, il s'agit de combler notre manque de connaissances sur la réticence parce qu'elle constitue un obstacle à l'utilisation des services et, du même coup, à la prévention de l'épuisement physique et psychologique des personnes-soutien qui est, soit dit en passant, la priorité d'intervention auprès de cette population.

Compte tenu de l'absence de recherche sur la réticence des personnes-soutien, nous avons décidé d'explorer ce phénomène à partir du point de vue d'informateurs clés[3]. Plus précisément, l'objectif de ce texte est de répondre aux questions suivantes :

---

1. Par cette expression, nous entendons «une personne qui manifeste dans son discours et son comportement une réserve face à l'utilisation des services formels. Cette réticence peut se retrouver tant chez les utilisateurs de services que les non-utilisateurs qui connaissent les services ou en soupçonnent l'existence. Cette réticence peut prendre la forme d'un refus des services ou d'une acceptation obligée en raison du contexte de l'assistance ou de la condition de santé de la personne âgée et/ou de la personne-soutien» (Paquet, 1996a : 445).

2. Les services de soutien formels font ici référence aux services de répit institutionnels, communautaires ou à domicile, dispensés par le réseau des établissements publics ou communautaires.

3. Il s'agit de quatre spécialistes québécois : un anthropologue, un psychologue, un médecin et un professeur en sciences infirmières ayant une connaissance dans le champ de la recherche sur le soutien informel, de même que des dispensateurs de services de la région de Lanaudière (au nombre de 38). Ces derniers sont des professionnels (travailleurs sociaux, médecins, infirmières, auxiliaires familiales, etc.) et des cadres (gestionnaires œuvrant dans le domaine de la santé et des services sociaux). Ceux-ci sont rattachés au réseau public (CLSC, CA) et aux Centres d'action bénévole (CAB). Une analyse de contenu qualitative a été effectuée à partir du matériel recueilli par des entrevues individuelles et de groupes. Pour plus de détails sur la méthodologie, voir Paquet, 1996b.

1. Les personnes-soutien sont-elles vraiment réticentes à utiliser les services formels?

2. Sont-elles réticentes uniquement à l'égard des services formels?

3. Les personnes âgées aidées et les autres membres de la famille sont-ils aussi réticents?

4. La réticence varie-t-elle selon l'âge, le sexe, la proximité relationnelle et le milieu d'appartenance?

5. La réticence est-elle liée à la peur de la stigmatisation de la personne aidée et à des lacunes dans l'organisation des services?

Après avoir présenté les réponses à ces questions, nous proposons une conclusion qui fera ressortir les implications pratiques des différents constats que cette recherche permet d'établir.

LA RÉTICENCE ET LA PERSONNE-SOUTIEN

Les personnes-soutien sont-elles réticentes à utiliser les services formels?

Pour répondre à cette question, nous allons puiser dans un travail récent où nous avons démontré clairement l'existence du phénomène de la réticence des personnes-soutien face à l'utilisation des services de soutien formels. À cet égard, il ressort que:

> Le point de vue de la très grande majorité des informateurs clés rencontrés en entrevues appuie l'hypothèse de la réticence des personnes-soutien de personnes âgées dépendantes vis-à-vis l'utilisation des services de soutien formels. Il semble que la réticence n'est pas un phénomène isolé, mais une réalité avec laquelle le milieu de l'intervention doit composer quotidiennement. En effet, on observe la réticence chez plusieurs personnes-soutien. De plus, ces dernières ont tendance à peu utiliser les services disponibles même si elles en connaissent l'existence. Les personnes-soutien sont une «clientèle cible» particulièrement difficile à rejoindre. D'ailleurs, il est fréquent que celles-ci n'utilisent les services que lorsqu'il n'est pratiquement plus possible de faire autrement. Ainsi, pour faire face à la situation de la prise en charge, les personnes-soutien préfèrent choisir de se débrouiller avec les ressources de leur réseau informel (famille, entourage) avant de se tourner en définitive vers les services de soutien formels. (Paquet, 1995b: 45-46)

Cela étant dit, il faut indiquer que le recours au soutien formel comme choix potentiel de solution pour assurer la prise en charge de la personne âgée aidée ne se fait pas, normalement, en l'absence de celle-ci. Pour ce faire, il convient de se demander si la réticence ne serait pas aussi présente chez les personnes âgées aidées.

LA RÉTICENCE ET LA PERSONNE ÂGÉE AIDÉE

Les personnes âgées aidées sont-elles réticentes à utiliser les services formels ?

Le témoignage de nombre d'informateurs ne laisse pas de doute sur le caractère affirmatif de la réponse à cette question. Comme le fait remarquer l'un d'entre eux : « Quand on parle de réticence à accepter de l'aide, il y a l'opposition des personnes âgées. Elles ne veulent pas se faire aider par des intervenants étrangers. » (C2)[4] La réticence n'est donc pas un phénomène exclusif aux personnes-soutien. La personne aidée peut aussi être réticente à utiliser les services (C. CA).

Par rapport à l'opposition de la personne aidée, un informateur explique en prenant l'exemple de sa propre mère malade dont sa sœur était la personne-soutien principale. Alors que le CLSC lui avait offert un soutien pour l'entretien, la réponse de sa mère fut catégorique : « Pas question que je demande ça ; quand je ne serai plus capable d'entretenir ma maison, j'aimerais mieux mourir. » (C1) Pour la personne-soutien, il s'est avéré impossible de convaincre sa mère de recevoir du soutien à domicile de sorte que la situation était beaucoup plus difficile pour celle-ci. Décédée à 93 ans, cette dame appartenait à une génération où la norme était de se débrouiller seule dans la vie, où recevoir du soutien extérieur signifiait ne plus être en mesure de s'arranger soi-même, ce qui n'est pas facile à accepter.

Même si la personne-soutien a atteint le seuil de l'épuisement, il est fréquent que l'opposition des personnes aidées s'exerce par des pressions sur celle-ci pour ne pas utiliser les services. En fait, quoiqu'elles en soupçonnent l'existence, les personnes âgées connaissent mal les services offerts d'où la peur de l'inconnu et, comme il a été dit, des « étrangers ». Souvent, la personne aidée n'accepte pas d'autres personnes que la personne-soutien pour s'occuper d'elle, et pas seulement dans le cas des conjoints. Pour démontrer à quel point la personne aidée est

---

4. **Codes des participants**
   C.= Spécialiste (C1, C2, C3, C4)
   C.CA = Cadre, centre d'accueil   I.CA = Intervenant, centre d'accueil
   C. CAB = Cadre, centre d'action bénévole   I. CAB = Intervenant, centre d'action bénévole
   C.CLSC = Cadre, CLSC   I.CLSC = Intervenant, CLSC

réticente à l'idée de se faire aider par une autre personne que l'aidant régulier, il arrive que même si la personne-soutien bénéficie d'une ressource de gardiennage à la maison, celle-ci s'empêche «de sortir parce que la mère est réticente à se faire garder par quelqu'un qu'elle ne connaît pas» (I. CAB).

Il faut ajouter la peur du placement. Il semble que, si la personne-soutien accepte un hébergement temporaire, il en aille autrement de la personne aidée. En effet, même avec toute l'assurance du monde qu'il s'agit d'un séjour temporaire, celle-ci craint de ne pas revenir chez elle, d'autant plus que d'aller séjourner avec d'autres «vieux», ce n'est pas évident parce qu'inhabituel. De plus, pour la personne âgée, l'idée de se faire aider est déstabilisant par rapport à son propre vieillissement et, de surcroît, à son acceptation : «ça voudrais-tu dire que je suis trop vieux?» (I. CLSC) Or, qui de la personne-soutien et de la personne aidée est plus réticente à utiliser les services? Difficile à dire, il y a des situations où c'est la personne aidée qui ne veut rien changer aux arrangements de la prise en charge, tandis que dans d'autres occasions, c'est la personne-soutien. Cela est bien varié et dépend du contexte de soin (I. CLSC).

LA RÉTICENCE ET LES AUTRES MEMBRES DE LA FAMILLE

Les autres membres de la famille sont-ils réticents à utiliser les services de soutien formels?

Aux dires d'un informateur : «À l'extérieur de la dyade aidant-aidé, tout élément est perturbateur.» (C2) Cet informateur retrace un cas précis où «les autres membres de la famille n'ont été que des obstacles dans la recherche d'aide extérieure» (C2). Ce qui lui fait dire que : «Dans la cellule familiale, toute intrusion dans la dyade est perturbant.»

Des membres de la famille ont tendance à exercer des pressions, même jusqu'à culpabiliser les personnes-soutien, pour éviter ou retarder le placement parce que, selon eux, cela n'a pas de bon sens (I. CLSC). Ces pressions se font dans un contexte où les autres membres de la famille sont souvent peu disponibles pour aider, mais enclins à suggérer ce qu'il faut faire à la personne-soutien. Le paradoxe, c'est que le refus du soutien extérieur est justifié dans certains cas par une disponibilité avouée à vouloir contribuer aux partages des responsabilités : «Écoute, on va t'aider. On est capable de s'en occuper de maman. On est capable de t'en donner de l'aide.» (C3) Ce refus trouve une autre justification dans le fait que, de toute manière, la disponibilité du soutien formel sera très négligeable. En plus, il ne sera probablement pas celui que l'on souhaite obtenir : « Le CLSC ne te donnera rien ou tu n'auras pas les services que tu veux. Ils vont venir pourquoi ? Changer une couche, donner un bain une fois par semaine ? » (C3)

LA RÉTICENCE ET LE SOUTIEN FAMILIAL ET INFORMEL

La réticence des personnes-soutien vise-t-elle uniquement les services formels ?

À cet égard, il est intéressant de signaler que des personnes-soutien refusent même le soutien des membres de la famille. Le soutien des proches est parfois perçu comme du soutien extérieur. Par exemple, beaucoup de conjointes âgées « considèrent leur fille comme du soutien extérieur et vont trouver toutes les excuses possibles pour ne pas bénéficier de l'aide des enfants » (C4). Pour d'autres conjoints, il est fréquent qu'on ne veut pas déranger les enfants. En ce qui regarde un enfant qui prend soin d'un parent, la tendance n'est pas de demander du soutien des membres de la famille : « C'est rare qu'il va aller demander de l'aide. » (I. CLSC) D'habitude, les enfants savent d'avance que le soutien sera difficile à obtenir. Au début de la prise en charge, les enfants ont le réflexe de faire appel aux autres. Cependant, avec le temps, ceux-ci se retirent quelquefois en prétextant que si la personne-soutien a accepté cette responsabilité, c'est à elle de l'assumer. Quoiqu'il ne faille pas généraliser, la personne-soutien, à force de se faire dire non, tient pour acquis la non-disponibilité des autres membres de la famille (C. CLSC).

Pour ce qui est du soutien informel, il est commun de ne pas y faire appel car : « C'est plus facile d'appeler mon frère que d'appeler Joe Bleau, ou d'appeler son fils que d'appeler un étranger. Il y a une espèce d'illusion à l'effet qu'ils n'utilisent pas les services du réseau formel, mais en même temps, ils n'utilisent pas non plus ceux du réseau informel, communautaires entre autres. » (C. CLSC)

LA RÉTICENCE ET L'ÂGE, LE SEXE, LA PROXIMITÉ RELATIONNELLE ET LE MILIEU D'APPARTENANCE

La réticence varie-t-elle selon l'âge ?

Selon un intervenant de CLSC, les personnes-soutien de cinquante ans et moins ont plus tendance à demander du soutien que les personnes de cinquante ans et plus. Quoique maintenant les personnes âgées s'informent plus qu'auparavant sur les services publics, il apparaît que les cinquante ans et moins ont aussi plus tendance à s'informer sur les services disponibles et sur l'état de santé de la personne âgée. De surcroît, elles connaissent mieux les services du système public et elles ont le réflexe de plus s'y fier. De plus, le système de santé a été instauré depuis assez longtemps pour être intégré dans la gestion courante des pratiques de soins. Pour les cinquante ans et plus, le système est encore un grand inconnu qui fait peur. La référence première en regard du système demeure le médecin. Tout passe par lui, y compris la confiance : « La personne âgée attend que le médecin l'informe. Elle attend d'être rendue à bout pour se confier, mais c'est toujours au médecin qu'elle va se confier. » (I. CLSC) La meilleure prédisposition des cinquante ans et moins face à l'utilisation des services est, en partie, due à un niveau d'instruction plus élevé ainsi qu'à un mode de vie plus individualiste.

> La réticence varie-t-elle selon le sexe ? Il appert que les hommes sont moins réticents que les femmes à solliciter du soutien. Les hommes sont en général plus « vulnérables » dans une situation de prise en charge parce qu'ils sont démunis dans des tâches qui traditionnellement ne leur ont pas été confiées. Culturellement, la répartition entre les sexes des responsabilités familiales fait qu'il est moins dans la « nature » des hommes de prendre soin : « l'homme est plus tourné vers l'extérieur. Quand il devient aidant, c'est quelque chose de tout nouveau pour lui ; ce n'est pas naturel et ce n'est pas évident qu'il devient automatiquement un bon aidant. » (C. CA)

La réticence varie-t-elle selon la proximité relationnelle ?

À cet égard, un informateur mentionne que : « plus il y a une relation intime dans la famille, plus c'est difficile de demander du soutien » (I. CLSC). Cela dit, il est opportun de parler du cas particulier des conjoints. « Il faut séparer les conjoints des enfants (fils et filles) car la problématique n'est pas la même. Pour les conjoints, prendre soin, c'est un défi à surmonter. En fonction de ce défi, ils s'imaginent qu'ils sont obligés de tout faire seuls. Ils ne peuvent pas s'imaginer que d'autres personnes peuvent aider. » (I.CLSC)

La réticence varie-t-elle selon le milieu d'appartenance ?

Il est permis de croire que oui, car pour dire comme une intervenante de CLSC, en milieu rural : « C'est totalement différent. » C'est comme le jour et la nuit par comparaison au milieu urbain. En ville, les personnes se connaissent beaucoup moins alors qu'en campagne, elles se connaissent peut-être trop. Dans ce milieu, tout se sait rapidement et l'intervenant est un « étrange » peut-être encore plus dérangeant qu'en milieu urbain parce que l'anonymat est difficile à préserver. Le commérage, le « placotage » ou le « mémérage », comme on dit, est redouté : « Il y a des difficultés à intervenir dans ce milieu. Les gens ne veulent pas demander du soutien puisqu'ils savent que la voisine ou d'autres personnes vont aller commérer sur leur dos dans le village. » (I. CLSC) La peur du commérage est tellement présente que si une personne doit dispenser un service, la préférence et, parfois même l'exigence, est que cette personne ne soit pas de la place. De plus, pour des personnes du milieu rural, demander du soutien est perçu comme « une position de faiblesse », c'est « quêter quelque chose ». C'est aussi associé à la dépendance et plus péjorativement, au bien-être social. Enfin, en milieu rural comme en milieu urbain, il ne faut pas penser qu'il règne une seule attitude à l'égard du soutien extérieur. Une personne peut accepter de se faire aider par un voisin en qui elle a confiance comme une autre personne peut refuser sous le prétexte suivant : « [personne ne] va entrer chez nous pour voir comment je fonctionne. » (I. CLSC)

LA RÉTICENCE ET LA PEUR DE LA STIGMATISATION

La réticence est-elle liée à la peur de la stigmatisation de la personne aidée ?

Pour les personnes-soutien qui prennent soin d'une personne aux prises avec un problème de déficience cognitive, il est possible que la réticence provienne de la peur de voir l'aidé se faire stigmatiser : « La crainte du stigma est peut-être l'élément qui est le plus distinctif des cas comme la maladie d'Alzheimer. » (C2) Jadis, on cachait les personnes atteintes de démence ou d'un problème de santé mentale. Maintenant, avec les campagnes d'information et les efforts de sensibilisation autour de ces maladies, ce problème tend à diminuer. Toutefois, il y a encore aujourd'hui de la gêne à sortir la personne aidée à l'extérieur parce que ses comportements peuvent paraître « curieux » ou « bizarres ». Ce type de maladie est pour certains toujours « honteux ». Dès lors, on cache les personnes pour ne pas être jugé puisqu'il est très important, surtout dans les petites communautés, de bien paraître. L'image à projeter est celle du bien portant : « C'est tellement important de bien paraître dans la communauté. Il faut que tu paraisses en santé et que tout aille bien. » (C. CAB) D'autant plus que lorsque cela va mal, « les gens savent plus ou moins l'accepter » (C. CAB). Du reste, la peur de la stigmatisation conduit presque inévitablement, à plus ou moins long terme, à l'isolement, entre autres, de la personne-soutien. «En effet, la prise en charge de personnes âgées avec des troubles cognitifs comporte le risque particulier de renforcer l'insularité des ménages concernés.» (C2)

LA RÉTICENCE ET L'ORGANISATION DES SERVICES

La réticence est-elle liée à des lacunes dans l'organisation des services?

Plusieurs informateurs dénoncent l'accessibilité, le coût, le manque de coordination des services comme des lacunes qui entravent l'utilisation des services. Si la personne-soutien «freak ben raide» à l'idée de remplir la «paperasse», on imagine aussi l'ampleur de la complexité du système, de même que sa lourdeur. Les démarches pour obtenir un service sont donc onéreuses à bien des égards (questionnaires à remplir, intrusion dans le privé, coûts des services, etc.) sans compter que cela n'a rien de valorisant, étant donné que «la bureaucratie renvoie l'image que tu n'es pas capable de t'en sortir seul» (I. CLSC).

Nombre de doléances ressortent du manque de souplesse des services: «On n'a pas la souplesse nécessaire pour répondre en temps et lieu aux besoins les plus criants.» (C4) Par exemple, quand la personne-soutien fait une demande d'hébergement temporaire parce qu'elle est épuisée, ce n'est pas dans un an qu'elle désire une réponse. De plus, le manque de souplesse est parfois accompagné de services mal adaptés aux besoins. Il arrive que si une personne-soutien obtient du gardiennage à domicile, celle-ci soit obligée de respecter une consigne qui ne lui convient pas toujours, soit de sortir de la maison durant le temps de répit accordé. Or, ce n'est pas l'exception que des personnes-soutien ne savent pas trop quoi faire de ce temps de répit passé à l'extérieur du domicile. D'ailleurs, plusieurs aimeraient profiter de cette période de relâche comme une opportunité de vaquer librement à des activités courantes de la vie quotidienne: «Moi, je voudrais rester à la maison et m'occuper de mes affaires personnelles, ou faire la cuisine sans être dérangé, mais ils m'obligent à sortir à l'extérieur.» (C1)

Par ailleurs, non seulement les intervenants arrivent souvent trop tard pour prévenir l'épuisement, mais aussi ils interviennent avec une formation inadéquate: «Nous n'avons pas la formation nécessaire en psychologie et en anthropologie pour être aptes à pénétrer dans les familles autrement qu'en étrangers.» (C4) Cet état de fait est probablement encore plus vrai dans le cas de maladies de dégénérescence cognitive: «Les qualifications requises pour intervenir auprès de personnes atteintes, par exemple, de la maladie d'Alzheimer peuvent constituer des obstacles à ne pas utiliser des services. » (C2)

DISCUSSION ET CONCLUSION

Les données décrites précédemment révèlent que la réticence à l'égard de l'utilisation des services formels n'est pas unique aux personnes-soutien. Ce phénomène s'observe aussi chez des personnes âgées aidées et d'autres membres de la famille. Pour ce qui est des personnes âgées, d'autres travaux, comme celui de Moen (1978), confirment la réticence de ces dernières tandis que la revue de la littérature de Lévesque et Théolis (1993) va dans le même sens et valide en plus une partie des données présentées en indiquant que :

> [...] dans l'étude de Caserta et al. (1987), 16 % des aidants évoquent la crainte de laisser leur proche à des personnes qui lui sont étrangères comme raison de ne pas recourir à des services. Dans cet ordre de pensée, il semble que l'opposition des personnes atteintes de démence constitue un obstacle à l'utilisation des services [...] (p. 72)

Si comme nous l'avons déjà souligné, « la gestion de la prise en charge est négociée dans un processus dynamique de liens d'interaction entre les acteurs des différents systèmes de soutien (famille, informel, formel) » (Paquet, 1996 : 437), il est donc logique de penser que la personne âgée et les autres membres de la famille ne sont pas des individus passifs dans la détermination des solutions pour faire face à la situation. Ils sont en effet partie prenante dans le choix des ressources privilégiées et mobilisées pour les aider dans la résolution des problèmes. En ce sens, le milieu de la pratique doit prendre note que le soutien auprès des personnes âgées n'implique pas uniquement la personne-soutien même si celle-ci y joue un rôle déterminant. Ce soutien s'inscrit dans une dynamique familiale et la réticence émerge comme une consé-quence de cette dynamique. Ainsi, lorsque la présence d'une réticence est retracée au regard d'une offre de services, l'intervenant, afin d'assurer une utilisation adéquate et optimale des services, devrait orienter sa stratégie d'intervention en fonction d'un certain nombre de questions, à savoir : qui est réticent au sein de la famille ? Pourquoi ? Comment prend forme la réticence dans les rapports familiaux de négociation de la prise en charge ? Par exemple, la réticence se manifeste-t-elle sous forme de pression pour ne pas utiliser les services ? En gros, l'intervenant doit s'imprégner de la dynamique familiale de soutien afin de connaître les enjeux et les personnes faisant obstacle à l'utilisation des services. Il ne s'agit pas ici de forcer l'utilisation des services, mais dans le respect des membres de la famille impliqués dans la gestion de la prise en charge, de faire en sorte d'assurer des conditions favorables à la prévention de l'épuisement de la personne-soutien.

Par ailleurs, il a été démontré que les personnes-soutien ne sont pas réticentes qu'à l'égard des services formels. Il arrive que des personnes-soutien refusent le soutien des proches de la famille. Ce constat est intéressant à souligner dans la mesure où la recherche démontre que c'est d'abord vers la famille que l'on préfère se tourner pour se faire aider. Cependant, cette préférence ne veut pas dire automatiquement qu'en cas de besoin, les personnes-soutien mobiliseront le soutien de la famille. Ainsi, quand une personne-soutien ne sollicite pas le soutien des membres de la famille, l'intervenant qui oriente son action dans un objectif de répartition des responsabilités de la prise en charge a intérêt à savoir pourquoi il en est ainsi. Par exemple, est-ce parce que le soutien est constamment refusé ou trop difficile à obtenir ? Est-ce parce que la personne-soutien insiste pour se débrouiller seule ou ne veut absolument pas déranger ?

En outre, on a noté qu'il y a réticence face au soutien informel (entourage, organismes communautaires). Cela vient renforcer notre propos présenté ailleurs et selon lequel il est « somme toute préférable de parler de réticence vis-à-vis de toute forme d'aide venant de l'extérieur qu'elle soit formelle (services publics) ou informelle (communauté, entourage, famille) que de se limiter à la réticence face à l'utilisation des services [formels] » (Paquet, 1992 : 14).

La réticence semble varier selon l'âge, le sexe, la proximité relationnelle et le milieu d'appartenance. Il apparaît que les personnes de moins de cinquante ans et les hommes sont plus enclins à utiliser les services. En ce qui concerne les hommes, il faut rappeler, pour comprendre la mesure dans laquelle ils sont face à des responsabilités de soin que : « [...] les femmes jouent un rôle central dans l'organisation de la vie domestique, étant prioritairement affectées à la sphère familiale en société industrielle, alors que les hommes sont prioritairement affectés à la sphère du travail salarié » (Dandurant et Ouellette, 1992 : 27). Les femmes sont encore aujourd'hui « le pivot de la famille » (*Ibid.*) pour ce qui est de la responsabilité des soins et demeurent aussi normativement les « productrices de la santé » comme l'a clairement expliqué Saillant (1992). Au regard de la proximité relationnelle et du milieu d'appartenance, il est loisible de croire, si les informations sont justes, que les conjoints comparativement aux enfants ainsi que les personnes vivant en milieu rural sont plus réticents à utiliser les services. Bref, les informations précédentes offrent des indications précieuses au milieu d'intervention en ce qui touche le profil type de la personne-soutien réticente. Grosso modo, elle peut se décrire comme suit : une femme conjointe âgée de cinquante ans et plus avec un faible niveau d'instruction connaissant mal les services et habitant en milieu rural.

La réticence des personnes-soutien est probablement accentuée par la peur de la stigmatisation des personnes aidées qui souffrent d'une dégénérescence cognitive ou d'un problème de santé mentale. Le milieu d'intervention doit accorder une attention particulière aux personnes-soutien qui prennent soin d'une personne avec ce genre de problème, car les conséquences de la peur de la stigmatisation les rendent susceptibles de vivre un plus grand isolement. Finalement, la réticence semble, en partie, reliée à la structure d'organisation des services. À l'instar de plusieurs chercheurs, nous avons également retracé des lacunes (Germain, 1991 ; Guberman, Maheu et Maillé, 1991 ; Lévesque, Rochette et Paquet, 1990 ; Montgomery, 1984 ; Zarit, 1990). Ces chercheurs suggèrent de planifier des services accessibles, flexibles et coordonnés de même que d'assurer une formation appropriée aux intervenants.

En terminant, il a été démontré au cours des vingt dernières années comment la personne-soutien était l'élément clé du maintien à domicile. Or, la réticence à l'égard de l'utilisation des services peut entraver, à plus ou moins long terme, les efforts soutenus pour assurer le maintien à domicile de la personne âgée dépendante, donc son bien-être, car la personne-soutien risque de s'épuiser. Pour le milieu de la pratique, la réticence empêche de faire bénéficier de services pouvant contribuer à prévenir l'épuisement physique et psychologique de la personne-soutien. Les données de cette recherche ont divulgué des informations sur la réticence qui permettent de juger en partie de la complexité d'une expérience familiale de soins. Il est souhaitable que celles-ci soient intégrées dans la compréhension de la dynamique familiale de soins pour qu'elles fassent contrepoids aux obstacles à l'utilisation des services.

Finalement, il est somme toute indiqué de mentionner que cette recherche s'est limitée au point de vue des dispensateurs de services. Cependant, cette limite nous semble relative, car comme nous l'avons signalé ailleurs :

> La pertinence de rencontrer des informateurs clés est apparue, en cours d'entrevue, d'autant plus intéressante et légitime que leur discours traduit non seulement une logique de pratique professionnelle, mais aussi un vécu de personnes-soutien. En effet, à plusieurs reprises, il est arrivé que le témoignage s'entrecoupe, soit parce que l'informateur était ou avait été lui-même personne-soutien, soit parce qu'il connaissait quelqu'un (famille, entourage) aidant ou ayant aidé une personne âgée. Le lecteur attentif fera

sans doute la découverte de l'entrecroisement de ces deux discours qui, selon nous, révèle une sensibilité et une empathie peu communes, mais nécessaires à la compréhension des phénomènes humains. (Paquet, 1996b : 211)

D'ailleurs, un projet de recherche, actuellement en cours de réalisation, poursuit l'objectif de valider auprès des personnes-soutien les données recueillies auprès des dispensateurs de services.

Bibliographie

DANDURAND, R.B. et F.R. OUELLETTE (1992). *Entre autonomie et solidarité : parenté et soutien dans la vie de jeunes familles montréalaises*, Montréal, Institut québécois de recherche sur la culture (IQRC).

GARANT, L. et M. BOLDUC (1990). *L'aide par les proches : mythes et réalités,* Revue de littérature et réflexion sur les personnes âgées en perte d'autonomie, leurs aidants et aidantes naturelles et le lien avec les services formels, Québec, Direction de l'évaluation, Ministère de la Santé et des Services sociaux, Gouvernement du Québec.

GERMAIN, E. (1991). *Malades chroniques et familles aidantes au Québec, Une revue de littérature*, Centre local de services communautaires de Matane, Département de santé communautaire, Centre hospitalier régional de Rimouski.

GUBERMAN, N., MAHEU, P. et C. MAILLÉ (1991). « Et si l'amour ne suffisait pas... », dans *Femmes, familles et adultes dépendants*, Montréal, Remue-ménage.

LÉVESQUE, L. et M. THÉOLIS (1993). *Recension des écrits sur les services de répit à domicile destinés aux aidants naturels de personnes atteintes de démence,* Université de Montréal, Faculté des sciences infirmières.

LÉVESQUE, L., ROCHETTE, N. et M. PAQUET (1990). *Revue des écrits sur les programmes d'hébergement temporaire et de centre de jour en fonction des personnes atteintes de maladies démentielles et de leurs aidants naturels,* Rapport présenté aux Centres d'accueil Sainte-Élisabeth et Saint-Thomas de la région de Lanaudière, Université de Montréal, Faculté des sciences infirmières.

MOEN, E. (1978). « The Reluctance of the Elderly to Accept Help », *Social Problem*, vol. 25, 293-303.

MONTGOMERY, R.J.V. (1984). « Services for Families of the Aged : Which Ones Will Work Best ? », *Aging*, vol. 47, 16-21.

PAQUET, M. (1992). « La problématique d'intervention auprès des personnes-soutien de personnes âgées ou le défi de la prévention en santé mentale », *Le Gérontophile*, vol. 14, n° 2, 3-7.

PAQUET, M. (1995a). « La prévention auprès des personnes-soutien de personnes âgées dépendantes. Quelle prévention ? », *Revue canadienne de service social*, vol. 12, n° 1, 45-71.

PAQUET, M. (1995b). « Coup de pouce et pédale douce ou la règle du gros bon sens comme repère éthique de la prévention auprès des personnes-soutien de personnes âgées dépendantes », *Le Gérontophile*, vol. 17, n° 1, 42-46.

PAQUET, M. (1996a). «La réticence des personnes-soutien de personnes âgées dépendantes vis-à-vis de l'utilisation des services de soutien formels : un défi pour le milieu de la recherche et de l'intervention», *Revue canadienne de gérontologie*, vol. 15 , n° 3, 442-462.

PAQUET, M. (1996b). «Logique familiale de soutien et réticence à recourir aux services formels», *Ruptures,* vol. 3, n° 2, 209-223.

SAILLANT, F. (1992). «La part des femmes dans les soins de santé, *Revue internationale d'action communautaire*, vol. 28, n° 68, 95-106.

ZARIT, S.H. (1990). «Interventions with Frail Elders and their Families : Are They Effective and Why ?» dans PARRIS, S.M.A. *et al.* (dir.), *Stress and Coping in Later-Life Families*, New York, Hemisphere Publishing Corporation, 241-265.

❖ # Personnes âgées et résidences privées : le partage recherché des responsabilités entre le secteur public et le secteur privé

Aline VÉZINA
Jacques ROY
Daniel PELLETIER
École de service social
Centre de recherche sur les services communautaires
Université Laval

Cette recherche a été réalisée dans la région de Québec, en collaboration avec la Régie régionale de la santé et des services sociaux, les CLSC, les propriétaires de résidences privées pour personnes âgées et le Centre de recherche sur les services communautaires de l'Université Laval. Quatre objectifs sont poursuivis, soit tracer un portrait de la clientèle âgée hébergée dans les chambres et pensions, connaître les attentes des propriétaires à l'égard des CLSC, cerner les responsabilités du secteur privé et du secteur public pour assurer le bien-être des personnes âgées et, finalement, élaborer les paramètres d'un cadre de référence.

Cette recherche puise ses origines dans la volonté de mieux connaître la clientèle âgée du réseau des résidences privées, notamment les résidences de type chambre et pension[1]. De plus, elle vise à amorcer les discussions et à alimenter la réflexion entourant le partage des responsabilités entre le secteur privé et le secteur public afin de maintenir et de favoriser le bien-être des personnes âgées en perte d'autonomie hébergées dans les résidences privées.

Au cours des dernières années, le secteur des résidences privées pour personnes âgées a connu une croissance rapide. Certains auteurs, dont Forest et al. (1990), Saucier (1989) et Vaillancourt et al. (1993), y voient l'effet combiné du nombre restreint de places disponibles dans le réseau d'hébergement public et des difficultés vécues par les CLSC qui, en raison d'une clientèle de plus en plus nombreuse et en perte de plus en plus importante d'autonomie, dispensent moins d'heures de service par client. Le développement du réseau des résidences privées pour personnes âgées reçoit nombre de qualificatifs : rapide, non contrôlé, clandestin, illégal et ainsi de suite. Ces qualificatifs visent principalement les résidences privées sans permis, c'est-à-dire non agréées par le ministère de la Santé et des Services sociaux, qui accueillent des personnes âgées présentant des pertes d'autonomie fonctionnelle et cognitive (Leroux et Dion, 1992). Cette situation soulève des interrogations quant au type et à la qualité des services offerts à cette clientèle qui nécessite souvent de l'aide et des soins professionnels. Il est important de souligner que les demandes de la part des propriétaires de résidences privées se font de plus en plus nombreuses et pressantes pour que les CLSC offrent des services de maintien à domicile à leur clientèle âgée en perte d'autonomie, au même titre qu'ils en dispensent aux personnes âgées qui habitent chez elles ou chez un membre de leur famille. Bien que la perspective de maintien des personnes âgées dans leur milieu naturel soit réaffirmée dans plusieurs documents gouvernementaux (MSSS, 1990 ; 1992 ; 1994a), il existe peu, voire pas de règles d'application précises entourant les responsabilités de l'État et des propriétaires de résidences privées, eu égard aux services qu'ils peuvent et doivent dispenser aux personnes âgées en perte d'autonomie hébergées dans le secteur privé.

Quatre objectifs guident notre démarche : 1) tracer un portrait de la clientèle âgée hébergée dans les résidences privées de type chambre et pension, 2) connaître les relations et les attentes des propriétaires des

---

1. Les résultats détaillés de l'étude sont présentés dans A. VÉZINA, D. PELLETIER et J. ROY (1994). *Les résidences privées et HLM pour personnes âgées de la région de Québec : profils des ressources et clientèles et paramètres d'un cadre de référence*, Québec, Centre de recherche sur les services communautaires, Université Laval, 120 pages.

résidences privées à l'égard des CLSC, 3) cerner les responsabilités du secteur privé (les propriétaires de résidences privées) et du secteur public (la Régie régionale de la santé et des services sociaux et les CLSC) pour assurer le bien-être des personnes âgées et 4) élaborer les paramètres d'un cadre de référence, c'est-à-dire quelques éléments ou balises à partir desquels pourrait se construire un cadre de référence entre les trois partenaires retenus pour les fins de notre recherche.

PORTRAIT DE LA CLIENTÈLE ÂGÉE HÉBERGÉE DANS LES CHAMBRES ET PENSIONS

Méthodologie

Le premier objectif de la présente étude est de dresser un portrait de la clientèle âgée hébergée dans les chambres et pensions de la région de Québec, en termes de caractéristiques sociodémographiques, de niveau d'autonomie, de types de services reçus et de relations avec la famille. Afin de répertorier les résidences privées pour personnes âgées, nous avons, en premier lieu, utilisé la liste de la Régie régionale de la santé et des services sociaux de Québec, préalablement vue et corrigée par les représentants de l'ensemble des CLSC de la région de Québec. À cette liste se sont ajoutés des noms de résidences fournis par la firme de conseillers Guay-Genest et Bernier Inc. de Québec. Bien que cette liste ne soit pas exhaustive et qu'elle soit susceptible de se modifier au cours des mois et des années, elle renferme tout de même la presque totalité des résidences privées pour personnes âgées connues par les divers intervenants de la région de Québec, en date du 15 octobre 1993. Nous avons recensé 124 chambres et pensions qui hébergent 2 894 personnes âgées. Afin d'obtenir un échantillon représentatif, avec un taux d'erreur scientifiquement acceptable de 10 %, nous avons sélectionné 96 personnes âgées (Krejcie et Morgan, 1970).

Dans un premier temps, 25 résidences privées sont sélectionnées au hasard, parmi les 124 recensées, sans tenir compte du nombre de pensionnaires. Le ratio équivaut à peu près à une résidence sur quatre. Cette procédure permet d'éviter que les résidences ayant le plus grand nombre de pensionnaires aient plus de probabilités d'être choisies. Dans un deuxième temps, 96 personnes âgées sont réparties au hasard parmi les pensionnaires des 25 résidences identifiées, en tenant compte du ratio entre le nombre de pensionnaires hébergés dans la résidence sur le nombre total de pensionnaires dans l'ensemble des 25 résidences.

Les propos des personnes âgées sont recueillis à l'aide d'un questionnaire construit spécialement pour les fins de la recherche. La très grande
majorité des questions comporte un choix de réponses (questions fermées)
qui sont cochées par l'interviewer. Quelques questions ouvertes se rappor-
tant entre autres aux motifs du choix de la résidence, à l'énumération des
problèmes de santé et aux stratégies envisagées pour faire face à un
problème urgent de santé, font l'objet d'une brève analyse de contenu.

Résultats

Voici, sous une forme synthétique, les principaux résultats qui ressortent
des analyses.

– Les personnes hébergées sont majoritairement des femmes et
  des veuves âgées en moyenne de 81,7 ans.

– Près des trois quarts des personnes âgées mentionnent avoir des
  problèmes de santé limitant leurs déplacements ; 38,5 % ne
  sortent pas de la résidence.

– Près de la moitié des personnes âgées constatent que leurs capacités ont diminué ou fortement diminué durant la dernière année.

– Pour 21 activités de la vie quotidienne et domestique sur les 23
  retenues lors des entrevues, les personnes âgées mentionnent
  que ce sont les employés de la résidence d'hébergement qui leur
  apportent de l'aide ou exécutent les activités à leur place.

– Les services de santé sont très majoritairement reçus à la résidence et dispensés par le personnel infirmier de la résidence.
  Les organismes communautaires interviennent à l'occasion pour
  offrir du transport ou des visites d'amitié.

– Les contacts avec la famille se font surtout par téléphone.

– Près du quart des personnes âgées mentionne ne recevoir
  aucune aide ou soutien moral des membres de leur famille.

LES RELATIONS ET LES ATTENTES DU SECTEUR PRIVÉ À L'ÉGARD DES CLSC

Méthodologie

Le deuxième objectif de la présente étude est de mieux connaître les
relations et les attentes des propriétaires ou responsables des résidences
privées à l'égard des CLSC. Afin de recueillir les informations pertinentes,

nous avons construit un bref questionnaire qui contient majoritairement des questions fermées entourant les services reçus du CLSC par les personnes âgées hébergées dans leur résidence ainsi que les collaborations souhaitées par les propriétaires ou responsables. Le questionnaire est expédié par la poste à l'ensemble des 124 propriétaires ou responsables de chambres et pensions recensés. Quatre-vingt-cinq d'entre eux ont retourné le questionnaire complété, ce qui donne un taux de réponse de 68 %, se répartissant sur l'ensemble des dix territoires de CLSC de la région de Québec.

Pour les fins de notre recherche, nous retenons, comme services de santé dispensés par le CLSC, les suivants : les prélèvements, les pansements, les services d'ergothérapie et les services de physiothérapie. Comme services psychosociaux, nous retenons la relocalisation dans un centre d'accueil public et le support psychosocial. En ce qui concerne les attentes à l'égard du CLSC, trois propositions sont explorées : que le CLSC organise des rencontres régulières pour faire le point sur les collaborations entre le secteur privé et public, que le CLSC favorise le regroupement des résidences privées pour personnes âgées du territoire et que le CLSC apporte de l'aide pour assurer la qualité des services.

Résultats

Voici, sous une forme synthétique, les principaux résultats.

- Plus de 90 % des propriétaires ou responsables de résidences privées mentionnent avoir actuellement ou avoir eu dans le passé des contacts avec le CLSC.

- En ce qui concerne les services dispensés par le CLSC, 80 % mentionnent que certaines personnes âgées hébergées dans leur résidence ont déjà fait faire des prélèvements par le CLSC et 60 % précisent que certaines personnes âgées ont déjà utilisé les services du CLSC pour être relocalisées dans un centre d'accueil public. Les autres services à l'étude ont été mentionnés par moins de 30 % des propriétaires ou responsables.

- Près de 80 % des propriétaires ou responsables sont favorables à l'idée de recevoir de l'aide de la part des CLSC pour assurer la qualité des services. Cependant, ils réaffirment la qualité des services qu'ils donnent et l'attention qu'ils portent au bien-être de leurs pensionnaires. L'aide du CLSC est bien accueillie lorsqu'elle s'inscrit dans un climat de collaboration.

– De nombreux propriétaires sont satisfaits de la relation qui existe actuellement avec le CLSC de leur territoire. Ils désirent que cette relation conserve son caractère de « au besoin » ou « sur appel » telle qu'elle est actuellement.

LES RESPONSABILITÉS DU SECTEUR PRIVÉ ET DU SECTEUR PUBLIC

Méthodologie

Le troisième objectif de la présente étude est de mieux cerner les responsabilités qui incombent au secteur privé et au secteur public, pour assurer le bien-être des personnes âgées en perte d'autonomie, hébergées dans les résidences privées. Afin de recueillir les données pertinentes, nous avons utilisé le *focus group* lors d'une rencontre d'une durée de trois heures tenue à l'Université Laval. Ont participé à cette rencontre deux représentants des CLSC et un représentant de la Régie régionale de la santé et des services sociaux de Québec ainsi que cinq propriétaires ou responsables de résidences d'hébergement de type chambre et pension. Les propriétaires des résidences d'hébergement ont été sélectionnés au hasard parmi les résidences répertoriées. Ils ont accepté de participer à la rencontre sur une base volontaire et non rémunérée. Les représentants du secteur public ont été nommés en raison de leur implication dans le dossier de l'hébergement de personnes âgées en résidences privées. Trois thèmes principaux ont été abordés lors de la rencontre : 1) l'alourdissement de la clientèle âgée hébergée dans les résidences privées, 2) le choix d'une résidence : les mécanismes de référence et l'accréditation, 3) la qualité des services et la qualité de vie.

Résultats

Voici, sous une forme synthétique, les principaux résultats de la rencontre. Le texte qui suit comprend tantôt des constats, tantôt des souhaits.

Les responsabilités des propriétaires de résidences privées

Il est constaté que :

– Les propriétaires des résidences privées fournissent certains services de base comme le gîte et le couvert et autres services connexes comme la literie, la buanderie. Lorsque la personne est en perte d'autonomie, ils font appel à plus de personnel pour offrir ces services de base. La gestion financière et la gestion du personnel sont plus difficiles. Cependant, les propriétaires mentionnent une « responsabilité morale » qui se traduisent par la garde de la personne âgée malgré ses pertes d'autonomie et cela, souvent à la demande de cette dernière et au-delà des intérêts pécuniaires.

– En plus des services de base, ils offrent un ensemble de services « à la carte » (aide pour le bain, se vêtir et se dévêtir, etc.). Les coûts de ces services sont bien souvent assumés par le client et sont tarifés à l'acte ou selon une entente de services. Cette tarification de services pose parfois certains problèmes avec la clientèle : préoccupations quant à leur capacité à payer, étonnement face à un tarif pour chaque service rendu, etc.

– Dans la plupart des résidences, une évaluation sommaire du niveau d'autonomie de la personne âgée est faite par la personne responsable de la résidence, lors d'une entrevue en vue de l'admission.

– Les propriétaires de résidences privées recrutent eux-mêmes leurs clientèles (publicité et feuillets d'information, le bouche à oreille). Ils peuvent également faire appel à des firmes privées spécialisées dans l'hébergement des aînés. L'utilisation de ces services soulève à l'occasion certains commentaires entourant les coûts.

Il est souhaité que :

– Les services de base et les services à la carte soient bien identifiés dans un bail type utilisé par l'ensemble des résidences privées.

– Les propriétaires assument de différentes manières l'évaluation de l'autonomie de leurs clientèles et qu'ils précisent, dans les feuillets publicitaires et lors de l'admission, le niveau d'autonomie de la clientèle visée.

– Ces derniers rapportent les problèmes de santé de la personne âgée aux membres de sa famille.

– Les propriétaires assurent la qualité des services offerts. Selon les propriétaires, la réputation de leur établissement est très importante autant en ce qui concerne les résidents que les intervenants du secteur public.

– Les propriétaires participent au processus d'évaluation des services dans une perspective de concertation.

– Les propriétaires signalent, au CLSC, les personnes âgées pour lesquelles les services offerts ne correspondent plus aux besoins.

Les responsabilités du CLSC

Il est constaté que :

- Les services du CLSC sont disponibles à toute personne résidant à domicile et / ou en résidence privée. Dans les faits, cela est vrai pour l'ensemble des soins de santé. Pour les services d'aide, la personne âgée doit répondre aux critères et aux priorités définis par chacun des CLSC.

- Dans les résidences privées, les services d'aide sont offerts tout particulièrement aux personnes en attente d'hébergement dans le secteur public.

- Le CLSC n'a pas un rôle défini quant à la référence vers des résidences d'hébergement privées. Essentiellement, certains CLSC offrent des listes d'adresses des résidences privées de leur territoire. Quelques CLSC ont développé un guide pour aider les personnes âgées qui sont à la recherche de résidences d'hébergement. Ce guide leur indique quelques critères de choix et des questions à poser au responsable de la résidence.

- Les représentants des CLSC ont surtout exprimé certaines préoccupations entourant leur rôle d'évaluateurs de la qualité des services dans les résidences privées : manque de ressources humaines et financières, manque de critères et d'instruments d'évaluation, malaise quant à un rôle de « police sociale ».

- Le CLSC reconnaît son mandat de protection sociale et son rôle de première ligne entourant le dépistage des situations à risque (résidences sans permis, personnes âgées en difficulté).

Les responsabilités de la Régie régionale de la santé
et des services sociaux

Il est souhaité que :

- Cette dernière suive le dossier de l'alourdissement des clientèles âgées et assume la responsabilité du développement des liens entre l'hébergement privé et l'hébergement public.

- La Régie assume la responsabilité de l'émission de permis touchant les résidences privées aptes à prendre en charge des personnes non autonomes ou en perte d'autonomie.

- La Régie veille au développement de modalités de financement telles que l'allocation directe, l'achat de services, l'achat de places en résidences privées, etc.

 – Cette dernière définisse, de façon opérationnelle, les critères qui permettent de déterminer les limites de l'autonomie et de la non-autonomie des personnes âgées, dans le contexte de l'hébergement privé.

ÉLÉMENTS D'UN CADRE DE RÉFÉRENCE ENTOURANT LE PARTAGE DES RESPONSABILITÉS ENTRE LE SECTEUR PRIVÉ ET LE SECTEUR PUBLIC

Cette dernière section aborde les différents éléments ou paramètres d'un cadre de référence entourant le partage des responsabilités entre les trois partenaires retenus pour les fins de notre étude. Ces éléments sont le résultat d'une synthèse des différentes données recueillies dans le cadre de notre recherche ainsi que de la consultation de divers documents pertinents. Cet exercice de synthèse a comme principal objectif d'alimenter la réflexion des instances impliquées dans ce dossier. Il est important de rappeler qu'il ne s'agit pas d'énoncés définissant un cadre de référence, mais plutôt de balises à partir desquelles pourrait se construire un cadre de référence.

Deux questions de fond

Comme il a été mentionné précédemment, la très grande majorité des services sociosanitaires reçus par les personnes âgées en perte d'autonomie hébergées dans les résidences privées sont dispensés par le personnel des résidences et ce, moyennant des coûts plus ou moins importants qui doivent être assumés par la personne âgée elle-même. Cela fait référence à ce qu'il est convenu d'appeler les services «à la carte». D'après les propos recueillis dans notre étude, les CLSC de la région de Québec offrent peu de services dans les résidences privées, sauf dans les cas où la personne âgée est en attente d'hébergement dans un centre d'accueil public. Ce constat soulève une première question à savoir : est-ce que les personnes âgées en perte d'autonomie, hébergées dans les résidences privées, devraient recevoir les services de soutien à domicile dispensés par le CLSC au même titre que les personnes âgées en perte d'autonomie qui habitent chez elles ou chez des parents ? En plus de l'accessibilité des services de soutien à domicile dans les résidences privées s'imposent les rôles de prévention et de protection sociale dévolus aux CLSC. Est-ce qu'il est de la responsabilité des CLSC de protéger les personnes âgées en perte d'autonomie hébergées dans les résidences privées, en leur assurant des services de qualité et un milieu de vie sécuritaire?

Les critères de perte d'autonomie: une interprétation élastique

Selon les dires des propriétaires de résidences privées, plusieurs personnes âgées hébergées dans les résidences privées sont en perte d'autonomie fonctionnelle et/ou cognitive. Le qualificatif de personne en perte d'autonomie est attribué bien souvent de manière très subjective. Notons qu'il n'existe pas de définition couramment acceptée et applicable, de manière uniforme, aux diverses situations qui se présentent au personnel et aux responsables des résidences privées. Dans un guide produit par le ministère de la Santé et des Services sociaux du Québec, nous retrouvons la définition suivante:

> La personne démontre normalement une perte d'autonomie lorsqu'elle requiert régulièrement de l'aide pour les activités de la vie quotidienne telles que manger, se lever, se laver, etc., pour faire contrôler sa prise de médicaments et lorsqu'elle nécessite des soins infirmiers réguliers, une stimulation pour manger, une surveillance pour ne pas s'égarer ou présente des signes de confusion ou un besoin de protection. Conséquemment [...] en deçà du seuil critique d'une heure/soins par jour pour déterminer la perte d'autonomie d'une personne à admettre en CHSLD [...] une personne ne se qualifiant pas à une admission en CHSLD peut demeurer à domicile ou dans une résidence privée d'hébergement selon les circonstances. (MSSS,1993a: 3)

Cette définition sommaire connaît, dans la pratique, une certaine extension dans son application. Les différents intervenants du réseau public définissent généralement la perte d'autonomie en fonction du seuil critique d'admission au réseau d'hébergement public, soit une heure de soins par jour, résultant d'une évaluation à partir de la CTMSP (EROS, 1987). Par ailleurs, on note que selon les données des comités d'admission-orientation du réseau public, le seuil critique d'admission au réseau d'hébergement public tend plutôt vers trois heures de soins par jour (Garand, 1994; Trahan et Bélanger, 1993).

En ce qui concerne les définitions de l'autonomie et de la non-autonomie, utilisées par les responsables des résidences privées, elles correspondent à des estimations approximatives. De ce fait, il est parfois difficile de statuer clairement si une personne âgée habitant en résidence privée est en réelle perte d'autonomie au sens de la loi.

**Avoir ou ne pas avoir un permis :
une pièce importante sur l'échiquier**

L'ensemble des données recueillies témoignent de la charge de travail
et des responsabilités sans cesse croissantes qui incombent aux responsables des résidences privées, en raison de l'alourdissement des clientèles.
Cette situation soulève l'importance d'une meilleure sélection de leur
clientèle afin de préserver leur vocation de milieu de vie pour personnes
âgées autonomes. En général, les responsables des résidences privées
assument seuls l'évaluation sommaire de l'autonomie des personnes
âgées, lors de l'admission ou dans un suivi plus ou moins informel de
l'état de santé de leurs résidents. Cette évaluation permet de déterminer
les services complémentaires, c'est-à-dire « à la carte », nécessités par
l'état de santé de la personne âgée ainsi que les possibilités du personnel
engagé de dispenser ces services. Cette situation présente des aspects
litigieux particulièrement pour les résidences sans permis. En effet, pour
reprendre les termes d'un document du ministère de la Santé et des
Services sociaux du Québec concernant les interventions effectuées dans
les ressources sans permis en vertu des dispositions de l'article 489 de
la *Loi sur les services de santé et les services sociaux* (L.R.Q., chapitre
S-4.2) :

> Nous entendons par ressource sans permis, la ressource qui héberge des
> personnes [...] en perte d'autonomie fonctionnelle ou psychosociale,
> requérant [...] de l'assistance, du soutien et de la surveillance ainsi que des
> services de réadaptation, psychosociaux, infirmiers, pharmaceutiques et
> médicaux. (MSSS, 1993b : 9)

Rappelons en terminant que les responsables des résidences
privées pour personnes âgées sont souvent très mal instrumentés pour
faire une évaluation appropriée du degré d'autonomie de leur clientèle.
De plus, l'état de santé des personnes hébergées peut se détériorer très
rapidement dans les semaines et les mois suivant leur admission.

LES SERVICES OFFERTS PAR QUI,
À QUI ET À QUEL PRIX ?

Aux portes de l'iniquité

Comme il a été mentionné à plusieurs reprises dans les pages précédentes, les CLSC de la région de Québec dispensent peu de services
sociosanitaires aux personnes âgées en perte d'autonomie hébergées
dans les résidences privées. Ils interviennent à l'occasion, selon certaines

priorités propres à chacun des CLSC, particulièrement auprès de personnes âgées en attente d'hébergement public. Les données recueillies nous permettent de croire que la clientèle âgée des résidences privées a un accès plus limité aux services de soutien à domicile que les autres clientèles âgées vivant dans la communauté. Selon la loi, les CLSC sont responsables de la prestation des services de première ligne au domicile des personnes. Dans le document intitulé « Les services à domicile de première ligne. Cadre de référence », le domicile est défini comme :

> Le lieu où réside la personne, au sens d'un logement privé ou d'un établissement domestique autonome, ce qui comprend la maison privée, le logement ou l'appartement, la chambre, le logement dans un HLM. Les logements situés dans des conciergeries ou dans des résidences privées offrant des services à des personnes retraitées ou semi-retraitées sont considérés comme des domiciles seulement pour les services non couverts dans les baux ou contrats convenus entre les promoteurs ou propriétaires et les locataires. (MSSS, 1994a : 10)

Cette définition soulève la nécessité d'identifier clairement et de façon uniforme, pour l'ensemble des résidences privées, les services essentiels qui doivent être dispensés aux locataires. Pour les autres services sociosanitaires nécessaires au bien-être de la personne âgée en perte d'autonomie, les CLSC, dans le cadre de leur programme de maintien à domicile, devront établir des critères uniformes d'admissibilité aux services qui permettront de guider les intervenants dans l'élaboration des plans de services.

L'ÉVALUATION DE LA QUALITÉ DES SERVICES : LE MALAISE DES CLSC

Le rôle du CLSC, partagé avec la Régie régionale de la santé et des services sociaux, se définit également en termes de protection sociale des personnes âgées en perte d'autonomie qui peuvent être victimes d'abus. Dans le contexte des relations avec les résidences privées, ce mandat s'accompagne d'un rôle de prévention et de dépistage des situations à risque, particulièrement en ce qui concerne les foyers clandestins. (L.R.Q., Loi 120, art. 80) Cette tâche est définie dans plusieurs documents (Bohémier *et al.*, 1992 ; Lemasson, 1993, 1994 ; MSSS, 1990, 1992) et peut se résumer ainsi :

> Tel qu'annoncé dans le cadre de la réforme du système de santé et des services sociaux, les CLSC devront, afin d'éviter la présence de foyers clandestins – recenser les résidences privées d'hébergement sur leur territoire ; – prendre arrangement avec les municipalités pour obtenir l'information sur tout permis de chambre délivré pour l'hébergement de

personnes âgées sur leur territoire, – visiter régulièrement les résidences pour évaluer le degré d'autonomie des personnes hébergées – considérer les personnes habitant ces résidences comme admissibles aux programmes de maintien à domicile ; – rapporter au Ministère, aux fins de poursuite pénale ou de fermeture, toute résidence à l'intérieur de laquelle seront constatées des conditions pouvant causer de graves préjudices aux personnes âgées qui y sont hébergées. (MSSS,1990 :27)

En juin 1994, un premier inventaire des résidences privées de l'ensemble de la province a été réalisé par le ministère de la Santé et des Services sociaux du Québec. Le plan d'action concernant les résidences privées pour personnes âgées non titulaires d'un permis du ministère de la Santé et des Services sociaux publié récemment mentionne à l'égard de l'évaluation des besoins des personnes âgées :

Le Ministère de la santé et des services sociaux entend donc prendre des mesures pour s'assurer que la personne âgée requérant des soins, de l'aide ou de l'assistance, trouve réponse à ses besoins. À cet égard, les CLSC identifieront les personnes ayant des besoins de services et procéderont à une évaluation sommaire afin de définir le type et l'ampleur des services requis. (MSSS, 1994b :13)

Les tâches précédemment citées soulèvent l'ambiguïté du rôle des CLSC dans le dossier de l'évaluation des services dispensés par les résidences privées. Une part du malaise ressenti par les intervenants des CLSC vient de l'absence de directives claires concernant le type de relations qu'ils doivent entretenir avec les résidences privées. Rappelons ici la crainte exprimée par les représentants des CLSC rencontrés dans le cadre de notre étude quant au rôle de police sociale qui se dégage de l'évaluation des résidences privées. Notons également que le manque de ressources humaines et financières dans le secteur des services de soutien à domicile dispensés par les CLSC rend difficile, sinon impossible, la réalisation de visites régulières des résidences pour l'évaluation du degré d'autonomie des personnes âgées et encore plus difficile une évaluation de la qualité des services offerts dans ces résidences. Les intervenants des CLSC sont peu instrumentés pour évaluer la qualité des services offerts dans les résidences privées.

DISCUSSION

Ce questionnement entourant les responsabilités du secteur public et du secteur privé, eu égard au bien-être des personnes âgées en perte d'autonomie, s'inscrit au cœur même de la réforme québécoise entourant la prestation des services publics en matière de santé et de services sociaux. Bien que le nombre de résidences privées pour personnes âgées ait

progressé rapidement au cours des dernières années, leur apport, dans
le maintien des personnes âgées en perte d'autonomie dans la communauté, est devenu incontournable, particulièrement depuis la mise en
place des mesures visant le virage ambulatoire. Les décisions politiques
entourant la non-institutionnalisation des personnes âgées, la réduction
du temps d'hospitalisation et le support souvent insuffisant des CLSC
qui dispensent les services à domicile font en sorte qu'un nombre de plus
en plus important de personnes âgées, en perte importante d'autonomie,
font face aux difficultés d'être hébergées dans une institution publique
et, de ce fait, les familles soignantes s'épuisent à la tâche. Les enjeux
politiques et économiques actuels accentuent l'urgence d'envisager de
nouvelles pratiques qui ouvrent la porte à la collaboration avec d'autres
partenaires tel le réseau des résidences privées.

Aborder l'évaluation des services offerts par les résidences privées
aux personnes âgées en perte d'autonomie est un sujet difficile. Les
difficultés tiennent, entre autres, au fait que les intervenants des services
publics et les propriétaires de résidences privées peuvent avoir, chacun
de leur côté, des images biaisées, souvent généralisantes envers l'autre.
Ainsi, pour le secteur public, d'aucuns peuvent percevoir les propriétaires
de ressources privées comme des « exploiteurs », des gens sans scrupule,
qui abusent de la confiance des personnes âgées, en leur offrant des
services de qualité douteuse, à des coûts exorbitants. Cette image est
trop souvent celle qui nous est montrée par les médias d'information.
Il existe très certainement des personnes âgées maltraitées dans les
résidences privées et des actions s'imposent pour y remédier rapidement.
Cependant, il faut éviter le piège d'une généralisation outrancière qui
aurait pour effet d'accoler une fausse identité au réseau des résidences
privées et, de ce fait, de fermer la porte à d'éventuelles collaborations
fructueuses. De l'autre côté, les services publics peuvent être perçus par
les propriétaires de résidences privées comme des « polices sociales » qui
surveillent leurs moindres gestes et exigent d'eux une qualité de services
que même les centres d'accueil publics ne respectent pas.

La démarche réalisée dans le cadre de cette recherche interpelle
directement les rôles et les responsabilités dévolus à la Régie régionale
de la santé et des services sociaux, soit assumer la planification et l'évaluation de l'ensemble des services et voir à l'opérationnalisation et à
l'harmonisation des mécanismes d'évaluation des besoins de la clientèle.
L'élaboration d'un cadre de référence devrait assurer la mise en place
de mesures qui favorisent et actualisent la coordination et la concertation
entre les résidences privées qui accueillent des personnes âgées en perte
d'autonomie et les organismes publics, dans la région de Québec. Selon
les partenaires interrogés dans le cadre de notre étude, il est de la

responsabilité de la Régie régionale de la santé et des services sociaux de faire évoluer ce dossier.

Bien que notre recherche eût comme objectif de mieux connaître la clientèle hébergée dans les résidences privées de Québec et d'échanger avec les propriétaires concernant leurs attentes à l'égard des CLSC, un élément a constitué la toile de fond de notre démarche : maintenir et favoriser le bien-être des personnes âgées hébergées dans les résidences privées. Cette notion de bien-être s'inscrit directement dans la problématique de la violence et des abus faits aux personnes âgées, que ce soit en résidences privées, à domicile, ou dans les centres d'accueil publics. Nos données ne nous permettent pas de cibler les personnes âgées violentées ou à risque d'être violentées dans les résidences privées de la région de Québec. Par contre, en favorisant la mise en place de moyens efficaces pour évaluer les services offerts dans les résidences privées, nous espérons que soient ainsi réduites les situations qui portent atteinte à la santé physique et psychologique des personnes âgées qui y sont logées.

En ce qui concerne de futures avenues de recherche, les participants à notre étude ont mentionné à certaines reprises le rôle que jouent la famille et les organismes communautaires auprès des personnes âgées hébergées dans les résidences privées. Comment la famille peut-elle assurer le bien-être de ses proches hébergés dans les résidences privées et prévenir la violence et les abus ? Comment favoriser le maintien des liens familiaux indispensables pour la qualité de vie des personnes âgées ? Quels rôles les organismes communautaires jouent-ils et pourront-ils jouer dans l'avenir eu égard à l'intégration sociale de ces personnes âgées ? Des services de santé, d'hygiène et d'alimentation de qualité, c'est bien ; mais qu'en est-il de la participation sociale des personnes âgées hébergées dans les résidences privées ? Il nous apparaît essentiel que ces dernières demeurent socialement actives le plus longtemps possible. Il s'agit à n'en pas douter d'un indicateur important du bien-être des personnes âgées. Bien que non documentées dans notre étude, ces questions de recherche nous apparaissent importantes.

Bibliographie

BOHÉMIER, P., LAMOTHE, S., LANCOP, C. et M. RENAUD (1992). *L'utilisation des ressources d'hébergement privées non agréées et la pratique professionnelle des travailleurs sociaux*, Montréal, Corporation professionnelle des travailleurs sociaux du Québec.

ÉQUIPE DE RECHERCHE OPÉRATIONNELLE EN SANTÉ (EROS) [1987]. *La détermination des services requis et la mesure des ressources requises par le bénéficiaire*, Québec, Ministère de la Santé et des Services sociaux, Direction générale de la réadaptation et des services de longue durée.

FOREST, Pierre Gellier *et al.* (1990). *L'alourdissement des clientèles : la perception des membres des comités d'orientation-admission*, Rapport 5, Montréal, EROS, Université de Montréal.

GARANT, Louise (1994). *Synthèse d'un programme d'évaluation sur la réponse aux besoins de longue durée des personnes âgées ayant des limitations fonctionnelles*, Québec, Ministère de la Santé et des Services sociaux.

KREJCIE, Robert et Daryle MORGAN (1970). «Determining Sample Size for Research Activities», *Educational and Psychological Measurement*, 30, 607-610.

LEMASSON, Mireille (1993). *Rôle des CLSC à l'égard des personnes âgées vivant ou désirant vivre en résidences de retraite*, Montréal, Fédération des CLSC.

LEMASSON, Mireille (1994). « Des services de soutien à domicile fragiles pour une clientèle vulnérable», *Service social*, vol. 43, n⁰ 1, 47-65.

LEROUX, Pierre et Jean-François DION (1992). *Enquête sur le marché des résidences pour personnes âgées, région métropolitaine de Québec*, Québec, Société canadienne d'hypothèques et de logement.

MINISTÈRE DE LA SANTÉ ET DES SERVICES SOCIAUX (1990). *Une réforme axée sur le citoyen*, Québec, Gouvernement du Québec.

MINISTÈRE DE LA SANTÉ ET DES SERVICES SOCIAUX (1992). *La politique de la santé et du bien-être*, Québec, Gouvernement du Québec.

MINISTÈRE DE LA SANTÉ ET DES SERVICES SOCIAUX (1993a). *Guide d'information sur l'ouverture d'une résidence pour personnes âgées autonomes*, Québec, Gouvernement du Québec.

MINISTÈRE DE LA SANTÉ ET DES SERVICES SOCIAUX (1993b). *Les interventions effectuées dans les ressources sans permis en vertu des dispositions de l'article 489 de la « Loi sur les services de santé et les services sociaux » (L.R.Q., Chapitre S-4.2)*, Québec, Gouvernement du Québec.

MINISTÈRE DE LA SANTÉ ET DES SERVICES SOCIAUX (1994a). *Les services à domicile de première ligne, Cadre de référence*, Québec, Gouvernement du Québec.

MINISTÈRE DE LA SANTÉ ET DES SERVICES SOCIAUX (1994b). *Les résidences privées pour personnes âgées, non titulaires d'un permis du Ministère de la Santé et des Services sociaux, Plan d'action*, Québec, Gouvernement du Québec.

SAUCIER, Alain (1989). *Synthèse de l'alourdissement des clientèles placées dans les programmes offrant des services de longue durée*, Québec, Gouvernement du Québec, Ministère de la Santé et des Services sociaux, Direction de l'évaluation.

TRAHAN, Louise et Lucie BÉLANGER (1993). *Une évaluation de la prestation de services dans les CLSC et les centres hospitaliers ; Pour des services de qualité aux personnes âgées en perte d'autonomie*, Québec, Gouvernement du Québec, Ministère de la Santé et des Services sociaux, Direction générale de la planification et de l'évaluation.

VAILLANCOURT, Y., MATHIEU, R., JETTÉ, C. et R. BOURQUE (1993). *La privatisation des services de santé et des services sociaux au Québec en 1993*, Conférence présentée dans le cadre du colloque sur la privatisation dans le réseau de la santé et des services sociaux, Montréal, Holiday Inn Crown Plaza.

VÉZINA, A., PELLETIER, D. et J. ROY (1994a). *Les résidences privées et les HLM pour les personnes âgées de la région de Québec: profils des ressources et clientèles et paramètres d'un cadre de référence*, Rapport de recherche, Québec, Centre de recherche sur les services communautaires, Université Laval.

VÉZINA, A., PELLETIER, D. et J. ROY (1994b). *Les résidences privées et HLM pour personnes âgées de la région de Québec: profils des ressources et clientèles et paramètres d'un cadre de référence,* Résultats détaillés de la recherche, Québec, Centre de recherche sur les services communautaires, Université Laval, 120 pages.

Donner et signifier : de la bonne volonté à l'intérêt

Suzie ROBICHAUD
Département des sciences humaines
Université du Québec à Chicoutimi

La présente réflexion vise à montrer la permanence du don dans la gestion des rapports sociaux, bien que ses formes puissent varier considérablement d'une époque à l'autre, comme en témoignent les changements structurels de l'espace public ainsi que les attitudes des bénévoles eux-mêmes depuis les dix dernières années. À cet égard, les cadres sociaux de l'action bénévole et leur bouleversement récent révèlent que les usages de ce phénomène ne s'effectuent pas toujours en dehors de la logique des intérêts notamment ceux inhérents à la reconfiguration de l'État contemporain. Somme toute, partout une même préoccupation s'impose en toile de fond du bénévolat : les appels du cœur ne sont pas toujours compatibles avec les réponses de la raison, voire de la rationalité moderne elle-même.

INTRODUCTION

L'action bénévole contemporaine se trouve imprégnée par une gamme variée de ressources et de contraintes, notamment celles qu'apporte l'État. L'interaction entre ces deux acteurs publics que sont les instances bénévole et étatique modifie respectivement chacune d'elles, particulièrement la première, sans doute plus vulnérable aux décisions politiques que la deuxième ne l'est à l'égard de l'autre. L'examen de cette transformation a été conduit, au cours d'une recherche récente (Robichaud, 1994), en mettant l'accent sur l'évolution des rapports entre l'État et les groupes bénévoles œuvrant dans le domaine de la santé et des services sociaux. Un aperçu des répercussions que peut engendrer la valorisation du rôle de la gratuité au Québec a pu aider à comprendre les mutations qui s'y produisent. Le réaménagement de l'État dans l'espace social a permis de constater qu'il modifie le paysage des groupes bénévoles et les entraîne dans une logique d'institutionnalisation (incorporation, critères à respecter pour l'obtention de subvention, accentuation des relations avec les acteurs publics de l'environnement). Ils adoptent alors une forme de système intermédiaire, entre une structuration hiérarchique (appareil) et une autre non hiérarchique (réseau) ; forme intermédiaire que l'on nomme un quasi-appareil (embauche de permanents, spécialisation des acteurs, tendance à l'officialisation).

Mais les changements structurels qui surviennent au sein des groupes modifient moins l'existence du bénévolat que les cadres de son accomplissement. Malgré la diminution des effectifs bénévoles et le déclin de la séduction pour une spontanéité qui se modifie en s'institutionnalisant, les personnes interrogées sont plutôt enclines à affirmer qu'elles veulent persister dans l'action bénévole en dépit de la transformation des groupes. Aussi, dans un premier temps, il y aura lieu de s'interroger sur la fonction symbolique que le phénomène conserve et de tenter de montrer la permanence du don dans la gestion des rapports sociaux, bien que ses formes puissent varier considérablement d'une époque à l'autre, comme en témoignent les refontes systémiques de l'espace public, depuis les dix dernières années. Dans un deuxième temps, il s'agira d'étudier les modalités de la pratique du bénévolat et de vérifier sa capacité virtuelle à servir d'instrument de réalisation des politiques sociales.

PATHOS ET ETHOS : DIFFICULTÉ DU PARCOURS

La vie sociale est faite de symboles. Le bénévolat n'y échappe pas, d'autant plus que le principe de la charité demeure souvent pratiqué à travers une fonction d'exemplarité. La relation d'aide n'est pas réductible à un don : elle s'insère aussi dans la logique d'un témoignage, d'une pédagogie sur l'existence collective, que les individus et les groupes veulent bien dispenser pour le bénéfice du plus grand nombre possible, à travers la singularité d'un geste. Gurvitch disait que l'ambivalence du symbole est qu'il « voile en révélant et révèle en voilant ». C'est peut-être là toute sa force, davantage que son handicap. Donner à voir dans ce qui est tout ce qui n'est pas : c'est dans cette fonction emblématique de la charité que la société mercantile et rationnelle contemporaine trouve néanmoins l'opportunité de conserver à travers des figures aussi célèbres que celle de l'abbé Pierre, de Jean Vanier ou du cardinal Léger. Ces individus éveillent chez les gens un certain bagage d'émotion fait d'admiration, d'enthousiasme et peut-être aussi de compassion à l'égard de la condition des plus miséreux.

Ainsi, la mise en œuvre de solidarités diverses marque une permanence des idéaux et des comportements humains. Mais ce n'est pas par hasard qu'au cours des années 1980, le bénévolat occupe l'avant-scène. Alors que continue de fermenter le rêve d'une juste répartition des richesses, on découvre aujourd'hui de façon palpable les menaces de chômage – danger potentiel pour une fraction importante de la population – et les malaises qu'il soulève : l'insécurité, la précarité, l'angoisse de l'avenir, etc. Au terme de cette spirale, l'emploi pose un véritable défi aux sociétés actuelles. Comment aider l'homme à ne plus être prisonnier des circonstances comme d'une fatalité, afin qu'il puisse se prémunir contre les risques qui le menacent ? Il n'est pas possible de penser que l'attrait symbolique du bénévolat va aussi permettre de tout régler comme s'il s'agissait d'un décret collectif auquel on accepterait de se soumettre. L'histoire relate les événements du passé, qui rendent compte de l'utilisation de mesures radicales pour enrayer la pauvreté. À ce propos, Karl Marx rappelle, comment, jadis, Napoléon chargea ses services publics d'extirper la misère humaine, particulièrement la mendicité dans toute la France. Le 5 juillet 1808, un décret en promulgua la suppression. Par quel moyen ? Par les dépôts qui se muèrent si vite en pénitenciers que bientôt l'indigent ne parvint dans ces établissements qu'en passant par le tribunal correctionnel. En assurant un refuge à l'indigent et de la nourriture au pauvre, l'Empereur des Français fut considéré comme un héros. D'ailleurs, un des membres législatifs s'écria : « L'enfance ne sera plus abandonnée, les familles pauvres ne manqueront plus de ressources, ni les ouvriers d'encouragement et d'occupation. Nos pas ne seront plus arrêtés par l'image dégoûtante des infirmités et de la honteuse misère. » (Karl Marx, 1982 : 406-407)

Le décret napoléonien montre comment l'action sociale s'est parfois confondue avec le souci de l'ordre public. Des lois, des déclarations et des édits se succèdent pendant plusieurs siècles, si bien qu'en Europe, on a pu parler de législations concernant les mendiants. Quoi qu'il en soit, la lutte contre la mendicité allait donner naissance à des dispositions d'une extrême dureté. En effet, pour ne plus avoir à faire face au spectacle de la misère, un principe se généralise pour limiter cette calamité : le renfermement des pauvres. Ces procédures législatives présentent les dangers d'un volontarisme étatique. En effet, des lois humaines aussi draconiennes invitent à repousser une conception de la justice qui milite contre la détention des démunis et que, au demeurant, le XIXe siècle identifie souvent par les différents socialisme, utopisme et syndicalisme naissant. L'échec de l'État-providence est une reprise, sous une forme édulcorée, du décret napoléonien, et une telle conception incite à rejeter la légalisation des conditions de vie entre les hommes. Ainsi, ne court-on pas le risque d'assister à un recul constant de la sécurité sociale et des politiques égalitaristes? L'imaginaire collectif joue un rôle, et la tentative est grande de trouver, à l'heure des comptes, des boucs émissaires pour justifier la montée du coût du social.

LA PRATIQUE CONTEMPORAINE DU DON

Malgré quelques voies discordantes, la plupart des individus font actuellement chorus pour déclarer périmée la certitude selon laquelle l'État serait encore le grand pourvoyeur dans les situations d'insécurité économique. Mais comment redonner aux populations la responsabilité de leur existence? Les groupes bénévoles peuvent apporter une aide à autrui, certes, mais peuvent-ils servir d'instrument de réalisation des politiques sociales et des programmes institutionnels? Toutefois, peu importe la manière dont ce rôle leur est conféré, il importe d'en fixer les limites que sa signification même suggère. Car le bénévole n'a aucune obligation contractuelle envers les groupes à qui il donne de son temps. Il y a des modalités d'intervention à respecter, mais il peut mettre fin à son engagement au moment qu'il juge opportun. Le bénévolat, c'est donc un geste volontaire mais aussi temporaire, et il serait illusoire d'utiliser cette pratique sociale pour répondre d'une manière continue à toutes les nouvelles catégories de population en difficulté que la crise fait surgir. Des interventions ponctuelles et limitées semblent plus en harmonie avec leur mission. Un exemple l'atteste suffisamment : lorsqu'une cause exige l'engagement massif d'un jour, les bénévoles arrivent en grand nombre. La situation économique existante semble introduire le rêve d'un retour à des solidarités moins coûteuses, sur un mode néanmoins plus organisé qu'autrefois. Mais le bénévolat ne doit pas être là pour justifier le retrait massif de l'État-providence. La mise en veilleuse du volontarisme étatique n'autorise pas le recours à celui du bénévolat. Et à cela aussi, il faut être attentif pour évaluer la pertinence de donner au secteur bénévole la mission autrefois dévolue aux institutions publiques. Déjà, au milieu du siècle dernier, Alexis de Tocqueville (1986 : 39), dans sa réflexion sur l'idéal d'une société plus juste, annonçait les limites de l'assistance : «La charité individuelle, dit-il, est un agent puissant que la société ne doit point mépriser mais auquel il serait imprudent de se confier, elle est un des moyens et ne saurait être le seul.»

La crise actuelle crée une interdépendance entre les collectivités locales et politiques. Dans cette optique, plusieurs études permettent d'observer une réduction de l'écart entre ce qui caractérise les institutions publiques et les groupes bénévoles qui œuvrent dans le domaine de la santé et des services sociaux (Robichaud, 1996; Bechmann-Ferrand, 1992; Lamoureux, 1991; Laforest et Redjeb, 1989; etc.). Qui plus est, ces derniers réalisent que le développement du rôle de service leur donne un certain contrôle, permet de réaliser certaines activités et d'en créer de nouvelles. Cette conjoncture qui, en soi, apporte un dynamisme renouvelé peut-elle servir de prétexte pour remettre en cause le principe du partage collectif des risques sociaux? Les circonstances présentes ouvrent la voie au développement des solidarités de voisinage, mais toutes les communautés ne disposent pas de moyens analogues pour organiser leurs ressources et agir comme partenaires de l'État. En effet, les groupes bénévoles mettent en place des mécanismes pour venir en aide aux personnes dans le besoin. Congruent avec les problèmes concrets, il n'en demeure pas moins que l'arrangement des services varie d'un quartier à l'autre. En effet, tous les groupes ne jouissent pas de la même infrastructure financière leur permettant de se construire une assise particulière. Certains groupes démontrent une plus grande capacité à défendre leur budget et leur complémentarité avec les institutions. D'autres, par contre, sont plus vulnérables et dépendants des limites qu'imposent l'État et ses appareils. Sur la base de ce constat, il est possible de postuler que cette diversité dans l'organisation du travail bénévole peut conduire à des iniquités, à tout le moins à des disparités, entre les milieux. L'efficacité des uns à offrir une gamme variée de services se conjugue avec l'impossibilité des autres à donner une forme d'aide précise. Ces propriétés peuvent contribuer à l'accroissement des écarts qui séparent déjà les communautés en matière de soins et produire ainsi une instabilité, voire un déséquilibre chez le bénéficiaire, chez celui qui, somme toute, reçoit l'expression de la bonté. Au-delà de l'arbitraire découpage des subventions, et par voie de conséquence du financement des groupes, une perspective plus grande se développe sur la façon de s'entraider.

En effet, au fil des dernières années, les groupes bénévoles se sont taillé une place stratégique dans la dispensation de services à la collectivité. Leur originalité dans le panorama social contemporain réside moins dans la prétention de pouvoir contribuer à des changements que dans celle de soutenir activement des individus en difficulté. Ils font alors face à un double défi: se doter de structures pour offrir des services;

orienter continuellement ces mêmes structures sur leur mission qui est celle de secourir autrui. La stabilité institutionnelle semble plus attrayante que l'aventure de la révolution si chère aux bénévoles d'hier. Signe de souplesse ou d'un conservatisme stérile? Il y a peut-être une nouvelle sagesse à tenter de se reprendre en mains et à atténuer nos espoirs envers un État-tuteur. Le sens, c'est comme pluraliser et individualiser. Tous et chacun donnent l'impression d'en chercher un pour eux-mêmes et d'interdire de l'exporter à autrui. Le paradoxe, c'est que tout cela a produit en même temps que le foisonnement de la vie associative, une participation sociale apparemment incompatible avec l'individualisme. Ainsi, pour gérer les conditions de stabilité des pratiques sociales désenchantées, les actions coordonnées par les groupes incitent davantage à se structurer qu'à strictement contester le système social. Encore là, la ligne n'est pas tranchée, mais il faut simplement y voir des accentuations de tendance sans égard à la singularité du cas d'espèce. Devant tout événement, les groupes ne veulent pas seulement chercher quelque chose, mais aussi échapper à quelque chose en essayant de préserver leur originalité, à travers les multiples exigences qui les submergent. Ils arrivent à juguler de tels obstacles au succès, tantôt en dénonçant l'entrave à la liberté d'action, tantôt en affirmant avec persévérance leur vocation de réussir. Sans faire de prévisions, exercice toujours périlleux, on ne voit pas très bien comment, dans l'état des données existantes, les groupes bénévoles pourraient se créer des conditions susceptibles d'atténuer les difficultés qu'ils rencontrent dans une sorte d'harmonie. La situation actuelle révèle la présence d'impasses, même si les groupes ont le mérite d'offrir des services et de porter attention à la condition d'autrui. Aussi, dans le paysage québécois, la position des groupes oscille entre ceux qui, désespérés, décrètent une récupération, et ceux dont l'inclination première consiste à surnager entre la contrainte et le consentement.

CONCLUSION

Nonobstant les écueils liés au tracé d'une ligne de partage trop sommaire, les changements sociaux des dernières années montrent avec éloquence que les modes usuels de développement de l'action bénévole subissent actuellement des transformations accélérées. Car la seule bonne volonté ne peut se suffire à elle-même, se déployer sans une préoccupation du rendement social global : l'*homo benevolus* doit se faire *homo adaptatus* en nouant la pulsion du cœur à l'impératif de la raison. Qu'il y laisse de sa candeur en devenant plus soucieux de sa fonctionnalité n'est pas pour autant le signe qu'il s'y perde en s'intégrant dans des institutions.

Néanmoins, la concentration de la gestion du social et la multiplication des institutions traduisent des types de rapports plus organisés et hiérarchisés. Ces relations s'inscrivent toutefois dans un mouvement plus vaste et marqué par d'autres formes de structures. En effet, des réseaux évoluent dans le temps et dans l'espace en procurant de multiples possibilités de connexion qui alimentent les appareils. De plus, ces organisations non constituées apportent une diversité d'action dans la société. Parfois vulnérables, quelque peu mystérieuses, elles s'appuient sur une représentation du monde, constituée par une pluralité de sens qui, face à l'incertitude et au regain d'intérêt pour la quotidienneté, gagne une grande audience. Dans cette veine, Lemieux (1982 : 45) dégage l'importance des réseaux dans la configuration des modes d'exercice du social lorsqu'il écrit : « D'un certain point de vue, il importe peu que des réseaux soient contaminés par des appareils, car d'autres réseaux demeurent toujours en réserve, qui continuent d'être le potentiel des appareils. »

Bibliographie

BECHMANN-FERRAND, Dan (1992). *Bénévolat et Solidarité*, Paris, Gyros, Alternative, 413 pages.

LAMOUREUX, Henri (1991). *L'intervention sociale collective. Une éthique de solidarité*, Québec, Éditions du Pommier, 232 pages.

LAFOREST, Marcelle et Belhassen REDJEB (1989). *L'intervention sociale non salariée*, Étude exploratoire de diverses pratiques d'assistance bénévole auprès des personnes âgées dans la région de Québec, Québec, Université Laval, 181 pages.

LEMIEUX, Vincent (1982). « Problématique des appareils et des réseaux », *Communication et information*, vol. 4, n° 1, 33-45.

MARX, Karl (1982). *L'idéologie allemande*, Paris, Gallimard, La Pléiade, 1394 pages.

ROBICHAUD, Suzie (1994). *L'État et les solidarités bénévoles : les enjeux politiques de la gratuité*, Thèse de doctorat, Québec, Université Laval, 279 pages.

ROBICHAUD, Suzie (1996). « Du réseau à l'institution : le bénévolat en mouvement », *Revue suisse de sociologie*, vol. 22, 329-346.

TOCQUEVILLE, Alexis de (1966). *Mémoire sur le paupérisme*, Mémoire de la société académique de Cherbourg, 1835, Paris, PUF. Paru dans la *Revue internationale d'action communautaire*, vol. 16, n° 56, 24-40.

Impacts sociaux de l'ajustement structurel : cas de la Tunisie

Samira CHAKER
Département des sciences économiques
HEC – Tunis

L'ajustement structurel adopté par la Tunisie, réorientant la politique économique vers une réduction de la sphère économique de l'État au profit du marché, a permis, certes, la réalisation de bonnes performances macro-économiques. Mais elle a aussi entraîné un coût social dont le déséquilibre du marché du travail est le plus déterminant. L'objectif de cet article est d'analyser les attitudes et les nouvelles pratiques sociales engendrées par le PAS tant au regard de la réponse organisée de l'État qu'à celui des comportements des autres agents économiques.

La Tunisie a adopté en 1986 un vaste programme de réformes dont l'objectif ultime est de placer l'économie nationale sur une trajectoire de croissance forte dans un environnement de stabilité monétaire. Le programme en question répond au schéma classique de l'ajustement. Il associe à une politique d'austérité et budgétaire une panoplie de mesures incitatives pour stimuler l'offre. Ce programme prévoit également un recentrage du rôle de l'État qui voit sa sphère économique se réduire au profit du marché.

Cette réorientation de la politique économique depuis l'adoption de ce programme d'ajustement structurel (PAS) a permis, comparativement à la période antérieure, de réaliser des performances remarquables[1].

Le PIB réel a augmenté au taux moyen de 4,2 % au cours de la période de 1987 à 1994 contre un taux de 3,2 % au cours des dix années précédentes. Cette croissance s'est réalisée dans un contexte de rationalisation de la demande intérieure.

Le déficit budgétaire a ainsi passé d'une moyenne de 6 % du PIB durant le VIe plan, à 3,8 %, au cours du VIIe plan (de 1986 à 1991) et à 2,6 %, en 1994 ; la situation extérieure s'est, par ailleurs, améliorée. L'importante réduction en 1994 de la balance des opérations courantes, dont le niveau a représenté 2,6 % du PIB contre 6,9 %, en 1993, a permis de dégager une position de transfert net positive de 373 millions de DT. Ce qui a porté le niveau des réserves officielles de change à l'équivalent de 2,8 mois d'importations. Parallèlement, le taux d'endettement a baissé de près de 6 points de pourcentage du PIB passant de 59,6 % en 1986, à 53,6 % en 1994.

Dans le même intervalle, le coefficient de la dette est passé de 27,9 % à 17,5 % des recettes courantes. Le taux d'inflation de 4,7 %, en 1994, se rapproche progressivement du taux moyen prévalant dans les pays de l'Union européenne (4,1 %), principal partenaire économique de la Tunisie.

Ces performances sont en fait supérieures à ce qu'elles paraissent. Si l'on excluait l'agriculture, dont la contribution à la croissance en 1995 est négative (– 6 %) du fait de deux années consécutives de sécheresse, le taux de croissance de l'économie serait plus important et le taux d'inflation prévu serait encore plus faible. Cela signifie qu'il y a une diversification de l'économie nationale qui devient moins sujette aux chocs extérieurs (aléas climatiques par exemple). La plupart des secteurs ont effectivement contribué à la croissance, en partie tirée par la demande extérieure, avec une production manufacturière relativement importante qui a remplacé l'ancienne prépondérance des produits pétroliers et miniers.

Il serait cependant illusoire de penser que ces performances macroéconomiques ont été réalisées sans coût social. La rigueur budgétaire, notamment la réduction des subventions, conjuguée à la libéralisation des marges concernant le commerce intérieur, n'a pas manqué de peser

---

1. Les données proviennent de différentes publications de la Banque centrale de Tunisie, de l'Institut national des statistiques de la Banque mondiale.

lourdement sur les catégories sociales les plus défavorisées, surtout lors des premières années du PAS. L'évolution de la part des charges de compensation dans la consommation des ménages indique une baisse régulière. Elle atteint 3,2%, en 1993, contre 3,7%, en 1991 et 6%, en 1985, c'est-à-dire un an avant l'adoption du PAS. Au regard de la politique sociale, cette rigueur budgétaire signifie une réduction de la couverture sociale et des transferts sociaux. Cette tendance est très nette dans les domaines de la santé et de l'éducation qui sont devenus des services de plus en plus marchands.

Ainsi, dans le cadre de la restructuration du service public, la réforme de la santé vise un recouvrement des coûts plus poussé en contrepartie des services hospitaliers. Les tarifs ont été révisés à trois reprises de telle sorte qu'entre 1991 et 1993, les hôpitaux sont parvenus à augmenter les recettes provenant des patients d'au moins 64%, certains ayant même dépassé le taux de 100% (Banque mondiale).

Dans le domaine de l'éducation, nous assistons à la multiplication d'institutions d'enseignement et de formation privées qui viennent suppléer les défaillances du secteur public dont le rendement, mesuré par l'ampleur des déperditions, est de plus en plus faible. Pour la seule période de 1989 à 1994, le nombre d'élèves inscrits dans les institutions privées a augmenté de 45,7% contre 14% seulement dans le public. À ce phénomène s'ajoute l'augmentation des coûts éducatifs (Bedoui, 1994).

L'objet de ce texte n'est autre que de présenter dans un premier temps quelques caractéristiques du marché du travail en tant qu'indicateurs du coût social de l'ajustement, de dresser ensuite un tableau synoptique du programme d'encouragement à l'emploi et d'adaptation professionnelle en tant que réponse organisée de la part de l'État, pour préciser enfin les nouveaux comportements tant de l'État que des autres acteurs économiques, notamment les plus vulnérables, conséquences des bouleversements qu'a connus l'économie tunisienne depuis l'adoption du PAS.

LE MARCHÉ DU TRAVAIL
INDICATEUR DU COÛT SOCIAL DE L'AJUSTEMENT

Alors que l'ajustement doit normalement être synonyme de développement, on observe un coût social substantiel et mal réparti. Le marché du travail en constitue un indicateur important justifiant ainsi la nécessité d'appréhender les institutions du marché du travail non seulement sous l'angle de l'efficacité économique, mais également du point de vue de l'efficacité sociale (Lachaud, 1994). Le processus de développement, qui certes est apparent, en accélérant l'édification de l'économie et de la société, crée une dynamique sociale d'une longue période, entièrement nouvelle et difficilement maîtrisable. L'évolution complexe et multiforme du marché du travail urbain est un aspect essentiel de ce processus de transformation de la société.

La remise en cause de l'intervention de l'État dans le domaine économique et social engendre une nouvelle dynamique des systèmes sociaux. À cet égard, plusieurs éléments tendent à confirmer l'accentuation des déséquilibres sur le marché du travail à la fin des années 1980.

Au niveau macro-économique, on observe un déclin de la capacité d'absorption de la main-d'œuvre. Durant les trois dernières décennies, l'essentiel des emplois créés, soit plus des deux tiers, a été engendré par un nombre limité d'activités, à savoir les divers services autres que l'administration (22 %), le textile (14,5 %), le bâtiment et les travaux publics (8,2 %). Or ces activités risquent de ne plus pouvoir jouer un rôle aussi décisif dans la création d'emplois. Dans l'administration, une restructuration des recrutements demeure possible à cause d'une austérité budgétaire. Dans le BTP, l'emploi risque de pâtir de la compression des dépenses de l'État allouées à l'infrastructure de base et aux équipements (tendance à la saturation des besoins des ménages). Dans le textile de bas de gamme, la Tunisie risque de ne plus être compétitive. Quant aux créations d'emplois dans le commerce et autres services, elles représentent des créations induites, dont le volume dépend en principe du taux de croissance de l'économie. Dans le commerce et les services similaires, les créations d'emplois s'apparenteront davantage à du chômage déguisé, signe de malaise social plutôt que d'une prospérité économique.

Croissance de la population active, accélération de l'offre de travail. C'est ainsi qu'on observe un manque de capacité d'absorption de l'économie de diplômés de l'enseignement supérieur. Le nombre de diplômes universitaires a doublé entre 1992 et 1995 : 5 566 diplômés, en 1992, alors qu'ils sont près de 11 200, en 1995. D'une manière générale, les déterminants de ce déséquilibre se situent à la fois du côté de l'offre et de la demande. La croissance de la population, qui détermine sa structure par âge, les subventions accordées aux étudiants et l'attrait d'un emploi stable dans la fonction publique, ont maintenu la demande d'éducation à un niveau élevé. En revanche, la dimension du secteur productif et sa croissance ont été réduites sous l'impulsion des politiques d'ajustement. En outre, cette réduction de la demande des diplômés intervient dans une situation où le dynamisme du secteur privé ne suffit pas à absorber cet excédent.

Par ailleurs, alors que le système éducatif continue à produire des diplômés dans des spécialités relativement saturées, des compétences techniques nécessaires au système productif sont déficitaires. À cet égard, deux phénomènes sont couramment observés : le secteur privé emploie de nombreuses personnes sans formation dans des postes d'encadrement moyen ou supérieur, alors que les entreprises industrielles manquent de personnels techniques qualifiés du certificat d'aptitudes professionnelles ou du brevet de technicien, et cela dans beaucoup de spécialités. Les entreprises utilisent des techniques de plus en plus capitalistiques. Sous l'effet de l'exode rural, la proportion du « sous-emploi » est des plus élevées au sein de la population urbaine. La baisse de la part de l'agriculture dans le PIB s'accompagne d'un développement excessif des services. En général, un processus de développement de cette nature ne peut être poursuivi à long terme, car cela traduit l'incapacité des secteurs productifs à croître à un taux suffisant.

Compte tenu des coûts d'opportunités élevés qu'imposent les entreprises publiques à l'économie, l'État s'est désengagé du secteur productif. Certaines entreprises publiques ont été privatisées ou restructurées dans un souci d'améliorer les performances. D'autre part, une rationalisation des dépenses publiques en vue de réduire le déficit budgétaire a amené l'État à prendre des mesures ayant un caractère obligatoire qui ont contribué à réduire le nombre de fonctionnaires à son emploi. Il s'agit de l'élimination des emplois fictifs ou non autorisés, de la redéfinition des postes et des qualifications, du contrôle du versement des rémunérations, de la généralisation des concours d'entrée à la fonction publique, etc.

L'importance relative des emplois vulnérables semble avoir augmenté. Plusieurs indices tendent à mettre en évidence une précarisation de l'emploi : emplois occasionnels exercés par un nombre de plus en plus important de chômeurs avec ou sans expérience professionnelle, multiplication des activités secondaires, emplois temporaires dans les grandes entreprises, etc.

L'expansion de l'emploi dans le secteur informel, urbain et rural, a été un déterminant important de l'absorption de l'excédent de la main-d'œuvre urbaine auquel s'ajoute l'émigration vers l'étranger constituant ainsi un élément non négligeable d'ajustement du marché du travail. De tels ajustements ne sont pas étrangers à la persistance de la pauvreté et des écarts de revenus, impliquant par ailleurs autant des politiques d'accompagnement que des pratiques sociales.

LES POLITIQUES D'ACCOMPAGNEMENT, SOUTIEN AU MARCHÉ DU TRAVAIL

Dans le but de pallier les retombées négatives sur « les nouveaux pauvres » comme les « pauvres de longue date », des programmes d'aide ont vu le jour au cours de cette phase de transition[2]. La gamme de programmes de lutte contre la pauvreté ou « d'accompagnement social » est très large. Ils prennent la forme d'actions d'assistance directe (aide en nature, essentiellement alimentaire, et en espèce), d'actions de soutien (protection des personnes âgées sans soutien, des personnes handicapées) et de programmes régionaux de développement intégré (le programme de la famille productive, le programme d'aide aux petits agriculteurs, le fonds de solidarité nationale). De 1986 à 1992, le Programme national d'aide aux familles nécessiteuses a profité à 101 000 familles réparties sur l'ensemble des régions ; 57 % des bénéficiaires sont des femmes, 52 % sont âgés de plus de 60 ans, 17,5 % ont un handicap, 3 % bénéficient d'une couverture sociale et 18 % exercent une activité rémunérée (chantiers, secteur agricole, service, etc.).

À côté de ces programmes d'assistance, le traitement de la pauvreté se fait surtout par le développement d'activités génératrices d'emplois et de revenus, responsabilisant cette population défavorisée.

Par ailleurs, les tensions sur le marché de l'emploi proviennent en particulier des jeunes dont le poids devient de plus en plus important dans la structure du chômage. L'enquête population emploi de 1989 fait ressortir que les jeunes de 18 à 29 ans représentent 69,9 % et les jeunes de 18 à 24 ans, 48,5 % de la population en chômage. Des difficultés plus accentuées touchent plus particulièrement les jeunes de 20 à 24 ans, qui représentent à eux seuls 34,6 % de la population en chômage. Cette situation sociale se double d'un constat d'ordre économique.

En effet, les besoins des entreprises en main-d'œuvre sont devenus – à la faveur des réformes – de plus en plus urgents et à contenu professionnel élevé et polyvalent. C'est sous ce double aspect que, parallèlement au système de formation professionnelle, il a été mis en place progressivement, depuis 1981, un réseau de programmes spécifiques d'insertion permettant aux jeunes primodemandeurs d'emploi – de différents niveaux d'enseignement, et en particulier ceux présentant des difficultés particulières d'intégration – de réussir la transition du système éducatif au

---

2. Les actes du séminaire national sur « la planification des politiques alimentaires et nutritionnelles », organisé par le ministère de l'Agriculture et le ministère de la Santé publique, Tunis, octobre 1993.

système productif. À cette fin, des stages appropriés sont organisés dans le cadre du programme d'encouragement à l'emploi des jeunes qui compte le contrat Emploi-Formation et les stages d'Insertion à la vie professionnelle I et II.

Cet objectif social prioritaire est concilié avec l'objectif économique afin de répondre dans les délais relativement courts aux besoins du tissu économique et, par conséquent, d'améliorer le taux de technicité dans les entreprises. C'est ainsi que les programmes d'insertion s'inscrivent dans une vision dynamique du traitement de la demande d'emploi pour réduire la pression du chômage. Cette approche de la demande a été croisée par une approche de l'offre focalisant fondamentalement sur le traitement des besoins des entreprises par l'intermédiaire du Fonds d'insertion et d'adaptation professionnelle (FIAP).

Ce traitement actif des besoins des entreprises à travers des actions d'adaptation, de perfectionnement et de reconversion des ressources humaines, participe en définitive à la promotion de l'emploi et à la réduction des effets en termes de licenciement dans les secteurs les plus touchés par la restructuration, notamment dans le textile, la confection, l'agro-alimentaire et la micro-entreprise.

Par référence au nouveau cadre juridique en vigueur, soit la loi n° 93/17 du 22 février et le décret n° 93/1049 du 3 mai 1993, il est possible de cerner les principaux avantages qui prennent surtout la forme de subvention, de prime, en cas de recrutement définitif, d'exonération de charge de sécurité sociale. Ces avantages ont favorisé les réalisations qui atteignent en 1995, 66 649 contrats pour les programmes d'encouragement à l'emploi.

TABLEAU 1

Programme	Bénéficiaire			Pourcentage d'insertion
		Féminins	Masculins	
CEF	36 222	56,2 %	43,8 %	80
SIVP2	10 906	55,9 %	44,1 %	40
SIVP1	19 521	52,3 %	47,7 %	

Les actions du FIAP sont tout aussi nombreuses : elles atteignent en juin 1995, 2 542, avec un effectif de bénéficiaires de 34 161, dont 24 893 ont été insérés immédiatement après le cycle d'adaptation professionnelle. Une enquête de suivi réalisée sur un échantillon de 14 181 bénéficiaires relève l'étendue de l'intervention sociale du FIAP. Il s'adresse effectivement à toutes les catégories sociales et à tous les niveaux d'enseignement. Les femmes représentent 63 % de l'ensemble des bénéficiaires, cette prédominance féminine s'explique en grande partie par l'importance des besoins des secteurs du textile, de l'habillement et de l'artisanat.

LES PRATIQUES SOCIALES INDUITES

Le coût du PAS est évident pour certains groupes, les coûts transitoires de l'ajustement sont inévitables à court terme. Cependant, les changements de la structure économique ne manqueront pas d'exercer des effets d'adaptation en termes d'emploi, de comportements et d'attitudes.

Dans la mesure où, comme le note J.L. Lespes (1992), dans la plupart des PVD, la société ancienne fondée sur l'agriculture et les liens de parenté n'a pas été remplacée par la société marchande généralisée, le secteur informel, la création de micro-entreprises et les initiatives économiques axées sur l'entraide jouent un rôle d'amortissement des effets induits et d'accompagnement des transformations de la société.

La micro-entreprise et le secteur informel

La crise financière et les politiques d'ajustement ont fait disparaître les espoirs d'une croissance rapide de l'emploi dans le secteur moderne et ont entraîné un retournement dans les mentalités autant des responsables que des particuliers à l'égard du secteur informel. Pendant les années 1960 et 1970, les activités traditionnelles étaient considérées comme marginales et destinées à disparaître, parce que le secteur moderne allait créer de nombreux emplois rendus indispensables par l'urbanisation accélérée. Dans beaucoup de pays, la stratégie de croissance reposait sur le protectionnisme, l'interventionnisme et l'extension du secteur parapublic.

La politique d'ajustement et le coup d'arrêt porté aux investissements dans le secteur moderne par la crise financière ont provoqué un changement radical d'attitude : on a fait du secteur informel un secteur capable de se développer et de créer des emplois à la place du secteur moderne.

La confiance soudaine accordée à ce secteur marque un retournement politique important qui semble coïncider avec le succès des idées néolibérales. On a considéré l'État comme le premier responsable de la stagnation du secteur informel en raison des règlements et des pratiques administratives (Morrisson, Oudin et Soulignac Le Comte, 1994).

Ce qui caractérise la petite entreprise informelle, c'est précisément le fait que l'activité de production et l'activité du ménage sont indissolublement liées (Haudeville, 1992). C'est directement l'homme dans sa dimension sociale, c'est-à-dire totale, par opposition au réductionnisme de l'*homo economicus*, qui est pris en compte. De même, si on a pu dire que le secteur informel maximise la substitution du travail au capital, cela souligne bien le lien direct qui s'établit entre la production et la création des revenus. La petite entreprise apparaît ainsi comme le moyen de se procurer un revenu pour toute une fraction (considérable) de la population que le secteur moderne n'a pu absorber.

Toujours est-il qu'entre la diversité, le nombre, la densité et le mode de fonctionnement, les micro-entreprises varient considérablement suivant les pays et les milieux. Ces différences sont dues aux antécédents historiques, qui ont abouti à une plus au moins grande cohésion sociale, à l'existence préalable d'une industrie à domicile ou d'une tradition artisanale, à l'existence ou non d'un système économique axé sur le marché et, plus directement, à la grande diversité des structures économiques locales et des niveaux de développement global.

En Afrique, les micro-entreprises sont principalement implantées dans les zones rurales, où elles assurent l'essentiel de la production des besoins de consommation et de l'emploi non agricole. Elles garantissent généralement la transmission des compétences et du savoir-faire par des arrangements d'apprentissage. Selon J. Charmes (1991), elles constituent des liens et des points de passage essentiels entre les systèmes traditionnels et modernes, entre les zones urbaines et rurales, entre les secteurs agricole et industriel et entre les zones défavorisées et le reste du pays. En outre, elles représentent un lieu de formation et d'adaptation professionnelle privilégié pour l'apprenti. En effet, 70 à 90 % des apprentis qui apprennent un métier sur le tas le font dans une micro-entreprise. Si les externalités positives en termes de capital humain du secteur formel bénéficiaient peu au secteur informel (Charmes, 1990 ; Lubell, 1991), les marchés du travail ne sont pas très segmentés : la mobilité des travailleurs se manifeste tant du formel vers l'informel que dans le sens inverse.

« L'ajustement invisible »

Les vingt dernières années se caractérisent par le rôle croissant joué par les femmes dans l'activité économique. Cela résulte des efforts éducatifs, d'un bouleversement de la tradition conservatrice par la préoccupation du développement économique, d'une pénurie de main-d'œuvre masculine persistant dans les zones rurales et, surtout, d'une demande de main-d'œuvre féminine dans des secteurs étroitement associés au rôle féminin domestique ou demandant souvent un niveau élevé de flexibilité : textile, habillement, soins, éducation, etc. Toutefois, l'impact du PAS a directement touché l'emploi féminin du fait de sa concentration dans l'économie non protégée, sensible à la contraction économique.

On constate non'seulement une augmentation plus rapide du chômage féminin par rapport à celui des hommes, mais aussi une propension à la déqualification des emplois féminins. En effet, de 1984 à 1989, la population active féminine occupée, dans la population occupée totale, a vu sa part se réduire de 21,7 à 19,5 %. L'emploi est l'un des domaines dans lequel les disparités entre les hommes et les femmes sont particulièrement marquées, puisque sur cinq emplois en Tunisie, un seul est occupé par une femme. Ce ratio ne semble pas progresser dans le temps, puisqu'en 1989, il se situait au même niveau qu'en 1975, en dépit d'une légère progression en 1975 et en 1984.

Par ailleurs, ce choc, conjugué à l'abaissement des conditions de vie de la population, a modifié les attitudes des femmes envers l'activité économique ; nombre d'entre elles devenant « économiquement actives » afin de maintenir le niveau de vie de leur famille, d'autres se repliant sur le milieu domestique, d'autres enfin passant au secteur non structuré. Ainsi, l'entrée des femmes dans la vie active reflète leur réponse aux chocs économiques et leur contribution aux efforts déployés par la société pour s'adapter aux périodes de transformation économique. En termes d'emploi, la femme n'est pas typiquement une victime supportant passivement les effets des chocs économiques, mais un agent adaptant son comportement au nouveau climat économique et procurant ce que l'UNICEF (1987) a appelé « l'ajustement invisible ».

Solidarité sociale et lutte contre l'exclusion

La notion de solidarité sociale fait référence au concept de l'entraide économique en tant qu'intervention sociale de lutte contre la pauvreté. Traditionnellement, la lutte contre l'exclusion est axée essentiellement sur les actions d'un État-providence développant ainsi une situation « d'assistés ». L'entraide économique tenterait de provoquer le processus d'*empowerment,* point de convergence entre les objectifs et les pratiques sociales et ceux du développement économique (Ninacs, 1995). En ciblant la capacité des bénificaires, l'entraide économique peut contribuer à promouvoir une autonomie économique.

En Tunisie, l'essentiel de l'action sociale s'intègre dans les programmes d'emplois à travers la politique de promotion de revenus et de lutte contre la pauvreté. En plus des transferts sociaux, des programmes de développement sont mis en œuvre, permettant l'amélioration des conditions de vie ainsi que la consolidation et la création d'emplois au profit des catégories et des régions les plus défavorisées. Parmi ces programmes, citons les suivants : le Programme de développement régional, le Programme de développement intégré, le Programme de la famille productive, le Programme d'aide aux petits agriculteurs, le Programme de développement urbain intégré, le Fonds national de promotion de l'artisanat et de petits métiers et le Fonds de solidarité nationale « 2626 ». Ce dernier fonds, s'appuyant sur un lien étroit entre le politique, l'économique et le social, voulait au départ remédier à la situation des différentes agglomérations dépourvues des infrastructures élémentaires ; il s'étend à présent aux actions développant des activités génératrices de revenus. Cette entraide économique intègre autant des objectifs sociaux qu'économiques et s'insère dans une démarche d'autonomie économique et donc d'*empowerment*.

Par ailleurs, un autre phénomène induit est l'intervention de nouveaux acteurs, des organisations non gouvernementales agissant dans le domaine du développement et dont le fondement est l'entraide et la solidarité. Leurs interventions sont multiples et certaines visent l'implantation de projet de développement communautaire ciblant parfois des femmes sans emploi dans un milieu favorable à son développement. Leur généralisation et leur champ d'intervention amènent Desroche (1991) à noter que nous sommes dans l'économie du don et du contre-don et non dans l'économie d'échange.

L'implantation des ONG dans le processus de développement est sujet de débat et traduit dans une large mesure, pour certains auteurs, l'échec des politiques orientées essentiellement sur l'implantation d'un secteur moderne, capable d'exercer des effets d'entraînement. Cette implication porte en elle l'amorce d'un renouvellement des politiques de développement accordant une préoccupation plus large à l'ensemble de la population et l'initiative de groupements organisés (Haudeville, 1992).

CONCLUSION

Finalement, avec l'adoption du PAS, le fonctionnement de l'économie est profondément modifié et la société est en mutation. Le marché du travail est un des plus touchés. De nouvelles pratiques sociales, trouvant leur origine dans le bouleversement des marchés, ont vu le jour. Avec ces nouvelles pratiques, favorisant une plus importante segmentation du marché, nous assistons à côté des primodemandeurs d'emploi à un gonflement du secteur informel et à la création de micro-entreprises.

Cependant, il est sans doute illusoire de placer trop d'espoirs dans le développement de ces structures. En effet, celles-ci fonctionnent dans une politique de reproduction simple et ne réalisent pas ou très peu d'accumulation, s'exposant à des problèmes de sources de financement, de croissance et à la difficulté de créer de l'emploi.

Des mécanismes d'adaptation sont mis en place par les pouvoirs publics, mais ils nécessiteront certainement un continuel réajustement en fonction des conditions évolutives du contexte national et international, notamment devant l'impératif de la mondialisation de l'économie.

Bibliographie

BANQUE MONDIALE (1995). *En route vers le 21e siècle*, Mémorandum économique pour la Tunisie.

BEDOUI, A. (1994). « Analyse de la dynamique sociale dans le contexte de l'application du plan d'ajustement structurel en Tunisie », *Revue tunisienne d'économie*, n° 5, 253-314.

BEDOUI, M. et R. GOUIA (1995). *Patterns and Processes of Social Exclusion in Tunisia*, Copenhague, UNDP.

CHARMES, J. (1991). *L'emploi dans le monde arabe*, Paris, Centre français sur la population et le développement.

DESROCHE, H. (1969). *Le développement intercoopératif : ses modèles et ses combinaisons*, Librairie de cité universitaire.

HAUDEVILLE, B. (1992). « Logique économique et logique sociale : la double rationalité de l'entreprise informelle et ses implications en matière de financement », *Revue internationale PME*, vol. 5.

HURTUBISE, Yves (1994). « Post-providentialisme et émancipation : les possibles dans les services sociaux », *Possibles*, vol. 18, n° 3.

LACHAUD, J.P. (1994). « The Labour Market in Africa », *Research Series*, n° 102.

LESPES, J.L. (1992). « Les informalités tontinières : tradition et innovation », dans HAUDEVILLE, Bernard, « Logique économique et logique sociale », *Revue internationale PME*, vol. 5.

LUBELL, H. (1991). *Le secteur informel dans les années 80 et 90*, OCDE, Centre de développement, Paris.

MORRISSON, C., OUDIN, X. et H.B. SOLIGNAC LE COMTE (1994). *Micro-entreprises et cadre institutionnel dans les pays en développement*, OCDE.

NINACS, W.A. (1995). « Entraide économique, création d'entreprises, politiques sociales et empowerment », *Nouvelles pratiques sociales*, vol. 8, n° 1, printemps, 97-119.

UNICEF (1987). *The Invisible Adjustement : Poor Women and the Economic Crisis*.

Impact des programmes d'ajustement structurel sur le secteur de la santé : cas du Togo

Tchabouré Aimé GOGUÉ
Programme de 3e cycle interuniversitaire
Burkina Faso

Après avoir affiché des performances remarquables, le Togo a connu une crise économique profonde qui l'a contraint à adopter une politique économique rigoureuse, à savoir les Programmes d'ajustement structurel (PAS). Si l'application des mesures préconisées n'a pas entraîné une chute remarquable des dépenses publiques de santé, la baisse du PIB causée par les réductions des dépenses gouvernementales, des investissements publics et la contraction des effectifs de la fonction publique ont eu des impacts négatifs sur la demande et l'offre des services sanitaires dans le pays conduisant ainsi à une détérioration de l'état de santé de la population.

INTRODUCTION

Les conditions et politiques économiques qui ont prévalu en Afrique depuis les indépendances ont conduit à des résultats le plus souvent catastrophiques. D'une manière générale, après des performances économiques relativement satisfaisantes, des déséquilibres économiques importants, qu'il s'agisse du budget de l'État, de la balance des paiements, de l'endettement extérieur ou de l'emploi, ont commencé à apparaître à partir du début des années 1980. Les raisons de ces mauvaises performances économiques sont à la fois internes et externes. En vue de stopper la dégradation conséquente du bien-être de la population, de rétablir les grands équilibres macro-économiques et de relancer la croissance économique, les responsables ont été contraints d'appliquer des réformes économiques profondes. Les pays appliquant les Programmes d'ajustement structurel (PAS) ont adopté, à partir de la deuxième moitié des années 1980, des mesures permettant de tenir compte de la dimension sociale de l'ajustement.

La présente étude vise à montrer l'impact des PAS sur le secteur de la santé au Togo. Dans une première partie, après avoir examiné la situation sanitaire dans le pays, nous présenterons les déterminants de l'état de santé de la population. Dans la deuxième partie, nous analyserons l'influence des PAS sur des variables explicatives de la santé. Aussi, dans la troisème partie, nous verrons que les politiques budgétaires restrictives ont contribué à la détérioration de l'état sanitaire de la population. Des recommandations de politiques constitueront l'essentiel de la conclusion. Compte tenu de la crise sociopolitique profonde qu'a traversée le pays à partir de 1992 et qui a aggravé la détérioration des conditions de vie de la population, l'étude ne prendra pas en compte les données postérieures à 1991.

LES CONDITIONS SANITAIRES AU TOGO

La situation sanitaire au Togo

Classé parmi les pays les moins avancés, le Togo présente des indicateurs sanitaires inquiétants. Ainsi, malgré quelques améliorations, la situation sanitaire dans le pays n'est pas des plus réjouissantes. En effet, selon le Programme des Nations Unies pour le développement ou PNUD (1993) :

- l'espérance de vie à la naissance est passée de 39,4 ans en 1960 à 54 ans en 1992 ;

- le taux de mortalité infantile (pour 1 000 naissances) est passé de 156 à 134 entre 1965 et 1970, puis à 86 en 1992 ;

- le taux de mortalité des moins de 5 ans était de 140 en 1992 ;

- le taux de mortalité maternelle était de 600 pour 100 000 naissances vivantes en 1988 ;

– l'insuffisance pondérale (en pourcentage des enfants de moins de 5 ans) a chuté de 25 à 18 % entre 1975 et 1990.

Le taux de croissance démographique, qui s'était stabilisé à 2,9 % en moyenne par an entre 1960 et 1981, est passé à 3,0 % et 3,1 % en 1986 et en 1991 respectivement. Plus de la moitié (50,6 %) de la population avait moins de 15 ans en 1980 contre 44,7 % en 1993. L'importance relative de la population en âge de travailler (15 à 64 ans) a par contre augmenté, passant de 45,5 % en 1981 à 52,9 % en 1993.

Cependant, comme l'indiquent les données du tableau suivant, l'état de la santé de la population togolaise se compare favorablement par rapport à celui des autres pays de l'Afrique au sud du Sahara (ASS). En effet, entre 1970 et 1993, le taux de mortalité brute a baissé au Togo de 35,5 % contre 28,6 % en ASS et dans l'ensemble des pays à faible revenu. Pour cette même période, l'espérance de vie à la naissance s'est accrue de 23,9 % pour les femmes au Togo et de 25,6 % pour les hommes ; en ASS, l'augmentation a été de 15,2 % pour les femmes et de 19,1 % pour les hommes.

TABLEAU 1
État de santé des pays en développement

	Taux de mortalité brute		Taux de mortalité infantile		Espérance de vie à la naissance (femme)		Espérance de vie à la naissance (homme)	
	1970	**1993**	**1970**	**1993**	**1970**	**1993**	**1970**	**1993**
Pays à faible revenu	14 %	10 %	108 %	64 %	54 ans	63 ans	53 ans	61 ans
ASS*	21 %	15 %	132 %	93 %	46 ans	53 ans	42 ans	50 ans
Togo	20 %	13 %	134 %	83 %	46 ans	57 ans	43 ans	54 ans

*ASS. : Afrique au sud du Sahara.
Source : Banque mondiale (1995).

Les statistiques sanitaires de la Direction générale de la santé (DGS) révèlent une grande instabilité dans la prévalence des maladies parasitaires, infectieuses et diarrhéiques au Togo. Les cas d'amibiase déclarés, qui étaient relativement faibles au cours des années 1970 (6 200 cas en moyenne par an entre 1973 et 1979), ont considérablement augmenté au cours de la deuxième moitié des années 1980, passant à plus de 22 000 cas en moyenne par an entre 1985 et 1990. Ainsi, en 1973, il y en avait environ 200 pour 100 000 habitants alors qu'en 1990, la situation s'étant considérablement détériorée, il y avait plus de 950 cas. Même s'il a légèrement baissé entre les deux périodes, le nombre de cas de diarrhée demeure toujours une préoccupation. En effet, il était de 136 800 en 1985 contre 133 200 en 1990, soit environ 4 300 cas pour 100 000 habitants contre plus de 6 400 en 1973.

Cependant, le paludisme demeure la maladie la plus courante au Togo avec 466 500 cas déclarés en 1985, soit 15,4 % de la population, contre 810 500 en 1990, soit 23,7 % de la population. Il y avait donc plus de 23 000 cas de paludisme pour 100 000 habitants en 1990. Ces données semblent indiquer une prévalence de cas de maladies liées au cadre de vie de la population qui se serait détérioré et une stratégie sanitaire du pays basée sur la médecine curative plutôt que sur la médecine préventive. Ce constat est confirmé par les données sur le cadre de vie de la population et sur l'accès à l'eau potable (Adéwussi, 1994).

En ce qui concerne l'assainissement, les proportions de population qui jouissent d'un service d'évacuation d'excrétas considéré comme hygiénique sont les suivantes :

- en milieu urbain, de 53,7 %, avec des variations allant de 15 % en région centrale à 68 % en région maritime ;

- en milieu rural, de 9,7 %, avec des variations allant de 1 % en région des savanes à 24 % en région maritime.

Il faut, toutefois, signaler que ces systèmes d'évacuation ne présentent pas, dans la majorité des cas, une sécurité sanitaire certaine. Les caniveaux et égouts destinés à l'évacuation des eaux usées et de pluies, et le système d'enlèvement des ordures ménagères, même s'ils sont inefficaces et insuffisants, n'existe que dans la capitale. Par conséquent, 72,3 % de la population urbaine a accès à l'eau potable contre 56,1 % de la population rurale. Néanmoins, il existe des disparités régionales très marquées : 88 % de la population urbaine de la région des plateaux disposent d'eau potable contre 49 % dans la région des savanes ; 63 % de la population rurale de la région maritime n'ont pas accès à l'eau potable contre seulement 23 % dans la région de la Kara.

Le privilège accordé au système de santé curative se vérifie dans la répartition du personnel de santé. Le pays ne disposait que de trois ingénieurs sanitaires jusqu'en 1988. Le nombre de techniciens supérieurs de génie sanitaire est inférieur à 40 alors que celui des assistants d'hygiène d'État après avoir augmenté de 122, en 1973, à 245, en 1983, a baissé à 215 en 1990 (Direction générale de la santé, 1990). Alors qu'en 1990, il y avait 11 328 et 2 543 habitants par médecin et infirmier d'État respectivement, il y en avait 193 156 par technicien du génie sanitaire.

La dégradation de l'état de santé de la population se perçoit encore mieux par l'examen de l'évolution de la malnutrition dans le pays. En effet, selon le ministère du Plan et des Mines (1989), le nombre de consultations pour malnutrition dans les centres de santé est passé de 3 726, en 1980, à 7 880 et 14 166, en 1983 et en 1987, respectivement. Les enfants âgés de 0 à 4 ans ont été plus affectés par ce fléau, le nombre de cas dans ce groupe d'âge étant passé de 2 246 à 13 213 entre 1980 et 1987, soit un pourcentage de 93,3 % de l'ensemble de la population atteinte de malnutrition en 1987 contre seulement 60,3 % en 1980. La région des savanes, la plus pauvre du pays, est également la zone géographique la plus touchée, puisqu'elle comptait en 1987, 78,1 % des cas de consultations pour malnutrition contre seulement 23,1 % en 1980.

Cette dégradation de l'état nutritionnel de la population coïncide avec une détérioration de la quantité d'éléments nutritionnels disponibles par jour et par habitant. En effet, de 100 qu'ils étaient entre 1978 et 1982, les indices des quantités de calories, de glucides et de fer disponibles par jour et par habitant ont diminué constamment prenant des valeurs de 93,9, 92,6 et 88,9, entre 1983 et 1987. Ces données semblent confirmer les résultats des études concluant que ce sont généralement les groupes sociaux les plus vulnérables qui ont le plus souffert des effets négatifs des PAS. Cette situation sanitaire dans le pays s'explique par l'évolution des déterminants de l'état de santé de la population.

Les déterminants de l'état de santé de la population

L'état de santé de la population d'un pays dépend de plusieurs variables, notamment du taux d'alphabétisation, du revenu et de son taux de croissance. Pour Preston (1980, 1983), 50 % de l'accroissement de l'espérance de vie à la naissance entre 1940 et 1970 est expliqué par le revenu, le taux d'alphabétisation et la disponibilité de calories. En outre, des études reconnaissent de façon unanime le rôle prépondérant de la femme dans l'état de santé de l'individu, du ménage et de la société dans les pays en développement. En effet, selon une étude menée entre 1975 et 1985 sur 13 pays africains et citée par la Banque mondiale (1993), un accroissement de 10 % du taux d'alphabétisation de la femme entraîne une réduction du taux de mortalité infantile de 10 % ; une augmentation de un à trois ans du niveau d'instruction de la mère permet une réduction du taux de mortalité infantile de 15 %. Selon Behrman et Wolfe (1987), cette influence de la scolarité de la mère sur l'état de santé du ménage s'explique par le fait qu'une femme mieux éduquée sera plus sensibilisée aux problèmes d'hygiène, à une alimentation plus équilibrée, aux bienfaits des consultations médicales et à l'utilisation plus rationnelle de médicaments.

La Banque mondiale (1993) estime qu'une amélioration du niveau de revenu, du taux de croissance économique du pays ainsi qu'une réduction du niveau de pauvreté permet à l'agent économique d'avoir de meilleures conditions de vie et de meilleurs soins de santé. En effet, on devrait s'attendre à ce qu'un revenu de ménage élevé permette à ce dernier de consacrer plus de ressources à la médecine préventive et d'améliorer l'état d'hygiène dans la maison, favorisant ainsi la réduction des maladies.

Sur le plan macro-économique, des variables externes au ménage affectent également l'état de santé du ménage et du pays. En effet, les services et le personnel de santé, les conditions d'accès à l'eau potable, les infrastructures d'hygiène et sanitaires, peuvent également améliorer les conditions de médecine préventive, donc l'état de santé de la population.

En dehors du signe positif du coefficient des dépenses publiques comme variable explicative du taux de mortalité infantile, les tests effectués par Calipel, Guillaumont et Guillaumont (1994) sur un échantillon de 52 pays en développement confirment les conclusions des études antérieures. Selon ces auteurs, le signe du coefficient des dépenses publiques (cependant non significatif) s'expliquerait par la mauvaise qualité des données, une substitution des dépenses privées aux dépenses publiques, les délais dans les effets des variations des dépenses publiques sur l'état de santé et une meilleure efficacité dans l'utilisation des ressources.

En conclusion, dans la mesure où ils ont un impact sur les autres facteurs explicatifs, le PIB et le revenu du ménage seront les variables les plus déterminantes de l'état de santé de la population. Dans ces conditions, pour une compréhension de l'évolution de l'état de santé, il faut donc examiner celle des revenus du pays et des ménages. Or, ces variables dépendent en grande partie de la situation et des politiques économiques suivies par le pays durant la période sous analyse.

LES PROGRAMMES D'AJUSTEMENT STRUCTUREL

La cause des PAS : la crise économique des années 1980

Après avoir été stable entre 1970 et 1980, le PIB réel par habitant (37 195 F CFA en 1970 contre 37 150 en 1980) a chuté à un rythme annuel moyen de 1,8 % au cours des années 1980. Les investissements bruts rapportés au PIB, après avoir augmenté de 23 à 30 % entre 1970 et 1980, ont baissé à 19 % en 1991 alors que l'épargne intérieure brute, qui représentait 26 % du PIB en 1970, s'est littéralement effondrée

(10 % du PIB) en 1991. Le taux annuel moyen d'inflation qui était de 2,9 % entre 1965 et 1973 est passé à 8,2 % entre 1973 et 1980, puis à 6,6 % entre 1980 et 1987.

L'accroissement sur le marché international, durant les années 1970, des cours des principaux produits de base exportés par le pays (cacao, café et phosphate) a permis à l'État, qui a le monopole de leur commercialisation, d'accroître sa part dans la dépense nationale ; les dépenses budgétaires sont alors passées de 10,9 % du PIB, en 1970, à 28,2 %, en 1980, puis ramenées à 20,8 %, en 1990, après avoir culminé à 36,7 %, en 1976. Le solde budgétaire de l'État, qui était de 1,6 % du PIB en 1970 est passé à moins de 8,4 % en 1979 alors que le déficit du compte courant s'est aussi aggravé, passant de 1,1 % du PIB, en 1970, à 21,3 %, en 1979.

De surcroît, le pays a commencé à connaître des difficultés en ce qui concerne le service de sa dette extérieure dès 1979. L'encours de la dette publique extérieure rapporté au PIB est passé de 16 %, en 1970, à 82 %, en 1980, alors que le service de la dette en pourcentage des exportations des biens et services évoluait de 3,1 à 8,2 puis à 18,2 %, en 1970, en 1980 et en 1989 respectivement.

Pour corriger les déséquilibres macro-économiques et permettre la reprise d'une croissance durable, il fallait, par des mesures appropriées, s'attaquer aux problèmes fondamentaux de politique économique, de gestion et d'aménagement du cadre juridique et institutionnel du pays en difficulté. C'est ainsi que le pays a été contraint à recourir à des réformes de politiques économiques, les PAS, avec le concours des institutions de Bretton Woods. Les mesures appliquées dans le cadre des PAS affectent en premier lieu les capacités et la nature des interventions du gouvernement dans la vie économique et sociale et ne sont pas neutres quant à l'évolution des déterminants de l'état sanitaire dans le pays.

Les mécanismes de transmission des PAS au secteur de la santé

Conçus en vue de permettre aux pays de rétablir les grands équilibres macro-économiques, les PAS favorisent les mesures suivantes :

– des politiques monétaire et fiscale restrictives en vue de maîtriser la demande globale à un niveau compatible avec l'offre globale, ainsi que des mesures visant à rétablir l'équilibre des finances publiques ;

- des contrôles plus rigoureux des procédures budgétaires ;
- le contrôle des subventions du secteur public ;
- des politiques visant à rétablir la vérité des prix en vue d'améliorer l'allocation des ressources pour rendre l'économie plus compétitive ;
- la libéralisation des mouvements internationaux des biens et des capitaux ;
- la dépréciation du taux de change en vue d'améliorer l'état de la balance des paiements.

Le rétablissement de l'équilibre des finances publiques constitue souvent l'élément incontournable des politiques proposées par le FMI dans la mesure où les interventions de cette institution s'inspirent de l'approche monétaire de la balance des paiements. Pour réduire leur déficit, les gouvernements sont contraints de diminuer leurs dépenses et d'augmenter les recettes budgétaires. C'est dans ce cadre que s'inscrivent les mesures visant une plus grande rationalisation des investissements publics, un resserrement des dépenses publiques, un contrôle plus rigoureux des dépenses de fonctionnement de l'État, notamment, la masse salariale et les effectifs du secteur public. Du côté des recettes, l'État augmente certaines taxes et procède à la privatisation de certaines entreprises publiques. L'impact des PAS sur l'état de santé de la population peut donc être saisi à travers l'effet de ces réformes sur les variables explicatives de l'état de santé de la population.

Toutes choses étant égales par ailleurs, ces réductions des dépenses publiques se traduiront par une baisse des ressources allouées aux secteurs sociaux, dont la santé. On peut distinguer ici les effets à court et à long terme :

- À court terme, en raison de l'effet multiplicateur, la baisse des dépenses publiques conduit à une chute du revenu et de la demande globale ; ce qui, à son tour, affectera négativement le revenu disponible des ménages et, par conséquent, les sommes consacrées à la santé et à l'éducation. En outre, la volonté d'équilibrer les finances publiques se traduit également par la compression des effectifs de la fonction publique. Enfin, la réduction probable du taux de croissance économique du pays sous ajustement contribuera à une détérioration de l'état de santé dans le pays.
- À long terme, c'est surtout la réduction des dépenses d'éducation et des investissements qui influera négativement sur l'état de santé dans le pays. La baisse des dépenses publiques d'éducation réduit les conditions d'offre d'éducation, ce qui affecte le rendement interne du système éducatif.

En résumé, si à court terme les PAS, par leurs effets sur l'état de la pauvreté, l'emploi, l'éducation et le taux de croissance économique, entraînent la détérioration de l'état de santé dans le pays, on devrait s'attendre qu'à long terme ils favorisent l'amélioration de la santé de la population.

IMPACT DES PAS SUR LES SECTEURS DE LA SANTÉ AU TOGO

Effets du contrôle du budget de l'État

L'élasticité des dépenses de l'État dans le domaine de la santé par rapport aux dépenses gouvernementales totales est passée de 0,62, entre 1970 et 1974, à 0,88, entre 1975 et 1979. Par contre, durant la période d'application des PAS, elle a augmenté à 1,97 indiquant ainsi que, au cours des années 1980, pour tout accroissement de 1 % des revenus de l'État, le gouvernement augmentait ses dépenses dans le secteur de la santé de près de 2 %. Cependant, compte tenu de l'évolution du PIB et en raison des restrictions budgétaires qui ont réduit les dépenses budgétaires de 30,5 % du PIB, en 1979, à 20,8 %, en 1990, on constate que les dépenses de l'État en matière sanitaire augmentaient à un rythme inférieur à celui du PIB au cours des années 1980 (élasticité de 0,85, entre 1980 et 1990, contre 1,5, entre 1975 et 1979).

TABLEAU 2
Budget de la santé publique

Année	Budget général de fonction- nement (1)	Budget de fonction- nement de la santé publique (2)	$\frac{(1)}{(2)}$	Contribu- tions aux CHU à Lomé (3)	$\frac{(3)}{(2+3)}$	Budget d'investis- sement public dans la santé (4)	Dépenses publiques totales (2+3+4) par habitant
1970	7 980	573	7,8	336	37	160	552
1974	16 245	1 091	6,7	558	33	102	801
1975	30 515	1 441	4,7	770	34	192	1 070
1979	64 616	2 496	3,9	1 232	33	116	1 546
1980	67 275	2 838	4,4	1 377	33	141	1 657
1984	76 890	3 298	4,3	1 284	28	129	1 609
1985	81 890	3 937	4,9	1 290	25	129	1 775
1986	87 283	3 974	4,6	1 352	25	241	1 794
1987	89 691	3 941	4,4	461	27	360	1 804
1990	92 490	4 769	5,2	2 353	33	1 088	2 414

Source : Direction générale de la santé.

Un accroissement des ressources publiques pour les centres de santé secondaires indiquerait que l'État accorde plus d'importance aux populations rurales et à celles vivant dans les zones périurbaines du pays. Dans la mesure où les couches les plus défavorisées sont plus nombreuses dans les zones rurales et périurbaines que dans la capitale, l'évolution de la répartition des ressources financières de l'État révèle ainsi que, durant la première moitié de la période d'application des PAS au Togo (1980-1985), le gouvernement a favorisé les couches sociales du monde rural alors que, durant la deuxième moitié, il a plutôt privilégié la population urbaine. Ainsi, la volonté de considérer la dimension sociale de l'ajustement dans les PAS répond beaucoup plus aux préoccupations des populations urbaines.

Les données du tableau 2 indiquent également qu'après une hausse de 90 % en 1975, les investissements publics ont chuté de 32 % entre 1975 et 1985 en francs courants, révélant une forte détérioration des infrastructures. C'est ainsi que le nombre de centres de santé est passé de 360, en 1980, à 310, en 1986. La tendance a toutefois été renversée, à partir de 1986, avec un accroissement des investissements publics dans le secteur à un taux annuel moyen de plus de 87,8 %, entre 1986 et 1990, entraînant une augmentation graduelle du nombre de centres de santé jusqu'à 417 en 1990. Les efforts consentis par le gouvernement à partir de 1986 ont permis d'améliorer et d'accroître les infrastructures sanitaires.

La répartition des dépenses par catégories montre que les dépenses de personnel continuent d'absorber plus de 70 % des ressources du ministère de la Santé contre seulement 11 %, en moyenne, pour les médicaments et les équipements sanitaires. On doit toutefois signaler qu'après avoir augmenté de plus de 500 %, entre 1970 et 1978, les ressources publiques allouées aux médicaments et autres produits sanitaires ont baissé à un rythme annuel moyen de 6,2 %, entre 1978 et 1983, avant de recommencer à augmenter. Il faut cependant attendre 1989 pour que les ressources allouées à cette rubrique dépassent leur niveau de 1978 en francs courants ! Cette orientation aura également un influence négative sur l'état de santé de la population.

Dépenses publiques dans les autres secteurs sociaux

Les autres dépenses sociales ont augmenté de 13,2 % du budget de l'État, en 1976, à 23,0 %, en 1990. Cette évolution révèle l'importance accordée à l'éducation dans l'allocation de ses ressources dans la mesure où, depuis 1976, les affaires sociales n'ont jamais drainé plus de 0,60 % des ressources publiques.

Si les ressources publiques destinées à l'éducation n'ont pas baissé, des mesures de resserrement des conditions d'accès aux cycles de formation et d'enseignement, et la réduction des effectifs dans la fonction publique ont affecté négativement le taux de scolarisation dans le pays, entre 1980-1981 et 1984-1985 (Gogué, 1996). C'est ainsi que les effectifs féminins ont baissé de 198 418, en 1980-1981, à 195 523, en 1986-1987, dans le premier degré, et de 27 570, en 1980-1981, à 22 332, en 1988-1989. En outre, pour freiner l'entrée sur le marché du travail d'un personnel formé, le gouvernement a fermé, pour une période donnée, des établissements de formation professionnelle comme l'École nationale des sages-femmes, l'École nationale des auxiliaires médicaux et l'École des infirmiers. Ces mesures ont eu un impact négatif notable sur la possibilité d'engager du personnel qualifié.

Compression des effectifs de la fonction publique

Les PAS, dans leur souci de réaliser l'objectif de contrôle des dépenses gouvernementales, ont également eu recours à la réduction du personnel de la fonction publique. Dans le cas du Togo, à partir de 1983, l'accès à la fonction publique est conditionné au succès préalable à un concours de recrutement à la fonction publique, alors que les employés qui quittent (pour cause de retraite, décès, etc.) ne sont plus remplacés. Ces mesures vont affecter le secteur de la santé de deux façons.

En premier lieu, la réduction conséquente des effectifs de la fonction publique va entraîner une diminution des revenus des ménages et une réduction de la demande globale, ce qui va conduire à une baisse des effectifs du personnel du secteur privé moderne. En effet, comme l'indiquent les données du tableau 2, l'effectif de la fonction publique a augmenté de 30 635 à 38 621, entre 1977 et 1981, alors que celui du secteur privé a augmenté de 34,23 % au cours de la même période. À partir de 1981, le marché de l'emploi a commencé à se détériorer. C'est ainsi que le personnel de la fonction publique a continuellement chuté pour se situer à 34 377, en 1988, alors que l'effectif du secteur privé moderne atteignait 40 126, en 1989. Malgré la reprise de l'emploi en 1987, l'effectif du personnel dans le secteur moderne en 1990 était toujours inférieur à son niveau de 1984.

Dans la mesure où l'emploi dans le secteur moderne est concentré en milieu urbain, nous pouvons alors conclure que ce sera surtout les pauvres des villes qui seront touchés par cette détérioration du marché de l'emploi au cours des années 1980. La réduction conséquente des revenus des ménages en milieu urbain renforcée par l'accélération de

TABLEAU 3
Évolution de l'emploi moderne au Togo

Année	Secteurs		
	Public	Privé et parapublic	Total
1977	30 635	36 843	67 478
1981	38 621	49 458	88 079
1982	34 601	48 306	82 904
1986	34 300	39 871	74 171
1987	34 520	51 768	83 288
1988	34 383	51 875	86 258
1989	33 777	46 823	80 600
1990	33 851	45 962	79 793
1991	33 631	47 894	81 525

Source : Programme des Nations Unies pour le développement (1994).

l'inflation se traduira par une baisse des ressources consacrées à la santé. Dans tous les cas, on devrait s'attendre à ce que les couches sociales les plus défavorisées restreignent encore davantage les ressources qu'elles allouent à la santé.

En second lieu, la réduction du personnel de la fonction publique affectera l'effectif du personnel de la santé, à moins que des mesures particulières ne soient prises afin de protéger ce secteur. Bien entendu, l'offre des services sanitaires sera également touchée. C'est ainsi qu'après une croissance régulière de 10 % en moyenne par an entre 1971 et 1983, les effectifs du personnel de santé ont baissé de 3 % en moyenne par an, entre 1983 et 1986, puis augmenté de 12,3 %, passant de 5 060, en 1986, à 5 680, en 1987.

Les centres de santé dans les petites villes et en milieu rural sont relativement mieux protégés durant les périodes de compression du personnel ; leur effectif rapporté à l'ensemble du personnel de la santé a augmenté de 55,7 %, en 1983, à 63,2 %, en 1986. La reprise du recrutement les a, par contre, défavorisés puisque leur part dans l'ensemble du personnel de la santé a baissé à 44,8 %, en 1990. Ces données montrent que les mesures de compression des effectifs de la fonction publique adoptées dans le cadre des PAS n'ont pas systématiquement affecté les conditions d'offre de santé en milieu rural durant les premières années d'application. On note encore ici que la prise en compte de la dimension sociale a profité plus aux pauvres de Lomé.

TABLEAU 4
Personnel de santé

Année	Personnel aux CHU* de Lomé	Personnel de cabinets privés	Personnel des autres services MSP**	Personnel à l'intérieur du pays	Total Personnel de la santé
1980	726	–	1 384	2 761	4 871
1983	1 098	36	1 415	3 209	5 758
1985	962	82	1 406	3 334	5 784
1986	960	77	822	3 201	5 060
1987	1 131	52	1 370	3 130	5 683
1988	1 267	77	1 465	3 333	6 142
1989	1 395	125	1 640	3 110	6 270
1990	1 519	244	1 715	2 825	6 303

* CHU : Centres hospitaliers universitaires.
** MSP : Ministère de la Santé publique.
Source : Direction générale de la santé (plusieurs années).

Politique d'accroissement des recettes budgétaires

Dans le domaine des recettes, le gouvernement a introduit l'impôt de solidarité représentant 5 % des revenus des contribuables. Le transport public urbain dans la capitale a été supprimé en 1981. En outre, à partir de la même année, toutes les entreprises publiques déficitaires devaient sortir du portefeuille du gouvernement. C'est ainsi que sur les 74 entreprises publiques que comptait le pays, 16 ont été liquidées, 17 privatisées, 2 mises en location et 2, en observation. La réduction des subventions, l'accroissement des impôts et des prix aux usagers des services publics ont diminué le revenu réel des ménages et l'emploi dans le secteur moderne renforçant ainsi les effets dépressifs des réductions des dépenses publiques sur la demande des services de santé. Dans ces conditions, les mesures prises pour contrôler le budget de l'État ont eu des répercussions défavorables aussi bien sur les conditions d'offre que sur celles de la demande de santé.

Effets des politiques de prix

Les PAS renferment aussi des mesures visant à favoriser la production agricole par l'accroissement des prix aux producteurs. Dans le cas du Togo, la faible intervention du gouvernement dans la détermination des prix des produits vivriers limite l'impact de cette politique sur les revenus et le niveau de consommation des populations. Cependant, les restrictions imposées aux exportations des produits vivriers, toutes choses étant égales par ailleurs, auront des effets dépressifs sur les prix. Toutefois, étant donné que ces mesures existaient déjà avant l'instauration des PAS, leurs effets ne peuvent pas leur être attribués.

En ce qui concerne les produits agricoles d'exportation, les PAS ont prescrit la réduction des subventions aux intrants compensée par un accroissement des prix aux producteurs. C'est ainsi que, dans le cas du coton, le taux de subvention pour les engrais est passé de 80,5 % en 1980-1981 à 11,5 % en 1984-1985 puis à 0 % à partir de 1985-1986 (Gogué, 1990). Le prix aux producteurs de coton est passé de 60 F CFA en 1980-1981 à 90 F CFA en 1985-1986, d'une part, et de 74 à 125 % du prix du maïs au cours de la même période, d'autre part, principale spéculation concurrente au coton, au cours de la même période (Gogué, 1990).

Si la politique des prix aux producteurs a favorisé la production et les revenus agricoles, elle a cependant eu des effets pervers sur la scolarisation entre 1981 et 1985. En effet, au cours de cette période, les effectifs scolaires ont chuté de près de 15 % (Gogué, 1996). Au primaire, la population scolarisée des filles a chuté de 11,7 % au cours de la période contre 9,5 % pour la population scolarisée des garçons.

Réaction de la population à la suite de la chute des revenus et de l'augmentation des frais de santé

Un phénomène qui existait déjà mais qui s'amplifie avec la dégradation des conditions de vie des populations et l'accroissement des coûts des services de santé est le recours à la médecine traditionnelle. C'est ainsi que les populations, surtout défavorisées, font de plus en plus appel aux services des guérisseurs traditionnels et utilisent plus fréquemment les prescriptions de ces derniers pour se soigner. Si cette pratique permet de réduire le coût de la médecine curative et d'obtenir parfois de bons résultats, l'inexistence de normes et de codes réduit son efficacité. En outre, la médecine traditionnelle a très peu d'effets sur la médecine préventive ; or, la détérioration du cadre de vie à la suite de la réduction des investissements publics devrait favoriser la promotion de cette forme de médecine.

CONCLUSION

Au cours des années 1980, le Togo a traversé une crise économique caractérisée par une chute de la production, une augmentation de l'inflation et du chômage ainsi qu'une détérioration de la situation financière et de l'endettement extérieur de l'État. Les mesures qui ont été prises dans le cadre des PAS, si elles n'ont pas donné les résultats attendus pour des raisons qui ne peuvent être explicitées ici, ont par contre eu des effets sur l'état de santé de la population.

Si le gouvernement n'a pas réduit sensiblement la part de ses ressources au budget de fonctionnement aux ministères de la Santé et des autres secteurs sociaux, on a toutefois noté une diminution des investissements publics dans la santé et des dépenses pour les médicaments, ce qui a contribué à détériorer les conditions d'offre de santé au cours des premières années d'application des PAS. Le principal impact des PAS sur la demande de santé de la population a été suscité par la baisse des revenus réels, conséquence de l'aggravation du chômage et des effets multiplicateurs de la baisse des dépenses gouvernementales.

Les mesures pour atténuer les effets pervers des PAS sur les couches sociales les plus démunies ont beaucoup plus favorisé les pauvres dans les villes, en général, et dans la capitale Lomé, en particulier, et cela peut-être pour tenir compte du fait qu'ils ont été les plus touchés par la crise des années 1980. L'aggravation de l'état nutritionnel des enfants âgés de moins de quatre ans et de la population de la région des savanes, région la plus pauvre du pays, a cependant été observée.

À la lumière de cette analyse, une amélioration de l'état de santé de la population n'est donc pas envisageable sans une reprise durable de la croissance économique et de l'emploi, d'une part, et sans un accroissement des revenus des populations les plus défavorisées, d'autre part. Or, comme l'a confirmé Wheeler (1980), la production nationale dépend, entre autres, de l'état de santé et, selon l'hypothèse du salaire d'efficience, l'état de santé et de nutrition est un déterminant de la productivité du travail. Il est donc important que les politiques gouvernementales, tout en cherchant à rétablir des équilibres macro-économiques, reprennent des mesures qui permettent la croissance tout en ayant un impact favorable sur l'état de santé de la population. Les données ont montré que les maladies les plus courantes sont liées au mauvais état du cadre de vie et qu'elles sont en partie le résultat d'une allocation des ressources publiques de santé qui favorise la médecine curative. Dans ces conditions, une réallocation des ressources au profit d'investissements dans les infrastructures en vue d'améliorer l'environnement et le cadre de vie de la population devrait être encouragée. Cette réorientation des ressources aura l'avantage de permettre un meilleur transfert des revenus aux couches sociales les plus démunies dans la mesure où la réalisation de ces travaux fait appel, en général, à des technologies intensives en main-d'œuvre.

Bibiographie

ADÉWUSSI, S.G. (1994). *Analyse des indicateurs sociaux du développement humain au Togo*, Lomé, PNUD.

BLARDONE, G. (1990). *Le Fonds monétaire international : l'ajustement et les coûts de l'homme*, Éditions de l'Épargne.

BANQUE MONDIALE (1993 et 1995). *Rapport sur le développement dans le monde*, Washington.

BEHRMAN, R.J. (1993). « Health and Economic Growth : Theory, Evidence and Policy », dans WORLD HEALTH ORGANIZATION, *Macroeconomic Environment and Health*.

BEHRMAN, R.J. et B. WOLFE (1987). « How Mother's Schooling Affect Family Health, Nutrition, Medicale Care Usage and Household Sanitation ? », *Journal of Economics*, 36.

CALDWELL, J. (1979). « Education as a Factor in Mortality Decline : An Examination of Nigeria Data », *Population Studies*, vol. 33, n° 3.

CALIPEL, S., P. GUILLAUMONT et S. GUILLAUMONT (1994). « L'évolution des dépenses publiques d'éducation et de santé : déterminants et conséquences », dans GUILLAUMONT, P. et S. GUILLAUMONT, *Ajustement et développement : l'expérience des pays ACP*, Paris, Economica.

COMITÉ DSA (1989). *Dimension sociale de l'ajustement : tendance de la production nationale des vivriers et de la malnutrition, avant et au cours de la période d'ajustement structurel (1978-1987)*, Ministère du Plan et des Mines, Lomé.

CORNIA, G.A. *et al.* (sous la direction de) [1987-1988]. *Adjustment with Human Face*, vol. 1 et 2, Oxford, Clarendon Press.

DE COOPER WEIL, P.A., ALICBUSAN, WILSON, M.J., REICH, R.M. et J.D. BRADLEY (1990). *The Impact of Development Policies on Health : A Review of the Literature*, World Health Organization.

DIOP, F., HILL, K. et I. SIRAGELDIN (1991). *Economic Crisis, Structural Adjustment and Health in Africa*, Working Paper 766, The World Bank.

DIRECTION GÉNÉRALE DE LA SANTÉ (1990). *Statistiques sanitaires*.

GELEWIVE, P. et D. DE TRAY (1988). *The Poor During Adjustment : A Case Study of the Côte d'Ivoire*, The World Bank.

GENBERG, H. (1993). « Macroeconomic Adjustment and the Health Sector : A Review », dans WORLD HEALTH ORGANIZATION, *Macroeconomic Environment and Health*.

GOGUÉ, T.A. (1990). *La politique cotonnière du Togo*, Université du Bénin (mimeo).

GOGUÉ, T.A. (1996). « Impact des programmes d'ajustement structurel sur les effectifs scolaires : cas du Togo », *Revue Canadienne d'Étude de Développement*.

GOMES-NETO, B.J., HANUSHEK, A.E., LEITE, H.R. et C.R. FROTA-BEZZERA (1992). *Health and Schooling : Evidence and Policy Implications for Developing Countries*, Working Paper 306, Rochester University Centre for Economic Research (mimeo).

JOLLY, R. et A.G. CORNIA (1984). *The Impact of the World Recession on Children : A Study Prepared for UNICEF*, Oxford, Pergamon Press.

PINSTRUP-ANDERSEN, P. (1993). «Economic Crisis and Policy Reforms During the 80s and their Impact on the Poor», dans WORLD HEALTH ORGANIZATION, *Macro-economic Environment and Health*.

PRESTON, H.S. (1980). «Causes and Consequences of Mortality Declines in Less Developed Countries During the Twentieth Century», dans EASTERLIN, R. (sous la direction de), *Population and Economic Change in Developing Countries*, Chicago University Press.

PRESTON, H.S. (1983). *Mortality and Development Revisited*, University of Pennsylvania (mimeo).

PROGRAMME DES NATIONS UNIES POUR LE DÉVELOPPEMENT (1993). *Rapport sur le développement humain*.

SAHN, E.D. (1990). «The Impact of Export Crop Production on Nutritional Status in Côte d'Ivoire», *World Development*, vol. 18, n° 12.

WHEELER, D. (1980). «Basic Needs Fulfillment and Economic Growth: A Simultaneous Model», *Journal of Development Economics*, vol. 7, 435-451.

Le rêve de Diane
et les projets d'Albertine

Pierre Jean
Étudiant à la maîtrise en intervention sociale
Université du Québec à Montréal

Compte rendu du 3ᵉ colloque de la revue *Nouvelles pratiques sociales*, tenu le 13 mars 1997 au Pavillon Judith-Jasmin de l'Université du Québec à Montréal sur le thème de : *L'économie sociale et les services sociaux et de santé : enjeux et perspectives.*

En plus de fournir une occasion de s'informer sur cette réalité à la fois ancienne et nouvelle de l'économie sociale et sur la façon dont elle évolue dans le champ du sociosanitaire et du social en général, le colloque NPS 1997 permettra d'explorer les enjeux que ces nouvelles pratiques soulèvent pour l'emploi dans le réseau public et en particulier pour les femmes et pour les communautés locales. On y discutera enfin des conditions requises, et de la faisabilité de celles-ci, pour que l'économie sociale puisse contribuer au développement d'un nouveau contrat social, plutôt que de constituer un faire-valoir des politiques néolibérales[1].

Il s'agissait là d'un ambitieux programme pour un colloque d'une seule journée où se sont retrouvés quelques centaines de participants, venus de tous les horizons de l'intervention sociale au Québec. Mais qu'ils aient été du monde communautaire, coopératif, syndical ou du réseau sociosanitaire étatique, c'est avec un enthousiasme manifeste qu'ils ont répondu, sous différents registres, à ce défi auquel ils étaient conviés.

---

1. Extrait du formulaire de présentation et d'inscription du Colloque NPS, 1997.

Accueillies en début de journée par M. Jean-François Léonard, vice-recteur au partenariat et aux affaires externes de l'UQAM, les personnes présentes ont rapidement été plongées au cœur de la question lorsque ce dernier a évoqué d'entrée de jeu l'importance *des partenariats dans une chaîne de solidarité* comme outil de développement de modalités inédites d'intervention en prise sur la société et les problèmes sociaux émergents. Pour M. Léonard, l'économie sociale se situe directement dans le champ de ces nouvelles modalités tout en faisant intervenir l'expertise des sciences humaines et sociales.

En conférence d'ouverture de la première séance de la journée, présidée par Mme Linda Vallée[2] , nous avons eu le loisir d'entendre (et de lire[3]) les points de vue convergents de Mme Diane Lemieux[4] et de M. Yves Vaillancourt [5] sur l'état de la situation et des enjeux que soulève l'économie sociale, précédés d'un énoncé sur les diverses perceptions de l'économie sociale qui diffèrent, ou se caractérisent, suivant les fenêtres par lesquelles on l'appréhende.

Ainsi, pour Mme Lemieux, le lieu à partir duquel on examine l'économie sociale colore la lecture que l'on en a. En effet, que ces espaces de perception soient ceux du monde patronal, du mouvement communautaire ou qu'ils s'inscrivent sous le prisme d'un projet étatique, deux grandes lectures de l'économie sociale prédominent : elle devient un sous-produit du courant néolibéral pour les uns et un mode d'emploi défini pour ceux qui la combattent. Voilà ce qui explique que tant de forces vives s'agitent autour de l'économie sociale et le soudain intérêt des décideurs de tout acabit pour cette dernière.

Quoi qu'il en soit, pour M. Vaillancourt, on doit d'abord être soucieux de la jonction entre la recherche et les organismes qui décident d'emprunter cette voie afin de développer une vision tendant à réconcilier l'économie et le social. Pour ce dernier, l'économie sociale devient un passage obligé qui, au-delà des obstacles juridiques, conduit à une authentique démocratisation parce que l'économie sociale porte en elle les germes d'une culture de solidarité et de partage des valeurs et des principes qui réunissent à nouveau travailleurs, usagers des services et l'ensemble de la société civile. Il faudra être attentif, par ailleurs, à ne pas « ghettoïser » l'économie sociale, mais au contraire s'efforcer de la

---

2. Organisatrice communautaire au CLSC Jean-Olivier-Chénier et membre de l'équipe technique du Groupe de travail sur l'économie sociale.

3. Notes pour la conférence d'ouverture faite au colloque NPS du 13 mars 1997 (version du 12 mars).

4. Présidente du Conseil du statut de la femme.

5. Professeur au Département de travail social (UQAM) et directeur de la Revue NPS.

rendre perméable aux autres agents économiques et sociaux afin qu'elle devienne exportatrice de cette culture démocratique, celle-ci permettant le cas échéant le déploiement d'une nouvelle cohésion sociale.

Voilà résumé le contenu de la conférence d'ouverture sur lequel Mme Danielle Fournier[6] et M. Yves Nantel[7] auront eu à réagir en qualité d'analystes.

Pour la première, l'économie sociale est une opportunité formidable pour enfin reconnaître le travail invisible des femmes. Toutefois, le véritable défi à relever pour l'économie sociale réside dans la revalorisation de certains types de tâches encore dévolues quasi exclusivement aux femmes, notamment dans le domaine de l'aide domestique. Bien que l'économie sociale représente un gisement d'emplois particulièrement fertile pour les femmes, elle doit se concevoir comme un lieu de mixité soucieux de contrer les dangers d'enfermement du travail féminin.

M. Nantel, quant à lui, croit que l'économie sociale s'offre à nous comme une autre solution à la crise de l'emploi, mais pas une solution en attendant, ni une variante des mesures d'employabilité. On doit construire l'économie sociale sur des bases solides et permanentes. Son leadership doit demeurer sous la responsabilité des services et organisations communautaires déjà porteurs de larges pans de sa culture. En outre, il est primordial d'assurer l'équilibre de ses objectifs. L'objectif social vise à satisfaire les besoins des personnes, des collectivités tout en protégeant l'environnement alors que l'objectif économique tend à créer des emplois valorisants, à salaires décents. Enfin, l'objectif politique est de redonner du pouvoir aux salariés et aux communautés au sein de structures démocratiques.

Par ailleurs, il faut développer la capacité des organismes communautaires à défendre régionalement et localement leur vision de l'économie sociale. Tout cela exige une entente sur des positions communes de façon à assurer leur défense au sein des différentes structures partenariales.

Un des moments forts de cette première séance fut le témoignage de trois panélistes qui réagirent à partir d'une expérimentation terrain de l'économie sociale à travers des modèles différents d'activités d'utilité sociale. Il s'agissait de M. Jacques Blain, directeur général de la Coopérative des techniciens ambulanciers de la Montérégie, de M. Marc De Koninck, organisateur communautaire au CLSC Basse-Ville–Limoilou, et

---

6. Professeure à l'École de service social, Université de Montréal et présidente de Relais-Femmes.

7. Agent de développement du Regroupement des organismes communautaires des Laurentides.

de Mme Claudette Pitre-Robin, présidente de Concertation interrégionale des garderies du Québec. À tour de rôle et avec une rigueur ne servant pas à masquer certains états d'âme, les panélistes nous ont fait part de leur vécu à implanter dans leur sphère respective les principes de l'économie sociale.

Pour l'un, il s'agissait de s'approprier un processus décisionnel tout en mettant en place des principes de justice sociale auxquels les membres d'une coopérative adhéraient. Donc une occasion de faire place aux valeurs personnelles et collectives et de rapprocher l'usager de la prise de décisions le concernant. L'objectif de rentabilité constituait un enjeu de premier plan puisqu'elle procure l'indépendance et que celle-ci engendre des liens réels de partenariat. Son mot d'ordre : passer à l'action sans attendre la situation idéale.

Pour l'autre, dans le domaine de l'aide domestique, «Le rêve de Diane et les projets d'Albertine», l'option était de tirer le monde qui évoluait dans ce domaine vers le haut, tant au regard des salaires et des conditions de travail que de la valorisation que stimule une qualité de services où le monde, travailleurs et usagers, sont au centre du projet.

Dans le dernier cas, on rapporta un exemple d'appropriation étatique d'un projet d'économie sociale concernant la mise sur pied de Centres de la petite enfance dont le but consistait à développer des actions intégrées de services à la petite enfance en tenant compte des besoins diversifiés des familles et des principes interventionnels de différents milieux de pratique. Les instigateurs de ce projet ont été dépossédés de leur initiative par une récupération politico-bureaucratique (Office des services de garde) des principes moteurs supportant une entreprise où les acteurs avaient investi une somme considérable d'énergie. «Ils veulent tout décider [les fonctionnaires], mais que l'on reste autonome parce que ça coûte moins cher.»

Ce témoignage aura suscité énormément de réactions en plénière et une prise de conscience des incontournables enjeux politiques qui sous-tendent le développement et l'organisation de l'économie sociale et de la vigilance qu'il faut exercer dans la mise en place de ses paramètres.

> La recherche doit aussi servir de tremplin pour les pratiques qui se développent. Les décisions qui ont pour objet de «diriger» l'économie sociale dans un sens ou dans l'autre doivent se baser non pas sur l'air du temps, sur les pressions des uns et des autres, mais bien sur les pratiques qui évoluent sur le terrain[8].

---

8. Diane LEMIEUX et Yves VAILLANCOURT. *L'économie sociale et la transformation du réseau des services sociaux et de santé : définitions, état de la situation et enjeux.* Notes pour la conférence d'ouverture faite au colloque NPS du 13 mars 1997 (version du 12 mars 1997).

Des commentaires ajoutés en fin de plénière précisent que l'économie sociale doit être structurée non seulement par l'offre, mais par le bas avec l'*empowerment* des mouvements populaires, coopératifs, associatifs et syndicaux. Par contre, cet *empowerment* pourra être neutralisé si une partie des forces progressistes fait barrage par peur de l'économie sociale ou si l'on en travestit les objectifs. Cependant, la force de l'idéologie (démocratique) et le besoin de solutions devraient l'emporter sur les résistances «naturelles» (et mal définies) au développement de l'économie sociale.

ACTE DEUX DU COLLOQUE

Deuxième séance

C'est avec diligence que M. Clément Mercier[9], présidant la deuxième partie du colloque, nous présenta le principal conférencier de l'après-midi, M. Jean-Louis Laville[10], sociologue au CNRS.

Ce dernier, après avoir esquissé la toile de fond de la rupture et de la mutation actuelle des services sociaux dans les pays européens en évoquant la fin d'une solidarité indexée sur la croissance des sociétés salariales nationales de consommation et de protection sociale par l'avènement, pour ces sociétés, d'une croissance faible, durable, attribuable à un contexte structurel, nous propose un nouveau modèle de *services de proximité*, relevant de *services relationnels* dans des domaines aussi variés que l'éducation, la santé, les services domestiques et l'environnement.

Partant de l'évidence que les industries et les services standar-disables, dans la foulée de la mondialisation, ne créent plus d'emplois notamment à cause du développement technologique, il n'en constate pas moins qu'*il existe un ensemble de besoins non satisfaits d'un côté et, de l'autre, un nombre important de chômeurs*[11], il lui semble alors logique de promouvoir les possibilités d'insertion dans des services répondant à de nouvelles demandes.

Mais comment faire en sorte que l'offre et la demande se rencontrent et surtout comment «solvabiliser» cette occurrence? De même que l'intervention redistributive de l'État ne suffit plus, ainsi il n'est plus

---

9. Professeur au Département de service social, Université de Sherbrooke et membre du comité de rédaction de NPS.

10. Centre de recherche et d'information sur la démocratie et l'autonomie (CRIDA), CNRS, Paris.

11. J.-L. LAVILLE (1997). Services de proximité: la construction sociale d'un champ d'activités économiques, LAREPPS, UQAM.

possible pour les intervenants sociaux de faire essentiellement du social et ces derniers doivent s'engager de plain-pied dans l'économique en échafaudant des services de proximité relationnels et en créant un nouveau paysage de marché.

Il s'agit d'un espace public de proximité, réfléchi à partir de dialogues locaux sur les besoins de services et non d'une vision monétariste (marchande) des besoins. Cet espace se définira dans un processus d'échange et d'élaboration collective dans le respect de l'intégrité des usagers. En d'autres termes, il faut procéder autrement au niveau de la production de services par l'articulation de l'offre et des services à travers une réflexion collective.

La solvabilisation se pense en termes de partenariat dans une combinaison durable entre les ressources (marchandes, non marchandes et non monétaires).

> Il conviendra de sortir des « petits boulots » au profit d'une offre industrielle, seule capable d'apporter l'innovation, la sécurité, la reproductibilité et l'homogénéité qui sont, de l'avis général, les principales attentes à l'égard de la qualité de « services » à la personne. Le succès dépend du « professionnalisme du comportement », c'est-à-dire de « compétences comportementales et relationnelles » que les entreprises de services ont su identifier, développer et qu'elles sont en mesure d'enseigner [...][12].

Il faut cependant réfléchir sur les limites historiques de l'économie sociale : vision de la démocratie économique en termes de propriété collective, division du travail se réintroduisant à tous les jours, concurrence dommageable à cause de la dimension territoriale, nécessité d'échange et de regroupement, dimension politique de l'action.

L'idéal est de tendre vers une économie plurielle qui, à la longue, pourrait permettre la déconstruction du fonctionnement actuel de l'économie de marché. L'économie sociale peut participer d'un nouveau contrat social mais ne peut pas suffire à en fournir toutes les clés.

Cette conférence a évidemment suscité des réactions directement proportionnelles en qualité de la part de Mme Lorraine Guay du regroupement des ressources alternatives en santé mentale du Québec et de M. François Lamarche de la CSN.

Pour la première, l'économie sociale et les services de proximité n'ont pas pour fonction de générer des biens et des services mais du sens à notre monde social. Nous ne voulons pas produire des clients,

---

12. *Ibid.*

des usagers, des bénéficiaires, mais des citoyens libres, responsables et critiques. Il en va de l'intérêt public sans que nous soyons dans le système public étatique.

Il faut créer des espaces publics organisés de débats et faire un travail sur la notion de citoyenneté. Il faut replanter la question du rôle de l'État et la façon dont les besoins sont identifiés par une communauté. Cela est au cœur de la contestation de la planification technocratique.

Il faut en finir une fois pour toutes avec les politiques gouvernementales qui sont exclusivement axées sur le traitement social du chômage (*workfare*) et l'économie sociale doit être un point de ralliement. Pour Mᵐᵉ Guay, il est temps de repolitiser le débat et de revoir la plateforme politique pour sortir de nos logiques sectorielles et aller jusqu'à créer des espaces de dialogues internationaux où nous pourrions remettre en question les institutions internationales dominantes. De plus, le secteur privé marchand à but lucratif devrait être complètement exclu du social parce que incapable de construire du sens et de la socialité.

Pour M. Lamarche, les syndicats ne tueront pas l'économie sociale, comme plusieurs l'appréhendent, pas plus que le mouvement communautaire n'a fait disparaître le secteur public. La crise de l'emploi relève d'une crise du social et il faut recomposer les liens de solidarité dans les communautés.

L'économie sociale permet de préciser un nouveau mode d'intervention dans lequel l'État, les acteurs et les groupes sociaux, à travers différents niveaux et différents espaces, apportent leur contribution à la question de l'emploi, au problème d'insertion et, plus largement, à la lutte contre les inégalités, contre la pauvreté et à la recomposition des liens sociaux. Il faut, par ailleurs, se hâter parce que l'économie marchande, à partir des É.-U., est de plus en plus présente dans le secteur des services de soins et d'aide à domicile et s'apprête à combler le vide d'une demande sur laquelle nous agissons peu pour toutes sortes de raisons dont notre peur de s'engager n'est pas la moindre.

L'allocution de clôture du colloque fut prononcée par Mᵐᵉ Nancy Neamtan[13] avec une force de conviction laissant présager une vitalité accrue pour l'économie sociale bien qu'elle soit une réalité du paysage socio-économique québécois depuis une centaine d'années et que ses

---

13. Directrice générale du Regroupement pour la relance économique et social du Sud-Ouest de Montréal (RÉSO) et présidente du Groupe de travail sur l'économie sociale, Chantier de l'économie et de l'emploi. Le texte de l'allocution de clôture du colloque sera publié dans le prochain numéro de la revue *Nouvelles pratiques sociales* (automne 1997).

interventions aient été le lieu d'émergence de nos plus grandes réussites collectives.

L'économie sociale nous permet d'être proactif, d'innover et d'apprendre de nos erreurs et nous sort de la mentalité de programme pour mettre en place un mode de développement qui mobilise au maximum les forces vives du Québec autour de nouvelles pistes d'action.

Même si elle ne constitue pas en soi un projet de société, elle suggère néanmoins une autre façon de faire du développement. Elle fait appel à notre créativité et à notre volonté de répondre aux besoins sociaux de nos milieux. Elle suscite notre adhésion à des valeurs de solidarité et de démocratie et stimule notre capacité d'entreprendre.

Cependant, nous devons apprendre à manipuler un certain nombre d'outils économiques et financiers afin de les adapter à nos fins et à nos objectifs. En bout de piste, elle précisera que :

> Si on croit que les solutions d'avenir passent nécessairement à la fois par une société civile organisée, engagée et en mouvement, par un État dynamique pro-actif et connecté sur les réalités quotidiennes de sa population. Si on croit que le renouvellement de la démocratie passe nécessairement par la réappropriation par la population, incluant les plus marginalisés, de leur propre développement individuel et collectif. L'économie sociale peut et doit se retrouver au carrefour de ces solutions.

* * *

Certains des participants de ce colloque auront eu l'occasion, lors des plénières, soit de questionner conférenciers et analystes sur certains aspects de l'économie sociale, soit d'apporter des commentaires et des témoignages eu égard à leur propre vécu dans un secteur d'activité économique qui s'enrichit de plus en plus d'expérimentations nouvelles soutenues notamment par le Groupe de travail sur l'économie sociale.

Plusieurs d'entre eux ont manifesté leur satisfaction de voir l'économie sociale devenir autre chose qu'un cadre conceptuel où les experts, universitaires ou autres, se «chicanent» sur ses aspects théoriques.

Les actions déjà entreprises doivent être soutenues et les milieux communautaires et coopératifs doivent prendre les devants dans le développement de l'économie sociale au Québec afin de ne pas rater l'occasion historique que nous offre le contexte actuel de crise, de renouveler et de renforcer nos assises démocratiques, non seulement dans les espaces d'actions et de pratiques sociales, mais aussi à l'intérieur d'une société civile qui se cherche de nouvelles voies de cohésion et un contrat social qui soit différent de ce que nous offrent les tendances néolibérales prégnantes.

Bibliographie

L'EMIEUX, D. et Y. VAILLANCOURT (1997). *L'économie sociale et la transformation du réseau des services sociaux et de santé : définitions, état de la situation et enjeux.* Notes pour la conférence d'ouverture faite au colloque NPS du 13 mars 1997 (version du 12 mars 1997), LAREPPS, UQAM.

LAVILLE, J.-L. (1997). *Services de proximité : la construction sociale d'un champ d'activités économiques*, LAREPPS, UQAM.

Maladie mentale et délinquance. Deux figures de la déviance devant la justice pénale

Danielle LABERGE, Pierre LANDREVILLE,
Daphné MORIN, Marie ROBERT
et Nicole SOULLIÈRE
De Boeck, Université de Bruxelles,
Les Presses de l'Université d'Ottawa,
Les Presses de l'Université de Montréal,
collection Perspectives criminologiques,
1995, 153 p.

Depuis quelques années déjà, la sociologie du crime ou criminologie a sensibilisé la communauté scientifique sur les personnes malades mentales qui commettent des crimes, sur les aléas du pronostic de dangerosité, sur la judiciarisation des problèmes sociaux et des troubles mentaux en particulier, sur les zones d'interférence entre délinquance et trouble mental, sur la gestion pénale des justiciables manifestant des troubles mentaux, voire sur les contradictions flagrantes en Cour des expertises médico-légales en psychiatrie. Depuis la codification médico-psychiatrique officielle de la folie au XIXe siècle, le fou, par sa conduite déviante, a eu affaire à la fois au système de santé et au système pénal. Au cours des temps, cependant, le système pénal a adopté diverses modalités pour gérer cette clientèle juridiquement «non responsable». Qui pourrait s'en étonner puisque, avant même que la folie ne fasse l'objet d'un discours particulier, elle était à la croisée de plusieurs discours, ceux de la littérature certes mais aussi ceux des trois grandes «sciences» universitaires : le droit, la médecine et la théologie. Dans un passé plus lointain encore, la médecine a entretenu des plages d'interférence avec le droit. Si dans le discours médical, le corps du fou est à soigner, à examiner, dans le discours juridique, il s'agit d'un corps à maîtriser, à emprisonner.

Ce livre se situe au confluent, dans la dialectique de deux identités déviantes, celui de « malade mental » et de délinquant. Les auteurs signataires de ce livre au sein de leur groupe de recherche et d'analyse sur les politiques et les pratiques pénales (GRAPPP) sont les patrons incontestés de ce champ. Comment différencie-t-on la délinquance de la maladie mentale ? Quels sont les déterminants et les processus de cette attribution d'identité ? Quel est le rôle des divers acteurs dans ce processus de définition des personnes prises en charge par le système pénal ? Telles sont les questions auxquelles on souhaite donner réponse dans ce livre qui constitue une synthèse de plusieurs études menées sur ce sujet depuis 1987, principalement de deux travaux de recherche. Le premier portait sur le traitement judiciaire des personnes manifestant des problèmes de santé mentale à la Cour municipale de Montréal, et le second, sur les problèmes de prise en charge et d'intervention auprès des clientèles « Psychiatrie-Justice » dans la région métropolitaine de Montréal.

L'ouvrage se divise en deux grandes parties. La première cherche à expliquer le recours à l'intervention pénale, c'est-à-dire la façon dont on arrive à adopter ce style de solution pour cette clientèle différente. Cette partie comprend deux chapitres. Par des scénarios types, le premier chapitre illustre les différentes dynamiques dont la judiciarisation représente l'amortissement ; le second dissèque les conditions qui mènent à l'orientation pénale. Quant à la seconde partie traitant de la situation au tribunal, elle comporte quatre chapitres : le premier constitue un résumé des prescriptions du Code criminel relativement aux troubles mentaux et décrit les diverses étapes d'une affaire devant le tribunal. Le second trace le profil de la population de justiciables étudiés au cours de la recherche à la Cour municipale de Montréal. Quelle idée les principaux intervenants (policiers, procureurs, psychiatres) se font-ils de cette clientèle et de leur pratique à leur égard ? C'est la question à laquelle répond le troisième chapitre. Suit au dernier chapitre une analyse approfondie de quelques cas axés sur certaines modalités de leur prise en charge pénale : l'ordonnance du lieutenant-gouverneur, la sentence d'emprisonnement, la sentence d'aliénation mentale, le retrait de la plainte et la sentence suspendue avec probation.

Dans ce livre, les auteurs s'intéressent à la transparence des normes, à leur création et à leur application. Pourquoi, dans certains cas, insiste-t-on sur la dimension de la maladie alors que, dans d'autres, on refuse d'en tenir compte et l'on envisage plutôt la répression pénale ? Les auteurs s'inscrivent dans la trame de l'idéologie constructiviste, de transformation des rapports sociaux. Selon le temps, l'espace, les acteurs en cause, les différentes perceptions des personnes, de leur comportement, changent dans le traitement de la déviance. L'opposition, la discordance entre les acteurs est manifeste et s'explique par les intérêts divergents en présence. Et c'est dans ce jeu de contrôle social que s'actualise la judiciarisation des personnes manifestant des troubles mentaux à l'ombre des politiques sociales contradictoires.

Henri DORVIL
Groupe de recherche sur les aspects sociaux
de la santé et de la prévention (GRASP)
Université de Montréal

Département de travail social
Université du Québec à Montréal

L'économie solidaire, une perspective internationale

Jean-Louis LAVILLE *(sous la direction de)*
Paris, Desclée de Brouwer,
1994, 336 pages.

Cet ouvrage dirigé par J.-L. Laville nous convie à une réflexion sur la composition des rapports entre économie et société dans les sociétés dites «développées». Cette réflexion est appuyée par des études de cas en Amérique du Nord et du Sud. Ainsi L. Favreau traite du développement économique communautaire aux États-Unis, P.R. Bélanger, J. Boucher et B. Lévesque décrivent l'expérience de l'économie solidaire au Québec et I. Larraechea et M. Nyssens aborde l'économie populaire au Chili, (variation de l'économie solidaire au Québec). En France, deux institutions en transformation sont examinées à partir de la thématique de l'économie solidaire : C. Martin fait état du rôle joué par la famille avec l'accentuation du chômage et de l'exclusion et M. Lallement, de la flexibilité obtenue dans les négociations collectives, en particulier, par la décentralisation.

J.-L. Laville entame son étude en soutenant que les équilibres sur lesquels étaient fondées les sociétés développées sont remis en cause. Selon l'auteur, la lame de fond du chômage et de l'exclusion vient submerger toutes les digues édifiées pour lui barrer la route. L'ampleur des transformations nécessite une réflexion sur la recomposition des rapports entre économie et société (p. 11).

À la double crise que vit la société, soit la crise des valeurs et la crise économique, vient s'ajouter l'effondrement de la société-providence (p. 61). Ainsi, il faut favoriser des approches qui permettent de revaloriser l'appartenance sociale des exclus et des chômeurs. Cela nécessite de prendre ensemble la crise de socialisation et celle de l'emploi en privilégiant trois préoccupations concomitantes : 1) assurer la recherche de l'emploi moins égalitaire en veillant à ce que les modalités de ce partage concourent au renforcement du lien social; 2) exploiter toutes les occasions de création d'emplois sous réserve que les conditions de ceux-ci soient socialement acceptables, autrement dit qu'elles permettent de garder à l'emploi sa dimension d'appartenance citoyenne et 3) favoriser des formes de travail, autres que l'emploi, contribuant à la socialisation et à la reconnaissance sociale (p. 70-71).

Laville nous montre que les sphères politique et économique sont les deux principales constituantes de l'économie solidaire. Sur le plan politique, les pratiques sociales de l'économie solidaire, en participant à l'émergence d'espaces publics autonomes, peuvent atténuer les effets dévastateurs pour la démocratie d'une «marchandisation» et d'une abstraction des relations sociales. Sur le plan économique, l'économie solidaire, en constituant une ouverture en direction d'une économie plurielle, peut renouer avec cet élan originel dans le passage à une société de services, en particulier en s'appuyant sur des formes plurielles de travail (qu'elle soit de création d'emploi, de droit au revenu ou de partage du travail, p. 76).

L'exemple des services de proximité en Europe, qu'il s'agisse d'aide à domicile, d'accueil de jeunes enfants, d'entretien de l'environnement, rendent service à des millions d'usagers et représentent des dizaines de milliers d'emplois et de bénévoles. Ces différentes interventions procèdent d'une forme de légitimité issue de l'expression collective qui les amène à s'engager dans la production et la distribution de services. Cette activité économique est basée sur la réciprocité et cherche à attester du lien social fondateur en même temps qu'elle le soumet à différentes tensions; elle débouche, dans la production, sur le recours à du travail à la fois bénévole et rémunéré, et dans la distribution des services, sur une combinaison avec les principes du marché et de distribution (p. 83).

Les services de proximité expliquent leur pertinence aux yeux des usagers par un rapport aux besoins et aux demandes plus fin que celui établi dans les études de marché pour les services privés ou les études de besoins pour les services publics. L'innovation dans les services solidaires s'appuie sur le recours à un principe de comportement économique différent du marché et de la redistribution : le principe de la réciprocité qui conduit le processus d'interactions à travers lesquelles les services sont élaborés. Ces projets réussissent là où le marché ou l'État ont échoué parce qu'ils comblent le déficit informationnel entre offreur et demandeur et parviennent ainsi à atténuer la méfiance des utilisateurs que suscite l'idée de voir des intervenants s'immiscer dans leur intimité (p. 85).

L'économie solidaire est ainsi vue comme une tentative d'articulation inédite entre économies marchande, non marchande et non monétaire dans une conjoncture qui s'y prête étant donné le rôle conféré aux services par la «tertiarisation» des activités économiques. Les règles régissant l'échange rejoignent ici celles gouvernant la production avec le recours à des formes plurielles de travail au premier rang desquelles figure le bénévolat. Ici, le travail bénévole ne se substitue pas au travail salarié, il peut au contraire multiplier les emplois en abaissant le prix de revient des services et en facilitant le maintien d'un lien étroit et durable avec les usagers et les autres partenaires locaux (p. 86-87).

DES EXEMPLES SUR LE PLAN INTERNATIONAL

Selon L. Favreau, l'économie solidaire aux États-Unis existe principalement à travers un réseau de plus de 2 000 organismes de développement économique communautaire appartenant au secteur associatif. Ces organismes s'attaquent à la revitalisation des quartiers en soutenant simultanément des projets ayant trait au logement et à la formation professionnelle des résidents, à l'éducation des jeunes et à l'insertion sociale par l'économie dans des quartiers défavorisés des grandes villes (p. 93). Bref, ils se caractérisent par une approche intégrée et territorialisée (quartiers, zones, etc.). Ce type d'approche repose sur un diagnostic de la pauvreté selon lequel la société américaine est en train de créer des citoyens exclus des activités de citoyenneté (travail décent, quartier et logement viables). Ainsi, nous dit Favreau, «le problème, économique à l'origine, devient socioculturel, car il introduit des ruptures dans le tissu social et l'affaiblissement du sentiment d'appartenance à une communauté. Il est aussi politique, car la participation active des citoyens à la vie démocratique de la société est relativement faible» (p. 119-120).

Cette économie s'inscrit, selon l'auteur, dans une nouvelle voie entre l'économie de marché et l'économie publique en esquissant un pas vers une économie nouvelle axée sur la solidarité. C'est de cette manière que se crée un nouveau mode de gestion des rapports sociaux, «celui de l'emploi en relation avec le territoire, des associations de quartier en rapport avec le développement» (p. 132-133).

L'expérience de l'économie solidaire au Québec remonte aux expériences des caisses d'épargne Desjardins en passant par les corporations de développement économique communautaire. Toutefois, selon P.R. Bélanger, J. Boucher et B. Lévesque, les groupes du mouvement populaire et communautaire au Québec au nombre de 4 000 « se tournent vers l'économie et se voient de plus en plus comme des agents de développement économique en même temps que social. De plus, ils sont en train d'expérimenter de nouveaux types de rapports entre eux, avec d'autres groupes sociaux comme les syndicats, mais aussi avec l'État et dans certains cas, avec des associations patronales.» Ainsi de poursuivre les auteurs, «il est de plus en plus question de partenariat et de concertation, tant du côté du mouvement populaire et communautaire que des syndicats, pour lutter contre le chômage, la pauvreté et l'exclusion sociale» (p. 140).

En ce sens, le partenariat et les alliances stratégiques entre les groupes progressistes, le patronat et l'État sont et demeurent de nouvelles formes d'économie solidaire qui ne sont pas négligeables dans le cadre de la démarche d'un Québec «toujours en quête d'un statut mieux défini» (p. 175).

Quant à l'économie populaire, elle est une réalité bien vivante dans les quartiers pauvres de Santiago au Chili. I. Larraechea et M. Myssens l'inscrivent dans l'ensemble des activités du développement local et communautaire, parce qu'elle mobilise des facteurs non valorisés, exclus par les autres sphères de l'économie. Elle comprend cinq catégories : des organisations d'économie populaire (mises sur pied par des groupes religieux après la chute d'Allende), des micro-entreprises familiales, des initiatives individuelles, des stratégies d'assistance et des activités illégales (p. 190-191). L'ensemble de l'économie populaire est imbriquée dans des réseaux sociaux, des tissus populaires locaux. Son identité est fortement liée au milieu populaire. «Bien qu'elle occupe 50 % de la population active au Chili, l'économie populaire se place dans les interstices d'un système dominé par une logique de modernisation guidée par une exigence d'intégration au modèle de transnationalisation de l'économie mondiale.» (p. 202)

C'est ainsi que Larraechea et Nyssens se demandent si l'économie populaire, basée sur la valorisation du travail du monde populaire, développant des relations de réciprocité, ne serait pas un acteur privilégié de développement d'une économie solidaire.

Face à la montée de la crise de l'État-providence en France, C. Martin fait état des mécanismes traditionnels d'intégration qui reviennent à l'avant-scène, d'où l'importance des travaux portant sur le lien social, les réseaux de sociabilité, la parenté, les solidarités intergénérationnelles et familiales (p. 227). En somme, écrit Martin, pour faire face au processus de l'exclusion, chacun dispose d'un certain nombre de ressources au centre desquelles se situe systématiquement le capital relationnel ou l'intégration dans une sociabilité primaire, que ce soit pour accéder au logement, à l'emploi, ou plus globalement, à l'information (p. 235). Un des problèmes de cette soudaine redécouverte de l'importance du rôle des solidarités familiales est qu'elle donne l'illusion d'un nouveau gisement de ressources pour atténuer les difficultés sociales que rencontre une part croissante de la population. Or, les enquêtes qui ont étudié les pratiques de solidarité familiale depuis le début des années 1950 montrent qu'elles sont toujours demeurées actives, l'élément nouveau est qu'elles pourraient être assez puissantes pour participer à compenser la crise de protection sociale (p. 249).

M. Lallement, pour sa part, révèle que la décentralisation des conventions collectives en Allemagne et en France est certes l'élément marquant de la décennie des années 1980 qui se poursuit dans les années 1990. Les accords d'entreprise et l'individualisation des salaires entraînent «une crainte accrue des salariés qu'une telle politique fragmente les collectifs de travail en aiguisant le sens de la compétition ou encore en accentuant des processus d'exclusion des salariés qui ne se conforment pas au modèle du travailleur parfait» (p. 271).

Malgré ces réserves, la décentralisation, poursuit l'auteur, permet de gérer localement les procédures de l'emploi ; elle est une ouverture pour une plus grande implication des partenaires à la vie démocratique de l'entreprise.

> [...] si l'on prend au pied de la lettre l'injonction démocratique et parti-cipative véhiculée par les nouveaux modèles de gestion des ressources humaines, alors l'émergence de nouveaux lieux de débats et de décisions aptes à intégrer de façon plus égalitaire les protagonistes (syndicats, asso-ciations d'usagers, collectifs de travailleurs) impliqués localement dans l'activité économique et la création d'emploi est certainement une des con-ditions sine qua non à la production de nouveaux compromis favorables à l'emploi et à la cohésion sociale. (p. 281)

À l'heure de la crise de la société salariale et de l'État-providence, le livre de Laville nous invite à porter un regard différent sur les notions de partage du revenu et de l'emploi, d'utilité sociale et d'intérêt général, de tiers secteur et d'économie sociale, bref, à adopter une autre approche que celle proposée par l'État et l'entreprise. Il s'agit de la construction des rapports entre économie et solidarité dans la modernité. Les pratiques décrites, que ce soit aux États-Unis, au Québec ou au Chili, montrent que le développement local bénéficie d'une dynamique comparable à bien des égards. En Europe, plusieurs milliers de salariés travaillent dans les services solidaires (aide à la petite enfance, aux personnes âgées, loisirs, etc.). La portée de l'économie solidaire, malgré ses limites, ouvre une voie qui nous permet d'envisager une société diversifiée, pleine d'activités.

Omer CHOUINARD
Département de sociologie
Université de Moncton

Histoire de l'Abitibi-Témiscamingue

Odette Vincent *(sous la direction de)*
Institut québécois de recherche
sur la culture, Québec,
1995, 763 p.

L'Institut québécois de recherche sur la culture (IQRC) publiait à l'automne 1995 l'*Histoire de l'Abitibi-Témiscamigue*. Il s'agit du septième volume d'une collection grand public qui vise à retracer l'histoire des différentes régions du Québec. Livre de facture agréable et de lecture aisée, abondamment illustré de photos et comprenant plusieurs cartes et tableaux, il brosse en un peu plus de 650 pages les grandes étapes du peuplement et du développement de cette région du nord-ouest québécois. Bien plus qu'une simple chronologie d'événements économiques et politiques importants, cette histoire régionale met en évidence à la fois les tendances lourdes et les conjonctures particulières qui ont modelé l'histoire témiscabitibienne. On retrouve également plusieurs repères concernant la vie socioculturelle de la région et les institutions qui ont marqué son développement.

Le livre est divisé en trois grandes parties, chacune retraçant une période précise de l'histoire de la région. La première partie porte sur le territoire et ses occupants avant la période de colonisation qui débute, au Témiscamingue, en 1884. Les auteurs commencent, dans le premier chapitre, par présenter le cadre géographique de la région et son façonnement géologique. Celle-ci, apprend-on, est composée de trois sous-régions : «l'Abitibi au nord, le Témiscamingue au sud et, entre les deux, la zone des collines que [les auteurs identifieront] comme les hautes terres de l'Abitibi» (p. 23). Par ailleurs, l'Abitibi-Témiscamigue, c'est aussi le lieu du partage des eaux. Au nord, les eaux coulent en effet vers la baie James tandis qu'au sud, elles coulent vers le Saint-Laurent. Cette ligne de partage des eaux, qui serpente dans les hautes terres de l'Abitibi, constituera pendant longtemps un obstacle à l'exploitation des ressources naturelles et à la colonisation de la région, conditionnant ainsi toute son histoire. En effet, les portages nombreux qu'elle commande compliqueront les transports et freineront la pénétration dans le territoire tandis que l'écoulement des eaux vers le nord n'autorisera pas le flottage du bois vers les usines du sud compliquant ainsi l'exploitation de la forêt.

Les trois chapitres suivants portent, quant à eux, sur les premiers habitants de la région. Bien que, comme le soulignent les auteurs, l'Abitibi-Témiscamingue est dans l'imaginaire collectif québécois une région neuve, à l'histoire récente, il n'en demeure pas moins que bien avant l'arrivée des Européens, la région était peuplée par des Amérindiens. Les récentes découvertes archéologiques, dont traite abondamment le chapitre deux du livre, permettent de retracer une occupation humaine continue sur plus de cinquante siècles. À partir du XVIIᵉ siècle, les chroniques des missionnaires et les récits des explorateurs permettent de retracer avec plus d'exactitude «certains aspects de la vie sociale et économique des Amérindiens du Nord-Ouest du Québec lors de la période du contact avec les Européens» (p. 99). C'est ce à quoi s'attarde le chapitre trois en traçant le portrait du mode de vie des Abitibis et des Témiscamingues qui peuplent alors respectivement le nord et le sud de la région. Le dernier chapitre de cette première partie du livre cherche à faire «l'autopsie d'un contact» (titre du chapitre 4), celui entre le monde des Amérindiens et le monde des Eurocanadiens. Trois périodes peuvent ainsi, selon les auteurs, être retracées. D'abord, la période de la traite des fourrures pendant laquelle quelques postes de traite sont construits et que commence l'occupation blanche du territoire. Ensuite, la période des missionnaires, surtout les Oblats et les Sulpiciens, qui cherchent à évangéliser les Amérindiens. Enfin, à partir du milieu du XIXᵉ siècle, la période de création des réserves. Bien qu'on puisse croire que ce contact entre les Amérindiens et les Eurocanadiens ait provoqué une forte acculturation des premiers, les auteurs de l'*Histoire de l'Abitibi-Témiscamingue* préfèrent parler «de cohabitation caractérisée par des rapports pacifiques et commerciaux entre voisins, ou encore de dualité culturelle, voire de sociétés distinctes adaptées à un milieu géographique et engagées dans une histoire» (p. 159).

La seconde période de l'histoire de l'Abitibi-Témiscamingue, dont rend compte la deuxième partie du livre, débute selon les auteurs à la fin de 1884 avec la fondation de la Société de colonisation du Témiscamingue et s'achève en 1950 alors que «l'Abitibi et le Témiscamingue sont reliés par des voies de communication et [que] leurs intérêts sont suffisamment communs pour leur permettre de former une entité particulière au nord-ouest du Québec» (p. 413). Durant les 65 ans que dure cette phase du développement de l'Abitibi-Témiscamingue, on assiste d'abord à l'émergence de trois sous-régions puis à la création de liens entre elles. Aussi, est-ce en fait à trois histoires que les auteurs nous convient ici : celle du développement du Témiscamingue au sud de la région, celle du développement de l'Abitibi rural au nord et celle du développement de l'Abitibi minier entre les deux qui participera à l'unification des deux autres sous-régions.

Les trois premiers chapitres (les chapitres 5, 6 et 7) de cette deuxième partie du livre traitent de la naissance et de la consolidation de l'Abitibi-Témiscamingue rural et nous permettent de bien comprendre à la fois les dynamiques particulières et les points de convergence du développement de l'Abitibi rural et du Témiscamingue. On voit ainsi toute l'importance du clergé, des élites traditionnelles et de l'État (surtout dans le développement de l'Abitibi) dans le peuplement de ces deux sous-régions. Voulant notamment contrer l'exode des populations du sud du Québec vers la Nouvelle-Angleterre, ils développeront un projet de colonisation ruraliste et agriculturaliste dans le Nord-Ouest québécois. Cependant, la forêt prendra rapidement de l'importance, son exploitation assurant un revenu d'appoint important au colon-agriculteur, devenant même en Abitibi rural le cœur du développement. Aussi, se développera-t-il rapidement en Abitibi-Témiscamingue une économie agro-forestière. La crise de 1929 a obligé les gouvernements à établir plusieurs plans de colonisation qui favoriseront, nous expliquent les auteurs, d'abord une croissance démographique importante puis la consolidation de la région, faisant en sorte que «le monde rural de l'Abitibi-Témiscamingue atteint [...] sa maturité au début des années 1950» (p. 278).

L'histoire du développement de l'Abitibi minier, dont traite le chapitre 8, est quelque peu différente. Elle débute en 1910 avec l'arrivée de quelques prospecteurs en provenance de l'Ontario. Ce sera cependant la mise en exploitation de la mine Horne (cuivre, or et argent) à Noranda par la société américaine Noranda Mines Limited en 1927 qui consistera en quelque sorte le coup d'envoi du développement de l'Abitibi minier. À la fin des années 1930, un deuxième pôle minier se sera constitué plus à l'est autour des mines de Val-d'Or, Malartic et Cadillac. L'exploitation de ces mines amènera de nombreux travailleurs dans la région. Jusqu'au milieu des années 1930, les «Fros» (foreigners – il s'agit d'immigrants d'Europe centrale et d'Europe orientale) constitueront le gros de la main-d'œuvre. Cependant, avec la crise économique, les Canadiens-français remplaceront ces premiers travailleurs, d'autant plus qu'un grand nombre d'entre eux ont été expulsés de la région à la suite d'une grève à la mine Horne en 1934. Une deuxième vague d'immi-gration européenne se produira après la Deuxième Guerre mondiale. En effet, plusieurs personnes déplacées par la guerre en Europe seront recrutées par les mines pour venir travailler en Abitibi. On comprendra dès lors, comme l'expliquent les auteurs, que va se créer autour des mines un monde urbain cosmopolite, qui tranche avec le reste de l'Abitibi-Témiscamingue rural et fortement canadien-français. Ces villes, à l'ex-ception de Noranda et de Bourlamaque (près de Val-d'Or) qui seront construites par les compagnies minières pour loger leurs travailleurs, seront «agitées et désordonnées à leur début» (p. 317), habitées qu'elles sont par une «population hétéroclite de prospecteurs, de géologues, d'aventuriers et de commerçants» (p. 314).

Après avoir fait ce portrait chronologique du développement démographique et économique de la région, l'*Histoire de l'Abitibi-Témiscamingue* fait ressortir en deux chapitres (les chapitres 9 et 10) quelques aspects du développement institutionnel et de la vie socio-culturelle de la région à cette époque des pionniers. Les auteurs nous parlent notamment, au niveau institutionnel, des premières églises tant catholiques, que protestantes, russes orthodoxes, grecques orthodoxes ou juives ; des premières écoles primaires et secondaires ; et de la mise en place des premiers jalons d'un système de santé. Le chapitre sur la vie socioculturelle met l'accent à la fois sur le développement d'une culture de frontière – culture de désorganisation sociale qui favorise le «sens de l'inventivité face au défi du recommencement à zéro» (p. 373) –, sur les loisirs, sur les sports ainsi que sur les journaux, la radio et le cinéma dans la région.

La troisième partie de cette *Histoire de l'Abitibi-Témiscamingue* porte sur la période la plus récente du développement de la région, celle qui s'étend de 1950 à nos jours. Encore ici, comme dans la partie pré-cédente, les auteurs optent pour deux découpages : un chronologique, qui retrace le développement économique et démographique de la région, et un autre thématique, qui aborde la vie culturelle et la vie politique dans la région.

L'analyse du développement économique fait essentiellement ressortir la situation de dépendance de la région face à l'extérieur et le peu d'emprise qu'ont les Témiscabitibiens sur le développement écono-mique de celle-ci. En fait, relèvent les auteurs, l'économie régionale est très fortement intégrée à l'économie continentale, situation faisant en sorte que «les choix concernant la vie économique au quotidien appar-tiennent [...], dans une grande proportion, à des non-résidants» (p. 420). L'État, en appuyant l'entreprise privée durant les années 1950 et en définissant lui-même dans les années 1960-1980 les axes de développement, ne fait que renforcer cette tendance lourde. Néanmoins, et malgré la mondialisation des échanges et la diminution de l'importance des ressources, les auteurs concluent à la fin de cette analyse que de nos jours « c'est la perspective d'un développement durable fortement ancré sur son territoire qui fait surface et qui s'impose aux habitants de la région » (p. 480).

Quant au développement démographique, les auteurs font remarquer différents phénomènes se produisant entre 1951 et 1991 et qui modifient les dynamiques intrarégionales. On retiendra notamment : la diminution importante de la part relative de la population témiscabitibienne par rapport à l'ensemble du Québec ; la répartition plus égale de la population entre l'est et l'ouest de la région ; l'urbanisation de la population et l'effondrement du monde rural qui l'accompagne. Les auteurs font également remarquer qu'apparaît une nouvelle génération de gens qui sont nés en région et qui se font une représentation différente de l'Abitibi-Témiscamingue. Ils sont conscients de vivre en région et ne perçoivent plus l'Abitibi comme un pays de passage, comme un « lieu de transition » (p. 525).

Les trois derniers chapitres (les chapitres 13, 14 et 15) du livre traitent de la vie socioculturelle et de la vie politique dans la région depuis les années 1950. Les auteurs relatent notamment l'apparition d'institutions régionales tant dans le domaine de l'éducation (cégep, université) que dans celui de la santé. Ils analysent également l'apparition et le développement d'une culture régionale qui dit dans ses chansons, ses livres, son cinéma, ses toiles, la richesse du Nord-Ouest québécois. Enfin, la vie politique tant sur la scène fédérale que québécoise ainsi que l'importance des mouvements sociaux dans la région sont analysées. Cette section se termine avec quelques commentaires sur les identités locale, sous-régionale et régionale qui prennent forme et se consolident dans la période la plus récente de l'histoire de l'Abitibi-Témiscamingue.

En définitive, il est heureux que l'IQRC ait décidé de produire l'*Histoire de l'Abitibi-Témiscamingue*. La publication de ce livre est sans aucun doute un événement important dans la vie collective des Témiscabitibiens. Il leur fournit tout à la fois des données pour mieux comprendre d'où ils viennent, des repères afin de saisir les enjeux sociaux économiques et politiques qui traversent leur région et des éléments qui contribueront à la constitution d'une identité collective forte leur permettant d'envisager l'avenir avec détermination. Cette histoire régionale intéressera également, bien entendu, les chercheurs en développement local et régional, car on y fait bien ressortir les contraintes au développement et le rôle des acteurs de la région et hors de la région. Enfin, ce livre saura plaire à quiconque veut comprendre l'histoire du Québec. En effet, en retraçant tant l'histoire amérindienne que l'histoire eurocanadienne de la région, c'est en fait toute l'histoire du Québec que l'on voit se profiler en filigrane. Un livre, donc, que l'on ne peut que recommander.

Patrice LeBlanc
Professeur invité
Université du Québec en Abitibi-Témiscamingue

❖ Guide pour la présentation des articles

Les personnes qui soumettent des textes à la revue sont priées de respecter les règles suivantes.

Longueur : Dactylographier le texte à double interligne (26 lignes par page) avec des marges de 2,5 centimètres (1 pouce). La longueur maximale est de 20 pages ou 35 000 caractères. (Dans certains cas, le Comité de rédaction se réserve le droit de commander des articles plus longs ou plus courts.)

Première page : Inscrire le titre de l'article, le nom des auteurs ainsi que le nom de l'organisme auquel ils sont associés. Si cet organisme est une université, préciser le département ou la faculté.

Féminisation : Féminiser le texte en suivant la politique du ministère de l'Éducation (Québec). Utiliser, dans la mesure du possible, les tournures neutres qui englobent les femmes autant que les hommes (par exemple, «le personnel enseignant» au lieu de «les professeur-eure-s») ; à l'occasion, utiliser le féminin et le masculin pour bien montrer que l'on fait référence tant aux femmes qu'aux hommes (par exemple : les intervenantes et intervenants consultés).

Références : Lorsqu'on renvoie à des auteurs, on placera les références dans le texte, immédiatement après la citation ou le mot auquel elles se rapportent. On indiquera entre parenthèses le nom de l'auteur, suivi d'une virgule, suivie de l'année de publication et, s'il y a lieu, on ajoutera un deux-points suivis de la page citée, comme dans l'exemple suivant : (Tremblay, 1986 : 7).

Si l'on cite deux pages ou plus, on insérera un trait d'union entre la première et la dernière page citée, comme dans l'exemple suivant : (Tremblay, 1987 : 7-8).

Si l'on cite deux ouvrages publiés par le même auteur la même année, on les différenciera en ajoutant une lettre à l'année, comme dans l'exemple suivant : (Tremblay, 1987a, 1987b).

Si l'on cite des ouvrages distincts à l'intérieur de la même parenthèse, on les placera par ordre chronologique décroissant et on les séparera par un point-virgule, comme dans l'exemple suivant : (Tremblay, 1987 ; Lévesque, 1982). Si les années de publication sont identiques, utiliser l'ordre alphabétique.

Notes : Placer les notes en bas de page.

Citations : Utiliser les guillemets français («») pour les citations placées à l'intérieur d'un paragraphe. Ces citations ne doivent pas dépasser une longueur de trois lignes ; plus longues, on les détachera du texte sans mettre de guillemets.

Mettre entre crochets [ ] les lettres et les mots ajoutés ou changés dans une citation, de même que les points de suspension indiquant la coupure d'un passage […].

Tableaux et graphiques : Si les tableaux et graphiques ont été réalisés avec un logiciel autre que celui utilisé pour le texte, les présenter sur des feuilles distinctes en ayant soin d'indiquer le lieu d'insertion dans le corps du texte.

Bibliographie : La placer à la fin du texte. S'assurer que toutes les références indiquées dans le texte s'y retrouvent et que les dates de publication concordent. Classer les références par ordre alphabétique des noms d'auteurs ; ne pas écrire ces noms en lettres majuscules. Les titres de livres, revues et journaux doivent être en italique, mais les titres d'articles et de chapitres de livres doivent être entre guillemets. Ne pas oublier d'indiquer le lieu et la maison d'édition. Il est important que la bibliographie soit complète.

Exemples :

Fortin, Andrée (1991). «La participation : des comités de citoyens au mouvement communautaire», dans Godbout, Jacques T. (sous la direction de), *La participation politique*, Québec, IQRC, 219-250.

Lapeyronne, Didier (1988). «Mouvements sociaux et action politique. Existe-t-il une théorie de la mobilisation des ressources?», *Revue française de sociologie*, vol. 29, n° 4, 593-619.

Rémy, Jean, Voyé, Liliane et Émile Servais (1978). *Produire ou reproduire? Conflits et transaction sociale*, Bruxelles, Éditions Vie ouvrière, 383 pages.

Nombre d'exemplaires et résumé :   Remettre deux copies du texte ainsi qu'un résumé en français de 100 mots au plus.

Les dossiers parus

Vol. 7, n° 2 (automne 1994)
Dossier : **La recherche sociale et le renouvellement des pratiques**
Responsables : *Jean-Pierre Deslauriers et Jean-Marc Pilon*

Vol. 8, n° 1 (printemps 1995)
Dossier : **Les régions**
Responsables : *Louis Favreau et Juan-Luis Klein*

Vol. 8, n° 2 (automne 1995)
Dossier : **Les pratiques sociales des années 60 et 70**
Responsable : *Yves Vaillancourt*

Vol. 9, n° 1 (printemps 1996)
Dossier : **Spiritualité, Églises et religions**
Responsables : *Marie-Andrée Roy, Gregory Baum, et René Lachapelle*

Vol. 9, n° 2 (automne 1996)
Dossier : **Résurgence du social en prévention**
Responsables : *Lucie Fréchette et Doris Baril*

Vol. 10, n° 1 (printemps 1997)
Dossier : **10e anniversaire**
Responsables : *Francine Descarries et Christine Corbeil*

 ## Les dossiers à paraître

Vol. 10, n° 2 (automne 1997)
Dossier : **L'organisation du travail dans le réseau de la santé et des services sociaux**
Responsables : *Jacques Fournier et Paul Langlois*

Vol. 11, n° 1 (printemps 1998)
Dossier : **L'itinérance**
Responsables : *Danielle Laberge et Mario Poirier*

Vol. 11, n° 2 (automne 1998)
Dossier : **Le tiers secteur**
Responsables : *Yves Vaillancourt, Lucie Chagnon, Louis Favreau, Jean Gagné et Réjean Mathieu*

ABONNEMENT

Je m'abonne à la revue **NOUVELLES PRATIQUES SOCIALES**  à partir
du volume _____
numéro _____

	1 an (2 numéros)	**2 ans** (4 numéros)	**3 ans** (6 numéros)
Canada (taxes incluses)			
Individu	☐ 23 $	☐ 39$	☐ 49$
Étudiant	☐ 16 $	☐ 24$	☐ 33$
Institution	☐ 31 $	☐ 53$	☐ 73$
Étranger	☐ 35$	☐ 60$	☐ 83$

À l'unité : Chaque numéro des volumes 1 à 6 : **10$** (taxe incluse)
Chaque numéro des volumes 7 et suivants : **15$** (taxe incluse)

Veuillez me faire parvenir les numéros suivants déjà parus :
Volume _____ N° _____   Volume _____ N° _____   Volume _____ N° _____

Nom : _____

Adresse : _____

Ville : _____ Province : _____

Code postal : _____ Téléphone : (____) _____

Occupation : _____

☐ Chèque ou mandat postal ci-joint   ☐ Visa   ☐ Mastercard

N° de la carte : _____ Date d'expiration : _____

Signature : _____

Libellez votre chèque ou mandat postal en dollars canadiens à :

NOUVELLES PRATIQUES SOCIALES
Presses de l'Université du Québec
2875, boul. Laurier, Sainte-Foy (Québec) Canada, G1V 2M3
Téléphone :   (418) 657-4391
Télécopieur :   (418) 657-2096

Cahiers de recherche sociologique

numéro 29 :

La pauvreté en mutation

Bon de commande

JE DÉSIRE RECEVOIR

___ copies du numéro **La pauvreté en mutation**

($19,50 taxes et frais de poste inclus)

❑ chèque .... **Retourner à cette adresse :**
❑ Visa No .... Service des publications/CRS
Date d'expiration .... Université du Québec à Montréal
❑ Master Card No .... C.P. 8888, Succ. Centre-ville
Date d'expiration .... Montréal (Qc) H3C 3P8
Nom : ....
Organisme ou compagnie : ....
Adresse : ....
Ville : ....
Code postal ....

À paraître

numéro 30
La sociologie face au XXIe siècle
(printemps 98)

Abonnement

Prix de l'abonnement en dollars canadiens
(TPS et TVQ et frais de poste inclus)

	1 an (2 numéros)	2 ans (4 numéros)	3 ans (6 numéros)
au Canada	32,00$	58,00$	84,00$
à l'étranger	35,00$	64,00$	92,00$
institution au Canada	45,00$	82,00$	117,00$
institution étrangère	50,00$	91,00$	130,00$
étudiant	22,00$	40,00$	59,00$

À TOUTES LES INTERVENANTES ET TOUS LES INTERVENANTS SOCIAUX

Le département de travail social de l'UQAM, conjointement avec le département de sociologie, offre une

MAÎTRISE EN INTERVENTION SOCIALE

- Pour réfléchir sur sa propre pratique, sur les pratiques actuelles et sur les possibilités de les renouveler

- Pour se donner des outils de recherche appropriés au renouvellement de l'intervention sociale

- Pour développer une polyvalence en tant qu'intervenant(e) afin de faire face aux nouveaux enjeux sociaux et aux transformations des réalités sociales

Conditions d'admission :

1. Baccalauréat en travail social, en sociologie, en animation culturelle ou l'équivalent (moyenne cumulative de 3,2 sur 4,3);
2. Expérience de pratique de deux ans dans le domaine de l'intervention sociale;
3. Présenter un avant-projet de mémoire (de 3 à 5 pages).

Un programme souple qui part de votre expérience de l'intervention, de vos questionnements et prend en compte les enjeux de la pratique

Pour toute information :
appelez au secrétariat du programme de maîtrise en intervention sociale :
(514) 987-4822

AGMV
MARQUIS
Québec, Canada
1997